M. Paye Account

951.043-1709

sheriff

A04-346-7896

133-35520

Procedures in the Justice System

EIGHTH EDITION

CLIFF ROBERSON, LLM, PH.D.
Department of Criminal Justice
Washburn University

HARVEY WALLACE, J.D.
Department of Criminology
California State University, Fresno

GILBERT B. STUCKEY

PEARSON
Prentice
Hall

Upper Saddle River, New Jersey 07458

Library of Congress Cataloging-in-Publication Data

Roberson, Cliff
    Procedures in the justice system/Cliff Roberson, Harvey Wallace, Gilbert B. Stuckey.—8th ed.
      p. cm.
    Stuckey's name appears first on the previous editions.
    Includes bibliographical references and index.
    ISBN 0-13-173590-X
    1. Criminal procedure—United States.   2. Criminal justice, Administration
of—United States.   I. Wallace, Harvey   II. Stuckey, Gilbert B.   III. Title.
    KF9619.S8 2007
    345.73′05—dc22

                                                                    2006004215

Editor-in-Chief: Vernon R. Anthony
Executive Editor: Frank Mortimer, Jr.
Associate Editor: Sarah Holle
Marketing Manager: Adam Kloza
Production Editor: Karen Ettinger, TechBooks/GTS York, PA Campus
Production Liaison: Barbara Marttine Cappuccio
Director of Manufacturing and Production: Bruce Johnson
Managing Editor: Mary Carnis
Manufacturing Manager: Ilene Sanford
Manufacturing Buyer: Cathleen Petersen
Senior Design Coordinator: Mary Siener
Cover Designer: Lisa Klausing
Cover image: James Lemass; Picture Quest
Composition: TechBooks/GTS York, PA Campus
Printing and Binding: R.R. Donnelley & Sons

Pearson Education Ltd.   Pearson Education Australia Pty. Limited
Pearson Education Singapore Pte. Ltd.   Pearson Education North Asia Ltd.
Pearson Education Canada, Ltd.   Pearson Educación de Mexico, S.A. de C.V.
Pearson Education—Japan   Pearson Education Malaysia Pte. Ltd.

10 9 8 7 6 5 4
ISBN 0-13-173590-X

Contents

Preface

Thirty years ago, in 1976, Gilbert Stuckey published the first edition of *Procedures in the Justice System*. For the past twelve years, Cliff Roberson and Harvey Wallace have revised and updated the new editions. When the first edition was published, it contained 158 pages. The present edition contains almost three times that number. New to this edition are key term lists, new chapter headings, learning objectives, increased number of Law in Practice boxes, photos, and a glossary. This edition, like the four previous editions, is dedicated to our colleague, the late Gilbert B. Stuckey.

The eighth edition of *Procedures in the Justice System* continues the tradition of providing the reader with a thorough understanding of our justice system from the time of arrest through the sentencing of the criminal offender. Legal rules of procedure are presented in language that is easy to understand. The high crime rate continues to be one of society's major problems, not only in the United States but also throughout the world. It is the primary responsibility of those directly connected with the justice system, such as members of law enforcement agencies, the courts, and correctional officers, to fight crime. Yet to effectively curb crime, society needs the assistance of every law-abiding person.

By studying history, we often see the mistakes of the past and thus can make efforts not to repeat those mistakes in the future. One past mistake was the failure to recognize that the members of the justice system are a team who must work together. Yet, to work as a team, it is necessary for each member to understand his or her own responsibility as well as that of each of the other members.

In this eighth edition, the coverage of Supreme Court decisions and a new chapter on courtroom evidence have been added. This edition also contains actual copies of court documents, arrest warrants, and search warrants. These are submitted to provide the reader with a better idea of the practical issues involved in trying criminal cases. The discussions of the constitutional and civil rights of an accused, of the laws of arrest, and of search and seizure have also been expanded. We have also included additional court cases to provide the reader with experience in reading court decisions and to assist the reader in understanding the legal issues involved.

This book was written for those interested in our justice system, particularly police and correctional science students. It explains the duties and responsibilities of the law enforcement agencies, courts, and correctional departments in relation to law violators from the time of accusation until completion of the sentence. Criminal justice students should, however, study more than just judicial procedures. They should have some knowledge of why we have laws and why those laws are broken, should be cognizant of the constitutional rights of an accused, and should have a better understanding of the philosophy of correctional endeavors. Thus, material on these subjects is incorporated into the text. The information in this book will help the student, as well as others, attain a more thorough knowledge of our justice system and of the role that each member must play to achieve, through teamwork, law and order for all.

Special thanks to the following reviewers for their hard work and assistance on this edition; Elvira White, Prairie View A&M University, Prairie View, TX; Larry Vick, Fayetteville Technical Community College, Fayetteville, NC; Tina Fryling, Mercyhurst College, Erie, PA; and John Anderson, California State University–Fullerton, Fullerton, CA.

The invaluable assistance of associate editor Sarah Holle, editor Frank Mortimer Jr., and copy editor Helen Greenberg was necessary to accomplish this extensive revision to the text. Also a special thanks to the director of editorial development at Prentice Hall, Vernon Anthony, for his support and faith in the project.

To assist the instructor in presenting the material in this edition, an Instructor's Manual is provided, containing objectives, chapter outlines, and teaching aids. A Companion Website, TestGen, Test Item File, and a PowerPoint presentation are also available. Suggestions for improvement, corrections, and other comments are invited and may be forwarded to Cliff Roberson at Roberson37@aol.com.

Cliff Roberson, LLM, Ph.D.
Professor of Criminal Justice
Washburn University
Professor of Criminology (Retired),
California State University, Fresno

Harvey Wallace, J.D.
Professor of Criminology
California State University, Fresno

> The law embodies the story of a nation's development through many centuries, and it cannot be dealt with as if it contained only the axioms and corollaries of a book of mathematics.
> —Oliver Wendell Holmes, *The Common Law,* 1881

Historical Development of Law and the Justice System

1

Chapter Outline

Key Words

Abstract goals
Atonement
Code of Hammurabi
Court rules

Due process
Jurisdiction
Orientation goals
Pragmatic goals

Standards
Trial by ordeal
Venue

Learning Objectives

After completing this chapter, you should be able to:

1. Explain the development of the modern jury system.
2. Discuss the federal and state court systems.
3. Distinguish between jurisdictional issues and venue issues.
4. Describe the classifications of crimes and punishments.
5. Explain the basic structure of the justice system.
6. Identify the differences between court rules and standards.
7. Explain the various goals of the justice system.
8. Explain the foundational concepts in criminal procedure.

OVERVIEW

The study of our justice system should be viewed not as a set of rules for memorization, but as a cluster of ideas, principles, and values about which reasonable persons can and do disagree. The system is not fixed in stone; it is changing and flexible. Understanding our concept of justice requires a thoughtful comprehension of the historical background, social values, moral standards, and political realities that give direction to our system.

Both the state and federal governments have enacted statutes to regulate the administration of the criminal justice system. The primary state regulatory statute is the state code of criminal procedure that regulates procedure in state courts. The primary federal statute that governs the trial of criminal cases in federal court is Title 18 of the U.S. Code. Except for constitutional issues, federal procedural rules apply only to federal criminal cases. State procedural rules apply only to state cases.

Judicial Guidance

Judicial Opinions   Judicial opinions construe the constitutionality, meaning, and effect of constitutional and statutory provisions. The court decisions included in each chapter provide examples of the importance of judicial opinions in the justice system.

Court Rules   **Court rules** consist of the various standard procedures used by the courts that were developed as the result of a court's inherent supervisory power over the administration of the criminal justice system. Court rules regulate the guilt-determining process of the courts in the areas not regulated by other rules. Most students of the justice system fail to consider the importance of court rules in the trial of criminal cases.

Examples of court rules that impact on the courts follow.

Los Angeles County Municipal Court Rule 532.6:

> Each judge is required to list [report] all causes [cases] under submission for more than 30 days, with an indication of the length of time each has been pending (30 through 60 days, 61 through 90 days; or over 90 days).

California Supreme Court Rule 22 (regarding oral arguments before the court):

> Unless otherwise ordered: (1) counsel for each party shall be allowed 30 minutes for oral argument, except [that] in a case in which a sentence of death has been imposed each party shall be allowed 45 minutes. . . .

U.S. District Court (Eastern District California) Rule 5a:

> (1) The trial of a defendant held in custody solely for purposes of trial on a federal charge shall commence within 90 days following the beginning of continuous custody.

Goals of the Justice System

Most experts on the justice system agree that the most basic goal of the system is to protect society from crime. Beyond that, there is little agreement. There are several competing philosophies concerning the purposes of the justice system, each with its own specific goals. To help us understand some of the more commonly accepted goals of the justice system, the goals are classified as **orientation goals**, **pragmatic goals**, **abstract goals**, or **standards**.

Orientation Goals   Criminal justice professionals generally are oriented in one of two opposite directions—law and order or individual rights. The law and order orientation stresses the need to solve the crime problem. The individual rights orientation stresses the need to protect an individual's rights and considers this need greater than the need to punish offenders. Too great an emphasis on individual rights will restrict law enforcement and allow offenders to escape punishment. Arbitrary police practices that may occur under the law and order orientation may infringe on human and constitutional rights. As Chief Justice Earl Warren stated in *Miranda* v. *Arizona:*

> The quality of a nation's civilization can be largely measured by the methods it uses in the enforcement of the criminal law. . . . All of these policies point to one overriding thought: the constitutional foundation underlying the privilege is the respect a government—state or federal—must accord the dignity and integrity of its citizens. To maintain a fair state–individual balance, the government must shoulder the entire load.

Pragmatic Goals   The pragmatic goals of the justice system include:

Preventing Crime.   This goal includes providing potential criminals with conventional opportunities for success before they start a career of crime, building stronger social control units such as the family, providing guidance and counseling in our schools, and developing better environmental conditions in the neighborhoods that foster law-abiding behavior.

Diverting Offenders.   This refers to the efforts to remove offenders from the system and place them in nonpunitive treatment programs. The purpose of this effort is to correct offenders without placing the stigma of a criminal conviction on them.

Deterring Crime.   The justice system attempts to deter crime by making potential criminals believe that the punishments received for criminal behavior outweigh any potential benefit (i.e., crime does not pay).

Controlling Criminals.   The system attempts to control the behavior of known criminals by incarcerating the more serious offenders and placing the less serious ones in community correction programs.

Rehabilitating Offenders.   An objective of the system is to provide rehabilitation treatment to offenders in order to reduce the likelihood of future involvement in criminal behavior. The goal of rehabilitation was very popular in the 1960s. During the 1980s it was discounted because of the popular belief that existing rehabilitation programs were not effective. Today, rehabilitation is not a popular objective in most states.

Abstract Goals   Abstract goals are the underlying principles upon which our justice system is based. The most common abstract goals include:

Fairness.   The justice system should ensure that all persons involved in the criminal justice system are treated fairly and humanely. More specifically, socioeconomic status, ethnicity, and other factors should not determine the type of treatment or form of punishment one receives from various criminal justice agencies.

Efficiency.   The system should be organized and managed in a manner to ensure maximum utilization of personnel and resources.

Effectiveness.   The justice system should operate in an effective manner.

Justice. Justice is considered as the ideal goal of all governments and the disposition of a criminal matter in such a manner that the best interest of society is served. It is not measured solely by its application to the accused. Justice is the broad concept of reward and punishment currently accepted as proper by a society. A state court judge in an early Texas case defined justice as follows:

> Justice is the dictate of right, according to the common consent of mankind generally, or of that portion of mankind who may be associated in one government, or who may be governed by the same principles and morals.

Standards Organizations such as the American Bar Association and the American Correctional Association have developed detailed goals to improve the justice system. These goals are called standards. For the most part, standards are designed to protect individual rights and promote the efficiency of the justice process. (*Note:* Standards are goals, not binding rules.) Selected standards on criminal justice are as follows:

American Bar Association Standards *Relating to the Prosecution Function*

1.4 Duty to Improve the Law
It is an important function of the prosecutor to seek to reform and improve the administration of criminal justice. When inadequacies or injustices in the substantive or procedural law come to his or her attention, he or she should stimulate efforts for remedial action.

2.7 Relations with the Police
a. The prosecutor should provide legal advice to the police concerning police functions and duties in criminal matters.
b. The prosecutor should cooperate with police in providing the services of his or her staff to aid in training police in the performance of their function in accordance with the law.

National Advisory Commission on Criminal Justice Standards and Goals

4.11 Priority Case Scheduling
Cases should be given priority for trial where one or more of the following factors are present:
a. The defendant is in pretrial custody;
b. The defendant constitutes a significant threat of violent injury to others;
c. The defendant is a recidivist;
d. The defendant is a professional criminal;
e. The defendant is a public official.

6.5 Further Review
After a reviewing court has affirmed a trial court conviction and sentence, or after the expiration of a fair opportunity for a defendant to obtain a review with the aid of counsel, the conviction and the sentence generally should be final and not subject to further review in any state or federal court. Further review should be available only in unusual circumstances.

JUSTICE SYSTEM STRUCTURE AND PROCESS

We refer to the justice system as a system as if it were a formal system. It would be more accurate to refer to it as a nonsystem. The term system refers only to the interrelationship among all those agencies concerned with the prevention of crime in society. The systems approach to criminal justice sees a change in one part of the system affecting change in all the others. It implies that a closely knit, coordinated structure of organizations exists among the various components of the system.

The justice system, however, is not a close-knit, coordinated structure of organizations. It is actually three separate elements: police, courts, and correction institutions. Each operates almost independently of the others. In many cases, the goal orientations of the various elements within a local jurisdiction are in conflict with each other concerning the main functions of the criminal justice system. Thus the system can best be described as fragmented or divided. Accordingly, the criminal justice system is a group of agencies organized around various functions that each agency is assigned.

Evolution of Criminal Procedure

Our system of criminal justice is based on English common law. The colonists brought English traditions and concepts with them when they settled our country. Included was the English concept of justice on which our system is based. To this foundation, a bit of Spanish and French influence was added as the system was developed and changed to meet the requirements of our growing nation.

Foundational Concepts in Criminal Procedure

As an introduction to the study of criminal procedure, the foundational concepts in criminal procedure below should be considered. These concepts will be explained in the text and are listed here to create an awareness of their existence.

- The guarantees of the Bill of Rights in the U.S. Constitution apply directly only to the federal government.
- The Due Process Clause of the Fourteenth Amendment by selective incorporation applies most of the rights contained in the Bill of Rights to the states.
- State constitutions may provide rights to citizens in addition to those provided for in the U.S. Constitution but may not restrict the rights granted by the Constitution.
- The two questions regarding the burden of proof in criminal proceedings are: (1) Who has the burden of proving an issue? and (2) What is the magnitude of the burden? The magnitude may be (1) proof beyond a reasonable doubt, (2) clear and convincing evidence, or (3) preponderance of evidence.
- Charges in a criminal trial must first be formalized either by an indictment returned by a grand jury or by information prepared by a prosecutor.
- Prior to trial, both the prosecution and the defense may submit pretrial motions, and both have discovery rights imposed on them.
- Our system of criminal procedure is based on the adversarial process.

Two famous quotes from U.S. Supreme Court Justice Oliver Wendell Holmes should be noted:

- "Whatever disagreement there may be as to the scope of the phrase 'due process of law,' there can be no doubt that it embraces the fundamental conception of a fair trial, with opportunity to be heard." [*Frank* v. *Mangum,* 237 N.S. 309, 347 (1914).]
- "The life of the law has not been logic, it has been experience." [The Common Law (1881) 1.]

Supreme Court Justice Oliver Wendell Holmes (1841–1935), the son of the poet Oliver Wendell Holmes. He was appointed to the Supreme Court by President Theodore Roosevelt. Photo taken in 1920. (*Source:* Getty Images Inc.-Hutton Archive Photos.)

EARLY DEVELOPMENT OF LAWS

A law in its simplest form is merely a guideline for human behavior. Its purpose is to encourage people to do what is right and discourage them from doing what is wrong. A law has been described as a social tool to mold and regulate human conduct. Legally, a law is defined as an act of a legislative body written and recorded in some public repository, informing people of what is right and wrong. In the case of *Koenig* v. *Flynn,* it was stated as "that which must be obeyed and followed by citizens, subject to sanctions or legal consequences, is a law."[1]

The next question to be answered is, Are laws necessary today? It has been stated frequently that laws are made to be broken. Also, it has been alleged that if there were no laws, they would not be broken. In fairness to the declarant of this statement, it is only logical to assume that if there were nothing to break, nothing would be broken. So we return to the question, Are laws necessary? Before answering, it may be well to consider what the origin of laws is and why they came into being.

A human being comes into the world with certain basic needs that remain throughout his or her life. These are the needs for food, shelter, companionship, and sexual gratification. If untrained and uncontrolled, a person may attempt to satisfy these needs in a most animalistic manner. If one were completely isolated from all other human beings, the fashion in which one might try to satisfy personal needs would be relatively unimportant. However, the moment one comes in contact with another person, the needs of each individual must be considered, and each must respect the desires of the other. Each person must learn to realize that his or her liberties cease where the other's begin. Certain restraints upon activity must be imposed. Thus, there is a necessity for some guidelines about satisfying personal needs without infringing upon the rights of others.

People may agree upon a division of territory, and each will confine his or her activities to that territory. If this arrangement takes place, there is little reason for other guidelines, but if they agree to combine their efforts, further regulations must be made. It must be decided who will do what and how they will share. As more and more persons enter the picture, the necessity for more rules becomes apparent. Eventually, it will be necessary to choose a leader or chief to see that the rules are followed and to keep order within the tribe or society.

Undoubtedly, many of the early established guidelines came about through trial and error. When it was recognized that a tribal member committed an act that threatened the existence of the tribe, a restraint against that act was created, and a violation of that restraint was what we now know as a crime. It probably did not take long for members of a primitive tribe to learn that they could not kill each other and still have the tribe continue to exist. Therefore, rules against murder were established. To satisfy a person's need for food and shelter, that person devised certain tools that became his or her property. The taking of these tools by another, depriving the owner of their use, was a serious act, so a rule against theft was enacted. People took mates to satisfy their needs for companionship and sexual gratification. The mate was also personal property, and to violate that property right was an offense, so that rules against adultery were formed.

As tribes or societies grew in number and became somewhat more sophisticated, so did their regulations. As time passed, people developed the belief in a deity. Regulations respecting this belief were also established, and the violation of these regulations was a serious offense against the society.

Code of Hammurabi

The **Code of Hammurabi** is considered one of the first known attempts to establish a written code of conduct. King Hammurabi ruled Babylon in approximately 2000 B.C. He was the sixth king of the First Dynasty of Babylonia for about fifty-five years. Babylon during that period of time was a commercial center for most of the known and civilized world. Since its fortune lay in trade and other business ventures, the Code of Hammurabi provided a basis for the order and certainty that were essential for commerce. The code established rules regarding theft, sexual relationships, and interpersonal violence. It was intended to replace blood feuds with a system sanctioned by the state.

The Code of Hammurabi was divided into five sections:

A penal or code of laws

A manual of instruction for judges, police officers, and witnesses

A handbook of rights and duties of husbands, wives, and children

A set of regulations establishing wages and prices

A code of ethics for merchants, doctors, and officials

The code established certain obligations and objectives for the citizens of Babylon to follow. These included the following elements:

An Assertion of the Power of the State This was the beginning of state-administered punishment. The blood feuds that had occurred previously between private citizens were barred under the code.

Stele of Hammurabi—detail of the upper part. The sun god dictating his laws to King Hammurabi. Babylon relief from Susa c. 1760 B.C. (diorite: height of stele c. 2.1. m; height of relief 71 cm). Louvre, Paris, France. (*Source:* Copyright Giraudon/Art Resource, New York.)

Protection of the Weaker From the Stronger   Widows were to be protected from those who might exploit them, elder parents were protected from sons who would disown them, and lesser officials were protected from higher officials.

Restoration of Equity Between the Offender and the Victim   The victim was to be made as whole as possible and, in turn, he or she was required to forgive vengeance against the offender.

Of noteworthy importance in the code was its concern for the rights of victims. In reality, this code may have been the first victims' rights statute in history. Unfortunately, as will be seen, society began to neglect victims in its rush to punish the offenders, with the result that victims' rights would not resurface until the twentieth century.

Biblical historians tell us that when Moses led the Israelites out of Egypt, some thirteen hundred years before Christ, he quickly realized that these people must have some guidelines to follow if they were to continue to exist. Through an inspiration from God, ten basic rules known as the Ten Commandments were established. Included were not only those laws that earlier tribes found necessary for existence, that is, rules against murder, theft, and adultery, but also more sophisticated rules that pertained to admonitions against not respecting God. In addition were admonitions against certain thoughts that people may conceive that might lead them to greedy actions. Thus, a person should not covet his or her neighbor's property. When Moses gave these guidelines to the people of Israel, he commanded them to obey them, since they would ensure life and entrance into the possession of the land. He further indicated that these laws were not to be tampered with in the interest of human weakness. There was no mention that these laws were made to be broken. Nor has there been any suggestion by anyone in authority since that time that laws are made to be broken.

Because of the effect of ecclesiastical law on the nations of Europe, most of these commandments were incorporated into their laws and, in turn, were brought to this country by the colonists. Our early criminal laws included laws against murder, theft, adultery, working on Sunday ("blue laws"), profanity, and perjury, as well as rules describing family responsibilities. Although we have become a more permissive society and take some of the earlier guidelines less seriously, a few of the Ten Commandments are still found in the criminal laws of all the states of this nation, because they are necessary for the existence of any society. These are the laws against murder, theft, perjury, and adultery; other laws are added to these from time to time.

As societies become more complex, so do their laws. New restraints are placed upon people's activities. These laws are designed with the hope that people can and will live more peacefully and pleasantly with their fellow human beings. Again we see, from a sociological standpoint, that laws are necessary for humankind's existence. From a legal standpoint, laws are necessary to inform people of what is right and what is wrong. People must be made aware of the acts for which, if committed, they may be prosecuted. In our form of government, each criminal law must be spelled out in detail so that a person may know the exact act that, if committed, is a violation of the law. If a law is considered too vague, it will be declared null and void.

COMMON LAW

Much of the basic criminal law of this country originated from the common law of England. Originally, the common law of England was nothing more than a set of unwritten regulations and customs that acted as guidelines in settling disputes, determining the inheritance of property, and dealing with persons who committed misdeeds of a serious antisocial nature. As time passed, court decisions were made a part of the common law. Thereafter, the common law was further enlarged by legislative enactments and was brought to this country by the colonists to act as guidelines for conduct.

MODERN CRIMINAL LAW

Today, the criminal law of the various states is a written set of regulations that is largely the result of legislative action. These regulations are recorded in some official record within the states and are often referred to as the penal code. Criminal laws vary somewhat among the states. In some states, there is no reliance upon the common law to determine what is right and wrong. The statutes spell out specifically the act that is made a crime and the punishment that may be inflicted for the commission of such an act. For example, the law may state that manslaughter is the unlawful killing of a human being without malice. This definition will be followed by a statement that one convicted of manslaughter may be imprisoned for a period not to exceed four years. The statutes of other states provide that manslaughter is punishable by imprisonment not to exceed a prescribed number of years. But these latter statutes do not define what act constitutes manslaughter. The courts must then look to the common law to determine the interpretation of manslaughter.

CLASSIFICATION OF CRIMES AND PUNISHMENT

In our present form of jurisprudence, not only do we tell people what a criminal act is, but we also tell them the punishment they may be subjected to if they commit the act. The following definition is generally found in the statutes of the states: A crime or public offense is an act committed or omitted in violation of a law forbidding or commanding it and to which is annexed, upon conviction, one or more of several punishments. The basic forms of punishment are death, imprisonment, fines, removal from office, or disqualification to hold and enjoy any office of honor, trust, or profit. We have classified criminal laws in accordance with their seriousness to society and have stated the punishment that could be inflicted upon conviction. Earlier in our history, we classified criminal laws as treason, felonies, and misdemeanors. Most states eliminated treason as a category of crime and listed it merely as another felony violation. Thus, two classifications remained: felonies and misdemeanors. However, in recent years, many states have added a third and a fourth classification, an infraction and a state jail felony.

With the felony being the most serious crime, the violator is subjected to the most severe punishment either by death, imprisonment in a state prison, or a sentence of more than one year. The misdemeanor, being a less serious threat to the existence of a society, carries a lesser punishment, the most severe of which is usually not more than a year in

Television attorney "Eleanor" (C. Manheim) pleading a case in a courtroom in the television series *The Practice.* (*Source:* Photofest.)

jail. The infraction is the least serious crime, carrying a fine or probation but, in most states, no imprisonment. The state jail felony is a crime that is more serious than a misdemeanor but not as serious as a felony.

The procedure by which one accused of a crime is brought to trial and punished is known as a criminal action, and the one prosecuted is known as the defendant. Criminal actions are commenced with the filing of a formal written document with the appropriate court. In some states, there is no requirement to file a formal written document in cases involving infractions. The charging document is referred to as an accusatory pleading. In most felony prosecutions, the document will be an indictment or an information. In misdemeanor prosecutions, the accusatory pleading is generally a complaint, as explained in Chapter 4. When a criminal law is broken, it is done against society as a whole, so that the prosecutive action is brought in the name of the people; thus, the action is generally entitled "People versus [the defendant]," "State versus [the defendant]," or "Commonwealth versus [the defendant]," stating the defendant's name.

JUSTICE SYSTEM

When examining the criminal justice system, we will discover many technical rules and procedures that must be followed. These rules and procedures are the result of a long evolutionary process. The process is interesting, particularly the development of the right of an accused to a trial by jury. Trial by jury, for example, is regarded by many as one of the greatest achievements of our justice system.

When considering trial by jury, we immediately visualize a comfortable courtroom with a judge sitting behind a desk on a raised platform and presiding over the trial proceedings in a dignified and formal manner. We see the jury sitting in the jury box listening to the testimony of witnesses who have some knowledge about the facts of the case and the prosecuting attorney presenting evidence in an effort to prove the defendant guilty beyond a reasonable doubt. We also tend to see the defense attorney as an Eleanor in *The Practice*. We may also picture the defendant conferring with the attorney throughout the trial. At the conclusion of the trial, we visualize the jury deliberating on the evidence that has been presented and returning a verdict of guilt or innocence. The actual practice may, however, be quite different.

Guilt or innocence has not always been decided by a jury trial. In fact, the jury system as we know it today is of comparatively recent origin, coming into existence at the start of the eighteenth century. The early history of jurisprudence efforts to determine guilt or innocence were primarily calls upon the supernatural or for signs from God.

As we trace the development of trial by jury, we focus primarily on England, from which most of our judicial system came. Many blank spots are encountered in tracing the history of a jury trial because of the lack of records. But it is known that the Christian church played an important role in the development of much of the law and procedure of early England. Most of the early records available for study of the beginnings of the judicial system were prepared by the clergy and are largely incomplete. These records were not compiled as a history of the time but were merely a documentation of certain customs and events of the era.

Invasion of England

History states that Julius Caesar invaded England in 55 B.C. and that Christianity was taught there as early as A.D. 64. At that time, Christianity was not accepted by the Romans, and any activity of the Christian church throughout the Roman Empire had to be underground. Yet despite the persecution of Christians, their church continued to grow. Religious societies and new congregations were formed. Rules, regulations, and laws were established to be followed by the Christians, but they were unlawful in the eyes of the Romans. However, these laws were soon to become the laws of the continent

Roman Emperor Julius Caesar stands on a chariot overlooking his soldiers brandishing swords on a battlefield, as depicted in a sketch. (*Source:* Corbis/Bettmann.)

of Europe and England. By the year A.D. 200, Roman jurisprudence had reached its peak, and from that time on, Roman law began to decline. Instead of looking forward, the Roman leaders were looking backward to what had been. The Roman persecution of Christians terminated in A.D. 303: and in A.D. 313, Christianity was established as a lawful religion. Almost immediately the bishops of the Christian church involved themselves in politics, and they soon became as powerful as the emperor. The Church law, also known as the canon or ecclesiastical law, began to dominate the lives of people throughout Europe.

There is little doubt that Julius Caesar imported much of the Roman law to England, but the Romans did not have an easy life there because other people invaded England. The Saxons conducted raids on the coastal plains as early as the third century and continued to do so thereafter. The Romans are said to have abandoned England sometime before A.D. 429, and the Anglo-Saxon invasions began on a large scale in A.D. 449. The Anglo-Saxons are believed to have established laws, since they were known to have existed on the continent of Europe at the time, but records of the Anglo-Saxon laws and procedures are mostly fragmentary. Those that are available shed little light upon the judicial procedures of that time. It is known that kings established themselves and ruled until they were overthrown or died. A king formulated his own laws, which were known as the king's laws, laws of the land, temporal laws, or secular laws. The Anglo-Saxons held reign in England until the Norman Conquest in A.D. 1066. Prior to this time, England had experienced considerable strife. Much of the administration of justice was left to the bishops of the church, to be processed through the ecclesiastical courts, and the canon law continued to play a dominant role. But as kings began to establish themselves more securely, they continued to formulate more and more laws affecting the people.

These laws were enforced through the king's courts, known as secular or temporal courts. The king's court was presided over by the king's justices.

Although an effort was made to separate the jurisdiction of the secular courts and the ecclesiastical courts, rivalry still arose, particularly as it related to appeals. The ecclesiastical courts had jurisdiction over all matters pertaining to people's souls and church-related matters, including violations by the clergy. All laypeople were subject to both the ecclesiastical laws and the secular laws. The ecclesiastical laws regulated many affairs of the layperson's life, such as marriage, divorce, and the distribution of property after death. Through the ecclesiastical courts, laypeople could be tried and punished for various offenses, including such crimes as adultery, fornication, incest, bigamy, defamation, and blasphemy. Originally, the ecclesiastical courts were presided over by the bishops of the church, but as the caseload increased, charges were often heard by the bishops' assistants, known as archdeacons. Crimes of murder or theft and attacks on property or persons were violations of the secular laws, and the offender was tried and punished by the secular courts.

Magna Charta

When an offender was convicted, his or her property was usually forfeited. This forfeiture became a source of great revenue to the church or king, depending upon what law was broken. In order to increase their revenue, kings frequently made various acts a crime in order to confiscate the property of a landowner or merchant. How the people fared depended largely on the compassion of the king at the time. In tracing our judicial procedure, frequent mention is made of the Magna Charta (also spelled Magna Carta) and its influence on *people's* rights. This document is considered to be the forerunner of the present **due process** rights, since the Magna Charta granted to the people of England certain political and civil rights. The Magna Charta, which is the result of a king's being unduly oppressive to the people of England, was signed during the reign of King John, who was known as the cruel ruler.

King John took over the reign of England in A.D. 1199 after the death of his brother, King Richard, the "Lion Hearted." King John was described as being clever but greedy and tyrannical in ruling his people. Conditions under him became unbearable for both the nobleman and the commoner. In an effort to improve the situation, the noblemen gathered and prepared a document containing certain resolutions that they felt were in the best interest of the people. King John was maneuvered onto the Plains of Runnymede on June 15, 1215, where he was forced to sign the Magna Charta. Among other resolutions in the Magna Charta was the guarantee that, stated briefly, held that no free man shall be seized and imprisoned except by judgment of his peers or by the law of the land. Contrary to the beliefs of many, this guarantee did not give people the right to a trial by jury. Trial by jury, as we know it today, did not come into existence until the latter part of the seventeenth century. It merely meant that when a criminal accusation was made against a person, he or she was entitled to have the charge reviewed by a council consisting of members of the community. If the council concluded that the charge was well founded,

King John shown signing the Magna Charta (1215). Undated illustration, after a painting by Chapel. (*Source:* Corbis/Bettmann.)

they would command that the accused be held to answer for trial. Guilt or innocence was decided by the procedures of the time—**trial by ordeal** or trial by battle. This council, which became known as a grand jury, comprised between sixteen and twenty-four persons.

The right of an accused to appeal his or her case was practically unknown in early judicial procedure. But as time passed, a limited right of appeal was granted. Appeals in the ecclesiastical courts, in the twelfth century particularly, were taken to the bishop from the court presided over by an archdeacon, and from the bishop to the archbishop. The final appeal was to the pope in Rome. The final appeal from the king's court was to the king. Although the kings for the most part respected the jurisdiction of the ecclesiastical courts, this final appeal to the pope was upsetting to the kings. The inevitable result of this final appeal to the pope was to give recognition to the fact that the canon law was a worldwide system and was not limited to any national boundary. The kings were jealous of the pope's outside influence, over which the kings had little control, so that they often tried to restrict this influence. King William I declared that no one was to receive a letter from the pope unless it was first shown to him. Later, other kings declared that there should be no appeal to the pope without consent of the king. Yet with all the kings' jealousy of the pope, King John, in his desperation, sought the assistance of Pope Innocent III after he was forced to sign the Magna Charta on June 15, 1215. King John requested that the pope annul the Magna Charta, which he did on August 25, 1215. The pope further forbade the king to enforce the Magna Charta upon the grounds that this charter was extorted from King John by force and that the terms of the charter were "dishonorable, unjust, unlawful, and derogatory" to the king. But after the death of King John in October 1216, the Magna Charta was revised, and its provisions were again placed into operation. It was expected that kings thereafter would comply with these provisions.

Early Treatment of Offenders

With the church playing the paramount role in the administration of justice in the early history of England, it is only natural that the deity was called upon to assist when efforts were made to determine the guilt or innocence of one accused of a crime. From the time of the invasion of England by the Romans until the Norman Conquest, a person accused of breaking the law could be handled in one of four ways:

- The community could make war on the offender;
- the offender might be exposed to the vengeance of those he had offended;
- the offender might be permitted to make atonement for his crime; or
- the community might inflict upon the offender the penalty already established for the particular crime after his or her guilt had been determined.

Outlawry

Perhaps the earliest method of handling one who was accused of committing a crime was to wage war upon the accused. It was held that when one had gone to war with the community by committing a crime, the community was not only entitled to, but bound to, make war upon the offender. The accused was declared "outlawed," or without the protection of the law. Thus, the community was to pursue and slay the offender, burn the offender's house, ravage his or her land, and take his or her possessions. As time passed, this form of punishment was inflicted upon only the person of lowest status, the slave. The declaration was, in effect, the imposition of the death penalty, because without the protection of the community, the individual would soon be killed by others or by wild beasts.

Blood Feud

If the accused was not outlawed, the community might leave the accused unprotected against those he or she had offended, whereupon they might avenge themselves by taking whatever action they deemed appropriate in accordance with the crime committed, even to the slaying of the offender. Some of the offender's relatives might be slain also, since not all persons were of the same status in the early history of England. The lowest status was that of slave; next was the serf, who was bound to native soil instead of being the absolute property of a master like the slave; then status continued up to the highest, that of king. In between were a number of other classes of persons, such as the barons and knights, who were referred to as "thegns"; the freeman workers were known as "ceorls." It was alleged that six ceorls were the equivalent of one thegn. Thus, if a ceorl should slay a thegn, the slayer and five of his or her kinsfolk also would have to be slain. However, it might take time to locate the kinsfolk in order to slay them, and other members of the family might inherit the responsibility of avenging the crime; thus, the blood feud took place.

Atonement

There is no doubt that blood feuds were not the most popular method of settling a crime that had been committed, particularly when the blood feud reached a point where relatives of the offended or offender became involved in avenging the crime. It is only natural that the relatives would prefer to conduct some type of financial bargaining rather than engage in a lengthy hunt for the offender or the offender's relatives and then become involved in a bloody entanglement to avenge a crime. Frequently, a price of so many cows or horses, or a sum of money, was agreed upon, which the offender or the relatives could pay in order to bring about peace in the community. Thus, the system of atonement was established. Each particular crime developed a designated price that had to be paid when that crime was committed. Even murder could be atoned under certain circumstances, depending upon the status of the offender and the offended. **Atonement** was an accepted procedure in most instances, not only by the offended but also by the church and the king, since each would receive a portion of the atonement, depending upon the crime. For example, if a couple were caught committing adultery, the man paid the king in order to regain his peace in the community, whereas the woman paid the church for the sin she had committed. If the offender was without possessions, in order to make atonement, he or she might have to go into bondage or be subjected to a prescribed punishment. The system of atonement is the forerunner of the present procedures of fining persons for having committed certain crimes.

Trial by Ordeal

Since not all persons were permitted to make atonement, other procedures had to be devised to bring those guilty of having committed a crime to justice. One of the most prevalent methods utilized in determining the guilt or innocence of an accused was the trial by ordeal. The accused was required to perform some physical feat. This procedure was a call to the deity for assistance in determining the guilt or innocence of the accused. The theory was that if the accused were innocent, God would enable him or her to perform the required ordeal. If guilty, the accused would fail in his or her performance. The accused would then be subjected to the prescribed punishment for the crime committed. When punishment was inflicted, it was usually severe. The punishment may have been death by hanging, beheading, stoning, burning, or drowning. If the punishment did not amount to death, the guilty one might have one or both ears cut off, have the nose or upper lip severed, have a hand or foot cut off, be castrated, or be flogged, tarred, and feathered. People who had falsely accused someone might lose their tongues. In addition, they might be banished from the land (a punishment that was later referred to as outlawry) or be sold into slavery.

The ordeal that the accused might be subjected to varied greatly in procedure, but whatever it may have been, it was preceded by an oath by the accused; this was an oath of innocence to God. If found guilty by failing in the ordeal, the accused would not only suffer the punishment inflicted upon him or her but also would receive divine punishment according to the belief of the time. Most of the ordeals were supervised by priests.

The most prevalent ordeal used was that of the hot iron. The accused would appear before the altar, give the oath, and then have a hand sprinkled with holy water. A red-hot iron would be laid across the hand, and the accused would take nine paces and drop the iron. The accused would return to the altar, where a priest would bind the burned hand. Three days later, the accused would return to the priest and have the hand unbound. If the wound had healed, the accused was found innocent; if it had not healed, the accused was judged guilty and was then subjected to the prescribed punishment in accordance with the crime committed.

Another type of ordeal was that of the boiling pot of water from which the accused might be required to remove a large rock. The same binding procedure would be followed as in the ordeal of the hot iron. It would seem that under this system there would be few acquittals, but apparently many priests felt compassion for those accused and assisted God in determining guilt or innocence. Records reveal that in one period there were eighty-three acquittals out of eighty-four trials by ordeal. Upon viewing the wound, the priest declared that it had healed. This record of acquittals caused the king much displeasure because of the loss of revenue.

The accused might be subjected to other types of ordeals in addition to the hot iron and boiling pot of water. For example, the accused might be required to walk barefoot and blindfolded over nine red-hot ploughshares laid lengthwise at unequal distances, or the accused might have his or her thumbs tied to the toes and be thrown into a lake or pond. If the accused did not sink, he or she was declared innocent. Also used was the ordeal of the accursed morsel, whereby a piece of bread was prayed over. It was then given to the accused, who was to swallow it. If the person choked, he or she was found guilty. The decision of the cross involved laying two pieces of wood on an altar, one of which had been marked with a cross. After a prayer asking for a sign from God, a priest or young boy picked up one of the pieces of wood without looking at it. If it bore the mark of a cross, the accused was deemed to be innocent.

Trial by Battle

Another method of determining guilt or innocence was trial by battle. In this method, the accused and the accuser would go into actual combat with each other, usually using battle axes. Before the battle took place, both participants would swear to God that they were right. It is believed that the trial-by-battle procedure was brought to England by the Normans. It is known that trial by battle was used as a method of determining guilt on the continent before the Norman Conquest, and there is no record of its use in England before the Norman invasion. The church displayed less favor to trial by battle than to trial by ordeal because it involved a certain amount of pagan ceremony. However, trial by battle was tolerated because it also involved a call to God, and the one who came forth the victor did so not from brute force but through the assistance of God.

Trial by Compurgation

The church was always seeking ways to determine the guilt or innocence of an accused person without the tortures of the ordeal or the bloodshed of the battle, particularly when its own hierarchy was involved. It is believed that determining guilt by compurgation, through oath helpers or wager of the law, by which terms it was also known, originated within the church, but the method was not confined to church personnel. For a time, it was used for laypeople, since it related to violations of the secular and ecclesiastical laws. Trial by compurgation originated on the continent of Europe, but there are records indicating its existence in England before the Norman Conquest.

In the trial by compurgation, both the accused and the accuser would take an oath to God. The accused would swear to his or her innocence, and the accuser would swear that the accusation was true. Each would be assisted by oath helpers, or compurgators. The compurgators of the accused would swear to God that the oath given by the accused was a true oath. The accuser would be accompanied by oath helpers who would swear to his or her truthfulness.

Initially, the accused's oath helpers were often relatives, and if the accused failed in the oath-taking experience, the matter might turn into a blood feud; consequently, the relatives were usually very willing to assist, although their assistance frequently led to perjury. Because of the unreliability of the relatives as oath helpers, the accused soon had to select oath helpers from among persons in the community who were not relatives. If the accused had a bad reputation, he or she might experience difficulty in getting oath helpers. An oath helper might be compared with a character witness in our present judicial system. In some instances, the accused had to select oath helpers from a list supplied to him or her by the accuser or by one of the priests or justices involved. Many times the accused was unknown to these persons, so they were permitted to swear to the truthfulness of the accused's oath to the best of their knowledge and belief. The number of oath helpers that was called to assist varied considerably. Any number between four and sixty-six was called, but most frequently the number was twelve.

Although trial by compurgation was used for a time, it did not replace the trial by ordeal or the trial by battle. As time passed, the wording of the oath to be taken by the accused and the oath helpers became so complex that repeating it without error was almost impossible. If an error was made, the accused was automatically declared guilty, and the prescribed punishment was inflicted. Thus, with the technical language of the oath and the general unreliability of the oath helpers, trial by compurgation was somewhat of a farce. It therefore soon fell into decay and disuse, and other methods were adopted to determine guilt or innocence.

Establishment of Juries

As early as the ninth century, Frankish kings on the European continent would summon, through a public officer, the most trustworthy people of a community.

THE FIRST PETIT JURY IMPANELED TO TRY JEFFERSON DAVIS IN MAY, 1867

The first petit jury appointed to try Confederate President Jefferson Davis in 1867.
(*Source:* Library of Congress.)

These people were then placed under oath to answer truthfully all questions directed at them during sessions with the king. These sessions, which were called inquests, did not necessarily arise out of criminal activity or litigation but were often merely fact-finding meetings in which the king could gather information about the community. During the inquest, the king might ask the following kinds of questions: What were the rights of the king in their particular community? Who were the landowners, and how much land did they own? What were the customs of their area? Who had a better title to a piece of property, John or James? The number of people summoned to serve on this body varied from three to seventy-two, but twelve was the number most frequently called.

In addition to seeking the answers to these kinds of questions, the king would ask this body whom they suspected of having committed murder, rape, or robbery. This body was the first crude form of an accusatory jury. But the Frankish kings did not always use the jury merely to accuse a person of a crime; in fact, they often called upon the jury to render a verdict of guilt or innocence. In order to collect their revenue for crimes committed, these kings frequently preferred the verdict of this body of people over that of a trial by ordeal, battle, or compurgation. During the early use of the jury by kings, it is not inconceivable that people may have found themselves accused and convicted without even knowing that an accusation had been directed at them.

To collect the wages of sin, the Frankish bishops were also known to have used the inquest to determine who had committed crimes against the church. Records reflect that certain Frankish bishops selected a number of trustworthy men from an assembled laity, or congregation, who were administered an oath to tell the truth and conceal nothing for love or hate, reward or kinship, and to report their suspicions about their neighbors who might have sinned against the church. These suspected sinners then would be put through the ordeal.

There is little record of the inquest being used in England until after the Norman Conquest. However, Ethelred the Unready, King of England, is alleged to have decreed early in the eleventh century that a moot was to be held in every "wapentake," and that the twelve eldest thegns were to go out with the "reeve" and swear on a relic that they would neither accuse an innocent person nor conceal a guilty person. In our terminology, a meeting was to be held in every county subdivision where the eldest trustworthy members of that community were to go out with a local representative of the king and swear on some religious object that they would neither accuse an innocent person nor conceal one guilty of a crime.

Accusatory Juries

Hardly had England been conquered in A.D. 1066 when William the Conqueror summoned bodies of people from all the communities to assist him in obtaining general as well as criminal information concerning their respective areas. In the mid-twelfth century, King Henry II made great use of the juries to determine what cases his justices should hear as they rode their circuits through the kingdom. He summoned twelve of the most trustworthy noblemen of a hundred (or county) and four men from each township, who were sworn to hear accusations and determine whether they were well founded. If so, the accused was given an opportunity to prove his or her innocence by one of the various trial procedures.

King Henry II also suggested that the bishops of the ecclesiastical courts should not rely merely upon an accuser's unsworn suggestion that someone had committed a crime before subjecting the accused to the ordeal, battle, or compurgation. Rather, the bishops should have the sheriff summon twelve of the most lawful men of the neighborhood to hear an accusation to determine its reliability before the accused was put on trial.

The accusatory jury had become such an important part of justice by the beginning of the thirteenth century that when King John ignored its use and acted upon his own knowledge of accusations, the right to an accusatory jury was made a part of the Magna Charta. Included in the provisions of the Magna Charta was this guarantee: "No freeman shall be taken, or imprisoned, or disseized, or outlawed, or exiled, in any way harmed—nor will we go upon or send upon him—save by the lawful judgment of his peers or by the law of the land." It was expected that King John and all following kings would comply with this guarantee—the forerunner of our grand jury system.

Development of Trial by Jury

As time passed, greater use of the jury was made. It was called upon not only to decide whether an accusation was well founded but also, as in the case of some of the Frankish kings' juries, to render a verdict of guilt or innocence. It was eventually believed that a jury should not be both an accusatory jury and a trial or verdict jury. Consequently, one jury would be summoned to hear the accusation (later referred to as the grand jury), and another jury was summoned to render a verdict of guilt or innocence (known as the petit jury). The petit, or trial, jury, which usually consisted of twelve persons, initially functioned entirely differently from the juries of today. These early trial juries assembled and stated what they knew about a particular crime, or they might be assembled and commanded to go forth into the countryside and ascertain facts about the alleged crime. Then the jurors would talk to neighbors, pick up hearsay information and rumors, and undoubtedly be contacted by the accused and the accuser. After gathering their evidence, they would reassemble and draw a conclusion as to guilt or innocence. If the accused was found guilty, the prescribed punishment for the crime was inflicted upon him or her. Soon it was not just the jurors who stated what they had learned about the crime: witnesses might appear before the jury and relate what they knew about the accusation. Since the knowledge of the witnesses was often no more than rumor or hearsay, the jury might give little weight to their testimony and decide contrary to the general consensus of the witnesses. This outcome was particularly likely if the witnesses believed the accused to be innocent. The reason that the jury might decide contrary to the belief of the witnesses was that the jury was fearful of rendering a false verdict, thus denying the king his revenue. The jurors knew that the king's justices often had advance information about a crime because of reports from the sheriffs and the coroners. If the jurors made a false verdict in the eyes of the justices, they would be required to make atonement and were even punished in some instances.

Because of the danger of conviction in a trial by jury, an accused would frequently revert to the trial by ordeal. However, after the ordeal was abolished around A.D. 1215 and trial by compurgation had met with disfavor, the only procedure remaining was trial by battle. But if the accuser was a woman or a noncombatant, trial by battle was impossible, so it was unknown what should be done with the accused who refused a trial by jury or who put himself or herself upon the country, as the jury trial was sometimes referred to. Occasionally, under the circumstances, the accused was hanged immediately or, in other instances, was imprisoned for a year and given only a sip of water daily and a small morsel of bread. Sometimes the accused was imprisoned and weights were placed on his or her chest in increasing amounts until the person submitted to a trial by jury. Often the accused preferred being crushed to death in an effort to save his or her possessions for his or her family, rather than having them confiscated by the king, should the jury pass a conviction.

As time passed and the king could no longer confiscate property as payment for crimes and jurors were no longer punished or required to make atonement for possibly erroneous verdicts, greater reliance was placed on the testimony of witnesses. Accordingly, the development of trial by jury progressed to what we know today. However, it still had a way to go even when the colonists settled in this country. The Maryland Archives reveal that on September 22, 1656, a judge in Patuxent, Maryland, impaneled a jury of seven married women and four single women to determine the guilt of one Judith Catchpole, who was accused of murdering her child. She denied guilt and even denied having a child. The judge then commanded the jury to go forth and determine first whether Judith had a child and, if so, whether she had murdered it. At this time, the jury was to "go forth into the countryside and seek information" rather than depend upon the sworn testimony of witnesses. It is also interesting that a jury of eleven instead of twelve was impaneled, because long before that time, the number of twelve jurors for a trial was well established in England. By the thirteenth century, the usual number for a petit jury in England was twelve. By the fourteenth century, a jury of twelve persons was firmly established, and thereafter the number of twelve persons composing a trial jury seems to have developed some superstitious reverence.

Why a jury of twelve evolved is lost in the annals of history, but it is believed to have been based upon Christ's having chosen twelve apostles. It has been alleged that twelve was a popular number at the time of Christ, as witnessed by the twelve tribes of Israel, the twelve tablets, Solomon's twelve judges, and the twelve signs of the zodiac. Thus, it is highly likely that the jury comprising twelve persons is based upon that fact, especially since the church played a dominant role in the development of the judicial systems in both Europe and England. One of the ancient kings of Europe, Morgan of Gla-Morgan, is alleged to have adopted a form of trial by jury called the Apostolic Law, which declared that since Christ and his twelve apostles were finally to judge the world, so human tribunals should comprise the king and twelve wise men. Also at a later time, the following oath is alleged to have been required of a trial jury of twelve: "Hear this, ye justices, that I will speak of that which ye shall ask of me on the part of the king, and I will do faithfully to the best of my endeavor. So help me God, and these holy Apostles."

When the colonists came to North America, they were well indoctrinated with the view that a trial jury should comprise twelve persons, although it is known that one or two of the colonies permitted a jury to comprise fewer than twelve. It is not entirely clear from historical data whether permitting fewer than twelve was a conscious effort to break from tradition, a defiance of the king and England, or whether it was because of the small number of people in the colonies involved, making it difficult to find twelve qualified jurors. This situation may have accounted for the fact that the judge in the Catchpole case impaneled only eleven women instead of twelve. It was also a break with tradition to impanel women instead of men, since women were not generally considered to be qualified as jurors.

Historical Development of the Bill of Rights

As we approach the study of the judicial procedure followed today, it is important to review some of the rights and guarantees granted to one accused of a crime. These rights and guarantees are to be found either in the Constitution of the United States or in the constitutions and statutes of the various states. Some of these rights are based upon the common law of England, but others were developed over time as a result of dealing with accused persons.

Returning now to the Magna Charta, we find that it created no panacea, but it did ensure to the people certain liberties, which they had been denied previously, and made way for the establishment of due process of law. But the people of England continued to be subjected to many oppressive practices, and many were persecuted because of their religious beliefs. To escape these practices, a number of people left for North America to establish colonies. The king considered these colonies to be his possessions; the colonists were still under the rule of the king, and all too often that rule lay heavily upon them. They were taxed excessively and were generally oppressed. When they objected, they were often taken to England for trial. As time passed, the colonists increased their opposition. This became a source of irritation to the king, who sent his armies to enforce his rule. Suspected objectors were frequently subjected to searches and seizures without cause and imprisoned without justification.

As a result of the king's extreme actions, the colonists banded together and adopted a resolution declaring their political independence from England. This docu-ment is the Declaration of Independence, which announced to the world that the colonists were serious in their aim to become an independent nation, and it asked for understanding and compassion from other nations. The Declaration of Independence set forth the reasons for their actions and grievances against the king. Among the charges were that the king

> has refused to assent to laws, the most wholesome and necessary for the public good; . . . has obstructed the administration of justice; . . . has kept among us, in times of peace, standing armies without the consent of our legislatures; . . . has deprived many of the benefits of trial by jury; . . . has transported us beyond seas to be tried for pretended offenses.

By reviewing the Declaration of Independence, we are able to appreciate the conditions of the time and the conflicts experienced by the people of America. The Declaration became the basis of the guarantees later to be embodied in our Constitution.

The king did not take this Declaration of Independence lightly. He sent additional armies to subdue the colonies, resulting in the Revolutionary War. When peace was restored in 1783, the colonies became a self-governing nation. A governmental structure had to be formed, and laws had to be made for governing the people. Although various efforts at governmental structures were attempted, each revealed weaknesses. In 1787, representatives of the colonies, now referred to as states, met in Philadelphia to attempt again to formulate an acceptable and a workable governmental structure. The result of this conference, known as the Constitutional Convention, was the U.S. Constitution, which was finally adopted in 1789. It established three branches of government: executive, legislative, and judicial.

As the various state representatives reviewed this document, they felt that a vital weakness still remained in its structure: The people were not guaranteed protection against oppression should this central government become too strong and powerful. Therefore, it was agreed that certain additions should be made to the Constitution. Again representatives of the states met in Congress during 1789 and proposed twelve amendments to the Constitution. Ten of them were adopted in 1791 and are known as the Bill of Rights, which guarantees certain rights to the people. The two amendments that were not adopted did not pertain to guarantees but were related to the legislative structure of the government. Because of the importance of these amendments to the administration of justice, we review them next.

The Bill of Rights

> *Amendment I: Restriction on Powers of Congress.* Congress shall make no law respecting an establishment of religion, or prohibiting the free exercise thereof, or abridging the freedom of speech, or of the press; or the right of the people peaceably to assemble, and to petition the government for a redress of grievances.
>
> *Amendment II: Right to Bear Arms.* A well-regulated militia being necessary to the security of a free State, the right of the people to keep and bear arms shall not be infringed.
>
> *Amendment III: Billeting of Soldiers.* No soldier shall, in time of peace, be quartered in any house without the consent of the owner; nor in time of war, but in a manner to be prescribed by law.
>
> *Amendment IV: Seizures, Searches and Warrants.* The right of the people to be secure in their persons, houses, papers, and effects, against unreasonable searches and seizures shall not be violated, and no warrants shall issue but upon probable

cause, supported by oath or affirmation, and particularly describing the place to be searched and the persons or things to be seized.

Amendment V: Criminal Proceedings, Condemnation of Property. No person shall be held to answer for a capital or otherwise infamous crime, unless on a presentment or indictment of a grand jury, except in cases arising in the land or naval forces, or in the militia, when in actual service in time of war or public danger; nor shall any person be subject for the same offense to be twice put in jeopardy of life or limb; nor shall be compelled in any criminal case, to be a witness against himself; nor be deprived of life, liberty, or property, without due process of law, nor shall private property be taken for public use without just compensation.

Amendment VI: Mode of Trial in Criminal Proceedings. In all criminal prosecutions the accused shall enjoy the right to a speedy and public trial, by an impartial jury of the State and district wherein the crime shall have been committed, which district shall have been previously ascertained by law; and to be informed of the nature and cause of the accusation; to be confronted with the witnesses against him; to have compulsory process for obtaining witnesses in his favor, and to have the assistance of counsel for his defense.

Amendment VII: Trial by Jury. In suits at common law, where the value in controversy shall exceed twenty dollars, the right of trial by jury shall be preserved; and no fact tried by jury, shall be otherwise reexamined in any court of the United States than according to the rules of common law.

Amendment VIII: Involuntary Servitude. Excessive bail shall not be required, nor excessive fines imposed, nor cruel and unusual punishment inflicted.

Amendment IX: Certain Rights Not Denied to the People. The enumeration in the Constitution of certain rights shall not be construed to deny or disparage others retained by the people.

Amendment X: State Rights. The powers not delegated to the United States by the Constitution, nor prohibited by it to the States, are reserved to the states, respectively, or to the people.

Due Process of Law

As we study these amendments, we must remind ourselves that when they were adopted, the oppressive conditions that brought them into being were still vivid in the memory of the people. Thus, these guarantees were to protect the people against any action that might be attempted by the federal government and as such were applicable only to federal officers. The states, as provided in the Ninth and Tenth Amendments, were free to establish their own guarantees relating to the actions permitted by state and local officials. We will find that the Fourth, Fifth, Sixth, and Eighth Amendments are most significant in the administration of justice.

As time passed, slavery and involuntary servitude, such as forcing men to build public roads or to serve in a state militia without pay, were permitted in some states. After the Civil War, the Thirteenth Amendment, abolishing slavery, was added to the U.S. Constitution. To prohibit other oppressive and arbitrary actions by the states, the Fourteenth Amendment was adopted in 1868. This amendment held that:

All persons born or naturalized in the United States, and subject to the jurisdiction thereof, are citizens of the United States and of the State wherein they reside. No

State shall make or enforce any law which shall abridge the privileges or immunities of citizens of the United States; nor shall any State deprive any person of life, liberty, or property, without due process of law; nor deny to any person within its jurisdiction the equal protection of the laws.

It should be emphasized that this amendment was directed to the states to prevent them from depriving any person of life, liberty, or property without due process of law. However, the amendment raised a question regarding the interpretation of the term due process of law as it related to the administration of justice. The courts later concluded that if an accused had his day in court with the right to appeal a conviction, the due process of law clause of the Fourteenth Amendment had been satisfied. We will find in our study of the judicial procedure throughout this text that the U.S. Supreme Court has since placed a different interpretation on the meaning of the due process of law clause of the Fourteenth Amendment. The Supreme Court has ruled that the following particular Bill of Rights guarantees are applicable to the states: the Fourth Amendment right to be free from unreasonable searches and seizures and to have any illegally seized evidence excluded from criminal trials;[2] the Fifth Amendment privilege against self-incrimination[3] and the guarantee against double jeopardy,[4] and the Sixth Amendment rights to counsel,[5] to a speedy trial,[6] to a public trial,[7] to confront opposing witnesses,[8] and to an impartial jury.[9] Decisions making these guarantees applicable to the states will be discussed as the judicial procedure is further explained. For practical purposes, these amendments are as applicable to state and local officers as they are to federal officers.

In addition to the guarantees provided by the Bill of Rights, each state has furnished to the people within that state additional guarantees and rights, which are contained in the statutes of the state constitution. To ensure that the guarantees of the Bill of Rights and the state statutes are properly afforded the people, court structures have been established.

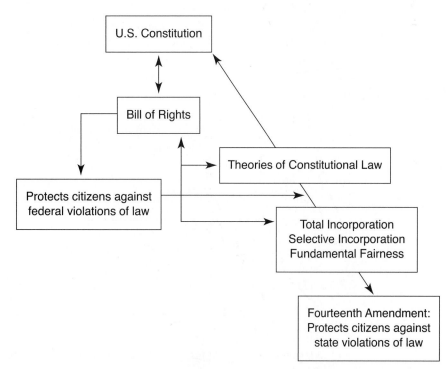

Relationship of the Bill of Rights and the Fourteenth Amendment to the Constitutional rights of the accused.

Annual Salaries of Federal Judges
By judicial office, as of Jan. 1, 2004

Chief Justice of the United States	$203,000
Associate justices of the Supreme Court of the United States	194,300
United States circuit judges	167,600
United States district judges	158,100
Judges, United States Court of International Trade	158,100
Judges, United States Court of Federal Claims	158,100
United States bankruptcy judges	145,452
United States magistrate judges (full-time)	145,452

Source: Sourcebook of Criminal Justice Statistics 2004, Table 1.80, p. 74.

COURT STRUCTURES

The court system in the United States is based upon the principle of federalism.[10] The first Congress established a federal court system, and the individual states were permitted to continue their own judicial structure. There was general agreement among our nation's founding fathers that individual states needed to retain significant autonomy from federal control. Under this concept of federalism, the United States developed as a loose confederation of semi-independent states, with the federal court system acting in a very limited manner. In the early history of our nation, most cases were tried in state courts, and it was only later that the federal government and the federal judiciary began to exercise jurisdiction over crimes and civil matters. **Jurisdiction** in this context simply means the ability of the court to enforce laws and punish individuals who violate those laws.

As a result of this historical evolution, a dual system of state and federal courts exists today. Therefore, federal and state courts may have concurrent jurisdiction over specific crimes. For example, a person who robs a bank may be tried and convicted in state court for robbery and then tried and convicted in federal court for the federal offense of robbery of a federally chartered savings institution.

The second characteristic of the American court system is that it performs its duties with little or no supervision. A supreme court justice does not exercise supervision over lower court judges in the same way that a government supervisor or manager exercises control over his or her employees. The U.S. Supreme Court and the various state supreme courts exercise supervision only in the sense that they hear appellate cases from lower courts and establish certain procedures for these courts.

The third feature of our court system is the specialization that occurs primarily at the state and local levels. In many states, courts of limited jurisdiction hear misdemeanor cases. Other state courts of general jurisdiction try felonies. Still other courts may be designated as juvenile courts and hear only matters involving juveniles. This process also occurs in certain civil courts that hear only family law matters, probate matters, or civil cases involving damages. At the federal level, there are courts, such as bankruptcy court, that hear only cases dealing with specific matters.

The fourth characteristic of the American court system is the organization of state and federal courts into geographic areas. In many jurisdictions, these are called judicial districts and contain various levels of courts. For example, on the federal level, the Ninth Circuit Court of Appeals has district (trial) courts that hear matters within certain specific boundaries and an appellate court that hears all appeals from cases within that area. Several studies have been conducted regarding the difference in sentences for the same type of crime in geographic district courts. For instance, in Iowa the average sentence for motor vehicle theft was forty-seven months, whereas the average sentence for the same offense in New York was fourteen months.[11] This observation shouldn't be taken as a criticism; rather, it may reflect different social values and attitudes within specific geographic areas.

After a person is arrested, unless the charge against him or her is dismissed, some prosecutive action must be taken, which will occur in the appropriate court. In order for students to have a clearer understanding of the judicial proceedings from the time of arrest through sentencing, a discussion of the court system follows. Although the court system may vary somewhat among the states, it is basically the same. The states are divided into territorial divisions known as counties, except in Louisiana, where they are called parishes, and in Alaska, which is divided into four judicial districts. Each county, parish, or district has its own trial court system. The chief trial court is known as the superior court, district court, or circuit court, depending upon the title that the court is given in a particular state. This court, in addition to trying civil matters, will hear trials involving felony cases and possibly some more serious, or high, misdemeanor charges. Generally, this court holds forth in the county seat. Although these courts are technically county courts, they are referred to in many books on judicial procedures as state courts, as distinguished from federal courts.

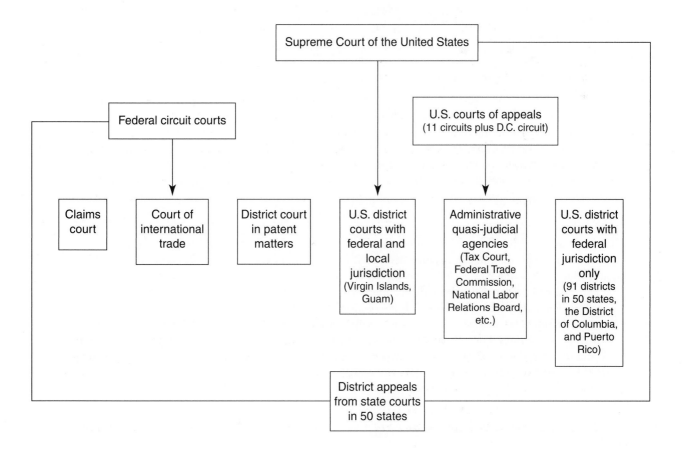

Table of Judicial Salaries of State Court Judges, April 2004

	Mean Salary	*Range*
Chief Justice, state supreme court	$130,461	$95,000 to 191,483
Associate Justice, state supreme court	126,159	95,000 to 175,575
Judge, intermediate court of appeals	122,682	94,212 to 164,604
Judge of general trial court	113,504	88,164 to 158,100

Source: Special Report by the National Center for State Courts, Volume 29, page 1, April 1, 2004, accessed at www.ncsonline.org/D_KIS//salary_Survey on November 9, 2005.

Law in Practice

U.S. Courts and the Death Penalty

The common belief that the U.S. Supreme Court and the U.S. courts of appeal base their decisions in death penalty cases on technicalities is wrong, according to James Liebman, professor at Columbia Law School, who headed a study that examined U.S. death penalty cases over twenty-three years. According to Liebman, the federal appellate courts are far more likely to overrule a lower court decision that ruled against the prosecution than to overrule a case in which the lower court ruled in favor of the prosecution.

Since the *Furman* decision in 1972, a yearly average of about 300 of the approximately 21,000 homicides committed in the United States have resulted in death sentences. These sentences are reviewed by state courts on state direct appeal and, if affirmed, in a state postconviction proceeding, and, if affirmed again, on federal habeas corpus. During the twenty-three-year period of a statistical study, 1973–1995, state appellate courts reversed about 47 percent of the capital judgments they reviewed.

[James Liebman, "The Overproduction of Death," *Columbia Law Review*, vol. 100, pp. 2030–2041, 2000.]

The 1996 Anti-Terrorism and Effective Death Penalty Act requires federal courts to defer to lower state court decisions unless there is a strong reason for overturning a decision. This is considered a high standard for appellate defense attorneys to overturn. Since the U.S. Supreme Court reviews only a small fraction of criminal cases each year, the U.S. courts of appeal make the final decision on federal issues in the vast majority of cases appealed to those courts. Of the courts of appeal, that of the Ninth Circuit is considered by most scholars as the most liberal and the most likely to overturn a death penalty case. The Ninth Circuit issued so many stays of execution during the 1990s that the high court ordered the judges in that circuit to stop. The most conservative circuit and the most likely to approve a death penalty case is the Fourth Circuit court, followed closely by the Fifth Circuit court.

It is assumed that when the Supreme Court issues an opinion, the U.S. courts of appeal adhere to the guidelines announced in the high court's decisions. That may not necessarily be the case. The Fifth Circuit court, which is based in New Orleans and serves Texas, Louisiana, and Mississippi, has a reputation for being unfriendly to death penalty appeals and, along with the Fourth Circuit court, is the most likely to uphold a death sentence. The Fifth Circuit court is also considered a circuit less likely to follow Supreme Court decisions. The Supreme Court has issued at least six opinions chastising the Fifth Circuit court for failing to follow the Court's rulings. For example, in a case involving defendant Thomas Miller-El, the Supreme Court issued a ruling telling the appellate court how it should rule. The appellate court reconsidered the case and reissued its opinion. In its revised opinion, the appellate court did not use the language from the Supreme Court's majority opinion, but instead lifted entire paragraphs from the dissenting opinion of Justice Clarence Thomas, the lone dissenter in the case.

[*Miller-El* v. *Dretke*, 125 S. Ct. 2317 (2005) and *Miller-El* v. *Dretke*, 361 F.3d 849 (2004).]

STATE COURT SYSTEM

Historically, each of the thirteen states had its own unique court structure. This independence continued after the American Revolution and resulted in widespread differences among the various states; some of these differences still exist today. Because each state adopted its own system of courts, the consequence was a poorly planned and confusing judicial structure. As a result, there have been several reform movements whose purpose has been to streamline and modernize this system.

Many state courts can be divided into three levels: trial courts, appellate courts, and state supreme courts. It is in trial courts that criminal cases start, evidence is presented, the defendant is found guilty or not guilty, and a sentence is imposed if the defendant is found guilty. The trial court conducts the entire series of acts that culminate in either the defendant's release or sentencing. State trial courts can be further divided into courts of limited or special jurisdiction and courts of general jurisdiction.

The nature and type of case determines which court will have jurisdiction. Courts that hear and decide only certain limited legal issues are courts of limited jurisdiction. Typically, these courts hear certain types of minor civil or criminal cases. Approximately 13,000 local courts exist in the United States. They are county, magistrate, justice, or municipal courts. Judges in these courts may be either appointed or elected. In many jurisdictions, these are part-time positions, and the incumbent may have another job or position in addition to serving as a judge.

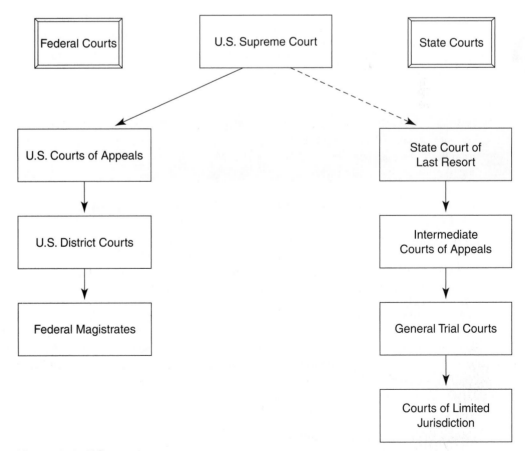

Hierarcy in the U.S. court system.

Coming to the county seat from outlying areas of the county has often created hardship and expense for many of those involved in a trial. To accommodate these persons and to relieve part of the caseload of the superior court, some counties have been divided into judicial districts, each containing a lower court. This lower court is often referred to as an inferior court, as opposed to the superior court, and is known in many places as the justice court. The judge is frequently called the justice of the peace. This court has limited jurisdiction, hearing certain misdemeanor charges and civil matters involving small amounts of money. Usually the judge is elected by the people within the district, and generally in the past there was no requirement that he or she have legal training. The reason for no such requirement was that in many outlying judicial districts, there were no attorneys; however, the people of those districts were entitled to some judicial assistance. Today, since more attorneys are available, many states have phased out the judges of the inferior courts who are not attorneys. However, the elimination of the layperson judge has met with resistance. Some contend that the local inferior, or lower, court can provide a form of justice that is convenient for both the accused and the accuser and that the layperson justice of the peace is part of the American heritage. Others contend that to subject an accused to possible imprisonment after a conviction in a trial presided over by a layperson judge is to deny the accused the right to due process of law. This matter was brought before the U.S. Supreme Court in the case of *North* v. *Russell* after North was convicted of drunk driving and sentenced to thirty days in jail by a lawperson sitting as a police court judge.[12] North contended that his conviction for drunk driving and sentencing to thirty days in jail was a violation of his right to due process of law as provided in the Fourteenth Amendment. The Court upheld the conviction upon the grounds that North could have taken his case to a higher court and had it completely tried again by a court presided over by an attorney judge. Therefore, North was not denied due process of law. The Court pointed out that there was an advantage to the accused in having the trial in a community near his residence rather than traveling to a distant court where a law-trained

Law in Practice

State Major Criminal Trial Courts

Circuit Court	Alabama, Arkansas, Florida, Hawaii, Illinois, Indiana, Kentucky, Maryland, Michigan, Mississippi, Missouri, Oregon, South Carolina, South Dakota, Tennessee, Virginia, West Virginia, and Wisconsin
Court of Common Pleas	Ohio and Pennsylvania
District Court	Colorado, Idaho, Kansas, Louisiana, Minnesota, Montana, Nebraska, Nevada, New Mexico, North Dakota, Oklahoma, Texas, Utah, and Wyoming
Superior Court	Alaska, Arizona, California, Connecticut, Delaware, District of Columbia, Georgia, Maine, Massachusetts, New Hampshire, New Jersey, North Carolina, Rhode Island, Vermont, Washington, and New York
Supreme Court	New York (New York also uses county courts and superior courts)

Source: David Rottman, Carol Flango, and R. Shedine Lockley, *State Court Organizations, 1993* (Washington D.C.: U.S. Department of Justice, Bureau of Justice Statistics, GPO, 1995).

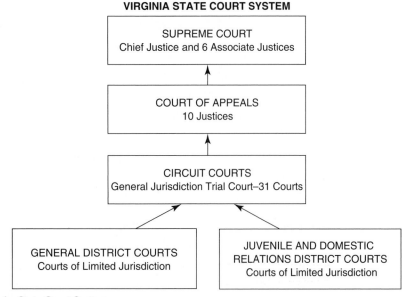

Sample of a State Court System.

judge was provided. The decision did not rule out all laypersons judges as being a denial of due process of law, but it should be noted that the judicial structures of some states do not provide for a conviction in a lower court to be taken to a higher court and the case started anew. Where such a procedure is not available, courts could hold that an accused would be denied the right of due process of law in a proceeding before a layperson judge.

However, simply because they handle minor civil and criminal matters does not mean that these courts do not perform important duties. Many times the only contact the average citizen will have with the judicial system occurs at this level. Courts of limited jurisdiction hear and decide issues such as traffic tickets or set bail for criminal defendants.

In addition, courts of limited jurisdiction may hear certain types of specialized matters such as probate of wills and estates, divorces, child custody matters, and juvenile hearings. These types of courts may be local courts or, depending on the state, courts of general jurisdiction that are designated by statute to hear and decide specific types of cases. For example, in California, a superior court is considered a court of general jurisdiction; however, certain superior courts are designated to hear only juvenile matters, thereby becoming courts of limited jurisdiction when sitting as juvenile courts.

Courts of general jurisdiction are granted authority to hear and decide all issues that are brought before them. These are the courts that normally hear all major civil or criminal cases. These courts are known by a variety of names, such as superior courts, circuit courts, district courts, or courts of common pleas. Since they are courts of general jurisdiction, they have authority to decide issues that occur anywhere within the state. Some larger jurisdictions such as Los Angeles or New York may have hundreds of courts of general jurisdiction within the city limits. Typically, these courts hear civil cases involving the same types of issues that courts of limited jurisdiction hear, although the amount of damages will be higher and may reach millions of dollars. These courts also hear the most serious forms of criminal matters, including death penalty cases.

Courts of general jurisdiction traditionally have the power to order individuals to do or refrain from doing certain acts. These courts may issue injunctions prohibiting certain acts or requiring individuals to perform certain functions or duties. This authority is derived from the equity power that resides in courts of general jurisdiction. Equity is the concept that justice is administered according to fairness, as contrasted to the strict rules of

---

A Comparison of Criminal and Tort Law

Similarities

- Goal of controlling
- Imposition of sanctions
- Some common areas of legal action—for example, personal assault, control of white-collar offenses such as environmental pollution

Differences

Criminal Law	Tort Law
Crime is a public offense.	A tort is a civil or private wrong.
The sanction associated with criminal law is incarceration or death.	The sanction associated with tort law is monetary damages.
The right of enforcement belongs to the state.	The individual brings the action.
The government ordinarily does not appeal.	Both parties can appeal.
Fines go to the state.	The individual receives damages as compensation for harm done.

---

law. In early English common law, such separate courts of equity were known as courts of chancery. These early courts were not concerned with technical legal issues; rather, they focused on rendering decisions or orders that were fair or equitable. In modern times, these courts have been merged with courts of general jurisdiction, allowing them to rule on matters that require fairness as well as the strict application of the law. The power to issue temporary restraining orders in spousal abuse cases comes from this authority.

Appellate Courts

Appellate jurisdiction is reserved for courts that hear appeals from both limited and general jurisdiction courts. Except for appeals from minor courts that are heard "de novo" (as a new trial), these courts do not hold trials or hear evidence. Instead, they decide matters of law on the basis of the record of trial and appellate briefs, and they issue formal written decisions, or opinions. In a few states, the intermediate-level appellate courts have limited authority to make findings of fact. There are two classes of appellate courts: intermediate and final.

The intermediate appellate courts are known as courts of appeals. Approximately half of the states have designated intermediate appellate courts. These courts may be divided into judicial districts that hear all appeals within their district. They hear and decide all issues of law that are raised on appeal in both civil and criminal cases. Since these courts deal strictly with legal or equitable issues, there is no jury to decide factual disputes. These courts accept the facts as determined by the trial courts. Most criminal cases end at either the trial or intermediate appellate court level; less than 1 percent of the cases are appealed to the state highest appellate court. However, whereas all states have appellate courts for criminal appeals, there appears to be no constitutional duty for states to have appellate courts. Intermediate appellate courts have the authority to reverse the decision of the lower courts and to send the matter back with instructions to retry the case in accordance with their opinion. They also may uphold the decision of the lower court. In either situation, the party who loses the appeal at this level may file and appeal to the next higher appellate court.

Supreme Courts

Final appellate courts are the highest state appellate courts. They may be known as supreme courts or courts of last resort. There may be five, seven, or nine justices sitting on this court, depending on the state. This court has jurisdiction to hear and decide issues dealing with all matters decided by lower courts, including ruling on state constitutional or statutory issues. Its decision is binding on all other courts within the state. In two states, Oklahoma and Texas, the state supreme courts do not have jurisdiction over criminal matters. In these two states, the highest court of appeal for criminal matters is the Court of Criminal Appeals.

Cases Incorporating Provisions of the Bill of Rights into the Due Process Clause of the Fourteenth Amendment

The information below indicates how the U.S. Supreme Court has applied the Due Process Clause of the Fourteenth Amendment to incorporate certain rights contained in the U.S. Constitution's Bill of Rights into state proceedings.

First Amendment

Establishment of religion	*Everson* v. *Board of Education* (1947)
Free exercise of religion	*Cantwell* v. *Connecticut* (1940)
Freedom of speech	*Gitlow* v. *New York* (1925)
Freedom of the press	*Near* v. *Minnesota* (1931)
Freedom to peaceably assemble	*DeJong* v. *Oregon* (1937)

Fourth Amendment

Unreasonable search and seizure	*Wolf* v. *Colorado* (1949)
Exclusionary rule	*Mapp* v. *Ohio* (1961)

Fifth Amendment

Grand jury	*Hurtado* v. *California* (1884) [Held not applicable to the states]
Double jeopardy	*Benton* v. *Maryland* (1969)
Self-incrimination	*Mallay* v. *Hogan* (1964)
Compensation for taking private property	*Chicago, Burlington and Quincy Railroad* v. *Chicago* (1897)

Sixth Amendment

Speedy trial	*Klopfer* v. *Worth Carolina* (1967)
Public trial	*In re Oliver* (1948)
Impartial jury	*Parker* v. *Gladden* (1966)
Jury trial	*Duncan* v. *Louisiana* (1968)
Confrontation of witnesses	*Pointer* v. *Texas* (1965)
Compulsory process	*Washington* v. *Texas* (1967)
Assistance of counsel	*Gideon* v. *Wainwright* [felony cases] (1963) *Argersinger* v. *Hanilin* [*misdemeanors involving confinement*] (1972)

Eighth Amendment

Excessive bail	*United States* v. *Salerno* (1987)
Cruel and unusual punishment	*Robinson* v. *California* (1962)

Once the highest state appellate court decides an issue, the conviction is considered final. The defendant may attack the judgment of a state court by filing a writ with a federal court. But before the federal court will accept a writ attacking a state court judgment, a federal issue must be involved. Normally, the federal issue is that the state court violated the federal constitutional rights of the defendant. This is regarded as a collateral attack.

The New York Unified Court System

The New York State court system is different from that of the other states. In New York, the Supreme Court is a trial court and the New York Court of Appeals is the court of last resort for the State of New York.

Mission
The mission of the New York Unified Court System is to promote the rule of law and to serve the public by providing just and timely resolution of all matters before the courts.

State Trial Courts in New York
The trial courts of superior jurisdiction are the supreme courts, the Court of Claims, the family courts, the surrogate's courts, and, outside New York City, the county courts. In New York City, the supreme court exercises both civil and criminal jurisdiction. Outside New York City, the supreme court exercises civil jurisdiction, while the county court generally handles criminal matters.

The trial courts of limited jurisdiction in New York City are the New York City Civil Court and the New York City Criminal Court. Outside New York City, the trial courts of limited jurisdiction are the city courts, which have criminal jurisdiction over misdemeanors and lesser offenses and civil jurisdiction over claims of up to $15,000. There are district courts in Nassau County and parts of Suffolk County. District courts have criminal jurisdiction over misdemeanors and lesser offenses and civil jurisdiction over claims of up to $15,000.

Upstate New York Trial Courts
The county court is established in each county outside of New York City. It is authorized to handle the prosecution of all crimes committed within the county. The county court also has limited jurisdiction in civil cases involving amounts of up to $25,000.

City courts outside of New York City exist in sixty-one cities, and have criminal jurisdiction over misdemeanors and lesser offenses and civil jurisdiction over claims of up to $15,000. Some city courts have separate parts to handle small claims or housing matters. City court judges act as arraigning magistrates and conduct preliminary hearings in felony cases.

Town and village courts have criminal jurisdiction over violations and misdemeanors and civil jurisdiction over claims of up to $3,000. As magistrates, town and village court justices hold arraignments and preliminary hearings for those charged with more serious crimes. Traffic infractions also are heard in these courts.

New York City Courts
The New York City Supreme Court is the trial court of unlimited original jurisdiction, but it generally only hears cases that are outside the jurisdiction of other trial courts of more limited jurisdiction. It exercises civil jurisdiction and jurisdiction over felony charges.

The Family Court hears matters involving children and families. Its jurisdiction includes custody and visitation, support, family offense (domestic violence), persons in need of supervision, delinquency, child protective proceedings (abuse and neglect), foster care approval and review, termination of parental rights, adoption, and guardianship.

The Surrogate's Court hears cases involving the affairs of decedents, including the probate of wills, the administration of estates, and adoptions.

The Civil Court of the City of New York has jurisdiction over civil cases involving amounts of up to $25,000 and other civil matters referred to it by the Supreme Court. It includes a small claims part for informal dispositions of matters not exceeding $5,000 and a housing part for landlord–tenant matters and housing code violations.

The Criminal Court of the City of New York has jurisdiction over misdemeanors and violations. Judges of the Criminal Court also act as arraigning magistrates and conduct preliminary hearings in felony cases.

State Appellate Courts

The appellate courts hear and determine appeals from the decisions of the trial courts. The appellate courts are the Court of Appeals (the highest court in the state), the appellate divisions of the Supreme Court, the appellate terms of the Supreme Court, and the county courts acting as appellate courts in the Third and Fourth Judicial Departments.

FEDERAL COURT SYSTEM

Although state courts had their origin in historical accident and custom, federal courts were created by the U.S. Constitution. Section 1 of Article III established the federal court system with the words providing for "one supreme Court, and . . . such inferior Courts as the Congress may from time to time ordain and establish." From this beginning, Congress has passed a series of acts that have resulted in today's federal court system. The Judiciary Act of 1789 created the U.S. Supreme Court and established district and circuit courts of appeals.

Federal district courts are the lowest level of the federal court system. These courts have original jurisdiction over cases involving a violation of federal statutes. Because these district courts handle thousands of criminal cases per year, questions have been raised regarding the quality of justice that can be delivered by overworked judges.

Federal circuit courts of appeals are the intermediate-appellate courts within the federal system. These courts are called circuit courts because the federal system is divided into eleven circuits. A twelfth circuit court of appeals serves the Washington, D.C., area. These courts hear all criminal appeals from the district courts. These appeals are usually heard by panels of three of the appellate court judges rather than by all the judges of each circuit.

The U.S. Supreme Court is the highest court in the land. It has the capacity for judicial review of all lower court decisions involving federal issues or federal questions. By exercising this power, the Supreme Court determines what laws and what lower court decisions conform to the mandates set forth in the U.S. Constitution, national treaties, and federal law. The concept of judicial review was first referred to by Alexander Hamilton in the *The Federalist* papers, where he referred to the Supreme Court as ensuring that the will of the people will be supreme over the will of the legislature.[13] This concept was firmly and finally established in our system when the Supreme Court asserted its power of judicial review in the case of *Marbury* v. *Madison*.[14]

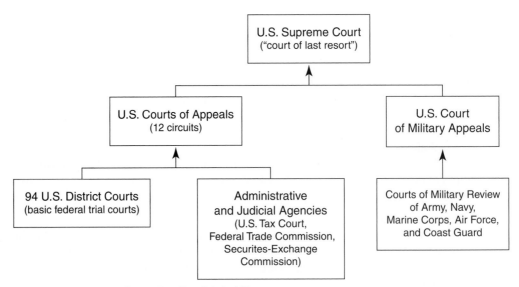

Organization of Federal Courts Handling Criminal Matters.

The U.S. Supreme Court has original jurisdiction in the following cases:

- cases between the United States and a state;
- cases between states; cases involving foreign ambassadors, ministers, and consuls; and
- cases between a state and a citizen of another state or country.

The Supreme Court hears appeals from lower courts, including the various state supreme courts (on issues involving federal questions). If four justices of the U.S. Supreme Court vote to hear a case, the Court will issue a writ of certiorari, which is an order to a lower court to send the records of the case to the Supreme Court for review. The Court meets on the first Monday of October and usually remains in session until June. The Court may review any case it deems worthy of review, but it actually hears very few of the cases filed with it. Of approximately 5,000 appeals each year, the Court hears about 100.

VENUE

Defined simply, **venue** is the geographic area in which a case may be heard. It is the place where a case is brought to trial and the area from which the jurors are selected. Usually, venue will lie within the county or judicial district in which a crime is committed. Venue may be waived by the defendant. There are times when a defendant may request that a trial be held in a county other than that where the crime was committed.

Occasionally, situations arise when it is difficult to determine in which county a crime was committed in order to have venue established. Many states have set forth guidelines to overcome this dilemma. They include such provisions as the following:

- When an offense is committed in part in one county and in part in another, the trial may be held in either county, and

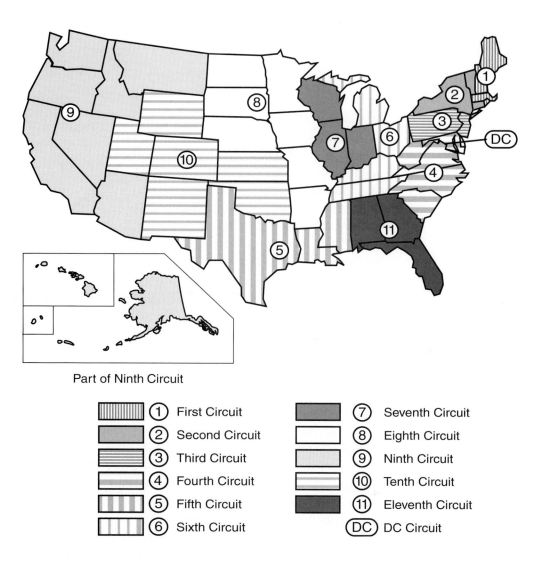

Part of Ninth Circuit

▥ ① First Circuit		▦ ⑦ Seventh Circuit	
▨ ② Second Circuit		☐ ⑧ Eighth Circuit	
▤ ③ Third Circuit		▦ ⑨ Ninth Circuit	
▤ ④ Fourth Circuit		▦ ⑩ Tenth Circuit	
▥ ⑤ Fifth Circuit		▦ ⑪ Eleventh Circuit	
▥ ⑥ Sixth Circuit		ⓓⓒ DC Circuit	

- when an offense is committed on the boundary of two or more counties, or within 500 yards (this distance may vary among states) of the boundary, the trial may be held in either jurisdiction.

Prior to the passage of such provisions, there was a joke among old-time sheriffs and prosecutors about wearing out bodies by dragging them across county lines to avoid the responsibility of investigations and prosecutions. It has also been held that when a crime is committed within the state in a boat, a motor vehicle, an aircraft, or a common carrier, the trial may be held in any county through which the trip passed or the one in which it was terminated.

JURISDICTION

Jurisdiction is the inherent power of a court to hear and decide a case, whereas venue designates a particular area in which a case may be heard and decided. Unfortunately, the statutes of some states use jurisdiction when in fact the statute refers to venue, thus creating confusion for the layperson. This dual use of the term jurisdiction stems from the fact that it is an all-encompassing word, embracing every kind of judicial action.

Federal versus Local Jurisdiction

Since we have learned that there are two court systems, that is, the state system and the federal system, it may be useful at this point to compare the jurisdiction of each. As we have previously stated, criminal laws enacted by the U.S. Congress are known as federal criminal laws and are enforced by federal officers. Criminal laws passed by the state legislatures are generally enforced by city police departments or sheriffs and their deputies, and are assisted by state officers where they have the authority to do so. Although most of the criminal laws within a state are state enacted, the violators are prosecuted in the county court or local system, since that is where the trial courts are located. Thus, our discussion of the jurisdiction of the two systems is directly related to the trial jurisdiction of the federal and county courts.

When a crime is committed, the violator may have broken either a federal law or a state law, depending upon the act. For example, a person may rob a liquor store, an act that would be a violation of a state statute, since all states have laws making robbery a crime. Or a person may violate the Sherman Antitrust Law, an act that would be a federal violation. The county court would have exclusive jurisdiction to try the case of robbery, whereas the federal government would have exclusive jurisdiction to try the antitrust violation. It is possible for a person to commit both a federal and a state violation with a series of acts arising out of a sequence of events. For example, a person may steal an automobile in one state and transport it to another state. Such an individual could be prosecuted in the local courts for the theft of the vehicle and prosecuted in the federal courts because it is a federal crime to transport a vehicle from one state to another knowing that it has been stolen. In this example, the offender has actually committed two violations as a result of two different acts—one being the theft and the other the transportation of the vehicle while knowing that it has been stolen. In these two examples, each court has its own trial jurisdiction exclusive of the other.

As stated, it is possible for an individual to violate both a federal and a state law by the same act. For example, an individual may kill a federal officer, thereby violating a federal statute, and the killing may also violate a state homicide statute. Under these circumstances, concurrent jurisdiction would exist. The question then would be whether the accused could be prosecuted in both the federal and the state courts. This question can best be discussed in Chapter 5, which deals with the plea of once in jeopardy. Where an act violates both federal and state statutes, the federal government can always take jurisdiction and prosecute the violation. In some states, like California, if the federal government prosecutes, the state prosecutor is barred by state statute from prosecuting for the same criminal act.

Although most crimes committed on government reservations are also local or state violations, the federal courts have exclusive jurisdiction to try those matters because they were committed on government reservations. It should be pointed out that government reservations are comparatively few in number. In order for a territorial area to be a government reservation, the land must have always been U.S. property, with the title still retained by the United States, or property acquired from a state for which all right and title was relinquished. Most military installations and national parks are government reservations; most post offices are not. Scattered throughout the United States are many national forests, but most of these are not government reservations, so that any crimes committed in these forests are within the jurisdiction of the local courts. However, any theft of the trees from these forests is a theft of government property, which would be a federal violation.

Foundational Concepts in Criminal Procedure

As an introduction to the study of criminal procedure, the foundational concepts in criminal procedure below should be considered. These concepts will be explained in the text and are listed here to create an awareness of their existence.

- The guarantees of the Bill of Rights in the U.S. Constitution apply directly only to the federal government.
- The Due Process Clause of the Fourteenth Amendment, by selective incorporation, applies most of the rights contained in the Bill of Rights to the states.
- State constitutions may provide rights to citizens in addition to those provided for in the U.S. Constitution but may not restrict the rights granted by the U.S. Constitution.
- The two questions regarding the burdens of proof in criminal proceeding are: (1) Who has the burden of proving an issue? and (2) What is the magnitude of the burden?
  - The magnitude may be proof beyond a reasonable doubt,
  - clear and convincing evidence, or
  - preponderance of the evidence.
- Formal charges in a criminal trial must first be formalized either by an indictment returned by a grand jury or by information prepared by a prosecutor.
- Prior to trial, both the prosecutor and the defense may submit pretrial motions, and both have discovery rights imposed on them.
- Our system of criminal procedure is based on the adversarial process.
- Two famous quotes from Oliver Wendell Holmes should be noted:
  - "Whatever disagreement there may be as to the scope of the phrase 'due process of law,' there can be no doubt that it embraces the fundamental conception of a fair trial, with opportunity to be heard." [*Frank* v. *Mangum*, 237 N.S. 309, 347 (1914).]
  - "The life of the law has not been logic, it has been experience." [The Common Law (1881) 1.]

The Interrelationship of the Criminal Justice System and the Criminal Justice Process

The System: Agencies of Crime Control	*The Process*
1. Police	1. Contact
	2. Investigation
	3. Arrest
	4. Custody
2. Prosecution and defense	5. Complaint/charging
	6. Grand jury/preliminary hearing
	7. Arraignment
	8. Bail/detention
	9. Plea negotiations
3. Court	10. Adjudication
	11. Disposition
	12. Appeal/postconviction remedies
4. Corrections	13. Correction
	14. Release
	15. Postrelease

In review, jurisdiction—as it relates to the administration of justice—refers to the right and the power of a particular court to try a case. It includes jurisdiction over the person and the subject matter of the issue to be tried. For example, inferior courts have jurisdiction, or the right, to hear misdemeanor matters. The superior or district court has jurisdiction, or the right, to hear felony cases. Jurisdiction is basic to the trial of a case, and it cannot be waived. It is a right of the court established by law.

Law in Practice

Drug Courts

With nearly 1,500 drug courts in existence or being planned, there is a great deal of bi-partisan interest in drug courts across the nation.

What Are Drug Courts and Why Do We Need Them?

A drug court is a special court given the responsibility to handle cases involving substance-abusing offenders through comprehensive supervision, drug testing, treatment services, and immediate sanctions and incentives.

Drug court programs bring the full weight of all intervenors (judges, prosecutors, defense counsel, substance abuse treatment specialists, probation officers, law enforcement and correctional personnel, educational and vocational experts, community leaders, and others) to bear, forcing the offender to deal with his or her substance abuse problem.

In addition, drug courts ensure consistency in judicial decision making and enhance the coordination of agencies and resources, increasing the cost effectiveness of programs.

Are All Drug Courts the Same?

The design and structure of drug court programs are developed at the local level to reflect the unique strengths, circumstances, and capacities of each community. Many sectors of the community are involved in the planning and implementation process of a drug court system, including criminal justice, treatment, law enforcement, educational, and community antidrug organizations. Not only do drug courts address issues in the criminal justice arena, but family dependency courts, driving under the influence (DUI) drug courts, juvenile drug courts, reentry courts, and mental health courts are all built around the drug court model. In these courts, issues such as juvenile delinquency, child abuse, and neglect, and repeat drunk driving are addressed. Offenders are treated holistically and smoothly reintegrated into society in these courts.

Do Drug Courts Work?

American University's Drug Court Clearinghouse reports that over 400,000 drug-using offenders have participated in drug court programs since their inception in 1989. In 1997, the Government Accounting Office (GAO) reported that 71 percent of all offenders entering drug courts since 1989 have either successfully completed their drug court program or are currently actively participating in their program.

In 2001, Columbia University's National Center on Addiction and Substance Abuse (CASA) concluded an updated study of its seminal 1998 review of drug court research and evaluations. It finds that drug courts continue to provide the most comprehensive and effective control of the drug-using offenders' criminality and drug usage while under the court's jurisdiction.

The revised study, based on a review of thirty-seven evaluations, finds that their results are consistent with the 1998 analysis and the 2000 update based on forty-eight other evaluations finding that "drug courts provide closer, more comprehensive supervision and much more frequent drug testing and monitoring during the program than other forms of community supervision" and that "drug use and criminal behavior are substantially reduced while offenders are participating in drug court." In fact, the average recidivism rate for those who complete the drug court program is between 4 and 29 percent compared to 48 percent for those who do not participate in a drug court program. Additionally, the 2003 National Institute of Justice (NIJ) recidivism report entitled "Recidivism Rates for Drug Court Graduates: National Based Estimates," representative of over 17,000 annual drug court graduates nationwide, finds that the recidivism rate for drug court participants one year after graduation is a mere 16.5 percent and only 27.5 percent after two years. The report also finds that participants from thirty-eight drug courts throughout the country have recidivism rates below 10 percent one year after graduation.

Who Is Eligible for Drug Courts?

Drug courts started out as diversionary programs dealing with less serious offenders, typically charged with simple drug possession or DUI charges. As these proved their effectiveness in controlling both the drug usage and criminality of drug-using offenders, communities successfully expanded drug court programs to probationers, including drug-using offenders charged with nondrug offenses. American University's Drug Court Clearinghouse reports that 70 percent of drug courts now include probation-based or post-plea programs, and the typical participant has at least a fifteen-year history of drug usage.

In 1995, the Bureau of Justice Statistics reported that 2 million probationers—two-thirds of all probationers—may be considered drug and alcohol involved.

Unfortunately, no more than 4 to 8 percent of drug-using offenders on probation and living in our communities are in drug court programs.

Drug Courts Provide a Viable Alternative

Drug courts provide one of the most viable options for addressing the substance-abusing offender today. Whether these persons enter the judicial system because of a criminal offense, delinquent behavior, or the neglect or abuse of their children, they can benefit from the enhanced supervision provided in the drug court system. Not only do offenders benefit, but public safety is also strengthened through the monitoring and accountability that occur in the drug court.

Will Drug Courts Provide More Jail Space for Serious Criminals?

With three-strikes-you're-out statutes proliferating and long-term incarceration for serious offenders increasing, drug court programs are needed to free up limited jail space for serious criminals.

Do Drug Courts Save Money?

Incarceration of drug-using offenders costs between $20,000 and $50,000 per person per year. The capital costs of building a prison cell can be as much as $80,000. In contrast, a comprehensive drug court system typically costs between $2,500 and $4,000 annually for each offender. Evaluations from the State of Oregon and Dallas County, Texas, have shown that for every $1 invested in drug court, $10 are saved by corrections.

Are Drug Courts Programs Soft on Crime?

Drug courts across the country control participants' drug usage and activity through frequent drug testing, intensive supervision and judicial monitoring, and immediate sanctions that include terms of incarceration in response to program violations. Drug courts also provide incentives to participants who comply with program requirements: reducing terms of probation, treatment, conditions, program fees, and other innovative rewards. Historically, this population has not been motivated by the threat of incarceration alone. In fact, drug court participants find drug court more challenging than jail or prison.

What Are DUI Drug Courts?

Given the phenomenal success of drug courts across the country, many courts are beginning to apply the drug court model to DUI cases. In doing so, DUI drug courts, like traditional drug courts, are making offenders accountable for their actions in a fair and just way, thus bringing about a behavioral change that ends DUI recidivism, stopping the abuse of alcohol, and protecting the public.

(Continued)

What Are Drug Court Systems?

Drug court systems deal with all drug-using offenders while they are on probation and supervised in the community (those not sent to state prison or incarcerated in county jail). Drug court systems place drug-using offenders in appropriate drug court tracks that tailor the level of intervention and resource commitment to the needs of the offender but, more importantly, to the public safety needs of the community.

All arrestees are drug tested, and those determined to have a drug abuse problem are supervised, drug tested, and monitored by the drug court team led by the drug court judge. Denver, Minneapolis, and Tampa are jurisdictions that have successful comprehensive drug court systems.

Statistics on Drug Courts

As of January 2005, there were 1,262 drug courts that were fully operational in the United States and 575 in the planning stages (Drug Court Activity Update: January 1, 2005, Office of Justice Programs Drug Court Clearinghouse and Technical Assistance Project, 2005).

As of January 2005, there were fifty-three tribal drug courts that were fully operational in the United States and sixty-five in the planning stages (Drug Court Activity Update: January 1, 2005, Office of Justice Programs Drug Court Clearinghouse and Technical Assistance Project, 2005).

According to the latest release in the Juvenile Court Statistics series, which describes the delinquency and status offense cases that were handled between 1990 and 1999 in U.S. courts with juvenile jurisdiction, "[t]he number of drug law violation cases increased 169% between 1990 and 1999" (Juvenile Court Statistics 1999, Office of Juvenile Justice and Delinquency Prevention, 2003).

According to data compiled by the Office of Justice Programs Drug Court Clearinghouse and Technical Assistance Project from 131 of the 150 juvenile drug court programs in operation as of January 1, 2001, 63 percent of juvenile drug court participants were living with one parent at program entry (52 percent with a biological mother, 8 percent with a biological father, and 3 percent with a stepparent) (Juvenile Drug Court Activity Update: Summary Information, Office of Justice Programs Drug Court Clearinghouse and Technical Assistance Project, 2001).

Between 1984 and 1999, the number of defendants charged with a drug offense in the federal courts increased from 11,854 to 29,306 (Federal Drug Offenders, 1999 with Trends 1984–99, Bureau of Justice Statistics, 2001).

According to the Office of National Drug Control Policy, the best estimates projected that in 2000 "Americans spent about $36 billion on cocaine, $10 billion on heroin, $5.4 billion on methamphetamine, $11 billion on marijuana, and $2.4 billion on other substances" ("What America's Users Spent on Illegal Drugs 1988–2000," Office of National Drug Control Policy, 2001).

[Information taken from NCJRS Fact Sheet, Drug Court, 2005.]

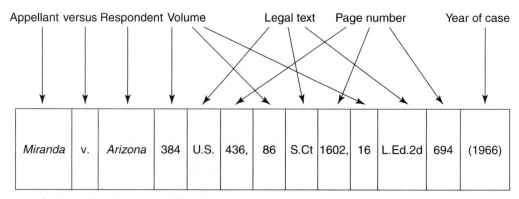

Legal Citations. (See discussion on Miranda cite on page 41.)

Law in Practice

The *Miranda* Citation

The full citation for *Miranda* is as follows: *Miranda* v. *Arizona*, 384 U.S. 436, 86 S.Ct. 1602, 16 L.Ed.2d 694 (1966). The lead name in the case usually refers to the party who lost in the lower court and is seeking to overturn that decision. That party is called the appellant. The second name refers to the other party (or parties) who won at the lower level (in this instance, the state of Arizona). The second party is called the appellee or the respondent. Miranda was seeking to overturn his conviction. The state of Arizona was named as the respondent because criminal prosecutions are brought in the name of the state.

After the names of the parties are three sets of references. All decisions of the U.S. Supreme Court are reported in the *Supreme Court Reports*, which is published by the U.S. Government Printing Office. It is the official reporting system and is abbreviated U.S. In addition, decisions of the Supreme Court are reported in two commercial reporting systems: the *Supreme Court Reporter*, which is abbreviated S.Ct., and *Lawyers Supreme Court Reports, Lawyers Edition*, which is abbreviated L.Ed.2d.

The numbers preceding the abbreviation for the volume refer to the volume number. Thus, *Miranda* can be found in volume number 384 of the *Supreme Court Reports*. The numbers after the abbreviation refer to the page number of the first page. Thus, the *Miranda* decision in volume 384 begins on page 436, in volume 86 of the *Supreme Court Reporter*, it is on page 1602, and so on.

Capstone Cases

Harmelin v. *Michigan*
111 S.Ct. 2680 (1991)

[Harmelin, an inmate, was convicted of possessing cocaine and sentenced to a mandatory term of life in prison without the possibility of parole. The Court of Appeals of Michigan affirmed the sentence, rejecting his argument that the sentence was cruel and unusual under the Eighth Amendment. The Michigan Supreme Court denied leave to appeal, and the inmate was granted certiorari by the U.S. Supreme Court. Before the Supreme Court, he claimed that his sentence was cruel and unusual because it was disproportionate to the crime and the sentencing judge was statutorily required to impose it.]

[The excerpts from this case provide the reader with a historical background of the "cruel and unusual" clause of the Eighth Amendment to the U.S. Constitution. The U.S. Supreme Court decided the case of *Ronald Allen Harmelin, Petitioner* v. *Michigan* on June 27, 1991.]

Justice Scalia announced the judgment of the Court. . . . [In this case, the defendant claims that his sentence was disproportionate and therefore in violation of the "cruel and unusual" clause of the Eighth Amendment. The Court denied his claim.]

(Continued)

Supreme Court Justice Antonio Scalia gestures while addressing the American Medical Association's National Leadership Conference in Washington, D.C., on March 9, 1998.
(*Source:* Susan Walsh/AP Wide World Photos.)

There is no doubt that the Declaration of Rights is the antecedent of our constitutional text. (This document was promulgated in February 1689 and was enacted into law as the Bill of Rights.) In 1791, five State Constitutions prohibited "cruel or unusual punishments," and two prohibited "cruel" punishments. The new Federal Bill of Rights, however, tracked Virginia's prohibition of "cruel and unusual punishments," which most closely followed the English provision. In fact, the entire text of the Eighth Amendment is taken almost verbatim from the English Declaration of Rights, which provided "[t]hat excessive Baile ought not to be required nor excessive Fines imposed nor cruell and unusuall Punishments inflicted."

Compare this case with a recent United States Supreme Court decision dealing with cruel and unusual punishment in the 21st Century.

Perhaps the Americans of 1791 understood the Declaration's language precisely as the Englishmen of 1689 did—though as we shall discuss later, that seems unlikely. Or perhaps the colonists meant to incorporate the content of that antecedent by reference, whatever the content might have been. Solem suggested something like this, arguing that since Americans claimed "all the rights of English subjects," "their use of the language of the English Bill of Rights is convincing proof that they intended to provide at least the same protection," . . . Thus, not only is the original meaning of the 1689 Declaration of Rights relevant, but also the circumstances of its enactment, insofar as they display the particular "rights of English subjects" it was designed to vindicate. . . . The Magna Charta provided that "[a] free man shall not be fined for a small offence, except in proportion to the measure of the offence; and for a great offence he shall be fined in proportion to the magnitude of the offence, saving his freehold. . . ." Most historians agree that the "cruell and unusual Punishments" provision of the English Declaration of Rights was prompted by the abuses attributed to the infamous Lord Chief Justice Jeffreys of the King's Bench during the Stuart reign of James II. . . . They do not agree, however, on which abuses.

Justices Jeffreys is best known for presiding over the "Bloody Assizes" following the Duke of Monmouth's abortive rebellion in 1685; a special Commission led by Jeffreys tried, convicted, and executed hundreds of suspected insurgents. Some have attributed the Declaration of Rights provision to popular outrage against those proceedings.

But the vicious punishments for treason decreed in the Bloody Assizes (drawing and quartering, burning of women felons, beheading, disemboweling, etc.) were common in that period—indeed, they were specifically authorized by law and remained so for many years afterwards. Thus, recently historians have argued, and the best historical evidence suggests, that it was not Jeffreys' management of the Bloody Assizes that led to the Declaration of Rights provision, but rather the arbitrary sentencing power he had exercised in administering justice from the King's Bench, particularly when punishing a notorious perjurer. Jeffreys was widely accused of "inventing" special penalties for the King's enemies, penalties that were not authorized by common-law precedent or statute.

The preamble to the Declaration of Rights, a sort of indictment of James II that calls to mind the preface to our own Declaration of Independence, specifically referred to illegal sentences and King's Bench proceedings. "Whereas the late King James the Second, by the Assistance of diverse Evil Councellors, Judges and Ministers imployed by him did endeavour to subvert and extirpate the Protestant Religion, and the Lawes and Liberties of this Kingdome."

"By Prosecutions in the Court of King's Bench for Matters and Causes cognizable onely in Parlyament and by diverse other Arbitrary and Illegall Courses. [E]xcessive Baile hath beene required of Persons committed in Criminal Cases to elude the Benefit of the Lawes made for the Liberty of the Subjects. And excessive Fines have been imposed. And illegall and cruell Punishments have been inflicted. All which are utterly and directly contrary to the knowne Lawes and Statutes and Freedome of this Realme."

The only recorded contemporaneous interpretation of the "cruell and unusuall Punishments" clause confirms the focus upon Jeffreys' King's Bench activities, and upon the illegality rather than the disproportionality of his sentences. In 1685 Titus Oates, a Protestant cleric whose false accusations had caused the execution of 15 prominent Catholics for allegedly organizing a "Popish Plot" to overthrow King Charles in 1679, was tried and convicted before the King's Bench for perjury. Oates' crime, "bearing false witness against another, with an express premeditated design to take away his life, so as the innocent person be condemned and executed" had, at one time, been treated as a species of murder, and punished with death. At sentencing, Jeffreys complained that death was no longer available as a penalty and lamented that "a proportionable punishment of that crime can scarce by our law, as it now stands, be inflicted upon him." The law would not stand in the way, however. The judges met, and, according to Jeffreys, were in unanimous agreement that "crimes of this nature are left to be punished according to the discretion of this court, so far as that the judgment extend not to life or member." Another Justice taunted Oates that "we have taken special care of you," . . . The court then decreed that he should pay a fine of "1000 marks upon each Indictment," that he should be "stript of [his] Canonical Habits," that he should stand in the pillory annually at certain specified times and places, that on May 20 he should be whipped by "the common hangman" "from Aldgate to Newgate," that he should be similarly whipped on May 22 "from Newgate to Tyburn," and that he should be imprisoned for life.

"The judges, as they believed, sentenced Oates to be scourged to death." Oates would not die, however. Four years later, and several months after the Declaration of Rights, he petitioned the House of Lords to set aside his sentence as illegal. "Not a single peer ventured to affirm that the judgment was legal; but much was said about the odious character of the appellant" and the Lords affirmed the judgment. A minority of the Lords dissented, however, and their statement sheds light on the meaning of the "cruell and unusuall Punishments" clause: "1st, [The King's Bench] being a Temporal Court, made it a Part of the judgment, That Titus Oates, being a Clerk, should, for his said Perjuries, be divested of his canonical and priestly Habit . . . ; which is a Matter wholly out of their Power, belonging to the Ecclesiastical Courts only. 2ndly, [S]aid Judgments are barbarous, inhuman, and unchristian; and there is no Precedent to warrant the Punishments of whipping and committing to Prison for Life, for the Crime of Perjury; which yet were but Part of the Punishments inflicted upon him. 4thly, [T]his will be an Encouragement and Allowance for giving the like cruel, barbarous and illegal Judgments hereafter, unless this Judgment be reversed. 5thly, . . . [T]hat the said Judgments were contrary to Law and ancient Practice, and therefore erroneous, and ought to be reversed. 6thly, Because it is contrary to the Declaration on the Twelfth of February last that excessive Baile ought not to be required, nor excessive Fines imposed, nor cruel nor unusual Punishments afflicted."

Unless one accepts the notion of a blind incorporation, however, the ultimate question is not what "cruell and unusuall punishments" meant in the Declaration of Rights, but what its meaning was to the Americans who adopted the Eighth Amendment. Even if one assumes that the Founders knew the precise meaning of that English antecedent, a direct transplant of the English meaning to the soil of American constitutionalism would in any case have been impossible.

There were no common-law punishments in the federal system, so that the provision must have been meant as a check not upon judges but upon the Legislature.

Wrenched out of its common-law context, and applied to the actions of a legislature, the word "unusual" could hardly mean "contrary to law." But it continued to mean (as it continues to mean today) "such as [does not] occu[r] in ordinary practice," "[s]uch as is [not] in common use," . . . According to its terms, then, by forbidding "cruel and unusual punishments." (*Continued*)

The Eighth Amendment received little attention during the proposal and adoption of the Federal Bill of Rights. However, what evidence exists from debates at the state ratifying conventions that prompted the Bill of Rights as well as the Floor debates in the First Congress which proposed it "confirm[s] the view that the cruel and unusual punishments clause was directed at prohibiting certain methods of punishment."

Atkins v. *Virginia*
122 S.Ct. 2242 (2002)

[Compare and contrast this case with *Harmelin* v. *Michigan*. Has the Supreme Court changed its fundamental position on cruel and unusual punishment? What is the effect of society's perception on the execution of the mentally retarded on the Court's decision?]

Justice John Paul Stevens was appointed to the Supreme Court by President Ford and has served from 1975 to the present. (*Source:* Joseph Bailey, National Geographic Society. Courtesy of the Supreme Court of the United States.)

Those mentally retarded persons who meet the law's requirements for criminal responsibility should be tried and punished when they commit crimes. Because of their disabilities in areas of reasoning, judgment, and control of their impulses, however, they do not act with the level of moral culpability that characterizes the most serious adult criminal conduct. Moreover, their impairments can jeopardize the reliability and fairness of capital proceedings against mentally retarded defendants. Presumably for these reasons, in the 13 years since we decided *Penry* v. *Lynaugh*, 492 U.S. 302 (1989), the American public, legislators, scholars, and judges have deliberated over the question [of] whether the death penalty should ever be imposed on a mentally retarded criminal. The consensus reflected in those deliberations informs our answer to the question presented by this case: whether such executions are "cruel and unusual punishments" prohibited by the Eighth Amendment to the Federal Constitution.

Petitioner, Daryl Renard Atkins, was convicted of abduction, armed robbery, and capital murder, and sentenced to death. At approximately midnight on August 16, 1996, Atkins and William Jones, armed with a semi-automatic handgun, abducted Eric Nesbitt, robbed him of the money on his person, drove him to an automated teller machine in his pickup truck where cameras recorded their withdrawal of additional cash, then took him to an isolated location where he was shot eight times and killed.

Jones and Atkins both testified in the guilt phase of Atkins' trial. Each confirmed most of the details in the other's account of the incident, with the important exception that each stated that the other had actually shot and killed Nesbitt. Jones' testimony, which was both more coherent and credible than Atkins', was obviously credited by the jury and was sufficient to establish Atkins' guilt. At the penalty phase of the trial, the State introduced victim impact evidence and proved two aggravating circumstances: future dangerousness and "vileness of the offense." To prove future dangerousness, the State relied on Atkins' prior felony convictions as well as the testimony of four victims of earlier robberies and assaults. To prove the second aggravator, the prosecution relied upon the trial record, including pictures of the deceased's body and the autopsy report.

In the penalty phase, the defense relied on one witness, Dr. Evan Nelson, a forensic psychologist who had evaluated Atkins before trial and concluded that he was "mildly mentally retarded." His conclusion was based on interviews with people who knew Atkins, a review of school and court records, and the administration of a standard intelligence test which indicated that Atkins had a full scale IQ of 59.

[The American Psychiatric Association's *Diagnostic and Statistical Manual of Mental Disorders* 41 (4th ed. 2000) defines "Mild" mental retardation as typically used to describe people with an IQ level of 50–55 to approximately 70.]

The Supreme Court of Virginia affirmed the imposition of the death penalty. Because of the gravity of the concerns expressed by the dissenters at the state supreme court, and in light of the dramatic shift in the state legislative landscape that has occurred in the past 13 years, we granted certiorari to revisit the issue that we first addressed in the Penry case.

The Eighth Amendment succinctly prohibits "excessive" sanctions. It provides: "Excessive bail shall not be required, nor excessive fines imposed, nor cruel and unusual punishments inflicted." In *Weems* v. *United States*, 217 U.S. 349 (1910), we held that a punishment of 12 years jailed in irons at hard and painful labor for the crime of falsifying records was excessive. We explained "that it is a precept of justice that punishment for crime should be graduated and proportioned to the offense." We have repeatedly applied this proportionality precept in later cases interpreting the Eighth Amendment. See *Harmelin* v. *Michigan*, 501 U.S. 957, (1991)].

As Chief Justice Warren explained in his opinion in *Trop* v. *Dulles*, 356 U.S. 86 (1958): "The basic concept underlying the Eighth Amendment is nothing less than the dignity of man. . . . The Amendment must draw its meaning from the evolving standards of decency that mark the progress of a maturing society."

Proportionality review under those evolving standards should be informed by " 'objective [[**16]] factors to the maximum possible extent,'" see *Harmelin*, 501 U.S., at 1000. We have pinpointed that the "clearest and most reliable objective evidence of contemporary values is the legislation enacted by the country's legislatures."

Thus, in cases involving a consensus, our own judgment is "brought to bear," by asking whether there is reason to disagree with the judgment reached by the citizenry and its legislators.

Guided by our approach in these cases, we shall first review the judgment of legislatures that have addressed the suitability of imposing the death penalty on the mentally retarded and then consider reasons for agreeing or disagreeing with their judgment.

The parties have not called our attention to any state legislative consideration of the suitability of imposing the death penalty on mentally retarded offenders prior to 1986. In that year, the public reaction to the execution of a mentally retarded murderer in Georgia apparently led to the enactment of the first state statute prohibiting such executions. In 1988, when Congress enacted legislation reinstating the federal death penalty, it expressly provided that a "sentence of death shall not be carried out upon a person who is mentally retarded." In 1989, Maryland enacted a similar prohibition. Responding to the national attention [regarding this issue], state legislatures across the country began to address the issue.

It is not so much the number of these States that is significant, but the consistency of the direction of change. The practice [of executing the mentally retarded], therefore, has become truly unusual, and it is fair to say that a national consensus has developed against it.

Our independent evaluation of the issue reveals no reason to disagree with the judgment of "the legislatures that have recently addressed the matter" and concluded that death is not a suitable punishment for a mentally retarded criminal. We are not persuaded that the execution of mentally retarded criminals will measurably advance the deterrent or the retributive purpose of the death penalty. Construing and applying the Eighth Amendment in the light of our "evolving standards of decency," we therefore conclude that such punishment is excessive and that the Constitution "places a substantive restriction on the State's power to take the life" of a mentally retarded offender.

(Continued)

The judgment of the Virginia Supreme Court is reversed and the case is remanded for further proceedings not inconsistent with this opinion.

It is so ordered.

DISSENT:

[Chief Justice Rehnquist] The question presented by this case is whether a national consensus deprives Virginia of the constitutional power to impose the death penalty on capital murder defendants like petitioner, i.e., those defendants who indisputably are competent to stand trial, aware of the punishment they are about to suffer and why, and whose mental retardation has been found an insufficiently compelling reason to lessen their individual responsibility for the crime. The Court pronounces the punishment cruel and unusual primarily because 18 States recently have passed laws limiting the death eligibility of certain defendants based on mental retardation alone, despite the fact that the laws of 19 other States besides Virginia continue to leave the question of proper punishment to the individuated consideration of sentencing judges or juries familiar with the particular offender and his or her crime.

In making determinations about whether a punishment is "cruel and unusual" under the evolving standards of decency embraced by the Eighth Amendment, we have emphasized that legislation is the "clearest and most reliable objective evidence of contemporary values." The reason we ascribe primacy to legislative enactments follows from the constitutional role legislatures play in expressing policy of a State. "'In a democratic society legislatures, not courts, are constituted to respond to the will and consequently the moral values of the people.'" Our opinions have also recognized that data concerning the actions of sentencing juries, though entitled to less weight than legislative judgments, "'is a significant and reliable index of contemporary values.'"

To further buttress its appraisal of contemporary societal values, the Court marshals public opinion poll results and evidence that several professional organizations and religious groups have adopted official positions opposing the imposition of the death penalty upon mentally retarded offenders. In my view, none should be accorded any weight on the Eighth Amendment scale when the elected representatives of a State's populace have not deemed them persuasive enough to prompt legislative action. Even if I were to accept the legitimacy of the Court's decision to reach beyond the product of legislatures and practices of sentencing juries to discern a national standard of decency, I would take issue with the blind-faith credence it accords the opinion polls brought to our attention. An extensive body of social science literature describes how methodological and other errors can affect the reliability and validity of estimates about the opinions and attitudes of a population derived from various sampling techniques. Everything from variations in the survey methodology, such as the choice of the target population, the sampling design used, the questions asked, and the statistical analyses used to interpret the data can skew the results.

Justice Scalia, with whom the Chief Justice and Justice Thomas join, dissenting.

Today's decision is the pinnacle of our Eighth Amendment death-is-different jurisprudence. Not only does it, like all of that jurisprudence, find no support in the text or history of the Eighth Amendment; it does not even have support in current social attitudes regarding the conditions that render an otherwise just death penalty inappropriate. Seldom has an opinion of this Court rested so obviously upon nothing but the personal views of its members.

Under our Eighth Amendment jurisprudence, a punishment is "cruel and unusual" if it falls within one of two categories: "those modes or acts of punishment that had been considered cruel and unusual at the time that the Bill of Rights was adopted," *Ford* v. *Wainwright*, 477 U.S. 399 (1986), and modes of punishment that are inconsistent with modern "standards of decency," as evinced by objective indicia, the most important of which is "legislation enacted by the country's legislatures."

The Court makes no pretense that execution of the mildly mentally retarded would have been considered "cruel and unusual" in 1791. Only the severely or profoundly mentally retarded, commonly known as "idiots," enjoyed any special status under the law at that time. They, like lunatics, suffered a "deficiency in will" rendering them unable to tell right from wrong. 4 W. Blackstone, Commentaries on the Laws of England 24 (1769).

The Court is left to argue, therefore, that execution of the mildly retarded is inconsistent with the "evolving standards of decency that mark the progress of a maturing society." Before today, our opinions consistently emphasized that Eighth Amendment judgments regarding the existence of social "standards" "should be informed by objective factors to the maximum possible extent" and "should not be, or appear to be, merely the subjective views of individual Justices."

[T]he Prize for the Court's Most Feeble Effort to fabricate "national consensus" must go to its appeal (deservedly relegated to a footnote) to the views of assorted professional and religious organizations, members of the so-called "world community," and respondents to opinion polls. I agree with the CHIEF JUSTICE, (dissenting opinion), that the views of professional and religious organizations and the results of opinion polls are irrelevant. Equally irrelevant are the practices of the "world community," whose notions of justice are (thankfully) not always those of our people. "We must never forget that it is a Constitution for the United States of America that we are expounding. . . . Where there is not first a settled consensus among our own people, the views of other nations, however enlightened the Justices of this Court may think them to be, cannot be imposed upon Americans through the Constitution."

Nothing has changed the accuracy of Matthew Hale's endorsement of the common law's traditional method for taking account of guilt-reducing factors, written over three centuries ago:

> "[Determination of a person's incapacity] is a matter of great difficulty, partly from the easiness of counterfeiting this disability . . . and partly from the variety of the degrees of this infirmity, whereas some are sufficient, and some are insufficient to excuse persons in capital offenses. . . .
>
> "Yet the law of England hath afforded the best method of trial, that is possible, of this and all other matters of fact, namely, by a jury of twelve men all concurring in the same judgment, by the testimony of witnesses . . . and by the inspection and direction of the judge." 1 Hale, *Pleas of the Crown*, at 32–33.

JUDICIAL DEFINITIONS

This section contains some key definitions used in the judicial system.

Aggravation or circumstances in aggravation. Facts that tend to justify the imposition of the more severe punishment.

Mitigation or circumstances in mitigation. Facts that tend to justify the imposition of a lesser punishment.

Civil contempt. Willful, continuing failure or refusal of any person to comply with a court's lawful writ, subpoena, process, order, rule, or command that by its nature is still capable of being complied with.

Complaint. A written statement made upon oath before a judge, magistrate, or official authorized by law to issue warrants of arrest, setting forth essential facts constituting an offense and alleging that the defendant committed the offense.

Constructive contempt. Any criminal or civil contempt other than direct contempt. [*See* Direct contempt.]

Criminal contempt. Either:

- Misconduct of any person that obstructs the administration of justice and that is committed either in the court's presence or so near thereto as to interrupt, disturb, or hinder its proceedings, or
- Willful disobedience or resistance of any person to a court's lawful writ, subpoena, process, order, rule, or command, where the dominant purpose of the contempt proceeding is to punish the contemptor.

Curtilage of a dwelling-house. A space, necessary and convenient and habitually used for family purposes and the carrying on of domestic employments. It includes the garden, if there is one, and it need not be separated from other lands by a fence.

Determination of guilt. A verdict of guilty by a jury, a finding of guilty by a court following a nonjury trial, or the acceptance by the court of a plea of guilty.

Direct contempt. Disorderly or insolent behavior or other misconduct committed in open court, in the presence of the judge, that disturbs the court's business, where all of the essential elements of the misconduct occur in the presence of the court and are actually observed by the court, and where immediate action is essential to prevent diminution of the court's dignity and authority before the public.

Duplicate. A counterpart produced by the same impression as the original, or from the same matrix, or by means of photography, including enlargements and miniatures, or by mechanical or electronic rerecording, or by chemical reproduction, or by other equivalent techniques which accurately reproduce the original.

Evidence relating to past sexual behavior. Such a term includes, but is not limited to, evidence of the complaining witness's marital history, mode of dress, and general reputation for promiscuity, nonchastity, or sexual mores contrary to the community standards and opinion of character for those traits.

Evidentiary hearing. A hearing held by the trial court to resolve contested factual issues.

Harmless error. Any error, defect, irregularity, or variance that does not affect substantial rights shall be disregarded.

Hearsay. A statement, other than one made by the declarant (person who makes the statement) while testifying at the trial or hearing, offered in evidence to prove the truth of the matter asserted.

Husband-wife privilege. A communication is confidential if it is made privately by any person to his or her spouse and is not intended for disclosure to any other person. An accused in a criminal proceeding has a privilege to prevent his spouse from testifying as to any confidential communication between the accused and the spouse. The privilege may be claimed by the accused or by the spouse on behalf of the accused. The authority of the spouse to do so is presumed. There is no privilege under this rule in a proceeding in which one spouse is charged with a crime against the other person or property of (1) the other, (2) a child of either, (3) a person residing in the household of either, or (4) a third person committed in the course of committing a crime against any of them.

Indictment. A written statement charging the defendant or defendants named therein with the commission of an indictable offense, presented to the court by a grand jury, endorsed "A True Bill," and signed by the foreman. The term indictment includes presentment.

Indigent. A person who is financially unable to pay for his or her defense.

Information. A written statement charging the defendant or defendants named therein with the commission of an indictable offense, made on oath, signed, and presented to the court by the district attorney without action by a grand jury.

Judgment. The adjudication of the court based upon a plea of guilty by the defendant, upon the verdict of the jury, or upon its own finding following a nonjury trial, that the defendant is guilty or not guilty.

Law enforcement officer and **officer.** Any person vested by law with a duty to maintain public order or to make arrests for offenses.

Magistrate. Includes magistrates, district judges, superior court judges, and any other judicial officer authorized by law to conduct a preliminary examination of a person accused of a crime or issue a warrant.

Mentally incompetent. Unable to stand trial or to be sentenced for an offense if the defendant lacks sufficient present ability to assist in his or her defense by consulting with counsel with a reasonable degree of rational understanding of the facts and the legal proceedings against the defendant.

Order to show cause. An order in response to a habeas corpus petition directing the respondent (warden) to file a return. The order to show cause is issued if the petitioner (prisoner) has made a prima facie showing that he or she is entitled to relief; it does not grant the relief requested. An order to show cause may also be referred to as "granting the writ."

Original. In regard to a writing or recording, the writing or recording itself or any counterpart intended to produce the same effect by a person executing or issuing it. An original of a photograph includes the negative or any print therefrom. If data are stored in a computer or a similar device, any printout or other output readable by sight, shown to reflect the data accurately, is an original.

Plain error. Plain errors or defects affecting substantial rights may be noticed, although they were not brought to the attention of the court.

Reasonable cause to believe. A basis for belief in the existence of facts that, in view of the circumstances under and purposes for which the standard is applied, is substantial, objective, and sufficient to satisfy applicable constitutional requirements.

Reasonable suspicion. A suspicion based on facts or circumstances that of themselves do not give rise to the probable cause requisite to justify a lawful arrest, but that give rise to more than a bare suspicion; that is, a suspicion that is reasonable as opposed to an imaginary or purely conjectural suspicion.

Release on own recognizance. Release of a defendant without bail upon his or her promise to appear at all appropriate times, sometimes referred to as personal recognizance.

Relevant evidence. Evidence having any tendency to make the existence of any fact that is of consequence to the determination of the action more probable or less probable than it would be without the evidence.

Return. The law enforcement officer executing an arrest warrant shall endorse thereon the manner and date of execution, shall subscribe his name, and shall return the arrest warrant to the clerk of the court specified in the arrest warrant.

Search. Any intrusion other than an arrest, by an officer under color of authority, upon an individual's person, property, or privacy, for the purpose of seizing individuals or things or obtaining information by inspection or surveillance, if such intrusion, in the absence of legal authority or sufficient consent, would be a civil wrong, criminal offense, or violation of the individual's rights under the Constitution of the United States or the state.

Search warrant. A written order, in the name of the state or municipality, signed by a judge or magistrate authorized by law to issue search warrants, directed to any law enforcement officer as defined by Rule 1.4(p), commanding him or her to search for personal property and, if found, to bring it before the issuing judge or magistrate.

Seizure. The taking of any person or thing or the obtaining of information by an officer pursuant to a search or under other color of authority.

Subpoenas. Orders issued by the clerk of the court in which a criminal proceeding is pending at any time for such witnesses as any party may require for attendance at trial and at hearings, for taking depositions, or for any other lawful purpose.

Summons. An order issued by a judicial officer or, pursuant to the authorization of a judicial officer, by the clerk of a court, requiring a person against whom a criminal charge has been filed to appear in a designated court at a specified date and time.

Victim. A person against whom a criminal offense has allegedly been committed, or the spouse, parent, lawful representative, or child of someone killed or incapacitated by the alleged criminal offense, except where the spouse, parent, lawful representative, or child is also the accused.

Waiver of error. No party may assign as error on appeal the court's giving or failing to give any instruction or portion thereof or to the submission or the failure to submit a form of verdict unless the party objects thereto before the jury retires to consider its verdict, stating distinctly the matter to which the party objects and the grounds of his or her objection.

Work product. Discovery cannot be required of legal research or of records, correspondence, reports, or memoranda to the extent that they contain the opinions, theories, or conclusions of the prosecutor, members of the prosecutor's legal or investigative staff or law enforcement officers, or of defense counsel or defense counsel's legal or investigative staff.

SUMMARY

- The law is merely a guideline for human behavior.
- The study of our justice system should be viewed as a cluster of ideas, principles, and values about which reasonable persons can and do disagree.
- Judicial opinions construe the constitutionality, meaning, and effect of constitutional and statutory provisions.
- Most individuals agree that the most basic goal of the criminal justice system is to protect society from crime.
- Criminal justice professionals are generally oriented toward one of two opposite goals—law and order or individual rights.
- The pragmatic goals include the goal of preventing crime.
- Organizations have developed standards, which are detailed goals for improving the system.
- Although the criminal justice system is referred to as a system, it is more accurate to refer to it as a nonsystem.
- Two important questions regarding the burden of proof in criminal proceedings are: Who has the burden of proving an issue? and What is the magnitude of the burden?
- The Code of Hammurabi is considered one of the first-known attempts to establish a written code of conduct.
- Most of our criminal law concepts and principles originated in the common law of England.
- Today the criminal laws of the states are largely the result of legislative action.
- The Magna Charta is considered the forerunner of the present due process rights.
- The court system in the United States is based upon the principle of federalism.
- A dual system of state and federal courts exists today.
- Appellate jurisdiction is reserved for courts that hear appeals from both limited and general jurisdiction courts. In many states, the appeals from minor courts are heard de novo.
- The Judiciary Act of 1789 created the U.S. Supreme Court and established district and circuit courts of appeal.
- Venue is the geographic area in which a case may be heard.
- Jurisdiction is the power of a court to hear and determine an issue.

REVIEW QUESTIONS

1. Why are laws necessary?
2. Define common law.
3. How do we classify laws?

4. What is civil law?
5. What is ecclesiastical law?
6. In what year was the Magna Charta signed?
7. What significant contribution did the Magna Charta make to the administration of justice?
8. How did the trial by ordeal and the trial by battle differ from each other?
9. Describe a trial by compurgation.
10. How did the English kings use early juries?
11. What was the accusatory jury?
12. The U.S. Bill of Rights is what part of what document?
13. What portions of the Bill of Rights are of particular significance to the administration of justice?
14. What amendment makes the Bill of Rights applicable to the states?
15. Define venue.
16. Define jurisdiction.
17. How do jurisdiction and venue differ from each other?

LOCAL PROCEDURE

Since judicial procedure differs slightly from state to state, the reader may wish to consult the local prosecuting attorney for the procedure within his or her state.

1. By what names are trial courts known in your state?
2. What are the trial jurisdictions of the trial courts in your state?
3. What are the qualifications of the judges presiding over the trial courts in your state?

ENDNOTES

1. 258 NY 292 (1932).
2. *Mapp* v. *Ohio,* 367 U.S. 643 (1961).
3. *Malloy* v. *Hogan,* 378 U.S. 1 (1964).
4. *Benton* v. *Maryland,* 95 U.S. 784 (1969).
5. *Gibdeon* v. *Wainwright,* 372 U.S. 335 (1963).
6. *Kloper* v. *N.C.,* 386 U.S. 335 (1967).
7. In re *Oliver,* 330 U.S. 257 (1942).
8. *Pointer* v. *Texas,* 380 U.S. 400 (1965).
9. *Duncan* v. *Louisiana,* 391 U.S. 145 (1968).
10. Portions of this section have been adapted from Harvey Wallace, "The Roles of Federal and State Law: The Judicial System and Victims of Crime in *The National Victim Assistance Academy Text* (OVC, Washington D.C.), 2001.
11. Pursley, *Introduction to Criminal Justice,* 6th ed. (Macmillan, New York), 1994.
12. 437 U.S. 328 (1976).
13. *The Supreme Court of the United States* (U.S. Government Printing Office, Washington, D.C.).
14. 1 Cranh 137 (1803).

The right of the people to be secure in their persons, houses, papers, and effects, against unreasonable searches and seizures, shall not be violated, and no Warrants shall issue, but upon probable cause, supported by Oath or affirmation and particularly describing the place to be searched, and the persons or things to be seized.

—Fourth Amendment of the U.S. Constitution (1791)

Search and Seizure

2

Chapter Outline

Key Words

Abandonment

Exclusionary Rule

Expectation of privacy zone

Fruits of the Poisonous Tree Doctrine

Independent state grounds

Magistrate

Open fields

Plain View Doctrine

Probable cause

Search

Learning Objectives

After completing this chapter, you should be able to:

1. Discuss the purpose of the Exclusionary Rule.
2. Explain the Fruits of the Poisonous Tree Doctrine.
3. Define the protected areas and interests.
4. Explain the requirements for obtaining a search warrant.
5. Identify the restrictions on inspections and regulatory searches.
6. List the exceptions to the Fourth Amendment.
7. Explain the purpose of the Fourth Amendment.

HISTORY AND PURPOSE
OF THE FOURTH AMENDMENT

From a criminal procedure perspective, the Fourth and Fifth Amendments contain the most important language in existence within the U.S. legal structure. It must be stressed that not all searches are prohibited, only those that are unreasonable. The issues surrounding searches and seizures can become quite complex, and many times students or even professionals in the field lose sight of the rationale and reasons for the Fourth Amendment. Asking the following questions any time that a **search** or seizure situation arises will assist in analyzing this complex area of constitutional law:

1. **Does the Fourth Amendment apply?** If it does not apply, the question of reasonableness and warrants and probable cause are irrelevant. For example, as will be discussed later in this chapter, there are certain situations, such as evidence found in open fields, that can be seized because the Fourth Amendment does not apply to property found in open fields.

2. **If the Fourth Amendment does apply, has it been complied with?** If all the requirements have been satisfied, then any evidence will be admitted. If it has not been complied with, go to question 3.

3. **If the Fourth Amendment does apply and has not been complied with, what sanctions will the court impose on any evidence seized in violation of the amendment?** The court has a range of options available to it if it determines that the officers or agents have violated the Fourth Amendment.

These are simple questions and a seemingly simple approach to the concepts of search and seizure, but using this approach will enable students to focus on the correct issues within this area of criminal procedure.

When the U.S. Constitution was being drafted and considered by our forefathers, very little, if any, thought was given to including a declaration of rights for individual citizens. At that time, the original state constitutions contained language that purported to protect individuals from undue oppression by the government. However, the ratification process produced a movement to include amendments in the form of a Bill of

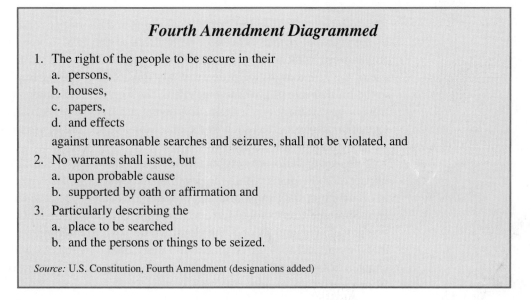

Fourth Amendment Diagrammed

1. The right of the people to be secure in their
   a. persons,
   b. houses,
   c. papers,
   d. and effects
   against unreasonable searches and seizures, shall not be violated, and
2. No warrants shall issue, but
   a. upon probable cause
   b. supported by oath or affirmation and
3. Particularly describing the
   a. place to be searched
   b. and the persons or things to be seized.

Source: U.S. Constitution, Fourth Amendment (designations added)

The twelve amendments submitted by the U.S. Congress in 1790 to safeguard the rights of individuals from the interference of the federal government. Ten of them were adopted in 1791 as the Bill of Rights. This document bears the signature of then Vice President John Adams. (*Source:* Getty Images Inc., Hulton Archive Photos.)

Rights, which would address individual rights and restrict government action in the area of the criminal justice process. The drafters of the U.S. Constitution and the Bill of Rights were influenced by a number of factors, including our English heritage, the misuse of the criminal justice process within the colonies during English rule, and a belief in the limited role of government.[1] Thus, the Fourth Amendment was based upon a distrust of government and a desire to prevent arbitrary actions by that government or its agents in personal areas such as the unreasonable seizure of persons, property, or other items without proper justification.

However, before the rights that are guaranteed in the Bill of Rights could have an impact on individuals within the criminal justice system, two critical events would have to occur: First, since most criminal prosecutions take place at the local or state level, the U.S. Supreme Court would have to make the Bill of Rights apply to local criminal justice procedures; and second, the Court would have to interpret those rights and the way that they impact local government and individual citizens. As will be seen later in this chapter, both of those events would occur, with the result that individuals are protected from invasive governmental action.

The Byron White Federal Court Building, Denver, Colorado. (*Source:* Cliff Roberson.)

The Fourth Amendment deals with the "seizures" of both persons and property. To properly understand its scope and ramifications within the criminal justice system, we should examine a concept known as the Exclusionary Rule.

EXCLUSIONARY RULE

In 1914, the U.S. Supreme Court decided *Weeks* v. *United States* that established the **Exclusionary Rule** and its applicability to the federal government.[2] In *Weeks,* local and federal law enforcement officers seized evidence from the home of the defendant. The Court excluded the evidence seized by the federal officers, holding that to allow it would defy the prohibitions of the Constitution that were intended to protect the people against such unauthorized actions. While the federal prohibition remained in effect, local police were still able to conduct searches and seizures according to the rules established by the individual states, since the Fourth Amendment applied only to federal action for the next thirty-five years.

In 1949, the Court issued its ruling in *Wolf* v. *Colorado.*[3] This was the first time the Supreme Court considered whether the Fourth Amendment should be imposed upon state proceedings by using the Fourteenth Amendment due process clause. In *Wolf,* the Court addressed the question of whether a conviction by a state court for a state offense denies due process of law as required by the Fourteenth Amendment solely because evidence admitted at the trial was obtained in a manner that would have rendered it inadmissible in a federal court, since such evidence would have been obtained in violation of the Fourth Amendment. Although acknowledging that individuals should be secure from arbitrary intrusion by police and that such security is basic to a free society, the *Wolf* Court reviewed the states' acceptance of the *Weeks* doctrine and pointed out that at the time of the decision, thirty states rejected the concept. The justices therefore held that the Fourteenth Amendment does not forbid admission of evidence obtained in violation of the Fourth Amendment. It would take another twelve years before the Court would overrule *Wolf* when it decided its landmark case of *Mapp* v. *Ohio*.[4]

In *Mapp* v. *Ohio,* the Court expressly overruled *Wolf* by acknowledging that *Wolf* was founded on factual considerations that lacked validity in today's society. The Court found that in the intervening years (since its decision in *Wolf*), a number of states had accepted the validity of the Exclusionary Rule, and experience had demonstrated that other options and remedies to prevent illegal searches were worthless and futile.

In *Mapp,* three Cleveland police officers arrived at Mapp's home to search for a person who was wanted for questioning in connection with a recent bombing. Miss Mapp and her daughter lived on the second floor of the two-family dwelling. Upon arrival at the home, the officers knocked on the door and demanded entry, but Miss Mapp, after telephoning her attorney, refused to admit them without a search warrant. Three hours later, after additional officers were on the scene, the officers forced a door in the house. By that time, Miss Mapp's attorney had arrived, but the officers would not allow him to enter the house or consult with Miss Mapp. Meanwhile, as the officers entered the house, Miss Mapp demanded to see their search warrant. One of the officers held out a paper and claimed that it was the warrant. Miss Mapp grabbed the paper and placed it in her bosom. The officers struggled with her, regained possession of the "warrant," and placed her under arrest. The officers searched the house, dressers, and trunks, finding some obscene material in a trunk. Miss Mapp was charged with and convicted of possession of obscene material. At the trial no search warrant was produced, nor was the failure to produce one explained. Miss Mapp was convicted, and she appealed.

In overturning her conviction, the Supreme Court stated:

> Moreover, our holding . . . is not only the logical dictate of prior cases but it also makes very good sense. There is no war between the Constitution and common sense. Presently, a federal prosecutor may make no use of evidence illegally seized [because of *Weeks*], but a State's attorney across the street may. . . . Thus the State, by admitting evidence unlawfully seized, serves to encourage disobedience to the Federal Constitution which it is bound to uphold. . . .
>
> Our decision, founded on reason and truth, gives to the individual no more than that which the Constitution guarantees him, to the police officer no less that that to which honest law enforcement is entitled, and, to the courts, that judicial integrity so necessary in the true administration of justice. . . .

The deterrence effect on unreasonable searches and seizure is a major purpose of the Exclusionary Rule. However, the rule also serves at least two other purposes. The judicial integrity approach is to ensure that courts will not become accomplices in violating the rules they were sworn to uphold. Another purpose is to ensure that citizens understand that the government will not profit by unlawful activity, thereby minimizing the lack of trust in our government.

What happens if the officers conducting the search were acting in good faith? This is exactly the situation in *United States* v. *Leon*.[5] This case presented the question of whether the Exclusionary Rule should be modified to allow the use of evidence obtained by officers acting in reasonable reliance on a search warrant issued by a detached and neutral magistrate but ultimately found to be unsupported by probable cause. During trial, respondents filed motions to suppress evidence seized pursuant to a warrant and said that motions were granted in part based on the conclusion that the warrant was not

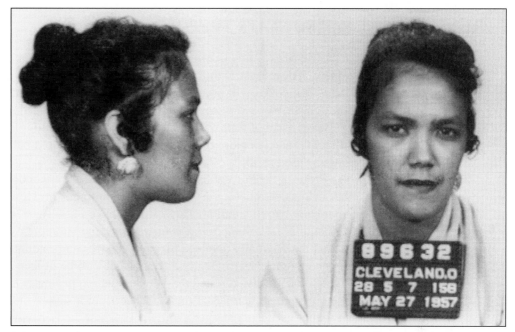

Police photo of Dolree (Dolly) Mapp. In *Mapp* v. *Ohio* (1961), the U.S. Supreme Court required states to apply the Exclusionary Rule in cases involving illegal searches. (*Source:* AP Wide World Photos.)

supported by probable cause despite the fact that the police officer was acting in good-faith reliance on what he believed to be a valid warrant. The lower court affirmed and held that there was no good-faith exception to the Exclusionary Rule. The U.S. Supreme Court reversed this decision and held that the Exclusionary Rule should be modified so as not to bar the admission of evidence seized in reasonable, good-faith reliance on a search warrant that was subsequently held to be defective. The Court concluded that the marginal or nonexistent benefits produced by suppressing evidence obtained in objectively reasonable reliance on a subsequently invalidated search warrant could not justify the substantial costs of exclusion.

Law in Practice

What If the Wrong Warrant Is Used in a Search and Seizure Case?

Suppose a detective investigating a homicide case needed a search warrant, but because it was Sunday, he could find only one that was used for controlled substances. He took it to a magistrate and pointed out the problems. The magistrate told him to cross out the language regarding controlled substances and to use the warrant; however, the detective neglected to make some of the changes. After the warrant was served, the defendant challenged its validity.

Should the warrant be declared valid under the principles set forth in *Leon*? In *Massachusetts* v. *Sheppard,* the court upheld such a process and allowed the seized evidence to be used against the defendant.

Source: 468 U.S. 981 (1984).

FRUITS OF THE POISONOUS TREE DOCTRINE

What happens if law enforcement violates the protections offered by the Fourth Amendment? The most straightforward explanation of the **Fruits of the Poisonous Tree Doctrine** is that courts will not allow the "fruit," or evidence obtained as a result of an illegal search, to be used against the accused. In explaining this doctrine, one court stated: "The essence of a provision forbidding the acquisition of evidence in a certain way is that not merely evidence so acquired shall not be used before the Court, but that it shall not be used at all."[6]

The Fruits of the Poisonous Tree Doctrine applies to searches, arrests, confessions, and other evidence-gathering activities of law enforcement. However, not all evidence is automatically barred simply because it may have initially been gathered in violation of the Constitution. In *Wong Sun* v. *United States,* the Supreme Court held that the issue was whether the originally obtained illegal evidence can be admitted because it could or was obtained by means sufficiently distinguishable to be purged of the primary taint of illegality.[7] *Wong Sun* also restated the rule that the Exclusionary Rule has no application when the government learned of the evidence from a source independent of any taint. Another theory used to cleanse or avoid the Fruits of the Poisonous Tree Doctrine is the so-called Inevitable Discovery Rule, which allows the admission of evidence if it would have been found and discovered legally at a later time.

PROTECTED AREAS AND INTERESTS

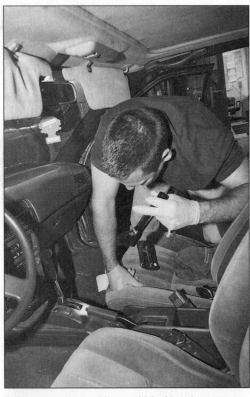

Police sergeant searching a vehicle driven by a suspected drug dealer. Police discovered 1 kilo (roughly 2 pounds) of powder cocaine in the vehicle in Kansas City, Missouri. (*Source:* Mikael Karlsson/Arresting Images.)

Exactly what interest is protected by the Fourth Amendment? The language in the Amendment states that persons, houses, papers, and effects shall be protected or secure against unreasonable searches. Does that mean that a person can carry a bomb on an airplane without being searched? Can a person commit a crime inside his or her home and be secure against a search? The courts have established a "zone of constitutional protection" that surrounds a person and moves with that person wherever he or she travels.

EXPECTATION OF PRIVACY ZONE

The older view was that a search required a physical intrusion into a "constitutionally protected area."[8] In the leading case of *Katz* v. *United States,* the Supreme Court expanded the scope of the Fourth Amendment by establishing an "**expectation of privacy zone**" that is protected by the Constitution.[9] In *Katz,* FBI agents had attached an electronic listening device to the outside of a public phone booth that the defendant used to make wagering calls. The Court held that the Fourth Amendment protects people, not places. Justice Harlen, in a concurring opinion, went on to state that the test for any expectation of privacy is based upon two requirements: (1) that a person exhibit an actual or subjective expectation of privacy and (2) that the expectation is one that society is prepared to recognize as reasonable. In this case, the defendant went to a public phone

Future Crime Concerns

At the 2005 National Conference on Preventing Crime sponsored by the National Crime Prevention Council, attendees were surveyed concerning the most critical law enforcement concerns over the next decade. On a 7-point scale, the percentage of respondents who rated the below issues at the highest two levels of importance were:

ID theft 54 percent

Gang crime 53 percent

School safety 53 percent

Drug trafficking 51 percent

Child safety 47 percent

Source: USA Today, p. 1, November 11, 2005.

booth, closed the glass door, and made a call. It is clear that while people could see him in the booth, he had an actual expectation that the phone call itself would not be overheard. It is also clear that society would deem that making any calls from a public phone booth with the door closed is a situation in which there is a reasonable expectation of privacy.

PRACTICUM

Using Justice Harlan's two-prong test for a citizen's expectation of privacy, answer the following questions regarding search and seizure:

> If a person leaves narcotics on his desk at work and that location is open to the public, is there any expectation of privacy?
> What if a criminal leaves plans for a burglary in a hotel room after she checks out of the hotel?
> If a person leaves a murder weapon in an open field, is there any expectation of privacy?

These and other questions will be discussed in the following section.

EXCEPTIONS TO THE FOURTH AMENDMENT

If the police activity is not a search, the Fourth Amendment does not apply. Therefore, the question becomes, How far does the protection of the Fourth Amendment extend? This section deals with areas and interests that are considered exceptions to the Fourth Amendment and therefore are considered outside the scope of protection of the Fourth Amendment.

Consent

If a party consents to a search, there are no Fourth Amendment protections. Whether the consent is valid is a question of fact to be determined from the totality of the circumstances.[10] The Supreme Court in *Schneckloth* v. *Bustamonte* held that although the subject's knowledge or a right to refuse is a factor to be taken into account, it is not a requirement to establishing a voluntary search.[11]

The Supreme Court held that individual consent could only be ascertained by analyzing all of the circumstances. The traditional definition of voluntariness, which the Court adhered to, did not require proof of knowledge of a right to refuse as the sine qua non of an effective consent to a search. In determining whether a defendant's will was overborne in a particular case, a court assesses the totality of all the surrounding circumstances—both the characteristics of the accused and the details of the interrogation. Some of the factors taken into account include the youth of the accused; his lack of education or his low intelligence; the lack of any advice to the accused of his constitutional rights; the length of detention; the repeated and prolonged nature of the questioning; and the use of physical punishment such as the deprivation of food or sleep.

Another issue that sometimes arises concerns consent obtained by deception. What if an undercover officer is invited into a home that is being used to distribute narcotics? When a criminal gives consent to another person to enter an area normally protected by the Fourth Amendment, knowing that as a result he will reveal to that person criminal activity, such consent is not invalid merely because the consent was given to an undercover police officer.[12]

What happens when a third party gives consent? The Supreme Court has adopted a common authority test for consent by third parties. Common authority rests upon the mutual use of the property by persons generally having joint access or control for most purposes, so that it is reasonable to recognize that any of the coinhabitants has the right to permit the inspection in his own right and that the others have assumed the risk that one of their number might permit the common area to be searched.[13]

Who can give consent? It is generally agreed that one spouse can give consent to search the family residence. If a son or daughter is a minor, parents are presumed to be able to consent to a search of the child's room. What happens if a child consents to a search of the parents' home? If the child is older, courts generally uphold such consent on the theory that older children acquire authority and discretion to admit whom they want into the family house. Property relationships raise special issues regarding consent. An owner may not consent to a search of the renter when the owner has given the renter exclusive possession of the property.

Plain View Doctrine

The Supreme Court has established an exception to the Fourth Amendment in the form of the **Plain View Doctrine**. This concept holds that the Plain View Doctrine authorizes seizure of illegal evidence visible to a police officer if the officer's access to the object has a Fourth Amendment justification. In *Horton* v. *California* the Court summed up this doctrine by stating, ". . . not only must the officer be lawfully located in a place from which the object can be plainly seen, but he or she must also have a lawful right to access to the object itself."[14] Compare and contrast the following situations: (1) The officer is standing on a public sidewalk and can see inside a home through an open window. He observes narcotics on a table. (2) The officer is responding to a loud party complaint, and after identifying herself to the owner, the officer is invited into the house. Once inside, she observes narcotics lying on the table in the room where she is standing. In the first situation,

Police sergeant searching the trunk of a vehicle after stopping the driver for suspected drug trafficking. (*Source:* Mikael Karlsson/Arresting Images.)

the officer is on a public sidewalk and therefore lawfully in a place from which he can observe the object, but to gain entrance to the house, he must obtain a search warrant.[15] In the second situation, the officer is lawfully located in a place from which the object can be seen, since she was given consent to enter the home; and once in the home, she has a lawful right to access to the object itself.

Notable Case Doctrines and Exceptions to the Fourth Amendment (Search and Seizure) and Fifth Amendment (Self-Incrimination) Clauses

	Case Decision	*Holding*
Fourth Amendment Doctrine		
Expectation of privacy	*Katz* v. *United States* (1968)	Electronic eavesdropping is a search.
Plain view	*Arizona* v. *Hicks* (1967)	Fourth Amendment may not apply when the object is in plain view.
Open fields	*Oliver* v. *United States* (1984)	To what extent can police search a field and curtilage?
Warrant Requirements		
Probable cause	*Illinois* v. *Gates* (1983)	Probable cause to issue a warrant is based on a "totality of circumstance."
Stop and frisk	*Terry* v. *Ohio* (1967)	Police are authorized to stop and frisk suspicious persons.
Consent	*Schneckloth* v. *Bustamonte* (1973)	There is consent to search and seizure.
Bus sweep	*Florida* v. *Bostick* (1991)	Police, after obtaining consent, may conduct a search of luggage without a search warrant or probable cause.
Exceptions to the Warrant Requirement		
Federal requirement of the Exclusionary Rule	*Weeks* v. *United States* (1914)	U.S. Supreme Court applied the Exclusionary Rule to federal prosecutions.
State application	*Mapp* v. *Ohio* (1961)	U.S. Supreme Court applied the Exclusionary Rule to state prosecutions.
Automobile search	*United States* v. *Ross* (1982)	Warrantless search of an auto is permissible when it is based on probable cause.
Search incident to arrest	*Chimel* v. *California* (1969)	Permissible scope for a search is the area "within the arrestee's immediate control."
Exceptions to the Exclusionary Rule		
Good faith	*United States* v. *Leon* (1984)	When police rely on "good faith" in a warrant, the evidence seized is admissible even if the warrant is subsequently deemed defective.
Good faith	*Arizona* v. *Evans* (1995)	Even though police arrested a man on the basis of an erroneous warrant that resulted from a court employee's computer error, the evidence they found in a subsequent search is admissible.
Fifth Amendment Doctrine		
Self-incrimination	*Miranda* v. *Arizona* (1966)	Defendant must be given the *Miranda* warning before questioning begins.
Miranda warning	*Dickerson* v. *United States* (2000)	Congress cannot overrule the requirements that *Miranda* rights be read to criminal suspects.

Is There a "Plain Feel" Rule?

In *State* v. *Ortiz* (Supreme Court of Hawaii; 67 Haw. 181; 683 P.2d 822; 1984 Haw. LEXIS 107) the Hawaii Supreme Court granted certiorari to determine whether a search warrant was required before a police officer opened a knapsack made of thin material through which the officer felt, after lawfully seizing the sack, what seemed to be the butt of a handgun. The trial court had suppressed the gun, ruling that the officer was not entitled to open the knapsack once it was removed from the immediate control of the defendant. The appellate court reversed, upholding the search under a plain feel rule. The Supreme Court affirmed the appellate court's result, but vacated its plain feel ruling and found that the warrantless search was a valid protective weapons search under *Terry.* The Court found that the officer's belief that the defendant was armed and that a search of the knapsack was necessary for his own protection was a reasonable belief when the defendant had made a quick grab for his allegedly empty knapsack; the officer was one-on-one with the defendant; it was late at night; the officer had no idea whether the defendant had a hidden confederate who might suddenly appear; and after feeling what seemed like a gun butt, the officer had a strong firsthand suspicion that the knapsack contained a gun.

How far does the expectation of privacy extend when dealing with the Plain View Doctrine? Does a defendant who is growing marijuana in a fenced backyard have a right of privacy from a plane flying over the property? In *California* v. *Ciraolo,* the Supreme Court held that the defendant did not have any reasonable expectation of privacy.[16] The officers were in a private plane flying at 1,000 feet when they saw the marijuana. They obtained a search warrant, seized the property, and charged the defendant. The court upheld the procedure, explaining that there was no reasonable expectation of privacy from aircraft flying overhead. This concept has been expanded to include helicopters flying at 400 feet over a partially enclosed greenhouse. In that case, the court upheld the search, reasoning that helicopters can lawfully fly lower than planes and that again there was no reasonable expectation of privacy.[17]

Abandonment

If a person abandons property, is there any continuing expectation of privacy regarding that property? **Abandonment** requires intent by the party abandoning the property to give up all claim of ownership to the item or items.[18] In *California* v. *Greenwood,* the Supreme Court held that evidence of the defendant's narcotic use obtained from his garbage bags left on the sidewalk for pickup by the trash collector was properly admitted, since the defendant had evidenced an intent to abandon the property.[19] The Court held that the defendant had no subjective expectation of privacy for garbage bags left on the sidewalk that society deems reasonable. It went on to state that such bags were readily accessible to animals, children, snoops, and other members of the public. What if a person checks out of a hotel room and leaves incriminating evidence in the room's trash container? Does the person have any expectation of privacy? Would the manager or a maid have a right to observe the material in the container? Could the manager of the hotel authorize the police to enter the vacant hotel room and seize the evidence? When someone checks out of a hotel and leaves property behind, there is no reasonable expectation of privacy. Furthermore, once having checked out, the person has no authority to prevent any member of the public or an employee from entering that room to clean it for the next guest or to inspect it for damage. Since technically the manager now controls the room, that person can grant police access to the abandoned room and any evidence in the trash container.[20]

Open Fields

In an early case dealing with the Fourth Amendment and seizure of evidence from an open field, Justice Holmes pointed out in *Hester* v. *United States* that the special protection offered by the Fourth Amendment to citizens in their persons, places, papers, and effects does not extend to open fields. He went on to point out that the distinction between **open fields** and the home is as old as the common law.[21]

The concept of the sanctity of a person's home developed during early times. Curtilage includes the home and the land immediately surrounding it.

What effect did *Katz* have on *Hester? Hester* was decided in 1924, and *Katz* established the expectation of privacy in 1967. Did *Katz,* by implication, overrule *Hester? Oliver* v. *United States* addressed this issue.[22] The Court in *Oliver* held that open fields do not provide the setting for those intimate activities that the Fourth Amendment was designed to protect.

Businesses

Does a business owner have any protection or expectation of privacy within a commercial establishment open to the general public? The question revolves around whether or not the activity engaged in by the police is classified as a search. This in turn depends on the physical characteristics of the business. An officer may enter a commercial business during the time it is open to the public and may go anywhere within that business that members of the public go, and that access will not be considered a search. However, if the officer opens a door marked private and observes criminal activity, that activity falls under the *Katz* zone of privacy rule, and it would be deemed an illegal search.

Federal rules do not recognize an expectation of privacy in business, financial, telephone, and post office box records. Accordingly, no warrant is required to search these records. Most states, including New York, California, and Texas, require a warrant or subpoena to search the records unless (1) exigent circumstances exist, (2) consent is obtained, or (3) the search is part of a valid inventory. [*People* v. *Chapman,* 36 Cal.3d 98 (1984).]

Vehicles

There is a lesser expectation of privacy when dealing with vehicles. If the officer is lawfully present at the vehicle (issuing a traffic ticket, for example) and the officer observes or smells what is inside the vehicle, or even examines the exterior of the vehicle, such activity is not considered a search within the meaning of the Fourth Amendment. However, if the officer intrudes into "protected" places, that activity may be classified as a search. Automobile Inventory Searches raise special issues.

Automobiles or motorcycles by their very nature are mobile and can be moved or relocated very easily. The Court addressed the issue of the scope of a search incident to a lawful arrest in *New York* v. *Belton,* where it held that when an officer has made an arrest, he may search the passenger compartment of that automobile including the contents of any containers found within the passenger compartment.[23] The courts have relied upon the fact that automobiles stopped on highways are movable (the so-called mobility factor), as well as stating that there is a lesser expectation of privacy for items carried within an automobile.

In *Illinois* v. *Caballes,* 125 S. Ct. 834 (2005), the U.S. Supreme Court held that police may use a drug-sniffing dog around the outside of a vehicle during a routine traffic stop even when police have no grounds to suspect illegal activity. A state trooper stopped Caballes for speeding. A second trooper drove to the scene with his dog and walked the dog around the respondent's car while the first trooper wrote a warning ticket. When the dog was alerted at Caballes's trunk, the officers searched the trunk and found marijuana. The Court held that the Fourth Amendment did not require reasonable, articulable suspicion to justify using a drug-detection dog to sniff a vehicle during a legitimate traffic stop. The Court noted that the use of a well-trained narcotics-detection dog—one that did not expose noncontraband items that otherwise would have remained hidden from public view—during a lawful traffic stop generally did not implicate legitimate privacy interests. The dog sniff was performed on the exterior of the respondent's car while he was lawfully seized for a traffic violation. Any intrusion on the respondent's privacy expectations did not rise to the level of a constitutionally cognizable infringement.

Tracking of Movements

Is it a search for law enforcement to monitor the movements of a suspect? Clearly, law enforcement officers may surveil or follow a suspect without his or her knowledge or consent on public roads and public property. The courts have stated that persons traveling in an automobile on public roads have no reasonable expectation of privacy in their movements from one place to another.[24] Additionally, the courts allow officers to attach electronic beepers to the exterior of cars and to follow the movement of those cars from a distance. In *United States* v. *Karo,* the Supreme Court held that the use of a beeper attached to the suspect's car was not a search within the scope of the Fourth Amendment because it did not infringe on any privacy interest and conveyed no protected information.[25] The court went on to state that no possessory interest had been interfered with in any meaningful way.

United States v. *Simms*

U.S. Court of Appeals, 11th Cir. 2004;
385 F.3d 1347; 2004 U.S. App. LEXIS 20293

A police officer observed a traffic violation by Simms, the defendant, and was subsequently alerted that Simms was suspected of drug activity and was being monitored with a tracking device in his vehicle, although the device was only authorized for use in another state. After a warning was issued and Simm's documents were returned to him, the officer obtained Simms's consent to search the vehicle and discovered the drugs in a hidden compartment. The appellate court first held that the alert concerning Simms and his apparent nervousness warranted prolonging the traffic stop, and there was no indication that his consent to search was involuntary. Further, the use of the tracking device outside the scope of a state warrant did not raise constitutional issues and was irrelevant to his guilt.

Random Drug Testing

In *Board of Education of Independent School Dist. No. 92 of Pottowotomie County* v. *Earls,* the Supreme Court upheld a school district's policy of requiring random drug testing as a condition for participating in interscholastic activities.[26] The Court held that the Fourth Amendment was not violated because the school's interest in protecting its students' health and safety and in deterring drug usage served an important governmental concern. The Court went on to state that there was a minimal invasion of privacy caused by the tests. The Court relied upon its earlier decision of *Vernonia School District* v. *Action* that allowed suspicionless drug testing of athletes.[27]

Student Searches by Educators

In *N.J.* v. *T. L. O.,* 469 U.S. 325 (1985), a student's purse was searched after she was suspected of having cigarettes. The principal discovered that the student had the cigarettes in her possession, and discovered evidence of marijuana and a list of alleged users from the school. The State of New Jersey brought delinquency charges against the student. The student alleged that the search of her purse violated her Fourth Amendment rights. The U.S. Supreme Court held that the search did not violate the Fourth Amendment. The Court stated that a search by a school official was permissible in its scope when the measures adopted were reasonably related to the objectives of the search and were not intrusive in light of the age and sex of the student.

The Court noted that school officials need not obtain a warrant before searching a student who is under their authority. The accommodation of the privacy interests of students with the substantial need of teachers and administrators for freedom to maintain order in the schools does not require strict adherence to the requirement that searches be based on probable cause to believe that the subject of the search has violated or is violating the law. The Court stated that under ordinary circumstances, a search of a student by a teacher or another school official will be justified at its inception when there are reasonable grounds for suspecting that the search will turn up evidence that the student has violated or is violating either the law or the rules of the school. Such a search will be permissible in its scope when the measures adopted are reasonably related to the objectives of the search and not excessively intrusive in light of the age and sex of the student and the nature of the infraction.

School locker searches made under the auspices of a previously promulgated school locker search policy have been upheld as constitutional [*Zamora* v. *Pomeroy,* 639 F.2d 662 (10th Cir. 1981)]. In the *Zamora* case, an appellate court held that school officials had authority to conduct a warrantless search of the student's high school locker after a drug detection dog's positive response provided reasonable cause.

Sobriety Checkpoints

The U.S. Supreme Court in *Michigan Department of State Police* v. *Sitz,* 496 U.S. 4 (1993), held that sobriety checkpoints were reasonable considering the increasing number of alcohol-related deaths and mutilations on the nation's roads. The Court considered that the state program was consistent with the Fourth Amendment, and that the balance of the state's interest in preventing drunken driving and the degree of intrusion upon individual motorists who were briefly stopped weighed in favor of the state program.

The Court noted that no allegations were made of unreasonable treatment of any person after an actual detention at a particular checkpoint. The Court noted that only the

State v. Michael G 106 N.M. 644; 1987

A swimming coach at a high school informed two assistant principals that an unidentified student had told him that another juvenile was selling marijuana. The assistant principals then searched the juvenile's locker and discovered two cigarettes that looked like marijuana joints. The cigarettes subsequently tested positive for marijuana. The court held that the assistant principals had reasonable grounds to suspect that the juvenile was violating the law or school rules. The information that provided the basis of the search was the specific statement of a student that the juvenile had tried to sell some marijuana to him. It was not a mere rumor or belief, but an eyewitness account of a breach of school rules and the law. Statements by eyewitness citizen-informants were subject to much less stringent credibility verification requirements. The fact that the principals did not know the identity of the complaining student did not affect the finding that this search was based upon reasonable grounds. The court further held that substantial evidence was present for the children's court to find that the juvenile was in possession of marijuana.

initial stop of each motorist passing through a checkpoint and the associated preliminary questioning and observation by checkpoint officers were before the court and stated that the detention of particular motorists for more extensive field sobriety testing may require satisfaction of an individualized suspicion standard.

INSPECTIONS AND REGULATORY SEARCHES

These are administrative searches that fall outside the scope of the day-to-day activities normally associated with law enforcement activities. They are considered outside the scope of the protection of the Fourth Amendment and therefore are judged by a different standard. The courts have established a reasonable legislative or administrative standard for use in these situations. This standard is less than the probable cause requirement used in Fourth Amendment situations. It is a test that balances the need to search against the invasion that the search entails. This balancing test considers (1) whether the practice has a long history of judicial and public acceptance, (2) whether the practice is necessary to achieve acceptable results, and (3) whether the practice involves a relatively limited invasion of privacy.[28]

Welfare Inspections

The courts have considered that a visit by caseworkers to a welfare recipient's home does not constitute a search within the meaning of the Fourth Amendment. In *Wyman* v. *James,* the U.S. Supreme Court reasoned that a welfare recipient may be required to consent to such visits as a condition of continued receipt of benefits.[29]

Inspections at Fire Scenes

Can a fire inspector or an arson inspector remain in a building after a fire to conduct an investigation without obtaining a search warrant? Clearly, fire personnel can enter a building to put out a fire. This is a form of emergency that is outside the protection of the Fourth Amendment. The courts have stated that whereas inspectors or fire fighters can remain in a building once the fire is extinguished, if they leave and desire to reenter, they must obtain a warrant.

Border Searches

The Supreme Court addressed the issue of competing rights and values in a border search in *United States* v. *Ramsey.*[30] The Court held that searches at the border are per se reasonable because of the right of a sovereign nation to protect itself by stopping and searching persons and property entering its soil. Therefore, searches of persons and property entering the country may be made without obtaining a warrant or establishing probable cause. This activity is a form of balancing the national interest in preventing illegal persons and goods from entering the United States against the limited intrusion that occurs when a person decides to cross the border.

Airport Searches

In the late 1960s, the United States began limited searches of persons traveling on airlines if they matched a predetermined profile. This process was abandoned in 1973, and then all persons traveling on airlines were required to pass through a magnetometer and have their carry-on luggage X-rayed and/or inspected. The courts have upheld such airport searches on the basis of balancing the need for the search with its limited scope. Additionally, the search is limited to a certain process, and passengers have advance notice of its existence. This notice allows them to avoid the search simply by choosing not to fly.

Searches of Prisoners

It has been said that prisoners do not lose all of their Fourth Amendment rights simply because they are incarcerated. However, the courts have ruled in favor of correctional institutions in a number of situations. For example, a prisoner's mail may be read; after a visit with friends or family, prisoners may be searched; and their religious practices may be curtailed. The courts balance the security of the institution against the rights of the inmate and in most situations find for the institution. It is said that courts are loath to second-guess prison administrators.

INDEPENDENT STATE GROUNDS

State constitutions may provide greater protection to an individual than that provided by the U.S. Constitution. A classic example is the *Sitz* case discussed under "Sobriety Checkpoints." After the U.S. Supreme Court determined that the checkpoints did not violate the Fourth Amendment, the state appellate court held that they violated Article I, Section 11 of the Michigan Constitution. On appeal, the Michigan Supreme Court affirmed, holding that the checkpoints were unconstitutional under the Michigan Constitution because there was no support in Michigan's constitutional history for the proposition that police were permitted to engage in warrantless and suspicionless seizures of automobiles in order to enforce criminal laws. The state court's review of cases construing Article II, Section 10 of the Michigan Constitution (1908) showed no support for the proposition that police could engage in warrantless, suspicionless seizures of automobiles. The state court also held that the Michigan Constitution offered more protection than the U.S. Constitution [*Sitz* v. *Department of State Police,* 443 Mich. 744 (1993)].

PROBABLE CAUSE

There are two parts to the Fourth Amendment. In the event that a warrant is not used, the first part of the amendment comes into play and requires that the people be secure "against unreasonable searches and seizures." However, when a warrant is used, the second part of the amendment requires that "no Warrants shall issue, but upon probable cause." Therefore, for a search warrant to be valid, the issuing authority must find that there are statements or other evidence that establishes probable cause.

The Supreme Court has a long history of expressing a strong preference for the use of search warrants. Warrants impose an orderly process with an independent review by the judiciary. This process has resulted in a slight shading or difference in evaluating searches with or without a warrant. The Court gives more deference to searches conducted with a warrant, holding that the reviewing court is not to conduct a de novo or an independent evaluation of the magistrate's probable cause determination; rather, the review is merely intended to decide whether the evidence taken as a whole forms a substantial basis for the magistrate's finding of probable cause.[31]

Probable cause is an objective test that requires the facts to be such as would warrant a belief by a reasonable person that criminal conduct has occurred or is about to occur.

Information received from informants can complicate evaluations by the courts of whether or not probable cause exists. An informant is a person who learns of criminal conduct by being involved in the criminal culture. The term does not refer to a citizen who is a witness or victim. In *Aguilar* v. *Texas,* the Supreme Court set forth a two-prong test to determine whether probable cause existed when dealing with information from an informant.[32] This test requires (1) that the informant have a basis of knowledge for his or her allegations that someone is committing a criminal act and (2) that there must be facts to support the credibility of the informant or his or her information.

In *Illinois* v. *Gates,* the Supreme Court later adopted a "totality of the circumstances" analysis that traditionally has been used in probable cause determinations.[33] The *Gates* court continued to state that an informant's veracity, reliability, and basis of knowledge are critical in determining whether probable cause exists in any given situation.

The Court views witnesses or victims in a different light. Witnesses or victims are not passing on rumor; rather, they are reciting information that they observed regarding criminal activity. The knowledge or veracity of witnesses or victims is seldom questioned for purposes of probable cause. Courts look at a variety of factors in determining whether statements by victims/witnesses establish probable cause, including the particularity of the description of the perpetrator.

SEARCH WITH A WARRANT

As indicated earlier in this chapter, the courts prefer that a law enforcement officer obtain a search warrant. The warrant process involves (1) a neutral and detached magistrate, (2) an oath or affirmation, (3) establishment of probable cause, (4) particular description of the place to be searched, (5) particular description of the items to be seized, and (6) the time of execution.

Importance of a Search Warrant

The U.S. Supreme Court has indicated a strong preference for obtaining a search warrant prior to conducting a search. The general rule is that the police must get a warrant unless they cannot. In the trial of a criminal case, searches conducted pursuant to a valid search warrant are presumed to be legal, and the party, normally the defendant, who attacks the validity of the search has the burden of proof to establish that the search was invalid. In the case of search without a warrant, the search is presumed to be invalid and the party, normally the prosecutor, who is attempting to enter into evidence the results of the search has the burden to establish that the search was legal.

A Neutral and Detached Magistrate

The court has stated that police and prosecutors cannot be expected to remain neutral when dealing with their own investigations. A neutral and detached **magistrate** provides a fresh, unbiased determination regarding the sufficiency of the evidence supporting the request for the warrant. The magistrate cannot receive any funds for issuing the warrant; otherwise, he or she has a financial interest in the case. Nor can the magistrate be involved in the execution of the warrant.

An Oath or Affirmation

Typically, warrants require a written record under an oath or affirmation. Courts are reluctant to allow other information to be brought in at a later date to rehabilitate an otherwise defective warrant. This rule should be distinguished from the oral or the telephonic issuance of warrants that is now common in many jurisdictions. Whether the information is presented in writing or over the telephone, it must be attested to by an oath or affirmation.

Establishment of Probable Cause

Once probable cause has been established in the warrant, it can be issued. What happens if the facts supporting the probable cause are false? In *Franks* v. *Delaware,* the Supreme Court allowed the defendant to present evidence to show that the information contained in the search warrant was false and therefore that no probable cause had been established.[34] The Court stated that banning such a process would destroy the probable cause requirement in a warrant because an officer could lie about the facts and there would be no way or method to counter such false allegations.

Particular Description of the Place to be Searched

The warrant does not have to describe every detail of the place to be searched. In urban areas, for single-family residences, the street address is usually sufficient. However, warrants must be more specific when dealing with multiple-family apartments. For example, there may be an apartment No. 3 on each floor, and if the warrant simply states "425 S. Swift, Apt 3" without stating the floor, the warrant may well be defective, since it does not describe the particular place to be searched. As a practical matter, many jurisdictions require that officers describe the place to be searched to avoid mistakes. "The address of the premise to be searched is 323 N. Apple Street. It is a single-family residence, with an attached two-car garage. The premise has white exterior stucco walls and a brown shingle roof with two tall trees in the front yard. It is the third house on the western side of the street in a northern direction from the cross street of S. Apple."

- The federal government does not recognize an expectation of privacy in business, financial, telephone, and post office box records.
- There is a lesser standard of probable cause for inspections and regulatory searches.
- The Supreme Court has upheld the use of sobriety checkpoints.
- There are two parts to the Fourth Amendment; the Warrant Clause and the Probable Cause Clause.
- State constitutions and statutes may provide greater protections to an individual than are provided by federal law.
- Only a neutral and detached magistrate may issue a valid search warrant.
- The general rule is that to conduct a search, you must get a warrant unless you cannot.
- A general search warrant is illegal.
- The search warrant must specifically describe the place to be searched and the items to be seized.

REVIEW QUESTIONS

1. Explain the purpose of the Fourth Amendment. Is it an absolute bar to all searches? Why? Why not?

2. What principle is the Exclusionary Rule based upon? Does it work? Can you list other ways that the objective of the Exclusionary Rule could be accomplished?

3. What is the zone of privacy? How does it work? Does it attach to places or persons?

4. List some of the exceptions to the Fourth Amendment. Which one is the most important in your opinion?

5. Describe the requirements for the issuance of a search warrant. Which one is the most important and which is the least important? Justify your answer.

ENDNOTES

1. Wayne LaFave et al., *Criminal Procdure,* 3rd ed. (West, St. Paul, Minn.), 2000.
2. 232 U.S. 383 (1914).
3. 338 U.S. 25 (1949).
4. 367 U.S. 643 (1961).
5. 468 U.S. 897 (1984).
6. *Silverhorne Lumber Co.* v. *United States,* 251 U.S. 385 (1920).
7. 371 U.S. 471 (1963).
8. See *Silverman* v. *United States,* 365 U.S. 505 (1961).
9. 389 U.S. 347 (1967).
10. *Schneckloth* v. *Bustamonte,* 412 U.S. 218 (1973).
11. Ibid.
12. See, for example, *On Lee* v. *U.S.,* 343 U.S. 747 (1952) and *Hoffa* v. *U.S.,* 385 U.S. 293 (1966).
13. *United States* v. *Matlock,* 415 U.S. 164 (1974).
14. 496 U.S. 128 (1983).
15. There are some situations in which police officers may enter the house without a warrant, but these are exceptions to the general rule.
16. 476 U.S. 207 (1986).
17. *Florida* v. *Riley,* 488 U.S. 445 (1989).
18. *Abel* v. *United States,* 362 U.S. 217 (1960).
19. 486 U.S. 35 (1988).
20. *Abel* v. *United States,* 362 U.S. 217 (1960).

21. 265 U.S. 57 (1924).
22. 466 U.S. 170 (1984).
23. 453 U.S. 454 (1981).
24. 460 U.S. 276 (1983).
25. 468 U.S. 705 (1984).
26. 122 S.Ct. 2559 (2002).
27. 515 U.S. 646 (1995).
28. See *Camara* v. *Municipal Court,* 387 U.S. 523 (1967).
29. 400 U.S. 309 (1971).
30. 431 U.S. 606 (1977).
31. *Massachusetts* v. *Upton,* 466 U.S. 727 (1984).
32. 378 U.S. 108 (1964).
33. 462 U.S. 213 (1983).
34. 438 U.S. 154 (1978).
35. 275 U.S. 192 (1927).
36. 403 U.S. 443 (1971).

Police officers find and remove a handgun from a suspect as he and another suspect lean against the exterior wall of a home and are frisked. (*Source:* Mikael Karlsson/Arresting Images.)

that the arrest is made. The ordinary, prudent person test has been criticized as being unrealistic because the officer, through training and experience, could recognize certain facts that would cause him or her to believe that a crime had been committed. Such facts may not be of a suspicious nature to the ordinary, prudent person. Yet the courts have consistently adhered to this test. However, most courts will consider the facts as seen by the officer before dismissing a charge because of lack of probable cause.

Arrest by a Law Enforcement Officer

We should define the terms law enforcement officer or peace officer before continuing this discussion. A law enforcement officer or peace officer is a person employed by some branch of the government and is sworn to uphold the laws of the United States and the state, county, or city by which he or she is employed. The statutes of some states specifically spell out who are law enforcement or peace officers within that state; if not listed in the statutes, a person is not a law enforcement officer within that state. Law enforcement or peace officers may be placed in four basic categories: federal officers, employed by the U.S. government; state officers, employed by the state; sheriffs, employed by the county or parish; and city police officers, employed by their respective cities.

ARRESTS AND WARRANTS

As we indicated earlier, the Fourth Amendment protects against unreasonable searches and seizures. This language makes it clear that the amendment applies both to searches of persons and places and to arrests of persons. An arrest may be made in two ways: with or without a warrant. As indicated, in both situations the arresting officer must have probable cause to arrest. There are two elements to probable cause to arrest: (1) there is reason to believe that a crime has been committed and (2) the person to be arrested committed the offense.[2]

Arrest without a Warrant

An arrest without a warrant is the most common form of arrest. Historically, warrantless arrests have always been allowed under the common law. The courts have held that requiring a warrant for every arrest is impractical.[3] However, there is one situation in which an arrest warrant is required. The Supreme Court held that unless there are exigent or emergency circumstances or consent, the police may not enter a private home to make a warrantless arrest.[4]

The courts have held that entry into a home is an extreme intrusion and that entry to make an arrest is very similar to entry to search a home; therefore the Fourth Amendment requires that a neutral magistrate make a determination that there is probable cause to make the arrest before such an intrusion is allowed. The exception to this warrant requirement is exigent or emergency circumstances. Courts have ruled that fresh or hot pursuit of a suspect as he or she runs into a home does not require a warrant.[5] Additionally, if the police believe that if they wait for the issuance of a warrant the suspect will destroy the evidence, they may enter and make an arrest without a warrant.[6]

Arrest with a Warrant

Even though officers may arrest a suspect without a warrant, there is legal preference for arrests made with a warrant. This is the case because it places the determination of finding of the existence of probable cause in the hands of a neutral magistrate. The Supreme Court, though upholding warrantless arrests, has stated that the deliberate determination of magistrates is preferred over the hurried actions of police officers.[7]

An arrest warrant is a written order issued by the proper judicial officer upon a showing of probable cause commanding the arrest of a particular person. Arrest warrants must conform to certain requirements. Although these vary from jurisdiction to jurisdiction, most warrants require the following information:

- The caption or title of the court from which the warrant is issued.
- The name of the person to be arrested. The warrant must describe with particularity the person to be seized. (Many warrants also require a detailed description of the person, including height, weight, and hair color.)
- A description of the offense. This normally is described in the language of the statute or law that the suspect violated.
- The date of issuance of the warrant.
- A command that officers take the suspect into custody and bring him or her before the proper judicial officer.
- The signature of the issuing official.

Many states require officers to have warrants of arrest for misdemeanors committed outside of their presence. This circumstance usually means that the officer must witness the criminal act. The officer doesn't have to see the offense; the courts have ruled that use of any of the officer's senses is sufficient. The officer may hear the offense (sounds of gunfire) or even smell the offense (marijuana burning). Recently, some states have enacted statutory exceptions to this requirement. Most notable is the duty of officers to arrest suspects in domestic violence cases, even if the officer did not see the suspect strike the victim.

Some jurisdictions allow for the use of telephonic arrest warrants. These warrants are most often used after normal working hours and when it is considered necessary to arrest the suspect immediately. In these jurisdictions, officers telephone a prosecuting attorney and explain why they need a warrant. The prosecutor then calls a judge at his or her home,

Reasonable Suspicion

A detention requires at least reasonable suspicion. (*Note:* Reasonable suspicion is less than probable cause. The officer must have reasonable suspicion that criminal activity is occurring, is about to occur, or has recently occurred and that the vehicle or a person in the vehicle is connected with that criminal activity.) The reasonable suspicion must be based on specific facts that can be articulated to a court. If the suspicion relates to any person in the vehicle (including a passenger), the officer may stop the vehicle.

In *People* v. *Remiro,* 89 C.A. 3rd 809 (1979), an appellate court upheld the stopping of the vehicle on the basis of the officer's reasonable suspicion. In this case, the officer saw a van he did not recognize that was driving slowly in a residential neighborhood at 1:30 A.M. The officer followed the van and noticed that it was traveling in a circle. He stopped the van. His stop was upheld on the basis of the following articulable facts:

1. The van's speed and route were suggestive of a casing operation.
2. The officer was familiar with the neighborhood, its vehicles, and its driving patterns.
3. He did not recognize the vehicle.
4. He knew that many residential burglaries had occurred in the neighborhood.
5. He knew that vans were frequently used in such burglaries.

In *People* v. *Dominguez,* 118 C.A. 3rd 1315 (1985), the Court upheld a detention of the vehicle when the identities of the persons within the vehicle were unknown and a warrant existed for the registered owner. The Court indicated that if none of the people could be the registered owner, that is, of a different race, then the legality of the detention would be questionable. While the *Remiro* and *Dominguez* cases are controlling only in California, their rationale appears to be accepted by most other states.

A stop based on a "wanted flyer" or a similar notice or bulletin issued by another jurisdiction and related to completed criminal activity is sufficient basis to detain a vehicle and its occupants if the other jurisdiction had a valid basis to issue the flyer, and so forth (*U.S.* v. *Hemsley,* 105 S Ct. 675, 1985).

Distinguishing an Arrest from a *Terry*-Type Detention

Often it is necessary to distinguish an arrest from a stop-and-frisk situation, especially if evidence is found during the detention. The leading Supreme Court decision on this question is *United States* v. *Sharp,* 470 U.S. 675 (1990). In that case, the length of the detention was considered. The Court indicated that a *Terry*-**level stop** will ordinarily be for a fairly short duration and that the detention will be no longer than necessary to effectuate the purpose of the detention. Other factors considered include the following: Did the police pursue the investigation diligently? Was the method of investigation likely to confirm or dispel the officer's suspicions quickly?

A warrantless protective sweep of a residence by the police who are making a lawful arrest in the residence is considered to be legal if the police have a reasonable suspicion that the residence may contain an individual who poses a danger to the officers or to others (*Maryland* v. *Buie,* 494 U.S. 325, 1985). The protective sweep should be a quick and limited search of the premises and narrowly confined to a cursory visual inspection of those places where an individual may be hiding.

TERRITORIAL JURISDICTION TO MAKE AN ARREST

From a procedural standpoint, it is important to determine if an officer has the authority to make an arrest, particularly when he or she has no warrant. If the officer does not have the authority, the arrest will be declared unlawful. One factor that becomes significant in determining the officer's authority is whether the officer was in his or her territorial jurisdiction. In most states, the territorial jurisdiction of the city police is confined to the city limits. Any arrest without a warrant made beyond the city limits would have to be made as a private person and meet the restrictions of a private person arrest. Similarly, the territorial authority of the sheriff of a county or parish is limited to the county or parish line. Some states limit the jurisdiction of the sheriff within the county, allowing arrests only in unincorporated areas. These states remove the sheriff's authority to make arrests within an incorporated city. However, in most states the sheriff is considered to be the chief law enforcement officer of the county and has authority to make arrests anyplace within the county. The sheriff, when within city limits, would have concurrent authority with the city police.

It was held for a long time that if an outlaw was able to outdistance a sheriff to the county line, the sheriff had to discontinue the pursuit since he had no authority to make an arrest in the adjoining county. To prevent the escape of an outlaw under these circumstances, the hot pursuit rule was developed. This rule provided that if an officer was in hot or fresh pursuit of an offender, the officer could follow the offender into another jurisdiction to make an arrest. The problem presented by this rule was, What would be interpreted as fresh pursuit? In early times when the local officer made the pursuit on horseback, it was concluded that if the officer could keep the outlaw in sight or still see the dust kicked up by the outlaw's horse, the officer was in fresh pursuit. With the advent of the motor vehicle as a means of escape, as well as pursuit, the in sight theory became impractical. Therefore, it is generally held today that if a pursuit is uninterrupted and continuous, it is a fresh pursuit. But even with this concept of fresh pursuit, the local officer had no authority to cross a state line to make an arrest. Thus, if the fleeing offender was able to reach the state line before apprehension, he or she had sanctuary in the next state. With rapid transportation available to criminals, new rules and regulations concerning the extent of pursuit had to be formulated.

Uniform Act of Fresh Pursuit

Today, most states have adopted what is known as the Uniform Act of Fresh Pursuit. This act provides that a peace officer of one state may enter another state in fresh pursuit to arrest an offender who has committed a felony in the state from which he or she fled. In adopting the Uniform Act of Fresh Pursuit, a few states have made the act applicable not only to felonies but also to certain misdemeanors, usually those involving moral turpitude. Moral turpitude has been defined as conduct contrary to justice, honesty, modesty, or good morals. There is no specific distance set forth in the act that the officer may travel within the state in order to make the arrest. The act does provide that after the arrest is made, the officer must take the arrested person before a local magistrate, without unnecessary delay, for a hearing to determine the lawfulness of the arrest. If the magistrate concludes that the arrest was lawful, the magistrate will either commit the accused or release him or her on bail pending extradition proceedings.

Limited Arrest Powers

A few states do grant local officers the right to make an arrest without a warrant anywhere in the state. This right is based on the theory that, when sworn as a peace officer within a city or county, the officer swears to uphold the constitution and laws of the state as well as local ordinances, thereby giving the officer statewide arrest powers. But as stated, in most states the local officer has authority to make arrests without a warrant only within the territorial jurisdiction in which he or she is employed, except in fresh pursuit instances. Some people in the justice system believe that this limited arrest power by local officers hampers law enforcement. As a result, statutes have been passed in some states extending the arrest power of local officers.

Although extended authority differs among states, the power to make arrests without a warrant beyond the territorial area in which an officer is employed is usually confined to one of three situations. Authority has been granted in some states permitting an officer to make a lawful arrest beyond the officer's area if the officer has prior permission from the chief or sheriff of the area in which the arrest is to be made. This granted authority is based upon an old posse comitatus right of a sheriff. The posse comitatus right came into being early in the history of this country and particularly in the western part of the United States. The sheriff was often the only law enforcement officer within the county and therefore frequently needed assistance in locating and apprehending a criminal. To obtain this assistance, the sheriff was authorized by law to call on citizens of the county and deputize them to assist in the location and apprehension of a dangerous felon. These deputies were formed into a posse. Under posse comitatus, the officer making the arrest, in a sense, is a temporary officer of the jurisdiction in which the arrest is made. Further, the right to make an arrest beyond the officer's area of employment has been granted in instances when the offender is wanted for a crime committed in the officer's area of employment. In other instances, authority has been granted to an officer to make arrests beyond the officer's jurisdiction with extended private person arrest power. This extended right permits the officer to arrest a person who has committed a crime or where there is reasonable cause to believe that a crime was committed in the presence of the officer and that lives may be in danger, property may be immediately damaged, or the offender may escape.

State Police Agencies

All states except Hawaii have some type of state police or law enforcement system. The state police agencies have statewide territorial jurisdiction, but states vary considerably in the power of the state police to make arrests. In some states, the state police have the power to enforce all state laws and have concurrent power throughout the state with local law enforcement agencies. In other states, the state police have limited jurisdiction that confines them to enforcing criminal laws only on state property. In addition to the state police, a number of investigative agencies in most states have limited authority and arrest powers and are employed to perform specific duties. Examples of persons with limited investigative authority and arrest powers are game wardens and drug law administrators. In some states, the state police not only enforce state laws generally but also patrol the highways; other states have a separate agency for this purpose: a highway patrol. Although the territorial jurisdiction of state police is restricted to the state boundaries, the Uniform Act of Fresh Pursuit is applicable to these agencies as well as to local officers.

Federal Law Enforcement Agencies

Technically, the only peace officers of the U.S. government are the U.S. marshals within the Department of Justice. But as with the states, a number of federal investigative agencies have emergency arrest powers. All federal officers have territorial jurisdiction throughout the United States and its possessions. Also within the U.S. Department of Justice is the Federal Bureau of Investigation (FBI), which was established in 1908 and has investigative jurisdiction over all federal violations not specifically assigned to some other federal agency. The FBI began in 1908 as the Bureau of Investigation.[8] It was created in part because of other law enforcement agencies' inability to investigate and arrest corrupt politicians and business leaders. The Bureau began as a small organization; however, it grew and became a household name under the guidance of J. Edgar Hoover. The FBI investigates a wide range of violations. Examples of FBI investigations include bank robberies; kidnapping when the victim has been, or is presumed to have been, transported across a state line; theft from interstate shipment; internal security matters; and interstate organized crime activities. The Federal Drug Enforcement Administration is now a part of the FBI. The Immigration and Naturalization Service, of which the Border Patrol is a part, is within the Department of Justice.

Within the U.S. Treasury Department is the Secret Service, created in 1865 to investigate and curtail counterfeiting of U.S. currency. After the assassination of President William McKinley in 1901, the Secret Service was charged with the duty of protecting the president of the United States. This duty has been expanded to include not only the president but also his immediate family, certain other high governmental officials, and some foreign dignitaries. Other agencies within the U.S. Treasury Department are the Customs Service; the Alcohol, Tobacco, and Firearms Service; the Internal Revenue Service; and the U.S. Postal Service. Among the duties of the Customs Service are investigations of smuggling operations. The Alcohol, Tobacco, and Firearms Service investigates violations pertaining to the illegal manufacture of alcoholic beverages, illegal possession of certain firearms, and tobacco infractions. The Internal Revenue Service oversees the collection of federal income taxes and violations of federal income tax law. U.S. Postal Service inspectors investigate violations pertaining to the mail, such as use of the mails to defraud and mail theft. There are a number of other investigative agencies of the federal government, but the foregoing are the ones most frequently encountered in law enforcement.

After the terrorist attacks of September 11, 2001, and in response to a number of factors, President George W. Bush created the Office of Homeland Security. He appointed Tom Ridge as its first director. The mission of the Department of Homeland Security is to do the following:

- Prevent terrorist attacks within the United States;
- Reduce America's vulnerability to terrorism; and
- Minimize the damage and recover from attacks that do occur.

The Department of Homeland Security has four divisions:

Border and Transportation Security. The department is responsible for securing our nation's borders and transportation systems, managing who and what enters our homeland, and working to prevent the entry of terrorists and the instruments of terrorism while ensuring the speedy flow of legitimate traffic.

Emergency Preparedness and Response. The department will ensure the preparedness of our nation's emergency response professionals, provide the federal government's response, and aid America's recovery from terrorist attacks and natural disasters.

Chemical, Biological, Radiological, and Nuclear Countermeasures. The department leads the federal government's efforts in preparing for and responding to the full range of terrorist threats involving weapons of mass destruction.

Information Analysis and Infrastructure Protection. The department merges under one roof the capability to identify and assess current and future threats to the homeland, map those threats against our current vulnerabilities, inform the president, issue timely warnings, and immediately take or effect appropriate preventive and protective action.

FORCE IN EFFECTING AN ARREST

The laws of the states are comparatively uniform as to the amount of force that may be used by a peace officer in making an arrest, but there seems to be some doubt as to the degree of force that may be used by a private person. The statutes of most states provide that any peace officer who has reasonable cause to believe that the person to be arrested has committed a public offense may use reasonable force to effect the arrest, to prevent escape, or to overcome resistance. It is also generally held that the officer may break open a door or window of a house in which the person to be arrested is, or is believed to be, located. Unless there is a danger to the life of the officer or others, the officer must first demand admittance and explain the purpose for which the admittance is desired.

Although the officer may use whatever force is reasonably necessary to overcome the resistance of the accused, the officer may not use force that is disproportionate to the resistance met. If undue force is used, the officer could be guilty of violating the civil rights of the accused and be prosecuted in a federal court under the Civil Rights Acts (see Title 18 U.S. Code, section 242, and Title 42 U.S. Code, section 1983). That is exactly what happened in *Tennessee* v. *Garner.*[9] In that case, Memphis police officers responded to a call of a burglary in progress. One of the officers went into the backyard of the house and saw Edward Garner flee from the house and attempt to climb a chain-link fence. The officer fired his weapon and killed the suspect. The perpetrator's father filed a federal civil rights lawsuit, and the U.S. Supreme Court held that the use of deadly force was a form of seizure protected by the Fourth Amendment and that it was unreasonable under these circumstances. The Court reasoned that the officer was not in fear for his safety and had no evidence that the suspect was armed or a danger to any other person. In its opinion in the *Garner* case, the Court created a new rule concerning the use of deadly force in an attempt to arrest an individual suspected of having committed a serious felony. The Court concluded that the use of deadly force while attempting to make an arrest or prevent an escape can be justified only as an absolute last resort if there are no other means of apprehending the felon and the failure to stop the felon creates a serious risk of bodily injury or death to others.

Whether excessive force was used in a particular instance is a matter of fact that would be determined by some board of inquiry, jury, or judge. The question to be determined is whether the force used was that which an ordinary, prudent person would have used under the circumstances. Any mistreatment of an accused person once he or she is under control could also be a violation of the accused's civil rights. In addition to having violated the federal laws on civil rights, the officer could possibly be charged with assault and battery under a state statute.

FOCUS: *Excessive Force and Videotapes*

In March 1991, several Los Angeles police officers were videotaped beating an African American male named Rodney King with their batons as he lay on the ground. The officers were charged with state crimes and tried in a superior court in Simi Valley, a suburb of Los Angeles. The state jury acquitted the officers, and they were then tried and found guilty of the federal crime of violating Mr. King's civil rights.

The videotape that was broadcast across the world shows the officers beating Mr. King for 19 seconds. The tape does not show that the officers had chased Mr. King for 8 miles, surrounded him, and used electronic darts carrying 50,000 volts that failed to subdue him. When he ran for the nearby park, the officers began to wildly beat Mr. King. That was the portion that was captured on videotape and shocked the world.

Approximately 11 years later, on July 6, 2002, Inglewood police officers were involved in an altercation with a young African American male that was also videotaped. The tape shows the officers pulling the handcuffed male to his feet and slamming his body onto the top of the police cruiser. Officer Jeremy More is then shown striking the male with his fist as he lay on the vehicle. The officer claims that the male was squeezing his testicles, so he had to apply force to make him let go.

When should an officer be able to use force to effect an arrest?
When does force become excessive?
What can be done to prevent officers from using excessive force?

More and more law enforcement agencies are using dogs in the location and capture of suspects. To avoid a possible excessive force accusation in the capture of a suspect, the dog handler should warn the suspect that a dog will be released unless the suspect surrenders peacefully. Also, the dog should be restrained when the suspect is under control.

Rodney King press conference. Lawyer Steven Berman showing a photo of a bruised Rodney King. (*Source:* Venegez/SIPA Press.)

Arrest Warrant

Scott Peterson's wife, Laci, a twenty-seven-year-old woman who was eight months pregnant, disappeared on Christmas Eve 2002, prompting a nationwide search. When her body and the body of her unborn child were found four months later, her husband was charged with two counts of murder. Scott Peterson was convicted and formally sentenced to death for the murders of the mother-to-be and the fetus. Following is a copy of the arrest warrant issued in the case.

PEOPLE OF THE STATE OF CALIFORNIA)		**PROBABLE CAUSE**
)		**WARRANT OF ARREST**
Plaintiff,)		
)		
vs.)		(P.C. §5814 and §1427
)		Peo. v. Ramey, 16 Cal. 3rd 263;
<u>Scott Lee PETERSON</u> Defendant)		Peo. v. Sesslin, 68 Cal. 2nd 418)

COUNTY OF STANISLAUS:

THE PEOPLE OF THE STATE OF CALIFORNIA

To any Peace Office of said State:

Complaint upon oath having been this day made before me by Detective Craig Grogan, I find that there is probable cause to believe that two counts of the crime of: 187 PC, homicide committed on or about Monday December 23, 2002 or Tuesday December 24, 2002, in the County of Stanislaus by Scott Lee Peterson, date of birth, 10/24/72.

YOU ARE THEREFORE COMMANDED forthwith to arrest the above-named Defendant and bring him/her before any magistrate in Stanislaus County pursuant to Penal Code Section 187.

The within named defendant may be admitted to bail in the sum of: _____*no bail*_____ Dollars.

WITNESS, my hand this ____*17ᵗʰ*____ day of ___*April*___ 2003.

_____*(signed by judge)*_____

Judge of the Superior Court

County of Stanislaus, State of California

[*Note:* The italicized words and figures were handwritten.]

But what about the private person? How much force may he or she use to effect an arrest? The statutes of many states are silent on this issue. Although it is generally conceded that a private person may also use that degree of force reasonably necessary to make the arrest and to overcome resistance, most states do not give a private person the right to break into a dwelling to make an arrest for a misdemeanor violation.

Calling for Assistance

In making an arrest, an officer or a private person may call upon as many persons as are deemed necessary for assistance in making the arrest. In general, no prosecutive action can be taken against anyone for refusing to assist the private person in making an arrest. However, the statute of one state provides that any person making an arrest may orally summon as many people as he or she finds necessary, and that all those failing to obey such a **summons** for assistance will be guilty of a misdemeanor. This provision implies that anyone failing to assist a private person will be subject to prosecution. Most states make it a violation for certain persons to refuse to assist an officer in making an arrest when summoned to do so. As was the case with states that allow officers to arrest outside their jurisdiction, this provision is based upon the old posse comitatus policy that a sheriff had the authority to deputize members of a community and demand that they assist him in the location and apprehension of an outlaw. In modern practice, it is not necessary in an emergency situation to deputize a person before requesting assistance. Many times an officer is confronted with circumstances in which immediate help is needed in making an arrest. Under these circumstances, an officer may orally summon those present to assist him or her, and a failure to come to the officer's aid may subject those persons to prosecution.

States differ considerably in who must assist an officer in making an arrest. The statutes of several states provide that an officer making a lawful arrest may command the aid of every male person over eighteen years of age to assist him or her, and any male failing to obey the command for assistance shall be guilty of a misdemeanor. This provision makes no mention of the male's being "able-bodied." This provision was excluded purposely. When an officer is presented with an emergency situation, he or she should not have to spend time determining who is physically capable of providing assistance. It also prohibits an individual from using the excuse that he is not physically able to assist. Not all requests for assistance entail a physical encounter with the accused. The assistance may be only a request that the individual radio for other police units to come to the aid of an officer, a task that could be performed by a person in a wheelchair.

The statutes of some states provide that every able-bodied person over the age of eighteen years who refuses to aid an officer in making an arrest after being commanded to do so is guilty of a misdemeanor. Such a provision makes both men and women subject to prosecution should they fail to assist in making an arrest after being summoned to do so by an officer. The problem created by the provision that the person be able-bodied is how to determine whether the person summoned was able-bodied. It has been held that the mere fact that there may be some danger involved in rendering assistance is not sufficient reason to refuse to assist. The statutes of a few states provide that every person who fails to obey a command by an officer to assist him or her in making an arrest shall be guilty of a misdemeanor. Such a provision is all-encompassing, since no mention is made of the person's being able-bodied, male or female, or within a specific age designation.

The statute of one state provides that the officer requesting assistance must be in uniform for prosecutive action to be applicable. This requirement is again designed to eliminate the possibility of an individual's using the excuse that he or she did not know that the person requesting assistance was an officer. However, this restriction is not without complications. In view of the wording of the statute, even if an individual knows that the person summoning assistance is an officer, unless the officer is in uniform when summoning aid, the individual cannot be prosecuted if he or she fails to assist the officer. This provision also raises the question, What is a uniform? Some law enforcement agencies have adopted the sport coat or blazer and sport pants style of uniform, which gives the appearance of civilian clothing. Would this be considered a uniform within the meaning of the statute?

When a person responds to an officer's call or demand for assistance, he or she has the same rights and privileges as the officer. Such a person is, in effect, a temporary law enforcement officer and has the right to use reasonable force to effect the arrest. If the person called upon to assist the officer acts in good faith, he or she is protected from civil liability.[10]

Resisting Arrest

Generally, it is a violation to willfully resist, delay, or obstruct a peace officer in the performance of his or her duty, including making an arrest. Yet, may an individual who is being arrested by a private person resist that arrest without being subjected to prosecution for the resistance? Most state statutes are silent on this point. Since there is no provision that an individual can be charged with an act of **resisting arrest** by a private person, presumably one is not subject to any additional charge except the one for which the arrest is being made, and the only peril is in meeting the resistance of the private person.

In this discussion, a question regarding the right of a person to resist an unlawful arrest must also arise. As previously stated, it is generally held that resisting an officer in the performance of his or her duty is a violation. But is an officer performing his or her duty by making an unlawful arrest? It was previously held at common law that a person could resist an unlawful arrest, and this view is followed in some of the states whether the arrest is being made by an officer or a private person. This situation results in many curbside court sessions and brawls between the accused and the arresting person, with each claiming to be right and with violent resistance taking place. Other states have provided that if a person is being arrested or has reasonable cause to believe that he or she is being arrested by an officer, the person is under the duty to refrain from using force or any weapon to resist such arrest. By court interpretation, it has been held that this provision refers to unlawful arrests as well as lawful ones. Note, however, that the provision pertains only to officers and is still silent about resisting arrest by a private person.

The justifications under the common law rule allowing for individuals to resist an unlawful arrest include:

- A state may not indiscriminately take away a person's liberty.
- Citizens are responsible for governing the governors (police).
- Innocent persons may resist by virtue of the injustice attempted to be placed on them.

Although a person may not resist an unlawful arrest in most states, he or she is not without recourse. One is entitled to seek immediate release from custody by a writ of habeas corpus proceeding and may sue those responsible for the illegal arrest for damages in civil court. Once the arrest of a suspect is completed, he or she should be searched for weapons and evidence. Depending upon the circumstances of the case, it may be advisable to search the immediate area where the arrest took place for any additional evidence, including instruments that may have been used in committing the crime. A search may also be made for any hidden weapons that the suspect might use to attempt an escape or to harm the arresting officer or others. These searches are considered reasonable as incidental to the arrest because if the search were not done at the time, evidence could be lost or destroyed.

MIRANDA AND ITS EFFECT

Before the U.S. Supreme Court decided *Miranda* v. *Arizona,* confessions and the accompanying interrogations were decided on a case-by-case method.[11] This approach reviewed the circumstances surrounding the interrogation to determine whether the suspect's will was broken by the police. The interrogation was considered improper if it violated the suspect's due process rights.

WARNING AS TO YOUR RIGHTS

You are under arrest. Before we ask you any questions, you must understand what your rights are.

You have the right to remain silent. You are not required to say anything to us at any time or to answer any questions. Anything you say can be used against you in court.

You have the right to talk to a lawyer for advice before we question you and to have him with you during questioning.

If you cannot afford a lawyer and want one, a lawyer will be provided for you.

If you want to answer questions now without a lawyer present you will still have the right to stop answering at any time. You also have the right to stop answering at any time until you talk to a lawyer.   P-4475

Since 1966, police have been required to advise an in-custody suspect using the *Miranda* warning. (*Source:* Getty Images Inc.-Hutton Archive Photos.)

Pre-*Miranda* Techniques

In *Brown* v. *Mississippi,* the defendant was taken to the crime scene, where he was questioned regarding his involvement in a murder.[12] After denying guilt, he was hung by a rope from a tree. He continued to claim innocence and was tied to the tree and whipped. Brown was released but subsequently seized again and whipped until he finally confessed. The court held that the confession was a product of coercion and brutality and therefore violated the defendant's Fourteenth Amendment due process rights.

In *Ashcraft* v. *Tennessee,* the defendant was taken to the police station and questioned continuously for two days regarding the murder of his wife.[13] The officers questioned Ashcraft in relays because they became exhausted during the interrogation; however, the defendant was denied rest and sleep during the entire time. The court held that the prolonged interrogation of Ashcraft was coercive, and therefore the confession was involuntary and inadmissible.

In *Spano* v. *New York,* the defendant was suspected of a murder.[14] Spano informed a friend who was a rookie police officer that he had in fact killed the victim. Spano was arrested, and the rookie officer was instructed to tell Spano that he (the officer) was in trouble and might lose his job unless Spano confessed. Spano finally confessed to the killing. The Supreme Court held that the use of deception as a means of psychological pressure to obtain a confession was a violation of the defendant's constitutional rights and that therefore the confession was involuntary and suppressed.

In *Escobedo* v. *Illinois,* the defendant was arrested for murder and interrogated for several hours at the police station.[15] During the interrogation, Escobedo repeatedly requested to see his attorney, who was also at the police station demanding to see his

Law in Practice

Handwriting Exemplars

Timothy McVeigh was arrested for bombing the Oklahoma City federal building, which caused many deaths. A federal grand jury issued a subpoena ordering him to furnish exemplars of his handwriting. He refused, contending that the subpoena was a violation of his Fifth Amendment privilege against self-incrimination. As a judge, how would you rule?

[*United States* v. *McVeigh*, 896 F. Supp. 1549 (W.D. Okla, 1995.]

client. The police refused both requests and finally obtained the confession. The court held that Escobedo was denied his right to counsel and that therefore no statement obtained from him could be used at a criminal trial.

The *Escobedo* decision was confusing because it is not clear when the right to counsel attaches during the interrogation. Trial courts began interpreting the meaning of *Escobedo* differently. Thus, the stage was set for the U.S. Supreme Court to clear up the confusion that had resulted from its previous rulings.

Miranda Safeguards

In *Miranda* v. *Arizona,* the U.S. Supreme Court established certain safeguards for individuals who are being interrogated by police.[16] Most people know that the *Miranda* decision requires police officers to advise defendants of their constitutional rights. In reality, *Miranda* established a four-prong test that must be satisfied before a suspect's statements can be admitted into evidence. The test requires affirmative answers to all four of the following questions:

1. Was the statement voluntary?
2. Was the Miranda warning given?
3. Was there a waiver by the suspect?
4. Was the waiver intelligent and voluntary?

Unless all these questions are answered in the affirmative, none of the suspect's statements can be admitted into evidence. In *Miranda,* the defendant was arrested at home in Phoenix, Arizona, in connection with the rape and kidnapping of a female and was taken to a police station for questioning. At the time, he was twenty-three years old, poor, and basically illiterate. After being questioned for two hours, he confessed to the crime. The Supreme Court issued its now famous **Miranda warning** requirement stating the following:

> We hold that when an individual is taken into custody or otherwise deprived of his freedom . . . the privilege against self-incrimination is jeopardized. . . . He must be warned prior to any questioning that he has a right to remain silent, that anything he says can be used against him in a court of law, that he has a right to an attorney, and that if he cannot afford an attorney one will be appointed for him prior to any questioning if he so desires.

Traffic stop in Des Moines, Iowa. The suspects were detained but later released. (*Source:* Mikael Karlsson/ Arresting Images.)

The *Miranda* decision has drawn a bright line for admissibility of confessions and admissions obtained during investigations. It changed the way police interrogated suspects. The decision was sweeping in its scope, but it still left questions unanswered.

In *Berkemer* v. *McCarty,* the Supreme Court held that the Miranda warning must be given during any custodial interrogation.[17] The Court held that a person subjected to a custodial interrogation must be given the warning regardless of the severity of the offense, but questioning a motorist at a routine traffic stop does not constitute custodial interrogation.

Law in Practice

Requirements of an Admissible Confession

- The confession must be given knowingly and not as the result of lies or deception.
- If in custody, the suspect must be informed of his or her rights.
- The confession must be voluntary.
- Confessions may not be obtained through threats, such as
  - threatening to turn an illegal foreign alien over to immigration authorities for deportation;
  - threatening to report a mother to child protective services for child abuse to have her children taken away from her;
  - threatening to report suspects to a welfare agency for the purpose of having their welfare benefits suspended.
- Confessions may not be obtained through use of pain or through constructive force.

Law in Practice

Using Psychological Tactics in Interrogation

The defendant Hawkins was arrested for rape and murder. While being interrogated by Officer LeFavers, he asked the police officer if he would be sentenced to death for his crime. The police officer stated: "Sam, to be honest with you, I would think that the courts in your situation would be very lenient. I really do. I think that they will observe the fact that you need help—you're trying to seek that help already, psychological, psychiatric help, and I think they would recommend a psychiatrist." The defendant was black and had professed a dislike for "honkies." The police used a black officer to interrogate him, hoping to obtain a psychological advantage. Taken together, does the statement of the police officer and use of the black officer establish improper psychological techniques and thus result in a confession that is not the result of the free will and rational choice of the defendant?

The court held in the above factual situation that the confession was admissible. The court stated that the comments were not a promise of leniency and that predictions about future events are not the same as a promise of leniency. The court also stated that there is nothing inherently wrong with the police's efforts to create a favorable climate for confession and that the use of the black police officer, even though designed to gain a psychological advantage, was not improper.

[*Hawkins* v. *Lynaugh*, 844 F.2d. 1132 (5th Cir. 1988).]

The *Miranda* decision has generated both support and criticism since its inception. Supporters argue that it protects the rights of those accused of crimes, whereas detractors claim that it allows the guilty to go free because the officer may not have followed all the rules. In recent years, the courts have begun to allow statements to be admitted into evidence despite the absence of the Miranda warning.

Eroding of *Miranda*

Miranda did not prevent statements obtained in violation of its rules from being used to impeach the credibility of a defendant who took the witness stand. In *Harris* v. *New York,* the U.S. Supreme Court held that it was proper to use such statements so long as the jury was instructed that the confession was not to be considered evidence of guilt but only to determine whether the defendant was telling the truth.[18] Voluntary statements made by the defendant without having received the Miranda warning are admissible even though the defendant is later advised of his or her rights and waives those rights. In *Oregon* v. *Elstad,* the defendant was picked up at his home as a suspect in a burglary and made incriminating statements without receiving his Miranda warning.[19] After being advised of his rights, he waived them and signed a confession. The Supreme Court held that the self-incrimination clause of the Fifth Amendment did not require suppression of the written confession because of the earlier unwarned admission.

In *Illinois* v. *Perkins,* the Supreme Court held that an undercover officer posing as an inmate need not give a jailed defendant the Miranda warning before asking questions that produce incriminating statements.[20] The Court held that no coercive atmosphere is present when an incarcerated person speaks freely to someone whom he believes is a fellow inmate. The Court added that the Miranda warning does not forbid strategic deception by taking advantage of a suspect's misplaced trust.

In *Arizona* v. *Fulminante,* the Supreme Court held that the harmless error rule is applicable to cases involving involuntary confessions.[21] The harmless error rule holds that an error made by the trial court in admitting illegally obtained evidence does not require a reversal of the conviction if the error was determined to be harmless. The burden of proving harmless error rests with the prosecution and must be proved beyond a reasonable doubt.

In *Davis* v. *United States,* the Supreme Court considered the degree of clarity that was necessary for a suspect to invoke his Miranda rights.[22] Agents of the Naval Investigative Service were questioning the defendant in connection with the death of a sailor. The defendant initially waived his rights, but approximately ninety minutes later he stated, "Maybe I should talk to a lawyer." The agents asked clarifying questions, and when the defendant stated that he did not want an attorney, the interrogation resumed and elicited incriminating statements. The Court held that an equivocal request for a lawyer is insufficient to invoke the right to counsel and that there is no need for clarifying questions before proceeding with the interrogation.

Two years after *Miranda* was decided, Congress passed Title 18 U.S. Code, Section 3501, which set forth only voluntariness as the touchstone of admissibility for statements. In 2000, the Supreme Court finally had a case before it that allowed it to examine this law. In *Dickerson* v. *United States,* the Court held that the *Miranda* decision was of constitutional orgin and that therefore Congress may not overrule its scope or effect.[23]

After years of allowing suspects to avoid police interrogation by invoking their Miranda rights, the Supreme Court is beginning to take a more reasonable and practical approach to this controversial issue.[24] However, police officers must still carefully tailor their interrogations so that they obtain information from the suspects while protecting their constitutional rights.

Accused wife murderer Scott Peterson (left) sits with attorney Mark Geragos during arraignment proceedings at the Stanislaus Superior Court in Modesto, California, December 3, 2003. (*Source:* Bart Ah You/CORBIS-NY.)

Law in Practice

Significant Cases Involving Interrogation

Brown v. *Mississippi* (1936)	The use of physical force (hanging in this case) to obtain a confession violated the Due Process Clause of the Fourteenth Amendment.
Ashcraft v. *Tennessee* (1944)	Psychologically coerced confessions are not voluntary and therefore not admissible in court.
Miranda v. *Arizona* (1966)	An in-custody suspect must be advised of his or her rights prior to being interrogated.
Harris v. *New York* (1971)	A voluntary statement taken from an in-custody defendant (without being advised, as required by *Miranda*) could be used at trial to impeach his in-court testimony.
New York v. *Quarles* (1984)	Public safety concerns justified the police officer's failure to provide a Miranda warning before asking about the location of a loaded weapon apparently abandoned immediately prior to arrest.
Duckworth v. *Eagan* (1989)	Advising a suspect that an attorney would be appointed only if he goes to court did not render the Miranda warning inadequate.
Illinois v. *Perkins* (1990)	When a police officer poses as a prison inmate and is placed in a cell with a defendant, there is no requirement that the officer advise the defendant of his or her Miranda rights prior to asking questions of the defendant.
Minnick v. *Mississippi* (1990)	Once a suspect invokes his or her right to counsel, the police may not resume interrogation unless the suspect has an attorney. (*Note:* This rule does not apply if the suspect initiates the latter questioning.)
Pennsylvania v. *Muniz* (1990)	Police officers are not required to give a Miranda warning prior to asking suspected drunken drivers routine questions and recording their answers.
Arizona v. *Fulminate* (1991)	The Court upheld a conviction even though the confession admitted may have been coerced. The Court noted that the evidence of guilt even without the confession was overwhelming.
Davis v. *United States* (1994)	Police were not required to stop questioning a suspect merely because the suspect made an ambiguous statement about wanting an attorney.
Dickerson v. *United States* (2000)	The Court noted that *Miranda* had become embedded in police practices and did not overrule *Miranda*.

IMMUNITY FROM ARREST

Certain classes of persons are immune from arrest because of statutory regulations. These include representatives of foreign countries, legislators, and out-of-state witnesses.

Diplomatic Immunity

International law and various agreements between nations exchanging representatives are the bases for **diplomatic immunity**. For example, in the United States, as provided by international law, diplomatic officers, their staff, members of their families, and their servants are free from local jurisdiction, and as such they should not be arrested or detained for any offense unless they are citizens of or permanent residents of the United States (Title

Prosecutors Rick Distaso, left, and David Harris confer during the Scott Peterson trial at the Stanislaus Superior Court in Modesto, California, January 23, 2004. (*Source:* AP Wide World Photos.)

22 U.S. Code, section 252). The diplomatic officers who enjoy this unlimited immunity are ambassadors, ministers, their assistants, and attachés. The purpose behind the doctrine of diplomatic immunity is to contribute to the development of friendly relations between nations and to ensure the efficient performance of the diplomatic missions.

Although these persons have complete immunity from arrest, detention, or prosecution, the immunity does not give them blanket authority to disregard the laws of the United States and of the individual states. As established by international law, it is the duty of all foreign representatives to respect the laws and regulations of the land. If a member of the diplomatic corps commits a crime, the offense should be brought to the attention of the U.S. Department of State, and if the crime is a serious one, the State Department may request that the member be recalled from the country.

Consular Immunity

Consuls and their deputies are also representatives of foreign nations but have only limited immunity. In all cases, however, they are to be treated with due respect. The consular officers are not liable for arrest or detention pending a trial except in cases of a serious felony having been committed. Since consular officers' immunity is limited to acts in performance of their duties, the immunity does not include members of their families or servants, but they too should be treated with proper respect. A police officer may treat a consular officer who commits a traffic violation the same as he or she does anyone else. The police officer may simply warn the consular officer, or the police officer may issue a citation, since this is not considered in violation of the immunity of arrest and detention.

Most diplomatic corps are stationed either in Washington, D.C., or with the United Nations in New York, but consular officers are assigned to stations in many large cities throughout the United States. Peace officers in the United States may encounter

Ernesto Miranda, twenty-seven, listens as the jury deliberates his case in Phoenix, Arizona, on February 24, 1967. The jury found Miranda guilty on charges of rape and kidnapping. His earlier trial was reversed by the U.S. Supreme Court because the police failed to advise him of his rights. (*Source:* AP Wide World Photos.)

members of these groups anywhere, since many of them travel extensively. Each member of these groups should have official identification in his or her possession, whereby a peace officer may determine the official status of the member and the immunity to which he or she is entitled.

Legislative Immunity

Most states have some type of provision in their statutes granting immunity to legislative members, but this immunity is limited. Many of the states hold that the immunity relates only to arrest arising out of some civil matter and that there is no immunity from arrest on a criminal charge.

Out-of-State Witnesses

The Uniform Act to Secure the Attendance of Witnesses from Without the State in Criminal Cases has been adopted by most of the states. This act provides that if a person enters a state in obedience of a subpoena to testify in that state, he or she shall not be subject to arrest in connection with any crime committed in the state prior to his or her entrance into the state to testify. The person is also granted a reasonable time to leave the state after testifying without being subject to such an arrest but is not granted any immunity from arrest for a crime that he or she may commit while in the state to testify. A similar immunity is given to persons passing through a state to testify in another state in obedience of a subpoena. One might question this immunity from arrest given to a witness. The reason is that the testimony is more important to a particular case than is the prosecution of a witness for some past violation of the law. In addition, if the prosecution were significant, there is no reason that extradition proceedings could not be brought against the witness.

BOOKING

When people are arrested, the usual procedure is to take them to the police station for booking. **Booking** consists of recording the arrest in official law enforcement records, fingerprinting, and photographing the accused. If the charge is a bailable offense, the accused is entitled to post bail at this time. If bail is not posted, the accused will be searched and placed in jail until he or she does post bail or until final prosecution takes place. Even though the accused was searched in the field at the time of the arrest, a more thorough search may be made at the time of booking for weapons or evidence that may have been missed during the field search.

Right to Telephone Calls

Whether an arrest is made by a law enforcement officer or by a private person, the accused is entitled to certain rights. One of these rights is to be informed of the offense for which the accused is being arrested. Another right provided by the statutes of some states is the right to make telephone calls. This right has been incorporated into the laws to prohibit individuals from being held indefinitely without anyone knowing that they have been arrested—in other words, to prevent them from being held incommunicado.

In those states in which the arrested person is permitted to make telephone calls, there are considerable differences in the rights afforded the arrested person. These rights differ as to the number of calls that may be made; to whom, how soon after the arrest, and at whose expense they may be made; whether the calls can be monitored; and whether the arrested person must be advised of the right to make the calls. It is generally held that the arrested person is entitled to make the calls immediately after being booked or, except where physically impossible, within a prescribed time, such as three hours, after the arrest. It is also generally provided that the arrested person is entitled to make at least one or more completed calls to an attorney, bail bondsman, relative, or other person. The calls are to be made free of charge to a local area; otherwise, they are made at the expense of the arrested person. Some jurisdictions require that the arrested person be advised of the right to make the calls; others merely require that the right be posted in a conspicuous place in the area of detention. This right is a continuing one and is not waived if the arrested person does not request to make the calls immediately after being booked. Some states also require that if the arrested person is physically unable to make the calls, he or she is entitled to the assistance of an officer.

ISSUANCE OF A CITATION

At one time in our history, all criminal offenders were brought to court with force. Even in civil matters, an arrest was frequently used to bring the defendant to court. Today, the defendant in a civil matter is not forced to appear in court. If the defendant fails to appear as requested, the person bringing the suit, who is known as the plaintiff, is given the judgment by default. Even in criminal matters, particularly involving minor violations, efforts are made to persuade the accused to come to court with as little inconvenience to all as possible. But when a warrant of arrest is issued, the person named in the warrant must be taken into custody, booked, and transported for arraignment unless he or she posts bail before arraignment. This same procedure is followed in most arrests made without a warrant. Each of these steps is time-consuming, and if the person does not post bail, he or she must be confined to jail pending the judicial proceedings. This detention often causes overcrowding of the jail facilities and, in some instances, an injustice to the accused. To alleviate this situation, many states have adopted legislation whereby an officer may issue a citation for a misdemeanor or an infraction violation instead of taking the person into custody.

A citation (sometimes referred to as a summons) is a written notice issued to a violator to appear in court. The citation lists the violator's name, address, and the offense committed. It also sets forth the time, place, and date that the violator is to appear in court. If the arrested person signs the citation agreeing to appear in court as directed, he or she is entitled to be released without further action being taken at that time.

In most instances, a citation will be issued for an infraction and for a traffic violation. But it is generally within the discretion of the law enforcement officer whether a citation will be issued for a misdemeanor violation. Many law enforcement agencies have established guidelines on which misdemeanor violations a citation may be issued for in lieu of taking the offender into custody. One reason for the selective practice is that it may be felt that the violator would not appear in court and that booking and confinement until he or she posts bail is the preferable procedure. Some law enforcement agencies have established a policy of taking an offender into custody, booking him or her, and then releasing the offender on a citation. This procedure defeats part of the purpose of issuing the citation in that the offender is taken into custody, transported to the station, and booked. Those following this process feel that the identifying data obtained from the booking justify the time consumed, particularly if the violator does not appear as agreed and must be sought on a bench warrant. To discourage the book-and-then-release practice, some jurisdictions require that the arresting agency conduct a background investigation to determine whether the person should be released on a citation. The investigation should include the person's name, address, length of residence at that address, length of residence in the state, marital and family status, current employment, length of current employment, prior arrest record, and such other facts as would bear on the question of the release of the individual.

Even though the violator is released in the field by signing the citation, most jurisdictions permit the law enforcement agency involved to request that the violator be booked prior to commencement of final judicial proceedings in order to get identifying data for future reference.

Citation Court Procedure

In some jurisdictions, a copy of the citation is filed with the appropriate court. This citation will become the accusatory document, eliminating the necessity of the officer's filing a complaint. In other jurisdictions, a copy of the citation is furnished to the prosecuting attorney, and on the basis of this citation, a complaint will be filed with the court that is to hear the case. After the citation has been issued and before the arraignment, the violator may post bail for his or her appearance. If the violator fails to appear as agreed, the bail may be forfeited. The judge, at his or her discretion, either may order that no further proceedings shall take place on the matter or may issue a bench warrant for the arrest of the violator. The judge will then proceed on the original charge for which the citation was issued, and in most jurisdictions, the violator can be charged with a misdemeanor for failure to appear.

CHARGING THE DEFENDANT WITH A CRIME

Misdemeanor—Brief judicial hearing and trial

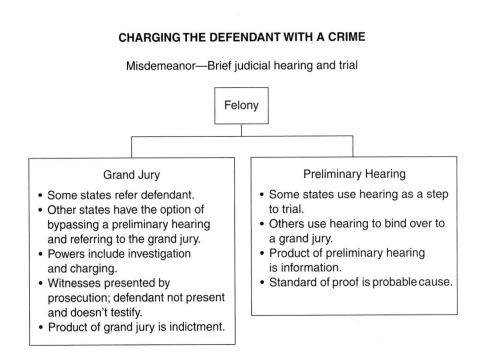

SUMMONS

Although a citation is sometimes referred to as a summons, technically a summons differs from a citation. The true summons is issued by a judge in lieu of a warrant of arrest. The summons commands the accused to appear in court at a specified time and eliminates the need for arresting the accused and bringing him or her before the court. The summons may be issued by a judge when he or she feels that the accused will appear as commanded without the need to make an arrest. The summons, like the warrant of arrest, is based upon a complaint filed with the court. After the summons is issued, it may be personally delivered or mailed to the accused. If the person named in the summons fails to appear as commanded, a warrant of arrest will be issued. A summons differs from a citation in that a summons is issued by a judge and either mailed to or served upon the accused personally, commanding his or her appearance; a citation is generally issued by an officer in the field.

Does *Miranda* Bear Poisonous Fruit?

Despite what lower courts might sometimes incorrectly rule, failing to mirandize a suspect does not violate the Fourth Amendment.

Devallis Rutledge

We're all painfully familiar with the fruit of the poison tree doctrine in the Fourth Amendment context: Evidence obtained by exploiting an unreasonable search or seizure is subject to suppression at trial. What judges and lawyers refer to as the derivative evidence exclusionary rule basically makes any evidence inadmissible if it was derived from an earlier violation of the defendant's constitutional rights [*United States,* 371 U.S. 471 (1963)].

But does that same consequence follow from the failure to follow the *Miranda* procedures? If you learn the whereabouts of contraband or evidence from a statement that doesn't comply with Miranda, must the contraband or evidence be suppressed as "poisonous fruit" of the inadmissible statement? Short answer: No.

Getting a Grip on Miranda

Ever since the 5-4 *Miranda* decision was issued in 1966, it has been the subject of considerable debate, litigation, and misunderstanding. More than a handful of judges, lawyers, and police officers mistakenly thought of Miranda as some sort of judicial rule about how police officers are required to conduct interrogations. But given the separation-of-powers structure of our Constitution, the judiciary has no inherent power to direct the functions of the executive branch (which includes law enforcement), as language from Supreme Court opinions has tried to make clear:

"*Miranda*'s purpose was not promulgation of judicially preferred standards for police interrogation, a function we are quite powerless to perform" [*Michigan* v. *Tucker,* 417 U.S. 433 (1974)].

"Nothing in the Constitution vests in us the authority to mandate a code of behavior for state officials [*Moran* v. *Burbine,* 475 U.S. 412 (1986)].

"The *Miranda* rule is not a code of police conduct. . . . It is not for this Court to impose its preferred police practices on law enforcement officials" (*United States* v. *Patane,* 542 U.S. 630 (2004)].

Then what exactly is the Miranda rule? It's an admissibility rule for criminal trial judges. All *Miranda* ever said was that courts could not admit as evidence of guilt a statement obtained by custodial interrogation unless the defendant had first been told of his or her rights and had agreed to waive them and talk. "*Miranda* conditioned the admissibility at trial of any custodial confession, on warning a suspect of his rights" [*Missouri* v. *Seibert,* 542 U.S. 600 (2004)]. "*Miranda* itself made clear that its focus was the admissibility of statements" (*United States* v. *Patane*). *(Continued)*

Although it is not unusual to see lower court opinions mistakenly describing a police officer's interrogation as "unlawful" or "unconstitutional" based on a finding that Miranda procedures were not followed, the Supreme Court has been careful to note that it is only the erroneous introduction of a statement in court that violates the Fifth Amendment—not the officer's noncoercive questioning of the suspect.

In *Chavez* v. *Martinez*, 538 U.S. 760 (2003), the Supreme Court ruled that because non-Mirandized questioning is not unlawful or unconstitutional, officers cannot be sued civilly for violating a suspect's Fifth Amendment rights on the basis of such questioning. The Court reaffirmed this distinction in the *Patane* case:

> A mere failure to give Miranda warnings does not, by itself, violate a suspect's constitutional rights or even the Miranda rule. Police do not violate a suspect's constitutional rights (or the Miranda rule) by negligent or even deliberate failures to provide the suspect with the full panoply of warnings prescribed by Miranda. Police cannot violate the Self-Incrimination Clause by taking unwarned though voluntary statements.

In other words, although Miranda procedures must be followed in order to ensure the admissibility of custodial statements at trial, they "are not themselves rights protected by the Constitution" (*Moran* v. *Burbine*). Therefore, non-coercive questioning that merely fails to meet Miranda's admissibility requirements is not unconstitutional. Because evidence derived from statements obtained without valid Miranda warnings and waivers is not the result of any constitutional violation, the derivative evidence exclusionary rule does not apply.

The **Patane** *Case*

Colorado Springs (Col.) police and Bureau of Alcohol, Tobacco, and Firearms agents were investigating Samuel Patane for violating a domestic violence restraining order and being a convicted felon in possession of a concealable firearm. After being taken into custody and without complete Miranda warnings (because Patane interrupted the officer who was trying to give him the warning), Patane told officers where he kept his Glock 40. The pistol was seized and used as evidence to convict him of the federal firearms offense. Patane appealed.

The federal court of appeals reversed the conviction and suppressed the gun under a "fruit of the poison tree" theory. The appeals court noted that in *Dickerson* v. *U.S.* the Supreme Court had called the Miranda rule a "constitutional rule," and interpreted this to mean that officers violate the Constitution when they do not comply with Miranda procedures, thus invoking the derivative evidence exclusionary rule.

The U.S. Supreme Court reversed this ruling and held that the fruit of the poison tree analysis does not apply to *Miranda* issues. As the *Patane* decision explains, the Miranda rule is indeed a constitutional rule—but that rule is simply that judges may not admit non-complying statements at trial. The constitutional rule of Miranda relates to admissibility of statements—not to any mandate that police give the warning and obtain a waiver. Therefore, if a statement is found to lack compliance with Miranda procedures, although that statement itself is inadmissible, evidence derived from it is not. Said the Court: "The exclusionary rule as articulated in cases such as *Wong Sun* does not apply."

Non-Complying Statements

Because statements taken without full compliance with Miranda's admissibility procedures have not been obtained "unlawfully" or "unconstitutionally," the statements themselves and information or evidence gained from them can legitimately be used for a variety of important purposes, such as clearing innocent suspects, recovering bodies or stolen property, identifying accomplices, and clearing unsolved cases.

A number of previous court decisions, grasping the distinction between Miranda and the Constitution, had already rejected a "fruit of the poison tree" extension of Miranda, allowing limited uses of statements and their derivative evidence. Examples of these limited uses include:

- Locating witnesses to the crime [*Michigan* v. *Tucker*]
- Impeaching the defendant's trial testimony [*Harris* v. *New York*, 401 U.S. 222 (1971); *Oregon* v. *Hass*, 420 U.S. 714 (1975)]
- Probable cause for arrest [*United States* v. *Morales*, 788 F.2nd 883 (CA2, 1986)]
- Probable cause for a search warrant [*United States* v. *Patterson*, 485 U.S. 922 (1988)]
- Recovery of physical evidence [*United States* v. *Villalba-Alvarado*, 345 F.3d 1007 (CA8, 2003)]

Precautions

It's obviously preferable to obtain statements that will be fully admissible at trial. This means that custodial interrogation should scrupulously adhere to the Miranda procedures wherever possible. Unfortunately, it's not always easy to predict which way a court will rule on many questions that arise about Miranda issues. As the [Supreme] Court itself has acknowledged, "In many cases, a breach of Miranda procedures may not be identified as such until long after full Miranda warnings are administered and a valid confession obtained" [*Oregon* v. *Elstad,* 470 U.S. 298 (1985)].

In cases where questioning occurs without satisfying Miranda's admissibility conditions, officers should be aware that a resulting statement and other evidence it leads to may still have legitimate investigative and prosecutorial value, so any such statements should be fully documented in arrest reports.

Always remember that actual coercion, such as mistreatment or the use of threats or overbearing promises of leniency, may make a statement and its derivative fruits completely inadmissible for any purpose, and may cause civil liability if found to be so egregious as to "shock the conscience."

[This article was originally printed in *Police Magazine,* September 2004, pp. 82–84. Reprinted by permission of *Police Magazine.*] [Attorney Devailis Rutledge, a former police officer and prosecutor, defends officers and agencies at Manning & Marder, Kass, Elrod, Ramirez in Los Angeles, California.]

Capstone Cases

Tennessee v. *Garner*
471 U.S. 1, 105 S.Ct. 1694, 85 L.Ed.2d 1 (1985)

Justice White delivered the opinion of the Court.

At about 10:45 P.M. on October 3, 1974, Memphis Police Officers Elton Hymon and Leslie Wright were dispatched to answer a "prowler inside call." Upon arriving at the scene they saw a woman standing on her porch and gesturing toward the adjacent house. She told them she had heard glass breaking and that "they" or "someone" was breaking in next door. While Wright radioed the dispatcher to say that they were on the scene, Hymon went behind the house. He heard a door slam and saw someone run across the back yard. The fleeing suspect, who was appellee-respondent's decedent, Edward Garner, stopped at a 6-feet-high chain link fence at the edge of the yard. With the aid of a flashlight, Hymon was able to see Garner's face and hands. He saw no sign of a weapon, and, though not certain, was "reasonably sure" and "figured" that Garner was unarmed. He thought Garner was 17 or 18 years old and about 5'5" or 5'7" tall. While Garner was crouched at the base of the fence, Hymon called out "police, halt" and took a few steps toward him. Garner then began to climb over the fence. Convinced that if Garner made it over the fence, he would elude capture,

Justice Byron R. White was appointed to the Supreme Court by President John F. Kennedy and served from 1962 to 1993. (*Source:* Joseph Bailey, National Geographic Society. Courtesy the Supreme Court of the United States.)

Hymon shot him. The bullet hit Garner in the back of the head. Garner was taken by ambulance to a hospital, where he died on the operating table. Ten dollars and a purse taken from the house were found on his body.

(Continued)

In using deadly force to prevent the escape, Hymon was acting under the authority of a Tennessee statute and pursuant to Police Department policy. The statute provides that "if, after notice of the intention to arrest the defendant, he either flee or forcibly resist, the officer may use all the necessary means to effect the arrest." The Department policy was slightly more restrictive than the statute, but still allowed the use of deadly force in cases of burglary. . . .

Garner's father then brought this action in the Federal District Court for the Western District of Tennessee, seeking damages under 42 U.S.C. 1 983 for asserted violations of Garner's constitutional rights. . . . The District Court . . . found that the statute, and Hymon's actions, were constitutional. . . . The Court of Appeals reversed and remanded. . . . The State of Tennessee, which had intervened to defend the statute, appealed to this Court.

Whenever an officer restrains the freedom of a person to walk away, he has seized that person. While it is not always clear just when minimal police interference becomes a seizure, there can be no question that apprehension by the use of deadly force is a seizure subject to the reasonableness requirement of the Fourth Amendment.

A police officer may arrest a person if he has probable cause to believe that person committed a crime. Petitioners and appellant argue that if this requirement is satisfied the Fourth Amendment has nothing to say about how that seizure is made. This submission ignores the many cases in which this Court, by balancing the extent of the intrusion against the need for it, has examined the reasonableness of the manner in which a search or seizure is conducted. . . . Because one of the factors is the extent of the intrusion, it is plain that reasonableness depends on not only when a seizure is made, but also how it is carried out. . . .

The same balancing process applied in the cases cited above demonstrates that, notwithstanding probable cause to seize a suspect, an officer may not always do so by killing him. The intrusiveness of a seizure by means of deadly force is unmatched. The suspect's fundamental interest in his own life need not be elaborated upon. The use of deadly force also frustrates the interest of the individual, and of society, in judicial determination of guilt and punishment. Against these interests are ranged governmental interests in effective law enforcement. It is argued that overall violence will be reduced by encouraging the peaceful submission of suspects who know that they may be shot if they flee. Effectiveness in making arrests requires the resort to deadly force, or at least the meaningful threat thereof. "Being able to arrest such individuals is a condition precedent to the state's entire system of law enforcement."

Without in any way disparaging the importance of these goals, we are not convinced that the use of deadly force is a sufficiently productive means of accomplishing them to justify the killing of nonviolent suspects. The use of deadly force is a self-defeating way of apprehending a suspect and so setting the criminal justice mechanism in motion. If successful, it guarantees that that mechanism will not be set in motion. And while the meaningful threat of deadly force might be thought to lead to the arrest of more live suspects by discouraging escape attempts, the presently available evidence does not support this thesis. The fact is that a majority of police departments in this country have forbidden the use of deadly force against nonviolent suspects. If those charged with the enforcement of the criminal law have abjured the use of deadly force in arresting nondangerous felons, there is a substantial basis for doubting that the use of such force is an essential attribute of the arrest power in all felony cases. Petitioners and appellant have not persuaded us that shooting nondangerous fleeing suspects is so vital as to outweigh the suspect's interest in his own life.

The use of deadly force to prevent the escape of all felony suspects, whatever the circumstances, is constitutionally unreasonable. It is not better that all felony suspects die than that they escape. Where the suspect poses no immediate threat to the officer and no threat to others, the harm resulting from failing to apprehend him does not justify the use of deadly force to do so. It is no doubt unfortunate when a suspect who is in sight escapes, but the fact that the police arrive a little late or are a little slower afoot does not always justify killing the suspect. A police officer may not seize an unarmed, nondangerous suspect by shooting him dead. The Tennessee statute is unconstitutional insofar as it authorizes the use of deadly force against such fleeing suspects.

It is not, however, unconstitutional on its face. Where the officer has probable cause to believe that the suspect poses a threat of serious physical harm, either to the officer or to others, it is not constitutionally unreasonable to prevent escape by using deadly force. Thus, if the suspect threatens the officer with a weapon or there is probable cause to believe that he has committed a crime involving the infliction or threatened infliction of serious physical harm, deadly force may be used if necessary to prevent escape, and if, where feasible, some warning has been given. As applied in such circumstances, the Tennessee statute would pass constitutional muster.

It is insisted that the Fourth Amendment must be construed in light of the common-law rule, which allowed the use of whatever force was necessary to effect the arrest of a fleeing felon, though not a misdemeanant.

The State and city argue that because this was the prevailing rule at the time of the adoption of the Fourth Amendment and for some time thereafter, and is still in force in some States, use of deadly force against a fleeing felon must be "reasonable." It is true that this Court has often looked to the common law in evaluating the reasonableness, for Fourth Amendment purposes, of police activity. On the other hand, it "has not simply frozen into constitutional law those law enforcement practices that existed at the time of the Fourth Amendment's passage." Because of sweeping change in the legal and technological context, reliance on the common-law rule in this case would be a mistaken literalism that ignores the purposes of a historical inquiry.

It has been pointed out many times that the common-law rule is best understood in light of the fact that it arose at a time when virtually all felonies were punishable by death. . . . Courts have also justified the common-law rule by emphasizing the relative dangerousness of felons.

Neither of these justifications makes sense today. Almost all crimes formerly punishable by death no longer are or can be. And while in earlier times "the gulf between the felonies and the minor offenses was broad and deep," today the distinction is minor and often arbitrary. Many crimes classified as misdemeanors, or nonexistent, at common law are now felonies. These changes have undermined the concept, which was questionable to begin with, that use of deadly force against a fleeing felon is merely a speedier execution of someone who has already forfeited his life. They have also made the assumption that a "felon" is more dangerous than a misdemeanant untenable. Indeed, numerous misdemeanors involve conduct more dangerous than many felonies.

There is an additional reason why the common-law rule cannot be directly translated to the present day. The common-law rule developed at a time when weapons were rudimentary. Deadly force could be inflicted almost solely in a hand-to-hand struggle during which, necessarily, the safety of the arresting officer was at risk. Handguns were not carried by police officers until the latter half of the last [nineteenth] century. Only then did it become possible to use deadly force from a distance as a means of apprehension. As a practical matter, the use of deadly force under the standard articulation of the common-law rule has an altogether different meaning—and harsher consequences—now than in past centuries.

One other aspect of the common-law rule bears emphasis. It forbids the use of deadly force to apprehend a misdemeanant, condemning such action as disproportionately severe.

In short, though the common-law pedigree of Tennessee's rule is pure on its face, changes in the legal and technological context mean the rule is distorted almost beyond recognition when literally applied.

In evaluating the reasonableness of police procedures under the Fourth Amendment, we have also looked to prevailing rules in individual jurisdictions. The rules in the States are varied. Some 19 States have codified the common-law rule, though in two of these the courts have significantly limited the statute. Four States, though without a relevant statute, apparently retain the common-law rule. Two States have adopted the Model Penal Code's provision verbatim. Eighteen others allow, in slightly varying language, the use of deadly force only if the suspect has committed a felony involving the use or threat of physical or deadly force, or is escaping with a deadly weapon, or is likely to endanger life or inflict serious physical injury if not arrested. Louisiana and Vermont, though without statutes or case law on point, do forbid the use of deadly force to prevent any but violent felonies. The remaining States either have no relevant statute or case-law, or have positions that are unclear.

It cannot be said that there is a constant or overwhelming trend away from the common-law rule. In recent years, some States have reviewed their laws and expressly rejected abandonment of the common-law rule. Nonetheless, the long term movement has been away from the rule that deadly force may be used against any fleeing felon, and that remains the rule in less than half the States.

This trend is more evident and impressive when viewed in light of the policies adopted by the police departments themselves. Overwhelmingly, these are more restrictive than the common-law rule. . . . Overall, only 7.5% of departmental and municipal policies explicitly permit the use of deadly force against any felon; 86.8% explicitly do not. In light of the rules adopted by those who must actually administer them, the older and fading common-law view is a dubious indicium of the constitutionality of the Tennessee statute now before us.

Actual departmental policies are important for an additional reason. We would hesitate to declare a police practice of long standing "unreasonable" if doing so would severely hamper effective law enforcement. But the indications are to the contrary. There has been no suggestion that crime has worsened in any way in jurisdictions that have adopted, by legislation or departmental policy, rules similar to that announced today.

(Continued)

Nor do we agree with petitioners and appellant that the rule we have adopted requires the police to make impossible, split-second evaluations of unknowable facts. We do not deny the practical difficulties of attempting to assess the suspect's dangerousness. However, similarly difficult judgments must be made by the police in equally uncertain circumstances. Nor is there any indication that in States that allow the use of deadly force only against dangerous suspects, the standard has been difficult to apply or has led to a rash of litigation involving inappropriate second-guessing of police officers' split-second decisions. Moreover, the highly technical felony/misdemeanor distinction is equally, if not more, difficult to apply in the field. An officer is in no position to know, for example, the precise value of property stolen, or whether the crime was a first or second offense. Finally, as noted above, this claim must be viewed with suspicion in light of the similar self-imposed limitations of so many police departments.

Officer Hymon could not reasonably have believed that Garner—young, slight, and unarmed—posed any threat. Indeed, Hymon never attempted to justify his actions on any basis other than the need to prevent an escape.

The dissent argues that the shooting was justified by the fact that Officer Hymon had probable cause to believe that Garner had committed a nighttime burglary. While we agree that burglary is a serious crime, we cannot agree that it is so dangerous as automatically to justify the use of deadly force. The FBI classifies burglary as a "property" rather than a "violent" crime. Although the armed burglar would present a different situation, the fact that an unarmed suspect has broken into a dwelling at night does not automatically mean he is physically dangerous. This case demonstrates as much. In fact, the available statistics demonstrate that burglaries only rarely involve physical violence. During the 10-year period from 1973–1982, only 3.8% of all burglaries involved violent crime.

The judgment of the Court of Appeals is affirmed.

Justice O'Connor, with whom the chief justice and Justice Rehnquist join, dissenting. . . .

Because burglary is a serious and dangerous felony, the public interest in the prevention and detection of the crime is of compelling importance. Where a police officer has probable cause to arrest a suspected burglar, the use of deadly force as a last resort might well be the only means of apprehending the suspect. With respect to a particular burglary, subsequent investigation simply cannot represent a substitute for immediate apprehension of the criminal suspect at the scene. Indeed, the Captain of the Memphis Police Department testified that in his city, if apprehension is not immediate, it is likely that the suspect will not be caught. Although some law enforcement agencies may choose to assume the risk that a criminal will remain at large, the Tennessee statute reflects a legislative determination that the use of deadly force in prescribed circumstances will serve generally to protect the public. Such statutes assist the police in apprehending suspected perpetrators of serious crimes and provide notice that a lawful police order to stop and submit to arrest may not be ignored with impunity. . . .

[The dissent notes also that three-fifths of all rapes in the home, three-fifths of all home robberies, and about a third of home assaults were committed by burglars.]

Illinois v. Perkins
496 U.S. 292 (1990)

JUSTICE KENNEDY delivered the opinion of the Court.

An undercover government agent was placed in the cell of respondent Perkins, who was incarcerated on charges unrelated to the subject of the agent's investigation. Respondent made statements that implicated him in the crime that the agent sought to solve. Respondent claims that the statements should be inadmissible because he had not been given Miranda warnings by the agent. We hold that the statements are admissible. Miranda warnings are not required when the suspect is unaware that he is speaking to a law enforcement officer and gives a voluntary statement.

I.

In November 1984, Richard Stephenson was murdered in a suburb of East St. Louis, Illinois. The murder remained unsolved until March 1986, when one Donald Charlton told police that he had learned about a homicide from a fellow inmate at the Graham Correctional Facility, where Charlton had been serving a sentence for burglary.

Justice Anthony M. Kennedy signs the oath of office during his swearing-in ceremony as former Chief Justice William Rehnquist looks on. In the background is Associate Justice Antonin Scalia. (*Source:* Ken Heinen/AP Wide World Photos.)

The fellow inmate was Lloyd Perkins, who is the respondent here. Charlton told police that, while at Graham, he had befriended respondent, who told him in detail about a murder that respondent had committed in East St. Louis. On hearing Charlton's account, the police recognized details of the Stephenson murder that were not well known, and so they treated Charlton's story as a credible one.

By the time the police heard Charlton's account, respondent had been released from Graham, but police traced him to a jail in Montgomery County, Illinois, where he was being held pending trial on a charge of aggravated battery unrelated to the Stephenson murder. The police wanted to investigate further respondent's connection to the Stephenson murder, but feared that the use of an eavesdropping device would prove impracticable and unsafe. They decided instead to place an undercover agent in the cellblock with respondent and Charlton. The plan was for Charlton and undercover agent John Parisi to pose as escapees from a work release program who had been arrested in the course of a burglary. Parisi and Charlton were instructed to engage respondent in casual conversation and report anything he said about the Stephenson murder.

Parisi, using the alias "Vito Bianco," and Charlton, both clothed in jail garb, were placed in the cellblock with respondent at the Montgomery County jail. The cellblock consisted of 12 separate cells that opened onto a common room. Respondent greeted Charlton who, after a brief conversation with respondent, introduced Parisi by his alias. Parisi told respondent that he "wasn't going to do any more time" and suggested that the three of them escape. Respondent replied that the Montgomery County jail was "rinky-dink" and that they could "break out." The trio met in respondent's cell later that evening, after the other inmates were asleep, to refine their plan. Respondent said that his girlfriend could smuggle in a pistol. Charlton said: "Hey, I'm not a murderer, I'm a burglar. That's your guys' profession." After telling Charlton that he would be responsible for any murder that occurred,

(Continued)

Parisi asked respondent if he had ever "done" anybody. Respondent said that he had and proceeded to describe at length the events of the Stephenson murder. Parisi and respondent then engaged in some casual conversation before respondent went to sleep. Parisi did not give respondent Miranda warnings before the conversations.

Respondent was charged with the Stephenson murder. Before trial, he moved to suppress the statements made to Parisi in the jail. The trial court granted the motion to suppress, and the State appealed. The Appellate Court of Illinois affirmed, 176 Ill. App. 3d 443, 531 N. E. 2d 141 (1988), holding that *Miranda* v. *Arizona*, 384 U.S. 436 (1966), prohibits all undercover contacts with incarcerated suspects that are reasonably likely to elicit an incriminating response.

We granted certiorari, 493 U.S. 808 (1989), to decide whether an undercover law enforcement officer must give Miranda warnings to an incarcerated suspect before asking him questions that may elicit an incriminating response. We now reverse.

II.

In *Miranda* v. *Arizona,* supra, the Court held that the Fifth Amendment privilege against self-incrimination prohibits admitting statements given by a suspect during "custodial interrogation" without a prior warning. Custodial interrogation means "questioning initiated by law enforcement officers after a person has been taken into custody. . . ." Id., at 444. The warning mandated by Miranda was meant to preserve the privilege during "incommunicado interrogation of individuals in a police-dominated atmosphere." Id., at 445. That atmosphere is said to generate "inherently compelling pressures which work to undermine the individual's will to resist and to compel him to speak where he would not otherwise do so freely." Id., at 467. "Fidelity to the doctrine announced in Miranda requires that it be enforced strictly, but only in those types of situations in which the concerns that powered the decision are implicated." *Berkemer* v. *McCarty,* 468 U.S. 420, 437 (1984).

Conversations between suspects and undercover agents do not implicate the concerns underlying Miranda. The essential ingredients of a "police-dominated atmosphere" and compulsion are not present when an incarcerated person speaks freely to someone whom he believes to be a fellow inmate. Coercion is determined from the perspective of the suspect. *Rhode Island* v. *Innis,* 446 U.S. 291, 301 (1980); *Berkemer* v. *McCarty,* supra, at 442. When a suspect considers himself in the company of cellmates and not officers, the coercive atmosphere is lacking. *Miranda,* 384 U.S., at 449 ("[T]he 'principal psychological factor contributing to a successful interrogation is privacy—being alone with the person under interrogation'"); Id., at 445. There is no empirical basis for the assumption that a suspect speaking to those whom he assumes are not officers will feel compelled to speak by the fear of reprisal for remaining silent or in the hope of more lenient treatment should he confess.

It is the premise of Miranda that the danger of coercion results from the interaction of custody and official interrogation. We reject the argument that Miranda warnings are required whenever a suspect is in custody in a technical sense and converses with someone who happens to be a government agent. Questioning by captors, who appear to control the suspect's fate, may create mutually reinforcing pressures that the Court has assumed will weaken the suspect's will, but where a suspect does not know that he is conversing with a government agent, these pressures do not exist. The state court here mistakenly assumed that because the suspect was in custody, no undercover questioning could take place. When the suspect has no reason to think that the listeners have official power over him, it should not be assumed that his words are motivated by the reaction he expects from his listeners. "[W]hen the agent carries neither badge nor gun and wears not 'police blue,' but the same prison gray" as the suspect, there is no "interplay between police interrogation and police custody." *Kamisar, Brewer* v. *Williams, Massiah and Miranda:* What is "Interrogation"? When Does It Matter?, 67 Geo. L. J. 1, 67, 63 (1978).

Miranda forbids coercion, not mere strategic deception by taking advantage of a suspect's misplaced trust in one he supposes to be a fellow prisoner. As we recognized in *Miranda:* "Confessions remain a proper element in law enforcement. Any statement given freely and voluntarily without any compelling influences is, of course, admissible in evidence," 384 U.S., at 478. Ploys to mislead a suspect or lull him into a false sense of security that do not rise to the level of compulsion or coercion to speak are not within Miranda's concerns. Cf. *Oregon* v. *Mathiason,* 429 U.S. 492, 495–496 (1977) (per curiam); *Moran* v. *Burbine,* 475 U.S. 412 (1986) (where police fail to inform suspect of attorney's efforts to reach him [496 U.S. 292, 298], neither Miranda nor the Fifth Amendment requires suppression of prearraignment confession after voluntary waiver).

Miranda was not meant to protect suspects from boasting about their criminal activities in front of persons whom they believe to be their cellmates. This case is illustrative. Respondent had no reason to feel that undercover agent Parisi had any legal authority to force him to answer questions or that Parisi could affect respondent's future treatment. Respondent viewed the cellmate-agent as an equal and showed no hint of being intimidated by the atmosphere of the jail. In recounting the details of the Stephenson murder, respondent was motivated solely by the desire to impress his fellow inmates. He spoke at his own peril.

. . . We hold that an undercover law enforcement officer posing as a fellow inmate need not give Miranda warnings to an incarcerated suspect before asking questions that may elicit an incriminating response. The statements at issue in this case were voluntary, and there is no federal obstacle to their admissibility at trial. We now reverse and remand for proceedings not inconsistent with our opinion.

It is so ordered.

[Concurring opinion of JUSTICE BRENNAN and dissenting opinion of JUSTICE MARSHALL are omitted.]

SUMMARY

- The arrest by a private person is sometimes referred to as a citizen's arrest.
- Thousands of arrests are made by private persons in this country.
- An arrest is the taking of a person in custody in a manner authorized by law.
- Probable cause to arrest exists when there is evidence that a crime has probably been committed and that the person to be arrested committed it.
- An arrest with a warrant is presumed to be legal.
- There is a legal preference for arrests made with a warrant.
- The *Terry* v. *Ohio* case developed the concept of stop and frisk.
- A mere temporary detention is not considered an arrest.
- A detention requires at least reasonable suspicion.
- A nonfederal law enforcement officer's jurisdiction to make an arrest is determined by state law.
- The Uniform Act of Fresh Pursuit has been adopted by most states. It permits a continuous pursuit of a fleeing person across jurisdictional lines.
- Generally, federal law enforcement officers have jurisdiction to arrest anywhere within the United States.
- An officer may use reasonable force to effect an arrest.
- Under most circumstances, it is illegal to willfully resist, delay, or obstruct a peace officer in the performance of his or her duty, including making an arrest.
- The *Miranda* rule requires that before a suspect is interrogated while in custody, the suspect must be advised of his or her Miranda rights.
- Certain individuals are immune from arrest because of statutory regulations.

REVIEW QUESTIONS

1. Define an arrest.
2. Define probable cause for an arrest.
3. Who are peace officers?
4. What is meant by fresh pursuit?
5. What charges may be brought against an officer who uses excessive force in making an arrest?
6. What is meant by diplomatic immunity?

7. Which officials fall within the diplomatic immunity provisions?

8. For what reason is an arrested person entitled to make telephone calls?

9. What is a citation?

10. How does the procedure followed in issuing a citation differ from that used in executing a warrant of arrest?

LOCAL PROCEDURE

1. Do peace officers have statewide arrest powers?
2. Who, if anyone, must come to the aid of an officer in making an arrest when called upon to do so or else be subject to prosecution?
3. Does an arrested person have the right to make telephone calls, and, if so, to whom and how many calls may he or she make? Must the person under arrest be advised of this right to make the calls?
4. Has your state adopted the Uniform Act of Fresh Pursuit? If so, does the act apply to felony violations only, or has it been made applicable to misdemeanors? If applicable to misdemeanors, what types?

ENDNOTES

1. 20 Ky. 539.
2. *Wong Sun* v. *U.S.,* 371 U.S. 471 (1963).
3. *U.S.* v. *Watson,* 423 U.S. 411 (1976).
4. *Payton* v. *New York,* 445 U.S. 573 (1980).
5. *U.S.* v. *Santana,* 427 U.S. 38 (1976).
6. *U.S.* v. *Davis,* 461 F.2d 1026 (3d Cir. 1972).
7. *Aguilar* v. *Texas,* 378 U.S. 108 (1964).
8. See Wallace, Roberson, and Steckler, *Fundamentals of Police Administration* (Prentice Hall, Upper Saddle River, N.J.), 1995.
9. 471 U.S. 1 (1985).
10. See *Peterson* v. *Robison,* 277 P.2d 19, 24 (Cal. 1954).
11. This section has been adapted from Harvey Wallace, Cliff Roberson, and Craig Steckler, *Written Interpersonal Communication Methods for Law Enforcement* (Prentice Hall, Upper Saddle River, N.J.), 1997.
12. 297 U.S. 278 (1936).
13. 322 U.S. 143 (1944).
14. 360 U.S. 315 (1959).
15. 378 U.S. 748 (1964).
16. 384 U.S. 436 (1966).
17. 468 U.S. 420 (1984).
18. 401 U.S. 222 (1971).
19. 470 U.S. 298 (1985).
20. 495 U.S. 292 (1990).
21. 111 S.Ct. 1246 (1991).
22. 114 S.Ct. 2350 (1994).
23. 539 U.S. 428 (2000).
24. *Kimberly* A. Crawford, "Invoking the Miranda Right to Counsel," *FBI Law Enforcement Bulletin,* 3, pp. 27–31 (March 1995).

To implement the Fourth Amendment's protection against unfounded invasions of liberty and privacy, the Court has required that the existence of probable cause be decided by a neutral and detached magistrate whenever possible.

—Justice Powell in *Gerstein* v. *Pugh* 420 U.S. 103 (1975)

It's better to enter the mouth of a tiger than a court of law.

—Old Chinese proverb

Initial Appearance

4

Chapter Outline

Key Words

Arraignment
Bail
Bounty hunters

Complaint
Demur
Exoneration of bail

Initial appearance
Material witness
Pretrial diversion

Learning Objectives

After completing this chapter, you should be able to:

1. Describe the purpose of an initial appearance.
2. Understand the legal requirements of a complaint.
3. Discuss the restrictions on bail.
4. Explain the various pretrial release mechanisms.
5. Discuss the problems with bounty hunters.
6. Explain what happens when the defendant violates the conditions of his or her bail.

PURPOSE OF THE INITIAL APPEARANCE

Although there is no mention of the **initial appearance** in our Bill of Rights, it is a basic right of an arrested person to be taken before a magistrate without unnecessary delay. This right is included in the federal rules of procedure and in the laws of the states. The initial appearance consists of the accused's appearing before a magistrate to be advised of certain rights to which he or she is entitled. A magistrate may be defined as anyone having the authority to issue an arrest warrant or a search warrant. From a practical standpoint, a magistrate generally is a judge of one of the inferior courts who spends much of his or her time conducting initial appearance hearings. The initial, or first, appearance is sometimes referred to as an arraignment. The term **arraignment** is used in many areas, and even the U.S. Supreme Court in the landmark cases of *McNabb* v. *United States*[1] and *Mallory* v. *United States*[2] referred to the initial appearance as an arraignment. In some states, the accused is permitted to enter a plea at the initial appearance, which adds to the tendency to call the initial appearance an arraignment.

At the initial appearance, the accused will be officially informed of the charge against him or her. Although the person is entitled to be informed of the charge at the time of the arrest, the charge is often changed between the time of the arrest and the initial appearance. For example, a person may be arrested on a charge of aggravated assault, but between the time of the arrest on that charge and the initial appearance, the victim dies. The charge is usually changed from aggravated assault to homicide. Further, at the initial appearance, if the offense is one for which bail may be posted, a bail amount is set and the accused will be informed of the right to make bail if he or she is not already out on bail. If the accused is not represented by an attorney, the rights to the assistance of counsel and to remain silent will be explained. Each of these rights is discussed in detail.

Steps in the Pretrial Process

1. **Arrest:** suspect taken into custody
2. **Booking:** administrative record of arrest
3. **Initial appearance:** notice of charge, advice of rights, setting of bail
4. **Preliminary hearing:** test of evidence against defendant
5. **Grand jury/information:** review of evidence by grand jury; charge filed by prosecution
6. **Arraignment:** appearance for plea; defendant elects trial by jury or judge
7. **Guilty plea/trial:** plea accepted, or trial scheduled

Defendants Henry Keith Watson, Antonio Miller, and Damian Williams stand in a security cage during their arraignment. The three were arrested for the beating of Reginald Denny. In front of the barrier is Watson's attorney. (*Source:* Douglas C. Plane/AP Wide World Photos.)

Time of the Initial Appearance

One of the more troublesome problems involved in an initial appearance concerns when it must be held once the arrest is made. For many years, neither the courts nor law enforcement agencies were particularly concerned about the timing of the initial appearance. As a result, many arrested persons were held incommunicado in jail for days and sometimes weeks before being taken before a magistrate. To overcome the injustice of this procedure, it is now provided that an arrested person must be taken before a magistrate without unnecessary delay. However, this provision is not without its complications. What will the courts accept, if anything, as necessary or reasonable delay in taking the defendant before a magistrate, and what penalties will be attached if there is an unnecessary delay deemed in the initial appearance? To assist officers in determining time limits, most states have enacted provisions setting forth the time within which the initial appearance must take place. The time limit varies considerably among the states, but the following is typical of the wording of such statutes:

> The arrested person must be taken before a magistrate without unnecessary delay, and in any event no longer than two days, Sundays and holidays excluded. If the two-day period expires when the Court is not in session, the time for the initial appearance will be extended until the next regular court session.

This provision implies that the two-day period is actually based on a forty-eight-hour limit. It is pointed out that the forty-eight-hour restriction does not provide blanket authority to hold all arrested persons for that time without taking them before a magistrate. A delay in the initial appearance for a much shorter time could be interpreted as an unnecessary delay. Some states have a seventy-two-hour limit, and a few states merely provide that an arrested person must be taken before a magistrate without unnecessary delay. If an arrested person is not taken before a magistrate within the prescribed time, he or she must be released. Whether the person could be arrested again after the release is doubtful; much would depend on the facts of the particular case and the reason for the delay in the initial appearance. In some instances, the release of the accused will result in a dismissal of the charge and will bar further prosecutive action, particularly in misdemeanor cases.

The time within which an initial appearance must occur and the penalties that may be attached for the delay were given particular emphasis by the landmark decision handed down by the U.S. Supreme Court in 1943 in the case of *McNabb* v. *United States*. The facts of that case reveal that some of the defendants were held for six days after the arrest before being arraigned, during which time confessions were obtained from them. These confessions were introduced against the defendants in their trial for the murder of a federal officer. The conviction was appealed to the U.S. Supreme Court upon the grounds that the confessions had been involuntarily given. The Court concluded that there was an unnecessary delay in the arraignment, during which time these confessions were obtained. To discourage unnecessary delay in arraignments, the Court held that any confession obtained during an unnecessary delay would be inadmissible as evidence in a court proceeding. This was an entirely new approach to the admissibility of confession. Prior to the *McNabb* decision, the test of admissibility was voluntariness in giving the confession. So the Court, in that case, attached a very significant penalty to a delay in arraigning an arrested person.

Although this decision pertained only to federal officers, several states have adopted the rule set forth in the *McNabb* decision by maintaining that confessions obtained by local officers during a delay in arraignment are inadmissible as evidence. It becomes important to determine what, if anything, might be considered a necessary delay in arraigning an arrested person. Following the *McNabb* case, the U.S. Supreme Court handed down other decisions relative to the time factor in arraignments. It was indicated in one case that the Court took into consideration that an arrested person should be booked before being arraigned. In another case, it was held that some investigative activity to verify information furnished by the defendant before being arraigned would be tolerated (see *Mallory* v. *United States*).

The U.S. Supreme Court cases mentioned are of little assistance in furnishing guidelines on how long an accused may be held within the prescribed time limit before the initial appearance and still have the delay considered necessary. The courts have held that if the delay is solely for the purpose of interrogating the accused, such delay is not considered necessary. Yet it is recognized that some questioning after an arrest may be in order, followed by a reasonable investigation to verify or refute information given by the arrested person. Such questioning could assist in the early release of an innocent person or could act as a justification for the arrest. For example, in one case, the delay in initial appearance for almost the entire prescribed time was upheld. In that case, the owner of an old model car took the car to a garage to be repaired. The mechanic told the owner that the car would be ready in three days. When the owner did not return for the car for more than a week, the mechanic checked the car in an effort to locate some identification in order to notify the owner that the car was ready. The mechanic found no identification, but he did find $1,500 in the glove compartment. He became suspicious and notified the local authorities. The officers were also unable to determine the owner and asked to be called if he returned for the car. Upon returning for the car a few days later, the owner was questioned by the officers but gave evasive answers. He was arrested for reasonable cause to believe that a crime had been committed since it was thought that an ordinarily prudent person would hold such a belief under the circumstances. But what crime should he have been booked for? Had he committed robbery, burglary, grand theft, or some other crime? He was arrested for grand theft, but there were no facts to verify such a crime in the area. He was further questioned by the officers but refused to reveal his identity or place of residence. The investigation revealed no damaging evidence. As the forty-eight-hour limit approached, the authorities realized that the accused would have to be released, yet they believed that he had been involved in some type of crime because an innocent person would have assisted in getting his own release much earlier. Just before the time limit was reached, the officers received a call from a woman reporting her husband as missing. The description of the missing husband fit that of the man in custody. It was learned that the accused had cashed a number of forged checks and that the money in the glove compartment was from his check-cashing activity. He had forgotten that it was in the glove compartment when he took the car to the garage. It is interesting that he stated that he was cashing the forged checks to get enough money to buy a small ranch where he could raise his children in a wholesome atmosphere.

Generally, a delay in an initial appearance or arraignment is not sufficient grounds for a reversal of a conviction on appeal unless it can be shown that the delay deprived the defendant of a fair trial. A few states have adopted the *McNabb* rule of excluding a confession obtained during a delay in arraignment. But there are other penalties besides the procedural one pertaining to the admissibility of a confession that may be attached to a delayed arraignment. Many states hold that a public officer who willfully delays bringing a defendant before a magistrate for the arraignment is guilty of a misdemeanor. It has also been held that once the time limit has been reached wherein an arrested person must be taken before a magistrate, any detention beyond that period is illegal, and that the officer responsible for such detention is subject to a civil suit for damages on a false imprisonment allegation.

Judge, court reporter, defense counsel, and prosecuting attorney at work during a trial. (*Source:* Peter Byron/ PhotoEdit Inc.)

Accepting the Accused for the Initial Appearance

Whether the accused was arrested by a private person or by an officer, he or she must be taken before a magistrate. The laws of many states provide that a private person who arrests another must take that person before a magistrate without unnecessary delay or deliver the arrested person to a peace officer who will in turn see that the accused is taken before a magistrate. The usual procedure is that the private person will deliver the arrested person to a peace officer rather than take the person before a magistrate personally. This situation creates the problem of how far the officer should go in determining the legality of the arrest before accepting the accused. There seems to be no uniformity in the answer to this problem. The courts of some states have held that if a competent private person informs the officer of the charge for which the arrest was made and demands that the officer take the accused, the officer has no right to refuse. This approach is reinforced by the further provision in some states that an officer who willfully refuses to accept one who has been charged with a crime is also subject to prosecution. Under the circumstances, an officer is not civilly liable for false arrest by accepting one arrested by a private person. The officer in reality is only a transportation officer and not an arresting one.[3] Other states permit the officer to make a determination concerning the legality of the arrest by the private citizen before accepting the accused. Such a ruling places a tremendous burden upon the officer. The officer is partially acting as a court in making a determination as to the legality of the arrest. If the officer incorrectly concludes that the arrest was legal, he or she could possibly be held civilly liable for accepting the accused.

COMPLAINT

Prior to the initial appearance, a legal document must be filed with the court setting forth the charge against the accused, who will be referred to as the defendant hereinafter in relation to the judicial procedure. In most instances, this legal document will be a **complaint**. The complaint is comparatively simple. It sets forth the name of the defendant, the date and place that the offense took place, and the nature of the offense. The complaint must contain enough facts to enable the judge to determine whether a crime has been committed and whether there is reasonable cause to believe that the defendant committed it. If the defendant is not in custody, a warrant of arrest will be issued on the basis of this complaint. The complaint is sometimes referred to as an accusatory pleading. As we discuss the judicial procedure further, it will be determined that other accusatory pleadings follow the complaint in felony cases, but in misdemeanor matters, it is usually the only accusatory pleading filed with the court.

Demurrer to Complaint

In most states, a person named as the accused in an accusatory pleading (indictment, information, or complaint) may demur to the pleadings. A **demur** is the formal mode of disputing the sufficiency in law of the pleadings. The grounds upon which a demur may be based include:

- The grand jury that issued the indictment had no legal authority to inquire into the offense charged or, in the case of information or a complaint, that the court had no jurisdiction for the offense charged.
- The accusatory pleadings do not conform to required provisions of the state's penal code.

> ### *What Are the Most Common Reasons for Rejection or Dismissal of a Criminal Case?*
>
> Many criminal cases are rejected or dismissed because of:
>
> 1. **Evidence problems**—a failure to find sufficient physical evidence linking the defendant to the offense, insufficient evidence that a crime was committed, or the existence of a defense apparent from the available evidence.
> 2. **Witness problems**—for example, when a witness fails to appear, gives unclear or inconsistent statements, is reluctant to testify, or is unsure of the identity of the offender, or when a prior relationship exists between the victim/witness and the offender.
> 3. **The interests of justice**—deciding not to prosecute certain types of offenses, particularly those that violate the letter but not the spirit of the law (for example, offenses involving insignificant amounts of property damage).
> 4. **Due process problems**—violations of the constitutional requirements for seizing evidence and for questioning the accused.
> 5. **A plea on another case**—for example, when the accused is charged in several cases and the prosecutor agrees to drop one or more of the cases in exchange for a plea of guilty on another case.
> 6. **Pretrial diversion**—agreeing to drop charges when the accused successfully meets the conditions for diversion, such as completion of a treatment program.
> 7. **Referral for other prosecution**—when there are other offenses, perhaps of a more serious nature, in a different jurisdiction, or deferring to a federal prosecution.

- More than one offense is charged (in those states that require a separate pleading for each charge).
- The facts stated in the pleading do not constitute a public offense (crime).
- The pleading contains matter that, if true, would constitute a legal justification or excuse for the offense charged or another legal bar to prosecution.

A demur must be in writing, signed either by the defendant or by his or her counsel, and filed with the court. It must distinctly specify the grounds of objection to the pleading. When a demur is filed with the court, generally the court will hold a hearing and then make an order overruling (denying) or sustaining (approving) it. Generally if the demur is overruled, a court must then allow the defendant to plead. If the demur is sustained, a court must, if the defect can be corrected, allow the indictment to be resubmitted to the grand jury or in the case of other pleadings to the prosecutor to amend the pleadings. If the demur is sustained and the pleading is not correctable, the court must dismiss the charge.

BAIL

The Right to Post Bail

The right of an arrested person to post bail to obtain release from custody is an inherent right. As stated in the case of *Stack* v. *Boyle:*[4]

> This traditional right to freedom [by posting bail] before conviction permits the unhampered preparation of a defense, and serves to prevent the infliction of punishment prior to conviction. . . . Unless this right to bail before trial is preserved, the presumption of innocence, secured only after centuries of struggle, would lose its meaning.

Setting Bail Amount

The amount of bail necessary to secure the defendant's presence at trial varies according to the circumstances of each case. Generally, the following factors are considered by judges in setting bail amounts:

1. Seriousness of the offense charged—some crimes, such as capital murder, may be assumed to be nonbailable offenses
2. Weight of the evidence against the defendant
3. Defendant's ties to the community, family, and employment
4. Defendant's prior criminal record
5. Any history of failure to appear

The right to be released before trial is conditioned upon the accused's giving adequate assurance to the court that he or she will return to stand trial. The assurance is often in the form of bail. Since the function of bail is the limited purpose of ensuring attendance at trial, the amount of bail varies with each defendant. Bail set at a figure higher than an amount reasonably calculated to fulfill this purpose is considered to be excessive under the Eighth Amendment.

[*Stack* v. *Boyle*, 342 U.S. 1 (1951).]

But the right to post bail is not a guarantee included in our Bill of Rights. The Eighth Amendment to the Constitution merely provides that "excessive bail shall not be required," implying that not all offenses are bailable. By constitutional provision or by statute, the right to post bail by someone arrested under certain conditions is granted by all states. If the defendant has not been released on bail by the time of the initial appearance, the right to post bail will be explained to him or her at that time.

Historical Development of Bail

The origin of the term **bail** has been obscured by time. Some believe that the term is from the old French word *baillier,* meaning to deliver. Others hold that it originated from the common law procedure of bailments. A bailment is the deposit of something of value with another for a particular purpose. In the case of bail, the deposit was for the release of one in custody. The right to post bail is found in the early history of England. By the time of the Norman Conquest in A.D. 1066, the posting of a form of security to obtain the release of an accused was a common practice on the continent of Europe, and it became part of the common law of England. It was developed as a humanitarian procedure. Previously, people accused of crimes were thrown into the dungeons of local noblemen to make sure that they would be available for trial when the judge made his circuit. This custom was important to the king. If the charge was serious and the accused was convicted, his or her property was confiscated, thus providing a lucrative source of revenue for the king. Often by the time of the trial, the accused would have died from malnutrition and neglect. To prevent this from happening, relatives or friends of the accused sought his or her release to their custody upon a promise that they would produce the accused for the trial. To make certain that the relatives or friends would fulfill their promise, they were required to post some security in the form of chattels or objects of value. If the accused was not produced for trial, these chattels would be confiscated by the king. In addition, the persons posting the security had to suffer the punishment that the accused would have been subjected to had he or she been convicted. As time passed, the practice of punishing those who had posted security was discontinued, and they lost only the security.

Purpose of Bail

Today, we continue to place persons who are arrested in jail. We do so not as a form of punishment, because one cannot be punished or imprisoned until found guilty of a crime. We confine arrested persons to make sure that they will be available for trial. If we can obtain that surety by permitting accused persons to post bail, they are entitled to be released from custody until found guilty of the accusation. Thus, the only purpose of bail is to secure the release from custody of one who has been arrested upon his or her promise to appear at the various court proceedings related to the offense. These may include the arraignment, the preliminary hearing, the trial, and other such proceedings that the court may direct.

At common law, it was felt that there was no way to ensure the trial presence of one who was charged with a capital offense, so bail was denied to that type of offender. A capital offense is one for which the death penalty may be inflicted. The statutes of many states have included similar provisions, holding that one charged with a capital offense may be denied bail if the proof of guilt is great. Even in those states in which capital punishment has not been made a penalty, bail may be denied to one arrested for murder if the proof of guilt is evident.

Denial of Bail for Protective Reasons

In the past, a few jurisdictions held that bail may be denied to an arrested person if his or her release on bail would cause a danger to the public. This policy is based upon an interpretation of the Eighth Amendment to the Constitution by the U.S. Supreme Court in the case of *Carlson* v. *Lando*.[5] In review, the Eighth Amendment guarantees that "excessive bail shall not be required." In the *Carlson* case, the Court rested its interpretation of the Eighth Amendment on the common law, stating the following:

> The bail clause was lifted with slight changes from the English Bill of Rights Act. In England that clause has never been thought to accord a right to bail in all cases, but merely to provide that bail shall not be excessive in those cases where it is proper to grant bail. When this clause was carried over into our Bill of Rights, nothing was said that indicated any different concept. The Eighth Amendment has not prevented Congress from defining the classes of cases in which bail shall be allowed in this country. Thus in criminal cases bail is not compulsory where the punishment may be death. Indeed, the very language of the Amendment fails to say [that] all arrests must be bailable.

Thus, it was concluded that the Eighth Amendment does not grant the right to bail. The Eighth Amendment can be construed to mean only that bail shall not be excessive in those cases in which it is proper and that the denial of bail in certain cases is permissible. In recognition of the Court's interpretation of the Eighth Amendment and in response to the alarming problem of crimes committed by persons released on bail, Congress enacted an elaborate plan of preventive detention by enactment of the Bail Reform Act of 1984 (Title 18 U.S. Code, section 3242). This act provides that a federal officer may detain, pending trial, an arrestee who may be a danger to another person or a community. But before such an arrestee can be detained, a hearing must be held to determine "by clear and convincing evidence" that no condition exists that will assure the safety of a person or community if the arrestee were released on bail.

The constitutionality of this act was questioned by the defendant in the case of *United States* v. *Salerno.*[6] The defendant Salerno alleged that the act violated his right to the Due Process of Law clause embodied in the Fifth Amendment of the Constitution, which provides that "No person shall . . . be deprived of life, liberty or property without Due Process of Law. . . ." The U.S. Supreme Court did not agree with this contention, and stated that the act limits its application to those arrested on the most serious offenses and that the arrestee is entitled to a prompt hearing. During this hearing, the arrestee has the right to be represented by an attorney, to cross-examine witnesses, and to testify in his or her own behalf. In the opinion of the Court, this procedure fulfills the Due Process Clause of the Constitution.

The defendant also alleged that the act violated his right against excessive bail provided in the Eighth Amendment of the Constitution. To this allegation, the Court reiterated that the Eighth Amendment does not guarantee bail in all instances. When community safety is at stake, the government may deny bail and detain individuals believed to be dangerous to society.

Since the U.S. Supreme Court has upheld the "protective detention" of certain individuals arrested by federal officers, many states have enacted similar statutes permitting the detention pending trial of individuals arrested by state officers, who are believed to be dangerous. However, to abide by the Due Process Clause, those acts are required to provide for a prompt detention hearing similar to the Bail Reform Act of 1984.

Form of Bail

To post bail is to deposit an acceptable object of value with the appropriate court to ensure the appearance of the accused in court. Generally, the acceptable object of value is cash, U.S. or state bonds, or an equity in real property. If real property is pledged as security, most states require that the value of the property be twice that of the amount of bail. This requirement is made because of the possible fluctuation of real estate values and the difficulty of converting the real property into cash.

Since most arrested persons do not have these forms of security, they must rely upon someone to post bail for them. This person, known as a surety, may be a friend or relative, but in many cases, the person depositing the security will be one in the business of posting bail—a bail bondsperson. For a fee, the bail bondsperson will post the required security, which is usually a surety bond issued by some reliable company. Should the accused fail to appear as promised, the surety bond guarantees the bail payment in cash to the appropriate court. The fee that the bail bondsperson charges for this service is about 10 percent of the amount of the bail. A bail bondsperson who has some doubt about whether the accused will appear if released on bail may request relatives of the accused to deposit collateral funds to reimburse him or her if the accused does not appear. If the risk of the accused's not appearing is too great and no one will come to the aid of the accused by depositing collateral funds, the bail bondsperson may refuse to post the bail, and the accused will be detained until the judicial proceedings are completed. But once bail has been deposited, the accused is entitled to immediate release from custody. The law is silent in most jurisdictions on the amount of time that a defendant may be free on bail, but it is generally assumed that he or she is entitled to be free throughout all the proceedings up to the time of conviction. However, at his or her discretion, a judge may commit a defendant during the trial. Also, the defendant is not guaranteed the right to be free during an appeal time. Upon conviction, the defendant is no longer presumed to be innocent but rather to be guilty. But again, a judge, at his or her discretion, may permit a defendant to post bail during the appeal proceedings.

In some states, a bail bond is issued by a professional bond agency, which will issue the bond for a limited period of time and require renewal of bail. The usual period for which a professional bail bonds person or ageny will issue a bond is one year, after which the bond must be renewed. This time limitation may be a problem in a lengthy trial.

Amount of Bail

The bail required to be posted is that amount that will ensure the court appearance of the accused. Anything above that amount could be considered excessive. This amount is not easy to determine. The amount that would guarantee the appearance of one person may be entirely different for another. Also, the amount that would ensure the appearance on one charge may differ from the amount for another charge. In determining the amount of bail, a judge may consider the seriousness of the crime; the criminal record of the defendant; his or her employment record; family ties; whether the defendant was a fugitive at the time of arrest; whether he or she is wanted in any other jurisdiction; how great the evidence of guilt may be; the financial burden that he or she may suffer by not appearing; and whether the defendant has more to gain than to lose by not appearing.

The amount of bail set by a judge will not necessarily remain the same throughout the proceedings. Circumstances may arise that justify an increase or decrease in the amount. If the defendant has been released on bail and the amount is increased, he or she must post the amount of the increase or be placed in custody again.

In some cases, especially those involving drug offenses or fraud, the trial court will require that the defendant establish that the money to secure the bail is from a legitimate source and is not fruits of the crime.

Excessive Bail

As has been stated, the Eighth Amendment to the Constitution provides that "excessive bail shall not be required"; however, what constitutes excessive bail is not easily determined. What is excessive for one defendant may not be excessive for another. Whether the wealth or poverty of a defendant should be considered in determining the amount of bail is a difficult question to answer. There is no doubt that a wealthy defendant could more readily post bail, flee the country, and live elsewhere in comfort, whereas a poverty-stricken defendant may be unable to post even the smallest amount of bail. However, the mere fact that one cannot post bail does not mean that it is excessive. The courts have held that for bail to be excessive, it must be unreasonably great and clearly disproportionate to the offense involved. A defendant who believes that his or her bail is excessive may apply to the court for a reduction and, if this attempt fails, may appeal the matter to an appellate court for review on a writ of habeas corpus.

Bail Schedules

Since the amount of bail required largely depends on judicial discretion, it varies extensively. To establish uniformity in the amounts required, many states have adopted a procedure whereby judges of a county agree upon the amount of bail that is considered to be equitable on each misdemeanor violation. These amounts are listed in a schedule and act as guidelines for judges of the county. The amounts may still vary among counties. It has been recommended that a similar schedule be prepared for felony charges. But as we have pointed out, it is difficult to determine the amount that will ensure the appearance of a defendant in court, particularly in felony matters, so that such a schedule could be most unrealistic. A few states, however, have adopted a schedule for felony charges.

Forfeiture of Bail

Once the defendant is released on bail and if, without sufficient cause, he or she fails to appear when lawfully required to do so, the bail will be forfeited. Forfeiting bail means that the security posted by the defendant, or someone in his or her behalf, is confiscated by the court and deposited in an official fund. The confiscation is justified on the grounds that the security will be used to pay additional court costs and costs involved in locating the defendant. In felony cases particularly, if the defendant does not appear as agreed, the court will issue a bench warrant for the immediate arrest of the accused. When arrested, the defendant will be tried on the original charge and, in some jurisdictions, can also be charged with violation of "failing to appear" or, as it is more commonly known, bail-jumping. If a defendant does not appear on some minor misdemeanor charges or on most traffic violations, a judge may forfeit the bail, considering it the equivalent of the fine, dismiss the charge, and order that no further action be taken on the matter.

Surrender of Defendant by Surety

The surety who posted bail for a defendant may surrender him or her to the court having jurisdiction over the case any time before bail is forfeited. Upon surrendering the defendant, the surety is relieved of all responsibility and is entitled to have the security returned to him or her. For the purpose of surrendering the defendant, the surety may arrest the defendant. This arrest is an extension to the power of arrest by a private person. It is based upon the old theory that one posting bail has indirect custody of a defendant, and the surety may be relieved of that obligation by seizing the defendant and surrendering him or her to the court.

Exoneration of Bail

If the defendant appears in court at all times required, the bail has served its purpose, and the surety is entitled to have it returned. This return is known as the **exoneration of bail**.

Release on Own Recognizance

In the past, judges developed a practice of releasing defendants charged with minor offenses without posting bail—merely upon their promise to appear. This procedure became known as releasing one on his or her own recognizance or OR release. The statutes of most states have extended this practice to any bailable offense, including felony charges. The laws provide that a judge may release a defendant on his or her own recognizance if it appears that the defendant will comply with the agreement to appear as directed. However, these laws do not give the defendant the right to be released merely on his or her own recognizance. Even though a defendant is released on his or her own recognizance, a judge may later require the defendant to post bail or even to be committed to actual custody.

Pretrial Release Mechanisms

Stage	Mechanism	Description
Police	Field citation release	An arresting officer releases the arrestee on a written promise to appear in court, at or near the actual time and location of the arrest. This procedure is commonly used for misdemeanor charges and is similar to issuing a traffic ticket.
Police	Station house citation release	The determination of an arrestee's eligibility and suitability for release and the actual release of the arrestee are deferred until after he or she has been removed from the scene of an arrest and brought to the station house or police headquarters.
Police/pretrial	Jail citation release	The determination of an arrestee's eligibility and suitability for citation release and the actual release of the arrestee are deferred until after he or she has been delivered by the arresting department to a jail or other pretrial detention facility for screening, booking, and/or admission.
Pretrial/court	Direct release authority by pretrial program	To streamline release processes and reduce the length of stay in detention, courts may authorize pretrial programs to release defendants without direct judicial involvement. Where court rules delegate such authority, the practice is generally limited to misdemeanor charges, but felony release authority has been granted in some jurisdictions.
Police/court	Bail schedule	An arrestee can post bail at the station house or jail according to amounts specified in a bail schedule. The schedule is a list of all bailable charges and a corresponding dollar amount for each. Schedules may vary widely from jurisdiction to jurisdiction.
Court	Judicial release	Arrestees who have not been released either by the police or the jailer and who have not posted bail appear at the hearing before a judge, magistrate, or bail commissioner within a set period of time. In jurisdictions with pretrial release programs, program staff often interview arrestees detained at the jail prior to the first hearing, verify the background information, and present recommendations to the court at arraignment.

Prior to being released on his or her own recognizance, the defendant must agree in writing to appear at all times and places as ordered by the court, and if he or she does not appear and is apprehended in another state, the defendant waives extradition proceedings. In most states, it is provided that if the defendant who is released on his or her own recognizance fails to appear as agreed, he or she can be charged with the failure to appear. If the original charge was a felony, the defendant can be charged with a felony for failure to appear. If the original charge was a misdemeanor, the defendant can be charged with a misdemeanor for failure to appear. It has been recommended that greater use be made of OR releases, particularly in minor offenses, to obtain the release of those who are unable to post bail for financial reasons.

Bail for a Material Witness

The laws of most states permit a judge to demand that a **material witness** to a felony violation deposit security for his or her appearance at the trial if the judge believes that the witness will otherwise not appear. If the witness is unable to post the security (bail) for his or her appearance, the witness may be held in custody. The detention of a witness who is unable to post bail is unusual in our form of judicial procedure, since it permits the incarceration of one not charged with a crime. For this reason, it is not used extensively. To further overcome the inconvenience of a material witness's being detained, many jurisdictions provide that if a material witness cannot deposit security to ensure his or her appearance at the trial, his or her testimony may be incorporated into a deposition. A deposition is a written statement of a witness taken under oath before a magistrate, with both the prosecution and the defense having the right to be present.

BOUNTY HUNTERS

Bounty hunter Michael Kole has nabbed more than 100 fugitives from justice. But he was arrested on burglary charges when he went into the home of a third party without permission. The state law (Ohio) provided that a bounty hunter could arrest a defendant at any time and any place. One of the prosecutors in the case stated that "the sancity of the American home just doesn't go out the window when somebody gets out on bond." The Ohio court approved the right of Mr. Kole to enter the home of a third party to arrest a defendant. Recently courts in Indiana, Iowa, Maryland, Minnesota, Missouri, New Mexico, New York, and North Carolina have ruled against the rights of bounty hunters and in favor of third-party rights (as reported in the *Dayton Daily News,* Dayton, Ohio, Monday, April 16, 2001).

Bail bondspersons provide criminal defendants a bond to get them out of jail pending trial. They hire **bounty hunters** to track down defendants who skip out on court appearances and leave the bondsperson liable for the bond money. Bounty hunters may pursue a fugitive into another state; may arrest him or her; and, if necessary, may break into and enter his or her house for that purpose according to the 1872 U.S. Supreme Court case of *Taylor* v. *Taintor.* The common law dating to medieval England included the right of bounty hunters to arrest bail jumpers.

Most states require bounty hunters to receive state-approved training of arrest procedures and the use of firearms. Ex-convicts are excluded from being bounty hunters. In some states, the bounty hunter must give the police advance warning before making an arrest. The actual number of bounty hunters is unknown. Most are part-timers with past law enforcement experience. Bounty-hunting information may be found on the Internet. For example, one company sells computer program "Bounty Hunter Computer Tracking & Recovery Software" to help bounty hunters.

Capstone Cases

United States v. Salerno
481 U.S. 739 107 5 Ct. 2095, 95 L.Ed.2d 697 (1987)

Chief Justice Rehnquist delivered the opinion of the Court.

I

Responding to "the alarming problem of crimes committed by persons on release," Congress formulated the Bail Reform Act of 1984, 18 U.S.C.3141 et seq., as the solution to a bail crisis in the federal courts. The Act represents the National Legislature's considered response to numerous perceived deficiencies in the federal bail process. By providing for sweeping changes in both the way federal courts consider bail applications and the circumstances under which bail is granted, Congress hoped to "give the courts adequate authority to make release decisions that give appropriate recognition to the danger a person may pose to others if released."

To this end, Section 3141(a) of the Act requires a judicial officer to determine whether an arrestee shall be detained. Section 3142(e) provides that "if after a hearing pursuant to the provisions of subsection (f), the judicial officer finds that no condition or combination of conditions will reasonably assure the appearance of the person as required and the safety of any other person and the community, he shall order the detention of the person prior to trial." Section 3142(f) provides the arrestee with a number of procedural safeguards. He may request the presence of counsel at the detention hearing, he may testify and present witnesses in his behalf, as well as proffer evidence, and he may cross-examine other witnesses appearing at the hearing. If the judicial officer finds that no conditions of pretrial release can reasonably assure the safety of other persons and the community, he must state his findings of fact in writing, and support his conclusion with "clear and convincing evidence."

The judicial officer is not given unbridled discretion in making the detention determination. Congress has specified the considerations relevant to that decision. These factors include the nature and seriousness of the charges, the substantiality of the government's evidence against the arrestee, the arrestee's background and characteristics, and the nature and seriousness of the danger posed by the suspect's release. Should a judicial officer order detention, the detainee is entitled to expedited appellate review of the detention order.

Respondents Anthony Salerno and Vincent Cafaro were arrested on March 21, 1986, after being charged in a 29-count indictment alleging various Racketeer Influenced and Corrupt Organizations Act (RICO) violations, mail and wire fraud offenses, extortion, and various criminal gambling violations. The RICO counts alleged 35 acts of racketeering activity, including fraud, extortion, gambling, and conspiracy to commit murder. At respondents' arraignment, the Government moved to have Salerno and Cafaro detained pursuant to Section 3142(e), on the ground that no condition of release would assure the safety of the community or any person. The District Court held a hearing at which the Government made a detailed proffer of evidence. The Government's case showed that Salerno was the "boss" of the Genovese Crime Family of La Cosa Nostra and that Cafaro was a "captain" in the Genovese Family. According to the Government's proffer, based in large part on conversations intercepted by a court-ordered wiretap, the two respondents had participated in wide-ranging conspiracies to aid their illegitimate enterprises through violent means. The Government also offered the testimony of two of its trial witnesses, who would assert that Salerno personally participated in two murder conspiracies. Salerno opposed the motion for detention, challenging the credibility of the Government's witnesses. He offered the testimony of several character witnesses as well as a letter from his doctor stating that he was suffering from a serious medical condition. Cafaro presented no evidence at the hearing, but instead characterized the wiretap conversations as merely "tough talk."

The District Court granted the Government's detention motion, concluding that the Government had established by clear and convincing evidence that no condition or combination of conditions of release would ensure the safety of the community or any person. . . .   *(Continued)*

Respondents appealed, contending that to the extent that the Bail Reform Act permits pretrial detention on the ground that the arrestee is likely to commit future crimes, it is unconstitutional on its face. Over a dissent, the United States Court of Appeals for the Second Circuit agreed. Although the court agreed that pretrial detention could be imposed if the defendants were likely to intimidate witnesses or otherwise jeopardize the trial process, it found Section 3142(e)'s authorization of pretrial detention [on the ground of future dangerousness] repugnant to the concept of substantive due process, which we believe prohibits the total deprivation of liberty simply as a means of preventing future crimes. The court concluded that the Government could not, consistent with due process, detain persons who had not been accused of any crime merely because they were thought to present a danger to the community. It reasoned that our criminal law system holds persons accountable for past actions, not anticipated future actions. Although a court could detain an arrestee who threatened to flee before trial, such detention would be permissible because it would serve the basic objective of a criminal system—bringing the accused to trial. The court distinguished our decision in *Gerstein* v. *Pugh* in which we upheld police detention pursuant to arrest. The court construed Gerstein as limiting such detention to the "administrative steps incident to arrest." The Court of Appeals also found our decision in *Schall* v. *Martin*, 467 U.S. 253 (1984), upholding post arrest pretrial detention of juveniles, inapposite because juveniles have a lesser interest in liberty than do adults.

A facial challenge to a legislative Act is, of course, the most difficult challenge to mount successfully, since the challenger must establish that no set of circumstances exists under which the Act would be valid. The fact that the Bail Reform Act might operate unconstitutionally under some conceivable set of circumstances is insufficient to render it wholly invalid, since we have not recognized an "overbreadth" doctrine outside the limited context of the First Amendment. We think respondents have failed to shoulder their heavy burden to demonstrate that the Act is "facially" unconstitutional.

Respondents present two grounds for invalidating the Bail Reform Act's provisions permitting pretrial detention on the basis of future dangerousness. First, they rely upon the Court of Appeals' conclusion that the Act exceeds the limitations placed upon the Federal Government by the Due Process Clause of the Fifth Amendment. Second, they contend that the Act contravenes the Eighth Amendment's proscription against excessive bail. We treat these contentions in turn.

A

The Due Process Clause of the Fifth Amendment provides that "No person shall . . . be deprived of life, liberty, or property, without due process of law. . . ." This Court has held that the Due Process Clause protects individuals against two types of government action. So-called "substantive due process" prevents the government from engaging in conduct that "shocks the conscience," or interferes with rights "implicit in the concept of ordered liberty." When government action depriving a person of life, liberty, or property survives substantive due process scrutiny, it must still be implemented in a fair manner. This requirement has traditionally been referred to as "procedural" due process.

Respondents first argue that the Act violates substantive due process because the pretrial detention it authorizes constitutes impermissible punishment before trial. The Government, however, has never argued that pretrial detention could be upheld if it were "punishment." The Court of Appeals assumed that pretrial detention under the Bail Reform Act is regulatory, not penal, and we agree that it is.

As an initial matter, the mere fact that a person is detained does not inexorably lead to the conclusion that the government has imposed punishment. To determine whether a restriction on liberty constitutes impermissible punishment or permissible regulation, we first look to legislative intent. Unless Congress expressly intended to impose punitive restrictions, the punitive/regulatory distinction turns on "whether an alternative purpose to which the restriction may rationally be connected is assignable for it, and whether it appears excessive in relation to the alternative purpose assigned. . . ."

We conclude that the detention imposed by the Act falls on the regulatory side of the dichotomy. The legislative history of the Bail Reform Act clearly indicates that Congress did not formulate the pretrial detention provisions as punishment for dangerous individuals. Congress instead perceived pretrial detention as a potential solution to a pressing societal problem. There is no doubt that preventing danger to the community is a legitimate regulatory goal.

Nor are the incidents of pretrial detention excessive in relation to the regulatory goal Congress sought to achieve. The Bail Reform Act carefully limits the circumstances under which detention may be sought to the most serious of crimes. See 18 U.S.C.3142(f) (detention hearings available if [the] case involves crimes of violence, offenses for which the sentence is life imprisonment or death, serious drug offenses, or certain repeat offenders). The arrestee is entitled to a prompt detention hearing, and the maximum length of pretrial detention is limited by the stringent time limitations of the Speedy Trial Act. Moreover, as in *Schall* v. *Martin*, the conditions of confinement envisioned by the Act appear to reflect the regulatory purposes relied upon by the government. As in Schall, the statute at issue here requires that detainees be housed in a "facility separate, to the extent practicable, from [that of] persons awaiting or serving sentences or being held in custody pending appeal." We conclude, therefore, that the pretrial detention contemplated by the Bail Reform Act is regulatory in nature, and does not constitute punishment before trial in violation of the Due Process Clause.

The Court of Appeals nevertheless concluded that "the Due Process Clause prohibits pretrial detention on the ground of danger to the community as a regulatory measure, without regard to the duration of the detention." Respondents characterize the Due Process Clause as erecting an impenetrable "wall" in this area that "no governmental interest—rational, important, compelling or otherwise—may surmount."

We do not think the Clause lays down any such categorical imperative. We have repeatedly held that the government's regulatory interest in community safety can, in appropriate circumstances, outweigh an individual's liberty interest. For example, in times of war or insurrection, when society's interest is at its peak, the government may detain individuals whom the government believes to be dangerous. Even outside the exigencies of war, we have found that sufficiently compelling governmental interests can justify detention of dangerous persons. Thus, we have found no absolute constitutional barrier to detention of potentially dangerous resident aliens pending deportation proceedings. We have also held that the government may detain mentally unstable individuals who present a danger to the public, and dangerous defendants who become incompetent to stand trial. We have approved of post arrest regulatory detention of juveniles when they present a continuing danger to the community. . . . Even competent adults may face substantial liberty restrictions as a result of the operation of our criminal justice system. If the police suspect an individual of a crime, they may arrest and hold him until a neutral magistrate determines whether probable cause exists. *Gerstein* v. *Pugh*. Finally, respondents concede and the Court of Appeals noted that an arrestee may be incarcerated until trial if he presents a risk of flight or a danger to witnesses.

Respondents characterize all of these cases as exceptions to the "general rule" of substantive due process that the government may not detain a person prior to a judgment of guilt in a criminal trial. Such a "general rule" may freely be conceded, but we think that these cases show a sufficient number of exceptions to the rule that the congressional action challenged here can hardly be characterized as totally novel. Given the well-established authority of the government, in special circumstances, to restrain individuals' liberty prior to or even without criminal trial and conviction, we think that the present statute providing for pretrial detention on the basis of dangerousness must be evaluated in precisely the same manner that we evaluated the laws in the cases discussed above.

The government's interest in preventing crime by arrestees is both legitimate and compelling. In Schall, we recognized the strength of the State's interest in preventing juvenile crime. This general concern with crime prevention is no less compelling when the suspects are adults. Indeed, "the harm suffered by the victim of a crime is not dependent upon the age of the perpetrator." The Bail Reform Act of 1984 responds to an even more particularized governmental interest than the interest we sustained in Schall. The statute we upheld in Schall permitted pretrial detention of any juvenile arrested on any charge after a showing that the individual might commit some undefined further crimes. The Bail Reform Act, in contrast, narrowly focuses on a particularly acute problem in which the government interests are overwhelming. The Act operates only on individuals who have been arrested for a specific category of extremely serious offenses. Congress specifically found that these individuals are far more likely to be responsible for dangerous acts in the community after arrest. Nor is the Act by any means a scattershot attempt to incapacitate those who are merely suspected of these serious crimes. The government must first of all demonstrate probable cause to believe that the charged crime has been committed by the arrestee, but that is not enough. In a full-blown adversary hearing, the government must convince a neutral decision maker by clear and convincing evidence that no conditions of release can reasonably assure the safety of the community or any person. While the government's general interest in preventing crime is compelling, even this interest is heightened when the government musters convincing proof that the arrestee, already indicted or held to answer for a serious crime, presents a demonstrable danger to the community. Under these narrow circumstances, society's interest in crime prevention is at its greatest.

(Continued)

On the other side of the scale, of course, is the individual's strong interest in liberty. We do not minimize the importance and fundamental nature of this right. But, as our cases hold, this right may, in circumstances where the government's interest is sufficiently weighty, be subordinated to the greater needs of society. We think that Congress' careful delineation of the circumstances under which detention will be permitted satisfies this standard. When the government proves by clear and convincing evidence that an arrestee presents an identified and articulable threat to an individual or the community, we believe that, consistent with the Due Process Clause, a court may disable the arrestee from executing that threat. Under these circumstances, we cannot categorically state that pretrial detention "offends some principle of justice so rooted in the traditions and conscience of our people as to be ranked as fundamental."

Finally, we may dispose briefly of respondents' facial challenge to the procedures of the Bail Reform Act. To sustain them against such a challenge, we need only find them "adequate to authorize the pretrial detention of at least some persons charged with crimes," whether or not they might be insufficient in some particular circumstances. We think they pass that test. As we stated in Schall, "there is nothing inherently unattainable about a prediction of future criminal conduct."

Under the Bail Reform Act, the procedures by which a judicial officer evaluates the likelihood of future dangerousness are specifically designed to further the accuracy of that determination. Detainees have a right to counsel at the detention hearing. They may testify in their own behalf, present information by proffer or otherwise, and cross-examine witnesses who appear at the hearing. The judicial officer charged with the responsibility of determining the appropriateness of detention is guided by statutorily enumerated factors, which include the nature and the circumstances of the charges, the weight of the evidence, the history and characteristics of the putative offender, and the danger to the community. The government must prove its case by clear and convincing evidence.

Finally, the judicial officer must include written findings of fact and a written statement of reasons for a decision to detain. The Act's review provisions provide for immediate appellate review of the detention decision.

We think these extensive safeguards suffice to repel a facial challenge. The protections are more exacting than those we found sufficient in the juvenile context, see Schall, and they far exceed what we found necessary to effect limited post arrest detention in *Gerstein* v. *Pugh*. Given the legitimate and compelling regulatory purpose of the Act and the procedural protections it offers, we conclude that the Act is not facially invalid under the Due Process Clause of the Fifth Amendment.

B

Respondents also contend that the Bail Reform Act violates the Excessive Bail Clause of the Eighth Amendment. . . .

The Eighth Amendment addresses pretrial release by providing merely that "Excessive bail shall not be required." This Clause, of course, says nothing about whether bail shall be available at all. Respondents nevertheless contend that this Clause grants them a right to bail calculated solely upon considerations of flight. They rely on *Stack* v. *Boyle* in which the Court stated that "Bail set at a figure higher than an amount reasonably calculated to ensure the defendant's presence at trial is excessive under the Eighth Amendment." In respondents' view, since the Bail Reform Act allows a court essentially to set bail at an infinite amount for reasons not related to the risk of flight, it violates the Excessive Bail Clause. Respondents concede that the right to bail they have discovered in the Eighth Amendment is not absolute. A court may, for example, refuse bail in capital cases. And, as the Court of Appeals noted and respondents admit, a court may refuse bail when the defendant presents a threat to the judicial process by intimidating witnesses. Respondents characterize these exceptions as consistent with what they claim to be the sole purpose of bail—to ensure integrity of the judicial process.

While we agree that a primary function of bail is to safeguard the courts' role in adjudicating the guilt or innocence of defendants, we reject the proposition that the Eighth Amendment categorically prohibits the government from pursuing other admittedly compelling interests through regulation of pretrial release. The above-quoted dicta in *Stack* v. *Boyle* is far too slender a reed on which to rest this argument. The Court in Stack had no occasion to consider whether the Excessive Bail Clause requires courts to admit all defendants to bail, because the statute before the Court in that case in fact allowed the defendants to be bailed. . . .

The holding of Stack is illuminated by the Court's holding just four months later in *Carlson* v. *Landon*, 342 U.S. 524 (1952). In that case, remarkably similar to the present action, the detainees had been arrested and held without bail pending a determination of deportability. The Attorney General refused to release the individuals, "on the ground that there was reasonable cause to believe that release would be prejudicial to the public interest and would endanger the welfare and safety of the United States." The detainees brought the same challenge that respondents bring to us today: the Eighth Amendment required them to be admitted to bail. The Court squarely rejected this proposition:

> The bail clause was lifted with slight changes from the English Bill of Rights Act. In England that clause has never been thought to accord a right to bail in all cases, but merely to provide that bail shall not he excessive in those cases where it is proper to grant bail. When this clause was carried over into our Bill of Rights, nothing was said that indicated any different concept. The Eighth Amendment has not prevented Congress from defining the classes of cases in which bail shall be allowed in this country. Thus, in criminal cases bail is not compulsory where the punishment may be death. Indeed, the very language of the Amendment fails to say all arrests must be bailable.

Carlson v. *Landon* was a civil case, and we need not decide today whether the Excessive Bail Clause speaks at all to Congress' power to define the classes of criminal arrestees who shall be admitted to bail. For even if we were to conclude that the Eighth Amendment imposes some substantive limitations on the National Legislature's powers in this area, we would still hold that the Bail Reform Act is valid. Nothing in the text of the Bail Clause limits permissible government considerations solely to questions of flight. The only arguable substantive limitation of the Bail Clause is that the government's proposed conditions of release or detention not be "excessive" in light of the perceived evil. Of course, to determine whether the government's response is excessive, we must compare that response against the interest the government seeks to protect by means of that response. Thus, when the government has admitted that its only interest is in preventing flight, bail must be set by a court at a sum designed to ensure that goal, and no more. We believe that when Congress has mandated detention on the basis of a compelling interest other than prevention of flight, as it has here, the Eighth Amendment does not require release on bail.

II

In our society liberty is the norm, and detention prior to trial or without trial is the carefully limited exception. We hold that the provisions for pretrial detention in the Bail Reform Act of 1984 fall within that carefully limited exception. We are unwilling to say that this congressional determination, based as it is upon that primary concern of every government's concern for the safety and indeed the lives of its citizens, on its face violates either the Due Process Clause of the Fifth Amendment or the Excessive Bail Clause of the Eighth Amendment.

Justice Marshall, with whom Justice Brennan joins, dissenting.

. . . The majority approaches respondents' challenge to the Act by dividing the discussion into two sections, one concerned with the substantive guarantees implicit in the Due Process Clause, and the other concerned with the protection afforded by the Excessive Bail Clause of the Eighth Amendment. This is a sterile formalism, which divides a unitary argument into two independent parts and then professes to demonstrate that the parts are individually inadequate.

On the due process side of this false dichotomy appears an argument concerning the distinction between regulatory and punitive legislation. The majority concludes that the Act is a regulatory rather than a punitive measure. The ease with which the conclusion is reached suggests the worthlessness of the achievement. The major premise is that "unless Congress expressly intended to impose punitive restrictions, the punitive/regulatory distinction turns on whether an alternative purpose to which it may rationally be connected is assignable for it, and

Justice Thurgood Marshall (shown here in his chambers) was appointed to the Supreme Court by President Lyndon Johnson and served from 1969 to 1991. (*Source:* Deborah L. Rhode. Collection of the Supreme Court of the United States.)

(Continued)

whether it appears excessive in relation to the alternative purpose assigned to it. . . ." The majority finds that "Congress did not formulate the pretrial detention provisions as punishment for dangerous individuals," but instead was pursuing the "legitimate regulatory goal" of "preventing danger to the community." Concluding that pretrial detention is not an excessive solution to the problem of preventing danger to the community, the majority thus finds that no substantive element of the guarantee of due process invalidates the statute.

This argument does not demonstrate the conclusion it purports to justify. Let us apply the majority's reasoning to a similar, hypothetical case. After investigation, Congress determines (not unrealistically) that a large proportion of violent crime is perpetrated by persons who are unemployed. It also determines, equally reasonably, that much violent crime is committed at night. From amongst the panoply of "potential solutions," Congress chooses a statute which permits, after judicial proceedings, the imposition of a dusk-to-dawn curfew on anyone who is unemployed. Since this is not a measure enacted for the purpose of punishing the unemployed, and since the majority finds that preventing danger to the community is a legitimate regulatory goal, the curfew statute would, according to the majority's analysis, be a mere "regulatory" detention statute, entirely compatible with the substantive components of the Due Process Clause.

The absurdity of this conclusion arises, of course, from the majority's cramped concept of substantive due process. The majority proceeds as though the only substantive right protected by the Due Process Clause is a right to be free from punishment before conviction. The majority's technique for infringing this right is simple: merely redefine any measure which is claimed to be punishment as "regulation," and, magically, the Constitution no longer prohibits its imposition. Because, as I discuss in Part III, infra, the Due Process Clause protects other substantive rights which are infringed by this legislation, the majority's argument is merely an exercise in obfuscation.

The logic of the majority's Eighth Amendment analysis is equally unsatisfactory. The Eighth Amendment, as the majority notes, states that "excessive bail shall not be required." The majority then declares, as if it were undeniable, that: "this Clause, of course, says nothing about whether bail shall be available at all." If excessive bail is imposed the defendant stays in jail. The same result is achieved if bail is denied altogether. Whether the magistrate sets bail at $1 billion or refuses to set bail at all, the consequences are indistinguishable. It would be mere sophistry to suggest that the Eighth Amendment protects against the former decision, and not the latter. Indeed, such a result would lead to the conclusion that there was no need for Congress to pass a preventive detention measure of any kind; every federal magistrate and district judge could simply refuse, despite the absence of any evidence of risk of flight or danger to the community, to set bail. This would be entirely constitutional, since, according to the majority, the Eighth Amendment "says nothing about whether bail shall be available at all."

But perhaps, the majority says, this manifest absurdity can be avoided. Perhaps the Bail Clause is addressed only to the judiciary. "We need not decide today," the majority says, "whether the Excessive Bail Clause speaks at all to Congress' power to define the classes of criminal arrestees who shall be admitted to bail." The majority is correct that this question need not be decided today; it was decided long ago. Federal and state statutes which purport to accomplish what the Eighth Amendment forbids, such as imposing cruel and unusual punishments, may not stand. The text of the Amendment, which provides simply that "excessive bail shall not be required, nor excessive fines imposed, nor cruel and unusual punishments inflicted," provides absolutely no support for the majority's speculation that both courts and Congress are forbidden to inflict cruel and unusual punishments, while only the courts are forbidden to require excessive bail.

. . . The majority concedes, as it must, that "when the government has admitted that its only interest is in preventing flight, bail must be set by a court at a sum designed to ensure that goal, and no more." But, the majority says, "when Congress has mandated detention on the basis of a compelling interest other than prevention of flight, as it has here, the Eighth Amendment does not require release on bail." This conclusion follows only if the "compelling" interest upon which Congress acted is an interest which the Constitution permits Congress to further through the denial of bail. The majority does not ask, as a result of its disingenuous division of the analysis, if there are any substantive limits contained in both the Eighth Amendment and the Due Process Clause which render this system of preventive detention unconstitutional. The majority does not ask because the answer is apparent and, to the majority, inconvenient.

III

The essence of this case may be found, ironically enough, in a provision of the Act to which the majority does not refer. Title 18 U.S.C.3142 provides that "nothing in this section shall be construed as modifying or limiting the presumption of innocence." But the very pith and purpose of this statute is an abhorrent limitation of the presumption of innocence. The majority's untenable conclusion that the present Act is constitutional arises from a specious denial of the role of the Bail Clause and the Due Process Clause in protecting the invaluable guarantee afforded by the presumption of innocence. "The principle that there is a presumption of innocence in favor of the accused is the undoubted law, axiomatic and elementary, and its enforcement lies at the foundation of the administration of our criminal law." Our society's belief, reinforced over the centuries, that all are innocent until the state has proven them to be guilty, like the companion principle that guilt must be proved beyond a reasonable doubt, is "implicit in the concept of ordered liberty," and is established beyond legislative contravention in the Due Process Clause.

The statute now before us declares that persons who have been indicted may be detained if a judicial officer finds clear and convincing evidence that they pose a danger to individuals or to the community. The statute does not authorize the government to imprison anyone it has evidence is dangerous; indictment is necessary. But let us suppose that a defendant is indicted and the government shows by clear and convincing evidence that he is dangerous and should be detained pending a trial, at which trial the defendant is acquitted. May the government continue to hold the defendant in detention based upon its showing that he is dangerous? The answer cannot be yes, for that would allow the government to imprison someone for uncommitted crimes based upon proof not beyond a reasonable doubt. The result must therefore be that once the indictment has failed, detention cannot continue. But our fundamental principles of justice declare that the defendant is as innocent on the day before his trial as he is on the morning after his acquittal. Under this statute an untried indictment somehow acts to permit a detention, based on other charges, which after an acquittal would be unconstitutional. The conclusion is inescapable that the indictment has been turned into evidence, if not that the defendant is guilty of the crime charged, then that left to his own devices he will soon be guilty of something else.

To be sure, an indictment is not without legal consequences. It establishes that there is probable cause to believe that an offense was committed, and that the defendant committed it. Upon probable cause a warrant for the defendant's arrest may issue; a period of administrative detention may occur before the evidence of probable cause is presented to a neutral magistrate. . . . Once a defendant has been committed for trial he may be detained in custody if the magistrate finds that no conditions of release will prevent him from becoming a fugitive. But in this connection the charging instrument is evidence of nothing more than the fact that there will be a trial, and release before trial is conditioned upon the accused's giving adequate assurance that he will stand trial and submit to sentence if found guilty. Like the ancient practice of securing the oaths of responsible persons to stand as sureties for the accused, the modern practice of requiring a bail bond or the deposit of a sum of money subject to forfeiture serves as additional assurance of the presence of an accused.

The finding of probable cause conveys power to try, and the power to try imports of necessity the power to assure that the processes of justice will not be evaded or obstructed. "Pretrial detention to prevent future crimes against society at large, however, is not justified by any concern for holding a trial on the charges for which a defendant has been arrested." The detention purportedly authorized by this statute bears no relation to the government's power to try charges supported by a finding of probable cause, and thus the interests it serves are outside the scope of interests which may be considered in weighing the excessiveness of bail under the Eighth Amendment.

IV

Honoring the presumption of innocence is often difficult; sometimes we must pay substantial social costs as a result of our commitment to the values we espouse. But at the end of the day the presumption of innocence protects the innocent; the shortcuts we take with those whom we believe to be guilty injure only those wrongfully accused and, ultimately, ourselves.

I dissent.

Justice Stevens, dissenting:

There may be times when the government's interest in protecting the safety of the community will justify the brief detention of a person who has not committed any crime. . . . It is clear to me that a pending indictment may not be given any weight in evaluating an individual's risk to the community or the need for immediate detention.

If the evidence of imminent danger is strong enough to warrant emergency detention, it should support that preventive measure regardless of whether the person has been charged, convicted, or acquitted of some other

(*Continued*)

offense. In this case, for example, it is unrealistic to assume that the danger to the community that was present when respondents were at large did not justify their detention before they were indicted, but did require that measure the moment that the grand jury found probable cause to believe they had committed crimes in the past. It is equally unrealistic to assume that the danger will vanish if a jury happens to acquit them. Justice Marshall has demonstrated that the fact of indictment cannot, consistent with the presumption of innocence and the Eighth Amendment's Excessive Bail Clause, be used to create a special class the members of which are, alone, eligible for detention because of future dangerousness.

County of Riverside v. *McLaughlin* *500 U.S. 44 (1991)*

[The Supreme Court granted certiorari review of a judgment of the U.S. Court of Appeals for the Ninth Circuit, which ordered the petitioner county to provide probable cause determinations within thirty-six hours of an individual's arrest except in exigent circumstances. A class action suit was brought under 42 U.S. Code section 1983 challenging the manner in which the county provided probable cause determinations to persons arrested without a warrant.]

JUDGES: O'CONNOR, J., delivered the opinion of the Court, in which REHNQUIST, C. J., and WHITE, KENNEDY, and SOUTER, JJ., joined. MARSHALL, J., filed a dissenting opinion, in which BLACKMUN and STEVENS, JJ., joined. SCALIA, J., filed a dissenting opinion.

JUSTICE O'CONNOR delivered the opinion of the Court.

In *Gerstein* v. *Pugh,* 420 U.S. 103 (1975), this Court held that the Fourth Amendment requires a prompt judicial determination of probable cause as a prerequisite to an extended pretrial detention following a warrantless arrest. This case requires us to define what is "prompt" under Gerstein.

Justice Sandra Day O'Connor was the first female U.S. Supreme Court justice. She retired in 2005. (*Source:* Mike Mergen/AP Wide World Photos.)

This is a class action brought under 42 U.S.C. §1983 challenging the manner in which the County of Riverside, California, provides probable cause determinations to persons arrested without a warrant. At issue is the County's policy of combining probable cause determinations with its arraignment procedures. Under County policy, which tracks closely the provisions of Cal. Penal Code Ann. § 825 (West 1985), arraignments must be conducted without unnecessary delay and, in any event, within two days of arrest. This 2-day requirement excludes from computation weekends and holidays. Thus, an individual arrested without a warrant late in the week may in some cases be held for as long as five days before receiving a probable cause determination. Over the Thanksgiving holiday, a 7-day delay is possible.

The parties dispute whether the combined probable cause/arraignment procedure is available to all warrantless arrestees. Testimony by Riverside County District Attorney Grover Trask suggests that individuals arrested without warrants for felonies do not receive a probable cause determination until the preliminary hearing, which may not occur until 10 days after arraignment. Before this Court, however, the County represents that its policy is to provide probable cause determinations at arraignment for all persons arrested without a warrant, regardless of the nature of the charges against them. We need not resolve the factual inconsistency here. For present purposes, we accept the County's representation.

In March 1989, plaintiffs asked the [federal] District Court to issue a preliminary injunction requiring the County to provide all persons arrested without a warrant a judicial determination of probable cause within 36 hours of arrest. The District Court issued the injunction, holding that the County's existing practice violated this Court's decision in Gerstein. Without discussion, the District Court adopted a rule that the County provide probable cause determinations within 36 hours of arrest, except in exigent circumstances. The court "retained jurisdiction indefinitely" to ensure that the County established new procedures that complied with the injunction.

The Ninth Circuit thus joined the Fourth and Seventh Circuits in interpreting Gerstein as requiring a probable cause determination immediately following completion of the administrative procedures incident to arrest. By contrast, the Second Circuit understands Gerstein to "stres[s] the need for flexibility" and to permit States to combine probable cause determinations with other pretrial proceedings. We granted certiorari to resolve this conflict among the Circuits as to what constitutes a "prompt" probable cause determination under Gerstein.

In Gerstein, this Court held unconstitutional Florida procedures under which persons arrested without a warrant could remain in police custody for 30 days or more without a judicial determination of probable cause. In reaching this conclusion we attempted to reconcile important competing interests. On the one hand, States have a strong interest in protecting public safety by taking into custody those persons who are reasonably suspected of having engaged in criminal activity, even where there has been no opportunity for a prior judicial determination of probable cause. 420 U.S. at 112. On the other hand, prolonged detention based on incorrect or unfounded suspicion may unjustly "imperil [a] suspect's job, interrupt his source of income, and impair his family relationships." We sought to balance these competing concerns by holding that States "must provide a fair and reliable determination of probable cause as a condition for any significant pretrial restraint of liberty, and this determination must be made by a judicial officer either before or promptly after arrest."

The Court thus established a "practical compromise" between the rights of individuals and the realities of law enforcement. Under Gerstein, warrantless arrests are permitted but persons arrested without a warrant must promptly be brought before a neutral magistrate for a judicial determination of probable cause. Significantly, the Court stopped short of holding that jurisdictions were constitutionally compelled to provide a probable cause hearing immediately upon taking a suspect into custody and completing booking procedures. We acknowledged the burden that proliferation of pretrial proceedings places on the criminal justice system and recognized that the interests of everyone involved, including those persons who are arrested, might be disserved by introducing further procedural complexity into an already intricate system. Accordingly, we left it to the individual States to integrate prompt probable cause determinations into their differing systems of pretrial procedures.

In so doing, we gave proper deference to the demands of federalism. We recognized that "state systems of criminal procedure vary widely" in the nature and number of pretrial procedures they provide, and we noted that there is no single "preferred" approach. We explained further that "flexibility and experimentation by the States" with respect to integrating probable cause determinations was desirable and that each State should settle upon an approach "to accord with [the] State's pretrial procedure viewed as a whole." Our purpose in Gerstein was to make clear that the Fourth Amendment requires every State to provide prompt determinations of probable cause, but that the Constitution does not impose on the States a rigid procedural framework. Rather, individual States may choose to comply in different ways.

Inherent in Gerstein's invitation to the States to experiment and adapt was the recognition that the Fourth Amendment does not compel an immediate determination of probable cause upon completing the administrative steps incident to arrest. Plainly, if a probable cause hearing is constitutionally compelled the moment a suspect is finished being "booked," there is no room whatsoever for "flexibility and experimentation by the States." Incorporating probable cause determinations "into the procedure for setting bail or fixing other conditions of pretrial release"—which Gerstein explicitly contemplated—would be impossible. Waiting even a few hours so that a

(Continued)

bail hearing or arraignment could take place at the same time as the probable cause determination would amount to a constitutional violation. Clearly, Gerstein is not that inflexible.

Notwithstanding Gerstein's discussion of flexibility, the Court of Appeals for the Ninth Circuit held that no flexibility was permitted. It construed Gerstein as "requiring a probable cause determination to be made as soon as the administrative steps incident to arrest were completed, and that such steps should require only a brief period." This same reading is advanced by the dissents. The foregoing discussion readily demonstrates the error of this approach. Gerstein held that probable cause determinations must be prompt—not immediate. The Court explained that "flexibility and experimentation" were "desirable"; that "there is no single preferred pretrial procedure"; and that "the nature of the probable cause determination usually will be shaped to accord with a State's pretrial procedure viewed as a whole." The Court of Appeals and JUSTICE SCALIA disregard these statements, relying instead on selective quotations from the Court's opinion. As we have explained, Gerstein struck a balance between competing interests; a proper understanding of the decision is possible only if one takes into account both sides of the equation.

Given that Gerstein permits jurisdictions to incorporate probable cause determinations into other pretrial procedures, some delays are inevitable. For example, where, as in Riverside County, the probable cause determination is combined with arraignment, there will be delays caused by paperwork and logistical problems. Records will have to be reviewed, charging documents drafted, appearance of counsel arranged, and appropriate bail determined. On weekends, when the number of arrests is often higher and available resources tend to be limited, arraignments may get pushed back even further. In our view, the Fourth Amendment permits a reasonable postponement of a probable cause determination while the police cope with the everyday problems of processing suspects through an overly burdened criminal justice system.

But flexibility has its limits; Gerstein is not a blank check. A State has no legitimate interest in detaining for extended periods individuals who have been arrested without probable cause. The Court recognized in Gerstein that a person arrested without a warrant is entitled to a fair and reliable determination of probable cause and that this determination must be made promptly.

Unfortunately, as lower court decisions applying Gerstein have demonstrated, it is not enough to say that probable cause determinations must be "prompt." This vague standard simply has not provided sufficient guidance. Instead, it has led to a flurry of systemic challenges to city and county practices, putting federal judges in the role of making legislative judgments and overseeing local jailhouse operations.

Our task in this case is to articulate more clearly the boundaries of what is permissible under the Fourth Amendment. Although we hesitate to announce that the Constitution compels a specific time limit, it is important to provide some degree of certainty so that States and counties may establish procedures with confidence that they fall within constitutional bounds. Taking into account the competing interests articulated in Gerstein, we believe that a jurisdiction that provides judicial determinations of probable cause within 48 hours of arrest will, as a general matter, comply with the promptness requirement of Gerstein. For this reason, such jurisdictions will be immune from systemic challenges.

This is not to say that the probable cause determination in a particular case passes constitutional muster simply because it is provided within 48 hours. Such a hearing may nonetheless violate Gerstein if the arrested individual can prove that his or her probable cause determination was delayed unreasonably. Examples of unreasonable delay are delays for the purpose of gathering additional evidence to justify the arrest, a delay motivated by ill will against the arrested individual, or delay for delay's sake. In evaluating whether the delay in a particular case is unreasonable, however, courts must allow a substantial degree of flexibility. Courts cannot ignore the often unavoidable delays in transporting arrested persons from one facility to another, handling late-night bookings where no magistrate is readily available, obtaining the presence of an arresting officer who may be busy processing other suspects or securing the premises of an arrest, and other practical realities.

Where an arrested individual does not receive a probable cause determination within 48 hours, the calculus changes. In such a case, the arrested individual does not bear the burden of proving an unreasonable delay. Rather, the burden shifts to the government to demonstrate the existence of a bona fide emergency or other extraordinary circumstance. The fact that in a particular case it may take longer than 48 hours to consolidate pretrial proceedings does not qualify as an extraordinary circumstance. Nor, for that matter, do intervening weekends. A jurisdiction that chooses to offer combined proceedings must do so as soon as is reasonably feasible, but in no event later than 48 hours after arrest.

For the reasons we have articulated, we conclude that Riverside County is entitled to combine probable cause determinations with arraignments. The record indicates, however, that the County's current policy and practice do not comport fully with the principles we have outlined. The County's current policy is to offer combined proceedings within two days, exclusive of Saturdays, Sundays, or holidays. As a result, persons arrested on Thursdays may have to wait until the following Monday before they receive a probable cause determination. The delay is even longer if there is an intervening holiday. Thus, the County's regular practice exceeds the 48-hour period we deem constitutionally permissible, meaning that the County is not immune from systemic challenges, such as this class action.

As to arrests that occur early in the week, the County's practice is that "arraignment[s] usually take place on the last day" possible. There may well be legitimate reasons for this practice; alternatively, this may constitute delay for delay's sake. We leave it to the Court of Appeals and the District Court, on remand, to make this determination.

The judgment of the Court of Appeals is vacated, and the case is remanded for further proceedings consistent with this opinion.

It is so ordered. [Dissenting opinions omitted.]

SUMMARY

- The initial appearance of a defendant is sometimes referred to as an arraignment.
- At the initial appearance, the defendant will be informed of the charges against him or her and advised of his or her rights.
- An accused should be taken before a magistrate without unnecessary delay.
- Prior to the initial appearance, a legal document must be filed with the court setting forth the charge or charges against the accused.
- A demurrer to a complaint is a formal mode of disputing the sufficiency in law of the pleadings.
- Originally, the purpose of bail was to ensure the presence of the accused at trial. Presently, bail can be denied for protective reasons.
- There are several types of bail. The most common is money bail.
- Excessive bail is a violation of the U.S. Constitution.
- Bail may be forfeited if the defendant does not appear as promised.
- If the defendant makes his or her required court appearances, bail may be exonerated.

REVIEW QUESTIONS

1. What is the purpose of the initial appearance?
2. Why is the initial appearance important?
3. How soon after an arrest must the accused be furnished with an initial appearance?
4. What is the purpose of bail?
5. In what form may bail be posted?
6. How much bail should a defendant be required to post?
7. What does forfeiture of bail signify?
8. What is the significance of the phrase "released on one's own recognizance"?

PRELIMINARY HEARING

Many states use a preliminary hearing in lieu of a grand jury. It also is referred to as a preliminary examination. At the **preliminary hearing**, a magistrate decides whether there is adequate cause to require an accused to stand trial for the offense or offenses charged. The preliminary hearing is conducted before a magistrate. A magistrate has been described as any officer of the court who has the power to issue a warrant of arrest. Generally, a preliminary hearing is held before a judge of an inferior court—for example, a municipal court.

Before a preliminary hearing may be held, the defendant must have a complaint filed against him or her charging the defendant with a felony. In some jurisdictions, the complaint is known as an information. If the defendant enters a plea of not guilty, the judge will set the case over for a preliminary hearing. At the preliminary hearing, the prosecuting attorney presents evidence against the accused. This evidence may consist of witnesses and such physical evidence as the prosecutor deems appropriate. In most states, the evidence may be in the form of sworn statements of witnesses, and formal rules of evidence do not apply to preliminary hearings. Most jurisdictions allow inadmissible hearsay evidence in the form of statements taken by a police officer to be considered in determining if there is sufficient evidence to hold the defendant over for trial. After the prosecution has presented its case, the defense may present a case. A defendant may waive a preliminary hearing in most jurisdictions. In most states, if there is a grand jury indictment, no preliminary hearing is required.

Bound Over for Trial

If the magistrate concludes that the evidence presented establishes probable cause that the defendant committed the crime(s) charged, the magistrate will bind or hold the defendant over for trial. If the magistrate concludes that the evidence supports only a misdemeanor charge, the magistrate will reduce the charges to the lesser offense. In some states, the magistrate has the authority to then handle the misdemeanor. In some states, if the defendant pleads guilty, the magistrate has the authority to accept the guilty plea in a felony case and then forwards the case to the felony trial court for sentencing. If the magistrate determines that probable cause does not exist to hold the defendant over for trial, the magistrate will dismiss the charges. (*Note:* When the magistrate dismisses the charges, jeopardy has not attached and the prosecutor may refile the charges and submit the case in another court. Most of the time, a prosecutor will not refile unless there is additional evidence of the defendant's guilt. Trial judges, in general, do not like to overrule another trial judge unless there are additional or new factors to consider.)

The magistrates dismiss the charges in about 15 percent of the cases and reduce the charges to misdemeanors in about 10 percent of the cases. The remaining 75 percent of the defendants are bound over for trial.

Waiver of Preliminary Hearing

Although the preliminary hearing is a safeguard established for the benefit of the defendant, he or she may waive it if he or she so desires. However, in most jurisdictions, the waiver must be agreed to by the prosecuting attorney and the judge. There are advantages and disadvantages to both the defendant and the prosecution in the waiver of the preliminary hearing. If the defendant is unable to make bail, a waiver of the hearing results in an earlier trial date being set. On the other hand, by demanding a preliminary hearing, a defendant might bring about a dismissal of the charge and his or her release from custody. The judge might conclude as a result of the hearing that there is insufficient cause to hold the defendant for trial. Another advantage to the defendant in having a preliminary hearing is that he or she may discover evidence held by the prosecution as it is unfolded during the hearing. This outcome is particularly likely in those jurisdictions where the right of the defendant to examine the evidence held by the prosecution before the trial is not recognized. This right is known as the **right of discovery** or the right of inspection. It is granted to defendants in order that they may better prepare their defense.

A waiver of the hearing also limits the charges against the defendant to those existing in the complaint at the time of the waiver. Accordingly, the prosecution may not amend later without starting the process again or obtaining a new waiver from defendant.

As it relates to the prosecution, there may be advantages in holding a preliminary hearing because it gives the prosecuting attorney an opportunity to obtain the testimony of the witnesses on an official record or transcript at a time when the facts are fresh in their memories and they are less likely to falsify. This record can be used during the trial should a witness become unavailable. In those states in which the right of discovery is not recognized, the prosecuting attorney may agree with the waiver so that he or she will not have to reveal evidence to the defense. The waiver will also eliminate a dilemma for the prosecuting attorney. In a preliminary hearing, the prosecuting attorney must present enough evidence to convince the judge that the accused should be held for trial, but the prosecuting attorney does not want to reveal any more evidence than is necessary in order to prevent the defense from endeavoring to obtain perjured testimony to meet the prosecution's case.

Although the grand jury system was established to safeguard the accused, this system has been under attack by defendants. Some professionals contend that a preliminary hearing better fulfills the Due Process Clause of the Fourteenth Amendment. The reasoning behind this position is that the grand jury meets in secret and the defendant is not permitted to be present, nor can the defendant demand to present evidence in his or her own behalf. Generally, the courts have held that either the grand jury hearing or the preliminary hearing system may be adopted by the states, as they see fit, and both satisfy the due process of law requirement.

ARRAIGNMENT

When an indictment is returned or an information is filed with the trial court, the accused will be arraigned upon that accusatory pleading. At the arraignment, the accused will be permitted to enter a plea to the charge set forth in that accusatory pleading. If a plea of not guilty or not guilty by reason of insanity is entered, a trial must take place. If the accused was not arrested before the indictment was returned, this arraignment may be the initial appearance for the accused. At the arraignment, the accused will again be advised of his or her constitutional rights. Even though the accused may have been taken before a magistrate after a complaint was filed, the accused is still entitled to he arraigned after the filing of the indictment or information. In a sense, the indictment or information is a separate formal charge. The arraignment under these circumstances is not to be confused with the initial appearance even though, in some areas, the initial appearance is referred to as an arraignment.

During the arraignment, the defendant is given an opportunity to enter a plea to the charge alleged in the complaint. The defendant may either enter the plea at that time or request time to consider the plea to be entered. Depending upon the jurisdiction, the defendant may enter any one or more of the following pleas: (1) guilty, (2) not guilty,

(3) nolo contendere, (4) not guilty by reason of insanity, (5) former jeopardy, or (6) former judgment of acquittal or conviction. Generally, the law provides that if a defendant does not plead not guilty by reason of insanity, he or she shall be conclusively presumed to have been sane at the time the crime was committed.

Guilty Plea

At one time in our history, defendants were not permitted to enter guilty pleas, since it was thought that the only way justice could be accomplished was by a trial. A plea of guilty is an admission of every element of the offense charged, and no proof of the crime needs to be presented.[1] A plea of guilty is more than a confession that admits that the accused did various acts; it is itself a conviction; nothing remains but to give judgment and determine punishment. Thus the plea of guilty cannot be accepted lightly by a judge.

Generally, in felony cases, a plea of guilty must be made by the defendant in open court either orally or in writing. The purpose behind the requirement that the defendant personally enter the plea is to ensure that it is his or her own plea. Most states provide that a judge may not accept a plea of guilty, particularly in felony cases, unless the defendant is informed of his or her right to the assistance of counsel. If the defendant understands this right to counsel and waives the right, the judge may then accept the plea of guilty. However, some states will not permit a judge to accept a guilty plea to a capital offense charge, or one in which the punishment is life imprisonment without the possibility of parole, unless the defendant is represented by counsel. A few states will not permit a defendant to enter a guilty plea to a capital offense even with the assistance of counsel. In lesser offenses (misdemeanors and infractions), most states allow counsel to enter guilty pleas on behalf of their clients in open court and on the record.

In accordance with the U.S. Supreme Court's *Boykin* v. *Alabama* decision, before a judge may accept a guilty plea to any charge, misdemeanor or felony, the judge must inform the defendant of the significance of the guilty plea. The defendant must be informed that by pleading guilty, he or she waives all right against self-incrimination, the right to a jury trial, and all right to be confronted by his or her accusers. Even though the defendant is represented by counsel at the time of the guilty plea, the records of the case in felony cases must reflect that the judge advised the defendant of the guarantees that would be waived by the plea of guilty.

The defendant must be advised of all the major consequences of his or her plea of guilty including, if applicable, the period of confinement, the period of probation, and any registration requirements. In most cases, before the trial judge takes the defendant's plea of guilty in open court, the prosecutor will provide written waiver forms advising the defendant of the rights that he or she is waiving by pleading guilty and the range of punishment that may be adjudged in the case. The waiver forms are then witnessed by the defense counsel and submitted to the trial judge as exhibits to be attached to the trial record.

The laws of some states provide that before the judge may accept a guilty plea, an inquiry must be made to make certain that the accused has actually committed a crime serious enough to justify the guilty plea. The extent of the inquiry will depend largely upon the facts of each case. The judge may confine the inquiry to the facts in the transcript of the preliminary hearing or of the grand jury. Or the judge may use whatever procedure is best under the circumstances, including interrogating the attorneys involved in the case. The accused does not have to admit guilt expressly at the time of the guilty plea. In some states, a guilty plea may be accepted even though accompanied by a claim of innocence.[2] A judge does not have to accept a guilty plea, particularly if the judge feels that the defendant does not understand the significance of the plea or if there is some question about the plea being voluntarily given. Most jurisdictions hold that defendants who are not citizens of the United States must be advised that if they plead guilty, they may be subject to deportation.

After a plea of guilty is accepted, the next step is to sentence the defendant. If the charge is a misdemeanor, the judge of the inferior court has the authority to mete out the sentence, but if the charge is a felony, the case must be transferred to the superior court for sentencing. A judge of an inferior court has the authority to accept a guilty plea to a felony charge in most jurisdictions, and the plea will have the same effect as if it had been entered in the superior court. A few jurisdictions do not permit a defendant to enter a plea to a felony charge in the inferior court, and the case must be transferred to the superior court for both the acceptance of the plea and the sentencing.

Withdrawal of Guilty Plea

In most jurisdictions, a defendant, upon showing a good cause, may withdraw a guilty plea and enter a not guilty plea or one of the other pleas at any time before the pronouncement of sentence. A few jurisdictions hold that if the defendant was not represented by counsel at the time the guilty plea was entered, the judge must permit the defendant to withdraw the guilty plea upon showing good cause. For this reason, most judges are reluctant to accept a plea of guilty if the defendant was not represented by counsel, particularly in felony cases. The request of a defendant to withdraw a guilty plea is not taken lightly. If the withdrawal is permitted, then the defendant is entitled to a trial on one of the other pleas that may have been entered. This action could inconvenience witnesses, crowd court calendars, and cause additional expense. But if the defendant can show sufficiently good cause, the withdrawal should be permitted by the trial judge; otherwise, the denial of the withdrawal may be overturned by an appellate court. The problem created by this procedure is determining what would be considered good cause.

It has been held that if the defendant did not understand the meaning or significance of the guilty plea, this allegation is sufficient showing of good cause. In *Henderson* v. *Morgan*,[3] the U.S. Supreme Court permitted the withdrawal of a guilty plea nine years after it was originally entered upon the grounds that the plea had been involuntarily given. In that case, the trial court accepted a guilty plea to a charge of second-degree murder. The defendant later attempted to withdraw the guilty plea on the grounds that he did not know that "intent" was a necessary element of second-degree murder and, further, that he had not been sufficiently informed of the sentence he would receive if he pleaded guilty. The appellate courts of New York upheld the judge's denial of the withdrawal, and the case was appealed to the U.S. Supreme Court upon the grounds that the defendant had been denied due process of law. The Supreme Court held that since the defendant had not been advised by either the judge or the attorneys involved that intent was a necessary element of the crime of second-degree murder, his plea of guilty was "as a matter of law involuntary and must be set aside." It was stated that a plea could not have been voluntarily given unless the defendant had "received real notice of the true nature of the charge against him, the first and most universally recognized requirement of due process." But it was felt that the defendant had been sufficiently informed of the sentence that he might receive if the guilty plea was received. In most jurisdictions, there is no requirement that a defendant be advised of the exact sentence that the court may impose if the guilty plea is accepted, but he or she must be informed of the potential maximum sentence and any mandatory minimum sentence that must be imposed. The acceptance of a guilty plea upon the basis of the sentence that may be imposed is discussed in Chapter 9 under the heading "Plea Negotiation."

An additional reason some states require a judge to make an inquiry concerning the facts surrounding a guilty plea is to prevent a defendant from later challenging the plea as

Denver, Colorado's prearraignment detention facility. (*Source:* Cliff Roberson.)

being a free and voluntary act, as was successfully done by Morgan some nine years after his guilty plea in the *Henderson* v. *Morgan* case. The dissenting justices in that case felt that the withdrawal of the guilty plea should have been denied. It was their opinion that the trial judge had held a factual inquiry and that the inquiry revealed that the defendant had sufficient knowledge of the elements of the crime. Thus, these justices believed that the guilty plea had been voluntarily given. The facts in *Parker* v. *North Carolina*[4] present an interesting attempt to withdraw a guilty plea. The defendant argued that his guilty plea was the product of a coerced confession. The court stated that even on the assumption that the confession had been coerced, the court could not believe that the alleged police conduct during the interrogation period was of such a nature or had such an enduring effect as to make involuntary a plea of guilty entered over a month later. According to the appellate court, the trial judge was within his rights to refuse the request for withdrawal of the guilty plea.

Not Guilty Plea

When a plea of not guilty is entered by the defendant, the case will start proceeding toward a trial. If the plea is to a misdemeanor charge, the case may be set immediately for trial, which, in most instances, will take place in the minor court. If the not guilty plea is to a felony charge, further proceedings must take place either by a grand jury hearing or by a preliminary hearing before the case can be set for trial in the superior or district court. This procedure protects the accused from being held for trial without sufficient cause. The grand jury and preliminary hearings will be discussed later. Most jurisdictions permit a defendant to withdraw a not guilty plea and to enter a plea of guilty at any time during the trial. This possibility eliminates much trial time, particularly if the change of plea takes place early in the trial proceedings.

Occasionally, a defendant will refuse to enter any plea and stand mute before the court. History reveals that when this behavior occurred in early common law, the defendant was returned to the prison from which he or she had been brought and made

A dead man lies face down on a sidewalk in New York City near a puddle of his blood surrounded by police officers. (*Source*: City of New York Police Department Photo Unit.)

to lie naked on his on her back on the floor. Great weights of iron were placed on the defendant, who was fed only three "morsels of the worst bread" the first day and three sips of stagnant water the next, with this diet alternating daily until the prisoner died or entered a plea. In later years, a more humane procedure was followed. When the defendant stood mute before the court, the silence was treated as a guilty plea. Today, if the defendant refuses to plead, a plea of not guilty is entered for him or her, followed by a trial. By entering a plea of guilty, the defendant admits that he or she is the person named in the indictment or information.

Nolo Contendere Plea

A plea of **nolo contendere**, meaning "I will not contest it," or "no contest," is essentially equivalent to a plea of guilty. In some states, the nolo contendere plea is known as "non volt contendere" and is sometimes abbreviated as "non volt." As with the plea of guilty, the judge must inform the defendant of those rights that he or she is entitled to and of those that he or she waives by such a plea. In some jurisdictions, the nolo contendere plea may not be used against the defendant in a civil matter because the defendant has not admitted guilt. As pointed out, a plea of guilty is a formal type of confession of the act charged. Not all states permit a nolo contendere plea to be entered by a defendant. In those states in which the plea has been adopted, there is a variance in who must agree to accept the plea. In some states, only the judge must agree to accept the plea; in others, the prosecuting attorney also must agree before the nolo contendere plea may be accepted.

This plea has been adopted to satisfy the thinking of two types of defendants charged with a violation. Some defendants will admit to committing a particular act but will refuse to admit that the act was a crime, so they enter the "no contest" plea of nolo contendere. For example, a person may be charged with speeding on a freeway. She may admit to excessive speed but allege that, since no one was injured or endangered, no crime was committed. Thus, she merely enters the plea of nolo contendere.

Other defendants have committed acts that may subject them to civil suits for damages or restitution as well as to criminal prosecution. They feel that the evidence against them is so great that it would be useless to contest the criminal charges, but they do not want to permit the guilty plea to be introduced against them in a civil trial. Under these circumstances, they may wish to enter the nolo contendere plea. As an example, this plea is frequently entered by a defendant who has been arrested for driving under the influence of alcohol after being involved in a serious accident in which persons were injured or killed. The defendant may know that the evidence against him is strong enough that a trial would result in a conviction. To save the expense of a trial and to prevent the conviction from being used against him in a civil suit, the defendant will attempt to enter a plea of nolo contendere. In this instance, the judge may refuse to allow the defendant to enter the nolo contendere plea, since it could be an injustice to the victims of the accident. A defendant may not plead nolo contendere as a matter of right but must have the consent of the judge, its acceptance being entirely a matter of grace.

Not Guilty by Reason of Insanity Plea

By entering a plea of not guilty by reason of insanity, the defendant is admitting the commission of the act for which he or she is charged, but the defendant alleges that he or she cannot be held responsible for the crime because he or she was not sane at the time the act was committed. The whole issue of the ensuing trial is whether the defendant was sane or insane at the time the crime was committed.

Most states provide that if the defendant enters this plea, he or she has the burden of proving that he or she was insane at the time the offense was committed, and the prosecution may endeavor to meet that allegation by introducing evidence to prove that the defendant was sane at the time of the offense. A few states hold that the burden of proving beyond a reasonable doubt that the defendant was sane at the time he or she committed the act still rests with the prosecution. The defendant has only to meet the prosecution's case by creating a doubt of his or her sanity. If the defendant is found to have been sane at the time he or she committed the crime, the only procedure to follow is sentencing the defendant because he or she has already admitted that he or she has committed the acts at issue by the plea of not guilty by reason of insanity. If the defendant is found to have been insane at the time the offense was committed, then technically he or she is entitled to be set free because his or her present sanity is not in question. However, most jurisdictions provide that the judge hearing the case may demand that the defendant be confined for a period, usually not less than ninety days, for observation to determine that the defendant is not a danger to society. If, after the confinement period, it is determined that the defendant is not a danger, he or she must be released from custody.

John W. Hinckley, Jr., being taken to a detention center at Quantico, Virginia. He was charged with the attempted assassination of President Ronald Reagan and pleaded not guilty by reason of insanity.
(*Source:* Larry Rubenstein/Corbis/Bettmann.)

A few states permit a defendant to enter dual pleas. He or she may enter a plea of not guilty and at the same time enter a plea of not guilty by reason of insanity. This procedure has been criticized, since the pleas are actually inconsistent. Upon entering the plea of not guilty, the defendant is denying his or her guilt. In the second plea, the defendant is confessing guilt but alleging that he or she cannot be held responsible for the offense because of his or her insanity at the time. Where this procedure is permitted, the trial on the not guilty plea takes place first. If the defendant is found not guilty, he or she is entitled to be released without further action being taken. If the defendant is found to be guilty, the trial on the plea of not guilty by reason of insanity must follow. If the defendant is found to be sane at the time of committing the act, the sentencing procedure will take place. But if the defendant is found to have been insane at the time he or she committed the offense, the same procedure for release or observation will be set in motion as was previously described.

Not all states permit a plea of not guilty by reason of insanity to be entered, but insanity may be raised as a defense to the crime charged. Appendix B consists of an actual psychological report entered in trial at a case involving the issue of not guilty by reason of insanity.

Plea of Once in Jeopardy

The guarantee against being placed twice in jeopardy, also referred to as the right against double jeopardy, is of ancient origin, having been found in procedures of early Greek and Roman jurisprudence. It was established in the common law of England and brought to this country by the colonists. The guarantee is embodied in the Fifth Amendment to the U.S. Constitution and the laws of all the states. Basically, the guarantee provides that no person shall be placed in jeopardy of his or her life or liberty more than once for the same offense. It prohibits undue harassment and oppression by those in authority. If it were not for this guarantee against double jeopardy, an accused could be tried and retried until found guilty. Likewise, he or she might be retried if it was felt that the sentence resulting from the first trial was not severe enough.

If an accused is charged with a crime and believes that he or she has been previously placed in jeopardy by court action on that same charge, the accused may enter the plea of once in jeopardy. But many ramifications are involved in this plea, such as what comprises jeopardy and under what conditions an accused may be placed twice in jeopardy. Many persons are under the impression that an accused cannot be tried twice for the same offense. This is not always the case. There are situations in which a defendant may be tried two or more times for the same offense. Generally, if a defendant is acquitted of a crime, he or she cannot be tried again for that particular offense. But if a defendant is convicted, he or she may appeal the conviction to an appellate court. If the conviction is reversed upon appeal, the case may be retried. Upon appealing the conviction, the defendant is in a sense waiving his or her guarantee against double jeopardy. In the same manner, if the defendant requests a new trial after being convicted, he or she is waiving the double jeopardy guarantee. Furthermore, it has been held that if the jury cannot arrive at a verdict, the case may be retried by a different jury without the second trial's being a violation of the double jeopardy right.

The determination of when an accused has been placed in jeopardy involves complications. The Fifth Amendment guarantee against double jeopardy is of little assistance, since it merely provides that an accused shall not "be subject for the same offense to be twice put in jeopardy of life or limb." As the courts began to grant the guarantee against double jeopardy, it became necessary to determine when jeopardy

A judge and jury listen as an attorney questions a witness in an Orange County, California, superior court. (*Source*: Spencer Grant/PhotoEdit Inc.)

attaches. In making this determination, the courts looked to the common law of England. The common law rule at the time that the Fifth Amendment was adopted was comparatively simple, merely providing that a defendant had been placed in jeopardy only when there had been a conviction or an acquittal after a complete trial. The early English history of jurisprudence reveals that, once commenced, most trials were completed. It is stated that the traditional practice was to keep the jury together, unfed and without drink, until they delivered a unanimous verdict. As late as 1866, an English court stated that the rule seemed to command the confinement of the jury until death if it did not agree on a verdict. At the time of the enactment of the Fifth Amendment, most criminal prosecutions in this country proceeded until a verdict was reached. At that time, neither the defendant nor the prosecution had any right to appeal an adverse verdict. The verdict in such a case was unquestionably final and barred further prosecution for the same offense.

But as time passed, this strict rule was relaxed through U.S. Supreme Court decisions. One of the first relaxations was the right granted to one convicted of a crime to be able to appeal the conviction if some error was committed during the trial. If the conviction was reversed upon appeal because of some error during the trial, the prosecution could retry the case. As stated, the appeal by the defendant amounted to a waiver of the right against double jeopardy. However, the U.S. Supreme Court in *Burks* v. *United States*[5] held that once a jury's verdict of acquittal is returned, that acquittal is a bar against further prosecutive action against the accused for the offense charged. The Court stated that the acquittal is an absolute bar "no matter how erroneous its [the jury's] decision" may be. In the past, some states held that if the jury returned an erroneous verdict of acquittal, the defendant could be retried because jeopardy did not set in until a just verdict had been rendered. The *Burks* decision has eliminated such a contention.

Since it was believed that jeopardy did not set in until the verdict stage was reached, many trials were commenced but did not reach the verdict state. A judge often would stop a trial if he or she believed that the defendant was guilty and that the jury selected would not return a guilty verdict. The judge would dismiss that particular jury and have the trial started over with a new jury. This procedure could be repeated until the judge and prosecution felt that the jury selected would return a guilty verdict. Since this procedure resulted in injustices, to prevent such injustices, rules were established that held that if a jury was dismissed without sufficient cause after the trial began, the defendant would have been placed in jeopardy and could not be retried.

The reason behind this rule was expressed by the U.S. Supreme Court in the *Burks* v. *United States* decision. The Court stated as follows:

> The Double Jeopardy Clause forbids a second trial for the purpose of affording the prosecution another opportunity to supply evidence which it failed to muster in the first proceeding. This is central to the objective of the prohibition against successive trials. The Clause does not allow the state to make repeated attempts to convict an individual for an alleged offense since the constitutional prohibition against double jeopardy was designed to protect an individual from being subjected to the hazards of trial and possible conviction more than once for an alleged offense.

The Court further stated in the case of *Crist* v. *Bretz:*[6]

> The basic reason for holding that a defendant is put in jeopardy even though the criminal proceeding against him terminated before verdict was perhaps best stated in Green v. United States, 355 US 184: "the underlying idea, one that is deeply ingrained in at least the Anglo-American system of jurisprudence, is that the State with all its resources and power should not be allowed to make repeated attempts to convict an individual for an alleged offense, thereby subjecting him to embarrassment, expense and ordeal and compelling him to live in a continuing state of anxiety and insecurity, as well as enhancing the possibility that even though innocent he may be found guilty."

The ruling that held that a defendant had been placed in jeopardy once the jury trial began created the problem of determining at what point the jury trial commenced. The legislatures and courts of the various states tried to establish guidelines to solve this problem, but there was no uniformity among the states. Some states held that a jury trial began once the jury was selected and sworn to do its duty in arriving at a verdict. Other states held that a jury trial did not commence until after the jury was selected and the first witness was sworn. The U.S. Supreme Court settled the problem in *Crist* v. *Bretz* by holding that a jury trial commences once the jury is selected and sworn. The Court stated as follows:

> . . . the federal rule that jeopardy attaches when the jury is empaneled and sworn is an integral part of the constitutional guarantee against double jeopardy. . . . The reason for holding that jeopardy attaches when the jury is empaneled and sworn lies in the need to protect the interest of an accused in retaining a chosen jury. That right was described in *Wade* v. *Hunter* as a defendant's valued right to have his trial completed by a particular tribunal. It is an interest with roots deep in the historic development of trial by jury in the Anglo-American system of criminal justice. Throughout that history there ran a strong tradition that once banded together a jury should not be discharged until it had completed its solemn task of announcing a verdict.

The rule provides that the defendant will have been placed in jeopardy if, once the trial begins, the jury is dismissed without sufficient cause before the verdict stage is reached.

There is no clear criterion concerning what is considered sufficient cause for a trial not to continue to the verdict stage. A sufficient cause may result from a mistrial having been declared by a judge. Often during a trial, a situation such as misconduct by a juror or some improper remark by a witness while testifying may cause a judge to believe that the defendant could not receive a fair trial if the trial was allowed to proceed. Even when a mistrial is declared primarily for the benefit of the defendant, the defendant usually must agree to the mistrial's being declared; otherwise, an appellate court may conclude that jeopardy had set in and the defendant could not be retried.

The U.S. Supreme Court in *Crist* v. *Bretz* indicated that a court trial (that is, a trial by the judge without a jury) begins when the first witness is sworn. Unless the trial is continued to the verdict stage, the defendant will be placed in jeopardy. Remember that the defendant may be retried if the trial is discontinued for good cause.

Plea of Former Judgment of Conviction or Acquittal

The plea of former conviction or **former acquittal** is not included in the statutes of all states. However, it has been held by some states that a defendant is not properly protected by the plea of double jeopardy in some instances. When a defendant commits an act and breaks both state and federal criminal laws, the defendant could be prosecuted by either the state or the federal government. The question arises, May the defendant be prosecuted by both without a violation of the double jeopardy guarantee? This question was answered by the U.S. Supreme Court in the case of *United States* v. *Lanza*[7] and re-iterated in *Abbate* v. *United States,*[8] in which cases the Court concluded that a defendant could be tried by *both* federal and state governments. The Court based its decisions upon the fact that a citizen of this nation owes a duty to both the federal and state governments. When an act is committed that violates the laws of both sovereignties, both may prosecute. About half of the states have statutory provisions that hold that if a defendant is prosecuted by the state government, prosecution by the local court in that state for the same act is prohibited. The plea of former judgment of conviction or acquittal would be the proper plea under the circumstances.

The protection against double jeopardy extends to the conduct of an accused, not just to the charged crimes. Once jeopardy has attached, the prosecutor may not file new and different charges against the defendant based on the same conduct.

The plea of former judgment would also be proper if a defendant were acquitted of one charge and retried on a lesser charge arising out of the same act. However, most states hold that the plea of once in jeopardy covers this situation and have not included the former judgment of conviction or acquittal plea in their statutes.

GRAND JURY

A **grand jury** is a group of persons representing a cross section of a community, usually a county, whose primary purpose is to hear certain types of criminal accusations in order to determine whether there are sufficient facts to hold the accused for trial. As was stated in the U.S. Supreme Court case of *Wood* v. *Georgia:*[9]

> Historically, this body [the grand jury] has been regarded as a primary security to the innocent against hasty, malicious and oppressive persecution; it serves the invaluable function in our society of standing between the accuser and the accused, whether the latter be an individual, minority group, or other, to determine whether a charge is founded upon reason or was dictated by an intimidating power or by malice and personal ill will.

The grand jury procedure came into being early in the common law of England. The Magna Charta provided that no freeman was to be seized and imprisoned except by the judgment of his or her peers. This provision established the procedure that before a person could be held for trial on a serious charge, the accusation had to be presented to a council comprising the accused's peers to determine whether the charge was well founded. The council later became known as a grand jury, as opposed to the petit or trial jury. The grand jury consisted of no fewer than sixteen persons and no more than twenty-three. There is really no logical reason for these numbers having been selected, except that it was thought that since a person was accused of a serious crime, a reasonable number of his or her peers should hear the accusation and determine whether the accused should be held for trial. Also, to prevent the body from becoming too large and unwieldy, a maximum of twenty-three was selected.

The grand jury was created as a safeguard for the accused. It prevented the accused from being held on a serious charge without sufficient cause or justification. The idea of the grand jury was brought to this country from England, and it was embodied in the Fifth Amendment of the U.S. Constitution. This amendment provides that "no person shall be held to answer for a capital or otherwise infamous crime, unless on presentment or indictment of a grand jury." A capital offense is one punishable by death; an infamous crime has been defined as one punishable by hard labor or imprisonment for more than one year. For all practical purposes, an infamous crime is any felony. This amendment was applicable only to federal charges, and the states were free to establish their own safeguards. Approximately one-half of the states hold that all felonies, and in some instances serious misdemeanors, must be presented to a grand jury. The remaining states provide that the accusation may be presented to a judge or magistrate in the form of a preliminary hearing in lieu of grand jury action.

Selection and Qualification of Grand Jurors

The selection of grand jurors varies greatly from state to state. In some states, they are selected at random, often using the list of voters for the territorial jurisdiction. The clerk of the court will cut the names from the list and place them in a box from which the required number of names will be drawn. In other states, the trial judge, or judges, of the county will furnish to the clerk of the court the names of prospective jurors. These names will be placed in a box from which the required number will be drawn. In some areas, the grand jury comprises persons who volunteer their services because it is considered to be an honor to serve on a grand jury.

Following the common law tradition, grand juries in this country vary from sixteen to twenty-three persons, but most grand juries consist of nineteen persons. They are usually selected at the beginning of the calendar or fiscal year and generally serve for one year. The qualifications necessary to serve on the grand jury are very similar to those of a petit jury. The individual must be eighteen years of age or over, a citizen of the United States, a resident of the jurisdiction for at least one year, and have sufficient knowledge of the English language to properly communicate. After the grand jurors have been selected, they are given an oath in which they promise to do their duty and to keep their proceedings secret and confidential. The oath is generally administered by a superior court judge. At this time, the grand jury is considered to be impaneled. After the grand jury is impaneled, the judge either will appoint a member of the grand jury to act as foreperson or may instruct the grand jury to select one of their members to act as foreperson. When the appointment of a foreperson is completed, the grand jury is authorized to hear criminal charges to determine whether an accused should be held for trial.

Differences in Procedure in the Charging Process When Using a Grand Jury or Preliminary Examination

Grand Jury Proceedings	Preliminary Examination
Primary duty is to determine if there is probable cause to believe that the defendant committed the crimes or crimes charged.	Same.
If probable cause is found, an indictment is returned against the defendant.	If probable cause is found, the defendant is bound over for trial. (*Note:* In a few states, the defendant may be referred to a grand jury.)
Grand jury sessions are closed hearings.	Held in open court.
Proceedings are secret.	Proceedings are open to the public.
Proceedings are informal.	Formal judicial proceedings occur.
Nonadversarial proceedings—grand jury normally hears only evidence presented by the prosecutor.	Adversarial proceedings—both prosecution and defense may present evidence.
A judge does not preside over the sessions.	A judge presides over the hearings.
Defendant has no right to be present or to present evidence.	Defendant has a right to be present and to present evidence.
Grand jury has power to conduct its own investigations.	No investigative authority is granted.
Grand jury can subpoena witnesses and documents.	No subpoena power at preliminary examination.
Grand jury has power to grant immunity.	No immunity power at hearing.

Indictment

Prior to the grand jury hearings, the prosecuting attorney will prepare a formal document setting forth the charge against the accused. This document is known as an **indictment**. It is also referred to as a bill of indictment in some jurisdictions. At one time in our history, the indictment was a very technically worded document, and any failure to word it properly would give a judge the right to dismiss the charge. In fact, the wording became ridiculously technical. For example, if the charge was for murder and if the indictment did not particularly designate the deceased as a human being, the indictment was considered faulty. Or if the initials A.D. did not accompany the date, it was held that the indictment did not reflect that the charge had not been outlawed by the passage of time. Today, the indictment is a comparatively simply worded instrument. It is very similar in form to the complaint. The indictment sets forth the name of the accused, the crime that is alleged to have been committed, the date and place of the alleged crime, and a few pertinent facts about the crime.

The indictment serves several purposes. First, it informs the grand jury of the charge about which they will receive evidence during the hearing. Second, if the required number of grand jurors votes in favor of holding the accused for trial, they will so designate that fact by having the foreperson sign the indictment, or as it is known, "endorse the indictment." In some states, the grand jury in upholding the indictment find it a "true bill of indictment." The indictment is then filed with the court in which the trial will take place. Third, if the accused is not in custody when the indictment is endorsed and filed with the court, the indictment will enable the judge to issue a warrant of arrest. The indictment is also an accusatory pleading and is the document that sets the trial in motion in the superior court. Finally, the indictment informs the defendant of the charge against which he or she must defend himself or herself. If the accused is charged with more than one crime, these additional crimes may be included in the same indictment, and they are referred to as counts.

Grand Jury Hearings

The frequency with which the grand jury meets depends upon the number of criminal charges that must be heard. In highly populated areas, the grand jury may meet daily, Monday through Friday. In other areas, it may meet only when there is an occasion to do so, which could be only once a month or less frequently. Although the grand jury may call a hearing on its own, the members usually meet at the request of the prosecuting attorney. The grand jury meets in closed hearings, and the procedure is secret. In determining whether an accused should be held for trial, jury members will question witnesses and receive the evidence that is deemed pertinent by the prosecuting attorney. Before testifying, each witness takes an oath to tell the truth and not to reveal the proceedings that take place during his or her presence before the grand jury. During the examination of the witnesses, the prosecuting attorney is usually present to assist in questioning. A court reporter who records the testimony of the witnesses is also usually present.

After hearing all the witnesses and receiving the evidence of the case, the grand jurors will deliberate on the facts of the matter among themselves. After deliberating on the facts, they will vote to determine whether in their minds there are sufficient facts to believe that a crime has been committed and whether the accused committed it. They do not have to believe beyond a reasonable doubt as to guilt; they require only sufficient probable cause to believe that the accused is guilty of the act. Only the grand jurors may be present during the deliberation and voting. Jurisdictions vary somewhat on the number who must vote to hold the accused for trial, or "vote for the indictment." If the grand jury comprises nineteen members, some states require only twelve to vote in favor of the indictment, whereas other states require fourteen. If the grand jury comprises twenty-three persons, some states require fourteen to vote in favor of the indictment, and others require sixteen. If the required number vote in favor of holding the accused for trial, the foreperson of the grand jury will endorse the indictment indicating that the grand jury believes in the truthfulness of the charge. Thus, we get the true bill as a name for an indictment that is returned by the grand jury holding an accused for trial. In some states, if a grand jury investigates a criminal charge that was not referred to them by the prosecuting attorney, the accusatory pleading is known as a presentment rather than an indictment.

If the required number does not vote in favor of holding the accused for trial, the foreperson will so designate on the indictment. At one time in our history, the foreperson would write the word "ignoramus" on the indictment, indicating that the grand jury ignored the indictment. Today, the foreperson will usually write on the indictment that the grand jury does not believe in the charge, or in other words, that there is no bill of indictment forthcoming, or a no bill.

The defendant is not entitled to be present during a grand jury hearing, and there is some doubt whether the defendant may demand to present evidence in his or her own

Grand Jury Indictment

[The following grand jury indictment was taken from a case in Texas. The defendant was indicted for capital murder. He was charged with committing murder in a state prison while serving a sentence for another murder. Note that he is charged in two separate counts with the same murder. After the evidence is admitted, the State will generally move to dismiss one count, depending on how the evidence is developed at trial. Also note that at the end of the indictment, the crime is alleged as "against the peace and dignity of the state." Most states require that all crimes be against the peace and dignity of the state. This case ended with a plea bargain for a guilty plea to Count 1 and an agreed sentence of thirty-five years to be served at the end of his present prison term of thirty years.]

The State of Texas *v.* Eric Roberto Acosta *Charge: Capital Murder, Penal Code 19.03(a)(6)(A)*

In the Name and by Authority of the State of Texas:

The Grand Jury, for the County of Bee, State of Texas, duly selected, impaneled, sworn, charged, and organized as such at the July Term A.D., 1999, of the 156th Judicial District Court for said County, upon their oaths present in and to said court at said term that:

Eric Roberto Acosta

Count 1

Hereinafter styled Defendant, on or about the 13th day of July A.D., 1996, and before the presentment of this indictment, in the County and State aforesaid, Eric Roberto Acosta while in a penal institution to-wit: The Garza East Unit of the Texas Department of Criminal Justice, Institutional Division and serving a sentence for the offense of Murder; did then and there intentionally and knowingly cause the death of another, Daniel Vela, by kicking the said Daniel Vela on or about the head and facial area with Eric Roberto Acosta's shoe clad feet.

Count 2

And hereinafter styled Defendant, on or about the 13th day of July, A.D., 1996, and before the presentment of this indictment, in the County and State aforesaid, Eric Roberto Acosta while in a penal institution to-wit: The Garza East Unit of the Texas Department of Criminal Justice, Institutional Division and serving a sentence for the offense of Murder, did then and there, intending to cause serious bodily injury to an individual, Daniel Vela, commit an act clearly dangerous to human life, to-wit: by kicking the said Daniel Vela on or about the head and facial area with Eric Roberto Acosta's shoe clad feet thereby causing the death of said Daniel Vela, against the peace and dignity of the state.

[Signed by Presiding Grand Juror chairperson]

behalf. If the grand jurors feel that other witnesses besides those presented by the prosecution would be helpful in determining the truth of the indictment, the grand jurors have the authority to call additional witnesses, including the accused. The accused does not have to answer any questions that might subject him or her to punishment.

If a grand jury fails to hold the accused for trial, the question arises whether the facts may be presented to a new grand jury. The answer varies from state to state. Most states permit the indictment to be submitted to a different grand jury. Some states have statutory regulations prohibiting this practice. Other states are silent on the matter, thereby indicating that there is no bar to presenting the case again, since a grand jury hearing is not an action in which jeopardy will attach.

Secret Indictment

If the defendant is not in custody at the time the indictment is returned, a warrant of arrest will be issued on the basis of this indictment. Under these circumstances, no public record is made of the indictment and warrant in order that the defendant will not be alerted to the fact that he or she is wanted, thereby making his or her location and apprehension more difficult. The indictment in this case is referred to as a secret indictment or sealed indictment.

Open Hearings

Frequently, a grand jury is called on to investigate and hold hearings concerning alleged acts of misconduct by public officials. In these situations, most jurisdictions permit the hearing to be open to the public when it is believed to be in the best interest of justice. To hold an open hearing usually requires that a request be made to the presiding judge by the prosecuting attorney and by the foreperson of the grand jury.

Dismissal of Indictment

Prosecution does not necessarily follow even though an indictment has been returned by a grand jury. The indictment may be dismissed. In many jurisdictions, the prosecuting attorney is permitted to dismiss the indictment. This procedure is referred to as a "nolle prosequi action," a formal entry on the record of the case stating that no further prosecutive action will be taken in the matter. Other jurisdictions hold that only the presiding judge may dismiss the indictment. The presiding judge may dismiss the indictment on his or her own if he or she does not believe that the facts will support a conviction, or the judge may dismiss the indictment upon the recommendation of the prosecuting attorney. It may seem to be somewhat paradoxical for the prosecuting attorney to seek an indictment and then dismiss it. But the prosecuting attorney may take this action because a material witness has become unavailable or if facts have been developed that, in the best interest of justice, indicate that the case should not go to trial.

Additional Functions of the Grand Jury

In many states, the sole function of the grand jury is to hold hearings on criminal charges to determine whether a crime has been committed and whether the accused should be held for trial. But in a few states, the grand jury performs other functions, such as investigating public expenditures. It may also inspect jails, prisons, and mental institutions within its territorial jurisdiction to determine whether these facilities are complying with safety and health regulations.

Criticism of the Grand Jury System

Many legal scholars have severely criticized the grand jury system. It has been alleged that the grand jury is not a safeguard of the accused but is merely a rubber stamp of the prosecuting attorney. Another allegation is that the grand jury is not representative of the peers of the accused, as was indicated to be necessary by the Magna Charta. The term peers seems to weave its way into the legal language of criminal procedure, but it is seldom found in the qualifications necessary for being a member of either a petit or a grand jury. The dictionary definition of peers reflects that they are one's equals or associates. Under this definition, a grand jury of one's peers could result in the impaneling of an odd group of persons, particularly if the accused had spent much of his or her life in prison. Generally, it is held that if the grand jury is a representative group of citizens from throughout the county, or a cross section of the county, it is the equivalent of one's peers, and such a group will fulfill the due process of law provision. However, greater emphasis is being placed on what determines a representative group when a member of a minority society is the accused. The cross section of the county provision has also been challenged by younger defendants, particularly since the age qualification for service on juries has been changed from twenty-one to eighteen.

Although the argument that the grand jury does not represent a cross section of society is valid, it is most difficult to obtain a truly representative group. Most grand jurors receive little or no compensation for their services. In those areas in which the grand jury holds frequent hearings, most persons cannot afford to serve on a grand jury. This circumstance results in many grand jurors who are retired or wealthy individuals who can afford to give their services. It has also been alleged that the grand jury is a cumbersome system because it cannot do anything that a magistrate could not do more efficiently at less cost. Those advocating the retention of the grand jury system in lieu of a preliminary hearing by a magistrate often quote Justice Harlan's dissenting opinion in the case of *Hurtado* v. *California*.[10] Justice Harlan stated the following:

> . . . nothing stands between the citizen and prosecution for his life, except the judgment of a justice of the peace [in a preliminary hearing]. Anglo-Saxon liberty would, perhaps, have perished long before the adoption of our Constitution, had it been in the power of government to put the subject on trial for his life whenever a justice of the peace, holding his office at the will of the crown, should certify that he had committed a capital crime. That such officers are, in some of the States, elected by the people, does not add to the protection of the citizen; for, one of the peculiar benefits of the grand jury system, as it exists in this country and England [the grand jury system has since been abolished in England] is that it is composed, as a general rule, of a body of private persons, who do not hold office at the will of the government, or at the will of voters. In many if not in all of the States civil officers are disqualified to sit on grand juries. In the secrecy of the investigations by grand juries, the weak and helpless—proscribed perhaps, because of their race, or pursued by an unreasoning public clamor—have found, and will continue to find, security against official oppression, the cruelty of mobs, the machination of falsehood, and the malevolence of private persons who would use the machinery of the law to bring ruin upon their personal enemies.

Thus, we find the grand jury system continuing to function in many states; however, as time passes, it is highly possible that more states will adopt the preliminary hearing procedure.

GRANTS OF IMMUNITY FOR WITNESSES

The government may compel the testimony of a witness if he or she has been granted immunity. When immunity is granted, the witness's testimony is not self-incriminating. There are two types of immunity: (1) **transactional** and (2) **use and derivative use**. If a person receives transactional immunity, he or she cannot be prosecuted for the transaction about which the witness was compelled to testify. It is the broadest type of immunity and gives the witnesses greater protection than is constitutionally required.

If a witness is granted immunity and still refuses to answer questions, he or she may be held in contempt of court. If the witness is on probation or parole, the refusal to answer may be grounds to revoke the probation or parole. In addition, the failure to provide information about a crime may in some jurisdictions make the witness an accessory after the fact to the crime.

Use and derivative use immunity restricts the government from using the testimony or any other information obtained directly or indirectly from the testimony. For example, the government may still prosecute a person who has use and derivative use immunity as long as the government establishes that the evidence it offers at trial was derived from a legitimate independent source. In *Kastigar* v. *United States,* 406 U.S. 441 (1972), the Supreme Court held that use and derivative use immunity was sufficient to compel a person to testify regarding an event. The Court noted that the burden was on the government to establish that the evidence used to convict the defendant was not obtained as a result of the compelled testimony. In *United States* v. *North,* 920 F.2d. 940 (D.C. Cir. 1990), a court of appeals held that the government did not fulfill its burden of showing that the evidence was free from the taint of immunized testimony where the government witnesses used at trial had seen Oliver North's immunized testimony on national television.

MEDICAL EXAMINER

> A coroner should go to the place where any person is slain or suddenly dead or wounded . . . summon a jury out of four or five neighboring towns to make inquiry upon view of the body; and the coroner should inquire into the manner of the killing. [Jarvis on Coroners, 1829]

From a sequential standpoint in the study of the administration of justice, the next procedure to be considered includes the various ramifications of the trial. Before entering that phase of the procedure, however, it is well to consider the medical examiner or county coroner and the important part he or she plays in the judicial process. The primary function of the coroner is to investigate the cause of certain deaths that take place within the county. In most jurisdictions, a medical examiner has replaced the coroner.

The coroner came into being in England shortly after the Norman Conquest, with the coroner's existence being traced as far back as A.D. 1194. The coroner was a direct representative of the king, or the crown or corona—thus coroner. The coroners were elected by the king's judges as they rode through the countryside. In the beginning, each county had four coroners. Their responsibility was to keep records on all that went on in the county as it concerned the administration of justice and to guard the revenues that might come to the king if justice was done. In the early history of England, as previously pointed out, if a person was convicted of a felony, his or her property was confiscated by the king, thereby resulting in sizable revenue for the king. It was in the king's interest to see that those accused of felonies were brought to trial and that their property was not dissipated before conviction. Thus, the office of the coroner was created. Around the beginning of the thirteenth century, the coroners began to investigate all sudden deaths that took place in their jurisdiction to determine whether they were brought about by criminal means. Although this investigation was primarily the duty of the sheriff, it was thought that since the sheriff was responsible only to the people of the county, the sheriff might be hesitant to bring the offender to trial. The sheriff knew that, if convicted, the accused would undoubtedly be put to death or banished from the county and his or her property confiscated.

Duties of the Medical Examiner or Coroner

As time passed and the king was no longer able to confiscate the property of a felon, the coroner should have disappeared from the judicial picture. But by that time, the coroner had become so entrenched in the judicial process that this person remained a public official, and the office was carried from England to the United States. The coroner is a part of most county governments throughout the United States, and his or her present duties deviate greatly from those first performed in this position.

The duties and power vary somewhat among the states, but the primary function is quite uniform among all the states. It is the duty and right of the coroner to inquire into and determine the circumstances, manner, and cause of all violent, sudden, and unusual deaths. In general, these are deaths believed to have been the result of hanging, suicide, burns, poisoning, cutting, stabbing, drowning, vehicular accidents, industrial accidents, explosion, gunshot, electrical shock, alcoholism, drug addiction, strangulation, suffocation, criminal means, illegal abortion, starvation, or contagious disease. In most jurisdictions, the coroner will also inquire into the cause of a death that occurs when no one else is present, when in a penal institution, when a physician has not been in attendance for ten days or some similar number of days depending upon the jurisdiction, or when the attending physician is unable to state the cause. It is the duty of any law enforcement officer, physician, funeral director, or other person knowing of such an aforementioned death to report it to the medical examiner or coroner.

Upon receiving such a report, the coroner's inquiry may be very informal if he or she determines that the death was the result of natural causes, or that no negligence by another or by criminal means was involved. If the cause of death cannot be readily determined, the coroner has the authority to take possession of the deceased body, to have an autopsy performed, and to conduct such other investigation as may be necessary to assist him or her in determining the cause of death. The coroner also may hold an inquest as a further aid. Most jurisdictions permit the coroner, at his or her discretion, to hold the inquest sitting alone or before a coroner's jury. During the inquest, witnesses who have some knowledge concerning the cause and manner of the death will be questioned. Physical evidence, including the body of the deceased, may be viewed if deemed pertinent. If the coroner decides to use a jury, the members of the jury will be selected from among persons in the community who could qualify as petit jurors. The number selected varies among the states, but between nine and fifteen people will usually be called, at least six or more of whom will serve on the jury.

The purpose of the inquest is to determine the name of the deceased; the time and place that the death took place; the medical cause of the death; and whether the death was by natural causes, suicide, accident, or at the hands of another. Some jurisdictions require that during the inquest, it not only be determined whether the death was at the hands of another, but also, if so, at whose hands and whether by criminal means. In those jurisdictions following this latter procedure, some permit the coroner to issue a warrant of arrest for the accused if it is determined that the death was caused by criminal means. Other jurisdictions hold that the inquest merely determines whether the death was brought about by the hands of another. Any arrest or prosecution that may follow will be at the discretion of the prosecuting attorney. Jurisdictions vary as to the admissibility of the information developed by the inquest.

Selection and Qualifications of the Medical Examiner or Coroner

In some jurisdictions, the medical examiner or coroner is appointed by the county governing body, and in other places, he or she is elected by the people of the county. Generally, no prescribed qualifications are set forth. Even though the coroner's responsibility is to determine the medical cause of death, in most jurisdictions there is no requirement that the coroner be medically trained. In this case, the coroner will have to rely upon a physician to perform the autopsies. In some jurisdictions, the sheriff is permitted to act in the capacity of coroner as well as that of sheriff. By legislative action, other jurisdictions have authorized county governments to replace the coroner with a medical examiner. The law sometimes provides that the coroner will act as the sheriff, should the sheriff become incapacitated or unable to perform his or her duties. In those jurisdictions where the sheriff and the coroner are the same individual, this dual capacity creates an awkward situation if the sheriff is unable to act. Most jurisdictions, however, provide that if the sheriff becomes incapacitated, the undersheriff, or the next in line, will act until the sheriff can be replaced. Even though the coroner may not function as a sheriff, the coroner does have the status of a peace officer in many states.

The medical examiner or coroner is often required, in addition to his or her other duties, to take custody of the personal property in the immediate possession of the deceased. This usually includes the property on the person of the deceased, but it may also include taking the necessary precautions to see that the property in a residence is secured if no relative or other responsible person is available. The property is then released to the legal representative of the deceased when that person is determined.

Capstone Cases

North Carolina v. Alford
400 U.S. 25, 91 S.Ct. 160, 27 L.Ed.2d 162 (1970)

Justice White delivered the opinion of the Court.

[*Note:* Alford was indicted for the capital crime of first-degree murder. At that time, North Carolina law provided for the penalty of life imprisonment when a plea of guilty was accepted to a capital crime and the punishment for second-degree murder was imprisonment for two to thirty years. Alford's attorney, because of the strong evidence against him, recommended that he plead guilty. The prosecutor agreed to accept a plea to second-degree murder. The trial court heard damaging evidence from certain witnesses before accepting the plea. The appellee pleaded guilty, although disclaiming guilt, because of the threat of the death penalty, and was sentenced to thirty years' imprisonment. The court of appeals, on an appeal from a denial of a writ of habeas corpus, found that the appellee's guilty plea was involuntary because it was motivated principally by fear of the death penalty.]

We held in *Brady* v. *United States,* 397 U.S. 742 (1970), that a plea of guilty which would not have been entered except for the defendant's desire to avoid a possible death penalty and to limit the maximum penalty to life imprisonment or a term of years was not for that reason compelled within the meaning of the Fifth Amendment. . . . The standard was and remains whether the plea represents a voluntary and intelligent choice among the alternative courses of action open to the defendant. . . . That he would not have pleaded except for the opportunity to limit the possible penalty does not necessarily demonstrate that the plea of guilty was not the product of a free and rational choice, especially where the defendant was represented by competent counsel whose advice was that the plea would be to the defendant's advantage. The standard fashioned and applied by the Court of Appeals was therefore erroneous and we would, without more, vacate and remand the case for further proceedings with respect to any other claims of Alford which are properly before that court, if it were not for other circumstances appearing in the record which might seem to warrant an affirmance of the Court of Appeals.

As previously recounted after Alford's plea of guilty was offered and the State's case was placed before the judge, Alford denied that he had committed the murder but reaffirmed his desire to plead guilty to avoid a

(*Continued*)

possible death sentence and to limit the penalty to the 30-year maximum provided for second-degree murder. Ordinarily, a judgment of conviction resting on a plea of guilty is justified by the defendant's admission that he committed the crime charged against him and his consent that judgment be entered without a trial of any kind. The plea usually subsumes both elements, and justifiably so, even though there is no separate, express admission by the defendant that he committed the particular acts claimed to constitute the crime charged in the indictment. Here Alford entered his plea but accompanied it with the statement that he had not shot the victim.

If Alford's statements were to be credited as sincere assertions of his innocence, there obviously existed a factual and legal dispute between him and the State. Without more, it might be argued that the conviction entered on his guilty plea was invalid, since his assertion of innocence negatived any admission of guilt, which, as we observed last Term in Brady, is normally "central to the plea and the foundation for entering judgment against the defendant. . . ."

In addition to Alford's statement, however, the court had heard an account of the events on the night of the murder, including information from Alford's acquaintances that he had departed from his home with his gun stating his intention to kill and that he had later declared that he had carried out his intention. Nor had Alford wavered in his desire to have trial court determine his guilt without a jury trial. Although denying the charge against him, he nevertheless preferred the dispute between him and the State to be settled by the judge in the context of a guilty plea proceeding rather than by a formal trial. Thereupon, with the State's telling evidence and Alford's denial before it, the trial court proceeded to convict and sentence Alford for second-degree murder.

State and lower federal courts are divided upon whether a guilty plea can be accepted when it is accompanied by protestations of innocence and hence contains only a waiver of trial but no admission of guilt. Some courts, giving expression to the principle that "[o]ur law only authorizes a conviction where guilt is shown," require that trial judges reject such pleas. But others have concluded that they should not "force any defense on a defendant in a criminal case," particularly when advancement of the defense might "end in disaster. . . ." They have argued that, since "guilt, or the degree of guilt, is at times uncertain and elusive," "an accused, though believing in or entertaining doubts respecting his innocence, might reasonably conclude a jury would be convinced of his guilt and that he would fare better in the sentence by pleading guilty. . . ."

This Court has not confronted this precise issue, but prior decisions do yield relevant principles. In *Lynch* v. *Overholser*, 369 U.S. 705 (1962), Lynch, who had been charged in the Municipal Court of the District of Columbia with drawing and negotiating bad checks, a misdemeanor punishable by a maximum of one year in jail, sought to enter a plea of guilty, but the trial judge refused to accept the plea since a psychiatric report in the judge's possession indicated that Lynch had been suffering from "a manic depressive psychosis, at the time of the crime charged," and hence might have been not guilty by reason of insanity. Although at the subsequent trial Lynch did not rely on the insanity defense, he was found not guilty by reason of insanity and committed for an indeterminate period to a mental institution. On habeas corpus, the Court ordered his release, construing the congressional legislation seemingly authorizing the commitment as not reaching a case where the accused preferred a guilty plea to a plea of insanity. The Court expressly refused to rule that Lynch had an absolute right to have his guilty plea accepted, but implied that there would have been no constitutional error had his plea been accepted even though evidence before the judge indicated that there was a valid defense.

The issue in *Hudson* v. *United States*, 272 U.S. 451 (1926), was whether a federal court has power to impose a prison sentence after accepting a plea of nolo contendere, a plea by which a defendant does not expressly admit his guilt, but nonetheless waives his right to a trial and authorizes the court for purposes of the case to treat him as if he were guilty. The Court held that a trial court does have such power, and except for the cases which were rejected in Hudson, the federal courts have uniformly followed this rule, even in cases involving moral turpitude. Implicit in the nolo contendere cases is a recognition that the Constitution does not bar imposition of a prison sentence upon an accused who is unwilling expressly to admit his guilt but who, faced with grim alternatives, is willing to waive his trial and accept the sentence.

These cases would be directly in point if Alford had simply insisted on his plea but refused to admit the crime. The fact that his plea was denominated a plea of guilty rather than a plea of nolo contendere is of no constitutional significance with respect to the issue now before us, for the Constitution is concerned with the practical consequences, not the formal categorizations, of state law. Thus, while most pleas of guilty consist of both a waiver of trial and an express admission of guilt, the latter element is not a constitutional requisite to the imposition of criminal penalty. An individual accused of crime may voluntarily, knowingly, and understandingly consent to the imposition of a prison sentence even if he is unwilling or unable to admit his participation in the acts constituting the crime.

Nor can we perceive any material difference between a plea that refuses to admit commission of the criminal act and a plea containing a protestation of innocence when, as in the instant case, a defendant intelligently concludes that his interests require entry of a guilty plea and the record before the judge contains strong evidence of actual guilt. Here the State had a strong case of first-degree murder against Alford. Whether he realized or disbelieved his guilt, he insisted on his plea because in his view he had absolutely nothing to gain by a trial and much to gain by pleading. Because of the overwhelming evidence against him, a trial was precisely what neither Alford nor his attorney desired. Confronted with the choice between a trial for first-degree murder, on the one hand, and a plea of guilty to second-degree murder, on the other, Alford quite reasonably chose the latter and thereby limited the maximum penalty to a 30-year term. When his plea is viewed in light of the evidence against him, which substantially negated his claim of innocence and which further provided a means by which the judge could test whether the plea was being intelligently entered, its validity cannot be seriously questioned. In view of the strong factual basis for the plea demonstrated by the State and Alford's clearly expressed desire to enter it despite his professed belief in his innocence, we hold that the trial judge did not commit constitutional error in accepting it. . . .

Justice Black . . . concurs in the judgment and in substantially all of the opinion in this case. Justice Brennan, with whom Justice Douglas and Justice Marshall join, dissenting.

It is sufficient in my view to state that the facts set out in the majority opinion demonstrate that Alford was "so gripped by fear of the death penalty" that his decision to plead guilty was not voluntary but was "the product of duress as much so as choice reflecting physical constraint."

[*Note:* Footnote 11 to the court's opinion stated: "Our holding does not mean that a trial judge must accept every constitutionally valid guilty plea merely because a defendant wishes so to plead. A criminal defendant does not have an absolute right under the Constitution to have his guilty plea accepted by the court, although the States may by statute or otherwise confer such a right. Likewise, the States may bar their courts from accepting guilty pleas from any defendants who assert their innocence. . . ."]

SUMMARY

- During arraignment, the defendant is given the opportunity to enter a plea to the charge alleged in the complaint.
- At one time, defendants could not enter a guilty plea based on the belief that the only way justice could be accomplished was by a trial.
- Many states use a preliminary hearing in lieu of a grand jury.
- The purpose of a preliminary hearing is to determine if there is sufficient evidence to hold the accused for trial.
- Inadmissible evidence may be used in the preliminary hearing in most states.
- If the magistrate determines that there is sufficient evidence, the accused is bound over for trial.
- The grand jury system was established to safeguard the accused, but the system has been under attack by some attorneys and charged with being a tool of the prosecutor.
- When an indictment is returned or an information is filed with the trial court, the accused will be arraigned upon the accusatory pleadings.
- In most jurisdictions, the defendant may withdraw a guilty plea upon a showing of good cause.

- Before a guilty plea is accepted by the court, the judge must advise the accused of his or her rights as required by the *Boykin* v. *Alabama* decision.
- A defendant does not have a constitutional right to have his or her guilty plea accepted by the court.
- A plea of nolo contendere means that the defendant does not contest the charge. Some courts do not accept nolo contendere pleas.
- Whether a defendant may enter a plea of not guilty by reason of insanity depends on the law of the state involved.
- The defendant is required to assert a plea of double jeopardy or it will be waived.
- A grand jury's primary purpose is to hear criminal accusations in order to determine whether there are sufficient facts to hold the accused for trial.
- A grand jury may also investigate public agencies and public officers.
- Grand jury hearings are not open to the public.

REVIEW QUESTIONS

1. What is a guilty plea?
2. Before a guilty plea may be accepted, of what must the defendant be advised?
3. What is the next procedural step after the acceptance of a guilty plea?
4. What is the significance of a nolo contendere plea?
5. Define double jeopardy.
6. What is a grand jury?
7. List the qualifications for being a grand juror.
8. What is an indictment?
9. Who may be present during a grand jury's deliberation on an indictment?
10. What is a no bill?
11. What is a secret indictment?
12. Explain a nolle prosequi action.
13. What criticisms have been made of the grand jury system?
14. What is the purpose of the preliminary hearing?
15. What is an information?
16. Describe the primary function of the coroner.

LOCAL PROCEDURE

1. What pleas may a defendant enter in your jurisdiction?
2. May a defendant enter a plea of guilty to a capital punishment charge? If so, under what circumstances?
3. How many members compose a grand jury in your state?
4. May a defendant be brought to trial on a felony charge by an information, or must he or she be indicted?
5. How are grand jurors selected?
6. May the prosecuting attorney enter a nolle prosequi?
7. In your state, is the accused entitled to a preliminary hearing even though indicted?

ENDNOTES

1. *Boykin* v. *Alabama,* 395 U.S. 238 (1969).
2. *North Carolina* v. *Alford,* 400 U.S. 25 (1970).
3. 426 U.S. 637 (1976).
4. 397 U.S. 790 (1970).
5. 437 U.S. 1 (1978).
6. 437 U.S. 28 (1978).
7. 260 U.S. 377 (1922).
8. 359 U.S. 187 (1959).
9. 370 U.S. 375 (1962).
10. 110 U.S. 516 (1884).

> In all criminal prosecutions, the accused shall enjoy the right to a speedy and public trial, by an impartial jury of the State and district wherein the crime shall have been committed. . . .
>
> —U.S. Constitution, Amendment VI, 1791

Place and Time of Trial 6

Chapter Outline

Key Words

Change of venue
Competency
Constitutional right
  to a speedy trial

Continuance
Insanity
Statute of
  limitations

Statutory right
  to a speedy trial

Learning Objectives

After completing this chapter, you should be able to:

1. Discuss the constitutional requirements concerning the place of trial.
2. Explain when a defendant may want a change of venue.
3. Distinguish between insanity and competency issues.
4. List the issues involved in determining if the defendant's constitutional right to a speedy trial has been violated.
5. Explain the differences between the constitutional and statutory right to a speedy trial.
6. Describe the differences between speedy trial and statute of limitations.
7. Explain the issues that a trial judge must consider in determining whether to grant a motion for a continuance.
8. Discuss the steps that a state must take when the defendant is confined in another state.

PRETRIAL ACTION

Before the trial phase of the administration of justice begins, many decisions must be made. It must be determined when and where the trial will take place, whether the trial will be by the judge alone or by a jury, whether the defendant will represent himself or herself or be assisted by counsel, what witnesses will be called, what physical evidence will be presented, and whether a pretrial hearing will be held. In view of the importance of each of these processes, we will discuss each in some detail. These decisions and the trial procedure are largely the same whether the charge involved is a felony or a misdemeanor. Appendix A contains an outline of the stages of a criminal trial.

COMPETENCY TO STAND TRIAL

The defense of **insanity** refers to the defendant's mental state at the time that the alleged crime was committed. **Competency to stand trial** refers to the defendant's mental state at the time of the trial. The due process clauses of the Fifth and Fourteenth Amendments of the U.S. Constitution prohibit the trial of an individual who is incompetent. A defendant is considered incompetent if he or she lacks the capacity to understand the nature and object of the proceedings against him or her, or lacks the ability to consult with the defense counsel or to assist the defense counsel in preparing a defense.

If no issue is raised as to the competency of the defendant to stand trial, then it is assumed that he or she is competent. If the defendant's competency is at issue, the burden of presenting the evidence as to his or her competency is on the defense. The U.S. Supreme Court in *Cooper* v. *Oklahoma*, 517 U.S. 348 (1996), held that it was permissible for a state

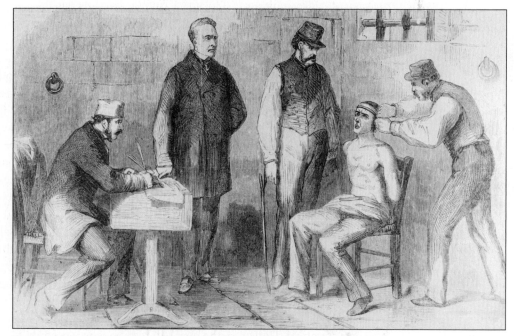

Guards at a Sicilian prison tighten the band around the head of a prisoner by small degrees, inflicting great pain and often driving the victim insane. (*Source:* Escho (AG)/Getty Images Inc. Hulton Archive Photos.)

to place the burden on the defendant to establish his or her lack of competency but that Oklahoma's requirement that the defense establish the incompetency by clear and convincing evidence was too much of a burden on the defense. Most states require that the defendant establish incompetency by the preponderance of the evidence, a lower level of proof.

If the defendant is determined to be incompetent, the state may detain him or her for a reasonable period of time necessary to determine whether there is a substantial probability that he or she will attain competency in the near future [*Jackson* v. *Indiana,* 406 U.S. 715 (1972)]. Unlike the insanity defense, if the defendant regains his or her competency, he or she may then be prosecuted.

PLACE OF THE TRIAL

Venue

The Sixth Amendment to the U.S. Constitution guarantees to an accused the right to a speedy and public trial, by an impartial jury of the State and district wherein the crime shall have been committed. This guarantee was placed in the Sixth Amendment as a result of the colonists' having been dragged from their homes to some secret place, often to England, and tried away from their peers. This guarantee applies to the states through the Due Process Clause of the Fourteenth Amendment. Thus, the place of the trial, or venue, lies within the judicial district in which the crime occurred. The term venue is derived from the French word *visne* meaning neighborhood. If the charge is a felony, the judicial district is the county; if it is a misdemeanor, the judicial district is the specific area of the county so designated and established by law. The burden is on the prosecution to present evidence during the trial to prove that the crime was committed within the judicial district in which the trial is being held. Proving venue may be accomplished merely by an investigating officer's testifying on the specific location within the county where the crime was committed. If venue is not established by the prosecution, a conviction may be reversed on appeal because it is the right of the defendant to have the jury chosen from the judicial district in which the crime was committed.

Motion to Change Venue Although the defendant is entitled to have the trial in the district where the crime occurred, that right may be waived and a request made that the trial be held in some other district. This outcome is particularly true in felony cases. The defendant often believes that a fair and impartial trial cannot be had in the county in which the crime was committed. This viewpoint is usually based on a belief that adverse publicity, the nature of the crime, or community hostility makes it impossible for the defendant to obtain an impartial jury. Under these circumstances, the defendant will file with the trial court a written request, known as a motion to change venue. The trial judge will hold a hearing on this request, at which time the defendant will present evidence in an effort to convince the judge that a **change of venue** should be granted. It may be alleged that, because the defendant is an outsider and the victim of the crime was popular, there is adverse feeling toward the accused. Or it may be alleged that because of the widespread publicity given to the crime, most persons in the county already believe in the defendant's guilt. In most instances, the prosecuting attorney will oppose the change of venue because of the inconvenience to witnesses and staff and because of the cost involved. However, the cost is not to be considered by the judge in granting or denying a change of venue because the accused is entitled to a fair and impartial trial, regardless of cost. The prosecuting attorney will oppose the change of venue on grounds other than cost in most instances. Also, the prosecuting attorney may contend that even though many persons have formed opinions unfavorable to the defendant as a result of what was published, it does not follow that persons without such views could not be found within the county to act as jurors or that those who have adverse opinions could not set those opinions aside and try the case in a fair and impartial manner on the basis of the evidence. Or the prosecuting attorney may contend that because of the widespread publicity given to the crime, it would be equally difficult to obtain an impartial jury in another county. Another contention may be that the emotional involvement with the crime has subsided sufficiently by trial time so that an impartial jury could be selected.

If, from the evidence presented during the hearing, the judge feels that a change of venue should be granted, the trial will be held in a county in which it is believed that a fair trial can be had. In most instances, the trial will be moved to an adjoining county. The cost of the trial will be borne by the county where the crime occurred. If the rule were otherwise, a county could impose on an adjoining county a terrific cost burden for trials of crimes not taking place within that adjoining county. If the judge does not grant a change of venue and the defendant is convicted, the refusal to grant a change of venue may be grounds for appeal. If the appellate court concludes that a change of venue should have been granted, the conviction will be reversed.

Time of Request for Change of Venue   Generally, a request for change of venue must take place before the date set for the commencement of the trial. A change may be made after the commencement date if the jury panel is exhausted without a jury's being selected or if there is danger of violence taking place within the district.

TIME OF THE TRIAL

The Sixth Amendment provision that the "accused shall enjoy the right to a speedy trial" is embodied in the laws of all the states. The **right to a speedy trial** is a fundamental right of an accused; otherwise, many injustices may be suffered. The people, or society, also have an interest in the guarantee that an accused will be brought to trial without unnecessary delay. This is the only way that society can be properly protected from the offender. These guarantees provide few guidelines on exactly when a trial must be held in order to comply with the speedy trial regulation, so the decision on when to hold a trial becomes a troublesome and difficult one to make. The right to a speedy trial does not permit the defendant to demand that a trial be held the same day as the arrest because the prosecution has the right to prepare its case against the defendant. But the prosecution may not take an indefinite time in its preparation. In setting the trial date, many factors must be considered, such as what is a reasonable length of time to permit each side to prepare its case and whether the accused is in jail or has posted bail. Further, the rules of procedure of most states require that criminal trials be set for those in jail ahead of those who have posted bail when other factors are equal. Even if a trial date is set, the trial may not necessarily begin on that date, since continuances may be granted that will cause delay.

The people or the state also has a right to a speedy trial. In most cases, it is the prosecution that is trying to bring a case to trial because it has the burden of establishing guilt, and delay generally weakens the case.

Continuances

Although the right to a speedy trial is primarily for the benefit of the accused, this right, like others rights, may be waived by the defendant, and often is. Defendants make frequent requests for **continuances** in bringing the case to trial. Often months pass between the time that an arrest is made and when the defendant is brought to trial, particularly in felony cases. Regardless of the hardships that may be suffered in not having a speedy trial, the defendant often will delay the trial date as long as possible. Delay often works to the advantage of the accused because, with the passage of time, witnesses for the prosecution are more likely to become unavailable and their memories are more likely to dull. In addition, physical evidence becomes difficult to identify and is likely to become lost or contaminated.

Although the defendant may suffer from continuances, others also suffer, particularly witnesses who must return to court many times only to find that the case has been continued. These witnesses usually receive no notice that a continuance will be granted. A continuance often is not granted until the case is called for trial, so notice is not possible. As a result, many witnesses must take time off from work, thus losing pay and experiencing the expense and inconvenience of traveling to and from court many times. It is understandable that people become reluctant to admit witnessing a crime. Delays also cause overcrowding of the court calendar, and other trials must be delayed, particularly civil trials.

Although the statutes of most states provide that a continuance may be granted only upon sufficient grounds and with sufficient notice, in most instances no specific grounds or time for the notice is stated. The most frequent ground alleged for a continuance is adequate time to prepare the case. Other grounds include obtaining witnesses or physical evidence, securing adequate and effective counsel for the defense, and ensuring the sound physical condition of the defendant. Delay may not be caused by inactivity of the defense in not preparing the case for trial. There is no set procedure to be followed in making a request for a continuance. It may be made orally in open court or by written request in advance of the trial date. Whether a continuance will be granted is at the discretion of the trial judge.

The U.S. Supreme Court, in the case of *Barker* v. *Wingo*,[1] discussed many of the ramifications of a speedy trial and the effect of delays on both the accused and the people. The Court also discussed some of the factors to be considered in determining whether the guarantee to a speedy trial had been violated. In view of the enlightening language of this decision, it is set forth in some detail for review by the reader. The facts of this case indicate that on July 20, 1958, in Christian County, Kentucky, an elderly couple was beaten to death by intruders wielding an iron tire tool. Two suspects, Silas Manning and Willie Barker, the petitioner, were arrested shortly thereafter. The grand jury indicted them on September 15. Counsel was appointed on September 17, and Barker's trial was set for October 21. The Commonwealth had a stronger case against Manning, and it believed that Barker could not be convicted unless Manning testified against him. Manning was naturally unwilling to incriminate himself. Accordingly, on October 23, the day Silas Manning was brought to trial, the Commonwealth sought and obtained the first of what was to be a series of sixteen continuances of Barker's trial. Barker made no objection. By first convicting Manning, the Commonwealth would remove the possible problem of self-incrimination and would be able to assure his testimony against Barker.

The Commonwealth encountered more than a few difficulties in its prosecution of Manning. The first trial ended in a hung jury. The second trial resulted in a conviction, but the Kentucky Court of Appeals reversed because of the admission of evidence obtained by an illegal search. At his third trial, Manning was again convicted, and the Court of Appeals again reversed because the trial court had not granted a change of venue. The fourth trial resulted in a hung jury. Finally, after five trials, Manning was convicted, in March 1962, of murdering one victim, and after a sixth trial in December 1962, he was convicted of murdering the other.

The Christian County Circuit Court holds three terms each year—in February, June, and September. Barker's initial trial was to take place in the September term of 1958. The first continuance postponed it until the February 1959 term. The second continuance was granted for one month only. Every term thereafter, for as long as the Manning prosecutions were in process, the Commonwealth routinely moved to continue Barker's case to the next term. When the case was continued from the June 1959 term until the following September, Barker, having spent ten months in jail, obtained his release by posting a $5,000 bond. He thereafter remained free in the community until his trial. Barker made no objection, through his counsel, to the first eleven continuances.

When on February 12, 1962, the Commonwealth moved for the twelfth time to continue the case until the following term, Barker's counsel filed a motion to dismiss the indictment. The motion to dismiss was denied two weeks later, and the state's motion for a continuance was granted. The state was granted further continuances in June 1962 and September 1962, to which Barker did not object. In February 1963, the first term of court following Manning's final conviction, the Commonwealth moved to set Barker's trial for March 19. But on the day scheduled for trial, the Commonwealth again moved for a continuance until the June term. It gave as its reason the illness of the ex-sheriff who was the chief investigating officer in the case. To this continuance, Barker objected unsuccessfully.

A lawyer questions a witness in a mock trial at the Rockville, Maryland, courthouse. (*Source:* Jim Pickerell/The Stock Connection.)

The witness was still unable to testify in June, and the trial, which had been set for June 19, was continued again until the September term, again over Barker's objection. This time the court announced that the case would be dismissed for lack of prosecution if it were not tried during the next term. The final trial date was set for October 9, 1963. On that date, Barker again moved to dismiss the indictment, and this time specified that his right to a speedy trial had been violated. The motion was denied; the trial commenced with Manning as the chief prosecution witness; Barker was convicted and given a life sentence.

Barker appealed his conviction through the Kentucky Court of Appeals and the U.S. District Court of Appeals. Both affirmed the conviction. The case was then appealed to the U.S. Supreme Court on the grounds that the Due Process Clause of the Fourteenth Amendment of the Constitution had been violated because the defendant had been denied a speedy trial as provided by the Sixth Amendment now made applicable to the states through U.S. Supreme Court decisions.

if a defendant knows that he or she is wanted in another place for a crime committed, the failure to demand to be brought to trial could be interpreted as a waiver of the right to a speedy trial.

Statutory Regulations

To assist those involved in the administration of justice, most states have enacted statutes setting forth guidelines on when a trial should take place, but even these guidelines have much flexibility. For example, many states have passed statutes similar to the following:

> The welfare of the people requires that all proceedings in criminal cases shall be set for trial and heard and determined at the earliest possible time, and it shall be the duty of all courts and judicial officers and of all prosecuting attorneys to expedite such proceedings to the greatest degree that is consistent with the ends of justice. In accordance with this policy, criminal cases shall be given precedence over, and set for trial and heard prior to any civil matters. Also no continuance of a criminal trial shall be granted except upon sufficient cause shown in open court, and upon reasonable notice to the opposition. It is held also that cases of those accused of a crime who are in custody are to take precedence over those who have been released on bail. [CA. Penal 1050(a).]

In addition, most states have provisions stating that unless an accused is brought to trial within a set number of days after the filing of the appropriate accusatory pleading, the charge shall be dismissed, and, if in custody, the defendant shall be released or bail shall be exonerated. The period of time is usually 30 days if the charge is a misdemeanor or within a period of 60 to 120 days, depending upon the jurisdiction, if the charge is a felony. This period may be waived by the defendant. In most instances, if a misdemeanor charge is dismissed, further prosecution will be barred on that particular offense, but states vary in the effect of a dismissal of a felony charge. Some states hold that further prosecution is barred. Other states hold that the defendant must be released after the dismissal but may be rearrested upon the filing of a new accusatory document, and the time clock begins to run again. How many times such a procedure could take place before it would be considered a violation of the speedy trial guarantee is uncertain. If it can be proved that the refiling was for harassment purposes, even one refiling would undoubtedly be considered a denial of due process.

It has also been held that unless reasonable efforts are made to execute a warrant of arrest after it has been issued, the accused may have been denied the right to a speedy trial. In one case, for example, a felony warrant of arrest was issued for an accused, but no efforts were made to execute it even though the accused had resided at the address listed on the warrant for nearly six months after the warrant was issued. The accused left the area for a few months but returned and again lived at the address listed on the warrant for several months before being arrested on a minor charge. After the conviction on the felony charge, the appellate court held that because of the delay in executing the warrant of arrest, the accused had been denied a speedy trial. However, if a reasonable effort is made to execute a warrant of arrest and the accused cannot be located, the delay in the execution of the warrant will not be interpreted as a denial of a speedy trial. It has been held that if there is a good reason for not serving the warrant of arrest immediately after it is issued, the defendant's right to a speedy trial is not denied. In one case, there was a delay of five months between the time that the warrant of arrest was issued and the time of service. The court held that since the delay was for the purpose of identifying other members of a narcotic ring and this undertaking would have been hampered by an immediate arrest, the delay was justified. Similarly, it has been held that if there is a good cause for a delay in having a warrant of arrest issued after a crime is committed, the defendant has not been denied the right to a speedy trial.

Statute of Limitations

To further assure that one accused of committing a crime is afforded a speedy trial, a **statute of limitations** is incorporated into the laws of all the states. This has been termed a humanitarian statute, since it provides that some prosecutive action must be commenced against an accused within a reasonable time after the crime is committed. The statute prevents the state or society from holding the threat of prosecutive action for an indefinite period over the head of an offender. The statute has also been described as an act of grace, since there is a surrendering by the sovereignty of its right to prosecute.

The statute forces society to take some action from two perspectives. It gives law enforcement the responsibility of taking immediate and continuous action upon a reported crime in order to identify the perpetrator so that he or she may be afforded a speedy trial. The statute also gives the prosecutive officials the responsibility of commencing prosecution within a specified time after the identity of an offender is established. There are occasions when a crime is committed and the law enforcement agency involved is unsuccessful in identifying the perpetrators of that crime until after the time stated in the statute of limitations has lapsed. Under those circumstances, the perpetrators may not be brought to trial even if later identified. In most states, the statute of limitations is considered to be a jurisdictional matter and may not be waived. If the perpetrators of a crime are identified before the statutory period runs out and their whereabouts are unknown, some prosecutive action, such as filing a complaint or indictment, must still be commenced before the statutory time expires or future prosecutive action will be barred.

There was no statute of limitations, as we know it today, at common law in England. If a crime was committed at common law, it was a crime against the king, and it was presumed that prosecution might occur at any time. This was particularly true in murder cases. This background may be the reason that even today, in the United States, the statute of limitations never lapses on a murder charge. With most other crimes, there is a specified time within which prosecutive action must commence. The time varies among states. On a felony charge, the statute of limitations varies from three to six years, depending upon the state. On a misdemeanor charge, the period is between six months and one year. A few states list other felonies besides murder, such as the embezzlement of public funds or falsification of public records, for which there are not statutory periods. If, during the investigation of a case, it is determined that the perpetrator of the crime has left the state in which the crime was committed, the statute of limitations is suspended, or tolled, while the perpetrator is out of state.

For some crimes that are difficult to detect, the statute of limitations does not begin to run until it is discovered the crime has occurred. For example, in many jurisdictions, the statute of limitations for embezzlement does not begin to run until the act of embezzlement is discovered or should have been discovered. In a number of jurisdictions, the statute of limitations for crimes against minors does not start to run until the minor has reached the age of majority. For example, a stepfather has sex with his twelve-year-old stepdaughter; the statute does not start to run until the victim reaches eighteen years of age.

7. What effect, if any, does out-of-state incarceration have on a speedy trial?
8. What is the statute of limitations?

LOCAL PROCEDURE

1. In your home state, what is the statute of limitations for the following:

a. Misdemeanors?
b. Felonies?

2. In your home state, if a felony is dismissed for the failure to bring the defendant to trial within statutory limitations, may the charge be refiled?

ENDNOTES

1. 407 U.S. 514 (1972).
2. 393 U.S. 374 (1969).

> The majestic equality of the law forbids the rich as well as the poor to sleep under bridges, to beg in the streets, and to steal bread.
>
> —Anatole France, 1914

Trial

7

Chapter Outline

Key Words

Alternate jurors
Bench trial
Court trial
Gag orders

Impartial trial by jury
Locked-down jury
Petty offenses

Public trial
Public's right of access to a trial
Right to a trial by jury

Learning Objectives

After completing this chapter, you should be able to:

1. Explain the differences between a bench and a jury trial.
2. Discuss the right of the public and press to attend a criminal trial.
3. Identify what constitutes a public trial.
4. Explain the defendant's right to a jury trial.
5. Discuss the procedure for waiving a jury trial.
6. List what constitutes a petty offense.
7. Discuss the rules regarding the size of a jury.

BENCH TRIAL VERSUS JURY TRIAL

By the beginning of the eighteenth century, the accused was being confronted by the witnesses against him or her, and hearsay evidence was eliminated. Witnesses were placed under oath to relate facts of their own knowledge. Juries rendered their verdicts based upon the testimony of witnesses given in open court, not upon what the jurors had learned about an accusation outside of court. Rules of evidence were being formulated. The trial by jury as it is known today was rapidly becoming part of the judicial system in Great Britain and was adopted by the colonists. The colonists had deep reverence for trial by jury, and they strongly resented interference by the king of Great Britain in his efforts to subdue them. This resentment was manifested by the colonists in the Declaration of Independence. Among other provisions, they included in this Declaration the following: "The history of the present King of Great Britain is a history of repeated injuries. To prove this, let facts be submitted to a candid world. . . . For his [the King] depriving us in many cases, of benefits of trial by jury."

Accused's Right to Jury Trial

After the colonists gained their independence from Great Britain, a new government was established. To prevent possible future interference with the **right to a trial by jury** in this newly formed government, the Sixth Amendment to the U.S. Constitution contained the provision that all persons accused of a crime had the right to be tried by an impartial jury. The Sixth Amendment right to trial by jury is made binding on the states through the Due Process Clause of the Fourteenth Amendment, as is the right to a speedy trial. These rights are also contained in all state constitutions or statutes. Although the Sixth Amendment did not mention the number of persons required to constitute a jury, it was generally accepted that the common law rule of twelve persons would prevail. So strongly was it felt that a jury must consist of twelve persons in a criminal case that a trial by jury consisting of fewer than twelve would be a denial of due process of law. The idea of an accused's being permitted to waive a jury trial and have the case heard by a judge alone was practically unthought of. It was not until 1930 in the case of *Patton* v. *United States*[1] that the U.S. Supreme Court held that a verdict rendered by a jury comprising fewer than twelve members was not a violation of an accused's constitutional right to a trial by jury. In the *Patton* case, the trial started with a jury comprising twelve persons, but during the trial one of the jurors became incapacitated. The defendant agreed to continue the trial with only eleven jurors. He was convicted, and the case was taken to the U.S. Supreme Court to determine whether a defendant has the right to waive a jury trial. The defendant did not waive the entire jury in the *Patton* case, but even waiving one juror and continuing with only eleven was so foreign to the common law procedure that the U.S. Supreme Court felt that the matter was worth their consideration. The Court in the *Patton* case stated that, after an examination of Article III, section 2, and the Sixth Amendment of the U.S. Constitution, they had come to the conclusion that a jury trial was a right that the accused might "forego at his election" and that this right was a privilege and not an "imperative right." As such, the defendant could waive a jury comprising fewer than twelve persons. This decision gave an implied permission to waive the jury entirely and have the case heard by a judge sitting alone.

Even though the Court in the *Patton* case sanctioned the right of an accused to waive his or her right to a jury, it did emphasize the necessity of preserving the jury trial system. The Court stated as follows:

Not only must the right of the accused to a trial by a constitutional jury be jealously preserved, but the maintenance of the jury as a fact-finding body in criminal cases is of such importance and has such a place in our traditions that, before any waiver can become effective, the consent of government counsel and the sanction of the court must be had, in addition to the express and intelligent consent of the defendant.

The U.S. Supreme Court further emphasized the importance of the right of an accused to a trial by jury in the case of *Duncan* v. *Louisiana.*[2] The Court in that decision stated the following:

Providing an accused with the right to be tried by a jury of his peers gave him an inestimable safeguard against the corrupt or overzealous prosecutor and against the compliant, biased, or eccentric judge. If the defendant preferred the common sense judgment of a jury to the more tutored but perhaps less sympathetic reaction of the single judge, he was to have it. Beyond this, the jury trial provisions in the Federal and State Constitutions reflect a fundamental decision about the exercise of official power—a reluctance to entrust plenary powers over the life and liberty of the citizens to one judge or to a group of judges. Fear of unchecked power, so typical of our State and Federal Governments in other respects, found expression in the criminal law in this insistence upon community participation in the determination of guilt or innocence. The deep commitment of the Nation to the right of jury trial in serious criminal cases as a defense against arbitrary law enforcement qualities for protection under the Due Process Clause of the Fourteenth Amendment, and must therefore be respected by the States.

Trial by Judge Alone

Further advantages of a jury trial over a trial by a judge sitting alone, also referred to as a court trial, include the belief that a jury of twelve persons, representing a cross section of society, may be better able to evaluate the demeanor of witnesses than a judge sitting alone; that the group judgment of a jury is better than that of a single person, the judge; that there is a value in community participation in the administration of justice; and that the jury injects the common law test into the legal system instead of the legalistic viewpoint.

With all these listed advantages to a trial by jury, why would a defendant wish to waive a jury and be tried by a judge sitting alone? Situations arise in which it may be advantageous to the accused to waive his or her right to a jury trial in favor of a court trial. The crime of which the defendant is accused may be a heinous one. The emotional involvement of the people within the community may make the selection of an impartial jury very difficult. The defendant's general appearance may be such that a jury may become prejudiced. There may be a serious past criminal record subjecting the defendant to possible impeachment should the witness stand be taken as a defense, and the probability of the jury's convicting the defendant on his or her past record rather than on the evidence contended in the present charge is great. Or the defendant may be a part of an organized criminal syndicate or of a minority group that local feeling is against, and the jury may convict the accused by association rather than on the facts of the case. A judge is considered less inclined to be affected by any of these situations than would a jury.

Procedure in the Waiver of a Jury   Prior to the *Patton* decision, only a few states had considered allowing a defendant to waive a trial by jury. However, after the *Patton* decision, a large majority of the states began permitting the defendant to waive the right to a trial by jury. States differ considerably regarding the conditions and the procedure to

Prosecutors Christopher Darden, Marcia Clark, and William Hodgam confer in a Los Angeles courtroom following the acquittal of O.J. Simpson on October 3, 1995, in the double murder trial of his ex-wife, Nicole Brown, and Ronald Goldman. (*Source:* Myung Chun, Pool/AP Wide World Photos.)

be followed in permitting a waiver of a jury trial. A few states still do not permit the defendant to waive a jury trial. Others permit the waiver in misdemeanor cases but not on felony charges. Still others permit the jury to be waived in all cases except those with a maximum penalty of death. One state permits the defendant to waive the jury in capital cases and be tried by a panel of three judges. A few states permit the jury to be waived in any type of charge, including capital cases.

States also differ concerning who must give consent and how the consent is given. Some states provide that the waiver is solely the right of the defendant, whereas others hold that the waiver must be consented to by the prosecution as well as the defendant. A few states require that the defendant, the prosecution, and the judge all must agree to the waiver of the jury, and a few others provide that the defendant and the judge must agree to the waiver, but the consent of the prosecution is not required. This latter position has been criticized, since it is believed that the prosecution should be permitted to disagree with the waiver. The reasoning is that a judge may be known to be sympathetic to the defendant or may be under political pressure, making him or her feel forced to render a verdict in favor of the defendant. In most instances, the prosecution will agree with the waiver of the jury, since the waiver expedites the trial by eliminating the time-consuming selection of the jury. Time is also saved by not having to stop during a jury trial to explain the law of the case to the jury.

The form in which the waiver of the jury takes place also varies among states. In some states, the defendant must waive the jury in open court by an express statement to that effect. Other states require the defendant to consent to the waiver in writing before the date of the trial. Some states hold that unless the defendant demands a jury trial at the time that he or she enters the plea of not guilty, a jury trial is automatically waived.

If the waiver of a jury takes place, it is usually before the jury is selected, but a few states permit the defendant to waive the jury anytime before the verdict is rendered.

A question that sometimes arises is, After consent to a waiver of the jury, may the defendant later demand to be tried by a jury? Generally, unless there is sufficient evidence of a miscarriage of justice, the defendant may not demand a jury trial, particularly if the trial has begun. The reason is that a jury would have to be selected and the trial would have to start over. Once the trial has begun, the waiver of a jury creates no particular difficulty, since the judge will have heard all the evidence during the trial's progress and will be in a position to render the verdict. Whether the defendant is permitted to withdraw the waiver of the jury is within the discretion of the trial judge. In making the decision, the judge may consider such matters as the timeliness of the motion to withdraw the waiver, the reason for the requested withdrawal, and the possibility of undue delay of the trial or inconvenience to witnesses that would result from granting the withdrawal of the waiver.

May the Defendant Demand a Bench Trial?   As previously pointed out, there are times when a defendant may wish to be tried by a judge sitting alone. Under these circumstances, may the defendant waive the jury and demand a **bench trial**, also known as a **court trial**? This question was answered by the U.S. Supreme Court in the case of *Singer* v. *United States*.[3] In that decision, the Court held that although a defendant could waive the right to a jury trial, there is no correlative right to a bench trial. The Court recognized the fact that a prosecutor also has the right to demand a jury trial. The Court in the *Singer* decision stated:

> The ability to waive a constitutional right does not ordinarily carry with it the right to insist upon the opposite of that right. For example, although a defendant can, under some circumstances, waive his constitutional right to a public trial, he has no absolute right to compel a private trial. Although he can waive his right to be tried in the State and district where the crime was committed, he cannot in all cases compel transfer of the case to another district, and although he can waive his right to be confronted by the witnesses against him, it has never been seriously suggested that he can thereby compel the Government to try the case by stipulation. . . .

Trial by jury has been established by the Constitution as the "normal and . . . preferable mode of disposing of issues of fact in a criminal case."

In light of the Constitution's emphasis on jury trial, we find it difficult to understand how the petitioner can submit the bald proposition that to compel a defendant in a criminal case to undergo a jury trial against his or her will is contrary to his or her right to a fair trial or to due process. A defendant's only constitutional right concerning the method of trial is to an **impartial trial by jury**. We find no constitutional impediment in conditioning a waiver of this right on the consent of the prosecuting attorney and the trial judge when, if either refuses to consent, the result is simply that the defendant is subject to an impartial trial by jury—the very thing that the Constitution guarantees him or her.

The Court concluded that forcing a jury trial was not a violation of any constitutional right of an accused even though the defendant might feel that it was advantageous to have a court trial. In this regard, many states permit the judge to refuse to consent to a court trial in lieu of a trial by jury. Those states adopting this policy feel that protection against community criticism should be provided when the judge might have to render an unpopular verdict.

Denial of a Jury Trial: Petty Offenses

Although the right to a trial by jury is an established guarantee to one accused of a crime, it is not an absolute right in all instances. As early as 1937, the U.S. Supreme Court in the case of *District of Columbia* v. *Clawans*[4] sanctioned a nonjury trial to one accused of a **petty offense**. This same sanction has been reiterated from time to time by the Court.[5]

In the *Duncan* v. *Louisiana* decision, the Court stated the following:

So-called petty offenses were tried without juries both in England and in the Colonies and have always been held to be exempt from the otherwise comprehensive language of the Sixth Amendment's jury trial provisions. There is no substantial evidence that the Framers intended to depart from this established common-law practice, and the possible consequences to defendants from convictions for petty offenses have been thought insufficient to outweigh the benefits to efficient law enforcement and simplified judicial administration resulting from the availability of speedy and inexpensive non-jury adjudications. These same considerations compel the same result under the Fourteenth Amendment. Of course the boundaries of the petty offense category have always been ill defined, if not ambulatory.

Determining Petty Offenses   In determining whether an offense is a "petty" one, the courts have had to turn to some criteria upon which to work. Although the statutes of some states have designated certain offenses as petty ones, this designation is not conclusive, and the courts may render different interpretations of petty offenses.

As stated by the U.S. Supreme Court in the *Frank* decision, to determine whether a particular offense could be classified as petty, the Court sought objective indications of the seriousness with which society regarded the offense. The Court stated that the most relevant indication of the seriousness of an offense was the severity of the penalty that could be imposed for the commission of the offense. The severity of the penalty authorized by law, and not the penalty actually imposed by the judge, was to be the criterion.

In the *Frank* case, the Supreme Court implied that they were relying upon the criterion set forth in the *Cheff* decision for a definition of petty offense. The *Cheff* decision adopted the definition of a petty offense found in 18 U.S. Code, Section 1, where it is described as any misdemeanor the penalty for which does not exceed imprisonment for a period of six months or a fine of $500.

It would appear from these U.S. Supreme Court decisions that the states could pass statutes denying an accused the right to a trial by a jury for the commission of an offense for which the penalty would not exceed six months' imprisonment or a fine of not more than $500, and the accused would not be denied due process of law. A few states grant a defendant the right to a jury trial in all misdemeanor charges irrespective of the penalty but deny him or her the right to a jury trial on infractions—violations for which no imprisonment may be imposed.

Juries Comprising Fewer Than Twelve Persons

In line with the common-law tradition, the laws of the United States, as well as of most of the states, require that a criminal trial jury consist of twelve persons. There are a few states where the law provides that in misdemeanor violations, the jury may comprise any number fewer than twelve, agreed upon in open court by the defendant and the prosecution. How many fewer than twelve is not indicated, but the U.S. Supreme Court has not approved the use of a jury with fewer than six members. As in the *Patton* case, in some states it is held that a felony trial must commence with twelve persons in the jury, but if one should become incapacitated and unable to act as a juror, the trial may continue with fewer than twelve if agreed to by the defendant, his or her attorney, and the prosecution. If it is not agreed to, the judge must declare a mistrial, and the case will have to be heard again with a new jury.

Due to the difficulty of obtaining and managing twelve jurors and alternate jurors, some states have broken with the traditional number of twelve in a jury, even in felony cases, and have passed laws providing that a jury may comprise fewer than twelve both in misdemeanor and in felony cases. The problem that arises is whether trial by a jury comprising fewer than twelve when not consented to, particularly by the defendant, is a denial of the right to trial by jury. This question was answered in the case of *Williams* v. *Florida*,[6] in which the U.S. Supreme Court held that a jury comprising fewer than twelve persons, in accordance with the laws of the state involved, did not violate the Due Process Clause of the Fourteenth Amendment. The facts in the *Williams* case indicate that Williams was charged with robbery in the state of Florida. Williams, referred to as the petitioner by the Court, filed a pretrial motion to impanel a twelve-person jury instead of the six-person jury provided by Florida law in all but capital cases. The motion was denied, and Williams was convicted and sentenced to life imprisonment. He appealed his case to the U.S. Supreme Court upon the grounds that his right to a jury trial, as provided in the Sixth Amendment to the U.S. Constitution, made applicable to the states by the Fourteenth Amendment, had been violated by requiring him to submit to a trial by a jury comprising only six persons. The Court stated as follows:

> The question in this case is whether the constitutional guarantee of a trial by "jury" necessarily requires trial by exactly 12 persons, rather than some lesser number, in this case six. We hold that the 12-man panel is not a necessary ingredient of "trial by jury," and that respondent's [state's] refusal to impanel more than six members provided for by Florida law did not violate petitioner's Sixth Amendment rights as applied to the States through the Fourteenth.
>
> We had occasion in *Duncan* v. *Louisiana* to review briefly the oft-told history of the development of trial by jury in criminal cases. That history revealed a long tradition attaching great importance to the concept of relying on a body of one's peers to determine guilt or innocence as a safeguard against arbitrary law enforcement. That same history, however, affords little insight into the considerations which gradually led the size of that body to be generally fixed at 12. Some have suggested that the number 12 was fixed upon simply because that was the number of the presentment jury from the hundred, from which the petty jury developed. Other, less circular, but more fanciful reasons for the number 12 have been given, "but they were all brought forward after the number was fixed," and rest on little more than mystical or superstitious insights into the significance of "12." Lord Coke's explanation that the "number twelve is much respected in holy writ, as 12 apostles, 12 stones, 12 tribes, etc." is typical. In short, while sometime in the 14th century the size of the jury at common law came to be fixed generally at 12, that particular feature of the jury system appears to have been an historical accident, unrelated to the great purposes which gave rise to the jury in the first place. The question before us is whether this accidental feature of the jury has been immutably codified into our Constitution. . . .
>
> It might be suggested that the 12-man jury gives a defendant a greater advantage since he has more "chances" of finding a juror who will insist on acquittal and thus prevent conviction. But the advantage might just as easily belong to the State, which also needs only one juror out of twelve insisting on guilt to prevent acquittal. What few experiments have occurred—usually in the civil area—indicate that there

is no discernible difference between the results reached by the two different sized juries. In short, neither currently available evidence nor theory suggests that the 12-man jury is necessarily more advantageous to the defendant than a jury composed of fewer members.

Similarly, while in theory the number of viewpoints represented on a randomly selected jury ought to increase as the size of the jury increases, in practice the difference between the 12-man and the 6-man jury in terms of the cross section of the community represented seems likely to be negligible. Even the 12-man jury cannot ensure representation of every distinct voice in the community, particularly given the use of the peremptory challenge. As long as arbitrary exclusions of a particular class from the jury rolls are forbidden, the concern that the cross section will be significantly diminished if the jury is decreased in size from 12 to 6 seems an unrealistic one.

We conclude, in short, as we began: the fact that the jury at common law was composed of precisely 12 is an historical accident, unnecessary to effect the purposes of the jury system and wholly without significance "except to mystics."

Since the *Williams* decision has been handed down by the U.S. Supreme Court, it is highly possible that more and more states will enact laws permitting juries to comprise fewer than twelve members in all but capital cases. However, the U.S. Supreme Court, in *Ballew* v. *Georgia*,[7] held that a jury may not comprise fewer than six persons. Ballew was convicted of a misdemeanor charge by a jury of five persons, as provided for by a Georgia statute. The conviction was upheld by the Georgia appellate courts. Ballew appealed his case to the U.S. Supreme Court on the grounds that his constitutional guarantee of a trial by jury had been denied, thereby denying him due process of law. The U.S. Supreme Court stated that a jury of six persons had been upheld in the *Williams* case and that the "line between five and six member juries is not difficult to justify, but a line has to be drawn somewhere if the substance of the jury trial is to be preserved." The Court further stated that assembled research data

raise substantial doubt about the reliability and appropriate representation of panels smaller than six. Because of the fundamental importance of the jury trial to the American system of criminal justice, any further reduction that promotes inaccurate and possibly biased decision making, that causes untoward differences in verdicts, and that prevents juries from truly representing their communities, attains constitutional significance . . . and such reduction from six-member to five-member juries is not to be permitted.

Regardless of the size of the jury, many courts select **alternate jurors**. An alternate juror sits with the jury and is prepared to serve as a jury member if one of the regular jurors is excused or disqualified during the trial. Because only jury members may be present in the room when a jury is deliberating, alternate jurors are generally excused by the trial judge shortly before the jury is **locked down** for deliberations.

PUBLIC TRIAL

Not only does the Sixth Amendment to the U.S Constitution, as well as the laws of all the states, provide that an accused person is entitled to a trial by jury, but it also further provides that he or she is guaranteed a public trial. The purpose of this guarantee is to ensure that the accused is dealt with fairly and not unjustly convicted. As was stated by the U.S. Supreme Court in the case of *Estes* v. *Texas*:[8]

History has proven that secret tribunals were effective instruments of oppression. As our Brother Black so well said in *In re Oliver,* 333 US 257 (1948): the traditional

Anglo-American distrust for secret trials has been variously ascribed to the notorious use of this practice by the Spanish Inquisition, to the excesses of the English Court of Star Chamber, and to the French monarchy's abuse of the lettre de cachet. Whatever other benefits the guarantee to an accused that his trial be conducted in public may confer upon our society, the guarantee has always been recognized as a safeguard against any attempt to employ our courts as instruments of persecution.

Clearly the openness of the proceedings (the trial) provides other benefits as well (as a safeguard against oppression): it arguably improves the quality of testimony, it may induce unknown witnesses to come forward with relevant testimony, it may move all the trial participants to perform their duties conscientiously, and it gives the public the opportunity to observe the courts in the performance of their duties and to determine whether they are performing adequately.

What Makes a Trial "Public"?

Although an accused's guarantee to a **public trial** appears on the surface to be a clear and explicit right, it is not without complications. Just what constitutes a public trial is not defined either by the Sixth Amendment or by any of the laws of the states. The problems that arise are the following: What is a public trial? Who constitutes the public? How many persons must be in attendance to make a trial a public one? And since the right to a public trial is basically a right of the accused, may the right be waived, resulting in a private trial? Over time, partial answers to these questions have come from court decisions, but the answers to some questions have not been unanimous.

It is clear that a public trial is one that is not secret. The commonsense interpretation of a public trial is one that the general public is free to attend. The doors of the courtroom are expected to be kept open. However, if no member of the public is in attendance, there is no requirement that a trial be stopped in order to satisfy the guarantee of a public trial. Under ordinary circumstances, the public includes persons of all classes, races, ages, and both sexes.

In some cases, even though the trial is open to the public, certain items of evidence are not open for public view. For example, pictures of children involved in a sexual pornography case, if entered into evidence, would not be open for public view.

There are times when it may not be necessary to permit every person to attend trial proceedings in order for a trial to be a public trial. It has been held that to satisfy the constitutional guarantee to a public trial, it is not necessary to provide a stadium large enough to accommodate all who might want to attend a particular trial. Yet a courtroom should be large enough to permit a reasonable number of the public to observe the trial proceedings. It also has been held that a judge may limit the number of persons attending a trial to the seating capacity of the courtroom facilities without violating the right of a public trial. A judge may eject any spectator or member of the public who becomes unruly and disrupts the trial proceedings. The judge may even clear the courtroom of all spectators if they become disruptive. However, that action does not permit locking the courtroom doors and prohibiting other members of the public who conduct themselves properly from attending the trial.

Public Right to Attend

The courts were far from unanimous in answering the question of public exclusion from the courtroom. The issue is whether or not the public may be excluded in any situation without violating the guarantee to a public trial. The question usually surfaced when a trial involved salacious testimony. Two cases that addressed the exclusion of the

Law in Practice

Key Decisions on Jury Trials

Griffin v. *California* (1965)	Prosecutor cannot comment on defendant's failure to testify during trial. It violates the defendant's privilege against self-incrimination.
Sheppard v. *Maxwell* (1966)	Defendant's right to a fair trial was denied because of prejudicial press coverage.
Duncan v. *Louisiana* (1968)	The Due Process Clause of the Fourteenth Amendment incorporates the Sixth Amendment's right to a jury trial in state criminal courts.
Baldwin v. *New York* (1970)	There is no right to a jury trial in state courts for petty offenses.
Williams v. *Florida* (1970)	State juries are not constitutionally required to consist of twelve members.
Johnson v. *Louisiana* (1972)	Federal criminal jury verdicts must be unanimous.
Apodaca v. *Oregon* (1972)	There is no federal requirement that state jury verdicts must be unanimous.
Taylor v. *Louisiana* (1975)	Women cannot be excluded from juries.
Ballew v. *Georgia* (1978)	State juries must have at least six members.
Burch v. *Louisiana* (1979)	Six-member jury verdicts must be unanimous.
Chandler v. *Florida* (1981)	The right to a fair trial is not violated by electronic media and still photographic coverage of the trial.
Batson v. *Kentucky* (1986)	Peremptory challenges may not be used by the prosecutor solely to exclude a racial group from the jury.
Georgia v. *McCullum* (1992)	The defense may not use peremptory challenges to exclude jurors based on race.
Daulbert v. *Merrell Dow* (1993)	Scientific evidence must be both relevant and reliable.
J.E.B. v. *Alabama* (1994)	Peremptory challenges may not be used to exclude jurors based on their gender.
United States v. *Scheffer* (1998)	Lie detector test results are not admissible because of doubts about their accuracy.
Apprendi v. *New Jersey* (2000)	Any fact that increases the penalty for a crime beyond the prescribed statutory maximum must be submitted to a jury.

public from trial were *Richmond Newspapers Inc.* v. *Virginia*[9] and *Globe Newspapers Co.* v. *Superior Court for the County of Norfolk.*[10]

Closing the Entire Trial   The Court in the *Richmond Newspapers, Inc.* case recognized that the **right of the press and the public to access to criminal trials** was based on the First Amendment of the U.S. Constitution and not on the Sixth Amendment right of a defendant to a public trial. The defendant was charged with murder and had been brought to trial on three prior occasions, each time ending in a mistrial. At the time of the fourth trial, the defense attorney requested that the trial be closed to the public because of prior interference by spectators. The prosecution voiced no objection to a closed trial, and the judge granted the defense request to close the courtroom to the press and the public. This right was granted to judges by the Virginia statutes. Richmond Newspapers, Inc., filed an objection to being barred from the courtroom, and a hearing was held on the objection. The Virginia Appellate Court upheld the judge's ruling to close the courtroom. The case was appealed to the U.S. Supreme Court on the grounds that the First Amendment right to freedom of the press had been violated by barring the press from the trial. Since the defendant had requested that the trial be closed, the U.S. Supreme Court could not consider the case on the Sixth Amendment right to a public trial. Consideration of the case was then based on First Amendment rights. The Court pointed out that the First Amendment does not mention the right of public access to a criminal trial explicitly but held that the First Amendment is broad enough in scope to encompass certain rights not specifically mentioned, including the right of access to criminal trials. The Court stated the following:

> Underlying the First Amendment right of access to criminal trials [by the public] is the common understanding that a major purpose of that Amendment was to protect the free discussion of governmental affairs. By offering such protection, the First Amendment serves to ensure that the individual citizen can effectively participate in and contribute to our republican system of self-government. . . . Thus to the extent that the First Amendment embraces a right of access to criminal trials, it is to ensure that this constitutionally protected discussion of governmental affairs is an informed one.

Closing a Portion of a Trial   *The Richmond Newspapers, Inc.* decision pertained to the closing of the entire trial to the press and public, which the Court held was in violation of the First Amendment. That decision still left the question of whether the press and public can be excluded from a portion of the trial when it may be in the interest of fairness to make such an exclusion. The U.S. Supreme Court discussed this issue in the *Globe Newspapers Co.* case. In *Globe,* the Court stated the following:

> Although the right of access to criminal trials is of constitutional stature, it is not absolute. But circumstances under which the press and public can be barred from a criminal trial are limited; the State's justification in denying access must be a weighty one. Where, as in the present case, the State attempts to deny the right of access in order to inhibit the disclosure of sensitive information, it must be shown that the denial is necessitated by a compelling governmental interest, and is narrowly tailored to serve that interest.

In the *Globe Newspapers Co.* case, the defendant was charged with the rape of three teenage girls. The law of the state of Massachusetts required that under all circumstances, the press and public must be excluded during the testimony of a minor victim in a sex offense trial. In *Globe,* the Supreme Court focused on the reasons behind the mandatory exclusion. By passing this law, the state of Massachusetts tried to protect minor victims of sex crimes from further trauma and embarrassment and to encourage such victims to come forward and testify in a truthful and credible manner. The Court stated that it agreed with the state of Massachusetts's interest in safeguarding the physical and psychological well-being of a minor but that this interest did not justify a mandatory exclusion rule for all cases. The Court felt that the trial judge could determine case by case whether a closure is necessary to protect the welfare of a minor victim. Among the factors to be weighed by the judge are the minor victim's age, psychological maturity and understanding, the nature of the crime, the desires of the victim, and the interests of the victim's parents and other relatives.

The Court further stated in the *Globe Newspapers Co.* case that the identities of the victims were already a matter of public record and that there was no showing that they would not testify in the presence of the public and press. Additionally, there was no showing that a closure of a trial during the testimony of a minor victim would result in others' coming forth and reporting such crimes. For these reasons, the Court held that the mandatory exclusion of the press and public in all such matters violated the First

Amendment to the U.S. Constitution. The *Globe* decision would appear to allow a trial judge to exclude the press and public during the giving of testimony by a witness when it would be in the best interest of fairness to make that exclusion. The burden of showing that such an exclusion was in the best interest of all would be on the trial judge.

In a state court case, the trial judge's exclusion of the press and public during the testimony of the prosecution's principal witness, a sixteen-year-old pregnant girl, was upheld by the state appellate court. The exclusion order was based partly on concern for the welfare of the young expectant mother and her unborn child and partly on her own subjective fear of reprisal if she testified in public. In another state case, the exclusion of the press and public by the trial judge was upheld by the state appellate court during the testimony of an undercover police officer whose safety might have been endangered if his identity had been publicly exposed.

Public Exclusion from Pretrial Hearings   The *Richmond Newspaper, Inc.* and *Globe Newspapers Co.* cases are not to be confused with the case of *Gannett Co.* v. *DePasquale*[11] In *Gannett,* the U.S. Supreme Court held that the press and public may be excluded from pretrial hearings, such as a pretrial hearing on the suppression of evidence or a preliminary hearing. *Gannett* upheld the exclusion of the press and public from pretrial hearings on the grounds that adverse prepublicity given to such hearings could pose a risk to the defendant and prevent a fair trial. The Court pointed out that there is a difference between the trial itself and pretrial hearings. The Court in the *Gannett* case stated the following:

> Publicity concerning pretrial suppression hearings such as the one involved in the present case poses special risks of unfairness. The whole purpose of such hearings is to screen out unreliable or illegally obtained evidence and ensure that this evidence does not become known to the jury. Publicity concerning the proceedings at a pretrial hearing, however, could influence the public opinion against a defendant and inform potential jurors of inculpatory information wholly inadmissible at the actual trial. This Court has long recognized that adverse publicity can endanger the ability of a defendant to receive a fair trial.

The *Gannett* decision does not demand that all pretrial hearings be closed to the press and public, but should be done only on a request made to the trial judge or on the judge's own discretion. As a general rule, a court will not allow a closed hearing without a strong showing of prejudice to the requesting party.

Fair Trial versus Freedom of the Press

From the foregoing discussion, it may be concluded that the public is entitled to know that justice is taking place during a criminal trial. Therefore, the public, with some reservations, is permitted to attend trial proceedings. Since not all members of the public who may have an interest in a particular trial may be able to attend, the news media have assumed the responsibility of informing the public about what takes place during certain trials. The problem that arises is just how far the news media may go in obtaining information and reporting it to the public. The courts and the news media are often in conflict over the answer to this question. The news media rely upon the First Amendment to the U.S. Constitution for support of the uninhibited right to exercise their power in getting the news. This amendment provides, among other things, that "Congress shall make no law . . . abridging the freedom of speech, or of the press. . . ."

When the courts attempt to curtail the media in obtaining news, the media allege violation of their rights under the First Amendment. The courts, on the other hand, hold that an accused is entitled to a fair trial by an impartial jury, and when that right is interfered with by the news media, they have exceeded their prerogative. Because of the right of the public to be informed of what takes place during criminal trials, the courts generally have permitted reporters to be present during criminal trials; and in many instances, special areas in courtrooms are set aside for reporters in order that they may have a vantage point to assist them in obtaining the news. With the advent of the camera, radio, and television, conflicts have arisen over whether these types of equipment should be permitted in the courtroom. The courts concede that when the gathering of news during trial proceedings becomes too disruptive or otherwise denies the defendant a fair trial by an impartial jury, some control must be exercised.

This viewpoint was emphasized by the U.S. Supreme Court in the *Estes* case. Estes was convicted in the state court in Texas on an extensive swindling charge. His case was taken to the U.S. Supreme Court on the grounds that, because of massive pretrial and trial publicity, he had been denied the right of due process of law as provided by the Fourteenth Amendment to the U.S. Constitution. The Supreme Court concluded that the defendant had been denied a fair trial because of the live radio and television coverage, so the conviction was reversed. The Court set forth some pertinent arguments against permitting live news coverage of criminal trials; these arguments are still being presented by those opposing live coverage.

At the time the *Estes* case was heard by the U.S. Supreme Court, the attorneys representing the state of Texas contended that the television portions of the trial did not constitute a denial of due process, since there was no showing of prejudice of *Estes* resulting from the television coverage. The state also argued that the public has a right to know what goes on in the courts, and that televising criminal trials would be enlightening to the public and promote greater respect for the courts. To this argument, the Court stated the following:

> It is true that the public has a right to be informed as to what occurs in its courts, but reporters of all media, including television, are always present if they wish to be and are plainly free to report whatever occurs in open court through their respective media. . . .
>
> As has been said, the chief function of our judicial machinery is to ascertain the truth. The use of television, however, cannot be said to contribute materially to this objective. Rather its use amounts to the injection of an irrelevant factor into court proceedings. In addition experience teaches that there are numerous situations in which it might cause actual unfairness, some so subtle as to defy detection by the accused or control by the judge. We enumerate some in summary:
>
> 1. The potential impact of television on the jurors is perhaps of the greatest significance. They are the nerve center of the fact-finding process. . . . From the moment the trial judge announces that a case will be televised it becomes [a] *cause celebre.* The whole community, including prospective jurors, becomes interested in all the morbid details surrounding it. The approaching trial immediately assumes an important status in the public press and the accused is highly publicized, along with the offense with which he is charged. Every juror carries with him into the jury box these solemn facts and thus increase[s] the chance of prejudice that is present in every criminal case. And we must remember that realistically it is only the notorious trial which will be broadcast, because of the necessity for paid sponsorship. The conscious or unconscious effect on the juror's judgment cannot be evaluated,

but experience indicates that it is not only possible but highly probable that it will have a direct bearing on his vote as to guilt or innocence. Where pretrial publicity of all kinds has created intense public feeling which is aggravated by the telecasting or picturing of the trial, the televised jurors can not help but feel the pressures of knowing that friends and neighbors have their eyes upon them. If the community is hostile to an accused, a televised juror, realizing that he must return to neighbors who saw the trial themselves, may well be led "not to hold the balance nice, clear, and true between the State and the accused. . . ."

2. The quality of the testimony in criminal trials will often be impaired. The impact upon a witness of the knowledge that he is being viewed by a vast audience is simply incalculable. Some may be demoralized and frightened, some cocky and given to overstatement; memories may falter, as with anyone speaking publicly, and accuracy of statement may be severely undermined. Embarrassment may impede the search for the truth, as may a natural tendency toward overdramatization. Furthermore, inquisitive strangers and "cranks" might approach witnesses on the street with jibes, advice or demands for explanation of testimony. There is little wonder that the defendant cannot "prove" the existence of such factors. Yet we all know from experience that they exist.

3. A major aspect of the problem is the additional responsibilities the presence of television places on the trial judge. His job is to make certain that the accused receives a fair trial. This most difficult task requires his undivided attention. Still, when television comes into the courtroom he must also supervise it. . . . In addition, laying physical interruptions aside, there is the ever-present distraction that the mere awareness of television's presence prompts. Judges are human beings also and are subject to the same psychological reactions as laymen. Telecasting is particularly bad where the judge is elected, as is the case in all save a half dozen of our States. The distractions inherent in broadcasting divert his attention from the task at hand—the fair trial of the accused.

But this is not all. There is the initial decision that must be made as to whether the use of television will be permitted. This is perhaps an even more crucial consideration. Our judges are high-minded men and women. But it is difficult to remain oblivious to the pressures that the news media can bring to bear on them both directly and through the shaping of public opinion. Moreover, where one judge in a district or even in a State permits telecasting, the requirement that the others do the same is almost mandatory. Especially is this true where the judge is selected at the ballot box.

Finally, we cannot ignore the impact of courtroom television on the defendant. Its presence is a form of mental—if not physical—harassment. . . . A defendant on trial for a specific crime is entitled to his day in court, not in a stadium, or a city or nationwide arena. The heightened public clamor resulting from radio and television coverage will inevitably result in prejudice.

After the *Estes* decision, courts for a time generally prohibited live coverage of criminal trials. But the news media eventually renewed their pressure to permit live coverage of trials. Many judges and attorneys have resisted this pressure principally on the grounds presented in the *Estes* decision. Regardless of these strong arguments against live coverage, more and more courts are permitting live coverage of trials. In 1996, the nation watched the televised trial of O.J. Simpson. As in the results of the coverage of that trial, many in the justice system are seriously concerned about the effects of this type of coverage, not only from the standpoint of the defendant but also concerning the safety of witnesses. Great strides have been made to protect the victims in rape cases from embarrassment during trials in order to encourage victims to come forth and report

Court TV

According to Court TV's press release, Court TV, a television channel, is the leader in the investigation genre, providing a window on the American system of justice through distinctive programming that both informs and entertains. Court TV telecasts high-profile trials by day and original programs like *Forensic Files, Psychic Detectives, Masterminds,* and *Impossible Heists* in primetime. Court TV is 50 percent owned by Time Warner and 50 percent owned by Liberty Media Corporation. The channel is seen in over 83 million homes and can be assessed online at www.courttv.com.

Trial coverage is the focus of Court TV's daytime programming, emphasizing newsworthy and controversial legal proceedings and delivering powerful real-life drama that provides a window on the justice system. High-profile cases covered by Court TV Daytime include the Scott Peterson trial, the Kobe Bryant sexual assault charges, the Martha Stewart trial, the child molestation charges against Michael Jackson, the murder trials of record producer Phil Spector and actor Robert Blake, and many more.

Court TV operates three distinct websites. CourtTV.com provides network information, news and features on trials, video archives, chats and the Court TV store and bookstore, plus a special section on educational resources and public affairs. Their CrimeLibrary.com is a collection of fiction and nonfiction accounts of criminal justice. The Crime Library is a rapidly growing collection of more than over 600 nonfiction feature stories on major crimes, criminals, trials, forensics, and criminal profiling by prominent writers. The stories focus mostly on recent crimes, but an expanding collection also delves into historically notorious characters dating back to the 1400s. The Crime Library serves as a resource for students researching current and historical judicial subjects. The Court TV website for Canada may be accessed at www.courttvcanada.ca.

such offenses. It is believed that with live coverage of trials, many victims of all types of crime will refuse to report offenses rather than face embarrassment and possible harm from testifying before television cameras.

Gag Orders

Courts throughout the nation are aware that the news media are entitled to report events occurring during a trial as well as crimes taking place, and no effort is made to suppress this type of reporting. However, the courts have periodically issued orders limiting the information that may be given to the press. Referred to as **"gag orders,"** they are issued to prevent extensive pretrial or trial publicity that could deny a defendant a fair trial because of the resulting difficulty in selecting and maintaining an impartial jury. But the news media have strongly protested the issuance of gag orders on the grounds that such orders violate the First Amendment. Thus, balancing the right of a defendant to a fair trial with the right of freedom of the press has continually plagued the courts. In *Sheppard* v. *Maxwell,*[12] the U.S. Supreme Court criticized the trial judge for the failure to restrain pretrial publicity. The facts of that case reveal that Dr. Sheppard was accused of killing his wife. Prior to the trial, there were numerous newspaper stories concerning the questioning of the accused as well as articles about his personal life and love affairs. The jury list was published, and many of the prospective jurors received telephone calls concerning the case. Inaccurate news releases were given to the press by the police. The judge, who was coming up for election, permitted extensive live news coverage of the trial. Sheppard was convicted and eventually appealed the case to the U.S. Supreme Court on the grounds that due process of law had been denied during the trial. The Court reversed the conviction because it felt that pretrial publicity and extensive live coverage of the trial had kept the defendant from receiving a fair trial. The Court stated

> [that the trial judge] should have made some effort to control the release of leads, information, and gossip to the press by police officers, witnesses, and the counsel for both sides. . . . The courts must take steps by law and regulation that will protect their processes from prejudicial outside interference. Neither prosecutors, counsel for defense, the accused, witnesses, court staff nor enforcement officers coming under the jurisdiction of the court should be permitted to frustrate its function.

Although the Court in the *Sheppard* case stated that trial judges "have the duty of so insulating the trial from publicity as to insure its fairness," the Court did not set down any fixed rules to guide the trial judges and others on what could and could not be printed. But acting upon the suggestion of the *Sheppard* case, trial judges have occasionally issued gag orders. In *Nebraska Press Association* v. *Stewart,*[13] the U.S. Supreme Court discouraged, but did not rule out, the use of gag orders. The Court stated, "This Court has frequently denied that the First Amendment rights are absolute and has consistently rejected the proposition that a prior restraint can never be employed." The Court indicated that such prior restraint should be used only when absolutely necessary to assure a fair trial. As stated by one of the justices, before a prior restraint is to be used there must be "a showing that (i) there is a clear threat to the fairness of trial, (ii) such a threat is posed by the actual publicity to be restrained, and (iii) no less restrictive alternatives are available."

The U.S. Supreme Court in this case felt that the trial judge had overstepped his rights in issuing the gag order. He prohibited the publication of information brought out in an open preliminary hearing that the public was free to attend. The Court did not rule out the possible use of a gag order to prevent pretrial publicity concerning information not otherwise known that would prevent a fair trial from being obtained when other, less restrictive measures were unavailable. But the Court did not indicate what less restrictive measures might be substituted for the gag order.

One less restrictive measure suggested for use instead of issuing a gag order was the granting of a change in venue. But many crimes committed receive such extensive publicity that a change in venue would accomplish little. Under these circumstances, judges may still issue gag orders to prevent undue pretrial publicity and will undoubtedly receive the sanction of the U.S. Supreme Court.

Even before the *Sheppard* decision, law enforcement officers and prosecuting attorneys restricted the release of certain information to the news media. This restrictive action, taken even without a gag order, was the result of criticism directed at law enforcement officers in *Rideau* v. *Louisiana.*[14] The U.S. Supreme Court in that case was critical of the law enforcement agencies involved in permitting the televising of a confession while it was being given by the defendant. The facts of the case reveal the following: Some two months before the petitioner's (Rideau's) trial began and some two weeks before he was arraigned on charges of robbery, kidnapping, and murder, a local TV station broadcast three different times in the space of two days a twenty-minute film of the petitioner, flanked by the sheriff and two state troopers, admitting in detail the commission of the various offenses in response to leading questions by the sheriff.

Rideau was convicted of the charges against him, and his case was taken to the U.S. Supreme Court on the grounds that he had been denied due process of law when a change of venue request was denied by the trial judge. The Supreme Court reversed the conviction, stating the following:

> . . . we hold that it was a denial of due process of law to refuse the request for a change of venue, after the people of the Parish had been exposed repeatedly and in depth to the spectacle of Rideau personally confessing in detail to the crimes with which he was later to be charged. For anyone who has ever watched television the conclusion cannot be avoided that this spectacle, to the tens of thousands of people who saw and heard it, in a very real sense was Rideau's trial—at which he pleaded guilty to murder. Any subsequent court proceedings in a community so pervasively exposed to such a spectacle could be but a hollow formality.

After the *Rideau* decision, many law enforcement officers and prosecuting attorneys decided that it was generally best not to reveal to the press whether an accused person has confessed or to comment on the results of any tests that may have been given. Some officers will not reveal any criminal record of an accused. However, not all are in agreement with this viewpoint, since some contend that if an accused has been previously convicted, the court record of the conviction is a public record, and the news media should be able to obtain this information. But self-imposed restrictions by officers and prosecutors may help ensure a fair trial. Judges often impose further restrictions during a trial to prevent jurors from being influenced by comments made in the news media.

The Prosecutor and the Press

The prosecutorial role in a case, as stated by the Supreme Court, is to be an advocate of a sovereign "whose obligation to govern impartially is as compelling as its obligation to govern at all; and whose interest, therefore, in a criminal prosecution is not that it shall win a case, but that justice shall be done" [*Berger* v. *United States,* 295 U.S. 78, 88 (1935)].

The prosecutor has unique burdens placed upon him or her due to the nature of the position. One of the chief differences between a prosecutor and any other attorney is that a prosecutor represents the entire community, including the victim, police, governmental agencies or officials, and even the prosecutor's adversary, the defendant. Because of this, the prosecutor has certain ethical responsibilities when releasing information to the press. The prosecutor should consider whether the release of information to the press will change or affect:

- endangerment of the lives, physical safety or the reputation of others;
- protection of confidential informants;
- potential prejudice to pending investigations;
- potential prejudice to pending cases;
- preservation of the trust of law enforcement agencies and law enforcement strategies; and
- any other factors which will affect the fair administration of justice.

[Rachel Luna, "The Ethics of Kiss-and-Tell Prosecution: Prosecutors and Post-Trial Publications Fall," 26 *Am. J. Crim. L.* 165, 1998.]

in the courtroom engenders. When state actors exercise peremptory challenges in reliance on gender stereotypes, they ratify and reinforce prejudicial views of the relative abilities of men and women. Because these stereotypes have wreaked injustice in so many other spheres of our country's public life, active discrimination by litigants on the basis of gender during jury selection "invites cynicism respecting the jury's neutrality and its obligation to adhere to the law." The potential for cynicism is particularly acute in cases where gender-related issues are prominent, such as cases involving rape, sexual harassment, or paternity. Discriminatory use of peremptory challenges may create the impression that the judicial system has acquiesced in suppressing full participation by one gender or that the "deck has been stacked" in favor of one side.

In recent cases we have emphasized that individual jurors themselves have a right to nondiscriminatory jury selection procedures. Contrary to respondent's suggestion, this right extends to both men and women. All persons, when granted the opportunity to serve on a jury, have the right not to be excluded summarily because of discriminatory and stereotypical presumptions that reflect and reinforce patterns of historical discrimination. Striking individual jurors on the assumption that they hold particular views simply because of their gender is "practically a brand upon them, affixed by law, an assertion of their inferiority." It denigrates the dignity of the excluded juror; and, for a woman, reinvokes a history of exclusion from political participation. The message it sends to all those in the courtroom, and all those who may later learn of the discriminatory act, is that certain individuals, for no reason other than gender, are presumed unqualified by state actors to decide important questions upon which reasonable persons could disagree.

Our conclusion that litigants may not strike potential jurors solely on the basis of gender does not imply the elimination of all peremptory challenges. Neither does it conflict with a State's legitimate interest in using such challenges in its effort to secure a fair and impartial jury. Parties still may remove jurors whom they feel might be less acceptable than others on the panel; gender simply may not serve as a proxy for bias. Parties may also exercise their peremptory challenges to remove from the venire any group or class of individuals normally subject to "rational basis" review. Even strikes based on characteristics that are disproportionately associated with one gender could be appropriate, absent a showing of pretext. . . .

Failing to provide jurors the same protection against gender discrimination as race discrimination could frustrate the purpose of Batson itself. Because gender and race are overlapping categories, gender can be used as a pretext for racial discrimination. Allowing parties to remove racial minorities from the jury not because of their race, but because of their gender, contravenes well-established equal protection principles and could insulate effectively racial discrimination from judicial scrutiny.

Justice O'Connor, concurring.

I agree with the Court that the Equal Protection Clause prohibits the government from excluding a person from jury service on account of that person's gender. . . . I therefore join the Court's opinion in this case. But today's important blow against gender discrimination is not costless. I write separately to discuss some of these costs, and to express my belief that today's holding should be limited to the government's use of gender-based peremptory strikes.

Batson v. *Kentucky* itself was a significant intrusion into the jury selection process. Batson mini-hearings are now routine in state and federal trial courts, and Batson appeals have proliferated as well. Demographics indicate that today's holding may have an even greater impact than did Batson itself. In further constitutionalizing jury selection procedures, the Court increases the number of cases in which jury selection—once a sideshow—will become part of the main event.

. . . Our belief that experienced lawyers will often correctly intuit which jurors are likely to be the least sympathetic, and our understanding that the lawyer will often be unable to explain the intuition, are the very reason we cherish the peremptory challenge. But, as we add, layer by layer, additional constitutional restraints on the use of the peremptory, we force lawyers to articulate what we know is often inarticulable.

In so doing we make the peremptory challenge less discretionary and more like a challenge for cause. We also increase the possibility that biased jurors will be allowed onto the jury, because sometimes a lawyer will be unable to provide an acceptable gender-neutral explanation even though the lawyer is in fact correct that the juror is unsympathetic. Similarly, in jurisdictions where lawyers exercise their strikes in open court, lawyers may be deterred from using their peremptories, out of the fear that if they are unable to justify the strike the court will seat a juror who knows that the striking party thought him unfit. Because I believe the peremptory remains an important litigator's tool and a fundamental part of the process of selecting impartial juries, our increasing limitation of it gives me pause.

Nor is the value of the peremptory challenge to the litigant diminished when the peremptory is exercised in a gender-based manner. We know that like race, gender matters. A plethora of studies make clear that in rape cases, for example, female jurors are somewhat more likely to vote to convict than male jurors. Moreover, though there have been no similarly definitive studies regarding, for example, sexual harassment, child custody, or spousal or child abuse, one need not be a sexist to share the intuition that in certain cases a person's gender and resulting life experience will be relevant to his or her view of the case.

Today's decision severely limits a litigant's ability to act on this intuition, for the import of our holding is that any correlation between a juror's gender and attitudes is irrelevant as a matter of constitutional law. But to say that gender makes no difference as a matter of law is not to say that gender makes no difference as a matter of fact. . . . In extending Batson to gender we have added an additional burden to the state and federal trial process, taken a step closer to eliminating the peremptory challenge, and diminished the ability of litigants to act on sometimes accurate gender-based assumptions about juror attitudes. . . .

Accordingly, I adhere to my position that the Equal Protection Clause does not limit the exercise of peremptory challenges by private civil litigants and criminal defendants. This case itself presents no state action dilemma, for here the State of Alabama itself filed the paternity suit on behalf of petitioner. But what of the next case? Will we, in the name of fighting gender discrimination, hold that the battered wife—on trial for wounding her abusive husband—is a state actor? Will we preclude her from using her peremptory challenges to ensure that the jury of her peers contains as many women members as possible? I assume we will, but I hope we will not.

Chief Justice Rehnquist, dissenting.

Unlike the Court, I think the State has shown that jury strikes on the basis of gender "substantially further" the State's legitimate interest in achieving a fair and impartial trial through the venerable practice of peremptory challenges. The two sexes differ, both biologically and, to a diminishing extent, in experience. It is not merely "stereotyping" to say that these differences may produce a difference in outlook which is brought to the jury room. Accordingly, use of peremptory challenges on the basis of sex is generally not the sort of derogatory and invidious act which peremptory challenges directed at black jurors may be.

Justice Scalia, with whom the Chief Justice and Justice Thomas join, dissenting.

The core of the Court's reasoning is that peremptory challenges on the basis of any group characteristic subject to heightened scrutiny are inconsistent with the guarantee of the Equal Protection Clause. That conclusion can be reached only by focusing unrealistically upon individual exercises of the peremptory challenge, and ignoring the totality of the practice. Since all groups are subject to the peremptory challenge (and will be made the object of it, depending upon the nature of the particular case) it is hard to see how any group is denied equal protection. That explains why peremptory challenges coexisted with the Equal Protection Clause for 120 years. This case is a perfect example of how the system as a whole is even-handed. While the only claim before the Court is petitioner's complaint that the prosecutor struck male jurors, for every man struck by the government, petitioner's own lawyer struck a woman. To say that men were singled out for discriminatory treatment in this process is preposterous.

The situation would be different if both sides systematically struck individuals of one group, so that the strikes evinced group-based animus and served as a proxy for segregated venire lists. The pattern here, however, displays not a systemic sex-based animus but each side's desire to get a jury favorably disposed to its case. That is why the Court's characterization of respondent's argument as "reminiscent of the arguments advanced to justify the total exclusion of women from juries" is patently false. Women were categorically excluded from juries because of doubt that they were competent; women are stricken from juries by peremptory challenge because of doubt that they were well disposed to the striking party's case. . . .

Even if the line of our later cases guaranteed by today's decision limits the theoretically boundless Batson principle to race, sex, and perhaps other classifications subject to heightened scrutiny (which presumably would include religious belief), much damage has been done. It has been done, first and foremost, to the peremptory challenge system, which loses its whole character when (in order to defend against "impermissible stereotyping" claims) "reasons" for strikes must be given. And make no mistake about it: there really is no substitute for the peremptory. Voir dire (though it can be expected to expand as a consequence of today's decision) cannot fill the gap. The biases that go along with group characteristics tend to be biases that the juror himself does not perceive, so that it is no use asking about them. It is fruitless to inquire of a male juror whether he harbors any subliminal prejudice in favor of unwed fathers. . . .

(*Continued*)

Boykin v. *Alabama*
395 U.S. 238 (1969)

MR. JUSTICE DOUGLAS delivered the opinion of the Court.

In the spring of 1966, within the period of a fortnight, a series of armed robberies occurred in Mobile, Alabama. The victims, in each case, were local shopkeepers open at night who were forced by a gunman to hand over money. While robbing one grocery store, the assailant fired his gun once, sending a bullet through a door into the ceiling. A few days earlier in a drugstore, the robber had allowed his gun to discharge in such a way that the bullet, on ricochet from the floor, struck a customer in the leg. Shortly thereafter, a local grand jury returned five indictments against petitioner, a 27-year-old Negro, for common-law robbery—an offense punishable in Alabama by death.

Before the matter came to trial, the court determined that petitioner was indigent and appointed counsel to represent him. Three days later, at his arraignment, petitioner pleaded guilty to all five indictments. So far as the record shows, the judge asked no questions of petitioner concerning his plea, and petitioner did not address the court.

Justice William O. Douglas was appointed to the Supreme Court by President Franklin Roosevelt and served from 1939 to 1975. (*Source:* Harris & Ewing. Collection of the Supreme Court of the United States.)

Trial strategy may of course make a plea of guilty seem the desirable course. But the record is wholly silent on that point and throws no light on it.

Alabama provides that when a defendant pleads guilty, "the court must cause the punishment to be determined by a jury" (except where it is required to be fixed by the court) and may "cause witnesses to be examined, to ascertain the character of the offense." Ala. Code, Tit. 15, 277 (1958). In the present case, a trial of that dimension was held with the prosecution presenting its case largely through eyewitness testimony. Although counsel for petitioner engaged in cursory cross-examination, petitioner neither testified himself nor presented testimony concerning his character and background. There was nothing to indicate that he had a prior criminal record.

In instructing the jury, the judge stressed that petitioner had pleaded guilty in five cases of robbery, defined as "the felonious taking of money . . . from another against his will . . . by violence or by putting him in fear . . . [carrying] from ten years minimum in the penitentiary to the supreme penalty of death by electrocution." The jury, upon deliberation, found petitioner guilty and sentenced him severally to die on each of the five indictments.

Taking an automatic appeal to the Alabama Supreme Court, petitioner argued that a sentence of death for common-law robbery was cruel and unusual punishment within the meaning of the Federal Constitution, a suggestion which that court unanimously rejected, 281 Ala. 659, 207 So.2d 412. On their own motion, however, four of the seven justices discussed the constitutionality of the process by which the trial judge had accepted petitioner's guilty plea. From the order affirming the trial court, three justices dissented on the ground that the record was inadequate to show that petitioner had intelligently and knowingly pleaded guilty. The fourth member concurred separately, conceding that "a trial judge should not accept a guilty plea unless he has determined that such a plea was voluntarily and knowingly entered by the defendant," but refusing "[f]or aught appearing" "to presume that the trial judge failed to do his duty," 281 Ala., at 662, 663, 207 So.2d, at 414, 415. We granted certiorari.

Respondent does not suggest that we lack jurisdiction to review the voluntary character of petitioner's guilty plea because he failed to raise that federal question below and the state court failed to pass upon it. But the question was raised on oral argument and we conclude that it is properly presented. The very Alabama statute

(Ala. Code, Tit. 15, 382 [10] [1958]) that provides automatic appeal in capital cases also requires the reviewing court to comb the record for "any error prejudicial to the appellant, even though not called to our attention in brief of counsel." *Lee* v. *State,* 265 Ala. 623, 630, 93 So.2d 757, 763. The automatic appeal statute "is the only provision under the Plain Error doctrine of which we are aware in Alabama criminal appellate review." *Douglas* v. *State,* 42 Ala. App. 314, 331, n. 6, 163 So.2d 477, 494, n. 6. In the words of the Alabama Supreme Court: "Perhaps it is well to note that in reviewing a death case under the automatic appeal statute, . . . we may consider any testimony that was seriously prejudicial to the rights of the appellant and may reverse thereon, even though no lawful objection or exception was made thereto." [Citations omitted.] Our review is not limited to the matters brought to our attention in brief of counsel. *Duncan* v. *State,* 278 Ala. 145, 157, 176 So.2d 840, 851.

It was [an] error, plain on the face of the record, for the trial judge to accept petitioner's guilty plea without an affirmative showing that it was intelligent and voluntary. That error, under Alabama procedure, was properly before the court below and considered explicitly by a majority of the justices and is properly before us on review.

A plea of guilty is more than a confession which admits that the accused did various acts; it is itself a conviction; nothing remains but to give judgment and determine punishment. See *Kercheval* v. *United States,* 274 U.S. 220, 223. Admissibility of a confession must be based on a "reliable determination on the voluntariness issue which satisfies the constitutional rights of the defendant." *Jackson* v. *Denno,* 378 U.S. 368, 387. The requirement that the prosecution spread on the record the prerequisites of a valid waiver is no constitutional innovation. In *Carnley* v. *Cochran,* 369 U.S. 506, 516, we dealt with a problem of waiver of the right to counsel, a Sixth Amendment right. We held: "Presuming waiver from a silent record is impermissible. The record must show, or there must be an allegation and evidence which show, that an accused was offered counsel but intelligently and understandingly rejected the offer. Anything less is not waiver."

We think that the same standard must be applied to determine whether a guilty plea is voluntarily made. For, as we have said, a plea of guilty is more than an admission of conduct; it is a conviction. Ignorance, incomprehension, coercion, terror, inducements, subtle or blatant threats might be a perfect cover-up of unconstitutionality. The question of an effective waiver of a federal constitutional right in a proceeding is of course governed by federal standards. *Douglas* v. *Alabama,* 380 U.S. 415, 422.

Several federal constitutional rights are involved in a waiver that takes place when a plea of guilty is entered in a state criminal trial. First is the privilege against compulsory self-incrimination guaranteed by the Fifth Amendment and applicable to the States by reason of the Fourteenth [Amendment]. *Malloy* v. *Hogan,* 378 U.S. 1. Second is the right to trial by jury. *Duncan* v. *Louisiana,* 391 U.S. 145. Third is the right to confront one's accusers. *Pointer* v. *Texas,* 380 U.S. 400. We cannot presume a waiver of these three important federal rights from a silent record.

What is at stake for an accused facing death or imprisonment demands the utmost solicitude of which courts are capable in canvassing the matter with the accused to make sure he has a full understanding of what the plea connotes and of its consequence. When the judge discharges that function, he leaves a record adequate for any review that may be later sought (*Garner* v. *Louisiana,* 368 U.S. 157, 173; *Specht* v. *Patterson,* 386 U.S. 605, 610), and forestalls the spin-off of collateral proceedings that seek to probe murky memories.

The three dissenting justices in the Alabama Supreme Court stated the law accurately when they concluded that there was reversible error "because the record does not disclose that the defendant voluntarily and understandingly entered his pleas of guilty," 281 Ala., at 663, 207 So.2d, at 415.

Reversed.

MR. JUSTICE HARLAN, whom MR. JUSTICE BLACK joins, dissenting. [Omitted]

SUMMARY

- A bench or court trial is a trial by judge alone.
- The Sixth Amendment right to a jury trial applies to all federal criminal proceedings.
- States may deny an accused a jury trial in cases involving petty offenses.

- Petty offenses are defined by the Supreme Court as offenses for which the maximum period of confinement is six months and a fine of not more than $500.
- The defendant may not demand a bench or court trial.
- In noncapital cases, a defendant may be tried by a jury of fewer than twelve persons, depending on state laws.
- If there are fewer than twelve jurors, in most states the verdict must be unanimous.
- A public trial is a trial in which the public has a right to attend.
- The public has a limited right to attend criminal trials.
- The First Amendment gives the press a limited right to attend a criminal trial.
- A trial judge may issue a gag order that directs the parties to the trial not to talk to the press or otherwise release information that would jeopardize a fair trial.

REVIEW QUESTIONS

1. What amendment of the U.S. Constitution embodies the right to trial by jury?
2. List three advantages to an accused of a trial by jury over a court trial.
3. Why would an accused waive a trial by jury?
4. What reasons has the U.S. Supreme Court set forth in prohibiting the accused from demanding and receiving a court trial?
5. Some jurisdictions hold that an accused may be denied a jury trial on petty offenses. What criteria has the U.S. Supreme Court set forth in determining what qualifies as a petty offense?
6. What U.S. Supreme Court decision upheld that a trial by a jury comprising fewer than twelve persons was not a denial of the Due Process Clause of the Fourteenth Amendment?
7. What is considered a public trial?
8. Why is the accused guaranteed a public trial?
9. Must a demand by an accused for a private trial be granted?
10. Why did the *Richmond* case base the public right to access to criminal trials on the First Amendment of the U.S. Constitution instead of the Sixth Amendment?
11. In what way may a fair trial and the freedom of the press be in conflict?
12. What is meant by a gag order, and why may one be placed in effect?

LOCAL PROCEDURE

1. May a defendant waive a jury trial in your state? If so, are there any restrictions on the type of offense for which the jury trial may be waived?
2. If a jury trial may be waived, who must give consent to the waiver?
3. Can a jury comprise fewer than twelve persons in your state?
4. May a petty offense charge be tried without a jury in your state?

ENDNOTES

1. 281 U.S. 276.
2. 391 U.S. 145 (1968).
3. 380 U.S. 24 (1965).
4. 300 U.S. 617 (1937).

5. See *Duncan* v. *Louisiana,* 391 U.S. 145 (1968); *Cheff* v. *Schnackenberg,* 384 U.S. 373 (1966); and *Frank* v. *United States,* 395 U.S. 147 (1969).
6. 399 U.S. 78 (1970).
7. 55 L.Ed. 2d. 234 (1978).
8. 381 U.S. 532 (1965).
9. 448 U.S. 555 (1980).
10. 457 U.S. 596 (1982).
11. 443 U.S. 368 (1979).
12. 384 U.S. 333 (1966).
13. 427 U.S. 539 (1976).
14. 373 U.S. 723 (1963).

> Once I decide to take a case, I have only one agenda: I want to win. I will try, by every fair and legal means, to get my client off—without regards to the consequences.
>
> —Alan Dershowitz, *The Best Defense*, 1983

Confrontation and Assistance of Counsel

8

Chapter Outline

Key Words

Appointed counsel
Bench warrant
Conviction in absentia

Effective counsel
Farce or sham test
Indigent defendant
Public defender

Retained counsel
Right of confrontation
Self-representation
Standby counsel

Learning Objectives

After completing this chapter, you should be able to:

1. Describe the defendant's right to be present at trial.
2. Explain the defendant's right to counsel.
3. Discuss when the state has an obligation to provide defendant with a counsel.
4. List the duties of a defense counsel.
5. Distinguish between appointed counsel and retained counsel.
6. Explain the right of self-representation.
7. Discuss the functions of a standby counsel.
8. Explain the test for effective assistance of counsel.

PRESENCE OF THE DEFENDANT AT A TRIAL

In some countries, an accused person may be tried and convicted of a crime without being present and without knowing that a trial has taken place. This procedure is referred to as **conviction in absentia**. To prevent such action from taking place in the United States, the Sixth Amendment of the U.S. Constitution, as well as the laws of all the states, includes a provision entitling an accused to be confronted with the witnesses for the prosecution. This provision has a dual purpose. It guarantees that witnesses against a defendant must appear in person in court to present their facts, and it provides a defendant with the right to be present during every phase of trial proceedings.

For many years, the interpretation of the right of an accused to be present during a trial was so rigid that, if a defendant was not present, the trial had to be halted until he or she was in attendance. Knowing the court's rigid interpretation of this right, defendants occasionally took advantage of it by being so disruptive that the trial could not continue with their presence or by failing to appear in court while out on bail, thus preventing the trial from taking place. Many states included provisions in their statutes stating that in felony cases, the defendant had to be present during all phases of the trial. But as time passed, some courts relaxed the rule requiring the defendant's presence when he or she voluntarily was absent.

When representing a defendant who has been in confinement for an extended period of time, a defense counsel may submit a motion that the defendant not be tried in

Law in Practice

Motion Not to Be Tried in Jail Clothes or Restraints

To the Honorable judge of Said Court:

NOW COMES the Defendant in the above-entitled and numbered cause by and through his attorney of record and files this Motion not to be tried before the Jury in jail clothes and restraints and in support thereof would show the following:

I.

On Defendant's being placed in confinement, his regular civilian type clothing was taken from him and he has been compelled to be dressed in identifiable prison clothing. When Defendant is brought from the Prison to Court, he will be handcuffed and shackled or be required to wear other such restraints.

II.

Compelling the Defendant to be tried before a jury in such distinctive, identifiable attire and restraints will affect the jury's judgment and violates the Defendant's constitutional right of presumption of innocence.

WHEREFORE, PREMISES CONSIDERED, Defendant prays that the Court order the Sheriff or Warden not to bring the Defendant to the courtroom for the purpose of trial or into the presence of any member of the jury panel attired in a prison uniform or in restraints of any kind.

Respectfully submitted,
STATE COUNSEL FOR OFFENDERS

_____
Attorney for Defendant

jail or prison clothing or restraints (handcuffs, chains, etc.). The U.S. Supreme Court in *Estelle* v. *Williams,* 425 U.S. 501 (1976), stated that with few exceptions, an accused should not be compelled to go to trial in prison or jail clothing and/or with restraints because of the possible impairment of his or her presumption of innocence, which is basic to the adversary system.

Disruption of the Trial

A separate issue is raised when the defendant is present and demands to remain present but becomes so disruptive that the trial cannot take place. This question was answered in the case of *Illinois* v. *Allen,*[1] in which the U.S. Supreme Court held that a defendant had waived his right to be present at his trial by his own disruptive action.

The facts of the *Allen* case state that Allen was convicted of armed robbery by an Illinois jury and was sentenced to serve ten to thirty years in the Illinois State Penitentiary. During the trial, Allen insisted upon acting as his own attorney, and when the judge appointed an attorney for him, Allen began to argue with the judge in an abusive and disrespectful manner. The judge ordered Allen to remain silent and to let his attorney speak for him. Despite this admonition, the defendant continued to talk and argue with the judge, proclaiming that the appointed attorney was not going to act for him. Allen also informed the judge that "when I go out for lunchtime, you're going to be a corpse here." At the same time, Allen tore up his attorney's file and threw the pieces on the floor. The judge informed Allen that he would be removed from the courtroom if another disruption occurred. This warning had no effect upon Allen, and the judge had him removed from the courtroom. The jury was selected in his absence. Later in the day, Allen was permitted to return to the courtroom but became disruptive again, forcing the judge to remove him a second time. Allen remained out of the courtroom during most of the prosecution's presentation of the case but, on promising that he would conduct himself properly, was permitted to return and remain in the courtroom during the presentation by his attorney.

The *Allen* conviction was upheld by the Illinois appellate courts but was reversed by the U.S. District Court of Appeals. This court held that Allen's removal from the courtroom was a denial of his guarantee of confrontation as provided by the Sixth Amendment to the U.S. Constitution. The court stated that Allen could have been bound and gagged to prevent him from being disruptive and that the judge erred in removing Allen from the courtroom.

The case was then taken to the U.S. Supreme Court to determine whether Allen was denied due process of law because his Sixth Amendment guarantee of confrontation had been violated. The Supreme Court upheld the conviction and stated that the Sixth Amendment guarantee of confrontation could be "lost by consent or at times even by misconduct." The Court further stated the following:

> Although mindful that courts must indulge every reasonable presumption against the loss of constitutional rights . . . we explicitly hold today that a defendant can lose his right to be present at trial if, after he had been warned by the judge that he will be removed if he continues his disruptive behavior, he nevertheless insists on conducting himself in a manner so disorderly, disruptive, and disrespectful of the court that his trial cannot be carried on with him in the courtroom. Once lost, the right to be present can, of course, be reclaimed as soon as the defendant is willing to conduct himself consistently with the decorum and respect inherent in the concept of courts and judicial proceedings.

A lawyer questions a woman on the witness stand as the judge listens. (*Source:* John Neubauer/PhotoEdit Inc.)

It is essential to the proper administration of criminal justice that dignity, order, and decorum be the hallmarks of all court proceedings in our country. The flagrant disregard in the courtroom of elementary standards of proper conduct should not and cannot be tolerated. We believe trial judges confronted with disruptive, contumacious, stubbornly defiant defendants must be given sufficient discretion to meet the circumstances of each case. No one formula for maintaining the appropriate courtroom atmosphere will be best in all situations. We think there are at least three constitutionally permissible ways for a trial judge to handle an obstreperous defendant like Allen: (1) bind and gag him, thereby keeping him present; (2) cite him for contempt; (3) take him out of the courtroom until he promises to conduct himself properly.

Trying a defendant for a crime while he sits bound and gagged before the judge and jury would to an extent comply with that part of the Sixth Amendment's purposes that accords the defendant an opportunity to confront the witnesses at the trial. But even to contemplate such a technique, much less see it, arouses a feeling that no person should be tried while shackled and gagged except as a last resort. Not only is it possible that the sight of shackles and gags might have a significant effect on the jury's feelings about the defendant, but the use of this technique is itself something of an affront to the very dignity and decorum of judicial proceedings that the judge is seeking to uphold. . . . However, in some situations which we need not attempt to foresee, binding and gagging might possibly be the fairest and most reasonable way to handle a defendant who acts as Allen did here.

In citing the unruly defendant for contempt of court, the Court in the *Allen* case stated:

It is true that citing or threatening to cite a contumacious defendant for criminal contempt might in itself be sufficient to make a defendant stop interrupting a trial. If so, the problem would be solved easily, and the defendant could remain in the courtroom. Of course, if the defendant is determined to prevent any trial, then a court in attempting to try the defendant for contempt is still confronted with the identical dilemma that the Illinois court faced in this case. Any criminal contempt has obvious limitations as a sanction when the defendant is charged with a crime so serious that a very severe sentence such as death or life imprisonment is likely to be imposed. In such a case the defendant might not be affected by a mere contempt sentence when he ultimately faces a far more serious sanction. Nevertheless, the contempt remedy should be borne in mind by a judge in the circumstances of this case.

Another aspect of the contempt remedy is the judge's power, when exercised consistently with state and federal law, to imprison an unruly defendant such as Allen for civil contempt and discontinue the trial until such time as the defendant promises to behave himself. This procedure is consistent with the defendant's right to be present at trial, and yet it avoids the serious shortcomings of the use of shackles and gags. It must be recognized, however, that a defendant might conceivably, as a matter of calculated strategy, elect to spend a prolonged period in confinement for contempt in the hope that adverse witnesses might be unavailable after a lapse of time. A court must guard against allowing a defendant to profit from his own wrong in this way.

The trial court in this case decided under the circumstances to remove the defendant from the courtroom and to continue his trial in his absence until and unless he promised to conduct himself in a manner befitting an American courtroom. As we said earlier, we find nothing unconstitutional about this procedure. Allen's behavior was clearly of such an extreme and aggravated nature as to justify either his removal from the courtroom or his total physical restraint. Prior to his removal he was repeatedly warned by the trial judge that he would be removed from the courtroom if he persisted in his unruly conduct, and, as Judge Hastings observed in his dissenting opinion, the record demonstrates that Allen would not have been at all dissuaded by the trial judge's use of his criminal contempt powers. Allen was constantly informed that he could return to the trial when he would agree to conduct himself in an orderly manner. Under these circumstances we hold that Allen lost his right guaranteed by the Sixth and Fourteenth Amendments to be present throughout his trial.

It is not pleasant to hold that the respondent Allen was properly banished from the court for a part of his own trial. But our courts, palladiums of liberty as they are, cannot be treated disrespectfully with impunity. Nor can the accused be permitted by his disruptive conduct indefinitely to avoid being tried on the charges brought against him. It would degrade our country and our judicial system to permit our courts to be bullied, insulted, and humiliated and their orderly progress thwarted and obstructed by defendants brought before them charged with crimes.

Voluntary Absence from Trial

The *Allen* decision definitely established that a trial could take place in the absence of a defendant when he or she was so disruptive that his or her removal from the courtroom became necessary. This decision also provided that a defendant who voluntarily absented himself or herself waived all right to be present. Even before the *Allen* decision, the courts were beginning to accept that if a defendant was voluntarily absent from his or her trial, the trial could proceed in his or her absence. This viewpoint was expressed in the case of *Cureton* v. *United States.*[2] The Court concluded that "if a defendant at liberty remains away during his trial the court may proceed provided it is clearly established that his absence is voluntary. He must be aware of the processes taking place, of his right and of his obligation to be present, and he must have no sound reason for remaining away." This viewpoint is sometimes referred to as the *Cureton* test. In other words, the defendant must have "knowingly and voluntarily absented himself."

As a result of the *Allen* decision and the viewpoint expressed in the *Cureton* case, many states have passed provisions similar to that of the *Federal Rules of Criminal Procedure,* which provides that "in prosecutions for offenses, not punishable by death, the defendant's voluntary absence after the trial has been commenced in his presence shall not prevent continuing the trial to and including the return of the verdict." The federal rule, as well as the provisions of many states, holds that the trial may continue in the absence of the defendant if the trial was commenced in his or her presence. Under these circumstances, the trial cannot commence unless the defendant is present. After the trial date is set, a defendant out on bail could keep the trial from taking place merely by not showing up for the trial. Of course, the judge could issue a **bench warrant** for the defendant's arrest, but it could take time to locate the defendant, thus delaying the trial. To overcome this problem, several states have provisions stating that a trial may commence when the defendant, knowing that the case is set for trial, voluntarily fails to appear on that date.

In those states requiring a trial to begin in the defendant's presence, for it to continue if the accused is voluntarily absent, the court must establish that the trial actually began while the defendant was present. Remember that a jury trial begins once the jury is sworn, and a court trial begins when the first witness is sworn. In one case, the defendant was present during the selection of eleven jurors before court was adjourned for the day. The following day the defendant failed to appear for the trial. The judge concluded that the defendant had voluntarily absented himself. Over the objections of the defense attorney, the judge permitted a twelfth juror to be selected, and the trial continued to the verdict stage in the absence of the defendant. The defendant was convicted, and he appealed his conviction on the grounds that he had been denied due process. The conviction was reversed since the law of the particular state provided that a trial could continue only if it commenced in the presence of the defendant. Since the jury had not been selected and sworn in the presence of the defendant, the trial had not begun.

Even in those states that hold that a trial may continue only if it began in the presence of the defendant, this rule usually refers to felony charges. In a misdemeanor case, most states provide that if a defendant voluntarily fails to appear at the time the case is set for trial or is voluntarily absent during the course of the trial, the judge may proceed when the defendant has full knowledge that the trial was to be held. In most jurisdictions, whether the charge is a felony or misdemeanor, it is not necessary to advise the defendant that this action will take place in the event of voluntary absence.

The problem created by these rules is establishing that the defendant knowingly and voluntarily absented himself or herself from the trial. Establishing this could take time, and the judge would have to delay the progress of the trial until this could be determined. The delay might be only a few hours, but it could take several days. If the court cannot determine satisfactorily whether the defendant was absent knowingly and voluntarily, the judge must declare a mistrial or delay the present trial until the defendant can be located and arrested on a bench warrant. If it cannot be determined that the defendant was absent without cause and if a conviction results, a new trial must be granted unless a satisfactory reason for absence is given. Thus, the courts are cautious in continuing a trial in the absence of a defendant.

The Sixth Amendment provision that "an accused shall enjoy the right . . . to be confronted with the witnesses against him" has been interpreted to mean not only the right to be present during the trial against him or her but also the right of a face-to-face confrontation with the witnesses as held by the U.S. Supreme Court in the case of *Coy* v. *Iowa.*[3] The facts of the case indicate that the accused was charged with the sexual assault of two thirteen-year-old girls. In accordance with an Iowa state statute, a screen was placed between the accused and the girls during their testimony. The purpose of the statute was to protect young victims of sexual assault from the "fear and trauma of testifying in front of the accused" by placing a screen between the victim and the accused. The screen in this case was placed in such a way that the girls could be observed by the judge and the jury during their testimony. They could also be dimly seen by the accused, but the girls could not see the accused.

The accused was convicted of the assault, and he appealed his conviction to the U.S. Supreme Court on the grounds that his Sixth Amendment **right of confrontation** had been violated, since he had not been allowed the right to a face-to-face confrontation with the witnesses against him. The Court agreed with this contention, stating:

> There is something deep in human nature that regards face-to-face confrontation between accused and accuser as essential to a fair trial in a criminal prosecution. . . . It is more difficult to tell a lie about a person to his face than behind his back. . . . The screen issue [in this case] was specifically designed to enable the witnesses to avoid viewing the appellant [the accused] as they gave their testimony. . . . It is difficult to imagine a more obvious or damaging violation of the defendant's right to a face-to-face encounter.
>
> Thus, the conviction was reversed.

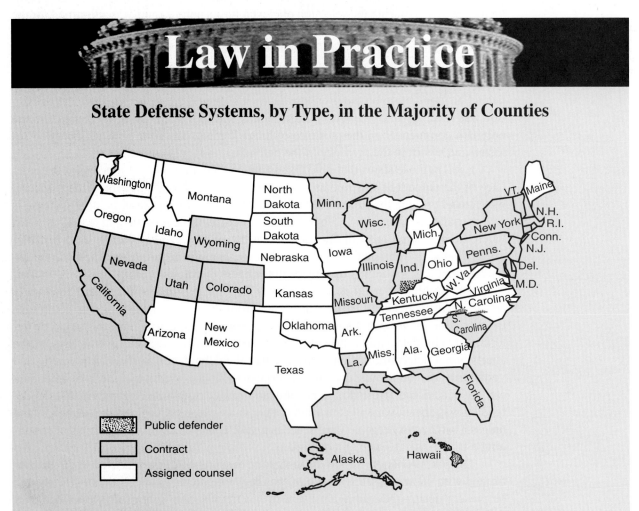

Law in Practice

State Defense Systems, by Type, in the Majority of Counties

Public defender

Contract

Assigned counsel

Source: Bureau of Justice Statistics, *Criminal Defense for the Poor, 1986* (Washington, D.C., U.S. Department of Justice, 1988).

Defense attorney Johnnie Cochran, Jr., puts on a pair of gloves during the O.J. Simpson trial on September 27, 1995, at the Los Angeles Criminal Courts Building. Many court observers believe that the high quality of the defense by the defense counsel was the primary reason that Simpson was acquitted on the murder charges. (*Source:* Vince Bucci/AP Wide World Photos.)

RIGHT TO COUNSEL

Under the common law of England, a person on trial for a felony was not entitled to the assistance of counsel. If the charge was a misdemeanor, however, the defendant had the right of counsel. Various reasons have been given for this paradoxical situation. In felony cases, it was thought that the judge would be sympathetic to the defendant because if the defendant were convicted, he would be subjected to severe punishment and might have his property confiscated by the king. In misdemeanor cases, the judge would have less interest in protecting the accused. Another theory is that because the property of a felon could be confiscated, the king knew that the chances for the defendant's conviction would be greater if the assistance of counsel was not allowed. Thus, the king did not permit the assistance of counsel in a felony trial.

The denial of the assistance of counsel in felony cases was rejected by the colonists, and in most of the colonies the right of counsel became a part of their due process of law. The right to counsel had become such an accepted practice that when the Bill of Rights was formulated, the following provision was included in the Sixth Amendment of the U.S. Constitution: "In all criminal prosecutions, the accused shall . . . have the assistance of counsel for his defense." This guarantee pertained only to federal prosecutions, but the states included similar provisions in their constitutions or statutes upon admittance to the Union. These provisions are usually worded similarly to that of the following: "In criminal prosecutions the accused shall have the right to appear and defend, and in person and with counsel."

For many generations, this right to the assistance of counsel was interpreted as meaning that if an accused appeared in court with an attorney, the accused could not be denied the assistance of the attorney. If, however, defendants were unable to afford an attorney to assist in their defense, it was their misfortune. Little thought was given to providing counsel for the accused. Nor was assistance of counsel considered essential for the accused prior to the time of the trial. But as time passed, new interpretations were placed upon the Sixth Amendment guarantee of counsel, particularly by the U.S. Supreme Court.

Providing the Accused with Counsel

One of the earliest decisions in which the U.S. Supreme Court held that in certain instances an accused must be provided with an attorney, if he or she cannot afford one, was the case of *Powell* v. *Alabama*.[4] The facts of this case indicate that ignorant and friendless black youths, strangers in the community without means to obtain counsel, were hurried to trial in an Alabama state court for a capital offense without appointment of counsel. The youths were convicted, and their case was taken to the U.S. Supreme Court on the grounds that the defendants had been denied due process of law. The Court agreed that the defendants had been denied due process of law in that they had not been provided with counsel to assist them in their defense. The Court stated:

> All that is necessary now to decide, as we do decide, is that in a capital case, where the defendant is unable to employ counsel, and is incapable adequately of making his own defense because of ignorance, feeblemindedness, illiteracy, or the like, it is the duty of the court, whether requested or not, to assign counsel for him as a necessary requisite of due process of law. . . .

In the *Powell* case, the charge was a capital offense, and the Court held that in capital offenses, the judge must appoint an attorney when the accused is unable to obtain counsel. This decision remained in effect until the case of *Gideon* v. *Wainwright*,[5] when the U.S. Supreme Court held that counsel must be provided for any defendant brought to trial irrespective of the charge. The facts of the *Gideon* case indicate that Gideon (the petitioner) was charged in a Florida state court with breaking into and entering a poolroom with intent to commit a misdemeanor. This offense is a felony under Florida law. Appearing in court without funds and without a lawyer, the petitioner asked the court to appoint counsel, but the judge informed him that under the laws of the state of Florida, the only time that the court could appoint counsel to represent a defendant is when that person is charged with a capital offense. Gideon attempted to conduct his own defense by making an opening statement, cross-examining prosecution witnesses, and presenting witnesses in his own behalf. Gideon was convicted and sentenced to five years in the state prison. The case was taken to the U.S. Supreme Court on the grounds that he had been denied due process of law in that his Sixth Amendment guarantee to the assistance of counsel had been denied. The Court agreed with this contention and reversed the conviction. The Court, in its decision, stated that

> reason and reflection require us to recognize that in our adversary system of criminal justice, any person hauled into court, who is too poor to hire a lawyer, cannot be assured a fair trial unless counsel is provided for him. This seems to us to be an obvious truth. Governments, both state and federal, quite properly spend vast sums of money to establish machinery to try defendants accused of crime. Lawyers to prosecute are everywhere deemed essential to protect the public's interest in an orderly society. Similarly, there are few defendants charged with crime, few indeed, who fail to hire the best lawyers they

Ex-convict and amateur legal scholar Clarence Gideon pores over a law book in a law library. His appeal to the U.S. Supreme Court in an important decision led the Court to rule that an indigent defendant charged with a felony in a state criminal court has the right to a court- or state-appointed attorney. (*Source:* Corbis/Bettmann.)

can get to prepare and present their defenses. That government hires lawyers to prosecute and defendants who have the money hire lawyers to defend are the strongest indications of the widespread belief that lawyers in criminal courts are necessities, not luxuries. The right of one charged with crime to counsel may not be deemed fundamental and essential to fair trials in some countries, but it is in ours. From the very beginning, our state and national constitutions and laws have laid great emphasis on procedural and substantive safeguards designed to assure fair trials before impartial tribunals in which every defendant stands equal before the law. This noble ideal cannot be realized if the poor man charged with crime has to face his accusers without a lawyer to assist him. A defendant's need for a lawyer is nowhere better stated that in the moving words of Mr. Justice Sutherland in *Powell* v. *Alabama:* "The right to be heard would be, in many cases, of little avail if it did not comprehend the right to be heard by counsel. Even the intelligent and educated layman has small and sometimes no skill in the science of law. If charged with crime, he is incapable, generally, of determining for himself whether the indictment is good or bad. He is unfamiliar with the rules of evidence. Left without the aid of counsel he may be put on trial without a proper charge, and convicted upon incompetent evidence, or evidence irrelevant to the issue or otherwise inadmissible. He lacks both the skill and knowledge adequately to prepare his defense, even though he has a perfect one. He requires the guiding hand of counsel at every step in the proceedings against him. Without it, though he be not guilty, he faces the danger of conviction because he does not know how to establish his innocence."

Right to Counsel in Petty Cases

Although the Court in the *Gideon* case held that any person haled into court who is too poor to hire a lawyer cannot be assured a fair trial unless counsel is provided for him or her, the charge in this case was a felony. Thus, there remained the question of whether counsel must be appointed for one brought to trial on a petty charge. This doubt was resolved in the case of *Argersinger* v. *Hamlin*,[6] in which the U.S. Supreme Court held that no person may be imprisoned for any offense, petty or otherwise, unless he or she is represented by counsel. The facts of the case show that Argersinger was charged in Florida with carrying a concealed weapon, an offense punishable by imprisonment for up to six months. Argersinger was tried before a judge and was not represented by counsel, since he could not afford one, and the state contended that since the charge was a petty one, counsel did not have to be appointed for the defendant. Argersinger was convicted and

Major U.S. Supreme Court Cases Granting the Right to Counsel

Case	Stage and Ruling
Moore v. *Michigan,* 355 U.S. 155 (1957)	The defendant has the right to counsel when submitting a guilty plea to the court.
Brady v. *United States,* 397 U.S. 742 (1970)	Counsel is required during the plea bargaining process.
Powell v. *Alabama,* 287 U.S. 45 (1932)	Defendants have the right to counsel at their trial in a state capital case.
Hamilton v. *Alabama,* 368 U.S. 52 (1961)	The arraignment is a critical stage in the criminal process, so denial of the right to counsel is a violation of due process of law.
Coleman v. *Alabama,* 399 U.S. 1 (1970)	The preliminary hearing is a critical stage in a criminal prosecution requiring the state to provide the indigent defendant with counsel.
United States v. *Wade,* 388 U.S. 218 (1967)	A defendant in a pretrial, postindictment lineup for identification purposes has the right to assistance of counsel.
Gideon v. *Wainwright,* 372 U.S. 335 (1963)	An indigent defendant charged in a state court with a noncapital felony has the right to the assistance of free counsel at trial under the Due Process Clause of the Fourteenth Amendment.
Argersinger v. *Hamlin,* 407 U.S. 25 (1972)	A defendant has the right to counsel at trial whenever he or she may be imprisoned, even for one day, for any offense, whether classified as a misdemeanor or a felony.
Faretta v. *California,* 422 U.S. 806 (1975)	The defendant has a constitutional right to defend herself or himself if her or his waiver of the right to counsel is knowing and intelligent.
Escobedo v. *Illinois,* 378 U.S. 478 (1964)	The defendant has the right to counsel during the course of any police interrogation.
Miranda v. *Arizona,* 384 U.S. 436 (1966)	Procedural safeguards, including the right to counsel, must be followed at custodial interrogation to secure the privilege against self-incrimination.
Massiah v. *United States,* 377 U.S. 201 (1964)	The defendant has the right to counsel during postindictment interrogation.
In re Gault, 387 U.S. 1 (1967)	Procedural due process, including the right to counsel, applies to juvenile delinquency adjudication that may lead to a child's commitment to a state institution.
Townsend v. *Burke,* 334 U.S. 736 (1948)	A convicted offender has a right to counsel at the time of sentencing.
Douglas v. *California,* 372 U.S. 353 (1963)	An indigent defendant granted a first appeal from a criminal conviction has the right to be represented by counsel on appeal.
Mempa v. *Rhay,* 389 U.S. 128 (1967)	A convicted offender has the right to assistance of counsel at probation revocation hearings where the sentence has been deferred.
Morrissey v. *Brewer,* 408 U.S. 471 (1972)	The defendant has the right to counsel in the court's discretion at parole revocation hearings.
Gagnon v. *Scarpelli,* 411 U.S. 778 (1973)	The defendant has a right to counsel in the court's discretion at probation revocation hearings.

sentenced to jail for ninety days. The conviction was upheld by the Florida Supreme Court, and the case was taken to the U.S. Supreme Court on the grounds that the defendant had been denied the right to counsel. The Court stated the following:

> . . . The Sixth Amendment, which in enumerated situations has been made applicable to the States by reason of the Fourteenth Amendment . . . provides specified standards for all criminal prosecutions.
>
> One is the requirement of a public trial . . . the right to a public trial was applicable to a state proceeding even though only a 60-day sentence was involved.
>
> Another guarantee is the right to be informed of the nature and cause of the accusation. Still another, the right of confrontation. And another, compulsory process for obtaining witnesses in one's favor. We have never limited these rights to felonies nor to lesser but serious offenses. . . .
>
> While there is historical support for limiting the deep commitment to trial by jury to serious criminal cases, there is no such support for a similar limitation on the right to assistance of counsel. . . .
>
> The assistance of counsel is often a requisite to the very existence of a fair trial. . . .
>
> The requirement of counsel may well be necessary for a fair trial even in a petty offense prosecution. We are by no means convinced that legal and constitutional questions involved in a case that actually leads to imprisonment even for a brief period are any less complex than when a person can be sent off for six months or more.
>
> The trial of vagrancy cases is illustrative. While only brief sentences of imprisonment may be imposed, the cases often bristle with thorny constitutional questions.
>
> Beyond the problem of trials and appeals is that of the guilty plea, a problem which looms large in misdemeanor as well as in felony cases. Counsel is needed so that the accused may know precisely what he is doing, so that he is fully aware of the prospect of going to jail or prison, and so that he is treated fairly by the prosecution.
>
> We hold, therefore, that absent a knowing and intelligent waiver, no person may be imprisoned for any offense, whether classified as petty, misdemeanor, or felony, unless he was represented by counsel at his trial.

Waiver of Counsel

Although the Sixth Amendment guarantees the right to counsel, may this constitutional guarantee, like most others, be waived, or is it mandatory that the defendant be represented by counsel? This question was answered in *Adams* v. *United States,*[7] in which the U.S. Supreme Court held that a capable defendant could waive the right to the assistance of counsel. But it must be determined first that the accused is capable of defense without counsel's assistance.

The right of a defendant to represent himself or herself was carried one step further by the U.S. Supreme Court in *Faretta* v. *California,*[8] where the Court held that when a defendant "knowingly and intelligently" waives the right to the assistance of counsel, the defendant has the constitutional right to **self-representation**. The facts reveal that Faretta was charged with grand theft. At the arraignment, the judge appointed a public defender to represent him, but before the trial, Faretta requested that he be permitted to represent himself. In an effort to determine whether Faretta was capable of representing himself, the judge questioned Faretta and learned that he had represented himself in a prior criminal prosecution, that he had a high school education, and that he did not want to be represented by the public defender. After further questioning at a later time, the judge concluded that Faretta had not intelligently waived his right to the assistance of counsel. The judge also ruled that Faretta did not have a constitutional right to self-representation. Faretta was represented by a public defender, and he was convicted and sentenced to prison. He appealed his case to the U.S. Supreme Court, which agreed to hear it to settle the question of whether an accused has a Sixth Amendment right to decline counsel. The Court ruled that there is such a constitutional right. The Court pointed out that in early common law, those accused of serious crimes had to represent themselves and that only later was an accused given the choice of receiving the assistance of counsel. This was the practice at the time that the colonists came to America and at the time that the Sixth Amendment was written. The Court stated that it recognized the advantages of an accused's having the assistance of counsel but was unable to find an instance where a colonial court required an accused to accept an unwanted attorney as his or her representative. The Court felt that when the framers of the Sixth Amendment included the right of an accused to have the assistance of counsel, they were not denying the accused the right of self-representation. The Court stated the following:

> . . . in most criminal prosecutions defendants could better defend with counsel's guidance than by their own unskilled efforts. But where the defendant will not voluntarily accept representation by counsel, the potential advantage of a lawyer's training and experience can be realized, if at all, only imperfectly. To force a lawyer on a defendant can only lead him to believe that the law contrives against him. Moreover, it is not inconceivable that in some rare instances, the defendant might in fact present his case more effectively by conducting his own defense. Personal liberties are not rooted in the law of averages. The right to defend is personal. The defendant, and not his lawyer or the State, will bear the personal consequences of a conviction. It is the defendant, therefore, who must be free personally to decide whether in his particular case counsel is to his advantage. And although he may conduct his own defense ultimately to his own detriment, his choice must be honored out of that respect for the individual which is the lifeblood of the law. When an accused manages his own defense, he relinquishes, as a purely factual matter, many of the traditional benefits associated with the right to counsel. For this reason, in order to represent himself, the accused must "knowingly and intelligently" forego those relinquished benefits. Although a defendant need not himself have the skill and experience of a lawyer in order competently and intelligently to choose self-representation, he should be made aware of the dangers and disadvantages of self-representation, so that the record will establish that "he knows what he is doing and his choice is made with eyes open." Here, weeks before trial, Faretta clearly and unequivocally declared to the trial judge that he wanted to represent himself and did not want counsel. The record affirmatively shows that Faretta was literate, competent, and understanding, and that he was voluntarily exercising his informed free will.

Knowing and Intelligent Waiver   The Court in the *Faretta* case stated that "in order to represent himself the accused must knowingly and intelligently" waive the right to the assistance of counsel. This statement placed a serious burden on trial judges in determining whether a defendant is capable of knowingly and intelligently waiving the right to the assistance of counsel. The problem created by this decision is that if a trial judge concludes that the defendant is capable of self-representation and the defendant is convicted, the defendant may appeal, and the appellate court may hold that the defendant was not capable of making an intelligent waiver of the right to counsel. On the other hand, as in *Faretta*'s case, if the judge concludes that the defendant was incapable of intelligently waiving the right to the assistance of counsel and is convicted, the appellate court may decide that the defendant had been denied the right of self-representation. The dissenting justices in the *Faretta* case pointed out that the majority of justices had created a problem that undoubtedly would cause confusion for trial courts, since no guidelines were set forth for the trial courts to follow in their efforts to determine when an accused was capable of self-representation.

Since the U.S. Supreme Court has held that an accused has the constitutional right of self-representation when the right to the assistance of counsel is knowingly and intelligently waived, a trial court must make a careful evaluation of the accused's ability to make the waiver. When an accused requests permission for self-representation, it is usually necessary for the trial judge to hold a hearing to determine the capability of the accused to make the waiver. This hearing has been referred to as a *Faretta* hearing. The time required to conduct this hearing varies with the circumstances of each case. It may become obvious to the judge after a short questioning of the accused that he or she has a limited educational background or knowledge of court procedure. The judge will conclude quickly that such an accused is not capable of making a knowing and intelligent waiver and will require representation by counsel. Other defendants who have some education and some knowledge of court procedures may insist on self-representation, and the hearing can be lengthy. The appellate courts have held that a "perfunctory hearing is improper. The record must show that the defendant made a knowing and intelligent election" to waive assistance of counsel. Further, "the actual conducting of a *Faretta* hearing may be difficult, time-consuming and trying of the patience of the trial judge, particularly if the defendant is eccentric, or prone to causing exasperation in others, or engages in the playing of games, or harassing the establishment. However the judge should not be misled by a confusion of the issue to be determined, that is, whether the defendant is capable of making the waiver."

Judges are inclined to conclude that a defendant is not capable of intelligently waiving the right to the assistance of counsel because of the many problems encountered by an untrained defendant attempting self-representation. The untrained defendant causes the trial to last longer, tries to introduce inadmissible evidence, makes improper objections to questions, and often argues with the judge over rulings. Deciding whether assistance should be provided by the trial judge for the self-represented defendant becomes a further issue. Many judges believe that with all the other duties to be performed during the trial, it is dangerous to try to assist the defendant because of the possibility of mistaken or misunderstood assistance. Yet, some appellate courts have stated that one of the major functions of the trial judge is to make certain that the "innocence or guilt of those accused of a crime is based upon the merits of the trial and not upon their inability to understand legal procedure." Therefore, the trial judge should render that assistance necessary for a fair trial.

The dissenting justices in the *Faretta* case recognized that these problems would be encountered by trial judges and believed that the majority justices had read into the Sixth Amendment something not intended by its framers.

Standby Counsel   The majority justices in the *Faretta* case did indicate that a trial judge, even over the objections of the defendant, could appoint a **standby counsel** to aid the defendant, if and when the defendant requests help, and to be available to represent the defendant in the event that termination of the defendant's self-representation should become necessary. The appointment of a standby attorney is not a practical solution, however, since trial judges may appoint standby attorneys in most instances, tying up the services of an attorney and increasing court costs.

In *McKaskle* v. *Wiggins*,[9] the U.S. Supreme Court reaffirmed the *Faretta* ruling that a trial judge may appoint a standby attorney over the objections of the defendant. The Court stated as follows:

> A defendant's Sixth Amendment rights are not violated when a trial judge appoints standby counsel even over the defendant's objection—to relieve the judge of the need to explain and enforce basic rules of courtroom protocol or to assist the defendant in overcoming routine obstacles that stand in the way of the defendant's achievement of his own clearly indicated goals.

The Court further stated the following:

> A defendant does not have a constitutional right to receive personal instruction from the trial judge on courtroom procedure. Nor does the Constitution require judges to take over chores for a *pro se* defendant [one representing himself] that would normally be attended to by trained counsel as a matter of course. The right of self-representation is not a license to abuse the dignity of the courtroom. Neither is it a license not to comply with relevant rules of procedure and substantive law.

Although the *McKaskle* decision reaffirmed a trial judge's right to appoint standby counsel over the defendant's objections, the decision did not solve all the problems connected with the appointment of a standby attorney. The trial judge is still faced with deciding how far a standby attorney may proceed over the defendant's objections without the assistance being a violation of the defendant's right to self-representation. The Court in the *McKaskle* case gave few guidelines in this respect but stated that a defendant's rights to self-representation

> are not infringed upon when standby counsel assists the defendant in overcoming routine procedural or evidentiary obstacles to the completion of some specific task, such as the introducing [of] evidence or objecting to testimony, that the defendant has clearly shown he wishes to complete. Nor are they infringed when counsel merely helps to ensure the defendant's compliance with basic rules of courtroom protocol and procedure. In neither case is there any significant interference with the defendant's actual control over the presentation of his defense.

Why an Accused Chooses Self-Representation

With the advantages to an accused in having the assistance of counsel and with the disadvantages of self-representation, one might ask why a defendant would insist upon self-representation rather than having the assistance of counsel. The saying is that an attorney who chooses self-representation has a fool for a client. Yet many defendants either do not trust attorneys or question their capabilities. One defendant, for example, conceded that an attorney had "more on the ball" than he himself did, but he also stated that there are certain questions "the attorney might not ask certain witnesses that are very potent, important, in regard to the case itself." Some defendants feel that attorneys do not have their client's best interests at stake or that attorneys are in collusion with the prosecuting attorney, with the result that the defendants will be railroaded into prison. Other defendants receive a certain gratification from representing themselves. Some are aware that by representing themselves they are entitled to confer with codefendants and witnesses in private, enabling them to conspire against the prosecution.

A defendant who represents himself or herself is referred to as "appearing in propria persona" ("in one's own proper person"), or in person. This circumstance is sometimes referred to by the courts as "pro per."

When the Right to Counsel Begins

For many years, the Sixth Amendment guarantee to the assistance of counsel was interpreted as meaning assistance at the time of trial. The *Gideon* decision did not materially change that interpretation, since that decision referred to the fact that "any person hauled into court, who is too poor to hire a lawyer, cannot be assured a fair trial unless counsel is provided for him." It was generally accepted that counsel need not be provided for the indigent defendant until the time of trial. However, later U.S. Supreme Court decisions established a new interpretation of when the right to counsel began and when counsel had to be provided for the indigent defendant.

In the case of *Escobedo* v. *Illinois,*[10] the U.S. Supreme Court held that the right to the assistance of counsel begins long before the time of the trial and may occur even before an arrest is made. The Court stated that when the investigation of a crime "shifts from . . . investigatory to accusatory," the accused is entitled to the assistance of counsel and such assistance could be very hollow if denied until the time of trial.

The facts of the *Escobedo* case indicate that Escobedo was arrested on a charge of murder. He was taken to a Chicago police station for interrogation. En route, Escobedo asked to consult with his attorney. Shortly after Escobedo arrived at the police station, his attorney arrived and requested permission to talk to Escobedo. Both were advised by the police that they could confer after the interrogation was completed. During the interrogation, Escobedo made certain admissions that implicated him in the murder charge. These admissions were used against him during the trial. Escobedo was convicted of murder, and his conviction was upheld by the Illinois Supreme Court. The case was taken to the U.S. Supreme Court upon the grounds that Escobedo was denied the assistance of counsel in violation of the Sixth Amendment guarantee. The attorneys for the State of Illinois argued that the right to counsel was not operative until the indictment stage of proceedings. To this argument, the Court stated that

in *Gideon* v. *Wainwright* we held that every person accused of a crime, whether state or federal, is entitled to a lawyer at trial. The rule sought by the State here, however, would make the trial no more than an appeal from the interrogation; and the "right to use counsel at the formal trial [would be] a very hollow thing if, for all practical purposes, the conviction is already assured by pretrial examination." *In re Groban,* 352 US 330 (1957) (Black, J., dissenting): One can imagine a cynical prosecutor saying: "Let them have the most illustrious counsel, now. They can't escape the noose. There is nothing that counsel can do for them at a trial."

It is argued that if the right to counsel is afforded prior to indictment, the number of confessions obtained by the police will diminish significantly, because most confessions are obtained during the period between arrest and indictment, and "any lawyer worth his salt will tell the suspect in no uncertain terms to make no statement to police under any circumstances." This argument, of course, cuts two ways. The fact that many confessions are obtained during this period points up its critical nature as a "stage when legal aid and advice" are surely needed. The right to counsel would indeed be hollow if it began at a period when few confessions were obtained. There is necessarily a direct relationship between the police in their quest for a confession and the criticalness of that stage to the accused in his need for legal advice. Our Constitution, unlike some others, strikes the balance in favor of the right of the accused to be advised by his lawyer of his privilege against self-incrimination.

We hold, therefore, that where, as here, the investigation is no longer a general inquiry into an unsolved crime but has begun to focus on a particular suspect, the suspect has been taken into police custody, the police carry out a process of interrogations that lends itself to eliciting incriminating statements, the suspect has requested and been denied an opportunity to consult with his lawyer, and the police have not effectively warned him of his absolute constitutional right to remain silent, the accused has been denied "the assistance of Counsel" in violation of the Sixth Amendment to the Constitution as "made obligatory upon the States by the Fourteenth Amendment," *Gideon* v. *Wainwright,* and that no statement elicited by the police be used against him at a criminal trial. . . .

Nothing we have said today affects the powers of the police to investigate "an unsolved crime" by gathering information from witnesses and by other "proper investigative efforts." We hold only that when the process shifts from investigatory to accusatory—when its purpose is to elicit a confession—our adversary system begins to operate, and, under the circumstances here, to consult with his lawyer.

The *Escobedo* decision provided that once suspicion is focused upon a particular suspect, he or she is entitled to consult with an attorney, but nothing was said about having to furnish the accused with an attorney. In the *Miranda* case, as previously stated, the Court held that before an accused can be interrogated, he or she must be advised of the right to the assistance of counsel. The accused must be advised of the right to remain silent and of the right to the assistance of counsel during the interrogation; and if the accused cannot afford an attorney, then one will be provided free.

Although both the *Escobedo* and *Miranda* decisions are more closely related to the field of evidence and the admissibility of confessions than to procedure, these decisions emphasized the importance of the assistance of counsel and set forth guidelines on when that right to assistance begins.

Effective Counsel

A defendant is entitled not only to the assistance of counsel but also to effective counsel. An **effective counsel** is one who has knowledge of the defendant's rights and who is capable of presenting the defenses to which the accused is entitled. Establishing the effectiveness of counsel is not easy. A counsel may be knowledgeable in one field but unfamiliar with crucial problems in another. If counsel does not effectively represent a defendant, whether through lack of knowledge or interest or because of mere carelessness, a conviction could be overruled upon appeal because of the denial of assistance of counsel. When attorneys are found to be ineffective, they are frequently sanctioned by the state bar association. This is a powerful incentive to diligently represent a client.

Farce or Sham Test   In determining whether a conviction should be reversed because of ineffective counsel, many state appellate courts have stated that it must appear that counsel's lack of diligence or competence reduced the trial to a **farce or sham**. Today's courts have rejected the traditional farce or sham test and have adopted a less stringent criterion for determining the competency of counsel. Counsel is considered ineffective if in representing the defendant, the counsel fails to meet the standard of competence expected of criminal case attorneys. Counsel is held to be ineffective when not exercising the customary skills and diligence that a reasonably competent attorney would have used under similar circumstances. Effective counsel has the duty to investigate carefully all defenses of fact and law of a case. If counsel's failure to do so results in the failure to present a crucial defense during the trial, the defendant has been denied proper assistance of counsel. Further, mere allegations by the defendant indicating a lack of preparation by or general incompetence of counsel are not enough to show ineffectiveness. The defendant must show acts or omissions resulting in a failure to present a crucial defense. Counsel does not have to interview or call every witness with knowledge of the case, since many witnesses may be of little assistance to the defense.

Crucial Error by Counsel   The effectiveness of counsel is usually considered when the court appoints an attorney to represent the defendant who cannot afford to choose an attorney. There are times when a defendant will complain about the effectiveness of chosen counsel (**retained counsel**). If an attorney selected by the accused is so ineffective that the defendant was denied a fair trial, the conviction will be reversed on appeal. For a time, courts were inclined to require a lesser degree of competence from an attorney of the defendant's own choosing. Today, it is accepted that whether an attorney is appointed for the defendant or is one of the defendant's own choosing, competence will be measured by the same degree. As stated by the U.S. Supreme Court in *Strickland* v. *Washington,*[11] "An accused is entitled to be assisted by an attorney, whether retained or appointed, who plays the role necessary to ensure that the trial is fair." A defendant may not expect an error-free attorney, but if an error is crucial to the defense, effective counsel has been denied. Determining whether an error was crucial has been a major problem for appellate courts. Defendants who have been convicted have successfully appealed on the allegation that effective counsel had been denied. Since no guidelines were set forth to measure the effectiveness of counsel, many convictions have been reversed. In *Strickland,* the Court endeavored to correct this situation by providing some criteria to measure effectiveness. The Court stated that "when a convicted defendant complains of the ineffectiveness of counsel's assistance, the defendant must show that counsel's representation fell below an objective standard of reasonableness. More specific guidelines are not appropriate."

Burden of Proof   The *Strickland* decision points out that the burden of proving ineffective assistance of counsel is on the defendant. When a convicted defendant claims that counsel's assistance was so defective as to require a reversal of a conviction or a death sentence, the defendant must prove two things. First, the defendant must show that counsel's performance was deficient. The defendant is thus required to show that the errors made were so serious that counsel did not function as a reasonably competent attorney. Second, the defendant must show that the deficient performance prejudiced the defense. Counsel's errors must be so serious as to deprive the defendant of a fair trial.

A defendant may allege ineffectiveness of counsel when there may have been acts or omissions such as the failure of counsel to enter a proper plea when applicable (such as a plea of not guilty by reason of insanity); the failure to raise the defense of diminished capacity; the failure to cross-examine prosecution witnesses; or the failure to object to the introduction of evidence improperly obtained. In one case, an appellate court overruled a conviction when the defense attorney's request for a continuance was denied, and the attorney thereafter refused to assist in the selection of the jury. The appellate court held that the defense counsel had reduced the trial to a sham.

Public Defender and Appointed Counsel

As has been stated, an accused is entitled to the assistance of counsel when that assistance is requested. If the accused is not in a position to employ private counsel, the court must appoint effective counsel. It is not always easy for a judge to obtain effective counsel to represent one accused of a crime. If effective counsel cannot be readily obtained, all prosecutive action must be suspended. To overcome this problem, many counties have established the **public defender**, whose function is representing those defendants who cannot afford an attorney of their own. These defendants are referred to as indigent persons or **indigent defendants**. The public defender, like the prosecuting attorney, is paid out of public funds. Many do not understand the use of public funds to employ a prosecuting attorney to prosecute offenders and, at the same time, to pay a public defender to defend the accused. But until the indigent defendant is furnished with the assistance of counsel, no prosecutive action can be taken. This delay can be expensive in time and money. If there is no public defender in a particular jurisdiction, the court must draw local attorneys from private practice. This necessity creates a problem, since most of these attorneys practice civil law and have little knowledge of the intricacies of a criminal trial; furthermore, in case of a conviction, the question of whether there was effective assistance of counsel could arise.

Before an accused may have the assistance of the public defender or an appointed private attorney, it must be established that the defendant is an indigent person, and this is sometimes difficult. Approximately 85 percent of all those arrested on felony charges are without question unable to afford an attorney. Determining which of the others can afford an attorney is difficult. Some courts have held that if the defendant can post bail, he or she is not indigent. Others have ruled that counsel is to be provided for any defendant who is unable to obtain counsel without serious financial hardship. The mere fact that friends or relatives have posted bail is not sufficient ground for denying the defendant free counsel. Another test is whether or not a private attorney would be interested in representing the defendant in his or her present economic circumstances. Undoubtedly, there have been defendants who have taken advantage of these tests to obtain free counsel, but with the large number of defendants who claim indigency, a thorough inquiry into each case is impossible. Judges who doubt the indigency status of a defendant have required the defendant to file a financial statement under oath. If it is determined later that the defendant was not indigent, prosecution for perjury as well as civil charges may be filed for the cost of the **appointed counsel**.

Capstone Cases

Faretta v. California
422 U.S. 806, 95 S.Ct. 2525, 45 L.Ed.2d 562 (1975)

Justice Stewart delivered the opinion of the Court.

The Sixth and Fourteenth Amendments of our Constitution guarantee that a person brought to trial in any state or federal court must be afforded the right to the assistance of counsel before he can be validly convicted and punished by imprisonment. This clear constitutional rule has emerged from a series of cases decided here over the last 50 years. The question before us now is whether a defendant in a state criminal trial has a constitutional right to proceed without counsel when he voluntarily and intelligently elects to do so. Stated another way, the question is whether a State may constitutionally hale a person into its criminal courts and there force a lawyer upon him, even when he insists that he wants to conduct his own defense. It is not an easy question, but we have concluded that a State may not constitutionally do so.

Anthony Faretta was charged with grand theft in . . . the Superior Court of Los Angeles County, California. At the arraignment, the Superior Court Judge assigned to preside at the trial appointed the public defender to represent Faretta. Well before the date of trial, however, Faretta requested that he be permitted to represent himself. Questioning by the judge revealed that Faretta had once represented himself in a criminal prosecution, that he had a high school education, and that he did not want to be represented by the public defender because he believed that that office was "very loaded down with . . . a heavy case load." The judge responded that he believed

Faretta was "making a mistake" and emphasized that in further proceedings Faretta would receive no special favors. Nevertheless . . . the judge, in a "preliminary ruling," accepted Faretta's waiver of the assistance of counsel. The judge indicated, however, that he might reverse this ruling if it later appeared that Faretta was unable adequately to represent himself.

Several weeks thereafter, but still prior to trial, the judge sua ponte held a hearing to inquire into Faretta's ability to conduct his own defense, and questioned him specifically about both the hearsay rule and the state law governing the challenge of potential jurors. After consideration of Faretta's answers, and observation of his demeanor, the judge ruled that Faretta had not made an intelligent and knowing waiver of his right to the assistance of counsel, and also ruled that Faretta had no constitutional right to conduct his own defense. The judge, accordingly, reversed his earlier ruling permitting self-representation and again appointed the public defender to represent Faretta. Faretta's subsequent request for leave to act as cocounsel was rejected, as were his efforts to make certain motions on his own behalf. Throughout the subsequent trial, the judge required that Faretta's defense be conducted only through the appointed lawyer from the public defender's office. At the conclusion of the trial, the jury found Faretta guilty as charged, and the judge sentenced him to prison. The California Court of Appeal affirmed the trial judge's ruling that Faretta had no federal or state constitutional right to represent himself, and the California Supreme Court denied review.

Justice Potter Stewart was appointed to the Supreme Court by President Dwight D. Eisenhower and served from 1959 to 1985. (*Source:* Ken Rarich. Collection of the Supreme Court of the United States.)

In the federal courts, the right of self-representation has been protected by statute since the beginnings of our Nation. Section 35 of the Judiciary Act of 1789, 1 Stat. 73, 92, enacted by the First Congress and signed by President Washington one day before the Sixth Amendment was proposed, provided that "in all the courts of the United States, the parties may plead and manage their own causes personally or by the assistance of . . . counsel. . . ." With few exceptions, each of the several States also accords a defendant the right to represent himself in any criminal case. The Constitutions of 36 States explicitly confer that right. Moreover, many state courts have expressed the view that the right is also supported by the Constitution of the United States. This Court has more than once indicated the same view. . . . [And] the United States Courts of Appeals have repeatedly held that the right of self-representation is protected by the Bill of Rights.

This Court's past recognition of the right of self-representation, the federal court authority holding the right to be of constitutional dimension, and the state constitutions pointing to the right's fundamental nature form a consensus not easily ignored. "The mere fact that a path is a beaten one," Mr. Justice Jackson once observed, "is a persuasive reason for following it." We confront here a nearly universal conviction, on the part of our people as well as our courts, that forcing a lawyer upon an unwilling defendant is contrary to his basic right to defend himself if he truly wants to do so. This consensus is soundly premised. The right of self-representation finds support in the structure of the Sixth Amendment, as well as in the English and colonial jurisprudence from which the Amendment emerged.

The Sixth Amendment includes a compact statement of the rights necessary to a full defense. . . . The rights to notice, confrontation, and compulsory process, when taken together, guarantee that a criminal charge may be answered in a manner now considered fundamental to the fair administration of American justice through the calling and interrogation of favorable witnesses, the cross-examination of adverse witnesses, and the orderly introduction of evidence. In short, the Amendment constitutionalizes the right in an adversary criminal trial to make a defense as we know it.

(Continued)

The Sixth Amendment does not provide merely that a defense shall be made for the accused; it grants to the secured personally the right to make his defense. It is the accused, not counsel, who must be "informed of the nature and cause of the accusation," who must be "confronted with the witnesses against him," and who must be accorded "compulsory process for obtaining witnesses in his favor." Although not stated in the Amendment in so many words, the right to self representation—to make one's own defense—is thus necessarily implied by the structure of the Amendment. The right to defend is given directly to the accused; for it is he who suffers the consequences if the defense fails.

The counsel provision supplements this design. It speaks of the "assistance" of counsel, and an assistant, however expert, is still an assistant. The language and spirit of the Sixth Amendment contemplate that counsel, like the other defense tools guaranteed by the Amendment, shall be an aid to a willing defendant—not an organ of the State interposed between an unwilling defendant and his right to defend himself personally. To thrust counsel upon the accused, against his considered wish, thus violates the logic of the Amendment. In such a case, counsel is not an assistant, but a master; and the right to make a defense is stripped of the personal character upon which the Amendment insists. It is true that when a defendant chooses to have a lawyer manage and present his case, law and tradition may allocate to the counsel the power to make binding decisions of trial strategy in many areas. This allocation can only be justified, however, by the defendant's consent, at the outset, to accept counsel as his representative. An unwanted counsel "represents" the defendant only through a tenuous and unacceptable legal fiction. Unless the accused has acquiesced in such representation, the defense presented is not the defense guaranteed him by the Constitution, for, in a very real sense, it is not his defense.

The Sixth Amendment, when naturally read, thus implies a right of self-representation. This reading is reinforced by the Amendment's roots in English legal history. In the long history of British criminal jurisprudence, there was only one tribunal that ever adopted a practice of forcing counsel upon an unwilling defendant in a criminal proceeding. The tribunal was the Star Chamber. That curious institution, which flourished in the late 16th and early 17th centuries, was of mixed executive and judicial character, and characteristically departed from common-law traditions. For those reasons, and because it specialized in trying "political" offenses, the Star Chamber has for centuries symbolized disregard of basic individual rights. . . .

In the American Colonies the insistence upon a right of self-representation was, if anything, more fervent than in England. The colonists brought with them an appreciation of the virtues of self-reliance and a traditional distrust of lawyers. When the Colonies were first settled, "the lawyer was synonymous with the cringing Attorneys-General and Solicitors-General of the Crown and the arbitrary justices of the King's Court, all bent on the conviction of those who opposed the King's prerogatives, and twisting the law to secure convictions." This prejudice gained strength in the Colonies where "distrust of lawyers became an institution." . . .

This is not to say that the Colonies were slow to recognize the value of counsel in criminal cases. Colonial judges soon departed from ancient English practice and allowed accused felons the aid of counsel for their defense. At the same time, however, the basic right of self-representation was never questioned. We have found no instance where a colonial court required a defendant in a criminal case to accept as his representative an unwanted lawyer. Indeed, even where counsel was permitted, the general practice continued to be self-representation. . . . After the Declaration of Independence, the right of self-representation, along with other rights basic to the making of a defense, entered the new state constitutions in wholesale fashion. The right to counsel was clearly thought to supplement the primary right of the accused to defend himself, utilizing his personal rights to notice, confrontation, and compulsory process. . . . At the time James Madison drafted the Sixth Amendment, some state constitutions guaranteed an accused the right to be heard "by himself" and by counsel; others provided that an accused was to be "allowed" counsel. The various state proposals for the Bill of Rights had similar variations in terminology. In each case, however, the counsel provision was embedded in a package of defense rights granted personally to the accused. There is no indication that the differences in phrasing about "counsel" reflected any differences of principle about self-representation. . . .

There can be no blinking the fact that the right of an accused to conduct his own defense seems to cut against the grain of this Court's decisions holding that the Constitution requires that no accused can be convicted and imprisoned unless he has been accorded the right to the assistance of counsel. See *Powell* v. *Alabama, Johnson* v. *Zerbst*, Gideon v. *Wainwright*, and *Argersinger* v. *Hamlin*. For it is surely true that the basic thesis of those decisions is that the help of a lawyer is essential to assure the defendant a fair trial. And a strong argument can surely be made that the whole thrust of those decisions must inevitably lead to the conclusion that a State may constitutionally impose a lawyer upon even an unwilling defendant.

But it is one thing to hold that every defendant, rich or poor, has the right to the assistance of counsel, and quite another to say that a State may compel a defendant to accept a lawyer he does not want. The value of state-appointed counsel was not unappreciated by the Founders, yet the notion of compulsory counsel was utterly foreign to them. And whatever else may be said of those who wrote the Bill of Rights, surely there can be no doubt that they understood the inestimable worth of free choice. It is undeniable that in most criminal prosecutions defendants could better defend with counsel's guidance than by their own unskilled efforts. But where the defendant will not voluntarily accept representation by counsel, the potential advantage of a lawyer's training and experience can be realized, if at all, only imperfectly. To force a lawyer on a defendant can only lead him to believe that the law contrives against him. Moreover, it is not inconceivable that in some rare instances, the defendant might in fact present his case more effectively by conducting his own defense. Personal liberties are not rooted in the law of averages. The right to defend is personal. The defendant, and not his lawyer or the State, will bear the personal consequences of a conviction. It is the defendant, therefore, who must be free personally to decide whether in his particular case counsel is to his advantage. And although he may conduct his own defense ultimately to his own detriment, his choice must be honored out of "that respect for the individual which is the lifeblood of the law."

When an accused manages his own defense, he relinquishes, as a purely factual matter, many of the traditional benefits associated with the right to counsel. For this reason, in order to represent himself, the accused must "knowingly and intelligently" forgo those relinquished benefits. Although a defendant need not himself have the skill and experience of a lawyer in order competently and intelligently to choose self-representation, he should be made aware of the dangers and disadvantages of self-representation, so that the record will establish that "he knows what he is doing and his choice is made with eyes open."

Here, weeks before trial, Faretta clearly and unequivocally declared to the trial judge that he wanted to represent himself and did not want counsel. The record affirmatively shows that Faretta was literate, competent, and understanding, and that he was voluntarily exercising his informed free will. The trial judge had warned Faretta that he thought it was a mistake not to accept the assistance of counsel, and that Faretta would be required to follow all the "ground rules" of trial procedure. We need make no assessment of how well or poorly Faretta had mastered the intricacies of the hearsay rule and the California code provisions that govern challenges of potential jurors on voir dire. For his technical legal knowledge, as such, was not relevant to an assessment of his knowing exercise of the right to defend himself.

In forcing Faretta, under these circumstances, to accept against his will a state-appointed public defender, the California courts deprived him of his constitutional right to conduct his own defense. . . .

Chief Justice Burger, with whom Justice Blackmun and Justice Rehnquist join, dissenting: [Omitted.]

Justice Blackmun, with whom the Chief Justice, and Justice Rehnquist join, dissenting.

I fear that the right to self-representation constitutionalized today frequently will cause procedural confusion without advancing any significant strategic interest of the defendant. [Although] the Court indicates that a pro se defendant necessarily waives any claim he might otherwise make of ineffective assistance of counsel, the opinion leaves open a host of other procedural questions. Must every defendant be advised of his right to proceed pro se? If so, when must that notice be given? Since the right to assistance of counsel and the right to self-representation are mutually exclusive, how is the waiver of each right to be measured? If a defendant has elected to exercise his right to proceed pro se, does he still have a constitutional right to assistance of standby counsel? How soon in the criminal proceeding must a defendant decide between proceeding by counsel or pro se? Must he be allowed to switch in mid-trial? May a violation of the right to self-representation ever be harmless error? Must the trial court treat the pro se defendant differently than it would professional counsel? I assume that many of these questions will be answered with finality in due course. Many of them, however, such as the standards of waiver and the treatment of the pro se defendant, will haunt the trial of every defendant who elects to exercise his right to self-representation. The procedural problems spawned by an absolute right to self-representation will far outweigh whatever tactical advantage the defendant may feel he has gained by electing to represent himself.

If there is any truth to the old proverb that "one who is his own lawyer has a fool for a client," the Court by its opinion today now bestows a constitutional right on one to make a fool of himself.

(Continued)

Associate Supreme Court Justice Ruth Ginsberg testifying during her confirmation hearings in Washington, D.C., in 1993. (*Source:* Rob Crandall/The Stock Connection.)

Halbert v. *Michigan*
2005 U.S. LEXIS 5012 (Decided June 23, 2005)

[In *Douglas* v. *California*, 372 U.S. 353 (1963), the U.S. Supreme Court held that, in criminal proceedings, a state must provide counsel for an indigent defendant in a first appeal as of right. Two considerations were key: (1) an appeal "of right" yields an adjudication on the "merits," and (2) first-tier review differs from subsequent appellate stages "at which the claims have once been presented by a lawyer and passed upon by an appellate court." Later, in *Ross* v. *Moffitt*, 417 U.S. 600 (1974), the Court held that a state need not appoint counsel to aid a poor person seeking to pursue a second-tier discretionary appeal to the state's highest court or thereafter. The *Douglas* rationale does not extend to second-tier discretionary review, the Court explained, because, at that stage, error correction is not the reviewing court's prime function. Principal criteria for state high court review, *Ross* noted, include whether the issues presented are of significant public interest, whether the cause involves legal principles of major significance to the state's jurisprudence, and whether the decision below is in probable conflict with the high court's precedent. Further, a defendant who has received counsel's aid in a first-tier appeal as of right would be armed with a transcript or another record of trial proceedings, a brief in the appeals court setting forth his or her claims, and, often, that court's opinion disposing of the case.

Michigan has a two-tier appellate system. Its Supreme Court hears appeals by leave only. The intermediate Court of Appeals adjudicates appeals as of right from criminal convictions, except that a defendant convicted on a guilty or nolo contendere plea who seeks intermediate appellate court review must apply for leave to appeal. Under Michigan law, most indigent defendants convicted on a plea must proceed pro se in seeking leave to appeal to the intermediate court. In *People* v. *Bulger*, 462 Mich. 495 (2000), the Michigan Supreme Court held that the Fourteenth Amendment's Equal Protection and Due Process Clauses do not secure a right to appointed counsel for plea-convicted defendants seeking review in the intermediate appellate court for these reasons: Such review is discretionary; plea proceedings are shorter, simpler, and more routine than trials; and a defendant entering a plea accedes to the state's fundamental interest in finality.]

JUDGES: GINSBURG, J., delivered the opinion of the Court, in which STEVENS, O'CONNOR, KENNEDY, SOUTER, and BREYER, JJ., joined. THOMAS, J., filed a dissenting opinion, in which SCALIA, J., joined, and in which REHNQUIST, C.J., joined.

Petitioner Halbert pleaded nolo contendere to two counts of criminal sexual conduct. During Halbert's plea colloquy, the trial court advised him of instances in which it "must" or "may" appoint appellate counsel, but failed to tell him that it could not appoint counsel in any other circumstances, including Halbert's own case. The day after his sentence was imposed, Halbert moved to withdraw his plea. Denying the motion, the trial court stated that Halbert's proper remedy was to appeal to the State Court of Appeals. Twice thereafter, Halbert asked the trial court to appoint counsel to help him prepare an application for leave to appeal to the intermediate court, stating that his sentence had been misscored, that he needed counsel to preserve the issue before undertaking an appeal, that he had learning disabilities and was mentally impaired, and that he had been obliged to rely on fellow inmates in preparing his pro se filings. The court denied Halbert's motion, citing Bulger. Halbert then filed a pro se application for leave to appeal, asserting sentencing error and ineffective assistance of counsel and seeking, inter alia, remand for appointment of appellate counsel. The Court of Appeals denied leave "for lack of merit in the grounds presented." The Michigan Supreme Court declined review.

Two aspects of the Michigan Court of Appeals' process following plea-based convictions compel the conclusion that Douglas, not Ross, controls here. First, in ruling on an application for leave to appeal, that court looks to the merits of the appellant's claims. Second, indigent defendants pursuing first-tier review in the Court of Appeals are generally ill equipped to represent themselves. A defendant who pleads guilty or nolo contendere in a Michigan court, although he relinquishes access to an appeal as of right, is entitled to apply for leave to appeal, and that entitlement is officially conveyed to him. Of critical importance, the intermediate appellate court, unlike the Michigan Supreme Court, sits as an error-correction instance. A court rule provides that the intermediate court may respond to a leave application in a number of ways: It may grant or deny the application, enter a final decision, grant other relief, request additional material from the record, or require a certified concise statement of proceedings and facts from the lower court. The court's response to the leave application by any of these alternatives—including denial of leave—necessarily entails some evaluation of the merits of the applicant's claims.

Whether formally categorized as the decision of an appeal or the disposal of a leave application, the intermediate appellate court's ruling on a plea-convicted defendant's claims provides the first, and likely the only, direct review the defendant's conviction and sentence will receive. Parties like Halbert, however, are disarmed in their endeavor to gain first-tier review. Ross emphasized that a defendant seeking State Supreme Court review following a first-tier appeal as of right earlier had the assistance of appellate counsel, who will have reviewed the trial court record, researched the legal issues, and prepared a brief reflecting that review and research. Such a defendant may also be armed with an opinion of the intermediate appellate court addressing the issues counsel raised. Without such guides keyed to a court of review, a pro se applicant's entitlement to seek leave to appeal to Michigan's intermediate court may be more formal than real. *Swenson v. Bosler*, 386 U.S. 258 (per curiam). Persons in Halbert's situation, many of whom have little education, learning disabilities, and mental impairments, are particularly handicapped as self-representatives. See *Kowalski v. Tesmer*, 543 U.S. __, __. Vacated and remanded.

Thomas J., dissenting.

Further, appeals by defendants convicted on their pleas may be "no less complex than other appeals." Michigan's complex procedures for seeking leave to appeal after sentencing on a plea, moreover, may intimidate the uncounseled. The State does have a legitimate interest in reducing its judiciary's workload, but providing indigents with appellate counsel will yield applications easier to comprehend. Michigan's Court of Appeals would still have recourse to summary denials of leave applications in cases not warranting further review. And when a defendant's case presents no genuinely arguable issue, appointed counsel may so inform the court.

The Court disagrees with Michigan's contention that, even if Halbert had a constitutionally guaranteed right to appointed counsel for first-level appellate review, he waived that right by entering a nolo contendere plea. At the time he entered his plea, Halbert had no recognized right to appointed appellate counsel he could elect to forgo. Moreover, the trial court did not tell Halbert, simply and directly, that in his case, there would be no access to appointed counsel.

SUMMARY

- The defendant has a right to be present at his or her trial.
- The defendant may waive the right by his or her conduct.
- The defendant has a right not to be tried before a jury in jail clothes.
- An unruly defendant may be gagged.
- After the trial has started, the accused may waive his or her right to be present by a voluntary absence from the proceedings.
- Under early English law, a person being tried for a felony had no right to counsel.
- The defendant has a right to counsel in all criminal proceedings, but whether the state is required to appoint a counsel for an indigent defendant depends on the nature of the charges and the possible punishment.
- An indigent defendant has the right to appointed counsel in any felony trial or in any trial where he or she faces confinement.
- While an accused has a right to counsel in petty cases, he or she does not have a right to appointed counsel even if indigent.
- An accused has the right to waive counsel and represent himself or herself. The waiver must be knowing and intelligent.
- The judge may appoint a standby counsel to assist the defendant when the defendant is self-represented.
- The right to counsel begins at all important stages of the criminal process.
- The defendant is entitled to the effective assistance of counsel.

REVIEW QUESTIONS

1. What is the significance of the constitutional guarantee that an accused must be confronted with the witnesses against him or her?
2. May a trial ever be conducted in the absence of the defendant? If so, under what circumstances?
3. What procedure, suggested by the U.S. Supreme Court, might be used against an unruly defendant during trial proceedings, and in what decision was the procedure suggested?
4. In what amendment to the U.S. Constitution is the right to the assistance of counsel embodied?
5. What was the significance of the *Gideon* v. *Wainwright* decision in reference to the assistance of counsel?
6. In the *Argersinger* v. *Hamlin* decision, what arguments were presented by the Court in granting the accused the assistance of counsel in the trial of a petty charge?
7. Under what circumstances, if any, may an accused waive the assistance of counsel and represent himself or herself during a trial?
8. When does the accused's right to counsel begin?
9. What is the significance of the term "effective assistance of counsel"?
10. What is the function of a public defender?

ENDNOTES

1. 397 U.S. 337 (1970).
2. 130 U.S. App. DC 22 (1968).
3. 101 L.Ed. 2d 857 (1988).
4. 287 U.S. 45 (1932).
5. 372 U.S. 335 (1963).
6. 407 U.S. 25 (1972).
7. 317 U.S. 269 (1942).
8. 422 U.S. 806 (1975).
9. 79 L.Ed. 2d 122 (1984).
10. 378 U.S. 478 (1964).
11. 466 U.S. 668 (1984).

confession was lawfully obtained. The defense may present evidence in an effort to prove that the evidence should be suppressed or not be introduced because of illegality.

Hearing to Suppress

The hearing to suppress evidence must be held prior to the trial time in some jurisdictions; the hearing is held before a judge alone and not before a jury. If the judge concludes that the evidence was illegally obtained, he or she will suppress it or hold that it is not admissible during the trial. If the judge believes that the material was lawfully obtained, it may be introduced against the defendant during the trial, and the jury will give the evidence the weight to which they feel it is entitled.

The hearing on the motion must be made prior to the trial in some jurisdictions because it is felt that the trial judge should not be required to stop in midtrial to determine whether evidence presented by the prosecution was lawfully obtained. If the evidence is ruled inadmissible, the prosecuting attorney may decide to dismiss the charge if a conviction would not be possible without the suppressed evidence. Thus, the time and expense of a trial would be saved.

Some jurisdictions permit the defense to object to the introduction of the evidence again at the trial, and the judge may consider at that time whether the evidence is admissible. A few jurisdictions require that the motion to suppress be made prior to trial, holding that unless the motion is made prior to the trial, the defendant waives the constitutional right to object to the method of obtaining evidence. In these instances, courts have held that there is no waiver if the defendant could not have reasonably made the motion prior to the trial. A reasonable cause may be that the defendant was unaware of the allegedly illegal search or seizure or did not have reasonable time to make the motion before the trial. Other states hold that a pretrial motion to suppress evidence is premature and that the objection should take place during the trial. Pretrial motions and hearings to suppress evidence unnecessarily delay setting the case for trial, and, since an objection to the introduction of the evidence may be made again in most jurisdictions during the trial, it is a duplication of effort.

In jurisdictions where the pretrial motion to suppress is not mandatory, many defense attorneys will not file a pretrial motion. They will wait and object to the introduction of the evidence at the preliminary hearings. It is the prosecution's responsibility to present testimony in an effort to prove that the evidence was lawfully obtained. Through cross-examination by the defense and the testimony of witnesses, efforts will be made to prove that the offered evidence was unlawfully obtained. If the judge holds that the evidence was illegally obtained, the defendant will be released unless other evidence causes the judge to reasonably believe that the defendant should be held for trial. If the evidence is lawfully obtained and the defendant is held for trial, a second objection to the introduction of the evidence may be made during the trial.

Grounds for Evidence Suppression

Obtaining confessions and unreasonable searches and seizures are two areas that include numerous grounds for challenging the introduction of evidence. A confession obtained through the psychological pressure of threats or promises would be suppressed. Search warrants may be improperly issued, or permission for consent searches involuntarily may be given. An officer exceeding the permissible area on a search incident to arrest provides grounds for a motion to suppress. A sample document for a typical motion to suppress evidence appears in the accompanying illustration.

MOTION TO DISMISS CHARGES

After a complaint, an information, or an indictment has been filed against a defendant, facts are sometimes revealed that, in the interest of justice, demand that the charge be dismissed. In some jurisdictions, this action may be taken by the prosecuting attorney and is known as "entering a nolle prosequi." Other jurisdictions do not grant the prosecuting attorney nolle prosequi authority. In these jurisdictions, a charge may be dismissed only by a judge, by judicial motion, or upon recommendation of the prosecuting attorney.

There are many reasons a prosecuting attorney may recommend that a charge be dismissed after it is filed. The original allegation may be unfounded; the evidence to be introduced may have been unlawfully obtained, making a conviction impossible; or a material witness may no longer be available to testify. Dismissals have also been granted to a defendant to allow testimony against codefendants. The defense may file a motion to dismiss on the grounds that the indictment or information was seriously defective or that a case was not brought to trial within the prescribed time.

A dismissal by a judge on judicial or defense motion is not always a bar to further prosecutive action on the matter, particularly if the charge is a felony. The prosecuting attorney may refile the charge. How many times this action may take place is not firmly established, but the right to a speedy trial prevents too many dismissals and refilings from taking place.

MOTION FOR CONTINUANCE

Criminal cases are to be heard as soon as reasonably possible, and they are to be given precedence over civil matters. Most state codes provide that no continuance of a criminal trial shall be granted except where the ends of justice require a continuance. The codes also provide that the continuance shall not be for a period longer than justice requires. Despite these provisions, perhaps no motion is made with greater frequency than the motion for a continuance, particularly by the defense. What is within the ends of justice and how long justice requires the continuance to be are primarily within the discretion of the trial judge.

Grounds for a Continuance

There are no specified grounds on which the continuance may be based. Justice requires that a continuance be granted to obtain a material witness. But before a continuance to obtain such a witness will be granted, the side making the request must present further evidence on why the witness is material, what effort has been made to locate the witness, and why the testimony of this witness is not available through any other witness. Continuances have been granted to defendants so that they may obtain effective counsel, and they often take advantage of this opportunity. Defendants have employed counsel and then, at trial time, they have discharged counsel and requested a continuance to obtain new counsel. There are cases in which this request was made as many as ten to thirteen times. Occasionally, the defendant will have employed new counsel just prior to the trial date, and the defense counsel will make a motion for continuance on the grounds that additional time is needed to prepare the defense. Continuances have been granted when a defendant is not physically able to attend the trial or when the defense attorney is ill or engaged in another trial. The length of time a trial may be delayed for these reasons is undetermined. If the defendant is not feigning illness, the court has no

---

(Title of Court)

Notice of Motion and Motion to Suppress Evidence

In the Matter of Property   Cr. No. _____

Seized from (<u>names of persons from whom the property was seized</u>)

To (<u>Names of all police officers known to have participated in the seizure of the property</u>)

PLEASE TAKE NOTICE that on _____, 20 _____ at _____.m., or as soon thereafter as the matter can be heard, at the courtroom of the Criminal District Court, Parish of Orleans at _____, City of New Orleans, State of Louisiana; Defendant Jon Notguilty will move the Court for an order directing various levying officers, including the above-named, to return to the movants forthwith certain personal property, _____ a schedule of which is attached to this motion, and which on _____ 19_____, at the premises known as _____, was unlawfully seized and taken from the movants by those levying officers, and directing that the property seized be suppressed as evidence against _____ in any criminal proceeding.

This motion is made on the grounds that:

1. _____.

2. _____.

This motion is based on this notice, the pleadings, records, and files in this proceeding, the attached memorandum of points and authorities and the attached supporting declaration of _____.

Dated: _____

_____ (signed)

Attorney for Defendant

---

alternative but to grant a continuance until the defendant recovers. But how long may defense counsel delay a trial? It has been held that unless a defense counsel is available for trial within a reasonable time, the defendant must obtain substitute counsel.

A continuance will not usually be granted for longer than thirty to sixty days. At the end of that period, a new request may be made, and frequently it is granted. As a result, many criminal trials are not heard for more than a year after the crime has been committed.

When a motion for a continuance is to be made, reasonable notice must be given to the trial judge and the opposing side. Reasonable notice is difficult to determine. Unfortunately, the notice may be given on the trial date. If a continuance is granted at that time, it is a hardship on everyone involved in the trial proceeding. It may be particularly inconvenient for witnesses who have taken time off from work and have traveled great distances to appear in court. The witnesses will have to reappear on the new date set for the trial. The defense makes these frequent requests for continuances because they usually work to the advantage of the defendant. The possibilities of prosecution witnesses' becoming unavailable and memories dulling increase with the passage of time.

MOTION FOR SEVERANCE OF OFFENSES

Criminals often commit a series of crimes in a relatively short period of time. For example, a burglar may commit a number of burglaries within a few days or weeks. If the burglar is caught and charged, it is logical to try the offender on all the charges at one time. Consolidating several charges into one trial saves time and expense by eliminating a separate trial for each crime. Most state laws permit a series of crimes committed in one jurisdiction to be combined into one accusatory pleading. Each of the crimes charged in the accusatory pleading is referred to as a count. Crimes must be of the same general nature to be consolidated. If the crimes are all similar, such as all burglaries or all robberies, there is no doubt about consolidating them into one accusatory pleading. It has also been held that if the crimes are of a different nature but are part of the same transaction, scheme, or plan, they may be consolidated. For example, if an offender commits a burglary and then commits arson to hide the burglary, these two offenses could be consolidated, since they are parts of the same transaction or plan. However, a crime of robbery and a crime of burglary could not be consolidated without being parts of the same transaction.

A defendant having a series of crimes consolidated into one trial has the advantage of avoiding a defense in separate trials. Yet there are times when a defendant will make a motion for a **severance** of offenses. This motion is based upon the premise that being tried on several counts during the same trial is prejudicial to the defendant. As stated in the case of *Cross* v. *United States:*[5]

> Prejudice may develop when an accused wishes to testify on one but not the other of two joined offenses which are clearly distinct in time, place and evidence. His decision whether to testify will reflect a balancing of several factors with respect to each count: the evidence against him, the availability of defense evidence other than his testimony, the plausibility and substantiality of his testimony, the possible effects of demeanor, impeachment, and cross-examination. But if the two charges are joined for trial, it is not possible for him to weigh these factors separately as to each count. If he testifies on one count, he runs the risk that any adverse effects will influence the jury's consideration of the other count. Thus he runs the risk on both counts, although he may benefit on only one. Moreover, a defendant's silence on one count would be damaging in the face of his express denial of the other. Thus he may be coerced into testifying on the count upon which he wished to remain silent.

Also, in *Drew* v. *United States,*[6] the Court stated the following:

> The justification for a liberal rule on joinder of offenses appears to be the economy of a single trial. The argument against joinder is that the defendant may be prejudiced for one or more of the following reasons: (1) he may become embarrassed or confounded in presenting separate defenses; (2) the jury, may use the evidence of one of the crimes charged to infer a criminal disposition on the part of the defendant from which is found his guilt of the other crime or crimes charged; or (3) the jury may cumulate the evidence of the various crimes charged and find guilt when, if considered separately, it would not so find. A less tangible, but perhaps equally persuasive, element of prejudice may reside in a latent feeling of hostility engendered by the charging of several crimes as distinct from only one. Thus, in any given case the court must weigh prejudice to the defendant caused by the joinder against the obviously important consideration of economy and expedition in judicial administration.

MOTION FOR SEVERANCE

The laws of most states hold that when two or more defendants are jointly charged with the same offense, they must be tried jointly unless the judge feels that in the best interest of justice separate trials should be granted. Jointly trying codefendants promotes economy and efficiency and avoids multiplicity of trials. But defendants often file a motion for severance to avoid the possibility of prejudice. The prejudice may stem from the fact that evidence against one defendant is not applicable to others, and a jury may have difficulty in separating the evidence. One defendant may have a particularly bad reputation, and a codefendant could be convicted by association. A defendant may have given a confession implicating other codefendants, and this confession is to be introduced during the trial. Under such circumstances, unless the identifying data concerning codefendants cannot be adequately deleted from the confession, they are not admissible. Otherwise, separate trials must be granted. The jury would then be expected to perform the overwhelming task of considering a confession in determining the guilt or innocence of the confessor and then ignoring the confession in determining the guilt or innocence of codefendants.[7]

Since the concern with joint trials stems principally from the fact that the jury might be prejudiced against the defendant, should a severance be granted if a jury is waived in favor of a court trial? Jurisdictions are divided on the answer to this question. Some hold that a judge is competent to separate evidence between codefendants, whether it be a confession, a testimonial, or physical evidence. Therefore, a severance of codefendants may be denied. Other jurisdictions hold that upon an allegation of prejudice, a defendant has an absolute right to a severance whether the trial is a court trial or a jury trial.

MOTION TO DETERMINE COMPETENCY

If the present mental state of the defendant is in question at any time prior to or during a trial, the defense counsel should make a motion for a hearing on competency. Insanity refers to the accused's mental state at the time of the act. Competency refers to the accused's mental state at trial time. A hearing may be ordered on the competency question if the actions of the defendant would cause doubt in the judge's mind. Competency of the defendant must be determined because a person cannot be tried, sentenced, or punished while insane. The procedure of determining competency is referred to as both a hearing and a trial. Usually the hearing is conducted before a judge sitting alone, unless the defense demands that a jury trial be held. In some states, like Texas, the accused has a right to a jury trial on the issue of competency.

The competency hearing should not be confused with a trial on a plea of not guilty by reason of insanity, as discussed later in the text. The hearing to determine the competency of the defendant has nothing to do with guilt or innocence; it ascertains the defendant's *present* mental capabilities. The test of competency determines the defendant's present ability to understand the nature and purpose of the proceedings, and it measures the capacity to assist in the defense in a rational manner. If the defendant is unable to understand the charge and possible defenses and is also unable properly to confer with counsel in regard to the conduct of the trial, the trial should not take place. The test to determine competency is not the same as that used in a trial on a plea of not guilty by reason of insanity.

Once the competency of the defendant is questioned, all prosecutive proceedings must be halted until the issue of competency can be determined. The next step is the competency hearing or trial. Prior to the hearing, the defendant will normally be examined by psychologists or psychiatrists appointed by the court and by those selected by the defense, if desired. During the hearing, these specialists and any other witnesses able to shed light on the defendant's competency may be called to testify. If the prosecution thinks that the defendant is presently able to defend himself or herself, evidence may be offered in an effort to prove that the defendant is competent. If determined incompetent, the defendant may be confined to a mental hospital until recovery. There is no formal procedure to determine that the defendant has recovered his or her competency other than certification to that effect by the hospital superintendent. After the defendant has recovered, he or she will be brought back for trial unless the recovery period is extensive and the charge has been dismissed in the interest of justice.

If the competency hearing determines that the defendant is presently sane, the prosecutive proceedings will commence again from the point where they stopped. This is the case unless the trial on guilt or innocence was in progress and the trial judge dismissed the jury and declared a mistrial. Under those circumstances, the trial would be resumed from the beginning with a new jury. Various other motions will be discussed as the trial proceedings unfold.

PRETRIAL CONFERENCE

Pretrial conferences in civil matters have been effectively used for years. These conferences are informal meetings, usually in the judge's chambers, between both attorneys and the judge. The strong and weak points of the case are discussed in an effort to arrive at a settlement without going to trial. With court calendars becoming more and more crowded, greater use is being made of the pretrial conference in criminal matters. As the trial date approaches, the trial judge will often call for a pretrial conference. During this conference, the judge will determine whether both sides will be ready for trial on the date set or if a continuance will be requested. The judge will also try to ascertain the approximate number of days each side anticipates taking to present its case. By gathering this information, the judge will be better able to set other cases for trial and decide whether alternate jurors should be selected.

The attorneys may try to arrive at some sequence in calling witnesses, particularly professional persons or expert witnesses. The attorneys will attempt to agree, or to stipulate, to certain testimony. There are advantages to each side in stipulating to certain facts that a witness may present if called to testify. The stipulation may concern some uncontroversial matter when the presentation of proof during the trial would be of little consequence—thus saving trial time. The stipulation of some fact that the prosecution can prove convincingly may be to the advantage of the defense because it prevents a witness from going into great detail to the detriment of the defendant. Those facts having a stipulation are brought to the attention of the jury at the appropriate time, and the jury considers those facts as though they had been presented in testimony during the trial. The presentation of facts by stipulation does not violate the defendant's right of confrontation, since the defendant has waived his or her right of confrontation of that particular witness, or witnesses, by agreeing to the facts.

PLEA NEGOTIATION

Plea negotiating, or plea bargaining, as it is more commonly known, is nothing more than agreement between the prosecuting attorney and the defense to reduce a charge to a lesser crime, to drop certain charges, or to receive a lessened sentence in return for a guilty or nolo contendere plea. Plea negotiating usually takes place shortly after the initial appearance or the arraignment of a defendant. In most jurisdictions, the negotiating can continue up to the time that the verdict is rendered. Plea negotiating is often discussed during the pretrial conference. Although it has been held that the judge should not be a part of the negotiation, he or she should be made aware of it, and in many instances must, by law, accept the conditions of the plea bargaining before the guilty or nolo contendere plea is acceptable.

Plea bargaining has been both praised and criticized. Some allege that plea bargaining is important in the administration of criminal law, is advantageous to the state by saving time and money, and increases efficiency and flexibility in the criminal process. The advantage to the defendant is reduced punishment. Plea bargaining has been criticized, particularly by some law enforcement officers, because it allows a criminal to take advantage of the justice system by not being convicted and sentenced for the crime actually committed. The result is a much lighter penalty.

Benefits of Plea Bargaining

Although the practice of accepting negotiated pleas has been criticized, many prosecuting attorneys state that the acceptance of a negotiated plea often is for more justifiable reasons than lightening caseloads and clearing crowded court calendars. Sometimes an offender is initially charged on a *more serious* crime than is warranted by the evidence. Or an offender may be charged with a more serious crime so that a higher bail will be set. Reducing the number of charges in exchange for a negotiated plea may be justified on the grounds that many judges tend to give concurrent sentences. There would be little advantage in going to trial on a larger number of charges over accepting a plea on a reduced number. As to accepting a negotiated plea on the promise of a lighter sentence, prosecutors point out that they have little or no control over the sentence that may be given one convicted of a crime. Even if the accused were convicted as a result of a trial, the sentence could be the same as that agreed to in the negotiated plea.

In the past, plea bargaining was not discussed openly since it was considered to be unethical, if not illegal. Judges seldom were aware of any agreements made by plea bargaining because, to be valid, a guilty or nolo contendere plea had to be freely and voluntarily given. If the plea was induced upon a promise of leniency, there was a question of its being freely and voluntarily given. The secrecy of plea bargaining was eliminated by legislative action and court decisions, and today plea bargaining is openly engaged in as part of the justice system.

Supreme Court and Plea Bargaining

Much of the change in viewpoint was brought about by the case of *Brady* v. *United States*,[8] in which the U.S. Supreme Court gave sanction to plea bargaining. The facts of the case show that Brady was charged with a kidnapping violation and faced a maximum penalty of death if the verdict of the jury should so recommend. Brady entered a plea of guilty to the charge and was sentenced to thirty years' imprisonment. The case was taken to the U.S. Supreme Court upon the grounds that the plea was not freely and voluntarily given because of representations of a reduction of sentence and clemency. Brady alleged that this inducement was compelling him to be a witness against himself in violation of the Fifth Amendment to the U.S. Constitution. The Supreme Court concluded that the guilty plea "was voluntarily and knowingly made" even though it may have been induced by representations with respect to reduction of sentence and clemency, and, as such, Brady's guarantee against self-incrimination had not been violated.

The Court in this decision stated the following:

. . . That a guilty plea is a grave and so solemn act to be accepted only with care and discernment has long been recognized. Central to the plea and the foundation for entering judgment against the defendant is the defendant's admission in open court that he committed the acts charged in the indictment. He thus stands as a witness against himself and he is shielded by the Fifth Amendment from being compelled to do so, hence the minimum requirement that his plea be the voluntary expression of his own choice.

The voluntariness of Brady's plea can be determined only by considering all of the relevant circumstances surrounding it. One of these circumstances was the possibility of a heavier sentence following a guilty verdict after a trial. It may be that Brady, faced with a strong case against him and recognizing that his chances for acquittal were slight, preferred to plead guilty and thus limit the penalty to life imprisonment rather than to elect a jury trial, which could result in a death penalty.

The state to some degree encourages pleas of guilty at every important step in the criminal process. For some people, their breach of a state's law is alone sufficient reason for surrendering themselves and accepting punishment. For others, apprehension and charge, both threatening acts by the government, jar them into admitting their guilt. In still other cases, the postindictment accumulation of evidence may convince the defendant and his counsel that a trial is not worth the agony and expense to the defendant and his or her family. All these pleas of guilty are valid in spite of the state's responsibility for some of the factors motivating the pleas; the pleas are no more improperly compelled than is the decision by a defendant at the close of the state's evidence at trial that he or she must take the stand or face certain conviction.

Of course, the agents of the state may not produce a plea by actual or threatened physical harm or by mental coercion overbearing the will of the defendant. But nothing of the sort is claimed in this case; nor is there evidence that Brady was so gripped by fear of the death penalty or hope of leniency that he did not or could not, with the help of counsel, rationally weigh the advantages of going to trial against the advantages of pleading guilty.

The issue we deal with is inherent in the criminal law and its administration, because guilty pleas are not constitutionally forbidden, because the criminal law characteristically extends to the judge or jury a range of choices in setting the sentence in individual cases, and because both the state and the defendant often find it advantageous to preclude the possibility of the maximum penalty authorized by law. For a defendant who sees little possibility of acquittal, the advantages of pleading guilty and limiting the probable penalty are obvious—his or her exposure is reduced, the correctional processes can begin immediately, and the practical burdens of a trial are eliminated. For the state, there are advantages: the more promptly imposed punishment after an admission of guilt may more effectively attain the objectives of punishment; and with the avoidance of trial, scarce judicial and prosecutorial resources are conserved for those cases in which there is a substantial issue of the defendant's guilt or in which there is substantial doubt that the state can sustain its burden of proof. It is this mutuality of advantage that perhaps explains the fact that at present, well over three-fourths of the criminal convictions in this country rest on pleas of guilty, a great many of them no doubt motivated at least in part by the hope or assurance of a lesser penalty than might be imposed if there were a guilty verdict after a trial to judge or jury.

Of course, that the prevalence of guilty pleas is explainable does not necessarily validate those pleas or the system that produces them. But we cannot hold that it is unconstitutional for the state to extend a benefit to a defendant who in turn extends a substantial benefit to the state and who demonstrates by his or her plea that the defendant is ready and willing to admit his or her crime and to enter the correctional system in a frame of mind that affords hope for success in rehabilitation over a shorter period of time than might otherwise be necessary.

were completely self-defeating in nature because of his extreme aggressiveness and distortion. These distortions are not viewed as psychotic but as merely very self-serving. Richard's presentation at this evaluation is consistent with his presentation when visited by his attorney who noted the following: that Richard had to be manipulated with food even to agree to see the attorney, that Richard said the attorney had no right to talk to him, and that Richard refused to talk with him. After review of his TDC record it is likely he will become competent for a reasonable period of time only if he is consistently on psychotropic medication.

(signed)

Robert J. Martin, Ph.D

SUMMARY

- Both the prosecutor and the defense have a right to pretrial discovery.
- The right of discovery was originally created primarily for the benefit of the defendant.
- There are limitations on what the defendant or defense may inspect.
- The defense has no right to look at the prosecutor's work product.
- The defense has no right to examine the prosecutor's trial folder.
- In a few states where the defendant's pretrial right of discovery is not recognized, the defendant must rely on the preliminary hearing for any assistance received in trial preparation.
- In federal trials, the prosecutor has an almost identical right to pretrial discovery.
- A motion to suppress evidence is used to determine the admissibility of evidence prior to trial.
- Whether to grant a motion for a continuance rests with the trial judge.
- There are no specified grounds on which a continuance may be based. Justice may require that a continuance be granted to obtain a material witness.
- A motion for the severance of offenses or defendants must be made before the start of the trial.
- If the mental state of the defendant is in question, during the pretrial the defense may request a competency hearing.
- A plea bargain is an agreement between the prosecutor and the defense.
- The Supreme Court has sanctioned plea bargaining.
- In some states, like California, there are statutory restrictions on plea bargaining.
- A guilty plea based on a plea bargain may be withdrawn if the bargain is not complied with.

REVIEW QUESTIONS

1. What is the right of discovery?
2. What is the theory behind the right of discovery as it relates to the defendant?
3. In general, what may the defendant expect by exercising his or her right of discovery?
4. What reasons have been presented by some states in denying the defendant the right of discovery?
5. What is the chief argument against permitting the prosecution the right of discovery?

6. In relation to the right of discovery by the prosecution, what was the significance of the *Williams* v. *Florida* decision?

7. In general, what is the chief argument presented by the defense in support of a motion to suppress evidence?

8. Explain the significance of the Exclusionary Rule on the admissibility of evidence.

9. List two reasons for granting a trial continuance.

10. List the advantages and disadvantages of granting a motion to separate offenses.

11. What is the primary purpose of a motion to determine the present sanity of an accused?

12. What is the purpose of the pretrial conference?

13. What is a negotiated plea?

14. What are some of the advantages and disadvantages in plea bargaining?

LOCAL PROCEDURE

1. Is the defendant granted the right of discovery in your state?

2. Is the prosecution afforded any right of discovery? If so, to what extent?

3. At what point must the motion to suppress evidence be made during a criminal proceeding?

ENDNOTES

1. 47 Cal.2d 566 (1956).

2. 291 F. 646 (1923).

3. 399 U.S. 78 (1970).

4. 367 U.S. 643 (1961).

5. 335 F.2d. 987 (1964).

6. 331 F.2d 85 (1964).

7. *Burton* v. *United States,* 391 U.S. 123 (1968).

8. 397 U.S. 742 (1970).

9. 12 CalRptr. 556 (1974).

> "Give me your evidence," said the King "and don't be nervous, or I'll have you executed on the spot."
> —Lewis Carroll, *Alice's Adventures in Wonderland*, 1865

Courtroom Evidence

10

Chapter Outline

Key Words

Character evidence
Daubert test
Declarant
Hearsay

Impeachment
Judicial notice
Lay witness
Limited admissibility

Preliminary questions
Rape shield laws
Relevant evidence

Learning Objectives

After completing this chapter, you should be able to:

1. Explain what constitutes hearsay testimony.
2. Describe the purposes of the Rules of Evidence.
3. Identify and discuss the various rulings on evidence.
4. Understand the concept of judicial notice.
5. Demonstrate how documents are introduced into evidence.
6. Explain what constitutes relevant evidence.
7. Discuss the concept of fairness as it relates to the admissibility of evidence.
8. Explain the difference between lay and expert witnesses.

INTRODUCTION

The study of evidence is a study of regulation of the process of proving facts. Evidence law was originally almost entirely decisional law. Now it is codified in statutes and court rules. In this chapter, we will examine evidence based on the Federal Rules of Evidence. The Federal Rules did not depart significantly from the common law decisions. Most state rules of evidence are based on the Federal Rules, with only slight differences among the states. Evidence is a very complex and difficult subject for attorneys in law school. In this chapter, we will cover only the highlights to acquaint the readers with the subject.

Evidentiary rules should be construed in a manner to attempt to secure fairness in administration, elimination of unjustifiable expense and delay, and promotion of growth and development of the law of evidence to the end that the truth may be ascertained and proceedings justly determined.

The two basic themes found in the Federal Rules are:

- The Rules favor admissibility of evidence.
- The trial judge has considerable discretion as to the admissibility of evidence.

A trial judge has the authority (discretion) to fashion evidentiary procedures to deal with situations not specifically covered by the rules. In interpreting the Rules, it is important for judges to differentiate when Congress or the legislatures have spoken and finally determined an issue and when they have left room for judicial interpretation. As the Third Circuit Court of Appeals stated in *United States* v. *Pelullo,*[1] while the Rules "are to be liberally construed in favor of admissibility, this does not mean that we may ignore requirements of specific provisions merely because we view the proffered evidence as trustworthy."

Federal Rule 102 establishes a principle of flexibility in the application of the Federal Rules of Evidence. Most states have a similar rule. The U.S. Supreme Court has stated that judicial flexibility has no place when the "plain meaning" of a Federal Rule of Evidence mandates a certain result. However, cases such as *Daubert* v. *Merrell Dow Pharmaceuticals Inc.*[2] and *United States* v. *Mezzanatto*[3] indicate that the Supreme Court is sometimes willing to employ a more flexible approach than a rigid adherence to plain meaning would seem to allow.

HEARSAY RULE

Evidentiary Definitions

Statement   A statement is (1) an oral or written assertion or (2) nonverbal conduct of a person if it is intended by the person as an assertion.

Declarant   A **declarant** is a person who makes a statement.

Hearsay   Hearsay is a statement, other than one made by the declarant while testifying at the trial or hearing, offered in evidence to prove the truth of the matter asserted.
A statement is not hearsay if

- The declarant testifies at the trial or hearing and is subject to cross-examination concerning the statement, and the statement is (a) inconsistent with the declarant's testimony and was given under oath subject to the penalty of perjury at a trial, hearing, or other proceeding, or in a deposition, or (b) consistent with the declarant's testimony and is offered to rebut an express or implied charge against the declarant of recent fabrication or improper influence or motive, or (c) one of identification of a person made after perceiving the person; or

- Admission by a party-opponent. The statement is offered against a party and is (a) the party's own statement in either an individual or a representative capacity or (b) a statement of which the party has manifested an adoption or belief in its truth, or (c) a statement by a person authorized by the party to make a statement concerning the subject, or (d) a statement by the party's agent or servant concerning a matter within the scope of the agency or employment, made during the existence of the relationship, or (e) a statement by a coconspirator of a party during the course and in furtherance of the conspiracy. The contents of the statement shall be considered but are not alone sufficient to establish the declarant's authority under subdivision (c), the agency or employment relationship and scope thereof under subdivision (d), or the existence of the conspiracy and the participation therein of the declarant and the party against whom the statement is offered under subdivision (e).

General Rule on Hearsay

Hearsay is inadmissible unless an exception is applicable. Exceptions to the hearsay rule include:

- Affidavits to show grounds for issuing warrants.
- Affidavits to determine issues of fact in connection with motions.
- A statement describing or explaining an event or condition made while the declarant was perceiving the event or condition or immediately thereafter.
- A statement relating to a startling event or condition made while the declarant was under the stress of excitement caused by the event or condition.
- A statement of the declarant's then existing state of mind, emotion, sensation, or physical condition (such as intent, plan, motive, design, mental feeling, pain, and bodily health), but not including a statement of memory or belief to prove the fact remembered or believed unless it relates to the execution, revocation, identification, or terms of the declarant's will.
- Statements made for purposes of medical diagnosis or treatment and describing the medical history, or past or present symptoms, pain, or sensations, or the inception or general character of the cause or external source thereof insofar as is reasonably pertinent to diagnosis or treatment.
- A memorandum or record concerning a matter about which a witness once had knowledge but now has insufficient recollection to enable the witness to testify fully and accurately, shown to have been made or adopted by the witness when the matter was fresh in the witness' memory and to reflect that knowledge correctly. If admitted, the memorandum or record may be read into evidence but may not itself be received as an exhibit unless offered by an adverse party.
- A memorandum, report, record, or data compilation, in any form, of acts, events, conditions, opinions, or diagnoses, made at or near the time by, or from information transmitted by, a person with knowledge, if kept in the course of a regularly conducted business activity, and if it was the regular practice of that business activity to make the memorandum, report, record or data compilation. The term business includes a business, institution, association, profession, occupation, and calling of every kind, whether or not conducted for profit.

- Evidence that a matter is not included in the memoranda reports, records, or data compilations, in any form, to prove the nonoccurrence or nonexistence of the matter, if the matter was of a kind of which a memorandum, report, record, or data compilation was regularly made and preserved, unless the sources of information or other circumstances indicate lack of trustworthiness.

- Records, reports, statements, or data compilations, in any form, of public offices or agencies, setting forth (a) the activities of the office or agency, or (b) matters observed pursuant to duty imposed by law as to which matters there was a duty to report, excluding, however, in criminal cases matters observed by police officers and other law enforcement personnel, or (c) in civil actions and proceedings and against the government in criminal cases, factual findings resulting from an investigation made pursuant to authority granted by law, unless the sources of information or other circumstances indicate lack of trustworthiness.

- Records of vital statistics. Records or data compilations, in any form, of births, fetal deaths, deaths, or marriages, if the report thereof was made to a public office pursuant to requirements of law.

- Absence of a public record or entry. To prove the absence of a record, report, statement, or data compilation, in any form, or the nonoccurrence or nonexistence of a matter of which a record, report, statement, or data compilation, in any form, was regularly made and preserved by a public office or agency, evidence in the form of a certification in accordance with Rule 902, or testimony, that diligent search failed to disclose the record, report, statement, or data compilation, or entry.

- Records of religious organizations. Statements of births, marriages, divorces, deaths, legitimacy, ancestry, relationship by blood or marriage, or other similar facts of personal or family history contained in a regularly kept record of a religious organization. Marriage, baptismal, and similar certificates. Statements of fact contained in a certificate that the maker performed a marriage or other ceremony or administered a sacrament, made by a clergyman, public official, or other person authorized by the rules or practices of a religious organization or by law to perform the act certified, and purporting to have been issued at the time of the act or within a reasonable time thereafter.

- Family records. Statements of fact concerning personal or family history contained in family Bibles, genealogies, charts, engravings on rings, inscriptions on family portraits, engravings on urns, crypts, or tombstones, or the like.

- Statements in ancient documents. Statements in a document in existence twenty years or more the authenticity of which is established.

- Judgment of previous conviction. Evidence of a final judgment, entered after a trial or upon a plea of guilty (but not upon a plea of nolo contendere), judging a person guilty of a crime punishable by death or imprisonment in excess of one year, to prove any fact essential to sustain the judgment, but not including, when offered by the government in a criminal prosecution for purposes other than impeachment, judgments against persons other than the accused. The pendency of an appeal may be shown but does not affect admissibility.

The following are not excluded by the hearsay rule if the declarant is unavailable as a witness:

1. **Former testimony.** Testimony given as a witness at another hearing of the same or a different proceeding, or in a deposition taken in compliance with law in the course of the same or another proceeding, if the party against whom the testimony

probative value, despite a limiting instruction, then the nonoffering party can argue that the evidence should be completely excluded because any limiting instruction would be inadequate.

A trial judge, in determining the prejudice to be suffered from the offered evidence, must necessarily take into account whether this prejudice can be sufficiently ameliorated by a limiting instruction. A trial judge is required to restrict the evidence to its proper scope and to instruct the jury accordingly if a request is made, but it does not articulate the requirements of a proper request.

Admission of Part of a Document

When a writing or recorded statement or part thereof is introduced by a party, an adverse party may require the introduction at that time of any other part or any other writing or recorded statement which ought in fairness to be considered contemporaneously with it. The rule is an expression of the rule of completeness. The rule is based on two considerations. The first is the misleading impression created by taking matters out of context. The second is the inadequacy of repair work when delayed to a point later in the trial.

The rule of completeness does not prevent the other party from developing the matter on cross-examination or as part of his or her own case. The rule is limited to writings and recorded statements and does not apply to conversations. The rule applies to separate writings and recordings as well as to excised portions of a single writing or recording.

Oral Statements

Where a party introduces a portion of an oral statement, the adversary is entitled to have omitted portions introduced at the same time, insofar as that is necessary to correct any misimpression that the initially proffered portion would create.[6]

Fairness

The fairness rule requires admission of completing evidence only when it ought "in fairness" to be considered with the admitted statement.[7] For example, the rule does not require that "portions of a writing which are neither explanatory of the previously introduced portions nor relevant to the introduced portions be admitted"; the rule does not mean that if any part of a statement is to be admitted, then the entire statement is to be admitted. Sometimes it is difficult to determine whether fairness mandates the admission of allegedly completing evidence.

A good example of the rule's fairness principle arose in *United States* v. *Haddad*.[8] Haddad was a prosecution for a firearms offense. In a postarrest confession, the defendant stated that he knew that marijuana was under his bed, but that he did not know that a gun was under the bed. At trial, the inculpatory statement was admitted as an admission, but the exculpatory statement was excluded as hearsay. The court of appeals found that the confession had been improperly (though harmlessly) redacted to exclude the exculpatory statement about the gun. The court noted that ordinarily, a defendant's self-serving, exculpatory, out-of-court statements would not be admissible. But here the exculpatory remarks were part of the very statement a portion of which the government was properly bringing before the jury, that is, the defendant's admission about the marijuana.

JUDICIAL NOTICE

The concept of **judicial notice** is used when a relevant fact is so well known that to require that it be proved would be a waste of time. For example, a trial judge may take judicial notice that July 4th is a court holiday. A judicially noticed fact must be one not subject to reasonable dispute in that it is either (1) generally known within the territorial jurisdiction of the trial court or (2) capable of accurate and ready determination by resort to sources whose accuracy cannot reasonably be questioned. A party is entitled upon timely request to an opportunity to be heard as to the propriety of taking judicial notice and the tenor of the matter noticed. In the absence of prior notification, the request may be made after judicial notice has been taken. Judicial notice may be taken at any stage of the proceeding.

RELEVANT EVIDENCE

Relevant evidence is where it has some tendency as a matter of logic and human experience to make the proposition for which it is advanced more likely than that proposition would appear to be in the absence of that evidence. To identify logically irrelevant evidence, ask, "Does the evidence assist in proving the fact that one party is trying to prove?"[9] Problems of relevancy call for an answer to the question of whether an item of evidence possesses sufficient probative value to justify receiving it in evidence. For example, evidence that a person purchased a revolver shortly prior to a fatal shooting with which he is charged is considered relevant because it may prove that the person was guilty of the fatal shooting if the gun used in the shooting is the same gun that was purchased.

Under the concept of conditional relevancy, probative value depends not only upon satisfying the basic requirement of relevancy, as described above, but also upon the existence of some matter of fact. For example, if evidence of a spoken statement is relied upon to prove notice, probative value is lacking unless the person sought to be charged heard the statement. Does the item of evidence tend to prove the matter sought to be proved?

Exclusion of Relevant Evidence on Grounds of Prejudice, Confusion, or Waste of Time

Although relevant, evidence may be excluded if its probative value is substantially outweighed by the danger of unfair prejudice, confusion of the issues, or misleading the jury, or by considerations of undue delay, waste of time, or needless presentation of cumulative evidence. Case law recognizes that certain circumstances call for the exclusion of evidence which is of unquestioned relevance. These circumstances entail risks which range all the way from inducing decision on a purely emotional basis, at one extreme, to nothing more harmful than merely wasting time, at the other extreme. Situations in this area call for balancing the probative value of and need for the evidence against the harm likely to result from its admission.

Exclusion for risk of unfair prejudice, confusion of issues, misleading the jury, or waste of time all find ample support in the authorities. Unfair prejudice within its context means an undue tendency to suggest decision on an improper basis, commonly, though not necessarily, an emotional one. Surprise is generally not a ground for exclusion under this concept, but unfair surprise may be a ground for exclusion if it is coupled with the danger of prejudice and confusion of issues.

Character Evidence Not Admissible to Prove Conduct, Exceptions, and Other Crimes

Evidence of a person's character or a trait of character is not admissible for the purpose of proving action in conformity therewith on a particular occasion, except:

- Character of the accused. Evidence of a pertinent trait of character offered by an accused, or by the prosecution to rebut the same, or if evidence of a trait of character of the alleged victim of the crime is offered by an accused and admitted, evidence of the same trait of character of the accused offered by the prosecution;
- Evidence of a pertinent trait of character of the alleged victim of the crime offered by an accused, or by the prosecution to rebut the same, or evidence of a character trait of peacefulness of the alleged victim offered by the prosecution in a homicide case to rebut evidence that the alleged victim was the first aggressor;
- Evidence of the character of a witness may be admissible to impeach the witnesses' testimony.
- Evidence of other crimes, wrongs, or acts is not admissible to prove the character of a person in order to show action in conformity therewith. It may, however, be admissible for other purposes, such as proof of motive, opportunity, intent, preparation, plan, knowledge, identity, or absence of mistake or accident, provided that upon request by the accused, the prosecution in a criminal case shall provide reasonable notice in advance of trial, or during trial if the court excuses pretrial notice on good cause shown, of the general nature of any such evidence it intends to introduce at trial.

Character questions arise in two fundamentally different ways: (1) Character may itself be an element of a crime, claim, or defense. A situation of this kind is commonly referred to as character in issue. Illustrations include the competency of the driver in an action for negligently entrusting a motor vehicle to an incompetent driver. No problem of the general relevancy of character evidence is involved, and the present rule therefore has no provision on the subject. (2) Character evidence is susceptible of being used for the purpose of suggesting an inference that the person acted on the occasion in question consistently with his character. This use of character is often described as circumstantial. Illustrations are evidence of a violent disposition to prove that the person was the aggressor in an affray or evidence of honesty to disprove a charge of theft. This circumstantial use of character evidence raises questions of relevancy as well as questions of allowable methods of proof.

In most jurisdictions today, the circumstantial use of character is rejected but with important exceptions: (1) an accused may introduce pertinent evidence of good character (often misleadingly described as putting his character in issue), in which event the prosecution may rebut with evidence of bad character; (2) an accused may introduce pertinent evidence of the character of the victim, as in support of a claim of self-defense to a charge of homicide or consent in a case of rape, and the prosecution may introduce similar evidence in rebuttal of the character evidence, or, in a homicide case, to rebut a claim that the deceased was the first aggressor, however proved; and (3) the character of a witness may be gone into as bearing on his credibility.

Character evidence is of slight probative value and may be very prejudicial. It tends to distract the jury from the main question of what actually happened on the particular occasion. It subtly permits the jury to reward the good man or to punish the bad man because of their respective characters despite what the evidence in the case shows actually happened.

RAPE SHIELD LAWS

Pursuant to Federal Rule 412 and similar state rules, the following evidence is not admissible in any civil or criminal proceeding involving alleged sexual misconduct of a victim except as otherwise provided in subdivisions Rule 412 (b) and (c):

1. Evidence offered to prove that any alleged victim engaged in other sexual behavior
2. Evidence offered to prove any alleged victim's sexual predisposition

Rule 412(b) Exceptions

In a criminal case, the following evidence is admissible, if otherwise admissible under these rules:

- Evidence of specific instances of sexual behavior by the alleged victim offered to prove that a person other than the accused was the source of semen, injury, or other physical evidence;
- Evidence of specific instances of sexual behavior by the alleged victim with respect to the person accused of the sexual misconduct offered by the accused to prove consent or by the prosecution; and
- Evidence the exclusion of which would violate the constitutional rights of the defendant.

Procedure to Determine Admissibility

A party intending to offer evidence under Federal Rule 412 (b) must

A. file a written motion at least fourteen days before trial specifically describing the evidence and stating the purpose for which it is offered unless the court, for good cause, requires a different time for filing or permits filing during trial; and
B. serve the motion on all parties and notify the alleged victim or, when appropriate, the alleged victim's guardian or representative.

Before admitting evidence under Rule 412, the court must conduct a hearing in camera and afford the victim and the parties a right to attend and be heard. The motion, related papers, and the record of the hearing must be sealed and remain under seal unless the court orders otherwise.

Federal Rule 412 was amended to also exclude all other evidence relating to an alleged victim of sexual misconduct that is offered to prove a sexual predisposition. This amendment was designed to exclude evidence that does not directly refer to sexual activities or thoughts but that the proponent believes may have a sexual connotation for the jury. Admission of such evidence would contravene Rule 412's objectives of shielding the alleged victim from potential embarrassment and safeguarding the victim against stereotypical thinking. Consequently, unless the exception is satisfied, evidence such as that relating to the alleged victim's mode of dress, speech, or lifestyle will not be admissible.

The reason for extending the rule to all criminal cases is obvious. The strong social policy of protecting a victim's privacy and encouraging victims to come forward to report criminal acts is not confined to cases that involve a charge of sexual assault. The need to protect the victim is equally great when a defendant is charged with kidnapping,

Oath or Affirmation

Before testifying, a witness is required to declare that he or she will testify truthfully, by oath or affirmation administered in a form calculated to awaken the witness's conscience and impress the witness's mind with the duty to do so. Along with cross-examination, the requirement of an oath is designed to ensure that every witness gives accurate and honest testimony. The idea behind the oath requirement is to preserve the integrity of the judicial process by awakening the witness's conscience and making the witness amenable to perjury prosecution if he fibs.[13] Federal Rule 603 states that a witness need not swear an oath, but may merely affirm that he or she will testify truthfully. The affirmation can be given in any form calculated to awaken the conscience of the witness and impress upon the witness the duty to tell the truth. By permitting affirmation as well as oath, many of the difficulties faced by certain members of some religious groups should be alleviated.

In *United States* v. *Ward*,[14] the defendant refused to testify because the trial judge did not permit him to take an altered version of the standard oath. The defendant would have taken an oath that substituted the term "fully integrated honesty" for the word "truth." The court of appeals held that the trial court was in error for refusing to accede to the defendant's demand. It found the defendant's objection to the standard oath to be based on "beliefs that are protected by the First Amendment." The court noted that there is no rigid formula for an acceptable oath. For example, a proffered oath that "I would not tell a lie to stay out of jail" has been properly rejected, since the witness could later say that he or she lied for some purpose other than to stay out of jail, such as to protect a relative.[15]

Impeachment of a Witness

Impeachment is a legal term referring to the process of attacking the credibility of a witness. The rules provide that the credibility of any witness may be attacked by any party, including the party calling the witness. At common law, a party who called a witness could not impeach that witness unless the court declared the witness to be a "hostile witness." This is no longer the rule in most jurisdictions. The rationale for the common-law rule rested on assumptions concerning a party's presumptive support of a witness called by that party and the need to protect the witness from harassment. The Federal Rules recognize that a party does not necessarily vouch for a witness; in fact, a party may have no choice but to call an adverse witness in order to prove a case.

Evidence of Character and Conduct of the Witness

The credibility of a witness may be attacked or supported by evidence in the form of opinion or reputation, but subject to these limitations: (1) the evidence may refer only to character for truthfulness or untruthfulness, and (2) evidence of a truthful character is admissible only after the character of the witness for truthfulness has been attacked by opinion or reputation evidence or otherwise.

Specific instances of the conduct of a witness, for the purpose of attacking or supporting the witness's character for truthfulness, may in the discretion of the court, if probative of truthfulness or untruthfulness, be inquired into on cross-examination of the witness (1) concerning the witness's character for truthfulness or untruthfulness or (2) concerning the character for truthfulness or untruthfulness of another witness as to which character the witness being cross-examined has testified.

Impeachment by Evidence of Conviction of Crime

Evidence that a witness other than an accused has been convicted of a crime is admissible if the crime was punishable by death or imprisonment in excess of one year by the law under which the witness was convicted; and evidence that an accused has been convicted of such a crime shall be admitted if the court determines that the probative value of admitting this evidence outweighs its prejudicial effect to the accused; and evidence that any witness has been convicted of a crime shall be admitted if it involved dishonesty or false statement, regardless of the punishment.

Evidence of a conviction is not admissible if a period of more than ten years has elapsed since the date of the conviction or of the release of the witness from the confinement imposed for that conviction, whichever is the later date, unless the court determines, in the interests of justice, that the probative value of the conviction supported by specific facts and circumstances substantially outweighs its prejudicial effect. However, evidence of a conviction more than ten years old, as calculated herein, is not admissible unless the proponent gives the adverse party sufficient advance written notice of an intent to use such evidence to provide the adverse party with a fair opportunity to contest the use of such evidence.

Evidence of a conviction is not admissible under this rule if the conviction has been the subject of a pardon, annulment, certificate of rehabilitation, or other equivalent procedure based on a finding of the rehabilitation of the person convicted, and that person has not been convicted of a subsequent crime which was punishable by death or imprisonment in excess of one year, or the conviction has been the subject of a pardon, annulment, or other equivalent procedure based on a finding of innocence.

Evidence of juvenile adjudications is generally not admissible. The court may, however, in a criminal case allow evidence of a juvenile adjudication of a witness other than the accused if conviction of the offense would be admissible to attack the credibility of an adult and the court is satisfied that admission in evidence is necessary for a fair determination of the issue of guilt or innocence.

Mode and Order of Interrogation and Presentation

The court exercises reasonable control over the mode and order of interrogating witnesses and presenting evidence so as to (1) make the interrogation and presentation effective for the ascertainment of the truth, (2) avoid needless consumption of time, and (3) protect witnesses from harassment or undue embarrassment.

Cross-examination should be limited to the subject matter of the direct examination and matters affecting the credibility of the witness. A court may, in the exercise of discretion, permit inquiry into additional matters as if on direct examination.

Leading questions should not be used on the direct examination of a witness except as may be necessary to develop the witness's testimony. Ordinarily leading questions should be permitted on cross-examination. When a party calls a hostile witness, an adverse party, or a witness identified with an adverse party, interrogation may be by leading questions.

A witness may be cross-examined on any matter relevant to any issue in the case, including credibility. In the interests of justice, the judge may limit cross-examination with respect to matters not testified to on direct examination.

Prior Statements of Witnesses

In examining a witness concerning a prior statement made by the witness, whether written or not, the statement need not be shown nor its contents disclosed to the witness at that time, but on request the same shall be shown or disclosed to opposing counsel. Evidence of a prior inconsistent statement by a witness is not admissible unless the witness is afforded an opportunity to explain or deny the same and the opposite party is afforded an opportunity to interrogate the witness thereon, or the interests of justice otherwise require.

One of the traditional ways of impeaching a witness is by introducing evidence of a prior inconsistent statement. Under common law, the examining party was required to lay an adequate foundation for the statement at the time the witness testified. This was referred to as "the rule in Queen Caroline's case." That rule required the cross-examining party to confront the witness directly on cross-examination with the inconsistent statement. At that point, the witness would have an opportunity to explain, repudiate, or deny the statement. If the witness denied making the statement, then the trial court could in its discretion permit the cross-examining party to prove that the statement was made.

Federal Rule 613 provides that when a witness is examined concerning a prior statement, this statement need not be shown to the witness at the time of the examination. However, before evidence of the statement can be introduced, the witness must be given some opportunity, at some point in the trial, to explain, repudiate, or deny the statement. On request of opposing counsel, the contents of the statement must be disclosed so that opposing counsel may protect his or her case against unwarranted insinuations that a statement has been made. The time for the showing or disclosure is when the witness is examined about the prior statement, assuming that a proper request is made.

Opportunity for Witness to Explain or Deny the Statement

The basic common-law foundation consists of affording the witness an opportunity for either admitting or denying that a prior inconsistent statement was made and, if he or she admits it, of explaining the circumstances of the statement. The traditional method of confronting a witness with his or her inconsistent statement prior to its introduction is the preferred method of proceeding. In fact, where the proponent of the testimony fails to do so and the witness subsequently becomes unavailable, the proponent runs the risk that the court will properly exercise its discretion to not allow the admission of the prior statement.

Exclusion of Witnesses (Invoking the Rule)

At the request of a party, the court shall order witnesses excluded so that they cannot hear the testimony of other witnesses, and it may make the order of its own motion. This rule does not authorize exclusion of (1) a party who is a natural person, or (2) an officer or employee of a party which is not a natural person designated as its representative by its attorney, or (3) a person whose presence is shown by a party to be essential to the presentation of the party's cause, or (4) a person authorized by statute to be present.

The sequestration of prospective witnesses is a common method of discouraging or preventing collusion and exposing inaccuracies in testimony. Federal Rule 615 provides that at the request of a party, or on its own motion, the court shall order witnesses excluded so that they cannot hear the testimony of other witnesses. Where a victim of a crime is a witness in the criminal case, the sequestration power set forth in Rule 615 has been substantially changed by legislation.

In a criminal case, the Sixth and Fourteenth Amendments entitle a defendant to be present, although the defendant may waive that right in several ways. It is generally held that the police officer in charge of the investigation is within the "officer or employee" exception provided in Rule 615. As noted by the appellate court in *United States* v. *Payan,*[16] a defendant has no right to sequestration of the officer in charge of the investigation.

Opinion Testimony by Lay (Nonexpert) Witnesses

If a witness is not testifying as an expert, the witness's testimony in the form of opinions or inferences is limited to those opinions or inferences which are (1) rationally based on the perception of the witness; (2) helpful to a clear understanding of the witness's testimony or the determination of a fact in issue; and (3) not based on scientific, technical, or other specialized knowledge. **Lay witnesses** often find it difficult to express themselves in language which is not that of an opinion or conclusion. While the courts have made concessions in certain recurring situations, necessity as a standard for permitting opinions and conclusions has proved too elusive and too unadaptable to particular situations for purposes of satisfactory judicial administration. For example, law enforcement agents could testify that the defendant was acting suspiciously without being qualified as experts; however, the rules on experts are applicable where the agents testify on the basis of extensive experience that the defendant was using code words to refer to drug quantities and prices. Courts have permitted lay witnesses to testify that a substance appeared to be a narcotic so long as a foundation of familiarity with the substance has been established. For example, two lay witnesses who were heavy amphetamine users were permitted to testify that a substance was amphetamine; but it was an error to permit another witness to make such an identification where she had no experience with amphetamines.[17] Such testimony is not based on specialized knowledge, but rather is based upon a layperson' s personal knowledge. If, however, that witness were to describe how a narcotic was manufactured, or to describe the intricate workings of a narcotic distribution network, then the witness would have to qualify as an expert.[18] In *State* v. *Brown,*[19] the trial court declared that the distinction between lay and expert witness testimony is that lay testimony "results from a process of reasoning familiar in everyday life," while expert testimony "results from a process of reasoning which can be mastered only by specialists in the field." The court in *Brown* noted that a lay witness with experience could testify that a substance appeared to be blood, but that a witness would have to qualify as an expert before he could testify that bruising around the eyes is indicative of skull trauma.

Testimony by Experts

If scientific, technical, or other specialized knowledge will assist the jury to understand the evidence or to determine a fact in issue, a witness qualified as an expert by knowledge, skill, experience, training, or education may testify thereto in the form of an opinion or otherwise if (1) the testimony is based upon sufficient facts or data, (2) the testimony is the product of reliable principles and methods, and (3) the witness has applied the principles and methods reliably to the facts of the case.

The fields of knowledge which may be drawn upon are not limited to the scientific and technical but extend to all specialized knowledge. Similarly, the expert is viewed not in a narrow sense, but as a person qualified by knowledge, skill, experience, training or education. Thus, within the scope of the rule are not only experts in the strictest sense of the word, such as, physicians, physicists, and architects, but also the large group sometimes called skilled witnesses, such as bankers or landowners testifying to land values.

The **Daubert** test set forth a nonexclusive checklist for trial courts to use in assessing the reliability of scientific expert testimony.[20] The specific factors explicated by the *Daubert* court are (1) whether the expert's technique or theory can be or has been tested—that is, whether the expert's theory can be challenged in some objective sense, or whether it is instead simply a subjective, conclusory approach that cannot reasonably be assessed for reliability; (2) whether the technique or theory has been subject to peer review and publication; (3) the known or potential rate of error of the technique or theory when applied; (4) the existence and maintenance of standards and controls; and (5) whether the technique or theory has been generally accepted in the scientific community.

The courts both before and after *Daubert* have found other factors relevant in determining whether expert testimony is sufficiently reliable to be considered by the trier of fact. These factors include:

- Whether experts are proposing to testify about matters growing naturally and directly out of research they have conducted independent of the litigation, or whether they have developed their opinions expressly for purposes of testifying.
- Whether the expert has unjustifiably extrapolated from an accepted premise to an unfounded conclusion.
- Whether the expert has adequately accounted for obvious alternative explanations.
- Whether the expert is being as careful as he would be in his regular professional work outside his paid litigation consulting.
- Whether the field of expertise claimed by the expert is known to reach reliable results for the type of opinion the expert would give.

A review of the case law after *Daubert* shows that the rejection of expert testimony is the exception rather than the rule. The court in *Daubert* stated: "Vigorous cross-examination, presentation of contrary evidence, and careful instruction on the burden of proof are the traditional and appropriate means of attacking shaky but admissible evidence."[21]

When a trial court rules that an expert's testimony is reliable, this does not necessarily mean that contradictory expert testimony is unreliable.

Bases of Opinion Testimony by Experts

The facts or data in the particular case upon which an expert bases an opinion or inference may be those perceived by or made known to the expert at or before the hearing. If they are of a type reasonably relied upon by experts in the particular field in forming opinions or inferences upon the subject, the facts or data need not be admissible in evidence in order for the opinion or inference to be admitted. Facts or data that are otherwise inadmissible shall not be disclosed to the jury by the proponent of the opinion or inference unless the court determines that their probative value in assisting the jury to evaluate the expert's opinion substantially outweighs their prejudicial effect.

Facts or data upon which expert opinions are based may, under the rule, be derived from three possible sources. The first is the firsthand observation of the witness, with opinions based thereon traditionally allowed. A treating physician is an example. The second source, presentation at the trial, also reflects existing practice. The technique may be the familiar hypothetical question or having the expert attend the trial and hear the testimony establishing the facts. The third source consists of presentation of data to the expert outside of court and other than by his or her own perception.

Disclosure of Facts or Data Underlying Expert Opinion

An expert may testify in terms of opinion or inference, and give reasons therefor without first testifying to the underlying facts or data, unless the court requires otherwise. The expert may in any event be required to disclose the underlying facts or data on cross-examination.

DOCUMENTS

Requirement of Original

To prove the content of a writing, recording, or photograph, the original writing, recording, or photograph is required, except as otherwise provided. Rule 1002 is the best evidence rule that requires the production of an original in order to prove the contents of a writing, recording, or photograph unless an exception is provided in another rule. The traditional rationale of the best evidence rule is that accuracy is promoted by production of the original because the process of copying creates a risk of error.

An exception to the best evidence rule is police testimony as to the contents of a confession. Officers who heard a defendant confess may testify to what they heard even if there is a recording of the confession and a transcript of that recording. A duplicate is admissible to the same extent as an original unless (1) a genuine question is raised as to the authenticity of the original or (2) in the circumstances it would be unfair to admit the duplicate in lieu of the original.

The original document is not required, and other evidence of the contents of a writing, recording, or photograph is admissible, if

1. The original has been lost or destroyed. The original is lost or has been destroyed, unless the proponent lost or destroyed it in bad faith; or
2. The original is not obtainable. No original can be obtained by any available judicial process or procedure; or
3. The original is in the possession of the opponent. At a time when an original was under the control of the party against whom offered, that party was put on notice, by the pleadings or otherwise, that the contents would be a subject of proof at the hearing, and that party did not produce the original at the hearing; or
4. Collateral matters. The writing, recording, or photograph is not closely related to a controlling issue.

Public Records

The contents of an official record, or of a document authorized to be recorded or filed and actually recorded or filed, including data compilations in any form, if otherwise admissible, may be proved by copy, certified as correct, or testified to be correct by a witness who has compared it with the original. If a copy that complies with the foregoing cannot be obtained by the exercise of reasonable diligence, then other evidence of the contents may be given.

Summaries

The contents of voluminous writings, recordings, or photographs which cannot conveniently be examined in court may be presented in the form of a chart, summary, or calculation. The originals, or duplicates, shall be made available for examination or copying, or both, by other parties at a reasonable time and place. The court may order that they be produced in court.

Requirement of Authentication or Identification

One of the general requirements of introducing real evidence, including writings, at trial is that the evidence must be authenticated. This means that someone must lay a sufficient foundation so that the jury is able to determine that the evidence is what it is supposed to be. Similarly, when a witness testifies to statements made by someone else, the witness must be able to identify the person from whom the statements emanated so that the trier of fact is able to properly attribute the statements.

The requirements for authenticating evidence are not burdensome, but they often require that foundational evidence be presented. Courts will not assume that evidence is what the proponent claims simply because on the face of the evidence it is apparent that it might be. In *United States* v. *Skipper*,[22] Skipper was charged with and convicted of possession of crack cocaine with intent to distribute. Police stopped the car that Skipper owned because he was changing lanes erratically. A plastic bag containing crack cocaine was thrown from the driver's side of the car shortly after the lights of the patrol car were activated. Skipper was arrested. At trial, the prosecution introduced criminal evidence of two other convictions for crimes allegedly committed by Skipper. Government Exhibit No. 3 was a certified copy of a judgment against "John Derrick Skipper" indicating that the defendant in that case had pleaded guilty to possession of a controlled substance. An expert testified that the fingerprints on this conviction matched Skipper's fingerprints. Government Exhibit No. 2 was a certified copy of a deferred adjudication order indicating that "John D. Skipper" was placed on ten-year probation for possession of a controlled substance. However, Exhibit No. 2 bore no fingerprints and the government did not otherwise identify Skipper as the person named in the order.

The court of appeals held that the trial judge erred, but the error was harmless in admitting Exhibit No. 2 because the prosecution failed to produce evidence proving that the defendant was the actual John D. Skipper named in the deferred adjudication order. The court held "that the mere similarity in name between a criminal defendant and a person named in a prior conviction alone does not satisfy the identification requirement."

San Diego, California, police evidence technicians and homicide detectives carry belongings out of a house of a neighbor of missing seven-year-old Danielle van Dam in a search for clues to the girl's disappearance on Tuesday, February 5, 2002, in San Diego. (*Source:* Fred Greaves/AP Wide World Photos.)

Chain of Custody

In criminal cases, a question of authenticity arises where something is seized from the defendant and then introduced at trial, and the defendant disputes that it is his or hers or argues that the thing has been altered in some way. One way for the prosecution to authenticate the evidence in these circumstances is to establish a chain of custody. Courts have been permissive in determining whether the government has established a sufficient chain of custody. The standard rule is that gaps in the chain of custody go to weight and not admissibility.[23] For example, a one-year gap in the chain of custody for contraband goes to the weight and not the admissibility of the evidence; there is no showing of bad faith on the part of government officials, who are entitled to a presumption that they did not alter the proffered evidence.

The most important chain of custody is the one from the original seizure of the evidence to the analysis of the substance. Given the fungibility of drugs, it is essential to make a connection between the substance seized from the defendant and the substance actually tested. Any substantial gap in this chain of custody or any indication of alteration should be treated as fatal, since otherwise there is an unacceptable risk that the test does not reflect the contents of the substance seized.[24] A gap in the chain occurring after testing can be treated more permissively, given the admissibility of the testing procedure itself and the fact that the only purpose for introducing the substance in court is to illustrate the testimony of government witnesses.

Testimony of a witness who has personal knowledge of a piece of evidence is a classic way of authenticating the evidence. Someone who is an eyewitness to the signing of a document may authenticate the document. A layperson can identify handwriting based upon familiarity with the handwriting. A signature may be the identified by the testimony of a person familiar with the signature. It is not essential for the witness to have been present when the signature was executed.

Handwriting, fingerprints, blood, hair, clothing fibers, and numerous other things can be authenticated by comparison with specimens that have been authenticated. Sometimes the comparison can be done by the jury; at other times, an expert witness will be required, especially when scientific knowledge is needed to make a valid examination of the samples. The trial judge has discretion to exclude specimens when questions as to their authenticity will be confusing and excessively time-consuming.

Sometimes the characteristics of an item will themselves serve to authenticate the item. A letter may be authenticated, for example, by its content and the circumstances indicating that it was a reply to a duly authenticated letter.

One who is familiar with the voice of another may authenticate a conversation or identify the speaker on a tape or other recording. However, if the tape or recording is offered for its truth, hearsay problems still will exist and must be solved following the satisfaction of the authentication requirement.

SUMMARY

- Evidence is a study of the regulations involving the process of proving facts.
- Two themes of the Federal Rules are that (1) the rules favor admissibility of evidence and (2) the trial judge has considerable discretion concerning the admissibility of evidence.
- Hearsay is a statement, other than one made by the declarant while testifying at the trial or hearing, offered in evidence to prove the truth of the matter asserted.
- Hearsay is inadmissible unless an exception is applicable.

ADVERSARY SYSTEM

Before discussing the actual trial proceedings, the roles of the other major participants in a criminal trial, in addition to the defendant, should be examined. These include the judge, prosecuting attorney, defense counsel, clerk of the court, bailiff, and court reporter. All are considered officers of the court. The function of the jury and the witnesses will be examined later. By the time of the trial, the law enforcement officer will have completed his or her major role in the administration of justice. The investigation will be finished, and the final duty will be serving as a witness and testifying in a truthful, convincing manner.

The criminal trial procedure varies little—whether the charge is a felony or misdemeanor or whether the trial is a court trial or jury trial. The defendant is entitled to a fair trial before an impartial judge and an honest jury in an atmosphere of judicial calm.

Our justice system is an **adversary system**, meaning that it has two sides. In a criminal trial, these are the prosecution and the defense. Each is permitted to present evidence in its own behalf. Theoretically, both sides come into the trial on an equal basis. But Justice White of the U.S. Supreme Court, in *United States* v. *Wade,* pointed out that our system is not a true adversary system with both sides entering the trial on an equal footing. He stated the following:[1]

> Law enforcement officers (and prosecuting attorneys) have the obligation to convict the guilty and to make sure they do not convict the innocent. They must be dedicated to making the criminal trial a procedure for the ascertainment of the true facts surrounding the commission of the crime. To this extent, our so-called adversary system is not adversary at all: nor should it be. But defense counsel has no comparable obligation to ascertain or present the truth. Our system assigns him a different mission. He must be and is interested in not convicting the innocent, but absent a voluntary plea of guilty, we also insist that he defend his client whether he is innocent or guilty. The State has the obligation to present the evidence. Defense counsel need present nothing, even if he knows

---

The Steps in a Jury Trial

Selection of the jury

Prosecutor's opening statement to the jury

Defense's opening statement to the jury

Prosecutor's presentation of evidence and direct examination

Defense's cross-examination of prosecutor's witness

Prosecution rests

Defense's presentation of evidence and direct examination

Prosecution's cross-examination of defense witnesses

Prosecution's case in rebuttal

Prosecution's closing argument

Defense's closing argument

Prosecution's argument in rebuttal

Judge's instructions to the jury

(*Note:* in some states this comes before arguments)

Jury deliberations and voting

Pronouncement of the verdict

Hearing on the sentence

what the truth is. He need furnish no witnesses to the police, reveal any confidences of his client, nor furnish any other information to help the prosecution's case. If he can confuse a witness, even a truthful one, or make him appear at a disadvantage, unsure or indecisive, that will be his normal course. Our interest in not convicting the innocent permits counsel to put the State to its proof, to put the State's case in the worst possible light, regardless of what he thinks or knows to be the truth. Undoubtedly there are some limits which defense counsel must observe but more often than not, defense counsel will cross-examine a prosecution witness, and impeach him if he can, even if he thinks the witness is telling the truth, just as he will attempt to destroy a witness who he thinks is lying. In this respect, as part of our modified adversary system and as part of the duty imposed on the most honorable defense counsel, we countenance or require conduct which in many instances has little, if any, relation to the search for truth.

JUDGE

Although the terms judge and the court are used interchangeably, they should be distinguished. The judge presides over the trial proceedings and exercises those duties and power imposed by law. The court is a judicial proceeding presided over by a judge. The judge plays a very important role both before and during the trial. There is a great deal of power and authority, and many decisions are solely at the judge's discretion. Since unscrupulous acts could seriously affect the administration of justice, the judge's actions are subject to review by appellate courts. This scrutiny avoids any abuse of power or authority by the judge. Fortunately, most judges are honest individuals who endeavor to do a conscientious job.

Superior or District Court Judges

In most states, the judges of the superior or district court, or its equivalent, are elected by the people of the judicial district where they serve. This district is often the county. These judges are attorneys with past experience in the practice of law. One might wonder why an attorney with a number of years in law practice would wish to become a judge. Probably the most prevalent reason is the prestige that the office holds. Judges are generally held in high esteem within a community. One might be fearful that a judge, being an elected official, would have political obligations that interfere with the ability to carry out his or her functions impartially. As practicing attorneys, most candidates for a judgeship are fairly well known to the people of the community. The campaigning is primarily through personal contacts and the assistance of friends and does not place the victorious judge in a position where he or she is bound to grant political favors. This situation does not mean that members of organized crime have not tried to influence elections, as well as judges, in some areas. But the great majority of judges have proven to be above this corrupt influence.

Inferior Court Judges

Like superior or district court judges, inferior court judges are elected in most states. They are elected by the people of the judicial district where they serve, but this district is only a portion of a county. The qualifications for this position vary greatly among states. In many outlying rural areas, there is not enough court business to justify a full-time judge, so the judge may be a local practicing attorney elected to act as the judge when court business is required. The judge may also be the operator of a local market or a service station, or may be a retired person who needs a part-time job, as usually there is no requirement that the judge of these courts be trained in law. The fact that these judges are

Law in Practice

Selection of State Judges

States where the judge is initially selected by a partisan election
Alabama, Arkansas, Illinois, Indiana, Louisiana, Mississippi, Missouri (in nonmetropolitan areas only), New York, North Carolina, Pennsylvania, Tennessee, Texas, and West Virginia

States where the judge is initially selected by a nonpartisan election
California, Florida, Georgia, Idaho, Kentucky, Michigan, Montana, Nevada, North Dakota, Ohio, Oklahoma, Oregon, South Dakota, Washington, and Wisconsin

States where the judge is initially selected based on merit
Alaska, Arizona, Colorado, Connecticut, Delaware, District of Columbia, Hawaii, Iowa, Kansas, Maryland, Massachusetts, Nebraska, New Mexico, Utah, Vermont, and Wyoming

States where the judge is initially appointed by the governor
Maine, New Hampshire, New Jersey, and Rhode Island

States where the judge is initially appointed by the state legislature
South Carolina and Virginia

Source: American Judicature Society, *Judicial Selection in the United States: A Compendium of Provisions,* 2nd ed. (Chicago: American Judicature Society, 1993).

often poorly paid encourages bribery. Some judges work on a commission, receiving a percentage of fines levied, often creating the temptation to fine excessively, particularly in traffic violation cases. The brand of justice meted out in such courts sometimes leaves a great deal to be desired. But again, like superior court judges, most inferior court judges are honest individuals elected because of the community's faith in their honesty and integrity. However, some inferior courts, like municipal courts in some districts, require the judge to be an attorney before acting in the capacity of judge, and the judges of these courts are capable of handling the responsibilities imposed on them.

Function of the Trial Judge

As pointed out in previous chapters, many duties have already been performed by the judge prior to the trial. With the judge sitting as magistrate, arraignments and preliminary hearings will have been held. Further, decisions will have been made on motions presented, appointments of counsel for indigent defendants will be completed, and the right to a speedy and fair trial will have been preserved. Though a fair trial is essential, a perfect trial is not expected.

During the trial, the judge has the primary responsibility for seeing that justice is carried out. The judge has a duty not only to protect the interests of the defendant but also to protect the interests of the public, ensuring that the guilty are convicted. The judge controls all proceedings during the trial and limits the introduction of evidence and arguments of counsel to relevant and material matters, with a view to the expeditious and effective ascertainment of the truth. The judge must control the conduct of the defendant and the spectators; determine the competency of witnesses and the admissibility of evidence; rule on objections made to questions asked by the attorneys; protect witnesses from harassment during cross-examination; interpret for the jury the laws involved in the particular case; and, in some jurisdictions, comment on the weight of the evidence presented and the credibility of witnesses. In many jurisdictions, the judge sentences the defendant after conviction. If the trial is a court trial, the judge renders a verdict of guilt or innocence. Additional duties during the trial will be enumerated as the discussion of the trial progresses.

Contempt of Court   A trial is to be conducted in a calm, dignified atmosphere. It is the responsibility of the judge to maintain such an atmosphere. Assisting in this regard is the authority to punish one who interrupts this atmosphere by declaring the offender in contempt of court. **Contempt** is an act that is disrespectful to the court or adversely affects the administration of justice. Any act that embarrasses, hinders, or obstructs the court in the administration of justice may be declared by the judge as contempt of court. Typical acts falling within this category include contemptuous or insulting remarks made to the judge and counsel's persistent arguments with the judge after an admonition to desist has been given. A judge may not go so far as to hold a defense counsel in contempt when counsel is merely defending his client vigorously. Disorderly conduct by a defendant or by the spectators may cause the judge to exercise the right of contempt. A witness who refuses to be sworn in and testify could be held in contempt of court. These acts generally take place within the presence of the judge and are known as direct contempt. The judge may punish the offender summarily—that is, there and then—without a hearing or any other procedure taking place. The punishment may be imprisonment and/or a fine.

Not only are insulting remarks made to a judge possible contemptuous acts, but also such remarks between the prosecuting attorney and the defense counsel. In *People* v. *Fusaro,* a case in which the two attorneys had exchanged a series of acrimonious remarks, the judge held both in contempt of court. The defense counsel accused the prosecuting attorney of "indulging in crap," to which the prosecuting attorney, according to the judge, "sank to the occasion by voicing an epithet denoting fecal matter of a male bovine."[2] On another occasion, a prosecuting attorney was held in contempt upon using an old southern colloquialism implying that the defendant was the incestuous son of a canine mother.

An interesting development arose out of the *Fusaro* case. The defense counsel was held in contempt and was imprisoned in the middle of the trial. The facts of the case reflect the following: "The record reveals an acrimonious five day trial in which the attorneys mistook bickering and side remarks for vigorous advocacy. The prosecutor . . . was guilty of at least one act of misconduct," and the defense attorney

> in his turn cluttered and interrupted the trial with frivolous objections. He aroused the trial judge's ire by permitting a witness to remain in the courtroom despite an exclusion order. He was twice late in returning to the trial after a recess.
>
> On the afternoon of the third day he was 15 minutes late, apologized and explained that the judge of another court had detained him. Outside the jury's presence the trial court held him in contempt for tardiness and imposed a one-day suspended jail sentence.

This exchange of remarks between the prosecuting attorney and defense counsel "indulging in crap" took place thereafter:

> At that point the judge recessed the trial, rebuked the attorneys, indicated that he wanted to consider their behavior and put the matter over to the next morning.
>
> The next morning, outside the jury's presence, the court found both attorneys in contempt.

The prosecuting attorney apologized, and the judge fined him $50. The defense counsel endeavored to justify the language. The judge

> imposed a 24-hour jail sentence on defense counsel, refused to stay the execution and committed him to jail immediately. In view of the jailing, defendant's trial was recessed until the following morning.

The defendant was convicted on four narcotics charges. The conviction was appealed on the grounds that the judge had abused discretion in holding the defense counsel in contempt and immediately imposing a jail sentence. The defendant alleged that the jailing of the counsel prejudiced the defendant in the eyes of the jury and that a speedy trial was denied because of the interruption. Although the appellate court upheld the conviction, the court took a dim view of jailing a defense counsel in the middle of a trial. The court stated the following:

> A trial court has inherent statutory power to exercise reasonable control over the trial in order to insure the orderly administration of justice and to maintain the dignity and authority of the court; it has power to punish summarily for contempts committed in its immediate view and presence. In accordance with the code of the State as punishment for contempt a court may impose a fine not exceeding $500 or up to five days imprisonment or both.

Attorneys as well as others may be held in contempt more than once during a trial and may be punished for each time they are so held. Offenders have been known to receive sentences lasting for years if the sentences are made to run consecutively. The U.S. Supreme Court has held that under these circumstances, the offender is entitled to a trial on the contempt charge. The Court stated that criminal contempt is a crime and that the offender is entitled to the same trial procedure as in any other crime. If the total sentence exceeds six months, the offender is entitled to a trial by jury. If the sentence is not more than six months, the offender may be tried by a judge sitting without a jury, but the Court stated that the trial should be conducted by a judge other than the one holding the offender in contempt because of the possible emotional involvement in the matter.[3] Some states grant a person accused of a crime a jury trial for all violations. The offender would then be entitled to a jury trial even though the sentence would not exceed six months.

The U.S. Supreme Court has considerably restricted the right of a trial judge to take summary contempt action and confused the action that may be taken. But the Court apparently did not eliminate the right entirely. The wording of the Court indicated that if it is necessary to preserve the calm atmosphere and dignity of the court, a judge may exercise the contempt action at the time of the misconduct and may even sentence the person involved. But if the judge waits until the conclusion of the trial to take the contempt action, the offender is entitled to a trial on the contempt charge.

Defense counsels are held in contempt more frequently than prosecuting attorneys. If a prosecuting attorney indulges in misconduct, the misconduct may be considered prejudicial error, and a conviction may be reversed on appeal.

In addition, acts not performed in the presence of the judge may also be declared as contempt. These acts are known as indirect, or constructive, contempt, and they are usually the result of failure to abide by court orders. For example, jurors may discuss the facts of the case during a recess—in violation of the judge's order not to discuss the case—a juror may refuse to appear in court without sufficient good reason after receiving a summons to appear, or a witness may not appear as directed. Since indirect contempt does not occur in the presence of the judge, a hearing is held to determine whether the alleged offender should be held in contempt. Prior to the hearing, the judge will issue an order requesting the offender to show cause why he or she should not be held in contempt of court. Witnesses both for and against will be questioned at the hearing to assist in determining whether the accused should be held in contempt. If the judge determines that the person should be held in contempt, it would appear that the offender is entitled to a trial on the contempt charge, since the act was not committed in the presence of the judge.

The right of contempt is a powerful weapon, and it is meant to be. It permits a judge to prohibit court proceedings from getting out of hand because of misconduct. It also protects those involved in the court proceedings. If a judge should abuse his or her power of contempt, appeals may be made to a higher court for review and possible remedy.

VICTIM AND PERPETRATOR

Victim

The victim of any crime is often the forgotten party in the criminal justice system. For many years, victims were perceived as simply another witness to the crime.[4] The prevailing attitude was that the real victim was the people of the state in which the crime was committed. Families of murder victims could not obtain information regarding the case and were often ignored by overworked and understaffed criminal justice personnel. Within the past twenty years, this attitude has begun to change as we have become more aware of the needs and desires of crime victims.

Law enforcement professionals dealing with crime victims must understand that these victims may be suffering emotional and/or physical trauma as a result of the offense.[5] Care must be taken to ensure that victims understand how the process works and what their rights are. It is also important to realize that there are individuals other than the original victim who have an interest in the process. These parties include the victim's family and friends and, in some situations, the victim's employer. All the appropriate parties should be notified of every significant event within the criminal justice process. Law enforcement professionals must also respect and protect the victim's right to privacy if that is the victim's desire.

Victims of crime will normally have a number of questions and concerns regarding the court system and their involvement in it. One of the most frustrating aspects of this process is the fact that victims often perceive that the defendant has more rights and faster access to the courts than they do.

Perpetrator

The perpetrator of a crime is guaranteed certain rights within our form of government. Many aspects of the criminal procedure process are controlled by the U.S. Constitution, specifically the Bill of Rights (the original ten amendments to the Constitution). These federal constitutional protections concerning individual rights are, for the most part, binding on state courts.[6]

These rights attach to the perpetrator early in the criminal procedure process, and violation of these rights may result in the case's being dismissed. For example, if the perpetrator confesses to the crime of murder and if that confession is obtained in violation of his or her constitutional rights, it may be suppressed.[7] If the confession is the only link connecting the defendant to the crime, the case may have to be dismissed. When these types of incidents occur, it is very difficult for the victim to understand why the defendant goes free when there has been a confession.

PROSECUTOR

The prosecuting attorney is known by a variety of names. In some places, he or she is known as the district attorney, or the D.A., and in other areas as the county attorney. In the federal system, the title is United States Attorney. The public official role of the prosecuting attorney is comparatively recent. For many years, it was the responsibility of the victim or relatives to prosecute when a crime was committed. Attorneys were employed by these persons to assist in the prosecution. As time passed, it was deemed advisable to have a full-time public prosecutor, since the offense was actually committed against society, and therefore the office of the prosecuting attorney was established.

In most states, the prosecuting attorney is an elected official of the county. In large urban areas, this is a sought-after position, since it holds prestige, it pays well, and the prosecuting attorney has a number of deputies for assistance. In many places, there may be no staff, and in sparsely settled counties, the position may be only a part-time job. When not engaged in handling official duties, the prosecuting attorney in such counties may have a private law practice. A few states have permitted several counties to form a judicial district and employ a single prosecuting attorney to handle the duties. Many attorneys have no interest in running for the position of prosecuting attorney, since their private practices are more lucrative. Others shun the idea of running as a candidate in an

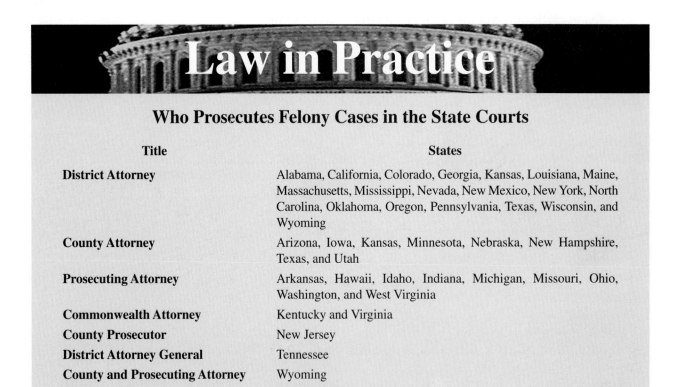

Law in Practice

Who Prosecutes Felony Cases in the State Courts

Title	States
District Attorney	Alabama, California, Colorado, Georgia, Kansas, Louisiana, Maine, Massachusetts, Mississippi, Nevada, New Mexico, New York, North Carolina, Oklahoma, Oregon, Pennsylvania, Texas, Wisconsin, and Wyoming
County Attorney	Arizona, Iowa, Kansas, Minnesota, Nebraska, New Hampshire, Texas, and Utah
Prosecuting Attorney	Arkansas, Hawaii, Idaho, Indiana, Michigan, Missouri, Ohio, Washington, and West Virginia
Commonwealth Attorney	Kentucky and Virginia
County Prosecutor	New Jersey
District Attorney General	Tennessee
County and Prosecuting Attorney	Wyoming
Solicitor	South Carolina
Circuit Attorney	City of St. Louis
Statewide prosecution	Alaska, Delaware, and Rhode Island

Note: Some states are listed more than once because different parts of the state use a different system.

Source: Carol DeFrances, Steven Smith, and Louise van der Does, "Prosecutors in State Courts, 1994" (Washington, D.C.: Bureau of Justice Statistics, National Institute of Justice, 1996).

election. As a result, in many counties, the office of the prosecuting attorney is a training ground for younger attorneys willing to run for the office to gain experience and to tide them over financially while building a private practice. In most counties, the prosecuting attorney is a capable and reputable local attorney who has a sincere interest in making certain that justice is done.

Responsibilities of the Prosecuting Attorney

The prosecuting attorney has a great deal of power, irrespective of personal capabilities or jurisdiction of service. The prosecuting attorney is charged with grave responsibilities to the public that demand integrity, zeal, and conscientious effort in the administration of justice. As stated by the U.S. Supreme Court in the *Gideon* decision, prosecuting attorneys "are everywhere deemed essential to protect the public's interest in an orderly society." The public prosecutor institutes proceedings before magistrates for the arrest of persons charged with or reasonably suspected of committing a public offense. In addition to acting as prosecutor, in most instances he or she represents the county on all civil matters.

The prosecuting attorney enters the justice procedural picture early in the prosecutive process. A great number of arrests are made by law enforcement officers on their own determination that there is reasonable cause to believe that a crime has been committed. Unless the alleged offender is released by the arresting agency without further action being taken, the prosecuting attorney must be consulted to determine whether prosecutive action will be taken against the arrested person. The prosecuting attorney evaluates the weight of evidence against the accused and the nature of the charge in deciding whether to prosecute. If the prosecuting attorney decides against prosecution, the accused will be released. If he or she decides that prosecutive action should be taken, a complaint will be prepared by the prosecuting attorney and filed with the appropriate court. The accused is then taken before a committing magistrate for the initial appearance, or arraignment, as it is referred to in some jurisdictions. Often law enforcement agencies conduct an investigation of alleged violations before making an arrest. In these instances, the prosecuting attorney is

Duty of a Prosecutor in a Criminal Case

The National District Attorneys Association states that it is the fundamental duty of prosecutors to seek truth and justice, not merely convictions. If you were the prosecutor, how would you handle the following situations?

You are assigned to prosecute a robbery case. The victim has identified the perpetrator in a photographic lineup and at the beginning of the trial. A detective has testified that the defendant has confessed to the crime. During a break in the trial, the victim tells you that he is not sure whether the defendant was the person who robbed him.

During cross-examination of a rape defendant, you start to doubt the testimony of the victim and begin to believe that the act may have been consensual in nature.

You are in charge of issuing cases, and you are screening one involving a terrorist who was found with explosives and plans to detonate an explosive device on a cruise ship. You discover that the arrest was invalid; therefore, if you do not issue a complaint, he will go free. If you issue the complaint, the investigating officer assures you that he can find other crimes to charge the terrorist with and keep him in confinement.

usually consulted to determine whether there is sufficient evidence against the accused to justify prosecutive action, whether a complaint should be filed, and whether a warrant of arrest should be obtained. As pointed out in Chapter 5, the prosecuting attorney may prefer to present the charge to the grand jury to determine whether prosecutive action should be taken or whether a secret indictment should be sought. This procedure is followed in felony charges. If the crime for which the arrest was made is a less serious misdemeanor, the prosecutive decision may be left to the discretion of the law enforcement agency involved. Even the preparation of the complaint and the prosecution during the trial may be handled by the officer, and the prosecuting attorney may not appear on the scene unless a special problem arises. In the more serious misdemeanor cases and on felony charges, the prosecuting attorney will be involved from the time of arrest through the appeal.

If the charge is a serious one and the prosecuting attorney decides to prosecute, there are many decisions and duties to perform. The first duty is to determine what charge or charges the evidence will support so that the appropriate accusatory pleading may be filed. The prosecuting attorney must decide whether the charges, when there is more than one, are to be separated into different trials or consolidated into one. In some jurisdictions, if the charge is a felony, it must be decided whether the facts are to be presented in a preliminary hearing or to a grand jury. The information or the indictment must be prepared depending on the type of hearing conducted. Where appropriate, the granting of motions requested by the defense must be disputed.

At the time of the trial, another responsibility is to present enough evidence to prove the defendant guilty beyond a reasonable doubt. The prosecuting attorney must also assist in the selection of the jury, decide what witnesses to call, and determine what physical evidence should be introduced. It is not necessary that every person who has some knowledge of the facts in the case be called, nor is it necessary that all physical evidence collected by the law enforcement officers during an investigation be presented during a trial. The prosecuting attorney must present enough witnesses and physical evidence to ensure the defendant a fair trial, and may not withhold any evidence that

Law in Practice

Significant Cases Involving the Prosecutor

Berger v. *United States* (1935)	Court notes that the prosecutor's primary interest is in doing justice, not simply winning cases.
Imbler v. *Pachtman* (1976)	Prosecutors enjoy absolute immunity from civil liability when making decisions about initiating and pursuing a criminal prosecution.
Morrison v. *Olson* (1988)	The federal independent counsel law is constitutional.
Burns v. *Reed* (1991)	Prosecutors have only qualified immunity from civil lawsuits concerning advice they give to police officers.
Buckley v. *Fitzsimmons* (1993)	Prosecutors have only qualified immunity from civil lawsuits for statements made during a news conference. They also have only qualified immunity for actions they take during criminal investigations.
Kalina v. *Fletcher* (1997)	A prosecutor may be subject to civil liability for making false statements of fact in an affidavit in support of an arrest warrant.

The Elected Prosecutor

The first election of a district attorney in Philadelphia occurred in 1850 [Carole Ramsey, "The Discretionary Power of 'Public' Prosecutors in Historical Perspective," 39 *Am. Crim. L. Rev.* 1309 (2002)]. In New York State, private lawyers ceased to represent victims at trial when the district attorney became an elected official in 1846. Private settlements were also eliminated. A complainant might approach the district attorney to urge investigation and prosecution; however, by the second half of the nineteenth century, the district attorney possessed sole discretion over whether to present the victim's charges to the grand jury [N.Y. Const. of 1846, art. X, § 1]. The election of district attorneys represented a move to subject a variety of local officials, including sheriffs and coroners, to the vote. The change ostensibly arose from a desire to increase accountability to the voters. What control should the public have over prosecutors? Consider the two quotes below.

> The . . . main remedy for prosecutorial misconduct [besides administrative supervision, trial court control, and appellate review] is public oversight. State district attorneys typically are elected officials. Misconduct within their offices—even by lawyers whom they have not directly supervised—becomes an issue during elections. Accordingly, media attention and political review by the voters may provide a deterrent or, at least, a reason for district attorneys to take corrective steps when misconduct is brought to their attention.

[Fred C. Zacharias, "The Professional Discipline of Prosecutors," 79 *N.C.L. Rev.* 721, 765 (2001)]

> I do not suggest that the honorable prosecutor be the slave of his electorate. Indeed, in many matters his duty clearly lies in the defiance of community pressures. But within the confines of the law, I would rather see his discretion guided by an honest effort to discern public needs and community concerns than by personal pique or moralistic impertinence.

[H. Richard Uviller, "The Virtuous Prosecutor in Quest for an Ethical Standard: Guidance from the ABA." 71 *Mich. L. Rev.* 1145, 1153 (1973)]

would be advantageous to the defendant. If the defense presents witnesses in its behalf, the prosecuting attorney must cross-examine them. The responsibilities of making recommendations to the judge on the severity of the sentence and of assisting the state attorney general with appeals also fall to the prosecuting attorney.

STATE ATTORNEY GENERAL

In most states, the attorney general has broad authority to coordinate local prosecutions. This authority includes the right to prosecute on his or her own and to supervise, assist, and consult local prosecuting attorneys. If a local prosecuting attorney needs assistance or fails to perform his or her duties, the attorney general is free to act. Unless called on by the local prosecutor or unless the local prosecutor fails to prosecute when the facts warrant it, the state attorney general does not ordinarily intervene. There are a few states where the attorney general has no authority over local prosecutions. If there is a malfeasance in office by the local prosecuting attorney in those states, the governor could be called to appoint a special prosecutor to perform the duties of the local prosecutor. When a case is appealed, in most jurisdictions it is the responsibility of the state attorney general to present the case to the appellate court. The attorney general will be assisted by the prosecuting attorney of the county in which the trial took place.

Law In Practice

State of New York Attorney General's Organizational Structure

Source: Office of the New York State Attorney General at www.org.state.ny.us. Accessed November 11, 2005.

DEFENSE COUNSEL

The defense attorney represents the rights and interests of the perpetrator. Unlike the prosecutor, who is concerned with justice, truth, and fairness, the defense attorney's obligation as established by the American Bar Association's General Standards of Conduct is to use all of his or her courage, devotion, and skills to protect the rights of the accused. Many defense attorneys interpret this obligation as requiring that they do everything possible to obtain an acquittal even if they know that the defendant in fact committed the offense.

The Sixth Amendment to the U.S. Constitution requires that those who are accused of crimes have a right to be represented by an attorney. The Supreme Court in the landmark case of *Gideon* v. *Wainwright* established the principle that all defendants have a right to counsel in all felony cases even if they cannot afford to hire their own attorney.[8] The Court extended this concept to misdemeanor cases in *Argersinger* v. *Hamilin,* holding that absent a waiver, no person may be imprisoned for any offense, either misdemeanor or felony, unless he or she has been represented by an attorney.[9]

There are basically four types of defense attorneys: public defenders, contract defense services, assigned defense counsel, and private defense counsel. Public defenders are hired and paid for by the government and are appointed to represent those persons charged with crimes who cannot afford to hire an attorney to represent them. Many counties have public defenders' offices that are staffed by very able, aggressive attorneys. However, there are instances when, for a variety of reasons, the public defenders office has a conflict of interest in a case. For example, this conflict might occur if there were two defendants in one case. In this situation, the court might appoint an attorney from the contract defense services to represent one of the two defendants. Contract defense services normally comprise a group of attorneys who have entered into an agreement with the county to represent indigent defendants for a specified amount of money. Assigned defense counsels exist in the majority of the counties in the United States.[10] Many of these counties are small and cannot afford the cost of maintaining a public defenders office. Under the assigned defense counsel format, the court maintains a list of attorneys who are willing to be appointed to represent indigent criminal defendants. When a defendant appears in court, the judge appoints the next attorney on the list to represent this person. The last form of defense attorney is the private defense counsel. These attorneys usually represent those defendants who are capable of paying for their services. Well-known examples of private defense counsel include attorneys such as Johnny Cochran, F. Lee Bailey, and Alan Dershowitz of the "Dream Team" who represented O.J. Simpson.

Not only do perpetrators have a right to an attorney, the courts have held that the attorney must be competent.[11] Although the Constitution requires competent counsel who will vigorously defend the perpetrator, there is no requirement or right to have an attorney who will knowingly present perjured testimony. In *Nix* v. *Whiteside,* the defense attorney, upon learning that his client was going to take the stand and commit perjury, informed the client that he could not permit such testimony and that if the client insisted upon giving this testimony, the attorney would disclose the perjury and withdraw from the case. The perpetrator testified and did not commit perjury; however, he did file an appeal claiming ineffective counsel. The court disagreed, holding that attorneys who follow their state's rules of professional (ethical) conduct do not violate the Sixth Amendment right to counsel.[12]

Right to Represent Oneself

The Supreme Court has held that the Sixth Amendment right to counsel allows a defendant to proceed pro se, that is, to represent himself or herself without counsel.[13] The rationale is that the right to counsel guaranteed by the Sixth Amendment is a personal right of the accused, not a right bestowed upon an attorney representing the accused. The defendant who desires to proceed pro se must make a knowing and an intelligent waiver of his or her right to an appointed counsel. The right to represent oneself does not mean that the defendant can engage in disrespectful or disruptive conduct in court. Additionally, the courts have stated that when a defendant knowingly waives the right to counsel, he or she cannot later raise the issue of ineffective representation; in essence, the accused has waived any appeal on this issue.

Privileged Communication

Defense counsels are often placed in a most awkward position because of the age-old relationship of **privileged communication** between attorney and client. This relationship provides that information furnished to an attorney in confidence by his or her client may not be revealed without the permission of the client. Law enforcement agencies may be unaware of crimes discussed by a client. In one instance, a client told his attorney about two murders that he had committed and where the bodies were buried. The problem created by receiving this information is whether the attorney should furnish it to the appropriate law enforcement agency or keep it in strictest confidence.[14] The answer to this question has been debated by many legal scholars, with no concrete answer forthcoming. It would appear that the better action would be to give the information to the appropriate law enforcement agency so that the bodies could be recovered and relatives notified. Society, as well as the criminal, is entitled to some consideration and justice. In most instances, prosecutive action cannot be taken, since the exclusionary rule would prohibit the use of the information as evidence.

If the facts of a case are such that an attorney cannot accept the responsibility of effectively defending a client, the case should be refused. Once the case is accepted, it is the attorney's duty to remain until it has been brought to a logical conclusion. The defense attorney has many functions to perform, both before and during the trial. A conference with the accused should be held as soon as practically possible. This conference should be private and unobserved even though the accused is in jail at the time. If there are codefendants, the defense counsel must decide whether all of them can be effectively represented without a conflict of interest. If either counsel or one of the defendants feels that being represented by just one counsel would result in prejudice, each defendant is entitled to and must be provided with individual counsel.

The defense counsel will advise the defendant on the plea that should be entered at the arraignment, and counsel will be present for the purpose of cross-examining witnesses at the preliminary hearing. Counsel also has a right to be present during an identification lineup procedure if the defendant has been formally charged; however, the attorney has no right to interfere with the lineup or to prohibit the defendant from participating. The counsel will file those motions that are in the best interest of the defendant. The defendant is entitled to sit with counsel at the counsel table during the trial so that they may confer on the defense. This assistance is another reason why a defendant is entitled to be present during a trial. Defense counsel will cross-examine prosecution witnesses when appropriate and will present such evidence on behalf of the defendant deemed necessary under the circumstances. Further duties of the defense counsel will be pointed out in the discussion of trial procedures.

CLERK OF THE COURT

With the judge, the prosecuting attorney, and the defense counsel all playing dramatic roles during a criminal trial, one could easily overlook the clerk of the court, or county clerk, as the position is also known. This official also has a most important function in the justice system, not only during the trial but before and after it as well. The main function of the court clerk is to maintain all records of a particular case. These records include items such as copies of all the accusatory pleadings and motions that have been filed. The clerk also issues subpoenas and, in many jurisdictions, prepares the jury panel. He or she attends trials to swear in witnesses, marks exhibits, and maintains the evidence that is introduced. The clerk also keeps copies of the court transcripts, judgments rendered, and motions for appeals.

BAILIFF

The court **bailiff** may be a permanent member of the justice system or an individual appointed to assist in a particular trial. In some jurisdictions, the bailiff is a member of the county government and carries the title of marshal. The bailiff assists the judge in maintaining order in the court and calls the witnesses to testify. If the defendant has not been released from custody, it is the duty of the bailiff to guard the defendant in the courtroom. When the jury is sequestered, it is the responsibility of the bailiff to make certain that the jurors are free from all contact with the public; the bailiff will return the jury to the courtroom after they have reached a verdict. In many jurisdictions, the bailiff serves court orders and other court papers.

COURT REPORTER

The responsibility of recording everything said during the trial proceeding belongs to the court reporter. This includes the testimony of all the witnesses, objections made to the attorney's questions, rulings made by the judge, and conferences between the attorneys and the judge. If the case is taken up on appeal, the recorded notes must be transcribed.

The court reporter must be highly skilled to record transactions as they take place, often at a rapid pace. The reporter may record the proceedings in shorthand or with a stenotype machine. When first used in the courtroom, tape recorders were not very reliable. However, today many jurisdictions are using audiotapes to record the trial proceedings. These recorders have increased both their reliability and the quality of recording.

COURT COMMISSIONER

In many judicial districts, court commissioners are appointed to assist trial judges. In most instances, they must possess the same qualifications as the judge, and a commissioner may substitute for a judge in an emergency situation. Otherwise, the commissioners hold hearings on motions filed, set and accept bail, and perform other duties that may be imposed on them by law.

Capstone Cases

Strickler v. *Greene*
527 U.S. 263; 119 S.Ct. (1999); 144 L.Ed. 2d 286 (1999)

The District Court for the Eastern District of Virginia granted petitioner's application for a writ of habeas corpus and vacated his capital murder conviction and death sentence on the grounds that the Commonwealth had failed to disclose important exculpatory evidence and that petitioner had not, in consequence, received a fair trial. The Court of Appeals for the Fourth Circuit reversed because petitioner had not raised his constitutional claim at his trial or in state collateral proceedings. In addition, the Fourth Circuit concluded that petitioner's claim was, "in any event, without merit." Finding the legal question presented by this case considerably more difficult than the Fourth Circuit, we granted certiorari, to consider (1) whether the State violated *Brady* v. *Maryland*, 373 U.S. 83, 10 L.Ed. 2d 215, 83 S.Ct. 1194 (1963), and its progeny. . . .

In the early evening of January 5, 1990, Leanne Whitlock, an African-American sophomore at James Madison University, was abducted from a local shopping center and robbed and murdered. In separate trials, both petitioner and Ronald Henderson were convicted of all three offenses. Henderson was convicted of first-degree murder, a noncapital offense, whereas petitioner was convicted of capital murder and sentenced to death.

(Continued)

testimony was prejudicial in the sense that it made petitioner's conviction more likely than if she had not testified, and discrediting her testimony might have changed the outcome of the trial.

That, however, is not the standard that petitioner must satisfy in order to obtain relief. He must convince us that "there is a reasonable probability" that the result of the trial would have been different if the suppressed documents had been disclosed to the defense. [T]he question is whether "the favorable evidence could reasonably be taken to put the whole case in such a different light as to undermine confidence in the verdict."

Even if Stoltzfus and her testimony had been entirely discredited, the jury might still have concluded that petitioner was the leader of the criminal enterprise because he was the one seen driving the car by Kurt Massie near the location of the murder and the one who kept the car for the following week. In addition, Tudor testified that petitioner threatened Henderson with a knife later in the evening.

More importantly, however, petitioner's guilt of capital murder did not depend on proof that he was the dominant partner: Proof that he was an equal participant with Henderson was sufficient under the judge's instructions. Accordingly, the strong evidence that Henderson was a killer is entirely consistent with the conclusion that petitioner was also an actual participant in the killing. Furthermore, there was considerable forensic and other physical evidence linking petitioner to the crime. The weight and size of the rock, and the character of the fatal injuries to the victim, are powerful evidence supporting the conclusion that two people acted jointly to commit a brutal murder.

We recognize the importance of eyewitness testimony; Stoltzfus provided the only disinterested, narrative account of what transpired on January 5, 1990. However, Stoltzfus' vivid description of the events at the mall was not the only evidence that the jury had before it. The record provides strong support for the conclusion that petitioner would have been convicted of capital murder and sentenced to death, even if Stoltzfus had been severely impeached. The jury was instructed on two predicates for capital murder: robbery with a deadly weapon and abduction with intent to defile.

Accordingly, the judgment of the Court of Appeals is Affirmed.

SUMMARY

- Our system of justice is based on the adversary system.
- The judge presides over the trial proceedings and performs those duties imposed upon him or her by law.
- The trial judge has the primary responsibility during a trial for ensuring that justice is carried out.
- A trial judge has contempt authority. Contempt is an act that is disrespectful to the court or adversely affects the administration of justice.
- The victim is often the forgotten person in the trial.
- The prosecutor's primary duty is to promote justice.
- The prosecutor institutes proceedings before magistrates for the arrest of persons charged with or reasonably suspected of committing a public offense.
- In most states, the state attorney general has broad authority to coordinate local prosecutions.
- The defense counsel has a duty to represent the defendant.
- There are four types of defense attorneys: public defenders, contract defense services, assigned defense counsel, and private retained counsel.

REVIEW QUESTIONS

1. What is the primary function of the judge?
2. List four duties of the judge during trial proceedings.
3. What is contempt of court?

4. Name three types of misconduct that might cause one to be held in contempt of court.
5. List five duties and/or responsibilities of the prosecuting attorney.
6. What are some of the problems that a defense attorney encounters with a client?
7. List four duties of a defense counsel.
8. Describe the functions of the following:
   a. the clerk of court
   b. the bailiff
   c. the court reporter

LOCAL PROCEDURE

1. Does the state attorney general have the authority to assist local prosecuting attorneys in handling prosecutions?

ENDNOTES

1. 388 U.S. 218 (1967).
2. See *People* v. *Fusaro,* 18 Cal App 3rd 877 (1971).
3. See *Taylor* v. *Hayes,* 418 U.S. 488 (1974) and *Codispoti* v. *Pennsylvania,* 418 U.S. 506 (1974).
4. This section has been adapted from H. Wallace, *Victimology: Legal, Psychological and Social Perspectives* (Allyn & Bacon, Boston), 1996.
5. M. Randell and L. Haskell, "Sexual Violence in Women's Lives," 1/1 *Violence Against Women* 6 (1995).
6. The Fifth Amendment's right to grand jury indictment and the Eighth Amendment's right regarding excessive bail have not been applied to the states. See *Hurtado* v. *California,* 110 U.S. 516 (1884).
7. If the confession was obtained by coercion, it may not be admitted even for impeachment purposes. See *Mincey* v. *Arizona,* 437 U.S. 385 (1978).
8. 372 U.S. 335 (1963).
9. 407 U.S. 25 (1972). See also *Scott* v. *Illinois,* 440 U.S. 367 (1979), where the U.S. Supreme Court held that the right to counsel only applies where imprisonment is actually imposed rather than merely authorized by statute.
10. Bureau of Justice Statistics Bulletin, *Criminal Defense Systems* (U.S. Department of Justice, Washington, D.C., August 1984), p. 6.
11. *Strickland* v. *Washington,* 466 U.S. 668 (1984).
12. 475 U.S. 157 (1986).
13. *Faretta* v. *California,* 422 U.S. 806 (1975).
14. Robert Garrow was arrested and charged with murder of a young girl. At the time of his arrest, police suspected that Garrow had committed at least two other murders. Garrow admitted these other murders to his defense counsel and told the lawyers where the bodies were. The victims were both teenage girls. Garrow's lawyers, following his directions, found the girls' bodies and photographed them. They did not provide information about their discovery of the bodies to the police. The father of one of the girls, thought it might be possible that Garrow was involved in the case of his daughter and approached one of the defense counsel to see if he could obtain information about his daughter. The attorney did not reveal to the father information he had learned from Garrow. After Garrow was convicted of murder, the district attorney brought charges against the defense attorneys. The charges were later dismissed. A state bar committee concluded that the attorneys were bound by the confidentiality of a lawyer-client relationship and that their failure to disclose the information was correct. See *Confidentiality and the Case of Robert Garrow's Lawyers,* 25 BUFFALO L. REV. 211, 213-14 (1975).

would be most difficult to find in some jurisdictions. If such a jury were possible, the chances of jury impartiality would be low. Fortunately, courts have not gone this far in selecting juries. As long as the jury is made up of persons representing a cross section of the community in which the trial takes place, it is regarded as comprising one's peers.

At one time, only white males were qualified to serve as jurors. In fact, most states did not permit women to serve on juries until they were granted the right to vote with the passage of the Nineteenth Amendment to the U.S. Constitution in 1920. Persons of certain races, religions, and national origins were excluded, if not by statutory provision, then by those making the **jury panel** selection. These exclusions were justified by those responsible for the jury panel, since they were to select only persons who were males, over twenty-one years of age, honest, intelligent, and of good character and sound judgment. It was alleged that members of minority groups did not meet these qualifications. To overcome this practice, the federal government passed legislation stating that no citizen shall be excluded from service on a federal grand jury or a federal petit jury because of race, color, religion, sex, national origin, or economic status and that persons are to be selected at random from a fair cross section of the community.[1]

Cross Section of the Community Standard

Many states have adopted the **cross section of the community standard** to meet the peer group regulation, particularly in view of U.S. Supreme Court decisions. In *Glasser* v. *United States*,[2] the Court stated, "The American tradition of trial by jury, considered in connection with either criminal or civil proceedings, necessarily contemplates an impartial jury drawn from a cross section of the community." The Court has also stated that it is part of the established tradition in the use of juries as instruments of public justice that the jury be a body truly representative of the community. However, what is a truly representative body? Does it pertain only to race, education, age, sex, religion, economic status, or philosophical thinking, or must *all* of these matters be considered when composing a jury panel? These questions were partially answered by the U.S. Supreme Court in *Fay* v. *New York*,[3] where the Court stated the following:

> There is no constitutional right to a jury drawn from a group of uneducated and unintelligent persons. Nor is there any right to a jury chosen solely from those at the lower end of the economic and social scale. But there is a constitutional right to a jury drawn from a group which represents a cross section of the community. And a cross section of the community includes persons with varying degrees of training and intelligence and with varying economic and social positions. Under our Constitution, the jury is not to be made the representative of the most intelligent, the most wealthy or the most successful, nor of the least intelligent, the least wealthy or the least successful. It is a democratic institution, representative of all qualified classes of people.

Only by being able to select a jury from among persons who truly represent a cross section of a community can the accused be assured of an impartial jury.

In order to have a truly representative cross section of a community on a jury panel, more and more jurisdictions are conducting surveys to determine the percentage of persons of minority races and different national origins within the community. In this way, a like percentage can be included on jury panels. Younger people make up a larger percentage of those selected to serve on jury panels. In the past, juries frequently comprised older persons, since they were less likely to suffer financially by serving on juries. As idealistic as it may be to have a truly representative cross section of the community, juries often are not truly representative because many classes of persons suffer financial hardships by serving and are thus excused. However, as long as there is no systematic

Forensic psychiatrist Dr. Park Dietz testifies regarding the mental state of Deanna Laney during her capital murder trial in Tyler, Texas, on Wednesday, March 31, 2004. (*Source:* AP Wide World Photos.)

exclusion of any class of persons, the cross-section requirement is fulfilled. As pointed out by the courts, it is not necessary that a jury include one of each class of persons to be truly representative of a cross section of a community.

When the courts use the term community, they generally mean the judicial district in which the crime was committed. In most instances, the judicial district is the county, but in the case of inferior courts, the judicial district may be only a portion of a county.

When a jury is challenged as not being a true representation of a cross section of a community, the challenge usually is made by a defendant who fails to find one of his or her particular sex, race, or group among those from whom the jury may be chosen. But in *Taylor* v. *Louisiana,*[4] the U.S. Supreme Court held that a defendant may object to the exclusion of a class of persons from the jury panel even though the defendant is not one of the excluded class. In that case, a male defendant objected to the exclusion of women from the jury unless they volunteered for jury duty. The Court pointed out that although 53 percent of persons eligible for jury duty in the judicial district were female, only 10 percent of these had volunteered, and thus there was not a true representation of the cross section of the community. The defendant had a right to object to the exclusion of women from his jury even though he was not a member of the excluded class.

JURY PANEL OR JURY LIST

The procedure of jury selection varies somewhat among states and even among districts within a state. In some larger metropolitan districts, a jury commissioner is often appointed, whose duty it is to select persons within his or her district to be available for jury duty. This group of persons is referred to as a **jury panel** or **jury list**. In other districts, the selection of the panel may fall to the court clerk. In most jurisdictions, the selection of a jury panel is made annually, usually at the beginning of the calendar year. Generally, no guidelines are set forth for selection. As noted, the federal government provided that no person was to be excluded from serving on a jury because of race, religion, and so forth, and that the persons were to be a community cross section picked at random. No procedure was set forth for how those persons were to be randomly selected. This regulation did provide that each federal judicial district must devise and place into operation a written plan for how the jurors were to be selected—whether from voter registration lists or some other source. In this way, the courts would have some record to verify that no class of persons had been systematically excluded.

The official making the selection has almost complete power over the selection of names to be placed on the jury panel, and in most districts, the sources from which he or she obtains the names are solely at his or her discretion. Whatever list is used, the names will be individually placed in a box from which the official will randomly pull those to be placed on the jury panel. For convenience, officials often use the voter registration list, but it is generally not required that a juror be a registered voter. However, this list is often utilized with greater frequency than any other list for two reasons. First, it is more likely to be representative of a cross section of the community than other lists. Second, the qualifications for voting more nearly coincide with those that a juror must possess. However, the supreme courts of some states have held that the use of only voter registration is too restrictive since many members of minority groups do not register to vote. These courts have suggested that other sources in addition to voter registration lists be utilized to get a better cross section of a community. Tax assessors' lists have been used, but this source has been criticized since it has been held that property owners are more likely to be convicting juries than nonproperty owners. Church membership lists have also been used, but with such lists, religious conflicts ensue. Some officials select names randomly from telephone books in the area, or they select every tenth name or some similar numerical sequence. In sparsely settled districts, officials have made selections through personal contact or by selecting names furnished by acquaintances. On one occasion, an official used the membership list of the area League of Women Voters to get a representative number of women on the panel. The use of this list was criticized as being too restrictive in the class of women selected and not a cross section of the women of the community (see *Glasser* v. *United States*). To assure that the jury panel is truly representative of a cross section of a community, some courts require the selection to be made from two lists, such as a voter registration list and a driver's license list.

Juror Qualifications

Although individual juror qualifications may vary somewhat among states, the general qualifications are the same. The person must be a citizen of the United States, eighteen years of age or over, and a resident of the judicial district for a specified time, usually one year. This last qualification has been criticized by some as being too restrictive and not representative of a community, because many residents of a community move more frequently than once a year. In view of this contention, the legislatures of some states have changed the residence requirement from one year to one month. Those upholding the one-year requirement contend that it takes at least a year for a person to learn the thinking and moral standards of a community. For this reason, many states still use the one-year residence requirement.

The person must be in possession of his or her natural faculties, meaning that the person must be able to see, hear, talk, feel, smell, and be comparatively mobile. Some states have passed legislation that a person is not disqualified as a juror because of loss of sight, hearing, or other disabilities that substantially interfere with mobility. This legislation is criticized as being unrealistic by many within the justice system. The belief is that the amount of physical evidence presented during a trial prevents a blind person from adequately functioning as a juror. Similarly, since most evidence presented during a trial is through testimony of witnesses, a person unable to hear the testimony would be unable to perform duties as a juror. A person with limited or impaired mobility may be in a better position to act as a juror unless that impairment prevents the person from sitting where the sights and sounds of the trial are adequate. The proponents of this legislation argue that such persons should not be deprived of the opportunity to perform their civic duty merely because of an impairment. They allege that if there is a reason that the impaired person cannot perform in a particular case, a challenge for cause could be made. This challenge, however, is not without its complications, as we will see later.

Some states hold that a decrepit person may not qualify as a juror. Although the law does not specify the characteristics that make a person decrepit, it appears to be aimed at someone who is of advanced age, cannot move about freely, and may be senile. Determining when one has reached this condition is difficult.

A person must also be of "ordinary" intelligence to qualify as a juror in most states. This is another nebulous term. What might be considered ordinary intelligence by some might not be considered ordinary by others. And by what standards is intelligence to be measured? This qualification has led to the exclusion of competent persons from the jury panel. To establish whether a prospective juror is of ordinary intelligence, many conscientious efforts have been made to devise tests to assist in making the determination. These tests have been challenged by many defendants. They maintain that words unfamiliar to many ethnic groups are included in the tests, thus preventing a jury from being truly representative of the community. Because of these challenges, most such tests have been eliminated. The prospective juror must have sufficient knowledge of the English language to communicate properly and to understand the trial proceedings. Not all persons on voter lists understand English, nor do all have the full use of their natural faculties. Thus, registered voters are not necessarily qualified as jurors. Aliens, those convicted of malfeasance in office, of any felony, or of other high crimes are excluded by most jurisdictions from jury duty. However, even this exclusion has been challenged as excluding a cross section of society.

Some jurisdictions exclude persons who have served as jurors during the preceding year. This is to discourage the professional jurors who continually hang around courthouses attempting to serve on juries because they have little else to do. Whether there is anything wrong with the professional juror is subject to debate.

Obtaining Jurors

Because of the number of persons in a community who do not qualify as jurors, are exempt, or are excused, obtaining a sufficient number of persons who are available for jury duty is not always easy. In one large metropolitan area, the jury commissioner selected 300,000 names in order to maintain a panel of 15,000 persons—the estimated need for the coming year in that district. Generally, it is the responsibility of the official in charge of the jury panel to determine whether the persons selected are qualified to serve or are exempt. To facilitate this determination, many officials will mail a questionnaire to the selected persons, requesting certain information. A sample questionnaire is presented in the accompanying illustration.

The procedure of mailing questionnaires to prospective jurors also has been challenged by defendants. They contend that many members of minority groups do not respond to the questionnaires and thus do not become eligible to be placed on the jury panel. Regardless of these challenges, many jurisdictions still send out questionnaires to assist in obtaining competent persons to act as jurors. The courts recognize that though there is no ideal way to select prospective jurors, the system used is acceptable if no groups of people are eliminated.

When the selection of prospective jurors is completed, those persons found to be competent are placed on the jury panel. As each trial date is set, a number of these persons will be notified to appear in court on that date. The notice is usually by legal document, referred to as a summons, served on the prospective juror by the sheriff, marshal, or other official of the district involved. If the person does not appear as directed after being personally served with the summons, a contempt charge may result unless good cause is shown for not appearing. For example, a prospective juror with a serious illness could not be expected to appear. From the group that appears in court, the trial jury is selected.

The number of persons called to appear in court varies with the type of crime charged and the amount of pretrial publicity that may have been given the case. Usually, no fewer than 25 persons will be summoned to appear in court, and if the charge is murder and the case has received wide publicity, as many as 100 persons may be summoned. There have been times when even with this number, a trial jury could not be picked, and additional persons from the panel had to be called to appear in court. The first twelve names called by the clerk at the time of the trial may not be those of the persons who will serve on the jury.

Typical Jury Questionnaire

Name _____ Address _____

1. Occupation _____ Employed by _____
   If retired, state former occupation _____

2. Do you own your own business? _____ (Yes or No) Firm name _____
   How many employees? _____

3. Age _____ Condition of hearing _____ Eyesight _____

4. Do you have any physical or mental disability that would interfere with or prevent you from serving as a juror? _____ (Yes or No) If so, describe fully.
   Doctor's name _____

5. Can you read and understand English? _____ (Yes or No)

6. Have you ever been convicted of any felony in a state or federal court? _____ (Yes or No) If your answer is yes, have your civil rights been restored by pardon or amnesty? _____ (Yes or No)

7. Have you been a resident of this County and State for one year immediately before this date? _____ (Yes or No)

8. Have you served as a juror in this State within the last two years? _____ (Yes or No) If yes, when? _____

9. Do you have minor children? _____ Ages: _____

10. Do you have dependents who require your personal constant care? _____
    If yes, please explain: _____

11. If you are entitled to legal exemption or have legal grounds for excuse from jury duty, do you claim it? _____ (Yes or No) If so, explain fully the ground for your claim.

I certify (or declare) under penalty of perjury that the answers to the foregoing questions are true and correct.

Executed in _____ County, State of _____, on the _____ day of _____, 20____.

Signature _____

In some districts, the official will not establish a jury panel very far in advance of a trial. As juries are needed, the official will have a number of persons summoned to appear in court on a particular day. At this time, it will be determined whether those summoned are qualified to serve on a jury. The difficulty with this procedure is that many of those summoned may not qualify for jury duty, and more will have to be notified to appear in order that a trial jury may be selected.

When it is established that those persons appearing in court qualify for jury duty, their names will individually be written on slips of paper and placed in a box. When the trial jury is selected, the clerk will pick, at random, twelve individuals (or fewer, depending upon the jurisdiction) who are to act as the trial jurors. They will take seats in an area provided for them, commonly known as the jury box. The prosecuting attorney and the defense counsel very closely scrutinize the jurors to determine whether this is the group with which they wish to rest their case. If not, the attorneys may decide to replace all or a few of the jurors.

EXEMPTION FROM JURY DUTY

Many persons have the qualifications to be a juror but are exempt from jury duty because of their occupations. It is believed that the functions they perform within a community outweigh their responsibility to serve on a jury. Included among those most often exempted from jury duty are members of legislative bodies; members of the armed services on active duty; attorneys and their staffs; ministers and priests; teachers; physicians; correctional officers; law enforcement officers; mail carriers; and most public officers of the county, state, or federal government. (*Note:* In New York City, owners of one-person businesses are not exempt.) However, those persons exempt from jury duty do not have to claim the exemption and are free to serve as jurors if they so choose. Some state statutes do not designate any class of persons who are exempt from jury duty but do include a provision that the court has the authority to excuse a person upon finding that jury service would entail undue hardship on the person or on the public. However, since it is a citizen's civic duty to serve on juries when called, a person may not be excused for a trivial cause or because of mere inconvenience. The courts are considerate of those for whom jury duty would create a real hardship. This group generally includes persons operating one-person businesses requiring individual attention, students in the midst of a school year, mothers with small children, and persons caring for sick dependents. Since jury duty is an inconvenience if not an actual hardship for most persons, many districts will excuse a person from further jury duty during the year if he or she has served for as many as twenty days, or some other predetermined number, as a juror. This does not mean that a juror may be excused in the middle of a trial after serving for twenty days. The juror must continue serving until that particular trial is completed, even if it takes several more weeks.

CHALLENGING JURORS FOR CAUSE

In most instances, by the time the jurors reach the jury box, it will have been determined that each possesses the qualifications necessary to act as a juror. If this has not been determined, the judge or prosecuting attorney will read to the jurors the qualifications necessary, and if anyone seated in the jury box does not possess those qualifications, that juror will be excused and another name will be pulled from the box to replace the excused juror. There have been instances where a person selected to act as a juror did not qualify yet refused to acknowledge the lack of qualification. If either the prosecuting attorney or defense attorney knows that the juror is not qualified, that attorney may challenge the juror's right to serve. For example, it may be known that one of the jurors has been convicted of a felony. That person could be challenged. These challenges are referred to as **challenges for cause**. In other words, there may be some cause why a person should not serve on the jury. There are a number of other reasons why a juror may be challenged for cause besides not being qualified. After viewing the jury, the defense counsel may conclude that it does not represent a cross section of the community because there is no member of the same race, national origin, or age level as the defendant. The defense counsel may then challenge the entire jury panel. If this challenge is made and the judge knows that there was no systematic exclusion of any class of persons, the judge will deny the challenge and the trial activities will proceed. If any other challenges are forthcoming, they will have to be made on other grounds. If the judge questions the possibility of certain classes of persons being excluded, a recess may be declared until doubt is resolved by determining the method used to select the panel.

Preconceived Ideas of Guilt or Innocence

One of the grounds for challenging a juror for cause is preconceived ideas about the guilt or innocence of the defendant. A juror is often asked how much he or she has heard or read about the case through newspapers, radio, and television. In many instances, the juror, or all jurors, may admit hearing or reading about the case. The juror will then be asked if he or she has formed an opinion regarding the guilt or innocence of the defendant. If the juror has, he or she will be challenged for cause, and the judge will undoubtedly excuse that juror unless there is an indication that his or her opinion could be changed as a result of evidence presented during the trial. The problem is whether a juror can in reality throw off an opinion of guilt or innocence already formed irrespective of how strong the evidence may be on either side. The questioning of a prospective juror on a challenge for cause is often referred to as a "voir dire examination."

In almost all instances, the prospective juror who has formed an opinion about the defendant's guilt or innocence prior to a trial has formed that opinion as a result of pretrial publicity given to the case. This circumstance creates a continuing battle between the freedom of the press and the defendant's right to a fair trial by an impartial jury. Publicity is given to many cases, particularly those involving murder charges, and it is almost impossible for prospective jurors not to have learned something about the case. As stated by U.S. Supreme Court Justice Clark in the case of *Irvin* v. *Dowd:*[5]

> It is not required . . . that the jurors be totally ignorant of the facts and issues involved [in a case]. In these days of swift, widespread and diverse methods of communication, an important case can be expected to arouse the interest of the public in the vicinity, and scarcely any of those best qualified to serve as jurors will not have formed some impression or opinion as to the merits of the case. This is particularly true in criminal cases. To hold that the mere existence of any preconceived notion as to the guilt or innocence of an accused, without more, is sufficient to rebut the presumption of a prospective juror's impartiality would establish an impossible standard. It is sufficient if the juror can lay aside his impression or opinion and render a verdict based upon the evidence presented in court.

In the *Irvin* case, pretrial newspaper stories described the defendant as a confessed slayer of six and a parole violator. Because of deep-seated preconceived opinions of the guilt of the defendant by members of the jury, the Court felt that the defendant had been denied a fair trial by an impartial jury.

Returning again to the *Sheppard* v. *Maxwell* case discussed in Chapter 7, the U.S. Supreme Court held that the defendant had been denied a fair trial, as in the *Irvin* case. In the *Sheppard* decision, extensive pretrial publicity accusing the defendant of the crime occurred even though he had not been arrested or charged with the crime. Headlines such as "Why Don't Police Quiz Top Suspect?" appeared, with a demand that Sheppard be taken to police headquarters for questioning. One newspaper described Sheppard in the following language:

> "now proved under oath to be a liar . . . still free to go about his business shielded by his family, . . . protected by a smart lawyer who has made monkeys of the police and authorities, . . . carrying a gun part of the time, . . . left free to do whatever he pleases." After the arrest of the defendant, the publicity intensified and continued throughout the trial. The Court felt that if the prospective jurors did not have a preconceived opinion of the guilt of the defendant, they reached that opinion during the trial primarily from the publicity given the case and not from the evidence presented. [*Sheppard* v. *Maxwell,* 384 U.S. 333 (1966).]

Although the trial judge in the *Sheppard* case endeavored to keep the jurors from being exposed to publicity, the effort was apparently not successful. At the beginning of the trial, the judge stated the following: "I would suggest to you and caution you that you do not read any newspapers during the progress of this trial, that you do not listen to radio comments nor watch or listen to television comments, insofar as this case is concerned. . . . After it is all over, you can read it all to your heart's content." At intervals during the trial, the judge repeated his suggestions. But the "jurors were thrust into the role of celebrities by the judge's failure to insulate them from reporters and photographers. The numerous pictures of the jurors, with their addresses, which appeared in the newspaper before and during the trial itself exposed them to expressions of opinion from both cranks and friends."

As a result of these U.S. Supreme Court decisions, local courts have been encouraged to control information released to the news media. This control does not interfere with the freedom of the press but assists in picking jurors without preconceived opinions on the guilt or innocence of the defendant because of pretrial publicity. The control is designed to prevent the jury from being influenced during the trial by extensive publicity, some of which may be inaccurate. Because of the freedom of the press in this country, much pretrial and during-the-trial publicity is given many cases, despite gag order controls. Because of pretrial publicity, extensive questioning of prospective jurors takes place to determine whether they have a deep-seated opinion of guilt or innocence that cannot be overcome by the evidence presented during the trial. In some of the more notorious cases, it has taken several weeks just to select a jury.

Challenging the Jurors for Bias

A preconceived opinion on guilt or innocence is not the only grounds for challenging a juror for cause. Another ground is bias, either implied or actual.

Implied bias is set by law and disqualifies a juror from serving. Implied bias may include consanguinity or affinity (that is, kinship or relationship) to within the fourth degree to the victim of the crime or to the defendant. Other examples of implied bias are having a relationship of employer and employee, or landlord and tenant, to either the victim of the crime or the defendant, or having served on a jury that tried another person for the offense charged. Actual bias is prejudice that a juror may admit to having because of a dislike for a particular race, religion, national origin, or class of persons. For example, the juror may admit to a bias against law enforcement officers that would create prejudice against the prosecution.

Since some states do not disqualify prospective jurors because of blindness, an attorney might challenge a blind person for cause if evidence will be presented during the trial requiring visual examination. However, because of the general sympathy for blind people, an attorney should be cautious in excusing a blind person for cause under these circumstances. That same sympathy might be given a prospective deaf juror, causing other jurors to become prejudiced against the attorney. Even though a challenge is made, complications in executing the challenge can occur, as in the following instance. A hearing-impaired person was challenged in a criminal case because of his inability to hear the testimony. He countered the challenge for cause, alleging an inherent right to be a juror. He stated that it was the court's responsibility to supply an interpreter capable of using sign language to translate the testimony for him. The judge concluded that persons could be challenged for cause on other grounds permitted by law and that there was no inherent right to be a juror in all circumstances. The judge further pointed out that even if an interpreter was a practical solution to the challenge, there was always the danger of misinterpretation of the testimony by the interpreter or misconception in the translation by the juror. To further complicate the matter, at the final deliberation, only jurors could be present. The judge's position was further supported by the fact that a person without a sense of smell or feeling could be excused for cause if these faculties were important to the examination of evidence.

Prospective Jurors Opposed to the Death Penalty

Prior to the U.S. Supreme Court decision in *Witherspoon* v. *Illinois,*[6] if a juror was against the death penalty, a challenge for cause could be made in cases carrying a maximum penalty of death. The facts of the *Witherspoon* case show that Witherspoon, the petitioner, was brought to trial in Cook County, Illinois, on a charge of murder. The jury found him guilty and fixed the penalty at death. At the time of trial, an Illinois statute provided the following: "In trials for murder it shall be a cause for challenge of any juror who shall, being examined, state that he has conscientious scruples against capital punishment or that he is opposed to the same."

During the trial, the prosecution eliminated approximately half of the jury panel on a challenge for cause when prospective jurors expressed any qualms about capital punishment. Those persons chosen for the trial jury were ones with no conscientious scruples against the death penalty. Witherspoon took the case to the U.S. Supreme Court on the grounds that a fair trial by an impartial jury representative of the cross section of the community had been denied. Witherspoon maintained that persons who were not against the death penalty were more likely to be convicting jurors. Since many persons were against the death penalty, eliminating those persons from a jury resulted in a jury that was not representative of the community. The Supreme Court agreed with Witherspoon and held that merely having conscientious scruples against capital punishment was not a sufficient cause to disqualify a person from serving on a jury. The Court did state that if a prospective juror advised that under no circumstances could he or she vote to convict a defendant if the death penalty was the sentence, that person could be excused on a challenge for cause.

In those states in which the death penalty may be imposed upon conviction of certain crimes, the prosecuting attorney may ask whether a prospective juror is opposed to the death penalty. If the juror indicates opposition, the prosecuting attorney may then ask whether the juror could vote for conviction knowing that the death penalty could be imposed. A prospective juror who states that he or she could vote for conviction may not be challenged for cause. The problem created by the *Witherspoon* decision is just what action may be taken against the prospective juror who merely indicates some reservations about being able to vote for conviction. Some appellate courts have held that the prospective juror must state positively that he or she could not consider a guilty verdict, if the penalty is death, in order to have the person challenged for cause. There were three dissenting justices in the *Witherspoon* decision who felt that permissible questioning of prospective jurors on the death penalty would not result in a different kind of jury and that prosecutors would be put to a great deal of trouble for nothing.

The *Witherspoon* decision has caused great complication in the voir dire examination of prospective jurors in capital punishment cases. Some appellate courts have adopted the view that the *Witherspoon* decision holds that to constitutionally excuse a prospective juror for cause due to opposition to the death penalty, the juror must make it unmistakably clear that, first, the juror would automatically vote against the death penalty without regard to evidence presented, or that, second, this attitude toward the death penalty would prevent the prospective juror from making an impartial decision on the defendant's guilt.

Prosecuting attorneys and judges have attempted to abide by the *Witherspoon* decision, but just how strong must the feeling be against the death penalty before a prospective juror is excused? In one case, a prospective juror stated on voir dire examination that she was against the death penalty. The judge asked, "Are you so against the death penalty that you would just automatically vote against the death penalty?" To this the prospective juror stated, "I think there might be a hypothetical case in which so heinous a crime was committed that I would consider the death penalty. But I have not been able to think of a hypothetical case that heinous." With this statement, the judge excused the prospective juror for cause. The defendant in that case was convicted, and the case was automatically appealed to the state supreme court, which reversed the death penalty on the grounds that the prospective juror had been improperly excused as not stating that she would automatically vote against the death penalty. There was a dissenting justice in that case who felt that the juror had been properly excused. The case indicates the difficulty facing the courts in determining when a prospective juror was properly excused for cause in being against the death penalty.[7]

Jurors taking a vote on a verdict as they sit at a round table in the jury room.
(*Source:* David Young-Wolff/Getty Images.)

In another state case, a prospective juror was asked whether any personal feelings might prevent his participation in the deliberation of a case carrying a possible death sentence. The prospective juror replied that he was a born-again Christian and did not think that he could have any part of sitting in on a case that would send anyone to the electric chair. With this reply, the judge excused the man. After the defendant was convicted and given the death penalty, the state supreme court in that case reversed the death penalty on the grounds that the prospective juror was improperly excused since it was not made unmistakably clear that the juror's participation in the deliberation of the case was not possible because of the penalty. The dissenting justice in that case felt that the court was only seeking a way to reverse death penalties. Justices who have personal feelings against the death penalty have been able to effectively overrule death penalty sentences by holding that a prospective juror was improperly excused in violation of the *Witherspoon* decision. This treatment has brought about criticism of those justices for not upholding the will of the people.

In the case of *Wainright* v. *Witt,*[8] the U.S. Supreme Court somewhat relaxed the strict rule of the *Witherspoon* decision. In this case, the Court set forth a new standard for determining when a prospective juror may be excused for cause because of his or her views on capital punishment: "That standard is whether the juror's views would prevent or substantially impair the performance of his duties as a juror in accordance with his instructions and his oath. . . . We [the Supreme Court] note that, in addition to dispensing with Witherspoon's reference to 'automatic' decision making, this standard likewise does not require that a juror's bias be proved with 'unmistakable clarity.' " Remember that state appellate courts have the power to make rules for their own trial courts. These rules may be more restrictive than the ones set forth by the U.S. Supreme Court and, as such, may still adhere to the strict rule set forth in the *Witherspoon* decision.

The voir dire examination of prospective jurors can be extensive in any type of case. To limit this examination, some states have passed legislation permitting the trial judge to conduct the voir dire examination. In other states, the trial judge will often call into the courtroom all members of the jury panel selected to appear for the particular trial, and the judge will conduct a portion of the voir dire examination. The panel will be asked whether they have any preconceived opinions on guilt or innocence as a result of pretrial publicity given to the case. The judge may also consider other phases of possible bias. Even though this procedure is followed, the prosecuting attorney and particularly the defense counsel are permitted a reasonable voir dire examination opportunity. Some judges conduct no voir dire examinations, since they believe that selecting the jury is the prerogative of the attorneys involved and that any interference with it is a denial of their rights. Most attorneys enjoy the privilege of conducting voir dire examinations in challenging for cause, since it gives them an opportunity to become better acquainted with the jurors who are finally selected. Some courts frown on this reason for voir dire examinations as having no place in the justice system. These courts hold that voir dire examinations by the attorneys are for determining whether a juror should be disqualified by a challenge for cause. In these courts, the attorneys are limited to questions pertinent to the cause for which they may be attempting to disqualify the juror. Other courts permit a certain amount of freedom when questioning a prospective juror. This aids the attorneys in determining whether a peremptory challenge should be exercised when an undesired juror cannot be disqualified for cause. As long as the attorneys' questions relate to a challenge for cause, the questioning can be almost limitless, particularly when the cause is for bias. For this reason, some judges try to limit the questioning to matters directly relating to the particular case involved. If a judge is too restrictive in permitting the questioning by the defense counsel, a conviction could be reversed on appeal through the allegation that the jury was not impartial.

PEREMPTORY CHALLENGE

After the prosecution and defense have exhausted their challenges for cause, there is one more opportunity to remove an undesired juror or jurors. Each attorney is given the right to excuse a juror whom he or she may not want on the jury. The right to excuse a juror under these circumstances is known as a **peremptory challenge**. Both the prosecution and the defense have a certain number of peremptory challenges that permit either attorney to excuse a juror without stating a reason. The challenges are granted based upon the theory that they assist the attorneys in more nearly selecting an impartial jury. A prosecuting attorney, for example, may exercise the right of peremptory challenge to excuse a juror who, during challenge for cause, indicated reservations against the death penalty but could vote for a conviction if the evidence against the defendant was strong enough. Even though this is the real reason the juror was excused, the attorney does not have to give the reason. A defense attorney may excuse a juror who stated during challenge for cause that he or she believed that the defendant was guilty but that this feeling could be controlled and the juror guided by the evidence of the case.

Prohibiting the Peremptory Challenge

Generally, the trial judge has no authority to prohibit a juror from being excused on a peremptory challenge. However, the U.S. Supreme Court in *Batson* v. *Kentucky*[9] held that an attorney may not use peremptory challenges to exclude persons from a jury solely on the basis of race. Batson was of the black race, and during the jury selection, the prosecuting attorney excluded all persons of this race from the jury by the use of his peremptory challenges. The Supreme Court stated the following:

> Although a prosecutor ordinarily is entitled to exercise permitted peremptory challenges for any reason at all as long as that reason is related to the outcome of the case to be tried . . . the Equal Protection Clause [of the Fourteenth Amendment] forbids the prosecutor to challenge potential jurors solely on account of their race or on the presumption that black jurors as a group will be unable impartially to consider the State's case against a black defendant.

The supreme court of one state held that "peremptory challenges may not be used to remove prospective jurors solely on the basis of presumed group bias. We define group bias as a presumption that certain jurors are biased merely because they are members of an identifiable group distinguished on racial, religious, ethnic, or similar grounds."[10]

The Court in the *Batson* case based its decision primarily on the violation of the Equal Protection clause of the U.S. Constitution. But some state courts have limited the use of peremptory challenges to exclude members of a certain group on the theory that a defendant is entitled to be tried by an impartial jury representative of a cross section of the community. The exclusion of members of a defined group by the use of peremptory challenges denies the defendant that right. The prosecution has the same right to question the use of peremptory challenges by the defense in the exclusion of certain classes of persons. The prosecution is also entitled to have the case tried by a jury representative of a cross section of the community.

The *Batson* decision did not eliminate all use of peremptory challenges to exclude from a jury persons of a defined group. But when it becomes apparent that such an attempted exclusion is taking place, the opposing side may question the procedure. The trial judge has the responsibility to determine whether there is a justification for the exclusions. If the offending attorney can establish a bona fide justification for the exclusions, the peremptory challenges will stand. The justification is generally based on some attitude displayed by the excluded juror, such as being unduly friendly toward the defendant or his attorney or displaying an unwholesome attitude toward law enforcement.

As in the challenge for cause, when a juror is excused by the peremptory challenge, the court clerk will pick another name from the jury panel box, and that prospective juror will take the seat of the excused juror in the jury box. That juror and any others who may replace excused jurors may be questioned to determine whether they should be challenged for cause. Thus, another time-consuming procedure occurs in the selection of the jury. The number of peremptory challenges for the prosecution and the defense varies among states. Some states grant the prosecution and defense an equal number of peremptory challenges, usually ten each. Other states grant the defense ten challenges and the prosecution only five. Some jurisdictions grant more peremptory challenges for felony trials than for misdemeanor trials. Where the maximum penalty is death, most jurisdictions permit twice as many peremptory challenges as in noncapital cases.

Holding Challenges in Reserve

Both the prosecuting attorney and the defense attorney will usually hold one or two of their peremptory challenges in reserve. The reason is that a person who is most unsatisfactory to one side or the other may have his or her name drawn from the panel, leaving no way to disqualify this person for cause. If all the peremptory challenges have been exhausted, there is no way of preventing that person from being a juror. The person may have a history of never having voted for conviction or having a known dislike for a particular race or religion, yet this dislike cannot be established in questioning for cause. Defense attorneys generally do not like to have law enforcement officers, either active or retired, on a jury, since such persons tend to assume guilt from the mere arrest and formal charging of the defendant. This tendency may be impossible to establish in order to excuse the officer on cause, but no cause is needed in the peremptory challenge.

U.S. Supreme Court Decisions Regarding the Peremptory Challenge

Case	Decision
Batson v. *Kentucky* (1986)	The Court ruled that under the Fourteenth Amendment, prosecutors are barred from using peremptory challenges to remove black jurors because of their race.
Powers v. *Ohio* (1991)	The Court concluded that a defendant has the standing to object to race-based exclusion of jurors by the use of peremptory challenges on the grounds of equal protection, even if the defendant is not of the same race as the challenged jurors.
Edmonson v. *Leesville Concrete Co.* (1991)	The Court held that the *Batson* ruling applies to attorneys in civil lawsuits. A private party in a civil action may not use peremptory challenges to exclude jurors on the basis of race.
Georgia v. *McCollum* (1992)	On the basis of *Batson,* the Court prohibited the exercise of race-based peremptory challenges by defense attorneys in criminal cases.
J.E.B. v. *Alabama* (1994)	The Court held that the Equal Protection Clause of the Fourteenth Amendment bars discrimination in jury selection on the basis of gender. Discrimination in jury selection, whether based on race or gender, causes harm to the litigants, the community, and the individual jurors who are wrongfully excluded from participation in the judicial process.

Both prosecuting attorneys and defense attorneys will question prospective jurors for cause as extensively as the court will permit. This questioning enables them to get a better idea of how a particular prospective juror may think or react in reaching a verdict. The attorneys may then utilize their peremptory challenges more effectively.

Accepting Jurors

All attorneys engaged in the trial of cases, whether civil or criminal, constantly try to analyze persons in an effort to determine who make the best jurors. There is no way to predict how a person will react in each instance, but attorneys feel that certain groups or classes of persons tend to react in more definite patterns than others. For example, defense attorneys feel that minority groups who have encountered hardships and discrimination tend to be more tolerant of defendants than members of white Anglo groups of medium or higher income. Younger persons are alleged to be more permissive and forgiving in their attitudes toward a defendant, particularly if the defendant is also a younger person. For that reason, defense attorneys try to have more persons between the ages of eighteen and twenty-one on jury panels as well as more members of minority groups. But obtaining these classes of people for jury duty is not easy. Many younger persons attending school are excused so that their school year will not be interrupted. If not in school, many are married and are in a lower-income bracket, as are many in minority groups who are excused from jury duty because of the extreme financial hardship that might be suffered. In most jurisdictions, the compensation for jury duty is meager, since it is considered to be a civic duty to serve on a criminal trial jury. Jurors in some areas receive only $5 a day plus a small mileage fee. It has been recommended that the compensation be increased in order that younger persons and members of minority groups in lower-income brackets can afford to serve on the jury. But court costs are already extremely high, and each increase in jury fees makes them that much greater, another burden on the taxpayer. A few jurisdictions have increased jurors' compensation to ease the financial hardship suffered by those who serve, as well as to obtain a wider selection of persons.

Many attorneys feel that the most satisfactory juror is one who takes pride in serving on a jury, takes the duty seriously, endeavors to conscientiously evaluate the evidence presented during the trial, and attempts to arrive at a just verdict. The financial burden upon the juror should not be great, and he or she should not have to worry about children or day-care issues.

After the prosecution and defense have exhausted their challenges for cause, have no desire to further exercise their right of peremptory challenges, and indicate to the judge that they are satisfied with the jury selected, the jury will be sworn to perform their duty. The oath administered to the jurors will in substance be that each of them will endeavor to reach a true and just verdict based on the evidence of the case. After the jurors have been sworn in, the trial begins. Some jurisdictions still swear jurors individually, but most jurisdictions administer the oath to the jury as a group once they have been selected and accepted by both sides and by the judge.

ALTERNATE JURORS

Records reveal that often during a lengthy trial, one or more jurors become incapacitated and cannot continue. If this happens and the defendant does not agree to continue the trial with those jurors who remain, the judge must declare a mistrial and the trial must be restarted. If several weeks have elapsed before the juror becomes incapacitated, having to start the trial again is frustrating as well as expensive. To avoid the possibility of having to start a new trial, most states have statutes providing that alternate jurors may be selected at the discretion of the trial judge. Determining the approximate time that the prosecution and defense plan to take in presenting their sides of the case enables the judge to decide whether and how many alternate jurors should be selected.

Alternate jurors are selected in the same manner as regular jurors. The alternates may be challenged for cause, and usually one additional peremptory challenge is granted for each alternate selected. The judge may decide that only one alternate will be necessary, or he or she may decide on more if the trial is to be extremely lengthy. Usually not more than four alternates are selected. If there is more than one alternate and one of the regular jurors becomes incapacitated, the clerk will draw the name of the alternate who will be substituted for the incapacitated juror. Some states permit an alternate to be substituted for the incapacitated juror up to the time that the case is given to the jury for deliberation. Other states permit an alternate to be substituted anytime before the verdict is reached. The alternate jurors must be situated in the courtroom where they can observe all the proceedings and can hear all that takes place. Usually, an area next to the jury box is reserved for alternate jurors to facilitate their ability to see and hear. After selection, the alternate jurors are given the same oath as the regular jury.

The use of the alternate juror system has been criticized by some legal scholars. They allege that the alternate juror creates a jury of thirteen instead of twelve, particularly if the alternate is substituted during the deliberation. It has been alleged that permitting a substitution during the deliberation handicaps the alternate juror, since he or she has not had the benefit of the group dynamics during the preceding deliberation. Because of these criticisms, some states do not permit substitution after the deliberation begins, and once the case is given to the jury for a verdict, the alternate juror or jurors are discharged. The problem created by discharging alternate jurors at the time of deliberation is that, after a lengthy trial, the deliberation could take several days and a juror could possibly become incapacitated during that time. If this happens, the jury would have to be dismissed and the trial started over, thus defeating the purpose of the alternate juror system. Those jurisdictions permitting the substitution of an alternate juror during deliberation either allow the deliberation to start anew or require that the alternate be thoroughly briefed on the deliberation up to the time of the substitution.

The alternate juror system has also been criticized as unfair to the defendant, because the alternate juror, knowing that chances of substitution are slight, may not take much interest in the case and be unable to properly evaluate the evidence during deliberation if substituted. To eliminate this possibility, it has been proposed that, if alternate jurors are to be selected, the entire jury—including alternates—should be selected at one time. At the time the case is given to the jury for deliberation, the court clerk would draw twelve names from the jury selection box. In this way, none of the jurors would know who were regulars or alternates until all the evidence of the case had been presented, and all would have an equal interest in the presentation.

Although the alternate juror system has been criticized by some as being unfair to the defendant, these criticisms seem shallow compared with the benefits gained by having a juror who can replace one who may become incapacitated. It must be remembered that the alternate juror system was established because, in most instances, a defendant will not agree to continue a trial with less than a full jury should one of the jurors become incapacitated. The refusal to continue with the trial is usually based on the belief that delays in a trial work to the defendant's advantage. In addition, it is impossible to make every situation arising in the justice system ideal for the defendant. In fact, many in the justice system feel that the system is already tilted heavily in favor of the defendant.

SEQUESTERING THE JURY

Once the jury has been selected and sworn in, the judge must decide whether it is to be sequestered, or locked up. When a jury is sequestered, it is segregated from all outside contact. The primary reason for **sequestering the jury** is to protect its members from possible outside influence in arriving at their verdict. When not in the courtroom, the jurors are kept together as a body at all times under the guard of a bailiff or some other court officer. They eat together and are housed in a hotel, motel, or some other convenient place until the trial is concluded. Even the newspapers that they may be permitted to read or the news broadcasts that they may listen to must be monitored to ensure that nothing that might affect their verdict is brought to their attention. As was pointed out in the *Sheppard* case, the jury was aware of the extensive news media publicity throughout the trial. According to the U.S. Supreme Court, the publicity influenced the jury in their opinion on guilt, and the Court reversed the conviction. The Court suggested that the judge should have had greater control over the news releases or should have sequestered the jury during the trial to prevent undue influence. Generally, it is held that when a jury is not sequestered, the judge has the authority to forbid the jurors from reading any newspapers or listening to any broadcasts about the case, and if they should inadvertently read about or listen to something about the case, they are to disregard it.

In a few states, the jury must be sequestered during a trial on certain charges; otherwise, sequestering is at the discretion of the judge. The jury may be sequestered at any time during the trial proceedings. It may be sequestered on the judge's own decision or at the request of either the prosecution or the defense. If the jury is not sequestered during the presentation of the evidence, it will usually be sequestered during the deliberation when the trial pertains to a serious charge. In a few jurisdictions, the jury must be sequestered during the deliberation. If the jury is sequestered, the alternate jurors are sequestered as well, but are generally sequestered separately from the regular jury. In those jurisdictions where the jury is sequestered at the judge's discretion prior to the time of deliberation, most judges hesitate to sequester the jury because of the hardship imposed. The jurors lose all contact with their families and friends during the period of sequestration. Most of the jurors are unacquainted with one another before the trial begins, yet they must be housed together. Often personality clashes occur, affecting their judgment during the deliberation. From the standpoint of the taxpayer, sequestering a jury is expensive because taxes pay for housing and feeding the jury during this period. Most jurors dislike being sequestered, and when that possibility is apparent, prospective jurors will do everything possible to be excused from that particular trial. Thus, in addition to the hardships experienced by the jurors themselves, selecting a jury becomes even more difficult than usual. When a jury is sequestered during a trial at the request of the prosecution or defense, it is the policy of the judge not to inform the jury which side made the request in order to avoid any prejudice by the jurors toward that side. Whether the jury is sequestered or not, each time the court is adjourned, the judge must advise the jurors against discussing the facts of the case among themselves or with others and against forming any opinions about the case until the time of deliberation.

FUTURE OF THE JURY SYSTEM

Interviews with persons who have accepted their duty to serve on criminal juries reveal that many become disenchanted with the jury system. The most common complaint concerns the time spent by prospective jurors waiting to be called for duty on a particular case. Many wait for hours in the uncomfortable surroundings of the courthouse halls.

a result, unadulterated equal protection analysis is simply inapplicable to peremptory challenges exercised in any particular case. A clause that requires a minimum "rationality" in government actions has no application to "an arbitrary and capricious right"; a constitutional principle that may invalidate state action on the basis of "stereotypic notions" does not explain the breadth of a procedure exercised on the "sudden impressions and unaccountable prejudices we are apt to conceive upon the bare looks and gestures of another."

That the Court is not applying conventional equal protection analysis is shown by its limitation of its new rule to allegations of impermissible challenge on the basis of race; the Court's opinion clearly contains such a limitation. . . . But if conventional equal protection principles apply, then presumably defendants could object to exclusions on the basis of not only race, but also sex, age, religious or political affiliation, mental capacity, number of children, living arrangements, and employment in a particular industry or profession.

In short, it is quite probable that every peremptory challenge could be objected to on the basis that, because it excluded a venireman who had some characteristic not shared by the remaining members of the venire, it constituted a "classification" subject to equal protection scrutiny. Compounding the difficulties, under conventional equal protection principles some uses of peremptories would be reviewed under "strict scrutiny and . . . sustained only if . . . suitably tailored to serve a compelling state interest," others would be reviewed to determine if they were "substantially related to a sufficiently important government interest," and still others would be reviewed to determine whether they were "a rational means to serve a legitimate end."

The Court never applies this conventional equal protection framework to the claims at hand, perhaps to avoid acknowledging that the state interest involved here has historically been regarded by this Court as substantial, if not compelling.

The Court also purports to express "no views on whether the Constitution imposes any limit on the exercise of peremptory challenges by defense counsel." But the clear and inescapable import of this novel holding will inevitably be to limit the use of this valuable tool to both prosecutors and defense attorneys alike. Once the Court has held that prosecutors are limited in their use of peremptory challenges, could we rationally hold that defendants are not? . . . Confronted with the dilemma it created, the Court today attempts to decree a middle ground. To rebut a prima facie case, the Court requires a "neutral explanation" for the challenge, but is at pains to "emphasize" that the "explanation need not rise to the level justifying exercise of a challenge for cause." I am at a loss to discern the governing principles here. A "clear and reasonably specific" explanation of "legitimate reasons for exercising the challenge will be difficult to distinguish from a challenge for cause. Anything short of a challenge for cause may well be seen as an "arbitrary and capricious" challenge, to use Blackstone's characterization of the peremptory. Apparently the Court envisions permissible challenges short of a challenge for cause that are just a little bit arbitrary but not too much. While our trial judges are "experienced in supervising voir dire," they have no experience in administering rules like this.

An example will quickly demonstrate how today's holding, while purporting to "further the ends of justice," will not have that effect. Assume [that] an Asian defendant, on trial for the capital murder of a white victim, asks prospective jury members, most of whom are white, whether they harbor racial prejudice against Asians. The basis for such a question is to flush out any juror who believes that [Asians] are violence-prone or morally inferior. . . . Assume further that all white jurors deny harboring racial prejudice but that the defendant, on trial for his life, remains unconvinced by these protestations. Instead, he continues to harbor a hunch, an "assumption" or "intuitive judgment," that these white jurors will be prejudiced against him, presumably based in part on race. The time-honored rule before today was that peremptory challenges could be exercised on such a basis. . . . The effect of the Court's decision, however, will be to force the defendant to come forward and "articulate a neutral explanation," for his peremptory challenge, a burden he probably cannot meet. This example demonstrates that today's holding will produce juries that the parties do not believe are truly impartial. This will surely do more than "disconcert" litigants; it will diminish confidence in the jury system. . . .

Today we mark the return of racial differentiation as the Court accepts a positive evil for a perceived one. Prosecutors and defense attorneys alike will build records in support of their claims that peremptory challenges have been exercised in a racially discriminatory fashion by asking jurors to state their racial background and national origin for the record, despite the fact that "Such questions may be offensive to some jurors and thus are not ordinarily asked on voir dire." This process is sure to tax even the most capable counsel and judges since determining whether a prima facie case has been established will "require a continued monitoring and recording of the group composition of the panel present and prospective. . . ."

SUMMARY

- The only qualification set forth in the Sixth Amendment is that a jury be an impartial jury.
- The concept of a jury of one's peers actually refers to a jury that is selected fairly and impartially from a cross section of the community.
- The procedures for selecting a jury vary from state to state.
- Jurors must be U.S. citizens, eighteen years of age or older, and residents of the judicial district for a specified period of time.
- Certain individuals are exempt from mandatory jury duty but may volunteer to serve on a jury.
- Potential jurors may be challenged for cause based on the concept that they will not be fair and impartial.
- Peremptory challenges may not be used to exclude a certain gender or racial group from a jury.
- A death-qualified jury is one in which the members have stated that, if appropriate, they would vote for the death penalty.
- The primary reason for sequestering a jury is to eliminate possible outside influence.

REVIEW QUESTIONS

1. Who are one's peers as the term relates to a jury?
2. In what amendment is found the right to trial by an impartial jury?
3. What is a jury panel or jury list?
4. List four qualifications for being a juror.
5. What persons may be exempt from jury duty, and why is the exemption granted?
6. What is meant by challenging a juror for cause?
7. List three possible challenges for cause.
8. What is the purpose of permitting a challenge for cause?
9. What is a peremptory challenge?
10. Who are alternate jurors, and why are they selected?
11. What is meant by sequestering the jury?
12. Explain the purpose of sequestering a jury.

LOCAL PROCEDURE

1. What are the qualifications for a juror?
2. If a juror becomes incapacitated, may he or she be replaced by an alternate during the deliberation?
3. Must the jury be sequestered? If so, at what point during the trial?
4. How many peremptory challenges are permitted to the prosecution and the defense?

ENDNOTES

1. See 18 U.S. Code, section 1861.
2. 328 U.S. 128 (1942).
3. 332 U.S. 261 (1947).

OPENING STATEMENTS

In order that the jury may be informed of both the charge against the defendant and the plea entered, it is the policy of most courts to have the accusatory pleading read to the jury. If the charge is a felony, the accusatory pleading will be an information or an indictment, depending on the circumstances. If the charge is a misdemeanor, the accusatory pleading is usually a complaint that may or may not be read, depending upon the custom of the jurisdiction.

Prosecuting Attorney Opening Statement

After the jury has been sworn in and the charge read to them, the prosecution is the first to present its evidence. The prosecution goes first because they have the burden of proof. Prior to calling the first witness, the judge will ask the prosecuting attorney whether he or she wishes to make an opening statement. An opening statement will be made in most instances, since it provides an opportunity to explain further the charge against the defendant. By making an opening statement, the prosecuting attorney is able to outline the evidence planned for the trial, thereby allowing the jury to follow more intelligently the presentation of the prosecution's side of the case. The opening statement is probably more important in jury trials than in court trials because it orients the jury to what is to follow and prepares them for the evidence.

The prosecuting attorney has considerable latitude in referring to the evidence that he or she plans to introduce during the trial, but the statements are not considered facts of the case. If for some reason the evidence is not admitted, the jury may not consider the attorney's statements as evidence of the case. It has been held to be prejudicial error for a prosecuting attorney to mention evidence known to be inadmissible. Prejudicial error may result from a statement or an act of misconduct by a prosecuting attorney or a witness that will prevent the defendant from getting a fair trial or that is so prejudicial that either a mistrial will be declared or a conviction will be reversed on appeal. It is also prejudicial error for a prosecuting attorney to refer to the defendant as an ex-convict or to imply that he or she has committed prior crimes. A defendant is entitled to be tried on the facts stated in the accusatory pleading; any reference to other crimes or prior convictions is considered to be so prejudicial against the defendant that the judge may declare a mistrial at that time. If the judge does not declare a mistrial and the defendant is convicted, the conviction may be reversed on appeal.

Defense Counsel Opening Statement

After the prosecuting attorney has completed the opening statement, the judge will often ask whether the defense attorney wishes to make an opening statement. In some jurisdictions, the judge may delay the defense attorney's opening statement until after the prosecution has presented its side of the case. Many defense attorneys believe that it is a mistake to make an opening statement before the prosecution has completed its side of the presentation of the evidence, since the defense strategy may change. If an opening statement is made before the prosecution presents its side of the evidence, statements may be made that will not conform with the defense strategy, and the jury may be confused about what happened or may question the innocence of the defendant. In making an opening statement immediately after the prosecuting attorney has made his or her opening statement, the defense attorney may alert the prosecution to an anticipated defense; most defense attorneys try to avoid this. Many defense attorneys waive the right of making an opening statement at any time, since they feel that the disadvantages outweigh the advantages. Often defense witnesses do not measure up to expectation or do not appear at all. If their testimony has been previously outlined, the jury may question the validity of the defense.

On the other hand, some defense attorneys believe that it is a mistake not to make an opening statement immediately following the opening statement of the prosecuting attorney. They theorize that the prosecuting attorney will have made a favorable impression on the jury and that it is dangerous not to challenge that statement immediately. These defense attorneys state that it is not necessary to go into any detail of the defense at that time. They can merely inform the jury that the defense plans to present evidence to prove that the facts of the case are not as alleged by the prosecuting attorney. These defense attorneys will request the jury to keep an open mind until the defense has the opportunity to present contrary evidence.

REASONABLE DOUBT

In our system of justice, the defendant in a criminal case is presumed to be innocent until proved otherwise. The U.S. Supreme Court has held in a number of cases proving a criminal charge *beyond a* **reasonable doubt** is constitutionally required though not included in the Bill of Rights. This Court stated the following in the case of *In re Winship:*

> . . . it is the duty of the Government to establish guilt beyond a reasonable doubt. This notion—basic in our law and rightly one of the boasts of a free society—is a requirement and safeguard of due process of law in the historic, procedural content of due process . . . that guilt in a criminal case must be proved beyond a reasonable doubt and by evidence confined to that which long experience in the common law tradition, to some extent embodied in the Constitution, has crystallized into rules of evidence consistent with that standard. These rules are historically grounded rights of our system, developed to safeguard men from dubious and unjust convictions, with resulting forfeitures of life, liberty and property. . . .
>
> The requirement of proof beyond a reasonable doubt has this vital role in our criminal procedure for cogent reasons. The accused during a criminal prosecution has at stake interests of immense importance, both because of the possibility that he may lose his liberty upon conviction and because of the certainty that he would be stigmatized by the conviction. Accordingly, a society that values the good name and freedom of every individual should not condemn a man for commission of a crime when there is reasonable doubt about his guilt. . . .

PROOF AND CRIMINAL JUSTICE ACTIVITIES

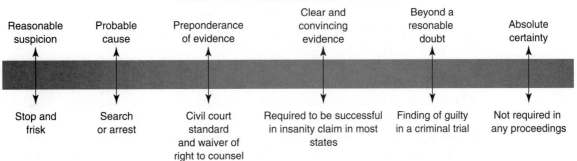

Moreover, use of the reasonable doubt standard is indispensable to command the respect and confidence of the community in application of the criminal law. It is critical that the moral force of the criminal law not be diluted by a standard of proof which leaves people in doubt whether innocent men are being condemned. It is also important in our free society that every individual going about his ordinary affairs have confidence that his government cannot adjudge him guilty of a criminal offense without convincing a proper factfinder of his guilt with utmost certainty.[1]

The term reasonable doubt is familiar to all. Yet many jurors are confused about the real meaning of the term and when reasonable doubt has been proved. They desire some explanation, but the more one tries to interpret the meaning of reasonable doubt, the more confusing it becomes. To further confuse the issue, some courts and statutes state that the defendant must be proved guilty beyond a reasonable doubt and to a moral certainty. A statute of one state defines reasonable doubt as follows:

It is not a mere possible doubt, because everything relating to human affairs, and depending upon moral evidence, is open to some possible or imaginary doubt. It is that state of the case, which, after the entire comparison and consideration of all the evidence, leaves the minds of jurors in that condition that they cannot say they feel an abiding conviction . . . of the truth of the charge.

After reading this definition, there is some question whether the jury would have any better understanding of the meaning of reasonable doubt than before. To state it in a simpler form, it is that doubt that a juror may have after weighing all the evidence of the case and is still not satisfied that the defendant is guilty of the crime charged.

WITNESSES

The defendant is entitled to be confronted by the witnesses against him or her. As stated by the U.S. Supreme Court in *California* v. *Green,* this confrontation

(1) insures that the witness will give his statements under oath thus impressing him with the seriousness of the matter and guarding against the lie by the possibility of a penalty for perjury; (2) forces the witness to submit to cross examination, the "greatest legal engine ever invented for the discovery of the truth"; (3) permits the jury that is to decide the defendant's fate to observe the demeanor of the witness in making his statement, thus aiding the jury in assessing his credibility.[2]

Since the defendant has the right to be confronted by opposing witnesses, most of the prosecution's evidence attempting to prove guilt beyond a reasonable doubt will be presented through the testimony of witnesses. As indicated earlier, the U.S. Constitution has been interpreted to require that a defendant has a right to confront and cross-examine all witnesses against him or her. However, this right is not absolute.[3] For example, hearsay statements of another person may be admitted against the defendant even though he or she does not have the opportunity to cross-examine the person making those statements. The U.S. Supreme Court also examined another aspect of this constitutional right when it addressed the issue of the use of closed-circuit television in child abuse cases in *Maryland* v. *Craig.*[4]

In October 1986, a Howard County grand jury charged Sandra Ann Craig with a number of child abuse offenses. The victim, Brooke, was a six-year-old girl who from August 1984 to June 1986 attended a prekindergarten and kindergarten center owned and operated by Craig. In March 1987, before the case went to trial, the state sought to invoke a Maryland statute that allowed the judge and jury to view the victim via closed-circuit television. The victim was to be located in a separate room outside the presence of the defendant. Although the defendant and her attorney could view the television and ask questions, they would not be allowed to physically confront the victim.

In support of its motion, the state presented expert testimony that Brooke, as well as a number of other children who were alleged to have been abused, would suffer serious emotional distress that they could not reasonably communicate if required to testify in the courtroom and face the defendant. Another expert testified that Brooke would probably stop talking and would withdraw and curl up into a ball if she were in the same room as the defendant. The trial court ruled that because of the possible distress that the victims would suffer in seeing the defendant, the closed-circuit television would be authorized.

In upholding such a procedure, the U.S. Supreme Court held that a strict reading of the Confrontation Clause would do away with every hearsay exception and that this was too extreme a result. Therefore, the Court held that the Confrontation Clause reflects a preference for face-to-face confrontations at trial but that this preference must occasionally give way to considerations of public policy and the necessities of the case. Thus, the holding in *Maryland* v. *Craig* allows the use of closed-circuit television under certain circumstances in child-abuse cases. Specifically, there must be a state statute that authorizes such a procedure, and the state must establish that the child is unable to face his or her accused molester in person.

There are two kinds of witnesses: the lay, or ordinary, witness and the expert witness. The lay witness is an individual who has some personal knowledge of the facts of the case derived from personal perceptions, that is, from what was seen, heard, or felt. An expert witness is an individual who has knowledge and skill in a particular field that is beyond the knowledge of the average person. The expert witness gives the judge and the jury the benefit of acquired knowledge, often in the form of an opinion, to assist them in arriving at the truth of a matter. The jury may either accept the opinion of the expert or reject it, as they see fit. Before an expert witness may testify, the side calling this witness must qualify him or her as an expert. By training, experience, or education, the expert witness must prove knowledge or skill in a particular field above that of the average person. This expertise is established by questioning the witness about his or her ability in a particular field. The judge must then declare the witness to be qualified as an expert before testimony or an opinion on the facts of the case can be given. Establishing the qualifications of the expert witness is referred to as a voir dire examination.

It is not necessary for the prosecution to call every person who has some knowledge about the facts of the case to be a witness. The prosecuting attorney must call enough witnesses to prove the defendant guilty beyond a reasonable doubt. It is difficult to determine how many witnesses this step will take in any given case. At first glance, it may appear that the prosecuting attorney should not gamble on how many witnesses should be called but should call all who may know something about the case. However, to accept testimony from every person who may have some personal knowledge about the case could be time-consuming and could cause the jury to become weary and lose interest in the prosecution's presentation. But the prosecution will call all the witnesses necessary to completely relate the story of what happened in the case. In addition, a few witnesses will probably be called to corroborate the testimony of other witnesses. The prosecution will have to present those witnesses necessary to establish that a crime was committed—that is, it will have to prove the elements of the crime. This process of proving that a crime was committed is known as establishing the corpus delicti.

The sequence in which the witnesses are called to testify may not result in the presentation of the events in the same sequence in which they occurred. The prosecuting attorney will decide the sequence in accordance with how the facts can best be presented in a logical, understandable manner.

SUBPOENA

Persons are officially notified to appear in court as witnesses by a legal document known as a subpoena. Subpoenas will be issued for the attendance of both prosecution and defense witnesses. Depending upon the jurisdiction, a subpoena may be issued by a judge, prosecuting attorney, clerk of the court, or public defender.

Occasionally, a witness will be commanded to bring books, papers, documents, or other physical evidence to court. If so, a "**subpoena duces tecum**" will be issued to the witness. The subpoena duces tecum follows the same general form as the subpoena, but it includes a description of the material that the witness is to produce in court and a statement of the relevance of the requested evidence to the trial.

Generally, a subpoena or subpoena duces tecum may be served by anyone, but most frequently it will be served by an officer of the court. Service is made by personally delivering a copy of the subpoena to the witness. After the service is made, the person serving the subpoena will make a written return on a copy of the subpoena stating the date, time, and place that the service was made.

It has been held that a person owes a duty to society to appear and testify as a witness in criminal cases when subpoenaed to do so. Because of this duty, witnesses generally are not compensated when appearing to testify. Yet it is recognized that a witness should not suffer undue financial hardship in performing duty as a witness. Since a subpoena is valid anyplace within the state in which it is issued, most jurisdictions provide for the payment of reasonable travel expenses to a witness who must travel a great distance to testify.

Before a witness can be compensated in some jurisdictions, the judge involved in the trial must endorse the subpoena with a statement that the witness is a material witness and that this attendance is absolutely necessary. Once a witness has appeared in court, it is common practice to have the judge order the witness back instead of issuing a new subpoena for a new date.

Witnesses Failing to Appear

The failure of a witness to appear as commanded in a subpoena can bring about contempt of court charges unless good cause for not appearing can be shown. In addition to being held in contempt, the witness, if subpoenaed by the defense, can in some states be civilly sued by the defendant for failure to appear. It is not necessary for a person to be served with a subpoena to be a witness. The witness may orally agree to appear but cannot be held in contempt for failing to be present at the trial.

In the past, since a subpoena was good only within the state in which it was issued, there was no way to command the appearance of a witness who was out of the state. Today, most states have adopted the Uniform Act to Secure the Attendance of Witnesses from without the State in Criminal Cases. This act enables a court to command the appearance of a material witness beyond the jurisdiction of the court because the witness resides in another state. The court in which the witness is needed to appear will issue a certificate naming this person as a material witness, the date and place

Photo of a Florida electric chair. The chair, built from oak by prison inmates in 1923, was nicknamed "Old Sparky." During its period of use, 233 men were executed in it. (*Source:* Mark Foley/AP Wide World Photos.)

at which he or she is to appear, and the approximate number of days that the person will be needed as a witness. This certificate is transmitted to the appropriate court in the state where the needed witness resides. The court in that state will order the witness to come before it for a hearing to determine whether the person is a necessary and material witness and whether any undue hardship will be caused by the person's appearing in the other state as a witness. If the judge concludes that the person is a necessary and material witness and that no hardship will be suffered, the person will be tendered expense money and ordered to appear in the demanding court as a witness. Should the person fail to appear as commanded, contempt of court charges may be filed in the state where the material witness resides. The witness is immune from arrest on any prior crimes committed in the demanding state while in the state to testify.

Excluding Witnesses

Prior to the time that any of the witnesses testify, the judge must decide whether the witnesses may remain in the courtroom or should be excluded until after they have testified. This decision may be made on the judge's own motion or on the request of either the prosecution or the defense. The primary purpose for excluding witnesses from the courtroom is to prevent them from trying to corroborate the testimony of other witnesses. The effort to corroborate another witness's testimony is not always done with an intent to falsify. It may be done because one witness may be uncertain of some of the facts. Although witnesses are excluded from the courtroom, it is almost impossible to keep them from conversing about their testimony even though the judge admonishes them against such action.

EXAMINATION OF WITNESSES

The Oath

Before being permitted to testify, an oath must be administered in which the witness promises to tell the truth. Throughout the history of trial by jury, witnesses have given an oath that their allegations are true. In the past, these oaths have involved a call to the deity to assist the oath giver in substantiating the truthfulness of the statements made, as well as a call for assistance in telling the truth. It was the general belief that, after giving such an oath, should one falsely testify, divine punishment would result. So strong was the belief in divine punishment at common law that if one did not believe in God, one was considered incompetent to testify.

Although most jurisdictions presently do not prescribe wording for the oath administered to a witness, generally a call to the deity to assist the witness in telling the truth is still included. Oaths that are administered to witnesses today are substantially as follows: "Do you hereby solemnly swear to tell the truth, and nothing but the truth, in the matter now pending before this court, so help you God?" At one time, while this oath was being administered, the witness was required to raise the right hand and lay the left hand on a Bible. Most jurisdictions have dispensed with the use of the Bible in administering the oath, but the witness is still required to raise his or her right hand during its administration.

Affirmation   Although there is no requirement that the word God be mentioned in the oath, it usually is included. Some persons consider it objectionable to "swear to God" to tell the truth. They feel this way either because they believe that the use of the word God under the circumstances is sacrilegious or because they do not believe in a God and object to swearing to something in which they have no belief. To accommodate these individuals, courts permit them to affirm to tell the truth. When either the court clerk or another court officer administers the oath or affirmation, or swears in the witness, as the procedure is known, the witness is asked to stand and be sworn. If the oath is found objectionable, the witness will advise the officer that the truth will be affirmed. The officer will then require the witness to raise the right hand, and the officer will state words to this effect: "Do you hereby solemnly affirm to tell the truth and nothing but the truth in the matter now pending before this court?" This procedure has been referred to as an affirmation. Whether a witness swears to tell the truth or affirms to tell the truth, both procedures are technically known as the "oath."

A few legal scholars argue that administering the oath is a useless procedure and a waste of time, since it does not guarantee that the witness will testify truthfully. But the great majority of persons engaged in the trial of cases believe that administering the oath to the witness gives a certain legal solemnity to the occasion and may cause the witness to reflect upon the necessity to tell the truth. As is stated in the Federal Rules of Criminal Procedure, the wording of the oath may be of any nature that will awaken the witness to the necessity of telling the truth.

Even though the oath may not guarantee that the truth will be told, the witness may be prosecuted for perjury if testimony is intentionally falsified after the oath is administered. This threat may be enough to encourage some witnesses to testify truthfully, when they might not otherwise do so.

Refusal to Be Sworn   If a witness refuses to be sworn, a contempt of court charge can be filed against the witness. The only exception to the administration of the oath to a witness is in the case of a small child or a mentally retarded person who may not understand the meaning of the oath. Under these circumstances, before the child or mentally retarded person is allowed to testify, the judge will conduct a voir dire examination to determine whether the prospective witness knows that it is wrong to tell a falsehood and that it is necessary to tell the truth. If this can be established by the judge through questioning the prospective witness, the oath will be eliminated.

Direct Examination

After the oath has been administered to the witness, the witness will begin his or her testimony; that is, facts will be related within the witness's knowledge of the case. Prior to making any statements about the case, the witness will be required to state his or her name and correct spelling of the name for identification purposes. Because of threats that have been made to law enforcement officers and their families, some jurisdictions permit the officers to give their headquarters address instead of their home address. After the identification data are furnished by the prosecution witness, the prosecuting attorney will start the examination. The questioning of the witness by the side that calls him or her is known as **direct examination**. The prosecuting attorney may approach the direct examination in one of two ways or in a combination of both. The prosecuting attorney may request the witness to relate in his or her own words the facts about the case. This procedure is sometimes referred to as the narrative approach. The prosecuting attorney may also use the short-question-and-answer approach. Both procedures have their advantages and disadvantages. The narrative approach permits the witness to tell the story in a more logical form so that the jury may be better able to follow the testimony. But unless the witness is familiar with the rules of evidence, irrelevant material and hearsay evidence may be included, or facts may be related that the prosecuting attorney wishes to avoid. By asking the witness short, direct questions, the prosecuting attorney has greater control over the facts to be related and can limit the testimony to relevant facts. The short-question-and-answer form of examination is frequently time-consuming, and sometimes this type of testimony becomes boring to the jury. If a witness is shy or perhaps somewhat reluctant to testify, it may be necessary to revert to the short-question-and-answer procedure.

During the direct examination, the attorney may not ask the witness leading questions. A leading question is one that indicates the desired answer to the witness. For example, the attorney may ask the witness, "You did see the defendant threaten the victim with a knife, didn't you?" Clearly, the attorney wants a yes answer. But by rephrasing the question, the witness may be asked, "Did you see the defendant threaten the victim with a knife?" Although the attorney may still desire a yes answer, that wish has not been indicated to the witness, and the witness is free to give either a yes or no answer. The mere fact that a question calls for a yes or no answer does not make it a leading one, but if phrased to indicate the answer desired, it is a leading question. The reason these questions are not generally permitted during direct examination is that the witness is usually favorable to the side that calls the witness, and thus there may be a tendency to assist that side irrespective of the truth if a desired answer is indicated.

Occasionally, a witness called by the prosecution will display hostility toward the prosecution, making the expected testimony difficult to obtain. Under these circumstances, the prosecuting attorney may request the judge to declare for the record that the witness is a hostile witness. If the witness is declared to be hostile, the prosecuting attorney may then ask leading questions. This type of questioning is permitted because it is assumed that the witness will answer truthfully, because of the displayed hostility, even though a desired answer is indicated. Although a hostile witness may be asked leading questions during direct examination, using that method does not mean that obtaining the desired testimony from the witness will become any less difficult. To be declared a hostile witness, a person must display hostility and uncooperativeness. The mere fact that a witness does not meet expectations or is reluctant to furnish information will not be sufficient grounds for the judge to declare the witness hostile.

A limited use of leading questions is permitted in the examination of children, senior citizens, and mentally retarded persons in order to assist them in telling their stories. Leading questions may also be asked concerning identifying matters, such as name, address, and place of employment of the witness, since these matters are usually not in controversy. Occasionally, a leading question may be permitted to assist in refreshing the memory of a witness.

Objections to Questions

During the direct examination by the prosecuting attorney, the defense attorney may object to some of the questions asked. If so, the objection will be indicated to the judge, who must rule upon the objection. After an objection is made, the witness should not answer the question until the judge has ruled on it. If the judge believes that the objection is well founded, he or she will sustain the objection, meaning that the witness may not answer the question. If the judge does not agree with the objection, he or she will overrule the objection, whereupon the witness must answer. There are many reasons the defense attorney may object to a question. The question may call for an answer that would be hearsay information; it may be leading; or it may require the witness to state an opinion about some matter. If the prosecution asks an improper question or one that calls for information that is not admissible, unless the defense attorney objects the answer is permitted to go into the record of the case and generally is not grounds for appeal should the defendant be convicted. For this reason, defense attorneys make frequent objections during the trial. From a psychological standpoint, defense attorneys may also inject objections from time to time in an effort to lessen the impact of the testimony of the prosecution's witnesses.

Occasionally, a witness will become overzealous in answering the prosecuting attorney's questions and will answer a question to which an objection is made before the judge is able to rule on it. If the objection is overruled, no serious consequences result, other than the judge's becoming irritated because the witness did not wait for the ruling. However, if the objection is sustained, the answer has been improperly given, and therefore it must be stricken from the record and the jury advised to disregard the answer. But the problem is, can a jury completely forget such a statement? Knowing the difficulty of disregarding some statements, especially if the answer is highly prejudicial against the defendant, the judge may declare a mistrial, and the case will have to be restarted with a different jury. In addition, the witness could be held in contempt of court, particularly if previously admonished against answering before the judge can rule on an objection.

Cross-Examination

After the prosecuting attorney has concluded questioning the witness on direct examination, the defense attorney is permitted to cross-examine the witness. The primary purpose of **cross-examination** is to assist in arriving at the truth. Cross-examination enables the opposition or adversary to challenge the witness's veracity, accuracy, and prejudices. One of the basic reasons that the accused is entitled to confront adverse witnesses is to enable cross-examination. This right was made mandatory on the states by the case of *Pointer* v. *Texas.*[5] The U.S. Supreme Court stated the following in the *Pointer* decision:

> . . . We hold today that the Sixth Amendment's right of an accused to confront the witnesses against him is likewise a fundamental right and is made obligatory on the States by the Fourteenth Amendment.
>
> It cannot seriously be doubted at this late date that the right of cross-examination is included in the right of an accused in a criminal case to confront the witnesses against him. And probably no one, certainly no one experienced in the trial of lawsuits, would deny the value of cross-examination in exposing falsehood and bringing out the truth in a trial of a criminal case . . . the right of cross-examination is one of the safeguards essential to a fair trial.

If the defense attorney believes that the witness told the truth during the direct examination and nothing is to be gained by cross-examining the witness, the right to cross-examine that particular witness may be waived. Cross-examination is at best a dangerous procedure for a defense attorney. Before deciding whether to cross-examine a witness, the defense counsel must carefully weigh whether there is more to be lost than gained by the cross-examination. If a witness was telling the truth during direct examination, the cross-examination may merely result in the witness's being able to reemphasize the story to the jury. There is also the possibility that the witness may become emotionally upset by vigorous cross-examination, thus often receiving the sympathy of the jury.

Impeachment   On the other hand, if a witness testified falsely during direct examination, has made prior inconsistent statements, or has colored the testimony because of some prejudice, these facts may be disclosed to the jury only through cross-examination. Cross-examination under these circumstances is necessary in order that the jury may disregard the testimony or give it the proper weight. This devaluation of the testimony by cross-examination is referred to as impeachment in the field of evidence.

Generally, cross-examination is an unpleasant experience for both the witness and the attorney. As we pointed out, if the witness told the truth during direct examination and cannot be upset by cross-examination, the defense attorney may suffer the unpleasantness of the witness's retelling the story to the jury. Many times a defense attorney does not receive the answer anticipated during cross-examination but is usually bound by the answer and thus often is powerless to overcome the damage the answer may cause. If a witness testifies truthfully during direct examination, there is usually little to fear from cross-examination. However, a few attorneys feel that the only way to properly represent the defendant in a criminal case is to vigorously cross-examine all witnesses. If the witness has given testimony particularly damaging to the defense, the defense attorney may endeavor to devalue the testimony by belittling or embarrassing the witness during cross-examination. Although having the responsibility of protecting a witness from overzealous cross-examination, the judge may not unduly restrict the defense attorney from vigorous cross-examination. Occasionally, a witness may have been indiscreet in some action or statement made that may be brought out during cross-examination, and the judge will be powerless to prevent this embarrassment. If the witness, and particularly the law enforcement officer, has testified discreetly in conduct and content, any attempt at embarrassment by the defense attorney may result in enhancing the officer's testimony. Juries often react unfavorably to this cross-examination tactic.

Although leading questions may not generally be asked during direct examination, they are permitted on cross-examination if the attorney feels that utilizing them is an advantage. Leading questions are frequently asked during vigorous cross-examination. The reason these questions are permitted during cross-examination is that usually the witness who is being cross-examined is not favorable to the side doing the cross-examining, and the witness will not give a desired answer, even though it is indicated, unless it is the truth.

Limited Cross-Examination   States differ in the extent of the cross-examination. A majority of the states limit the cross-examination to the facts brought out during direct examination. This procedure is referred to as limited or restricted cross-examination. Other states permit the witness to be cross-examined about any pertinent facts in the case that may be within the knowledge of the witness. This procedure is known as unlimited or unrestricted cross-examination. Those favoring restricted cross-examination allege that attorneys are able to control the material that is presented by a witness and may prepare the presentation in a more logical manner. This method enables the jury to follow more closely the facts as they unfold. Those who advocate unrestricted cross-examination allege that the unrestricted procedure saves time, in that a witness may be examined extensively while on the stand rather than being recalled at a later time. Also, the procedure eliminates objections by the opposing side that the questions asked during cross-examination did not pertain to matters brought out during direct examination. In those states following the restricted cross-examination procedure, witnesses are usually cautioned to confine their answers to questions asked during direct examination and not to volunteer additional information, since they may subject themselves to unnecessary and extensive cross-examination. This outcome is one of the dangers of permitting the story to be told in the witness's own words, since facts may be included that could be used to devalue the testimony during cross-examination. Whether the restricted or unrestricted procedure is followed, witnesses are seldom permitted to give the facts in their own way during cross-examination. The cross-examiner desires to control the testimony and can better do so by confining the questions to ones that require short answers, often only a yes or no.

Redirect Examination and Recross-Examination   After the defense attorney has completed his or her cross-examination, the judge will permit the prosecuting attorney to further question the witness. This questioning is known as redirect examination. The questioning must be confined to clarifying facts brought out during cross-examination. Sometimes the defense attorney will require that the witness answer a question with only a yes or no, but the answer does not reflect the true situation without further explanation. When the prosecuting attorney further questions the witness after cross-examination, the answers can be explained more fully by the witness. Seldom will a judge permit any new material to be brought forth during the redirect examination. To do so would start the whole questioning process again and could encourage sloppy practice by attorneys by not properly preparing the direct examination. Unless the prosecuting attorney believes that redirect examination will be beneficial, it may be waived.

If the prosecuting attorney further questions the witness on redirect examination, at the conclusion of this questioning the defense attorney is entitled to re-cross-examine the witness on facts stated on redirect examination. After this series takes place, the witness is excused and the next witness is called. The same sequence of examinations may take place with each prosecution and defense witness who is called, or the sequence could stop after the direct examination. When the whole series is repeated with each witness, criminal trials can become very lengthy.

Refusal to Answer Questions

The witness must answer all questions asked throughout the entire examination. The only exception is that if the answer to a question will incriminate the witness, the witness may refuse to answer. An incriminating answer is one that would subject the witness to prosecution. The Fifth Amendment to the U.S. Constitution provides that one may not be compelled to witness against oneself. But all other questions must be answered even though the answer may be embarrassing or life-endangering to the witness or his or her family. The degrading or endangering questions must be pertinent to the case, however, and not asked merely to embarrass the witness. Otherwise, the judge may not permit the question to be answered. Refusal to answer questions occurs more frequently during cross-examination than during direct examination. It is during cross-examination that the witness is questioned by the adversary, and it is then that questions may be asked that the witness would be hesitant to answer. If a witness persists in refusing to answer a question that is not incriminating, the entire testimony may be stricken from the record and the jury advised to disregard it. It is held that a witness may not testify to those facts that may be favorable and refuse to testify to matters that may be unfavorable. In addition to having the testimony stricken from the record, the witness could be held in contempt of court until the questions are answered.

There are times during a trial when arriving at the truth of what happened is more important than the prosecution of a witness incriminated by answering a question. Under these circumstances, the witness may be granted immunity from prosecution by the judge. If immunity is granted, the witness must answer all questions.

Examination by the Judge and Jury

Although it is the primary responsibility of the prosecution and defense to call and examine the witnesses whom they believe are necessary, witnesses may also be called by the trial judge if deemed necessary in the interest of justice. Most jurisdictions permit the judge to question prosecution and defense witnesses if such questioning may furnish information not brought forth by the prosecutor or defense counsel. Occasionally, a juror may wish to question a witness in order to clarify some point. Most judges will permit a limited amount of questioning by a juror if it is felt that the questioning is in good faith, but such questioning could very easily get out of hand, since some jurors may desire to get into the act and become counsels. The questioning of witnesses by jurors is generally not encouraged. When a juror wishes to ask a witness a question, the judge usually will require the juror to write the question on a slip of paper and have it handed to the judge, who will ask the question for the juror. This precaution keeps a juror from trying to become one of the questioning attorneys.

Introduction of Physical Evidence

During the investigation of a crime, officers will usually discover physical evidence, or material objects, that are pertinent to the crime. These objects, such as a latent fingerprint developed at a crime scene and identified as that of the defendant, often assist in connecting the defendant to the crime. Physical evidence may include objects taken during a robbery or burglary that were found in the possession of the defendant. These objects may be described by the officer who found them, and it is not necessary that they be presented in court. But in almost all instances, the prosecuting attorney will introduce these objects as evidence in order to substantiate the officer's testimony and to emphasize the facts of the case. These physical objects must be introduced by witnesses who can connect the objects with the crime charged. The witness will have to describe where the object was found, when, and under what circumstances. Who can forget the controversy surrounding the bloody glove in the O.J. Simpson murder trial? Once the object is introduced into evidence, the jury may examine it and consider it part of the facts of the case.

Viewing the Crime Scene

There are times when a judge may feel that a jury can better follow the testimony of the witnesses if they view the area in which the crime was committed. Under these circumstances, the judge will order the jury, as a body, to be taken to the crime scene by an officer of the court. Since viewing the crime scene is, in a sense, receiving facts of the case, the viewing in some jurisdictions is considered as evidence of the case. For that reason, the prosecuting attorney, defense attorney, defendant, and judge must accompany the jury. It has been established as improper for a jury, either as individuals or as a group, to view the crime scene without authorization from the judge.

In making the decision, the judge must consider several factors. If photographs of the crime scene are displayed to the jury, will that display accomplish as much as the actual viewing? Have material changes taken place in the crime scene that may cause more confusion than clarification?

Prosecution Rests

After presentation of all the prosecution witnesses and physical evidence that the prosecuting attorney believes is necessary, the prosecuting attorney will usually state,

These things he has not seen fit to take the stand and deny or explain. And in the whole world, if anybody would know, this defendant would know. Essie Mae is dead, she can't tell you her side of the story. The defendant won't.

The case was taken to the U.S. Supreme Court on a writ of certiorari to consider whether comment on the defendant's failure to testify violated the self-incrimination clause of the Fifth Amendment made applicable to the states by the Fourteenth Amendment. The Supreme Court pointed out that a defendant has a constitutional right to remain silent and not testify, and permitting the prosecuting attorney and judge to comment on the defendant's failure to testify was

> a penalty imposed by the courts for exercising a constitutional privilege. It cut down on the privilege by making its assertion costly. It is said, however, that the inference of guilt for failure to testify as to facts peculiarly within the accused's knowledge is in any event natural and irresistible, and that comment on the failure does not magnify that inference into a penalty for asserting a constitutional privilege. What the jury may infer, given no help from the court, is one thing. What it may infer when the court solemnizes the silence of the accused into evidence against him is quite another.

The defendant's Fifth Amendment right against self-incrimination and the fact that the exercise of that right may not be called to the attention of the jury were both clearly illustrated by the *Griffin* case. However, in most jurisdictions, if the defendant does take the stand and fails to explain certain facts that logically should have been explained, that failure may be commented on by the judge and the prosecuting attorney. The theory behind this permitted comment is that it is held that a defendant should not be able to testify on only those matters that are beneficial but fail to explain other facts that may be unfavorable. Another problem created for a defense attorney arises when the client insists on taking the stand and the attorney does not believe such action to be wise. Does a defendant have a right to testify in his or her own behalf over the objections of counsel? This question has not been answered in all jurisdictions, but a few have held that a defendant does have a right to present evidence in his or her own behalf, even to testifying over the objections of counsel. The court of one state made this comment concerning the right of a defendant to testify:

> We are satisfied that the right to testify in one's own behalf is of such fundamental importance that a defendant whose timely demands to take the stand contrary to the advice given by his counsel has the right to give an exposition of his defense before a jury. The defendant's insistence upon testifying may in the final analysis be harmful to his case, but the right is of such importance that every defendant should have it in a criminal case. Although normally the decision whether a defendant should testify is within the competence of the trial attorney where, as here, a defendant insists that he wants to testify, he cannot be deprived of that opportunity.[7]

However, the defendant does not have a right to have his or her attorney present perjured testimony. The courts have stated that there is no Sixth Amendment right to an attorney's knowingly presenting perjured testimony. In one case, the defendant told his attorney that although he never saw a gun in the victim's hand, he was going to take the stand and raise the issue of self-defense. His attorney told him that such conduct would be perjury, and if the defendant attempted to testify in that manner, the attorney would disclose the perjury and withdraw from the case. The defendant testified but did not raise the self-defense issue. He was convicted and appealed, claiming he was denied effective counsel since the attorney's refusal to allow him to testify in the way he wanted violated his right to counsel. The U.S. Supreme Court held that it was not a violation of the defendant's Sixth Amendment right for his counsel to act in accordance with state laws governing professional conduct.[8]

REBUTTAL BY THE PROSECUTION

After the defense has presented its side of the case and rests, the prosecution may present additional evidence to meet or rebut that presented by the defense. The presentation of **rebuttal evidence** is permitted because, in most instances, the prosecution will have no advance knowledge of the approach that the defense may take in an effort to prove the defendant not guilty. Although after resting the prosecuting attorney may have felt that the defendant was proved guilty beyond a reasonable doubt, the defense may have created some new doubt by presenting its evidence. The evidence presented by the defense may not have been based upon actual facts. For example, the defense may have tried to prove that the defendant was at some place other than that where the crime was committed, creating a doubt in the minds of the jury about the guilt of the defendant. This alibi evidence may have been attempted through perjured testimony. To allow this testimony to stand unchallenged by the prosecution would be an injustice to society. The only way that this testimony can be effectively challenged, except through cross-examination, is for the prosecution to present further testimony to prove that the defendant was at the scene of the crime.

Generally, no new evidence pertaining to the guilt of the defendant may be presented during the rebuttal. This is the case because permitting new evidence would cause the whole sequence of the trial examination procedure to take place again. The only time that additional evidence may be introduced is when new material evidence has been discovered. The prosecution must be in a position to convince the judge that the newly discovered evidence was not available when the prosecution first presented its side of the case and that its discovery was not due to carelessness, inadequate investigation, or poor preparation. In the interest of justice, the judge may permit the newly discovered evidence to be introduced, but the defense may again present evidence in an effort to overcome that presented by the prosecution. This presentation is sometimes referred to as the rejoinder in some jurisdictions and as the defense rebuttal in others.

After the prosecution has finished the rebuttal, the defense may again make a motion for a judgment of acquittal to be entered. If this motion is denied by the judge, the next procedure, depending upon the procedure of the jurisdiction, is either presentation of closing arguments by the prosecution and the defense or instruction to the jury on the law of the case.

Depositions

Sometimes during a trial, a witness for one side or the other is unable to attend court to testify, yet the testimony of that witness is material to the case. Rather than continuing the trial until the witness is able to appear in court, an out-of-court written statement, or **deposition**, given under oath, will be taken from the witness. Before a deposition may be taken, the opposing side must be notified that a deposition is to be taken at a particular time, date, and place. This notice is necessary so that the opposing side may be present to cross-examine the witness. The deposition is usually in a question-and-answer form much as the testimony would be given in court. The deposition will be read to the jury at the appropriate time during the trial, and the information will become part of the facts of the case. Because of the right of the defendant to be presented with the witnesses against him or her, some states do not permit the prosecution to introduce depositions in evidence.

NOT GUILTY BY REASON OF INSANITY

Because the procedure on the defense of not guilty by reason of insanity differs among states, a discussion of that defense is in order at this time. Not all states permit a separate plea of not guilty by reason of insanity. In those states where this plea is not permitted, the insanity defense is alleged by the defense after the prosecution rests in the same manner as other defenses that the defendant may utilize, such as the alibi of self-defense. Under these circumstances, the prosecution will present its evidence to prove the defendant guilty beyond a reasonable doubt.

After the presentation of this evidence, the defendant alleges that he or she cannot be held criminally liable for the crime, since he or she was insane at the time of committing the act. The defendant then presents evidence in his or her behalf in an endeavor to prove that he or she was insane at the time. This type of defense can catch the prosecution by surprise, and obtaining rebuttal evidence may be difficult. Further, with this type of defense being alleged, the prosecution has a double burden. Not knowing of the insanity defense in advance, the prosecution usually must present much evidence to prove that the defendant committed the crime, but by claiming the insanity defense, the defendant is in a sense admitting the act but alleging that there is no criminal liability. To rebut this allegation, the prosecution must prove that the defendant was sane at the time the crime was committed. Because of the element of surprise to the prosecution by the insanity defense and the double burden imposed upon the prosecutor, efforts have been made to have this defense included in the right of discovery by the prosecution. In those jurisdictions permitting a separate plea of not guilty by reason of insanity, the prosecuting attorney is not surprised and usually has ample opportunity to prepare the case to meet the allegation.

In those states where a separate plea of not guilty by reason of insanity is permitted, unless the defendant enters that plea, sanity is presumed at the time that the crime was committed, and no defense of insanity may be entered. As pointed out in Chapter 5, a few states permit the defendant to enter dual pleas. The defendant may enter a plea of not guilty and at the same time enter a plea of not guilty by reason of insanity. When the dual pleas are entered, the trial on the not guilty plea will be tried first. If the defendant is found not guilty, no further action may take place. But if the defendant is found guilty, a second trial takes place to determine the sanity of the defendant at the time the crime was committed. These trials may be heard by the same jury or different juries, depending on the wishes of the defendant or the procedure of the jurisdiction involved. In some states, the two trials are consolidated into one.

Burden of Proof

States differ in their approach regarding the burden of proof on the insanity issue. Some states contend that, by entering the plea of not guilty by reason of insanity, the defendant has admitted the conduct. Having admitted guilt, the defendant is not entitled to the presumption of innocence, and the prosecution has no burden of proof on the guilt issue. Since it is presumed that all persons are sane unless, and until, proved otherwise, in some states the defendant has the burden of proving insanity at the time the crime was committed. Having this burden, the defense will open the trial proceedings by presenting the defendant's evidence first, followed by the prosecution. In the effort to prove insanity, the defendant may produce expert witnesses in the field of psychology, who, after examining the defendant, may express their opinions on the defendant's mental state at the time the crime occurred. The defense counsel may call witnesses acquainted with the defendant to express their opinions on the defendant's sanity for corroboration with the opinions of the experts. The amount of proof that the defendant must present differs among states. Some states require the defendant to prove insanity by a **preponderance of evidence**; other states require that insanity be proved to the satisfaction of the jury. The line of demarcation between these proofs is very fine, but it is conceded that the defendant does not have to prove beyond a reasonable doubt that the crime was committed while he or she was insane.

After the defendant has presented evidence to prove insanity, the prosecution has the responsibility of going forward with the evidence and proving that the defendant was sane at the time of the act. How much evidence must the prosecution present to prove sanity? Merely going forward with the evidence generally implies meeting the evidence of the opposition. The consensus is that the prosecution must do more than meet the evidence. There must be more than a doubt about the sanity of the defendant before the jury can conclude that the defendant was sane at the time the crime occurred. Most jurisdictions contend that the prosecution still has the burden of proving the defendant sane beyond a reasonable doubt. In fact, in some jurisdictions, if the defendant enters the plea of guilty by reason of insanity, the prosecution opens the trial and presents evidence to prove the defendant sane beyond a reasonable doubt, and the defense may meet that evidence by merely creating a doubt about sanity at the time the act was committed.

Test for Sanity

Determining sanity is not easy. Whatever procedure is followed, the ultimate determination to be made is whether the defendant was in such a state of mind at the time the crime was committed that he or she cannot be held legally responsible. Some acceptable test must be applied. The problem becomes more complicated because it is not the defendant's present state of mind that is at issue. As has been previously pointed out, unless a defendant is mentally capable of defending himself or herself, the trial cannot take place. Since the case is going to trial, it has been adjudged that the defendant is presently sane. It is necessary then to go back in time in attempting to establish the sanity of the defendant. Even the most knowledgeable experts in the field of psychology can give only an opinion of the mental condition at the time of the crime unless the defendant was under a doctor's treatment.

Various Insanity Defense Standards

Test	Legal Standard of Mental Illness	Final Burden of Proof
M'Naghten	"Didn't know what he was doing or didn't know it was wrong."	Balance of probabilities
Irresistible impulse	"Could not control his conduct."	Beyond a reasonable doubt
Durham	"The criminal act was caused by his mental illness."	Beyond a reasonable doubt
Substantial capacity	"Lacks substantial capacity to appreciate the wrongfulness of his conduct or to control it."	Beyond a reasonable doubt
Present federal law	"Lacks capacity to appreciate the wrongfulness of his conduct."	Clear and convincing evidence

Devising a test that will accurately establish a defendant's mental condition months before has been very difficult. For many years in England, the "wild beast test" was used. This test has also been referred to as the good and evil test. It was held that if an accused did not know any more than a wild beast would when the crime was committed, then no criminal responsibility could result from the act. In other words, if the accused had no more conception of good and evil than a wild beast while committing the crime, he could not be held responsible. The good and evil test was used until it was replaced by the right and wrong test in 1843.[9] In that case, Daniel M'Naghten was indicted for the murder of Edward Drummond, private secretary to Sir Robert Peel, Prime Minister of Great Britain. M'Naghten mistook Drummond for Peel, whom M'Naghten felt was persecuting him. M'Naghten was found not guilty by reason of insanity. The acquittal generated so much public indignation in London, including that of the Queen, that the judges were called before the House of Lords and asked to explain the test that was used to determine the sanity of M'Naghten. The judges answered the inquiry with the following test, which the jury was to consider in determining the sanity of one accused of crime. The judges stated that

> the jurors ought to be told in all cases that every man is to be presumed to be sane, and possess a sufficient degree of reason to be responsible for his crimes, until the contrary be proved to their satisfaction; and that to establish a defense on the ground of insanity, it must be clearly proved that, at the time of the committing of the act, the party accused was laboring under such a defect of reason, from disease of mind, as not to know the nature of the act he was doing; or, if he did know it, that he did not know he was doing what was wrong. The mode of putting the latter part of the question to the jury on these occasions has generally been whether the accused at the time of doing the act knew the difference between right and wrong.

The test has been referred to as the M'Naghten test. It has since been followed in England and has been adopted by a majority of the states in this country. Although the test has been criticized by some legal scholars and psychologists, it has been replaced in only a few states. The M'Naghten test continues to have acceptance because it is generally felt that no better test has been devised and that the jury is better able to understand it than other tests that have been suggested.

Because of the confusion surrounding the M'Naghten test, in 1887 some jurisdictions adopted the Irresistible Impulse test. The landmark case in this area was *Parsons* v. *State,* where an Alabama court set forth the modern version of the Irresistible Impulse test.[10] This test holds that a person will be considered insane if, as a result of a disease of the mind, he or she was unable to control his or her behavior. Just as the name of this test implies, if the defendant could prove that he or she was suffering from a disease of the mind so that there was an impulse to commit criminal acts that he or she could not control, then the defendant would be considered insane. The current trend is to revert back to only the M'Naghten test.

This test also was controversial, and in 1954 the U.S. Court of Appeals in Washington, D.C., decided the case of *Durham* v. *United States.*[11] Although this decision was also controversial, some jurisdictions adopted its rationale as their test for insanity. The court stated that the "rule" to be followed in determining criminal responsibility is as follows:

> It is simply that an accused is not criminally responsible if his unlawful act was the product of mental disease or mental defect. . . .
>
> Whenever there is some evidence that the accused suffered from a diseased or defective mental condition at the time the unlawful act was committed, the trial court

must provide the jury with guides for determining whether the accused can be held criminally responsible. We do not, and indeed could not, formulate an instruction which would be either appropriate or binding in all cases. But under the rule now announced, any instruction should in some way convey to the jury the sense and substance of the following: If you the jury believe beyond a reasonable doubt that the accused was not suffering from a diseased or defective mental condition at the time he committed the criminal act charged, you may find him guilty.

The same problems inherent in the M'Naghten test regarding mental disease or defect were present in the *Durham* case. The Durham test has been severely criticized in the case of *United States* v. *Currens,* where the court said it is too vague and indefinite to be workable in the determination of criminal responsibility.[12] The Durham test does not give the jury any real guidelines to determine whether an unlawful act was the product of a mental disease or mental defect.

The other major test used is the American Law Institute's substantial capacity test (also known as the ALI test). The Model Penal Code uses the ALI test. It is also being used in a growing number of states. The test is found in Section 4.01 of the Model Penal Code and is as follows:

1. A person is not responsible for criminal conduct if at the time of such conduct as a result of mental disease or defect he lacks substantial capacity either to appreciate the criminality (wrongfulness) of his conduct or to conform his conduct to the requirements of the law.

2. As used in the Article, the terms mental disease or defect do not include abnormally manifested only by repeated criminal or otherwise antisocial conduct.

The primary difference between the M'Naghten and ALI tests is that the M'Naghten test requires the defendant to show total mental impairment, whereas the ALI test requires the defendant to show only that he lacked the "substantial capacity" to conform his or her conduct to the requirements of law, that is, lack of self-control.

A number of states now use the "guilty, but mentally ill" procedure for handling the insanity issue. Under this procedure, when an insanity defense is raised, the court, if the evidence permits, may find the defendant guilty but mentally ill. In most states, when the defense is raised, the case is tried without regard to the insanity defense. If a finding of guilty results, the jury is asked to determine whether the defendant is insane.

Syndromes

Starting in the 1980s, a range of **syndromes** that affect the mental state of the defendant have been presented to excuse or justify the conduct of the defendant. One of the most famous is the Twinkie defense. When considering nutrition and criminal behavior, consider that Americans buy 700 million Twinkies a year—80 percent of them on impulse. Over 50 billion Twinkies have been sold in the past sixty years.

On May 22, 1979, Dan White, a former San Francisco, California, county supervisor, was convicted of voluntary manslaughter for the November 1978 killing of San Francisco Mayor George Moscone and Supervisor Harvey Milk. White was originally charged with first-degree murder (a capital offense). The prosecutor argued to the jury that White was guilty of cold-blooded murder. It was established that White had gone to city hall to talk to the mayor. He had entered through a window to avoid the metal detector at the main entrance. At the time, he was carrying a snub-nosed revolver. He shot Mayor Moscone and Supervisor Milk nine times with the weapon, killing both of them.

White readily admitted killing both the mayor and the supervisor, the latter being his most vocal opponent on the San Francisco Board of Supervisors.

White's defense attorney, Douglas Schmidt, presented evidence to establish that White had suffered from "diminished capacity" caused by a "biochemical change" in his brain. According to the defense's theory of the case, White was incapable of the premeditation, deliberation, and malice required to obtain a murder conviction. Evidence at the trial indicated that White was a manic depressive with a high degree of stress caused by financial and other personal problems. A defense medical expert testified that White suffered from a "genetically caused melancholia," and at the time, he was "discombobulated." Defense witnesses, who comprised family members, friends and experts, testified about White's moods and his diet. One defense psychiatrist testified that White's compulsive diet of candy bars, Twinkies, and Cokes was evidence of a deep depression and resulted in excessive sugar intake, which either caused or aggravated a chemical imbalance in his brain. The Twinkie defense or syndrome apparently has not been successfully used since the Dan White trial. California has since abolished this defense.

XYY Syndrome   Some efforts have been made by defense attorneys to utilize the alleged effects of the XYY syndrome as an insanity defense. This defense is based upon the theory that individuals with an abnormal complement of chromosomes are legally insane and as such cannot be held criminally responsible for their acts. Generally, courts have been rejecting this defense, primarily because geneticists, in studying the extra Y chromosomes, differ in their opinions concerning the effects. It is generally conceded that not all individuals with an abnormal complement of chromosomes are, by nature, involuntarily aggressive. Also, these experts hold that it cannot be stated with certainty that a criminal act is the result of an abnormal complement of chromosomes.

PMS Syndrome   Another widely discussed defense is the premenstrual stress syndrome (PMS). The problems with the PMS defense are, first, that the defense must establish that PMS is a disease; second, that the defendant suffers from PMS; and third, that the PMS must cause the mental impairment that excuses the conduct. Premenstrual syndrome, or premenstrual tension (PMT), is believed to affect approximately 40 percent of American women between the ages of twenty and forty.[13] Normally, the symptoms begin ten to fourteen days prior to the onset of the menstrual period and become progressively worse until the onset of menstruation. In some women, PMS continues for several days after the onset. Common symptoms include irritability, anxiety, mood swings, depression, migraine headaches, fainting, dizziness, and allergies.

As one woman stated, "There is a pervasive sense of things always falling apart." Susan Lark, in her book *Premenstrual Syndrome Self-Help Book,* states that severely afflicted women are most vulnerable to extreme behavior during this time.[14] Katherine Dalton, an English physician, reports an increase in the likelihood of accidents, alcohol abuse, suicide attempts, and crimes committed by some women suffering from premenstrual tension. In "Menstruation and Crime," she states that in many cases, the affected women have Dr. Jekyll and Mr. Hyde personality splits; that is, they are "mean," "witchy," and "irritable" during the PMT period. They often yell at their children, pick fights with their husbands, and snap at friends and coworkers. After the symptoms end, they often spend the rest of the month trying to repair the damage done to these relationships.[15] There is a lot of skepticism regarding the PMS/PMT defense, which has generally not been successful.

Battered Spouse Syndrome   In recent years, wives who have killed their abusing spouses have attempted to use the battered spouse defense. In the 1980s, *The Burning Bed,* a popular film that was based on a real-life case, depicted a woman who killed her husband while he slept. The husband had apparently abused and threatened her. When he went to sleep, she set fire to the bed, killing him. Traditionally, self-defense is not available in these cases because at the time of the killings, the spouses were not in imminent danger. As one court stated, a battered woman cannot reasonably fear imminent life-threatening danger from her sleeping spouse. For the most part, courts have rejected the battered spouse syndrome as a defense for spousal killings. A growing minority of courts have, however, held that the fact that the other spouse was sleeping does not preclude self-defense. When courts allow persons who have been abused to use self-defense as a shield to liability, this practice is known as the imperfect self-defense plea.

The use of the imperfect self-defense plea received national attention when two sons claimed they had been sexually abused since childhood and therefore found it necessary to kill their mother and father. Eric and Lyle Menendez, along with a series of family violence experts, testified that, as a result of the continued sexual abuse, they believed that they were in imminent danger of death or great bodily injury.

More and more courts are accepting the use of the imperfect self-defense plea in battered women cases. There is a gradual acceptance that some women can be trapped emotionally in an abusive relationship and honestly believe that they must kill their abusers to survive.[16] However, a number of courts still do not recognize this syndrome. In *State* v. *Stewart,* evidence at trial indicated that Mike Stewart had abused Peggy Stewart during their marriage and had sexually abused her two daughters by an earlier marriage. On one occasion, he shot one of Peggy's cats and then held the gun to Peggy's head and threatened to pull the trigger.

Peggy left Mike and moved to Oklahoma. Because Peggy was suicidal, she was committed to a hospital. Mike came to the hospital, checked her out, and took her back home. As they drove back home to Kansas, Mike told Peggy that it was all in her head, and that from now on, he would decide what was right for her. When they arrived home, Mike forced her to have oral sex, and then he went to bed. Later that day, as Mike slept, Peggy heard voices in her head repeating over and over, "kill or be killed." She then took a gun that she had hidden in the house and killed him with it. The court ruled that the facts do not constitute self-defense and that the state does not recognize the battered spouse syndrome. To excuse a killing under these circumstances would be the same as permitting capital punishment to be used for spousal abuse.[17]

Irrespective of the sanity test or defense that is applied, if the jury finds the defendant to have been sane at the time the crime occurred, the only procedure left is sentencing. On the other hand, if the jury finds that the defendant was insane when the crime was committed, the accused is theoretically entitled to be released. As pointed out in Chapter 5, if the defendant was found to have been insane when committing the crime, in most jurisdictions confinement will be in a mental hospital under a civil commitment to make certain that there is no threat to society. One court went so far as to hold that "an accused person who is acquitted by reason of insanity is presumed to be insane and may be committed for an indefinite period to a hospital for the insane."[18] In another decision, it was stated that "even where there has been a specific finding that the accused was competent to stand trial and assist in his own defense, the court would be well advised to invoke the code provision so that the accused may be confined as long as the public safety and his welfare require."[19]

CLOSING ARGUMENTS

After both sides have presented their evidence, the next procedure in most jurisdictions is the closing arguments by the prosecuting attorney and the defense attorney. Closing arguments are merely a summarization of the evidence presented during the trial. Attorneys have mixed emotions regarding the value of closing arguments. Some attorneys allege that they have no effect on the jury and are a waste of time. Other attorneys feel that a closing argument may be the difference between losing a case and winning it. Irrespective of the viewpoints, in most criminal trials, both the prosecution and the defense will give closing arguments. There is no limit on the length of a closing argument. The attorneys may take only a few minutes or they may take several days, depending on the length of the trial. The judge does have the right to limit the time involved, but he or she cannot be too restrictive. With the possible exception of an insanity trial, the usual procedure is for the prosecuting attorney to give the closing argument first, followed by the defense. After the defense has completed its closing argument, the prosecuting attorney may give a rebuttal argument. Some jurisdictions reverse this procedure and permit the defense attorney to present the closing argument first, followed by the prosecution.

It is considered improper for the attorneys to appeal to the sympathy or emotions of the jurors, but frequently the closing arguments are a dramatic performance that results in an emotional appeal. In fact, during the questioning of the jurors for cause, attorneys may inject questions designed to later enable them to weave the personal lives of some of the jurors into the closing arguments. At this point in the trial, each side is endeavoring to sell the jury on the fact that its side is entitled to the verdict.

Closing Argument by the Prosecution

During the closing argument, the prosecuting attorney will summarize the evidence presented, emphasizing the strong points that indicate guilt. To substantiate the closing statements, the physical evidence already introduced may be displayed again. The prosecuting attorney may state that the evidence clearly proves that the defendant is guilty of the crime charged. It is held to be prejudicial error, however, for the prosecuting attorney to state that from personal knowledge, the defendant is known to be guilty, implying that information not brought forth during the trial is in his or her possession. The courts have stated that the right to discuss the merits of a case, regarding both the law and the facts, is very wide, and that the prosecuting attorney has the right to state what the evidence shows and what conclusions are to be drawn. The adverse party cannot complain if the reasoning is faulty and the deductions are illogical, since such matters are ultimately for the consideration of the jury. It has been held that the prosecuting attorney should be circumspect in remarks concerning the defendant and his or her counsel, but the use of derogatory epithets does not necessarily represent misconduct.

In the case of *People* v. *Jones,*[20] the prosecuting attorney referred to the defendant's behavior as consistent with animalistic and felonious tendencies, and also implied that there was a strange, twisted reason for the actions of the accused. The U.S. Supreme Court in that case stated the following:

> We recognize that prosecutors, like all others who have responsible roles in the trial of a criminal case, are human; as humans they may be affected by the tensions of a trial to the point of error and, on occasion, even to misconduct. We recognize, too, that the great increase in crime and the corresponding increase in the number of prosecutions in recent years has placed a heavy burden on district attorneys, who frequently must rely on inexperienced deputies to try cases. Be that as it may, prosecutors should be ever aware that in all they do and say they are representatives of the government of whom the public, including those who are prosecuted, are entitled to expect a high degree of ethical conduct.
>
> . . . while some of the references to the appellant (defendant), more particularly, "animalistic tendencies" and "felonious tendencies" were quite strong, we hold that, under the facts of this case, they were within the bounds of legitimate argument and did not constitute misconduct.

Following such arguments by the prosecuting attorney, the judge will often instruct the jury that the closing arguments are not to be considered as evidence in the case and that the jury is to disregard any statements not based on the evidence. If a prosecuting attorney does indulge in misconduct during the closing argument, the misconduct could lead to a mistrial being declared at the time or to a reversal of a conviction on appeal.

Closing Argument by the Defense

Technically, the same rules of conduct that apply to the prosecuting attorney also apply to the defense attorney. Since defense counsel misconduct is not appealable if the defendant is acquitted, the defense attorney often has considerable freedom in arguing the case to the jury. An appeal will often be made to the sympathy of the jury. It may be pointed out that in rendering a guilty verdict, the jury will deprive the defendant of freedom and companionship with his or her family. In one case, the defendant appeared in court wearing long hair and a shaggy beard. In the argument to the jury, the defense counsel stated that in looking over the jury, no member representative of the defendant's peer group could be seen. The defense attorney recalled a trial some 2000 years before at which the defendant also was wearing a beard, had long hair, and was tried without peer group representation. Keeping that fact in mind, the defense attorney felt that the appearance of the defendant would not deter the jury from rendering a verdict in favor of acquittal. Although the defense attorney may be dramatic in appealing to a jury, there are times when the jury may resent what they feel to be an insult to their intelligence in defense counsel arguments.

Even though represented by an attorney, occasionally a defendant will insist upon making a closing argument in addition to the one given by the attorney. Whether this will be permitted is at the judge's discretion. If the defendant is self-represented, a closing argument is always permitted.

Rebuttal Closing Argument

After the defense attorney has concluded the closing argument for the accused, the prosecuting attorney is entitled to make a rebuttal closing argument. Statements and challenges presented during the defense attorney's closing argument can be met.

Capstone Cases

Rock v. Arkansas
483 U.S. 44, 107 S.Ct 2704, 97 L.Ed.2d 37 (1987)

Justice Blackmun delivered the opinion of the Court.

The issue presented in this case is whether Arkansas' evidentiary rule prohibiting the admission of hypnotically refreshed testimony violated petitioner's constitutional right to testify on her own behalf as a defendant in a criminal case.

Petitioner Vickie Lorene Rock was charged with manslaughter in the death of her husband, Frank Rock, on July 2, 1983. A dispute had been simmering about Frank's wish to move from the couple's small apartment adjacent to Vickie's beauty parlor to a trailer she owned outside town. That night a fight erupted when Frank refused to let petitioner eat some pizza and prevented her from leaving the apartment to get something else to eat. When police arrived on the scene they found Frank on the floor with a bullet wound in his chest. Petitioner urged the officers to help her husband, and cried to a sergeant who took her in charge, "please save him" and "don't let him die." The police removed her from the building because she was upset and because she interfered with their investigation by her repeated attempts to use the telephone to call her husband's parents. According to the testimony of one of the investigating officers, petitioner told him that "she stood up to leave the room and [her husband] grabbed her by the throat and choked her and threw her against the wall and . . . at that time she walked over and picked up the weapon and pointed it toward the floor and he hit her again and she shot him." Because petitioner could not remember the precise details of the shooting, her attorney suggested that she submit to hypnosis in order to refresh her memory. Petitioner was hypnotized twice by Doctor Betty Back, a licensed neuropsychologist with training in the field of hypnosis. Doctor Back interviewed petitioner for an hour prior to the first hypnosis session, taking notes on petitioner's general history and her recollections of the shooting. Both hypnosis sessions were recorded on tape. Petitioner did not relate any new information during either of the sessions, but, after the hypnosis, she was able to remember that at the time of the incident she had her thumb on the hammer of the gun, but had not held her finger on the trigger. She also recalled that the gun had discharged when her husband grabbed her arm during the scuffle. As a result of the details that petitioner was able to remember about the shooting, her counsel arranged for a gun expert to examine the handgun, a single action Hawes .22 Deputy Marshal. That inspection revealed that the gun was defective and prone to fire, when hit or dropped, without the trigger's being pulled.

When the prosecutor learned of the hypnosis sessions, he filed a motion to exclude petitioner's testimony. The trial judge held a pretrial hearing on the motion and concluded that no hypnotically refreshed testimony would be admitted. The court issued an order limiting petitioner's testimony to "matters remembered and stated to the examiner prior to being placed under hypnosis." At trial, petitioner introduced testimony by the gun expert, but the court limited petitioner's own description of the events on the day of the shooting to a reiteration of the sketchy information in Doctor Back's notes. The jury convicted petitioner on the manslaughter charge and she was sentenced to 10 years' imprisonment and a $10,000 fine.

On appeal, the Supreme Court of Arkansas rejected petitioner's claim that the limitations on her testimony violated her right to present her defense. The court concluded that "the dangers of admitting this kind of testimony outweigh whatever probative value it may have," and decided to follow the approach of States that have held hypnotically refreshed testimony of witnesses inadmissible per se. . . . It ruled that the exclusion of petitioner's testimony did not violate her constitutional rights. Any "prejudice or deprivation" she suffered "was minimal and resulted from her own actions and not by any erroneous ruling of the court."

Petitioner's claim that her testimony was impermissibly excluded is bottomed on her constitutional right to testify in her own defense. At this point in the development of our adversary system, it cannot be doubted that a defendant in a criminal case has the right to take the witness stand and to testify in his or her own defense. This, of course, is a change from the historic common-law view, which was that all parties to litigation, including criminal defendants, were disqualified from testifying because of their interest in the outcome of the trial. The principal rationale for this rule was the possible untrustworthiness of a party's testimony. Under the common law, the practice did develop of permitting criminal defendants to tell their side of the story, but they were limited to making an unsworn statement that could not be elicited through direct examination by counsel and was not subject to cross-examination.

This Court in *Ferguson* v. *Georgia,* 365 U.S. 570 (1961), detailed the history of the transition from a rule of a defendant's incompetency to a rule of competency. As the Court there recounted, it came to be recognized that permitting a defendant to testify advances both the "detection of guilt" and "the protection of innocence," and by the end of the second half of the 19th century, all States except Georgia had enacted statutes that declared criminal defendants competent to testify.

The right to testify on one's own behalf at a criminal trial has sources in several provisions of the Constitution. It is one of the rights that "are essential to due process of law in a fair adversary process." *Faretta* v. *California.* The necessary ingredients of the Fourteenth Amendment's guarantee that no one shall be deprived of liberty without due process of law include a right to be heard and to offer testimony. . . .

The right to testify is also found in the Compulsory Process Clause of the Sixth Amendment, which grants a defendant the right to call "witnesses in his favor." . . . Logically included in the accused's right to call witnesses whose testimony is "material and favorable to his defense," *United States* v. *Valenzuela-Bernai,* 458 U.S. 858 (1982), is a right to testify himself, should he decide it is in his favor to do so. In fact, the most important witness for the defense in many criminal cases is the defendant himself. There is no justification today for a rule that denies an accused the opportunity to offer his own testimony. Like the truthfulness of other witnesses, the defendant's veracity, which was the concern behind the original common-law rule, can be tested adequately by cross-examination.

Moreover, in *Faretta* v. *California,* the Court recognized that the Sixth Amendment "grants to the accused personally the right to make his defense." Even more fundamental to a personal defense than the right of self representation, which was found to be "necessarily implied by the structure of the Amendment," *Faretta,* is an accused's right to present his own version of events in his own words. A defendant's opportunity to conduct his own defense by calling witnesses is incomplete if he may not present himself as a witness.

The opportunity to testify is also a necessary corollary to the Fifth Amendment's guarantee against compelled testimony. In *Harris* v. *New York,* 401 U.S. 222 (1971), the Court stated: "Every criminal defendant is privileged to testify in his own defense, or to refuse to do so." Three of the dissenting Justices in that case agreed that the Fifth Amendment encompasses this right: "[privilege against self-incrimination] is fulfilled only when an accused is guaranteed the right to remain silent unless he chooses to speak in the unfettered exercise of his own will. . . . The choice of whether to testify in one's own defense . . . is an exercise of the constitutional privilege."

The question now before the Court is whether a criminal defendant's right to testify may be restricted by a state rule that excludes her post-hypnosis testimony. This is not the first time this Court has faced a constitutional challenge to a state rule, designed to ensure trustworthy evidence, that interfered with the ability of a defendant to offer testimony. In *Washington* v. *Texas,* 388 U.S. 14 (1967), the Court [struck down] . . . a state statute that prevented persons charged as principals, accomplices, or accessories in the same crime from being introduced as witnesses for one another. . . . By preventing the defendant from having the benefit of his accomplice's testimony, "the State arbitrarily denied him the right to put on the stand a witness who was physically and mentally capable of testifying to events that he had personally observed, and whose testimony would have been relevant and material to the defense." . . . Just as a State may not apply an arbitrary rule of competence to exclude a material defense witness from taking the stand, it also may not apply a rule of evidence that permits a witness to take the stand, but arbitrarily excludes material portions of his testimony. In *Chambers* v. *Mississippi,* the Court invalidated a State's hearsay rule on the ground that it abridged the defendant's right to "present witnesses in his own defense."

Of course, the right to present relevant testimony is not without limitation. The right "may, in appropriate cases, bow to accommodate other legitimate interests in the criminal trial process." *Chambers.* . . . But restrictions of a defendant's right to testify may not be arbitrary or disproportionate to the purposes they are designed to serve. In applying its evidentiary rules a State must evaluate whether the interests served by a rule justify the limitation imposed on the defendant's constitutional right to testify. *(Continued)*

The Arkansas rule enunciated by the state courts does not allow a trial court to consider whether posthypnosis testimony may be admissible in a particular case; it is a per se rule prohibiting the admission at trial of any defendant's hypnotically refreshed testimony on the ground that such testimony is always unreliable. Thus, in Arkansas, an accused's testimony is limited to matters that he or she can prove were remembered before hypnosis. This rule operates to the detriment of any defendant who undergoes hypnosis, without regard to the reasons for it, the circumstances under which it took place, or any independent verification of the information it produced.

In this case, the application of that rule had a significant adverse effect on petitioner's ability to testify. It virtually prevented her from describing any of the events that occurred on the day of the shooting, despite corroboration of many of those events by other witnesses. Even more importantly, under the court's rule petitioner was not permitted to describe the actual shooting except in the words contained in Doctor Back's notes. The expert's description of the gun's tendency to misfire would have taken on greater significance if the jury had heard petitioner testify that she did not have her finger on the trigger and that the gun went off when her husband hit her arm.

In establishing its per se rule, the Arkansas Supreme Court simply followed the approach taken by a number of States that have decided that hypnotically enhanced testimony should be excluded at trial on the ground that it tends to be unreliable. Other States that have adopted an exclusionary rule, however, have done so for the testimony of witnesses, not for the testimony of a defendant. The Arkansas Supreme Court failed to perform the constitutional analysis that is necessary when a defendant's right to testify is at stake.

Although the Arkansas court concluded that any testimony that cannot be proved to be the product of prehypnosis memory is unreliable, many courts have eschewed a per se rule and permit the admission of hypnotically refreshed testimony. Hypnosis by trained physicians or psychologists has been recognized as a valid therapeutic technique since 1958, although there is no generally accepted theory to explain the phenomenon, or even a consensus on a single definition of hypnosis. The use of hypnosis in criminal investigations, however, is controversial, and the current medical and legal view of its appropriate role is unsettled.

Responses of individuals to hypnosis vary greatly. The popular belief that hypnosis guarantees the accuracy of recall is as yet without established foundation and, in fact, hypnosis often has no effect at all on memory. The most common response to hypnosis, however, appears to be an increase in both correct and incorrect recollections. Three general characteristics of hypnosis may lead to the introduction of inaccurate memories: the subject becomes "suggestible" and may try to please the hypnotist with answers the subject thinks will be met with approval; the subject is likely to "confabulate," that is, to fill in details from the imagination in order to make an answer more coherent and complete; and, the subject experiences "memory hardening," which gives him great confidence in both true and false memories, making effective cross-examination more difficult. See generally M. Orne, et al., Hypnotically Induced Testimony. . . . Despite the unreliability that hypnosis conceivably may introduce, however, the procedure has been credited as instrumental in obtaining investigative leads or identifications that were later confirmed by independent evidence.

The inaccuracies the process introduces can be reduced, although perhaps not eliminated, by the use of procedural safeguards. One set of suggested guidelines calls for hypnosis to be performed only by a psychologist or psychiatrist with special training in its use and who is independent of the investigation. See Orne, The Use and Misuse of Hypnosis in Court. . . . These procedures reduce the possibility that biases will be communicated to the hypersuggestive subject by the hypnotist. Suggestion will be less likely also if the hypnosis is conducted in a neutral setting with no one present but the hypnotist and the subject. Tape or video recording of all interrogations, before, during, and after hypnosis, can help reveal if leading questions were asked. Such guidelines do not guarantee the accuracy of the testimony, because they cannot control the subject's own motivations or any tendency to confabulate, but they do provide a means of controlling overt suggestions.

The more traditional means of assessing accuracy of testimony also remain applicable in the case of a previously hypnotized defendant. Certain information recalled as a result of hypnosis may be verified as highly accurate by corroborating evidence. Cross-examination, even in the face of a confident defendant, is an effective tool for revealing inconsistencies. Moreover, a jury can be educated to the risks of hypnosis through expert testimony and cautionary instructions. Indeed, it is probably to a defendant's advantage to establish carefully the extent of his memory prior to hypnosis, in order to minimize the decrease in credibility the procedure might introduce.

We are not now prepared to endorse without qualifications the use of hypnosis as an investigative tool; scientific understanding of the phenomenon and of the means to control the effects of hypnosis is still in its infancy. Arkansas, however, has not justified the exclusion of all of a defendant's testimony that the defendant is unable to prove to be the product of prehypnosis memory. A State's legitimate interest in barring unreliable evidence does not extend to per se exclusions that may be reliable in an individual case. Wholesale inadmissibility of a defendant's testimony is an arbitrary restriction on the right to testify in the absence of clear evidence by the State repudiating the validity of all posthypnosis recollections. The State would be well within its powers if it established guidelines to aid trial courts in the evaluation of posthypnosis testimony and it may be able to show that testimony in a particular case is so unreliable that exclusion is justified. But it has not shown that hypnotically enhanced testimony is always so untrustworthy and so immune to the traditional means of evaluating credibility that it should disable a defendant from presenting her version of the events for which she is on trial.

In this case, the defective condition of the gun corroborated the details petitioner remembered about the shooting. The tape recordings provided some means to evaluate the hypnosis and the trial judge concluded that Doctor Back did not suggest responses with leading questions. Those circumstances present an argument for admissibility of petitioner's testimony in this particular case, an argument that must be considered by the trial court. Arkansas' per se rule excluding all posthypnosis testimony infringes impermissibly on the right of a defendant to testify on his or her own behalf. The judgment of the Supreme Court of Arkansas is vacated and the case is remanded to that court for further proceedings not inconsistent with this opinion.

Chief Justice Rehnquist, with whom Justice White, Justice O'Connor, and Justice Scalia join, dissenting.

In deciding that petitioner Rock's testimony was properly limited at her trial, the Arkansas Supreme Court cited several factors that undermine the reliability of hypnotically induced testimony. Like the Court today, the Arkansas Supreme Court observed that a hypnotized individual becomes subject to suggestion, is likely to confabulate, and experiences artificially increased confidence in both true and false memories following hypnosis. No known set of procedures, both courts agree, can insure against the inherently unreliable nature of such testimony. Having acceded to the factual premises of the Arkansas Supreme Court, the Court nevertheless concludes that a state trial court must attempt to make its own scientific assessment of reliability in each case where it is confronted with a request for the admission of hypnotically induced testimony. I find no justification in the Constitution for such a ruling. In the Court's words, the decision today is "bottomed" on recognition of Rock's "constitutional right to testify in her own defense." While it is true that this Court, in dictum, has recognized the existence of such a right, the principles identified by the Court as underlying this right provide little support for invalidating the evidentiary rule applied by the Arkansas Supreme Court.

As a general matter, the Court first recites, a defendant's right to testify facilitates the truth-seeking function of a criminal trial by advancing both the "detection of guilt" and "the protection of innocence." Quoting *Ferguson* v. *Georgia.* Such reasoning is hardly controlling here, where advancement of the truth-seeking function of Rock's trial was the sole motivation behind limiting her testimony. The Court also posits, however, that "a rule that denies an accused the opportunity to offer his own testimony" cannot be upheld because, "Like the truthfulness of other witnesses, the defendant's veracity . . . can be tested adequately by cross-examination." But the Court candidly admits that the increased confidence inspired by hypnotism makes "cross-examination more difficult," thereby diminishing an adverse party's ability to test the truthfulness of defendants such as Rock. . . .

This Court has traditionally accorded the States "respect for establishment and implementation of their own criminal trial rules and procedures." Chambers. . . . One would think that this deference would be at its highest in an area such as this, where, as the Court concedes, "scientific understanding is still in its infancy." . . . The Supreme Court of Arkansas' decision was an entirely permissible response to a novel and difficult question. M. Orne et al., Hypnotically Refreshed Testimony. . . . As an original proposition, the solution this Court imposes upon Arkansas may be equally sensible, though requiring the matter to be considered res nova by every single trial judge in every single case might seem to some to pose serious administrative difficulties. But until there is a much more general consensus on the use of hypnosis than there is now, the Constitution does not warrant this Court's mandating its own view of how to deal with the issue.

SUMMARY

- One purpose of an opening statement is to orient the jury to evidence that will follow.
- Because the prosecution has the burden of proof, it presents its case first.
- The defense may present an opening statement immediately after the prosecutor's or may delay it until the defense presents its case.
- The defendant is presumed innocent until his or her guilt is established beyond a reasonable doubt.
- The term beyond a reasonable doubt is difficult to define and does not mean proof beyond a moral certainty.
- The defendant is entitled to confront the witnesses against him or her. The right of confrontation includes the right to cross-examine the witness.
- Witnesses are officially notified to appear as witnesses by the use of subpoenas.
- If a witness voluntarily appears, there is no requirement to have a subpoena issued.
- Witnesses who fail to appear as ordered by a subpoena are subject to sanctions for contempt of court.
- Prior to questioning a witness, an oath must be given. If the witness objects to being sworn in, the witness may affirm that his or her testimony will be truthful.
- There is no requirement that the word God be included in an oath.
- The order of examination of a witness is direct examination, cross-examination, redirect, and recross.
- Most states put the burden of establishing an insanity issue upon the defense.
- The purpose of closing arguments is to summarize the evidence.

REVIEW QUESTIONS

1. What is the purpose of the opening statement?
2. Define reasonable doubt.
3. What amendment guarantees a defendant the right to be confronted with the witnesses against him or her?
4. What is the purpose of a subpoena?
5. In what way does the oath differ from the affirmation?
6. Why was the affirmation adopted?
7. What is direct examination?
8. Define a leading question.
9. What is the primary purpose of cross-examination?
10. Must the defendant present evidence in his or her own behalf?
11. What is the purpose of rebuttal by the prosecution?
12. State the purpose of the M'Naghten test.
13. What purpose do closing arguments serve?

LOCAL PROCEDURE

1. In your home state, may a defendant enter a plea of not guilty by reason of insanity or is insanity raised only as a defense?
2. Is the M'Naghten test or some other test for insanity followed in your home state?

ENDNOTES

1. 397 U.S. 358 (1970).
2. 399 U.S. 149 (1970).
3. Portions of this section dealing with the use of closed-circuit television have been adapted from H. Wallace, *Family Violence: Legal, Medical, and Social Perspectives* (Allyn & Bacon, Boston), 1996.
4. 110 S.Ct. 3157 (1990).
5. 380 U.S. 400 (1965).
6. 380 U.S. 609 (1965).
7. See *People* v. *Robles,* 85 Cal.Rptr. 166 (1970).
8. *Nix* v. *Whiteside,* 475 U.S. 157 (1986).
9. 8 Eng. Reprint 718 (1843).
10. 81 Ala. 577, 2 So. 854 (1887). It should be noted that the Irresistible Impulse test actually predated the M'Naghten test. For an excellent historical discussion of the evolution of these early insanity rules, see Paul Keedy, "Irresistible Impulse as a Defense in Criminal Law," 100 *Univ. of Penn. Law Review* 956–961 (1952).
11. 214 F.2d 862 (D.C. Cir. 1954).
12. 290 E. 2d 751 (1961).
13. Susan Lark, *Premenstrual Syndrome Self-Help Book* (Forman, Los Angeles), 1984, p. 19.
14. Katherine Dalton, "Menstruation and Crime," *British Medical Journal* No. 3, 1961, p. 1752.
15. J. H. Morton et al., "A Clinical Study of Premenstrual Tension," *American Journal of Obstetrics and Gynecology,* No. 65, 1953, pp. 1182–1191.
16. H. Wallace, "Battered Women Syndrome: Self-Defense and Duress as Mandatory Defenses? The History and Acceptance of the Battered Women Syndrome in American Courts," *The Police Journal,* London, 1994, pp. 231–238.
17. *State* v. *Stewart,* 763 P.2d 572 (Kansas, 1988).
18. See *Orencia* v. *Overholser,* 82 U.S. App. D.C. 285 (1947).
19. See *Barry* v. *White,* 62 U.S. App. D.C. 69 (1933).
20. 86 Cal.Rptr 516 (1970).

> A jury verdict is a quotient of the prejudices of twelve people. . . .
>
> —Kenneth Grub, attorney

Instructions and Deliberation of the Jury

14

Chapter Outline

Key Words

Allen charge
Charging the jury

Consciousness of guilt
Deliberations

Foreperson
Hung jury

Learning Objectives

After completing this chapter, you should be able to:

1. Explain the judge's requirement to instruct the jury on various issues.
2. Discuss the deliberation process.
3. List the duties of the prosecutor and defense counsel in preparing jury instructions.
4. Explain the restrictions on a judge's ability to comment on the evidence.
5. List the materials that may be taken into the jury's deliberation room.
6. Discuss the Allen instructions and why a judge would give an Allen charge.
7. Explain the problems involved in less than unanimous verdicts.

INSTRUCTIONS TO THE JURY

On completion of the closing arguments, in most jurisdictions, the judge instructs the jury on the law applicable to the case. Instructing the jury is also known as **charging the jury** or as the charge to the jury. In a few states, the judge may instruct the jury prior to the closing arguments in order that the attorneys involved may include comments on the instructions during their closing arguments. Although the procedure of instructing the jury follows the presentation of the evidence, the judge has the responsibility of explaining the law to the jury as the trial progresses for their guidance in following the evidence. During the charge to the jury, the judge will summarize the points of law explained to them during the trial and instruct them on their function as jurors. Also, the judge will instruct the jury on any additional laws applicable that were not explained as the trial progressed.

Defense and Prosecution Recommendations

As a general rule, the prosecuting attorney and defense attorney prepare written instructions that they desire to be given to the jury. These instructions are furnished to the judge prior to the closing arguments. After reviewing these instructions, the judge selects those that appear to be applicable. Other instructions not suggested by the attorneys may also be given. The judge has the responsibility of instructing the jury on the laws applicable whether requested to do so or not.

The defendant is entitled to instructions being given on all pertinent evidence, regardless of its importance. The failure to give an instruction concerning pertinent evidence, whether requested or not by the defense, could be grounds for the reversal of a conviction on appeal. However, a judge does not have to give instructions that are repetitive or that include some statement of fact in the form of evidence in the case.

The judge also has the responsibility of instructing the jury in clear and understandable language. Too often the instructions are lengthy, complicated, and difficult for the jury to understand. For example, an instruction on the meaning of reasonable doubt may be confusing to the jury, but the defendant is entitled to an instruction on the presumption of innocence. The judge will read to the jury the definition of reasonable doubt as set forth in Chapter 13. The jury will be informed that a defendant in a criminal action is presumed innocent until the contrary is proved and that if there is a reasonable doubt of guilt, the defendant is entitled to an acquittal. The effect of this presumption places on the state the burden of proving guilt beyond a reasonable doubt.

The following are samples of additional instructions generally given to a jury. The jury will be informed that it is the function of the judge to interpret the law but that the jury is the exclusive judge of the facts. The jury must determine those facts only from the evidence presented in court, and it must conscientiously consider and weigh the evidence during the trial. It must also carefully determine the credibility of each witness. In measuring the credibility of a witness, the jury may consider the demeanor of the witness as he or she testifies; the opportunity of the witness to have gained the facts about which he or she testifies; and the witness's ability to observe, retain, and communicate the matters. The jury will be informed that it must not consider as evidence any statement made by the attorneys involved, nor is the jury to speculate on what an answer to a question may have been when an objection to the question was sustained. Nor may the jury consider in its deliberation on the verdict any statement that was stricken from the record. The jurors will be advised that they must not be governed by mere sentiment, sympathy, passion, or prejudice in arriving at a verdict and that they must reach a just verdict regardless of the consequences of that verdict. The jurors will also be informed that it is their duty to consult one another and to deliberate on a just verdict but that the verdict is to express the individual opinion of each juror. The jury will then be advised of the previously mentioned presumption of innocence and reasonable doubt instructions.

The foregoing instructions are applicable in all criminal trials but are not all-inclusive of those that may be given in a trial proceeding. In addition to these general instructions, more specific instructions applicable to the particular case will be included. Instructions may be given on the meaning of direct and circumstantial evidence. The jury will be informed that direct evidence directly proves the fact in issue, whereas circumstantial evidence proves a fact by an inference drawn from another set of facts having been proved. At this point in the instructions, the jury is often again hopelessly lost in the explanation. The right of an expert witness to give an opinion on controversial questions is explained. It is explained that the jury may consider the qualifications of the expert and must give the testimony the proper weight. The meaning of intent and motive may be explained. If an alibi defense was alleged, the judge will inform the jury that if they have reasonable doubt about the defendant's being present at the scene of the crime, an acquittal should result. The meaning of **consciousness of guilt** will be explained, as well as those acts that may fall within that category, such as a suspect's running from a crime scene.

The jury will be informed that the defendant has a right not to testify and that no inference of guilt is to be drawn from the failure to testify. Since most jurisdictions permit a jury to return a verdict to a lesser degree of crime than that charged in the accusatory pleading, the jury will be given an instruction to this effect. Most jurisdictions permit the jury to take the written instructions given by the judge with them during deliberations.

Comments by the Judge

States differ materially in permitting a judge to comment on the evidence of a case and the credibility of witnesses. About half of the states prohibit comments by the judge on the evidence and credibility of the witnesses, since it is believed that such comments are an invasion of the function of the jury. A few states and federal courts grant considerable freedom to a judge to comment on the evidence and the credibility of the witnesses. It has been stated that the judge should be a real factor in the administration of justice and not a mere referee of the adversary system. The judge must summarize the evidence in an impartial and instructive manner, but he or she may point out weaknesses in the evidence of the prosecution and defense or may question the credibility of witnesses. However, the judge's right to comment on the evidence and witnesses is not unlimited. Courts have stated that the judge must be fair, objective and impartial and must not ignore evidence favorable to the defendant. It has been held improper for the judge to directly state the belief that the defendant is guilty. Comments in one case were considered improper when the judge indicated to the jury that in viewing the evidence in its most favorable light to the defendant, one was still left with the conclusion that the defendant was guilty. The judge further stated that if he were deciding the case, the accused would be found guilty.

Comments to the jury may be made before or after the instructions, at the judge's discretion. Except in states where the judge gives the instructions to the jury prior to the closing arguments, the jury begins its deliberations once the instructions are given.

DELIBERATIONS

If the jury has not been sequestered prior to being given the case, the judge must decide whether or not to do so during **deliberations**. As we pointed out earlier, in some states the jury must be sequestered during the deliberations. In other states, it is at the discretion of the judge. The jury may decide on the verdict in the courtroom, but in most instances they will retire to some private and convenient place for deliberations. This place is generally referred to as the jury room.

Inside the Jury Room

While deliberating, the jurors will be under the guard of an officer of the court. The court officer will have been sworn to keep the jurors together, not permit any person to speak to them, and not speak to them himself or herself except on orders of the court. During the deliberation, no one—not even the officer in charge of the jury—may be present in the jury room except the jurors. On one occasion, an alternate juror was inadvertently given permission by the officer in charge of the jury to sit in the jury room merely to observe during the deliberation. On learning of this, the judge declared a mistrial although the alternate juror did not in any way engage in the deliberation. The courts of a few states, however, have permitted an alternate juror to be sequestered with the other jurors during the deliberation, but only after the judge has instructed the alternate juror not to participate in the deliberation.

In one case, the officer in charge of the jury was also a material witness for the prosecution. He and other officers transported the jury back and forth to their hotel while the jury was being sequestered, and these officers also ate at the same table with the jurors and conversed with them. Although it was alleged that there was no conversation about the facts of the case during these associations, the U.S. Supreme Court held that the presence of the officer interfered with the defendant's right to be tried by an impartial jury. The presence of the officer, according to the Court, may have established rapport with the jury that may have affected their verdict of guilty.[1]

In reference to only jurors being present during the deliberation, we return to the problem encountered by the hearing-impaired person who becomes a juror. By necessity, this juror's interpreter must be present during the deliberation to interpret the communication that takes place among the jurors as they attempt to arrive at a verdict. How may it be determined that the deliberation was accurately interpreted, or was that juror somehow influenced by the interpretation? Would it be held that the interpreter was an extra juror present during the deliberation? If the defendant was convicted, could the defense challenge on appeal the presence of the interpreter during the deliberation, or would this challenge have been waived by the lack of challenge for cause during jury selection? Only future cases will decide the answers to these questions.

Prior to beginning the deliberation, the jury will select one of their members to act as the **foreperson**—their leader and spokesperson. If, during the deliberation, the jury desires further instructions on the law or information concerning the case, the foreperson will advise the officer in charge, who in turn will notify the judge of the request. The judge, in most instances, will require that the jury be returned to the courtroom for the requested information. It is considered improper for the officer in charge to act as a messenger carrying information from the judge to the jury.

Materials Inside the Jury Room

On beginning the deliberation, the jury may take with them any and all documents introduced during the trial. However, in many jurisdictions, the jury may not take any depositions with them. The reason for this prohibition is that to permit the jury to take the depositions would possibly allow them to give greater weight to the testimony of a witness not present over one who was present. The rules of evidence in most states provide that the jury may take any document introduced and also permit the jury to take any exhibits or physical evidence, such as a gun, plaster of paris cast, or fingerprint, that may have been introduced. Courts in some jurisdictions have held that the jury should be permitted to take with them all evidence introduced, including depositions, any prepared transcript or recorded testimony, and personal notes as long as the defendant is not unduly prejudiced and the jury is not likely to use the evidence improperly.

A great majority of the states permit jurors to take notes at the discretion of the judge. Judges differ in their attitudes toward note-taking. Some judges argue that most jurors are not trained in the art of taking notes. Not being trained, they may take down trivial matters and overlook important facts, or they may try to take down everything and get hopelessly lost in the process, missing material testimony as it is presented. It is argued also that the better note-takers will tend to dominate the deliberation or that jurors will quarrel over whose notes are a correct record of the testimony. Those arguing in favor of note-taking by jurors allege that it is asking too much of a juror to remember all the testimony during a lengthy trial and that permitting notes to be taken enables the jurors to refresh their memory during the deliberation. Usually, the reporter's transcript is not available at the time of the deliberation, and unless the jurors have their notes, the only way that testimony may be recalled in some instances is to have the jury returned to the courtroom and the reporter's notes read to the jury. This procedure is time-consuming, and judges often frown on this activity when engaged in too frequently by a jury. It is argued that the benefits derived from a juror's taking notes during a trial far exceed any detriment that may be suffered.

The Judge's Instructions to the Jury in a Criminal Case

No. B-96-MO19-O-PR-B

The State of Texas	§	**In the 156th District**
v.	§	**Court of**
Michael Runnels	§	**Bee County, Texas**

Charge of the Court

LADIES AND GENTLEMEN OF THE JURY:

The Defendant, MICHAEL RUNNELS, stands charged by indictment with the offense of Assault on a Public Servant, alleged to have been made on a correctional officer on or about the 1st day of April A.D., 1996, in Bee County, Texas. The Defendant has plead[ed] not guilty.

1.

Our law provides that a person commits the offense of assault if he intentionally and knowingly causes bodily injury to another.

Such assault is aggravated assault when committed upon a guard employed by the Texas Department of Criminal Justice–Institutional Division in the lawful discharge of his official duty when the person committing the assault knows or has been informed that the person assaulted is such a guard.

2.

By the term "bodily injury" is meant physical pain, illness or any impairment of physical condition.

3.

A person acts intentionally, or with intent, with respect to a result of his conduct when it is his conscious objective or desire to cause the result.

A person acts knowingly, or with knowledge, with respect to a result of his conduct when he is aware that his conduct is reasonably certain to cause the result.

4.

Now, if you find, from the evidence, beyond a reasonable doubt that on or about the 1st day of April, 1996, in Bee County, Texas, MICHAEL RUNNELS TDCJ #698369, did then and there knowingly or intentionally cause bodily injury to Robert D. Hill, a public servant, to-wit: a Correctional officer with the Texas Department of Criminal Justice–Institutional Division, Garza East Unit, in Beeville, Bee County, Texas, by striking Robert D. Hill in the head and face with a closed fist, while Robert D. Hill was lawfully discharging an official duty and the defendant knew that Robert D. Hill was a public servant, then you will find the Defendant guilty of Aggravated Assault on a Correctional Officer.

Unless you so find beyond a reasonable doubt, or if you have a reasonable doubt thereof, you will find the defendant not guilty.

5.

A guard or Correctional Officer employed by the Texas Department of Correction is justified in using force against a person in custody when and to the degree the guard or Correctional Officer reasonably believes the force is necessary to maintain the security of the penal institution, the safety or security of other persons in custody or employed by the penal institution, or his own safety or security.

Therefore, if you find that Robert D. Hill used force against MICHAEL RUNNELS and that while doing so he did not reasonably believe that the use of force was necessary to maintain the security of the Penal Institution, the safety or security of other persons in custody or employed by the Penal Institution, or his own safety or security, you will next consider the defense of self-defense.

6.

"Reasonable belief" as used herein means a belief that would be held by an ordinary and prudent person in the same circumstances as Robert D. Hill.

Upon the law of self-defense, a person is justified in using force against another when and to the degree he reasonably believes the force is immediately necessary to protect himself against the other's use or attempted use of unlawful force. A person is under no obligation to retreat to avoid the necessity of repelling or defending with force less than deadly force, against an attack or threatened attack. The use of force against another is not justified if the actor provoked the other's use or attempted use of unlawful force, unless the actor abandons the encounter, or clearly communicates to the other his intent to do so reasonably believing he cannot safely abandon the encounter and the other nevertheless continues or attempts to use unlawful force against the actor.

"Reasonable belief" as used herein means a belief that would be held by an ordinary and prudent person in the same circumstances as defendant.

You are instructed that it is your duty to consider all the relevant facts and circumstances surrounding the alleged assault, including the previous relationship, if any, existing between the accused and Robert D. Hill, together with all relevant facts and circumstance going to show the condition of the mind of the defendant at the time of the alleged offense. In considering all the foregoing, you should place yourself in the defendant's position and view the circumstances from his standpoint alone, at the time in question.

Now if you find and believe from the evidence beyond a reasonable doubt that on the occasion in question the defendant, MICHAEL RUNNELS, intentionally and knowingly caused bodily injury to Robert D. Hill by

(Continued)

defendant was convicted of robbery by a nine-to-three verdict in the Criminal District Court of the Parish of Orleans. In the *Apodaca* case, the facts reveal that Robert Apodaca, Henry Morgan Cooper, Jr., and James Arnold Madden were convicted, respectively, of assault with a deadly weapon, burglary in a dwelling, and grand larceny, before separate Oregon juries, all of which returned less-than-unanimous verdicts. The vote in the case of Cooper was ten to two, the minimum requisite vote under Oregon law for sustaining a conviction. Johnson as well as the defendants in the Apodaca case took their convictions to the U.S. Supreme Court on the ground that they had been denied their guarantee of a trial by jury as provided by the Sixth Amendment and made applicable to the states by the Fourteenth Amendment. These defendants contended that permitting the conviction of a less-than-unanimous verdict did not constitute a trial by jury.

Johnson alleged that when a jury rendered such a verdict, the prosecution had failed to prove the defendant guilty beyond a reasonable doubt, thus violating the right to due process of law. The Court did not agree with this contention and stated the following:

> We conclude that as to the nine jurors who voted to convict, the State satisfied its burden of proving guilt beyond a reasonable doubt. The remaining question under the Due Process Clause is whether the vote of three jurors for acquittal can be said to impeach the verdict of the other nine and to demonstrate that guilt was not in fact proved beyond such doubt. We hold that it cannot.
>
> Of course, the State's proof could be regarded as more certain if it had convinced all 12 jurors instead of only nine; it would have been even more compelling if it had been required to convince and had, in fact, convinced 24 or 36 jurors. But the fact remains that nine jurors—a substantial majority of the jury—were convinced by the evidence. In our view disagreement of three jurors does not alone establish reasonable doubt, particularly when such a heavy majority of the jury, after having considered the dissenters' views, remains convinced of guilt. That rational men disagree is not in itself equivalent to a failure of proof by the State, nor does it indicate infidelity to the reasonable doubt standard. Jury verdicts finding guilt beyond a reasonable doubt are regularly sustained even though the evidence was such that the jury would have been justified in having a reasonable doubt; even though the trial judge might not have reached the same conclusion as the jury; and even though appellate judges are closely divided on the issue [of] whether there was sufficient evidence to support a conviction.

In the *Apodaca* decision, the Supreme Court further discusses the reasonable doubt argument as well as upholding the right of the states to permit a less-than-unanimous verdict and still uphold the Due Process Clause. In the *Apodaca* decision, the Court stated the following:

> In *Williams* v. *Florida,* we had occasion to consider a related issue: whether the Sixth Amendment's right to trial by jury requires that all juries consist of 12 men. After considering the history of the 12-man requirement and the functions it performs in contemporary society, we concluded that it was not of constitutional stature. We reach the same conclusion today with regard to the requirement of unanimity.
>
> Like the requirement that juries consist of 12 men, the requirement of unanimity rose during the Middle Ages and had become an accepted feature of the common-law jury by the 18th century.
>
> Our inquiry must focus upon the function served by the jury in contemporary society. As we said in *Duncan,* the purpose of trial by jury is to prevent oppression by the Government by providing a safeguard against the corrupt or overzealous prosecutor and against the compliant, biased, or eccentric judge. Given this purpose, the essential feature of a jury obviously lies in the interposition between the accused and

his accuser of the common sense judgment of a group of laymen. A requirement of unanimity, however, does not materially contribute to the exercise of this common sense judgment. As we said in *Williams,* a jury will come to such a judgment as long as it consists of a group of laymen representative of a cross section of the community who have the duty and the opportunity to deliberate, free from outside attempts at intimidation, on the question of a defendant's guilt. In terms of this function we perceive no difference between juries required to act unanimously and those permitted to convict or acquit by votes of 10 to two or 11 to one. Requiring unanimity would obviously produce hung juries in some situations where nonunanimous juries will convict or acquit. But in either case, the interest of the defendant in having the judgment of his peers interposed between himself and the officers of the State who prosecute and judge him is equally well served.

The defendants in the *Apodaca* case contended, as did Johnson, that a unanimous verdict was necessary in order to comply with the beyond-a-reasonable-doubt requirement for guilt, but the Court stated as follows:

> We are quite sure that the Sixth Amendment itself has never been held to require proof beyond a reasonable doubt in criminal cases. The reasonable doubt standard developed separately from both the jury trial and the unanimous verdict. As the Court noted in the *Winship* case, the rule requiring proof of crime beyond a reasonable doubt did not crystallize in this country until after the Constitution was adopted. And in that case, which held such a burden of proof to be constitutionally required, the Court purported to draw no support from the Sixth Amendment.
>
> Defendant's argument that the Sixth Amendment requires jury unanimity in order to give effect to the reasonable doubt standard thus founders on the fact that the Sixth Amendment does not require proof beyond a reasonable doubt at all. The reasonable doubt argument is rooted, in effect, in due process and has been rejected in *Johnson* v. *Louisiana.*

Mr. Justice Powell in his concurring opinion made some comments worthy of noting in upholding the less-than-unanimous verdict. Among other comments, he stated:

> . . . There is no reason to believe, on the basis of experience in Oregon or elsewhere, that a unanimous decision of 12 jurors is more likely to serve the high purpose of jury trial, or is entitled to greater respect in the community, than the same decision joined in the 10 members of a jury of 12. The standard of due process assured by the Oregon Constitution provides a sufficient guarantee that the government will not be permitted to impose its judgment on an accused without first meeting the full burden of its prosecutorial duty. . . .
>
> Removal of the unanimity requirement could well minimize the potential for hung juries occasioned either by bribery or juror irrationality. Furthermore, the rule that juries must speak with a single voice often leads, not to full agreement among the 12 but to agreement by none and compromise by all, despite the frequent absence of a rational basis for such compromise. . . .

The petitioners (defendants) contended that their right to a jury comprising a cross section of a community was interfered with by the less-than-unanimous verdict. Their petitions alleged that unless unanimity is required, the viewpoint of a minority of the jurors representing minority groups is excluded from discussion during the deliberation. They also alleged that whether the verdict is conviction or acquittal, it may be the unjust product of racism, bigotry, or an emotionally inflamed trial. To this contention, Mr. Justice Powell stated the following:

> Such fears materialize only when the jury's majority, responding to these extraneous pressures, ignores the evidence and the instructions of the court as well as the rational

arguments of the minority. The risk, however, that a jury in a particular case will fail to meet its high responsibility is inherent in any system which commits decisions of guilt or innocence to untrained laymen drawn at random from the community. In part, at least, the majority-verdict rule must rely on the same principle which underlies our historic dedication to jury trial; both systems are premised on the conviction that each juror will faithfully perform his assigned duty. . . . Even before the jury is sworn substantial protection against the selection of a representative but willfully irresponsible jury is assured by the wide availability of peremptory challenges and challenges for cause. The likelihood of miscarriage of justice is further diminished by the judges' use of full jury instructions, detailing the applicable burdens of proof, informing the jurors of their duty to weigh the views of fellow jurors, and reminding them of the solemn responsibility imposed by their oaths. Trial judges also retain the power to direct acquittals in cases in which the evidence of guilt is lacking, or to set aside verdicts once rendered when the evidence is insufficient to support a conviction. Furthermore, in cases in which public emotion runs high or pretrial publicity threatens a fair trial, judges possess broad power to grant changes of venue, and to impose restrictions on the extent of press coverage.

In light of such protections it is unlikely that the Oregon "ten-of-twelve" rule will account for an increase in the number of cases in which injustice will be occasioned by a biased or prejudiced jury. It may be wise to recall Mr. Justice White's admonition in *Murphy* v. *Waterfront Comm'n,* that the Constitution "protects against real dangers, not remote and speculative possibilities."

Since the U.S. Supreme Court has given sanction to less-than-unanimous verdicts, it is highly possible that other states in the future will adopt this verdict requirement.

It has been argued that there is no sound reason, other than tradition, for the requirement of the unanimous verdict. The origin of the unanimous verdict is unclear. By the latter part of the fourteenth century, the unanimous verdict was required, but it was not the jury verdict as we know it today. As pointed out in the history of the jury trial, in the fourteenth century, convicted persons were often subject to cruel and unusual punishment. It has been alleged that one of the reasons for the unanimous verdict at that time was to avoid such punishment as often as possible. Those who are for the less-than-unanimous verdict allege that since the convicted person is not subjected to cruel and unusual punishment today, there is no need for the unanimous verdict. The less-than-unanimous verdict would also eliminate many hung juries, resulting in fewer retrials and saving court costs.

The arguments of those who oppose the less-than-unanimous verdict are just as strong. It is stated that abolishing the unanimous verdict in order to prevent hung juries is a shallow argument and not sufficient reason for such an action. Some argue, as did Mr. Justice Douglas in his dissent in the *Johnson* case, that the less-than-unanimous verdict prohibits the minority members of the jury from presenting their arguments, which might prevent a conviction when the minority have a real doubt of guilt. It is also argued that if this verdict is permitted, the next step may be eliminating the presumption of innocence or proving the defendant guilty beyond a reasonable doubt. It should be pointed out that the Bill of Rights says nothing about twelve persons specifically being required to compose a jury, a verdict's being unanimous, proving the defendant guilty beyond a reasonable doubt, or presuming innocence. These rights of the accused have been established by tradition but allegedly have a constitutional standard, and any break with this standard will weaken our justice system.

The U.S. Supreme Court, however, in *Burch* v. *Louisiana,*[5] held that the verdict of a jury comprising only six persons must be unanimous for "nonpetty offenses." The Court stated that "to hold anything less than a unanimous verdict by a jury of only six persons would be a threat to the constitutional guarantee of a trial by an impartial jury."

Capstone Cases

Williams v. Florida
399 U.S. 78 (1970)

MR. JUSTICE WHITE delivered the opinion of the Court.

Prior to his trial for robbery in the State of Florida, petitioner filed a "Motion for a Protective Order," seeking to be excused from the requirements of Rule 1.200 of the Florida Rules of Criminal Procedure. That rule requires a defendant, on written demand of the prosecuting attorney, to give notice in advance of trial if the defendant intends to claim an alibi, and to furnish the prosecuting attorney with information as to the place where he claims to have been and with the names and addresses of the alibi witnesses he intends to use. In his motion petitioner openly declared his intent to claim an alibi, but objected to the further disclosure requirements on the ground that the rule "compels the Defendant in a criminal case to be a witness against himself" in violation of his Fifth and Fourteenth Amendment rights. The motion was denied. Petitioner also filed a pretrial motion to impanel a 12-man jury instead of the six-man jury provided by Florida law in all but capital cases. That motion too was denied. Petitioner was convicted as charged and was sentenced to life imprisonment. The District Court of Appeal affirmed, rejecting petitioner's claims that his Fifth and Sixth Amendment rights had been violated. We granted certiorari.

I.

Florida's notice-of-alibi rule is in essence a requirement that a defendant submit to a limited form of pretrial discovery by the State whenever he intends to rely at trial on the defense of alibi. In exchange for the defendant's disclosure of the witnesses he proposes to use to establish that defense, the State in turn is required to notify the defendant of any witnesses it proposes to offer in rebuttal to that defense. Both sides are under a continuing duty promptly to disclose the names and addresses of additional witnesses bearing on the alibi as they become available. The threatened sanction for failure to comply is the exclusion at trial of the defendant's alibi evidence—except for his own testimony—or, in the case of the State, the exclusion of the State's evidence offered in rebuttal of the alibi.

In this case, following the denial of his Motion for a Protective Order, petitioner complied with the alibi rule and gave the State the name and address of one Mary Scotty. Mrs. Scotty was summoned to the office of the State Attorney on the morning of the trial, where she gave pretrial testimony. At the trial itself, Mrs. Scotty, petitioner, and petitioner's wife all testified that the three of them had been in Mrs. Scotty's apartment during the time of the robbery. On two occasions during cross-examination of Mrs. Scotty, the prosecuting attorney confronted her with her earlier deposition in which she had given dates and times that in some respects did not correspond with the dates and times given at trial. Mrs. Scotty adhered to her trial story, insisting that she had been mistaken in her earlier testimony. The State also offered in rebuttal the testimony of one of the officers investigating the robbery who claimed that Mrs. Scotty had asked him for directions on the afternoon in question during the time when she claimed to have been in her apartment with petitioner and his wife.

We need not linger over the suggestion that the discovery permitted the State against petitioner in this case deprived him of "due process" or a "fair trial." Florida law provides for liberal discovery by the defendant against the State, and the notice-of-alibi rule is itself carefully hedged with reciprocal duties requiring state disclosure to the defendant. Given the ease with which an alibi can be fabricated, the State's interest in protecting itself against an eleventh-hour defense is both obvious and legitimate. Reflecting this interest, notice-of-alibi provisions, dating at least from 1927, are now in existence in a substantial number of States. The adversary system of trial is hardly an end in itself; it is not yet a poker game in which players enjoy an absolute right always to conceal their cards until played. We find ample room in that system, at least as far as "due process" is concerned, for the instant Florida rule, which is designed to enhance the search for truth in the criminal trial by

(Continued)

VERDICT

Derived from the Latin word *verdictum,* the word **verdict** means "a true declaration." In a court trial, the verdict is the decision of the judge. In a criminal trial, the verdict is the decision of the jury. Once the verdict in a criminal trial has been agreed on, the foreperson will so advise the bailiff, the officer who is in charge of the jury. The bailiff will then inform the judge, who will reconvene court in order that the verdict may be received. Since the deliberation often takes considerable time, the judge usually will adjourn court on the case while the jury is deliberating. This action permits the judge to perform other duties while being available at all times to furnish further instructions or information that the jury may request while deliberating. After the court is reconvened, the judge will instruct the bailiff to return the jury to the courtroom. On their arrival, the judge may request that their names be called to make certain that all the jurors are present. If a juror is missing, the judge may have to declare a mistrial unless the juror's whereabouts can be determined and his or her presence can be immediately obtained. After all the jurors are accounted for, the judge will ask the foreperson whether the jury has agreed on a verdict. If the foreperson answers in the affirmative, the judge may ask him or her to announce the verdict; if the verdict is in writing, the judge may request that it be given to the clerk of the court to read. Not all jurisdictions require that the verdict be in writing and signed by the foreperson. Whether it is required to be in writing or not, most jurisdictions furnish forms to the jury on which they may record their verdict. The defendant must be present at the time the verdict is announced in open court unless his or her whereabouts cannot be determined. In that case, the verdict may be announced in the absence of the accused.

After the verdict is announced, the prosecution or the defense may request that the jurors be polled individually to determine how each voted on the verdict. When the verdict must be unanimous, if one or more jurors allege that the verdict does not express all the jurors' opinions, the judge may instruct the jury to return to the jury room for further deliberation. If the facts warrant such action, the judge may discharge the jury and declare a mistrial.

If the jury finds the verdict to be not guilty, the defendant is entitled to immediate release if in custody. If the defendant is out on bail, the security will be returned to the person who posted it, since it will have served its purpose. In either event, the defendant is free from further prosecution on the crime charged.

If the defendant is found guilty, the next procedural step is sentencing. A few other matters should be considered before the discussion of the sentencing. The jury may have found the defendant guilty as charged in the accusatory pleading, or the jury may have found the defendant guilty of a lesser degree. It is possible that the jury found the defendant guilty on some of the charges stated in the accusatory pleading and not guilty on others. In addition to finding the defendant guilty, the jury may be called upon to determine whether the defendant was armed at the time that a crime was committed. All these matters may affect the sentence imposed. Once the verdict is announced in open court, it will be recorded in the record of the case. At this point, the jury is entitled to be discharged unless it is involved in the sentencing procedure. If it is a court trial, the judge has the responsibility of rendering the verdict.

Even though the jury returns a verdict of guilty, most jurisdictions permit the judge to modify the verdict. If the judge believes that the evidence shows the defendant was not guilty to the degree that the jury found him or her guilty, the judge may modify the verdict by finding the defendant guilty of a lesser degree or lesser crime included in the criminal act. A few states permit the judge to go one step further. The guilty verdict of a jury may be set aside and a judgment of acquittal entered, or the judge may set aside the verdict and dismiss the charge. In either event, the judge's action in this regard is usually a bar to any further prosecutive action against the defendant. The right of a judge to set aside the entire verdict is very powerful. But such action is permitted on the grounds that if the evidence is insufficient to establish the defendant guilty beyond a reasonable doubt, the judge must set aside the verdict in the interest of justice. However, a judge may not set aside a verdict of not guilty, since this action would deny the defendant the right of a trial by jury.

New Trial and Mistrial

If a judge believes that the prosecution has failed to prove the defendant guilty beyond a reasonable doubt, the judge may enter a judgment of acquittal in some jurisdictions. This action occurs before the case is turned over to the jury for deliberation and takes the case out of their hands. But if the judge is permitted to set aside the jury's guilty verdict, the case is taken from the jury after it has fulfilled its function. This action often draws criticism from jurors, since it voids their function. To avoid this criticism, judges will grant a motion for a new trial rather than enter the judgment of acquittal or set aside the verdict.

After a jury has returned a verdict of guilty, the defense may request that a new trial be granted. Generally, a new trial may be granted only on the motion, or request, of the defendant, and not on the judge's own motion. If a new trial is granted, the case will therefore be heard again from the beginning, usually before the same judge but with a new jury. The grounds for granting a new trial are specifically set forth in the codes of most states. These grounds usually include such matters as the jury's receiving evidence of the

Murder trial of Daniel McNaughten, 1843, Old Bailey, London. (*Source:* The Granger Collection.)

case out of court; the jurors separating without permission of the court after being sequestered; the verdict's being decided on by lot or by means other than a fair expression of opinion; misconduct of the jurors, preventing the defendant from receiving a fair trial; or a guilty verdict's being returned that was not supported by the evidence. Although it has been stated that a new trial may be granted only on statutory grounds, courts have held that new trials should be granted on nonstatutory grounds when a failure to do so would result in a denial of a fair trial to the defendant. In one case, the judge stated in comments to the jury that, in all his experience as a lawyer and judge, he had never seen so many defense witnesses, including the defendant himself, whose truthfulness was in doubt. Even though the judge informed the jurors that it was their duty to weigh the credibility of the witnesses, he felt that, after a guilty verdict was returned by the jury, a new trial should be granted in the interest of justice. In this way, the judge was correcting his own remarks that bordered on directing the jury to return a verdict of guilty.

One of the more frequent grounds used for granting a new trial is newly discovered evidence by the defense. In order for a defendant to take advantage of this ground, the defense must be in a position to prove to the satisfaction of the judge that the newly discovered evidence is material and that the evidence could not with due diligent search have been discovered by the time of the first trial. It has been held by some courts that the newly discovered evidence must be of sufficient importance to indicate a probable acquittal in a new trial. This evidence must be more than just a repetition of the evidence presented by the defense during the first trial unless the repetitive evidence would materially strengthen previously presented evidence.

The prosecution has the right to argue against the granting of a new trial. It may endeavor to prove that there was not due diligent search before the first trial to justify a new trial or it may argue against other grounds presented by the defense. It is not always necessary for the prosecution to argue against the motion for a new trial. The judge may deny the motion without any argument's being presented.

Granting a new trial is not to be confused with declaring a mistrial. The motion for a new trial may not be made until a verdict of guilty has been rendered. A mistrial may be declared anytime during the trial proceedings, on the judge's own motion or at the request of the defense. The right of the prosecution to request a mistrial is somewhat restricted and not permitted in all jurisdictions. A mistrial may be declared any time that there is misconduct that is so prejudicial that the defense would be denied a fair trial. The misconduct may occur early in the trial proceedings. For example, if, during the opening statement by the prosecuting attorney, he or she refers to the defendant as an ex-con or otherwise imply a past criminal record, the judge may decide that the remarks were so prejudicial that the defendant could not get a fair trial. The judge may at that time declare a mistrial. If the mistrial is declared at that point in the proceedings, not too much trial time is lost; but if the misconduct comes late in the trial, such as just before deliberation, much time, energy, and money will have been wasted.

Sometimes, rather than declare a mistrial, the judge will instruct the jury to disregard the misconduct and inform them that it is not to affect them in rendering a verdict. This admonition is not always effective, since jurors cannot always erase something that they have heard. If the defendant is convicted, the failure to declare a mistrial may be grounds for reversal on appeal. As stated, a judge may declare a mistrial when the jury cannot agree on a verdict. Defendants have argued that the inability of a jury to agree on a verdict indicates both that the prosecution has not proved the defendant guilty beyond a reasonable doubt and that the defendant is entitled to a judgment of acquittal. This argument has been rejected by the U.S. Supreme Court. The Court held that the defendant may be retried under these circumstances. The Court stated that it recognizes "society's interest in giving the prosecution one complete opportunity to convict those who have violated its laws."[1] However, before a mistrial may be declared when a jury cannot agree on a verdict, the judge must weigh the situation carefully. Courts have held that if a judge declares a mistrial too quickly when further deliberation would have resulted in a verdict, the defendant has been deprived of the "valued right to have his trial completed by a particular tribunal." But if the judge fails to declare a mistrial when the jury cannot agree on a verdict after lengthy deliberation, there is a risk that a verdict may result from pressure by some jurors on others that would deny the jurors an opportunity for individual expression.

If a mistrial is declared at the request of the defense, generally, the case can be tried again at the discretion of the prosecuting attorney. The retrial is not considered a violation of the double jeopardy guarantee, since the defendant, in requesting a mistrial, waives the guarantee against double jeopardy. However, some jurisdictions hold that unless there is sufficient cause to declare a mistrial or unless the defendant agrees to the mistrial, jeopardy may have set in, and the defendant cannot be retried. If the misconduct prejudicial to the prosecution was committed by defense counsel or by the accused, the prosecution may have little or no remedy.

However, in *Arizona* v. *Washington,* the U.S. Supreme Court did uphold the action of the trial judge in declaring a mistrial at the request of the prosecution when a defense attorney made improper statements to the jury during the opening argument. The trial judge concluded that the remarks were so prejudicial that the prosecution would be denied the right to have the case tried before an impartial jury. The Supreme Court stated that before a trial judge could declare a mistrial over the objections of the defense, it must be established that there was a "**manifest necessity**" for such action. In other words, there must be sufficient evidence to prove that such action should be taken. The Court stated the following:

> Because of the variety of circumstances that may make it necessary to discharge a jury before a trial is concluded, and because those circumstances do not invariably create unfairness to the accused, his valued right to have the trial concluded by a particular tribunal is sometimes subordinate to the public interest in affording the prosecutor one full and fair opportunity to present his evidence to an impartial jury. Yet in view of the importance of the right, and the fact that it is frustrated by any mistrial, the prosecutor must shoulder the burden of justifying the mistrial if he is to avoid the double jeopardy bar. His burden is a heavy one. The prosecutor must demonstrate "manifest necessity" for any mistrial over the objections of the defendant.

Yet in *Carsey* v. *United States,*[2] the U.S. Court of Appeals held that the improper remarks made by the defense attorney to the jury during the closing argument could have been corrected if the judge had instructed the jury to disregard the improper remarks of the defense attorney. The court held that declaring a mistrial was improper and that the defendant had been placed in jeopardy and could not be retried.

In a dissenting opinion in the *Carsey* case, Justice Tamm took the opposite view from that of the majority, stating as follows:

> When appellant's (defendant's) trial counsel, in his closing plea to the jury, advised the jury of two prior mistrials he did it deliberately for the purpose of creating doubt of the defendant's guilt in the minds of the jurors who, understandably, would ask themselves whether a reasonable doubt of guilt had not been established when two prior juries, upon the same evidence, had been unable to reach a verdict. If the prosecutor had made the same statement to the jury for the purpose of injecting into their thinking a fact completely outside of the evidence before them, we would label it as both a "foul blow" and an "improper method calculated to produce a wrongful

conviction." I am unwilling and unable to agree that the questioned statement herein was proper when made by defense counsel when it so obviously would have been improper if made by Government counsel. The statement would have been [an] adequate and proper basis for the granting of a mistrial if the prosecutor had made it, and I must conclude that it was proper and adequate for the trial judge's action when it was made by defense counsel. Defense counsel's initial statement created and triggered the factual situation resulting in the mistrial, despite the majority's feeble attempt to transfer the responsibility to the prosecuting attorney.

The majority opinion places a premium on chicanery and invites the defense counsel to engage in it by its "you cannot lose" result. If this opinion is to prevail, defense counsel may resort to trickery in the court room secure in the knowledge that if he gets by with it he will have the benefit of his misconduct, and if he does not a mistrial will be declared and thereby he reaps an even greater reward for his unethical behavior.

The facts of another case indicate that during the trial recess, the defendant, who was out on bail, approached a drinking fountain in the courthouse hall, drew a cup of water, and handed it to one of the women jurors, at the same time carrying on a conversation with her. Thereafter, the defendant proceeded to give other members of the jury drinks of water. This conduct was observed by an officer, who informed the judge. After court reconvened, the judge questioned the officer on the stand about the incident and declared a mistrial. The defense attorney endeavored to place the defendant on the stand to prove that no conversation pertaining to the facts of the case took place. The defense attorney also tried to accept the blame for the misconduct of the defendant by stating that he had failed to admonish the defendant against having any contact with the jury. The judge's opinion was that the defendant was endeavoring to make a favorable impression on the jury, and a mistrial was declared. In addition, the defendant was held in contempt of court. On retrial, the defendant entered a plea of once in jeopardy that the judge refused to accept, and the defendant was found guilty on the original charge of attempted robbery. The defendant appealed the conviction on the grounds that the guarantee against double jeopardy had been violated by the retrial. The appellate court agreed with the defendant. The court stated the following:

> Once a jury has been **impaneled** and sworn to try a defendant, jeopardy attaches, and its subsequent discharge when not authorized by law or by defendant's consent, is equivalent to an acquittal and constitutes former jeopardy barring retrial.
>
> As to what constitutes sufficient cause to authorize the discharge of a jury, the courts have required a showing that there exists some legal necessity resulting from physical causes beyond the control of the court.
>
> The determination as to whether the required legal necessity exists is a matter left to the discretion of the trial court. However, "the power of the Court to discharge a jury without the consent of the prisoner is not an absolute, uncontrolled discretionary power. It must be exercised in accordance with established legal rules and a sound legal discretion in the application of such rules to the facts and circumstances of each particular case, and in this State is subject to review by an appellate court."
>
> The trial court's action in summarily declaring a mistrial solely on the basis of the officer's testimony that he had observed defendant talking with two of the jurors during the recess on their way back to the court room from the water cooler was unjustified and constituted an abuse of discretion. Before the matter was ruled on defendant should have been given a reasonable opportunity to present his version of the incident and with proper participation by his counsel.[3]

This decision has been criticized by many legal scholars on the basis that the judge did have sufficient cause to declare a mistrial. It is alleged that the misconduct by the defendant in contacts with the jury could not help creating some favorable impression to the detriment of the prosecution. It is further alleged that if a material witness for the prosecution had made this contact with the jury, the judge undoubtedly would have declared a mistrial, since the defendant could not have received a fair trial from an impartial jury.

Arrest of Judgment and Pronouncement of Judgment

If a new trial is not granted after the verdict is rendered, the next procedure is the pronouncement of judgment by the judge. Pronouncement of judgment is usually thought of as the oral sentencing of the defendant by the judge. But technically, it entails more than the oral statement of what the sentence will be. The pronouncement of judgment is reduced to a written document generally known as the judgment. This judgment will set forth the plea entered, the verdict, and, if guilty, will reflect the sentence or other disposition of the case—all of which are entered in the case record. Technically, the pronouncement of judgment is made whether there is an acquittal or a conviction, but in many jurisdictions, it is synonymous with the pronouncement of the sentence. In misdemeanor cases, most jurisdictions permit the pronouncement of judgment in the absence of the defendant. In a felony conviction, the presence of the defendant is required unless he or she cannot be located after due diligent search; in this case, pronouncement of judgment may be made in his or her absence.

Jurisdictions vary somewhat in the time within which the pronouncement of judgment must take place after a guilty plea is entered or a guilty verdict is returned. In misdemeanor convictions in some jurisdictions, the pronouncement may be made immediately; if not, it must take place within a few days. Other jurisdictions provide that the pronouncement of judgment may not occur in fewer than six hours and not more than five days. The six-hour limit allows time for the convicted defendant to arrange personal affairs before serving time. In felony convictions, a considerable delay is usually permitted in the pronouncement of judgment. The delay permits time for a presentence investigation, conducted in order that a more equitable sentence may be imposed. The delay is usually not longer than one month. It is to the advantage of both society and the convicted defendant to have sentence pronounced without unnecessary delay. The defendant is entitled to know the sentence as soon as possible in order that the term may begin. As for society's interest, there is little comfort in having a felon free on bail who may be in a position to commit other crimes while awaiting the pronouncement of sentence.

Prior to the pronouncement of judgment, the defendant may file a motion in the arrest of judgment or, in most jurisdictions, the judge may enter the motion. In many jurisdictions, the law provides that at the time the convicted defendant is brought before the judge for pronouncement of judgment, the judge must inquire of the defendant, "Is there any legal reason why judgment should not be pronounced?" It is at this time that the defendant will show legal cause for the arrest of judgment. Some jurisdictions hold that making the inquiry of the defendant is a useless procedure, and the defendant is entitled to make a motion at any time after the verdict is rendered.

The motion for the arrest of judgment is made on statutory grounds. These grounds include such matters as present insanity of the defendant. If it is determined that the defendant is insane at the time of the pronouncement of judgment, it must be postponed until sanity has been restored, since a defendant may not be sentenced while insane. The motion may be on the grounds that there was some defect in the accusatory pleading that had not been successfully challenged previously, such as the failure to state that a crime had been committed. If the motion for arrest of judgment is denied or none is entered, the next procedure is the pronouncement of the sentence. In most jurisdictions, before the sentence is pronounced, the defendant is entitled to make a statement in his or her own behalf. This statement is generally a plea for leniency or consideration in the sentencing. If a judge fails to grant the defendant an opportunity to make a statement, the sentence may be set aside on appeal. The case does not have to be retried under the circumstances, but the sentence will be set aside and the case will be sent back to the trial court for resentencing after the defendant has been given an opportunity to speak. After the defendant has made a plea, if any, to the judge or jury, he or she will be sentenced. Before entering into the sentencing procedure, the appeals that may be taken by the defendant or the prosecution should be discussed. The outcome of the appeal could determine whether a defendant serves a sentence.

APPEALS

Appeal by the Defendant

If convicted, a defendant will usually appeal the conviction to the appropriate appellate court if there is any basis at all for the appeal. The defendant's appeal may be well founded, since some error may have been committed during the trial that was prejudicial. Or the defendant may attempt to appeal the case merely to delay serving the imposed sentence.

Freedom Pending Appeal Generally, the defendant must file a notice of appeal within a few days after the pronouncement of judgment. Whether the defendant remains free on bail pending the outcome of appeal is largely within the discretion of the judge. The defendant has no inherent right to remain free from custody once convicted, since

Appellate Court Structure of Various States

States with only a court of last resort
Delaware, Maine, Montana, New Hampshire, Nevada, Rhode Island, South Dakota, Vermont, West Virginia, and Wyoming

States with a court of last resort and one intermediate-level court of appeals
Alaska, Arizona, Arkansas, California, Colorado, Connecticut, Florida, Georgia, Hawaii, Idaho, Illinois, Iowa, Kansas, Kentucky, Louisiana, Maryland, Massachusetts, Michigan, Minnesota, Missouri, Nebraska, New Jersey, New Mexico, North Carolina, Ohio, Oregon, South Carolina, Utah, Virginia, Washington, and Wisconsin

States with a court of last resort and two intermediate-level courts of appeals
Alabama, New York, Pennsylvania, and Tennessee

States with a state supreme court and a court of criminal appeal (both courts of last resort) and one intermediate-level court of appeals
Oklahoma and Texas

Note: In Oklahoma and Texas, the state supreme court is the court of last resort for civil matters, and the court of criminal appeals is the court of last resort for criminal cases.

the presumption of innocence is lost. In determining whether a defendant should be free pending the appeal, the judge may consider whether the efforts to appeal were based on frivolous grounds; whether the appeal was merely a delaying tactic to avoid serving the sentence; whether there may be a temptation to flee the jurisdiction of the court pending the appeal; or whether the defendant may be a threat to the community if free on bail.

Whether the defendant remains free on bail or is incarcerated, the judge in most instances will have sentenced the defendant. If the defendant remains free on bail, no time will be served until the outcome of the appeal is determined. If the conviction is reversed, the defendant will not have served any time. But if the defendant is incarcerated pending the appeal, the sentence will have begun to be served. If the conviction is reversed and the defendant is not retried or cannot be retried, little can be done to compensate for the time spent in prison other than to clear the name of the accused. But if the conviction is affirmed or if the defendant is retried after a reversal, credit will be given for the time spent in incarceration pending the appeal. Not all appeals are made immediately after a conviction. An appeal may not be taken until several years of a sentence have been served. These appeals are usually based on the result of some U.S. Supreme Court decision that changes the justice procedure in some manner and is made retroactive; that is, the decision is applicable to all convictions irrespective of when the case was tried. If the decision is not made retroactive, it is applicable only to those defendants whose cases have not been decided previous to the U.S. Supreme Court's decision.

Not all efforts by a defendant to appeal a conviction to an appellate court are successful. Sufficient grounds must be alleged in order for the appellate court to hear the appeal. The grounds on which a defendant may appeal a case are numerous. Whatever grounds are alleged, it must be shown that the error committed during the trial was sufficiently prejudicial that the defendant was denied a fair trial or that there was a miscarriage of justice. Some of the grounds most frequently alleged on appeal are as follows: There was insufficient probable cause to make a lawful arrest; a confession that was improperly obtained was admitted as evidence; physical evidence was introduced that was unlawfully seized; a failure was made to grant a change of venue; there was insufficient representation of competent counsel; a failure to give pertinent instructions to the jury existed; a denial of a new trial was made; or there was a failure to declare a mistrial when there was prejudicial misconduct.

Method of Appeal   Upon appealing the case, the defendant, through counsel or on his or her own, will submit to the appropriate appellate court a brief that sets forth the alleged error committed during the trial with citations of appellate court decisions upholding the contended error. A transcript of the trial proceedings will accompany the brief. The prosecution will submit a brief in an effort to show why the conviction should be affirmed and not reversed. The appellate court will review the briefs and the transcript. After doing so, it may conclude that there is no ground for appeal, and the court will deny a hearing on the matter. A hearing date will be set if the appellate court feels that the appeal is worthy of a hearing. At the hearing, the defense attorney and the prosecution's representative, usually the state attorney general, assisted by the prosecuting attorney who was responsible for the conviction, will be present to argue their sides of the case. The defendant is usually not present, since he or she has no inherent right to be present at an appeal hearing. After the hearing, the appellate court justices will consider the matter and conclude whether the conviction should be affirmed or reversed. In making its determination, the appellate court will consider whether there was error or conduct that was so prejudicial that the defendant was denied a fair trial. Sometimes the appellate court will hold that there was error or misconduct during the trial but that this was not serious enough to deny the defendant a fair trial. Under these circumstances, the error is referred to as harmless error.

If the appellate court denies the defendant a hearing on the appeal, there is little the defendant can do about the decision. The appellate court may be called the court of last resort; its decision is usually final unless the defendant can prove that one of the constitutional guarantees was violated, and then the defendant may eventually appeal to the U.S. Supreme Court. The Supreme Court may or may not grant a hearing, depending upon the validity of the alleged violation. It may grant a hearing in an effort to determine whether there was a violation; if there was, the Supreme Court will reverse the conviction. If the Supreme Court denies the hearing or affirms the conviction, no further appeal can be taken by the defendant.

Retrial after Reversal   If a conviction is reversed by either the state appellate court or the U.S. Supreme Court, the states differ on whether the defendant may be retried. If the reversal is based on the fact that a law is unconstitutional, that jeopardy had attached, or that a law is too vague in wording to indicate the violation, there cannot be a retrial. But if the reversal is based on the introduction of illegally seized evidence or an improperly obtained confession, in many states the defendant may be retried, and the improperly introduced evidence will not be admissible during the retrial. The prosecuting attorney has to determine whether the other evidence was sufficient in obtaining a conviction. If not, the charge will undoubtedly be dismissed. A few states do not permit a retrial on reversal of a conviction, since it would be a violation of the guarantee against double jeopardy. Other states hold that on appealing a conviction, the defendant waives the double jeopardy guarantee. If a defendant is successful in getting a conviction reversed on appeal and is retried and convicted, may the judge impose an increased sentence after the new trial? This question was answered by the U.S. Supreme Court in the case of *North Carolina* v. *Pearce*.[4] The Court in that decision held that if identifiable misconduct by the defendant took place after the first trial, the judge might impose an increased sentence, but the increase should not be based on the fact that the defendant has appealed his or her case. The Court stated the following:

> Due process of law requires that vindictiveness against a defendant for having successfully attacked his first conviction must play no part in the sentence he receives after a new trial. And since the fear of such vindictiveness may unconstitutionally deter a defendant's exercise of the right to appeal or collaterally attack his first conviction, due process also requires that a defendant be freed of apprehension of such a retaliatory motivation on the part of the sentencing judge.
>
> In order to assure the absence of such a motivation, we have concluded that whenever a judge imposes a more severe sentence upon a defendant after a new trial, the reasons for his doing so must affirmatively appear. Those reasons must be based upon objective information concerning identifiable conduct on the part of the defendant occurring after the time of the original sentencing proceedings. And the factual data upon which the increased sentence is based must be made part of the record, so that the constitutional legitimacy of the increased sentence may be fully reviewed on appeal.

Justice White, who concurred in part with the majority opinion, stated that in his opinion, he would "authorize an increased sentence on retrial based on any objective, identifiable factual data not known to the trial judge at the time of the original sentencing proceeding." Only future decisions will tell whether the Court would sanction this reason for an increased sentence, rather than the majority's limited reason of "identifiable conduct" by the defendant after the original sentence. The Court did conclude that on an increased sentence after a new trial, the defendant must be given credit for the time served on the original sentence.

Steps in a Criminal Appeal

Appeal	A challenge to a decision or ruling by a lower court.
Mandatory Appeals	An appeal the appellate court is required to hear. Generally, the intermediate court of appeals is required to accept an appeal of a decision by a general trial court.
Discretionary Appeal	Appellate court may accept or reject the appeal.
Notice of Appeal	The party filing an appeal must submit a written notice of appeal to the court to which the party plans to appeal. Generally, the period of time in which a notice of appeal must be filed is short. Many states have a ten-day period after judgment is announced.
Trial Record	The party filing the appeal must make arrangements with the court reporter to prepare a transcript of the trial and the exhibits to be filed with the appellate court.
Appellate Brief	The party filing an appeal must submit a brief which consists of the written assignments of error, written arguments as to why the decision was wrong, and citations of authority relied on in the brief.
Rebuttal Brief	The opposing party submits a rebuttal brief stating why the decision should not be reversed.
Oral Arguments	The appellate court may or may not order the parties to present oral arguments on the case.
Written Decision	The appellate court will issue a written decision containing its decision and the reasons for it.
Disposition	The appellate court orders the case affirmed, remanded, and reversed and remanded.
Affirmed	The decision is upheld. The appellate court found no reversible error. *Note:* About 85 percent of criminal convictions are upheld.
Remanded	The appellate court returns the case to the lower court and orders the lower court to hold a hearing on a specific issue or make a determination on a specific issue.
Reversed and Remanded	The decision is set aside, and the case is returned to the trial court for either a new trial or a dismissal of the charges.

Appeal by Prosecution

States vary considerably concerning the prosecution's right of appeal. A few states deny the prosecution any right to appeal, since it would result in a violation of the guarantee against double jeopardy. Some permit a limited right of appeal by the prosecution when the appeal does not involve the double jeopardy guarantee. Generally, an appeal may be taken by the prosecution on a judge's order setting aside or dismissing an accusatory pleading. But the appeal may be taken only when the setting aside or dismissal was before the trial began; otherwise, jeopardy will have set in. An appeal may also be taken on a grant of a new trial, an arrest of judgment, or a modification of a verdict or punishment imposed. In most states, the prosecution has no right to appeal a case when an acquittal verdict has been rendered. As stated in *Washington* v. *Arizona,* a judgment of acquittal is final regardless of how erroneously it may have been arrived at. However, a few states do allow an appeal by the prosecution after a verdict of acquittal has been returned. The appeal is followed when the prosecution alleges that a serious error was made by the judge on a ruling of law or procedure. The appeal is permitted so that guidelines may be established for future cases, but the appellate court has no authority to reverse the acquittal.

An increasing number of states allow the prosecution to appeal a judge's order suppressing evidence. It is generally held that where such an appeal is permissible, the appeal may be taken only on an order suppressing evidence that was made before the trial began and may not be taken during the trial. Some states do not permit an appeal of an order suppressing evidence that was made even before the trial. The courts of these states hold that the prosecution is no more disadvantaged by an erroneous ruling before the trial than one during the trial when such ruling leads to an acquittal.

Appeal Involving a Guilty Plea

As we previously discussed, since a plea of guilty is equal to a conviction, this fact must be explained to the defendant before the plea may be accepted. Therefore, it is paradoxical to permit a defendant to appeal a conviction resulting from a voluntary plea of guilty, but some states do permit a defendant to appeal a guilty plea. The grounds for the appeal are based upon some alleged constitutional, jurisdictional, or other grounds concerning the legality of the proceedings. For example, the defendant may allege that the judge failed to explain the significance of the guilty plea as required by *Boykin* v. *Alabama,* that the judge denied the defendant the right to withdraw the guilty plea, or that there was a violation of the agreement pertaining to the plea bargain. There have been times when a defendant was denied a request for suppression of evidence and thereafter entered a plea of guilty, knowing that the trial would result in conviction. Under these circumstances, the defendant may appeal the guilty plea in an effort to determine whether the evidence should have been suppressed.

APPELLATE COURT CITATIONS

Judges of the appellate courts are generally referred to as justices. The number of justices composing an appellate court varies from one state to another as well as from one appellate court to another. Many states have only a single appellate court, which is generally referred to as the supreme court. Other states have a bilateral appellate court system in which there is an appellate court and a supreme court. Usually only three justices will compose an appellate court, whereas the supreme court varies, usually from five to nine justices. Not all justices must agree on the decision, only a majority. Once the decision is made, one of the justices agreeing with the majority will put the decision in writing, stating whether the conviction was upheld or reversed, and the reasoning behind the decision. A dissenting justice, if any, may or may not decide to write a dissenting opinion, setting forth the reasons for disagreement with the majority.

Recording Court Decisions

The decisions handed down by the appellate courts are recorded in official publications so that they may act as guidelines for future cases. Each decision is given a citation number in order that the decision may be filed, indexed, and located by attorneys, judges, and others having occasion to refer to a particular decision. The citation will include the name, or title, of the case; the name of the official record book; the volume and page number; and the year in which the decision was handed down by the appellate court.

The following is a typical example of an appellate court citation: *State* v. *Tison,* 142 Ariz. 446 (1999). *State* v. *Tison* is the title of the decision; 142 refers to the volume number of the official record; Ariz. is an abbreviation for the state of Arizona, indicating that the decision is that of the Arizona Supreme Court; 446 is the page number where the decision begins; 1999 is the date or year in which the decision was handed down by the Arizona Supreme Court. Sometimes the date will precede the volume and page number. The way that the titles of the decisions refer to the persons involved varies among the states. Instead of the title being *State* v. *Tison,* the title may be *Tison* v. *State,* depending on the manner in which the appeal was taken. In some states, the word *People* or *Commonwealth* is substituted for *State.*

In addition to the appellate decision's being published in official publications, the decisions, particularly those of the U.S. Supreme Court, are included in the publications of private companies. A different citation is reflected for these publications. In order that a particular decision may be more readily located by a judge or an attorney, both the official citation and the citation of private companies are included when a case decision is referred to. For example, the West Publishing Company in St. Paul, Minnesota, publishes the decisions of the supreme courts of the various states. These decisions are reported by geographic areas. This reporting system is known as the National Reporter System. The supreme court decisions of the states of Iowa, Michigan, Minnesota, Nebraska, North Dakota, South Dakota, and Wisconsin are published in the *North Western Reporter,* and the citation carries the abbreviation of NW. Returning to the case of *State* v. *Tison,* 142 Ariz. 446, there may be the additional citation of 690 P.2d 747 (1999). The P. indicates that the decision can be located in the *Pacific Reporter* of the National Reporter System. The 2d indicates the second series of the *Pacific Reporter* volumes. The supreme court decisions of the states of Connecticut, Delaware, Maine, Maryland, New Hampshire, New Jersey, Pennsylvania, Rhode Island, and Vermont are published in the *Atlantic Reporter,* abbreviated as A. The supreme court decisions of the states of Illinois, Indiana, Massachusetts, New York, and Ohio are published in the *North Eastern Reporter.* The decisions of the supreme courts of the states of Alaska, Arizona, California, Colorado, Hawaii, Idaho, Kansas, Montana, Nevada, New Mexico, Oklahoma, Oregon, Utah, Washington, and Wyoming are published in the *Pacific Reporter.* The *South Eastern Reporter* includes the supreme court decisions of the states of Georgia, South Carolina, Virginia, and West Virginia. The *Southern Reporter* publishes the decisions of the supreme courts of the states of Alabama, Florida, Louisiana, and Mississippi. The *South Western Reporter* publishes the decisions of the supreme courts of the states of Arkansas, Missouri, Kentucky, Tennessee, and Texas. If a decision is handed down by the U.S. Supreme Court on an alleged violation of a constitutional guarantee, the following is an example of the official citation that would be used: *Batson* v. *Kentucky,* 476 U.S. 79 (1986). The U.S. Supreme Court decisions are also published by the West Publishing Company in a publication known as the *Supreme Court Reporter,* abbreviated as S.Ct. The *Batson* decision would be cited as 106 S.Ct. 1712. The Lawyers Cooperative Publishing Company also publishes the U.S. Supreme Court decisions in a publication known as the *Supreme Court Reporter* Lawyer's Edition, abbreviated as L.Ed. Thus the *Batson* decision may be cited as 90 L.Ed.2d 69. Or a decision may carry all three citations as follows: *Batson* v. *Kentucky,* 476 U.S. 79, 106 S.Ct. 1712, 90 L.Ed.2d 69 (1986).

In those states in which there is an appellate court below the supreme court, the decisions of these appellate courts are also published in an official publication. These decisions can usually be distinguished from the decisions of the supreme court by the abbreviation App. appearing after the abbreviation of the state.

Capstone Cases

United States v. Scott
437 U.S. 82, 98 S.Ct. 2187, 57 L.Ed.2d 65 (1978)

Justice Rehnquist delivered the opinion of the Court.

On March 5, 1975, respondent, a member of the police force in Muskegon, Mich., was charged . . . with distribution of various narcotics. Both before his trial in the United States District Court and twice during the trial, respondent moved to dismiss the two counts of the indictment which concerned transactions that took place during the preceding September, on the ground that his defense had been prejudiced by preindictment delay. At the close of all the evidence, the court granted respondent's motion. . . .

The Government sought to appeal the dismissals of the first two Counts to the United States Court of Appeals for the Sixth Circuit. That court, relying on our opinion in *United States* v. *Jenkins,* 420 U.S. 358 (1975), concluded that any further prosecution of respondent was barred by the Double Jeopardy Clause of the Fifth Amendment, and therefore dismissed the appeal. . . . We granted certiorari to give further consideration to the applicability of the Double Jeopardy Clause to Government appeals from orders granting defense motions to terminate a trial before verdict. We now reverse. . . .

A detailed canvass of the history of the double jeopardy principles in *United States* v. *Wilson,* 420 U.S. 332 (1975), led us to conclude that the Double Jeopardy Clause was primarily "directed at the threat of multiple prosecutions," and posed no bar to Government appeals "where those appeals would not require a new trial." We accordingly held in Jenkins, that, whether or not a dismissal of an indictment after jeopardy had attached amounted to an acquittal on the merits, the Government had no right to appeal, because "further proceedings of some sort, devoted to the resolution of factual issues going to the elements of the offense charged, would have been required upon reversal and remand." If Jenkins is a correct statement of the law, the judgment of the Court of Appeals would in all likelihood have to be affirmed. Yet, though our assessment of the history and meaning of the Double Jeopardy Clause in *Wilson, Jenkins, and Serfass* v. *United States,* 420 U.S. 377 (1975), occurred only three Terms ago, our vastly increased exposure to the various facets of the Double Jeopardy Clause has now convinced us that Jenkins was wrongly decided. It placed an unwarrantedly great emphasis on the defendant's right to have his guilt decided by the first jury empaneled to try him so as to include those cases where the defendant himself seeks to terminate the trial before verdict on grounds unrelated to factual guilt or innocence. We have therefore decided to overrule Jenkins, and thus to reverse the judgment of the Court of Appeals in this case.

. . . At the time the Fifth Amendment was adopted, its principles were easily applied, since most criminal prosecutions proceeded to final judgment, and neither the United States nor the defendant had any right to appeal an adverse verdict. The verdict in such a case was unquestionably final, and could be raised as a bar against any further prosecution for the same offense.

It was not until 1889 that Congress permitted criminal defendants to seek a writ of error in this Court, and then only in capital cases. Only then did it become necessary for this Court to deal with the issues presented by the challenge of verdicts on appeal. And, in the very first case presenting the issues, *Ball* v. *United States,* 163 U.S. 662 (1896), the Court established principles that have been adhered to ever since. Three persons had been tried together for murder: two were convicted, the other acquitted. This Court reversed the convictions, finding the indictment fatally defective, whereupon all three defendants were tried again. This time all three were convicted and they again sought review here. This Court held that the Double Jeopardy Clause precluded further prosecution of the defendant who had been acquitted at the original trial but that it posed no such bar to the prosecution of those defendants who had been convicted in the earlier proceeding.

. . . These then, at least, are two venerable principles of double jeopardy jurisprudence. The successful appeal of a judgment of conviction, on any ground other than the insufficiency of the evidence to support the verdict, *Burks* v. *United States,* poses no bar to further prosecution on the same charge. A judgment of acquittal, whether based on a jury verdict of not guilty or on a ruling by the court that the evidence is insufficient to convict, may not be appealed and terminates the prosecution when a second trial would be necessitated by a reversal. What may seem superficially to be a disparity in rules governing a defendant's liability to be tried again is explainable by reference to the underlying purposes of the Double Jeopardy Clause. . . . The law attaches particular significance to an acquittal. To permit a second trial after an acquittal, however mistaken the acquittal may have been, would present an unacceptably high risk that the Government, with its vastly superior resources, might wear down the defendant so that even though innocent, he may be found guilty. (*Green* v. *United States,* 355 U.S. 184, 1957). On the other hand, to require a criminal defendant to stand trial again after he has successfully invoked a statutory right of appeal to upset his first conviction is not an act of governmental oppression of the sort against which the Double Jeopardy Clause was intended to protect. . . .

Although the primary purpose of the Double Jeopardy Clause was to protect the integrity of a final judgment, this Court has also developed a body of law guarding the separate but related interest of a defendant in avoiding multiple prosecutions even where no final determination of guilt or innocence has been made. Such interests may be involved in two different situations: the first, in which the trial judge declares a mistrial; the second, in which the trial judge terminates the proceedings favorably to the defendant on a basis not related to factual guilt or innocence. . . .

We turn now to the relationship between the Double Jeopardy Clause and re-prosecution of a defendant who has successfully obtained not a mistrial, but a termination of the trial in his favor before any determination of factual guilt or innocence. Unlike the typical mistrial, the granting of a motion such as this obviously contemplates that the proceedings will terminate then and there in favor of the defendant. The prosecution, if it wishes to reinstate the proceedings in the face of such a ruling, ordinarily must seek reversal of the decision of the trial court. . . .

It is quite true that the Government with all its resources and power should not be allowed to make repeated attempts to convict an individual for an alleged offense. This truth is expressed in the three common-law pleas of autrefois acquit, autrefois convict and pardon, which lie at the core of the area protected by the Double Jeopardy Clause. As we have recognized in cases from *Ball* to *Sanabria* v. *United States,* 437 U.S. 54 (1978), a defendant once acquitted may not be again subjected to trial without violating the Double Jeopardy Clause.

But that situation is obviously a far cry from the present case, where the Government was quite willing to continue with its production of evidence to show the defendant guilty before the jury first empaneled to try him, but the defendant elected to seek termination of the trial on grounds unrelated to guilt or innocence. This is scarcely a picture of an all-powerful state relentlessly pursuing a defendant who had either been found not guilty or who had at least insisted on having the issue of guilt submitted to the first trier of fact. It is instead a picture of a defendant who chooses to avoid conviction and imprisonment, not because of his assertion that the Government has failed to make out a case against him, but because of a legal claim that the Government's case against him must fail even though it might satisfy the trier of fact that he was guilty beyond a reasonable doubt.

We have previously noted that "the trial judge's characterization of his own action cannot control the classification of the action." . . . [A defendant is acquitted only when "the ruling of the judge," whatever its label, actually represents a resolution in the defendant's favor, correct or not, of some or all of the factual elements of the offense charged. Where the court, before the jury returns a verdict, enters a judgment of acquittal pursuant to Fed. Rule Crim. Proc. 29, appeal will be barred only when "it is plain that the District Court . . . evaluated the Government's evidence and determined that it was legally insufficient to support a conviction." *United States* v. *Martin Linen Supply Company,* 430 U.S. 564 (1977).

Our opinion in Burks necessarily holds that there has been a "failure of proof" requiring an acquittal when the Government does not submit sufficient evidence to rebut a defendant's essentially factual defense of insanity, though it may otherwise be entitled to have its case submitted to the jury. The defense of insanity, like the defense of entrapment, arises from "the notion that Congress could not have intended criminal punishment for a defendant who has committed all the elements of a proscribed offense," *United States* v. *Russell,* where other facts established to the satisfaction of the trier of fact provide a legally adequate justification for otherwise criminal acts. Such a factual finding does "necessarily establish the criminal defendant's lack of criminal culpability," post (Brennan, J., dissenting), under the existing law; the fact that "the acquittal may result from erroneous evidentiary rulings or erroneous interpretations of governing legal principles," ibid., affects the accuracy of that determination, but it does not alter its essential character. By contrast, the dismissal of an indictment for preindictment delay represents a legal judgment that a defendant, although criminally culpable, may not be punished because of a supposed constitutional violation. . . .

[I]n the present case, [defendant] successfully avoided a submission of [a part] of the indictment [to the jury] by persuading the trial court to dismiss it on a basis which did not depend on guilt or innocence. He was

(Continued)

HISTORY OF PUNISHMENT

In order to understand more fully the history of punishment and its severity, we begin by discussing early societies. The social world of early mankind comprised separate isolated groups, referred to as clans. These clans were an aggregate of families. Each family was a unit within the clan. The eldest male was the ruler in these ancient societies. If harm was done to some member of the clan by another member of the clan, it was the ruler's responsibility to right the wrong. If he was unable to right the wrong, other clan members were pressed into service for assistance. If the wrong was committed by a neighboring clan member, it was a religious duty of each wronged clan member to avenge the wrong. The belief was that an injury to any clan member was an injury to the entire clan. This philosophy of revenge usually ended with the clan's waging war on the offender. If the offender could not be located, the revenge could be inflicted on any other member of the neighboring clan.

The Blood Feud

As time passed, avenging the wrong became more of a family responsibility. The offended family member had the first and foremost responsibility to avenge the wrong. If the victim was killed by the offender or died before the crime had been avenged, other family members had the responsibility to avenge the wrong. Again, if the offender could not be located, then the revenge would be inflicted on other family members. This procedure resulted in what was known as the blood feud. Retaliation during a blood feud was often brutal and usually ended in the death of the offender.

In ancient days when the vengeance took the form of the blood feud, there was little that the offender could do to escape. Even the members of the offender's own family would provide little protection, since they would become the victims of the blood feud if the offender were not found. When time passed without a crime's being avenged, family members often became disenchanted with carrying on the blood feud, particularly when they were not personally offended. Consequently, members of the offended family became willing to accept money or property in return for not inflicting physical retaliation on the offender or on his or her relations. This procedure became known as atonement. By the twelfth century, atonement had grown in popularity and the blood feud had been all but abolished. In the beginning, atonement was primarily a family affair. But as families and clans were taken over by kingdoms, atonement became a source of revenue for kings or the church, depending on the crime. By this time, the church had begun to take a dominant role in the affairs of mankind and thus sought sources of revenue. Not all crimes could be atoned for, so the offender was required to stand trial. Trial could be by ordeal, battle, or compurgation. If found guilty by trial, the offender was subjected to the punishment prescribed for that particular crime. In many instances, the punishment was death. If the death penalty were not imposed, the convicted offender was often subjected to another form of severe physical punishment such as having a hand or ear amputated or an eye gouged out. On display in Marksburg Castle in Germany is a hinged metal helmet-type face mask that was heated red hot and applied to the head of anyone convicted of treason. If a person bearing the scars of such punishment was later seen in public, anyone could kill that person without recourse being taken against the slayer.

As late as the mid-twentieth century, certain primitive societies inflicted forms of unusual punishment on offenders. In New Guinea, for example, an unusual form of punishment was meted out to men caught in the act of adultery. The offended husband was permitted to shoot an arrow at the groin of the offender, who stood fifty paces away. If the wife got pregnant, the husband was permitted to chop off the offender's head. This method of avenging the wrong was probably a carryover from ancient societies. Adultery was considered to be the worst offense that could be committed among clan members. It was thought that adultery disrupted the family unit more than murder and threatened the foundation of the tribal religion.

Protection Within a Church

A study of early judicial procedure reveals that offenders in England were also subjected to many forms of severe punishment. Often to escape punishment, an offender entered a church for sanctuary from pursuers who were attempting to inflict punishment. The offender was safe as long as he or she remained inside the church. Sometimes the pursuers surrounded the church and remained there for days to prevent escape. Often the pursuers tried to have the priests or clergy starve the offender into submission. Usually, the priests would have nothing to do with matters that interfered with the holiness of the sanctuary. This practice was the beginning of what became known as the benefit of clergy. Generally, whatever punishment was imposed for conviction of a particular crime was a mandatory sentence carried out regardless of severity.

Imprisonment as Punishment

Imprisonment as a form of punishment was not used at that time. In fact, under Roman law, imprisonment as punishment was illegal. In early English history, imprisonment was a means of holding the offender for trial and sentencing but not for punishment. The imprisonment of convicted offenders was, and still is, a troublesome and an expensive form of punishment.

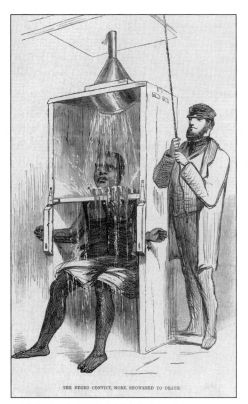

Punishment by a shower bath at the Auburn, New York, prison. (*Source:* CORBIS-NY.)

Thus, we find that in earlier times, swifter and less expensive forms of punishment were inflicted. Some imprisonment as a form of punishment was used at common law in England for a few minor offenses, such as vagrancy. The ecclesiastical courts also imposed imprisonment on convicted clergymen in some instances. But the death penalty, mutilation, and banishment were still the most frequently imposed forms of punishment. When a convicted person was banished from England, not only was the offender required to leave home, family, and friends, but his property was also confiscated by the king or the church. Banishment became another source of revenue for both king and church. It is alleged that as many as 100,000 persons were banished to the American colonies from England before the colonies received independence. As late as the early 1800s, England had more than 200 violations carrying a possible death penalty. But shortly thereafter, imprisonment and banishment to Australia were substituted for the death penalty as a form of punishment.

Punishment in Early America

As the colonies were being settled, the colonists brought with them much of the criminal procedure that they had known in England. At that time, retribution, or vengeance, was still the philosophy behind punishment. This philosophy was also brought to the colonies; consequently, the royal colonial governors continued to inflict cruel and unusual punishment on offenders. The death penalty was frequently inflicted, and the manner in which it was carried out was far more inhumane than it had been in England. Other forms of cruel and unusual punishment, such as mutilation, were also practiced. Much corporal punishment was inflicted—particularly whipping—and the pillory, stocks, and public cage were also used. It is little wonder that, with such practices existing, the framers of the U.S. Constitution included the Eighth Amendment guarantee against "**cruel and unusual punishment**." After a time, the colonists began substituting imprisonment for the death penalty, allegedly as a more humane form of punishment. But early imprisonment, in most instances, was far from humane, and most imprisoned offenders would probably have preferred other forms of punishment, even death, at that period in history. Since retribution was still the primary force behind punishment, little consideration was given to the imprisoned offender. The food that was furnished, if any, was meager; no thought was given to providing any comforts of warmth, lighting, ventilation, or sanitation. Prisoners often died of neglect. Each small community was responsible for providing places of confinement, which in many instances were abandoned stockades or fortresses.

William Penn, himself a prisoner for nine months in the Tower of London, is given credit for the first improvement in prison conditions, as well as for reforms in the types of punishment imposed. In 1681, Penn received the charter to a large tract of land, known as Pennsylvania, in payment of a debt owed to his father. Shortly thereafter, Penn moved to a new city that he named Philadelphia and established a government along the lines of republicanism and religious freedom. The death penalty was abolished for all offenses except murder. Around 1683, a jail was erected to replace the fort that had been used to confine offenders. Since this jail was nothing more than a boxlike room that soon became inadequate, other houses were erected to confine convicted offenders. Penn had further reforms in mind, but he died in 1718 before they could be completed. Almost immediately thereafter, Queen Anne reinstituted some of the harsh traditional penalties. The death penalty was imposed as the punishment for thirteen different crimes. Whipping and mutilation were again inflicted for a number of offenses.

Penalty reforms for convicted offenders began after the colonies achieved independence from England. Improvements were also made in the conditions of confinement. In 1786, an act was passed that provided for imprisonment at hard labor for many crimes that previously carried the death penalty or corporal punishment. Although the act was an improvement, much reform was still needed. Places of confinement soon became overcrowded. There was little supervision. There was no segregation according to sex, age, or offense committed. Liquor was freely sold to inmates, and prostitution was practiced. In 1790, a block of cells was added to the Walnut Street jail in Philadelphia. It was to house the more hardened criminals and was referred to as the penitentiary house. Inmates began to be separated according to sex, age, and offense committed, and they were sent to this jail from other parts of the state. It became a focal point of study by persons interested in prison reform.

Present Sentencing Procedure

Each rule of conduct written throughout history has required that a punishment be established for convicted violators. Usually, the more serious the crime, the more severe the punishment. But which punishments should be inflicted for each particular crime has plagued society for centuries. Even today, the sentencing of a convicted offender may be the most complex part of the judicial process. Convicting the offender may be easier

Sentencing Philosophies

Retribution	A person has infringed upon the rights of others and therefore deserves to be penalized to a degree commensurate with his or her criminal activity.
Incapacitation	To prevent crime, it is necessary to deprive the individual of the opportunity to commit crime (e.g., by confinement).
Deterrence	Punishing criminals to prevent future crimes. Punishment should focus on the crime committed, not on the defendant.
	Specific Deterrence: Punishment designed to prevent a specific person from committing a future crime.
	General Deterrence: Punishment designed to prevent others from committing future crime.
Rehabilitation	The concept that the criminal needs to be treated rather than punished. Punishment should be based on the needs of the defendant rather than the severity of the crime.

than deciding what should be done after the conviction. In primitive times, retaliation was the philosophy behind punishment, and the victim inflicted any punishment he or she desired. As more organized societies were developed, those in the judicial process began to make an effort to fit the penalty to the crime committed. Nevertheless, vengeance or retaliation against the offender was still prevalent in the thoughts of those trying to establish appropriate punishments. The problem became what penalty the offender should be subjected to in order to satisfy society's desire for vengeance and still have the penalty fit the crime. Thus, in the early sentencing process, a thief might have a hand cut off, a perjurer might have the tongue cut out, and a male adulterer might be castrated. The punishment continued to be cruel and severe.

As time passed, imprisonment became the generally accepted way of punishing an offender, and society turned from the retaliatory approach to the isolation philosophy of punishment. Instead of trying to get even with the offender, society attempted to protect itself by imprisonment. As long as the offender was confined, society would be free of recurrent harm. As a result, when penitentiaries were first built in the United States, they were built with the idea of confining the offenders in maximum security to isolate them from society for the prescribed length of the sentence. The offenders became known as inmates. These penitentiaries were fortresslike structures. There were high walls with gun towers surrounding the buildings and cell blocks. Inmates spent much time locked in their cells. They were required to wear a distinctive uniform; for a long time, the uniform was made of black and white striped material. Many of the penitentiaries built in the late 1800s and early 1900s are still in use.

Isolation as Punishment

With punishment based on the isolation theory, the problem was how long an offender should be isolated for society's protection. Early in our history, the sentencing of an offender to imprisonment was solely the responsibility of the trial judge. In most instances, there were no guidelines to assist in determining how long an offender should be confined. As a result, there was a great discrepancy among judges in the sentence imposed for the

Law in Practice

Key Court Decisions Regarding Imprisonment

Cooper v. *Pate* (1964)	Prisoners may sue state prison officials in federal court.
Estelle v. *Gamble* (1976)	Deliberate indifference to serious medical needs of inmates is a violation of the Eighth Amendment's prohibition against cruel and unusual punishment.
Ruiz v. *Estelle* (1980)	A federal district court held that the conditions of imprisonment in Texas prisons were unconstitutional.
Rhodes v. *Chapman* (1981)	Double-celling and overcrowding do not necessarily constitute cruel and unusual punishment.
Whitley v. *Albers* (1986)	A prisoner could not recover damages in federal court when he was shot in the leg during a prison riot if the shooting was part of a good faith effort to maintain discipline and not for the purpose of inflicting punishment.
Wilson v. *Seiter* (1991)	Before a prisoner can contest the living conditions of a state prison in federal court, the prisoner must establish that the prison officials acted with "deliberate indifference" to the prisoner's needs and living conditions.
Miller v. *French* (2000)	A Federal Prison Litigation Reform Act provision allowing a ninety-day limit to rule on prison conditions lawsuits was found to be constitutional.

same offense. Much depended on the judge's attitude and personal philosophy. When legislators began to establish appropriate penalties for each crime, they concentrated on the felony. There is considerable difference among states on the sentences that may be imposed. In some states, legislation has been passed providing a minimum and maximum number of years that an offender must serve for the conviction of a particular crime. For example, an offender convicted of burglary may receive a sentence of not less than one year in prison and not more than ten years. In other states, the law sets forth the maximum length of imprisonment that may be imposed. The law may provide that an offender may not be sentenced for a term longer than ten years. Under this system, an offender could be sentenced to a single hour in confinement, and this outcome has occurred in a few instances. As will be seen, under both systems, the trial judge has great leeway in deciding the sentence to be imposed. As legislators considered the penalties for felonies, misdemeanors were also considered. As with felonies, the length of the sentence to be imposed was usually left to the trial judge, with the maximum set forth in the state statutes.

Other Possible Penalties

Although imprisonment became one form of punishment, it is not the only penalty that may be imposed on a convicted offender. The types of sentences possible for criminal offenders are set forth in the codes of the various states. Penalty is still referred to as punishment in most codes. A penalty may be one or a combination of the following: imprisonment; fine; probation; suspended sentence; and in some states, the death penalty. Removal from public office and the disqualification to hold public office are also listed as forms of punishment in some states.

In a few jurisdictions, the terms punishment and sentence imply imprisonment. Therefore, probation is not considered to be a sentence but rather a disposition of the case. However, in most jurisdictions, the term sentence is the judgment of the court after conviction. The sentence is the final disposition of the trial, whether by imprisonment, suspended sentence, probation, or fine. But punishment is sometimes more closely associated with imprisonment than are other forms of sentence. Technically, punishment means any unpleasantness that the convicted offender may suffer. Any restrictions placed upon the offender, whether by imprisonment, suspended sentence, or probation, are forms of unpleasantness, as is the financial hardship imposed by a fine.

Deterrence

As reformists in the justice system continued to study punishment, its purpose shifted from isolation theory to **deterrence**. The movement to rehabilitate the offender followed. As our study will emphasize, the isolation approach has not been entirely abandoned, since there are inmates from whom society is safe only during their confinement. Neither deterrence nor rehabilitation is applicable to some hardened criminals.

Whatever sentence is imposed, its primary purpose is for the protection of society. The protection may be a result of isolating the offender from society or deterring the offender from committing future crimes, thus serving as an example to others inclined to commit crimes. The protection may also be through rehabilitation so that the offender will refrain from committing future crimes.

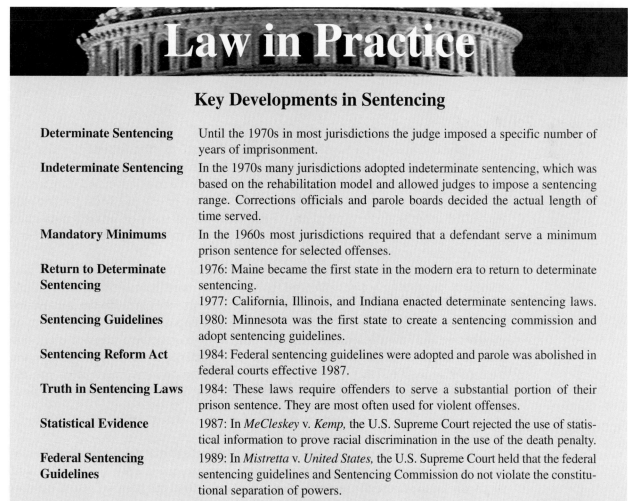

Law in Practice

Key Developments in Sentencing

Determinate Sentencing	Until the 1970s in most jurisdictions the judge imposed a specific number of years of imprisonment.
Indeterminate Sentencing	In the 1970s many jurisdictions adopted indeterminate sentencing, which was based on the rehabilitation model and allowed judges to impose a sentencing range. Corrections officials and parole boards decided the actual length of time served.
Mandatory Minimums	In the 1960s most jurisdictions required that a defendant serve a minimum prison sentence for selected offenses.
Return to Determinate Sentencing	1976: Maine became the first state in the modern era to return to determinate sentencing. 1977: California, Illinois, and Indiana enacted determinate sentencing laws.
Sentencing Guidelines	1980: Minnesota was the first state to create a sentencing commission and adopt sentencing guidelines.
Sentencing Reform Act	1984: Federal sentencing guidelines were adopted and parole was abolished in federal courts effective 1987.
Truth in Sentencing Laws	1984: These laws require offenders to serve a substantial portion of their prison sentence. They are most often used for violent offenses.
Statistical Evidence	1987: In *MeCleskey* v. *Kemp,* the U.S. Supreme Court rejected the use of statistical information to prove racial discrimination in the use of the death penalty.
Federal Sentencing Guidelines	1989: In *Mistretta* v. *United States,* the U.S. Supreme Court held that the federal sentencing guidelines and Sentencing Commission do not violate the constitutional separation of powers.

(Continued)

Megan's Law	1994: New Jersey adopted a law requiring convicted sex offenders to register with local police departments following the rape and murder of seven-year-old Megan Kanka. Other states quickly enacted similar laws.
Polly's Law	1994: California passed a three-strikes law named after murder victim Polly Klaas. By 1995 twenty-four states and the federal government had passed three-strikes laws.
San Diego County v. *Romero*	1996: The California Supreme Court held that judges have discretion in counting prior convictions for purposes of applying the three-strikes law.
Edwards v. *United States*	1997: The U.S. Supreme Court refused to hear a challenge that federal sentencing laws dealing with crack cocaine are racially discriminatory.
United States v. *Booker* and *United States* v. *Fanfan*	2005: The U.S. Supreme Court held that the federal sentencing guidelines established under the Federal Sentencing Reform Act were unconstitutional. The Court held that the guidelines were not binding on judges and that compliance by judges was discretionary.
Ropper v. *Simmons*	2005: The U.S. Supreme Court held that it was unconstitutional to impose the death penalty for a crime committed by an offender prior to his or her eighteenth birthday.

TYPES OF SENTENCING AND SENTENCES

To better understand the deterrence and rehabilitation theories of sentencing, we should discuss the type of sentence to be imposed. Perhaps in no other area of the justice system is there greater variance among states than in the sentencing phase of the justice proceedings.

Misdemeanor Sentencing

Upon conviction of a misdemeanor charge, the statutes of most states provide that the penalty imposed shall not exceed one year of imprisonment and/or a $1,000 fine. As stated, in most jurisdictions, the sentence is imposed by the trial judge, and if imprisonment is imposed, the time is generally served in a county or city jail. Most jurisdictions permit the judge to suspend the sentence and place the offender on probation; to grant probation with the provision that a certain amount of time must be spent in imprisonment; or merely to impose a fine.

Although the laws of most states provide that an offender convicted on a misdemeanor charge may not be sentenced for a period of more than one year, it is possible for him or her to serve more than a single year. This occurs when the offender is convicted on more than one misdemeanor charge. The judge may impose a sentence for one year on each charge and have the sentences run consecutively. A consecutive sentence is one that must be served before the next begins. A consecutive sentence for minor convictions is the exception; in most instances, if the offender is convicted on more than one charge, the judge will provide that the sentences are to be served concurrently, that is, at the same time.

Felony Sentencing

In a majority of the states, it is still the prerogative of the trial judge to impose the sentence. But in some states, the jury will impose the sentence, and in a few states, a jury must be impaneled to impose the sentence even though a jury trial has been waived. If the convicted offender is imprisoned, in some states the length of the sentence that must be served

A wood engraving at the Auburn, New York, prison, circa 1842. (*Source:* The Granger Collection.)

is determined by a board or committee appointed for that purpose. Generally, depending upon the jurisdiction, the types of imprisonment or sentence that may be imposed are the **definite sentence**, the **indefinite sentence**, or the **indeterminate sentence**. Although the sentences are classified as such, confusion has arisen because a definite sentence in one state may be known as an indefinite sentence in another state. Irrespective of their names, we will discuss each classification so that the reader will have some insight into the sentencing procedures followed in the various states.

Definite Sentence

As imprisonment began to be substituted for other forms of punishment, there were few guidelines to assist judges in deciding on the number of years to be imposed. Since retribution, or social retaliation, was still the primary purpose behind punishment, lengthy sentences were often imposed. Some judges became arbitrary and discriminatory in imposing sentences. To overcome this practice, legislation was passed in most states setting forth a prescribed sentence, or a definite mandatory sentence, to be required of one convicted of a particular offense. The theory behind the definite sentence was that it would be applied equally to all, irrespective of race, religion, or social or economic status. The judges no longer had any control over the length of time to be served. On conviction, the mandatory sentence was imposed, and the offender was required to serve that period of time. After serving the prescribed period of time, the offender was released back into society, but never was the offender released prior to that time. The first major change in the definite sentencing procedure came with the introduction of the conditional release. A few states passed legislation permitting the governing board of the penal system to grant time off from the definite sentence for good behavior. If, as an inmate, the convicted offender's behavior was proper, the sentence was reduced by a few days each month. Good behavior principally consisted of complying with prison rules.

The definite sentence was severely criticized by reformists as being inflexible. The definite sentence did not permit any aggravating or mitigating factors, such as age of the offender, prior criminal record, or other circumstances surrounding the commission of the crime to be considered. Since the definite, or mandatory, sentencing procedure was inflexible, judges often dismissed a charge against an offender rather than impose a severe definite sentence when there were mitigating circumstances. An offender was then permitted to go unpunished. Because of the inflexibility of the definite sentence, it has all but disappeared from the justice system.

Indefinite Sentence

As the definite sentence lost favor, it was replaced by the indefinite sentence. In some states, the indefinite sentence is referred to as the indeterminate sentence or as the determinate sentence. Technically, there is a difference in the application of the indefinite, or determinate, sentence and the indeterminate sentence. With the appearance of the indefinite sentence, legislative bodies passed statutes prescribing the maximum penalty that could be imposed on the convicted offender. For example, if an offender were convicted of armed robbery, the statute might state that the offender "shall not be imprisoned for a period of more than thirty-five years." Under the indefinite sentencing procedure, the imposition of the sentence was returned to the judge in most states. A few states provided for the jury to impose the sentence.

The theory behind the indefinite sentence was that it enabled the sentence to fit the offender and not the crime. The sentencing body would weigh the situation and impose the number of years deemed to be just under the circumstances. Since sentencing is far from an exact science, determining the number of years to be served was, and still is, a difficult problem. The problem is magnified because an individual's future conduct is difficult, if not impossible, to predict. Society's reaction to imposed sentences is also unpredictable. There are persons who would lead us to believe that vengeance plays no part in the sentencing procedure of our civilized society. However, realistically, society's vengeance may still be felt in a community when an atrocious crime is committed. Thus, in imposing a sentence, it must be of sufficient length to satisfy the desire for social retaliation but not so long as to discourage the offender from wanting to reform. In most instances, when legislation was passed prescribing the maximum sentence to be imposed, that time was long enough that the most vengeful individual could not take exception. It was the duty of the sentencing body to impose the exact length of a sentence. Since there were no guidelines on the length of an equitable sentence, it often reflected the judge's or the jury's feelings and philosophy. There were wide discrepancies between judges and juries in the sentences imposed for the same offenses. Also, some judges became very lenient in the sentences they imposed.

To overcome this leniency and to assist in establishing some sentencing guidelines, the legislatures of several states passed statutes that prescribed both a minimum and a maximum sentence. For example, on a conviction of armed robbery, the penalty prescribed may state that the offender "shall not serve less than five years' and not more than thirty-five years' imprisonment." It became the responsibility of the judge or jury to decide on an appropriate number of years between the minimum and the maximum allowed.

Presentence Investigations   To assist judges in attempting to arrive at an equitable sentence and to more nearly make the sentence fit the offender, many judges require a presentence investigation. The presentence investigation is usually conducted by a staff member of the probation department. It generally includes such matters as the offender's family status, educational background, work experience, and prior criminal record. It also includes circumstances surrounding the commission of the crime. Whether it was a crime of passion, a thrill, or an emotional involvement may have an impact on the sentence to be prescribed. The offender's attitude toward the crime will be reported. The investigation will also show whether the offender is remorseful over having committed the crime or is only unhappy about being caught. Even with the assistance of the information contained in a presentence report, the sentence to be imposed still involves a difficult decision for the judge. Not all judges have staffs

Inmates at the California State Prison at Salano, near Vacaville, California. Overcrowding has forced inmates to wait not only to eat, shower, and use the toilet but also to use the recreation yard. (*Source:* Rich Pedroncelli/ AP Wide World Photos.)

available to them to make presentence investigations, so in most instances, they must rely solely on their contact with the offender during the trial and their own insight regarding what sentence should be imposed. The judge may consider the mental state of the offender at the time the crime was committed. Was the offender in a state of diminished capacity? Was his or her mental condition so diminished by intoxication or drugs that the offender could not have formulated an intent, created a motive, or entertained malice toward the victim? If so, the judge may impose a lesser penalty. Some states have permitted diminished capacity to be pleaded as a defense to a criminal charge, but currently this use has been abolished in most states and may be considered only by the judge at the time of sentencing.

Juries Imposing Sentences   Juries generally do not have access to any presentence investigative material. When the jury imposes the sentence, it is too often nothing more than a calculated guess on what is appropriate. Often juries will be either extremely harsh or very lenient in sentencing, because of deep emotional involvement with a crime committed in their community. The sentence of the jury is often the result of a compromise brought about by bargaining over the verdict. Attempting to get a jury to arrive at what may be an equitable sentence is often more difficult than reaching a unanimous verdict. One may wonder why juries are permitted to impose the sentence in some states in view of the problems involved. This practice is a carryover from colonial days. The colonists frequently had unpleasant experiences with the royal judges, as well as some postindependence judges, who were too arbitrary and discriminatory in the imposition of sentences. To overcome these problems, a few state legislatures provided that the imposition of the sentence was to be the prerogative of the jury.

Whether a sentence is imposed by a judge or a jury, it will stipulate the exact number of years to be served. At first glance, it would appear that this sentencing procedure is of the definite type. Definite and indefinite sentences differ in that with the definite sentence, the law prescribes a definite mandatory number of years that must be served by all offenders on conviction of a particular crime. With the indefinite sentence, the law prescribes either a maximum amount of time that may be imposed or a minimum and a maximum, and from this indefinite period of time, the judge or jury will decide upon a definite amount of time for the sentence.

With the passing of time and the growing interest in rehabilitation, the indefinite sentence has become even more indefinite because, after serving a portion of the sentence, the inmate may become eligible for parole, thereby shortening the time to be served. Parole will be discussed more fully later in the chapter. Because the exact number of years that must be served is indefinite, or indeterminate, and because of the possibility of parole, this sentencing procedure is referred to as the indeterminate sentence in some states.

Indeterminate Sentence

The true indeterminate sentence removes the sentencing of a prescribed number of years from the hands of a judge or a jury. The length of the sentence is determined by a board or committee appointed for that purpose sometime after the imprisonment has been pronounced. The primary purpose of the indeterminate sentence is to permit the sentence to more nearly fit the offender and to assist in the rehabilitation process. But this was not the original purpose of the indeterminate sentence. On the continent of Europe during the seventeenth and eighteenth centuries, the indeterminate sentence was used to lengthen the sentences of dangerous criminals for protective detention after they had served their original sentences. This procedure eventually died out in Europe. The indeterminate sentence was adopted in this country, but for a different reason. This sentence permitted a mitigation of the sentence that might otherwise have been imposed with the view that the indeterminate sentence would assist the offender in reforming. When this sentence was first adopted in this country, the offender was imprisoned for an indeterminate time in order to accomplish physical, emotional, and mental rehabilitation so that his or her renewed freedom would no longer endanger the welfare of society. Once the offender arrived at this status, as decided by a board of managers of the penal system, he or she was entitled to be released. Thus, the inmate could be held for an indeterminate period, even for an entire lifetime—until reaching that point of physical, emotional, and mental rehabilitation where there was no threat to society on his or her release.

Very few states have adopted the true indeterminate sentencing procedure. Under this procedure, the legislature prescribes both the minimum and the maximum terms for each offense punishable by imprisonment in the state prison. Upon conviction of such an offense, and if neither a new trial nor probation is granted, the trial judge does not specify the length of imprisonment but merely sentences the defendant as prescribed by law. A board appointed by the governor then determines, within statutory limits, the length of time that the offender will actually be required to serve. This board is frequently referred to as the parole board.

The indeterminate sentence has been interpreted to mean that on being sentenced as prescribed by law, the offender has been sentenced to the maximum time prescribed by the statutes for the particular offense. But the indeterminate sentence process permits the shortening of the offender's sentence on a showing of rehabilitation. The theory behind the indeterminate sentence is to give the inmate a great incentive to reform so that the sentence will be reduced in length from the maximum prescribed.

When Is an Offender Rehabilitated?

Determining when an offender has been **rehabilitated** to a point where there is no longer a threat to society on release is an almost impossible task. Some never reach that point and have to serve the maximum time. However, each inmate is entitled eventually to have the length of his or her sentence determined by the board. In making the determination, the board will take many things into consideration. Each penal institution maintains a file or cumulative folder on each inmate. The board will study the file and hold a hearing at which the inmate may appear to plead the case. Generally, the hearing will not be held until the inmate has served six months to one year of the maximum time prescribed. By holding the hearing after the inmate has started serving a portion of the sentence, the board has an opportunity to study the inmate's reaction to incarceration, since these data, as well as much other information, will be included in the cumulative file. The file will contain the name and age of the inmate, the place and time of conviction, the charge for which the inmate was convicted, and the minimum and maximum sentence prescribed by the statutes. The presentence investigative report will be included to provide the board with background knowledge on the inmate. Also included may be the results of tests given to the inmate upon incarceration, as well as a record of the inmate's efforts to improve academically by attempting to learn some salable work skill. The board will consider the general attitude of the inmate toward society, law, and authority as expressed by the inmate in the appearance before the board.

After a review of the entire matter, the board will endeavor to arrive at some equitable length of time to be served. The board may conclude that the inmate should serve six years on a sentence prescribed by law to be not less than one year and not more than ten years. The board may conclude further that the inmate should serve four of those years in actual confinement and the other two years on parole. After the time has been set, if the inmate demonstrates an inability to conform to prison regulations or no attempt to reform has been made, the board has the authority to reset the length of the sentence, even requiring the inmate to serve the maximum time. For this reason, it has been interpreted that an offender sentenced under the indeterminate sentence procedure is sentenced to the maximum prescribed, and any time less than the maximum is based on the rehabilitation of the inmate. It has been held that the indeterminate sentence grants the inmate no vested right to a permanently fixed length of sentence at any time.

Advantages and Disadvantages of the Indeterminate Sentence

The indeterminate sentence has been attacked by inmates on the allegation that it violates the due process of law because of its uncertainty, and, as such, is cruel and unusual punishment. However, to date, these attacks have been unsuccessful, since the courts have found that the sentence is fixed at the maximum and that it is the inmate's reformation that permits the maximum to be reduced. The courts have held that as long as a minimum and a maximum sentence prescribed by the legislature are not disproportionate to the offense committed, the sentence is not cruel and unusual. It has been stated that whether a particular punishment is disproportionate to the offense is a question of degree. Courts have described a disproportionate punishment as one in which the length of the sentence is so disproportionate as to shock the moral sense of all reasonable people or the community.

The proponents of the true indeterminate sentencing procedure allege that a board is in a better position than a judge to determine the sentence that should be imposed. The board comes in contact with all convicted offenders who are imprisoned, whereas judges

period of imprisonment, but the execution of the sentence will be suspended, and the offender will be placed on probation for a prescribed time. The time that the offender may be placed on probation is generally at the discretion of the judge, but in most instances it is not for a period longer than the maximum time of imprisonment for the particular crime.

Conditions of Probation   The general condition imposed on the offender, when placed on probation, is that he or she be a law-abiding individual during the period of probation. Many other restrictions may also be imposed at this time. For example, the judge may restrict the offender's area of travel and associates, or the offender may be prohibited from patronizing bars. Restitution for damages or injuries caused while violating the law may be required. In some instances, as a condition of probation, the offender must agree to having his or her person or home searched without a warrant at any time by either a probation officer or a law enforcement officer. When these conditions are imposed, however, it is generally held that the search may not be a harassment procedure but that it is to be made only when there is probable cause to believe that the offender has violated probation. Whenever restrictions are placed on an offender, it has been stated that the restrictions should have some connection with the crime committed. For example, in one case, the defendant was convicted of grand theft. Prior to the conviction, the defendant had given birth to three illegitimate children fathered by different men. As a condition of probation, the judge advised the defendant that she was not to become pregnant out of wedlock again during the probation period. She did become pregnant out of wedlock, and the judge then revoked her probation and sentenced her to prison. She appealed the sentence as constituting cruel and unusual punishment. The appellate court agreed with her and reversed the case, sending it back to the judge for further consideration. The appellate court stated that the trial judge might be commended for the attempt to prevent illegitimacy but that the attempt should have been made in a different manner, since the restriction on pregnancy had no connection with the crime committed. However, judges frequently require a person placed on probation to do work for charity organizations, a requirement that appears to have no connection with the crime committed. There are times when a judge may grant probation with the stipulation that a short time be spent in imprisonment. Some reformists have criticized the use of imprisonment for one placed on probation as being a handicap to the rehabilitation process. Others justify the imprisonment as being a means of awakening the offender to the realization of what could happen if probation is violated.

There is a difference among states on the question of whether a convicted offender may refuse probation. In some states, it is held that the offender does not have to give consent to being placed on probation; therefore, there is no right to refuse to accept probation. In other states, it is held that the convicted offender must give consent to be placed on probation. Although probation is generally preferable to imprisonment, a judge, in granting probation, may impose certain restrictions that the offender may feel are intolerable. In this case, the offender may prefer a limited time of imprisonment. Since probation is not considered a form of punishment but a rehabilitation process, it is believed that the convicted offender should be willing to be placed on probation. Otherwise, the rehabilitative effect of probation is lost. There are a few states in which an offender may be placed on probation prior to conviction. On a complaint being filed, an offender can be placed on probation, thereby avoiding a conviction. It is felt that the consent of the offender is necessary under these circumstances. In some states, this procedure is known as diversion.

Revocation of Probation   If, during the period of probation, the offender, known as a probationer, violates the law or fails to abide by other restrictions that may have been imposed, the probation may be revoked and the probationer sentenced to imprisonment. Whether or not probation is revoked is at the discretion of the trial judge. In *Gagnon* v. *Scarpelli,* the U.S. Supreme Court held that before probation may be revoked, the probationer is entitled to a hearing, stating the following:

> Probation revocation, like parole revocation, is not a stage of a criminal prosecution, but does result in a loss of liberty. Accordingly, we hold that a probationer, like a parolee, is entitled to a preliminary and final revocation hearing, under the conditions specified in *Morrissey* v. *Brewer.* . . .

Criticism of Probation   Generally, one would not quarrel with the primary purpose of probation, which is rehabilitating the offender. But many persons both in and out of the justice system believe that judges grant probation too often. Probation has been granted to prevent overcrowding of prisons. It has also been granted to offenders who have no incentive to mend their ways. In one case, for example, an offender was convicted of burglary and placed on three years' probation. While on probation, the offender was convicted on another burglary charge, and the same judge again placed the offender on probation, to run concurrently with the probationary period of the prior conviction. For this reason, some states have passed legislation that prohibits an offender from being placed on probation after conviction for certain crimes or for using a gun while committing crimes. In spite of the efforts to curb the use of probation, it is still extensively utilized. At any given time, more than 2 million persons are on probation in the United States.

DEATH PENALTY

> The toughest part of this job is sentencing. I've lost all kinds of sleep over sentences. I find it dreadful.
> —Malcolm Muir, Judge, U.S. District Court, 1982

> I think a judge's education is very imperfect when it comes to the sentencing process.
> —Edward Davis, former Chief of Police, Los Angeles, 1973

Heated arguments have taken place over the years concerning the merits of the death penalty. Those who oppose the death penalty do so principally on the grounds that it has no place in a civilized society. They hold that the death penalty is a form of cruel and unusual punishment, and further allege that it does not act as a deterrent. An equal number contend that the death penalty is a deterrent and as such should be retained. But they concede that the deterrent effect does not function effectively, because, as previously pointed out, for any deterrent to be effective, the punishment must be swift and sure. In fact, the time interval between the imposition of the death penalty and the execution makes the death penalty anything but swift in coming and sure in being carried out.

Cruel and Unusual Punishment

The question of whether or not the death penalty is cruel and unusual punishment in violation of the Eighth Amendment was placed before the U.S. Supreme Court in the case of *Furman* v. *Georgia.*[1] The Court held in that case that the death penalty as such was not cruel and unusual punishment but that the indiscriminate manner in which it was applied made the death penalty cruel and unusual punishment in violation of the Eighth Amendment.

Law in Practice

States with and Without the Death Penalty

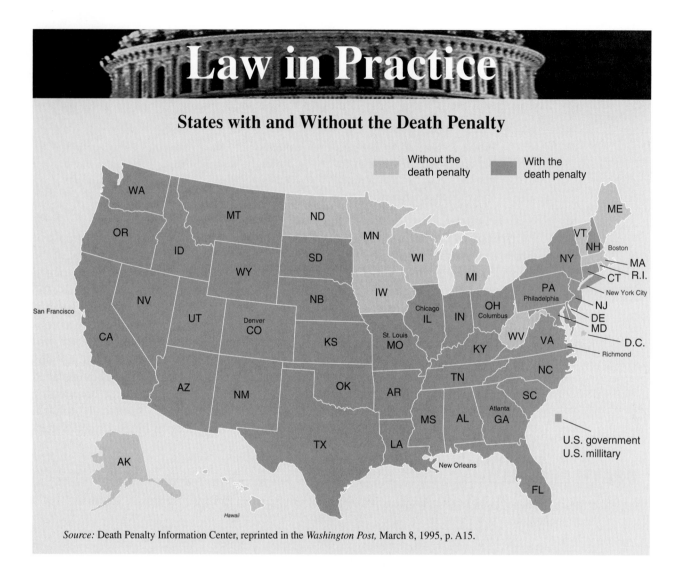

Source: Death Penalty Information Center, reprinted in the *Washington Post,* March 8, 1995, p. A15.

The Court in the *Furman* decision indicated that perhaps, if the death sentence was to be made mandatory for all of equal guilt, the sentence would not be discriminatory and thus would not violate the cruel and unusual punishment provision of the Eighth Amendment. As a result, many state legislatures passed statutes making the death penalty mandatory on conviction for certain crimes. This mandatory sentence took from the jury or judge the right to determine the sentence to be imposed on conviction for crimes previously carrying the alternate sentence of life imprisonment or death.

However, the U.S. Supreme Court, in *Woodson* v. *North Carolina,*[2] overruled as cruel and unusual punishment a North Carolina statute making the death penalty mandatory. The Court held that such a statute did not allow any consideration to be given to the character and record of the offender. The Court stated, "Consideration of both the offender and the offense in order to arrive at a just and appropriate sentence has been viewed as a progressive and humanizing development."

Consequently, those state statutes making the death penalty mandatory had to be revised to conform with the *Woodson* decision. Statutes were then passed allowing the jury or judge to take into consideration aggravating or mitigating circumstances in imposing the alternate sentence of life imprisonment or death. A Georgia statute of this nature was upheld by the U.S. Supreme Court in *Gregg* v. *Georgia.*[3] In reaffirming that the death penalty was not in violation of the Eighth Amendment guarantee against cruel and unusual punishment, the Court stated the following:

> The imposition of the death penalty for the Crime of murder has a long history of acceptance both in the United States and in England. The common-law rule imposed a mandatory death sentence on all convicted murderers. And the penalty continued to be used into the 20th century by most American States, although the breadth of the common-law rule was diminished, initially by narrowing the class of murders to be punished by death and subsequently by widespread adoption of laws expressly granting juries the discretion to recommend mercy.
>
> It is apparent from the text of the Constitution itself that the existence of capital punishment was accepted by the Framers. At the time the Eighth Amendment was ratified, capital punishment was a common sanction in every State. Indeed, the First Congress of the United States enacted legislation providing death as the penalty for specified crimes. The Fifth Amendment, adopted at the same time as the Eighth, contemplated the continued existence of the capital sanction by imposing certain limits on the prosecution of capital cases: "No person shall be held to answer for a capital, or otherwise infamous, crime unless on a presentment or indictment of a Grand Jury . . .; nor shall any person be subject for the same offense to be twice put in jeopardy of life or limb; . . . nor be deprived of life, liberty, or property, without due process of law. . . ." And the Fourteenth Amendment, adopted over three-quarters of a century later, similarly contemplates the existence of the capital sanction in providing that no State shall deprive any person of "life, liberty, or property" without due process of law.
>
> For nearly two centuries, this Court, repeatedly and often expressly, has recognized that capital punishment is not invalid per se.

In holding that the death penalty is not a violation of the guarantee against cruel and unusual punishment, the dissenting justices in the *Furman* case stated as follows:

> Punishments are cruel when they involve torture or a lingering death; but the punishment of death is not cruel, within the meaning of that word as used in the Constitution. It implies there something inhuman and barbarous, something more than the mere extinguishment of life. . . .
>
> The traditional humanity of modem Anglo-American law forbids the infliction of unnecessary pain in the execution of the death sentence. . . . The cruelty against which the Constitution protects a convicted man is cruelty in the method of punishment, not the necessary suffering involved in any method employed to extinguish life humanely.

The gas chamber, electric chair, hanging, lethal injection, and firing squad have all been sanctioned by the Court as humane means of carrying out the death penalty.

In the *Gregg* decision, the Court made some interesting comments on the death penalty as a deterrent as well as a necessary form of punishment to satisfy society's demand for justice. The Court stated the following:

> The death penalty is said to serve two principal social purposes: retribution and deterrence of capital crimes by prospective offenders.
>
> In part, capital punishment is an expression of society's moral outrage at particularly offensive conduct. This function may be unappealing to many, but it is essential in an ordered society that asks its citizens to rely on legal processes rather than self-help to vindicate their wrongs. "The instinct for retribution is part of the nature of man and channeling that instinct in the administration of criminal justice serves an important purpose in promoting the stability of a society governed by law. When people begin to believe that organized society is unwilling or unable to impose upon criminal offenders the punishment they deserve, then there are sown the seeds of anarchy—of self-help, vigilante justice, and lynch law." Retribution is no longer

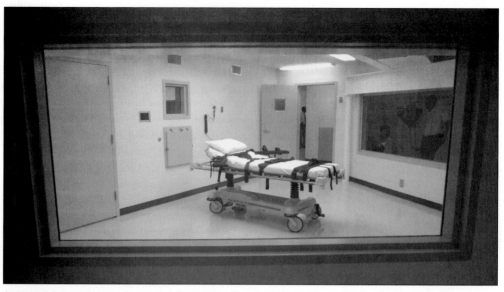

Alabama's lethal injection chamber at the Holman Correctional Facility in Atmore. (*Source:* Dave Martin/AP Wide World Photos.)

the dominant objective of the criminal law, but neither is it a forbidden objective nor one inconsistent with our respect for the dignity of men. Indeed, the decision that capital punishment may be the appropriate sanction in extreme cases is an expression of the community's belief that certain crimes are themselves so grievous an affront to humanity that the only adequate response may be the penalty of death.

Statistical attempts to evaluate the worth of the death penalty as a deterrent to crimes by potential offenders have occasioned a great deal of debate. The results simply have been inconclusive. Although some of the studies suggest that the death penalty may not function as a significantly greater deterrent than lesser penalties, there is no convincing empirical evidence either supporting or refuting this view. We may nevertheless assume safely that there are murderers, such as those who act in passion, for whom the threat of death has little or no deterrent effect. But for many others the death penalty undoubtedly is a significant deterrent.

Alternate Sentencing Procedure

Since the *Woodson* decision held that the alternate sentencing procedure must be followed, it is important to discuss the procedure's development. For many years, the death penalty was made mandatory upon the conviction of certain specified crimes in most states. Jurors aware of this situation knew that on voting for a guilty verdict, they were voting for the execution of a human being. Many jurors had reservations about the death penalty. When it came time to vote on the verdict, they could not bring themselves to vote guilty irrespective of the strength of the evidence of guilt. This inability to vote for a guilty verdict caused many trials to end with hung juries. In an effort to overcome this problem, the legislatures of many states enacted statutes setting forth alternate sentences of life imprisonment or death on conviction of certain crimes. The statutes further provided that the jury in the jury trial was to make the decision about which penalty was to be imposed. Under these circumstances, the juror with reservations about the death penalty could still vote for a guilty verdict but be in a position to vote for life imprisonment after the conviction. In 2002, the U.S. Supreme Court held that the factual determination about the existence of "aggravating factors" that make a convicted murder eligible for the death penalty must be made by the jury and not the judge.

When the alternate sentence was made possible, one of two procedures was generally followed. In some states, a trial was first held to determine the guilt or innocence of the accused. If the accused was found guilty, a second trial was held to determine whether the death penalty was to be imposed or whether the sentence was to be life imprisonment. In other states, only one trial was held. The jury would deliberate first on the guilt or innocence of the accused, and, if the jury voted a guilty verdict, then they would then deliberate on the penalty to be imposed. Both procedures have received the sanction of the U.S. Supreme Court. Under both procedures, the juror with reservations about imposition of the death penalty could still vote for a guilty verdict without voting for the death of the defendant.

During the trial or sentence determination hearing, the jury must consider both aggravating and mitigating circumstances, and weigh them against each other. The *Gregg* decision listed such aggravating circumstances as a murder committed by a convict under a sentence of imprisonment; a murder committed by one previously convicted of murder or a felony involving violence; a murder committed at the time the defendant committed another murder; a murder committed while committing or attempting to commit robbery, rape, arson, burglary, or kidnapping; a murder committed for the purpose of avoiding arrest; and a murder committed in an especially cruel or atrocious manner. As to mitigating circumstances, the Court suggested that it be taken into consideration whether the defendant had no significant prior criminal record; whether the murder was committed while the defendant was under some emotional stress; whether the defendant was an accomplice of another person who actually did the murder and whether the defendant's participation in the homicidal act was relatively minor; whether at the time of the murder the defendant was acting under a diminished capacity; and whether the defendant was of youthful age.

In most jurisdictions, when the death penalty is imposed, the case is automatically appealed to the highest appellate court within the jurisdiction. The court will review the facts of the case to determine whether the conviction should be affirmed and whether the death penalty is justified from the evidence presented. The appellate court may affirm both the conviction and the death penalty, or it may affirm the conviction but hold that the death penalty is not justified under the circumstances. In this instance, either the case will be returned to the trial court for revision of the sentence or, depending on the court, the life sentence may be imposed automatically. If the appellate court reverses the conviction, the penalty phase will not be considered.

The death penalty may be imposed in approximately two-thirds of the states and within the federal system, yet opponents undoubtedly will continue to attempt to have it abolished as being cruel and unusual punishment. In fact, in their dissenting opinions in the *Gregg* decision, Justices Marshall and Brennan were adamant in their contention that the death penalty is cruel and unusual punishment and thus a violation of the Eighth Amendment guarantee.

Death Penalty as Excessive Punishment for the Crime of Rape

Appellate courts have from time to time held that a particular sentence is excessive and disproportionate to the crime committed, and thus the sentence is cruel and unusual punishment. In such an instance, the sentence will be set aside and the case referred to the trial court for resentencing. What is considered excessive punishment is not easily determined and often rests largely upon the personal viewpoints of the justices involved. In *Coker* v. *Georgia*,[4] the U.S. Supreme Court held that the death penalty for the rape of an adult woman was excessive and disproportionate to the crime. The Court stated the following:

> We do not discount the seriousness of rape as a crime. It is highly reprehensible, both
> in a moral sense and in its almost total contempt for the personal integrity and

Law in Practice

Death Sentences and Executions in 2004

In 2004, 59 prisoners were executed, six fewer than in 2003. One hundred and twenty-five individuals, including five women, were sentenced to death in 2004. This was the smallest number for a year since 1973. For the year 2004, 22 prisoners on death row died of natural death or committed suicide. An additional 107 had their death sentences commuted, tossed out, or overturned. On December 31, 2004, there were 3,315 persons on death row compared to 3,378 on December 31, 2003.

Texas executed 23 prisoners in 2004, more than three times as many as any other state. The largest number of prisoners on death row on December 31, 2004, was in California, with 637 prisoners. California, Texas, and Florida account for 44 percent of the nation's death row population. Fifty-two women were on death row, an increase of five from 2003. The oldest prisoner on death row was 89 years old and the youngest was 18 years old.

[T]he 59 prisoners executed in 2004 . . . had spent an average of 11 years on death row. Thirty-six were white, 19 were black, 3 were Hispanic, and 1 was Asian.

Ten federal prisoners were sentenced to death in 2004, twice as many as in any other year since 1973.

Source: Death Penalty Information Center, reprinted in the *Houston Chronicle,* November 14, 2005, p. A3, and *USA Today,* November 14, 2005, p. A1.

autonomy of the female victim and for the latter's privilege of choosing those with whom intimate relationships are to be established. Short of homicide, it is the "ultimate violation of self." It is also a violent crime because it normally involves force, or the threat of force or intimidation, to overcome the will and the capacity of the victim to resist. Rape is very often accompanied by physical injury to the female and can also inflict mental and psychological damage. Because it undermines the community's sense of security, there is public injury as well.

Rape is without doubt deserving of serious punishment; but in terms of moral depravity and of the injury to the person and to the public, it does not compare with murder, which does involve the unjustified taking of human life. Although it may be accompanied by another crime, rape by definition does not include the death or even the serious injury to another person. The murderer kills; the rapist, if no more than that, does not. Life is over for the victim of the murderers; for the rape victim, life may not be nearly so happy as it was, but it is not over and normally is not beyond repair. We have the abiding conviction that the death penalty, which "is unique in its severity and irrevocability," is an excessive penalty for the rapist, who, as such, does not take human life.

Justice Powell, who voted with the majority in the *Coker* decision, dissented in one respect. He felt that the majority went beyond what was necessary in that decision when it held

that capital punishment always—regardless of the circumstances—is a disproportionate penalty for the crime of rape. . . .

The plurality (the majority) draws a bright line between murder and all rapes regardless of the degree of brutality of the rape or the effect upon the victim. I dissent because I am not persuaded that such a bright line is appropriate. There is extreme variation in the degree of culpability of rapists. The deliberate viciousness of the rapist may be greater than that of the murderer. Rape is never an act committed accidentally. Rarely can it be said to be unpremeditated. There is also wide variation in the effect on the victim. The plurality opinion says that "life is over for the victim of the murderer; for the rape victim, life may not be nearly so happy as it was, but it is not over and normally is not beyond repair." But there is indeed extreme variation in the crime of rape. Some victims are so grievously injured physically or psychologically that life is beyond repair.

Thus it may be that the death penalty is not disproportionate punishment for the crime of aggravated rape. Final resolution of the questions must await careful inquiry into objective indicators of society's "evolving standards of decency, particularly legislative enactments and the responses of juries in capital cases. The plurality properly examines these indicia, which do support the conclusion that society finds the death penalty unacceptable for the crime of rape in the absence of excessive brutality or severe injury. But it has not been shown that society finds the penalty disproportionate for all rapists. In a proper case a more discriminating inquiry than the plurality undertakes well might discover that both juries and legislatures have reserved the ultimate penalty for the case of an outrageous rape resulting in serious, lasting harm to the victim. I would not prejudge the issue.

This statement indicates that if legislation were passed making it possible to impose the death penalty in aggravated rape cases, such a penalty might not be declared excessive. However, the *Coker* decision, in which four justices declared the death penalty excessive in all instances except where murder was involved, may make the passage of such legislation difficult. And even if such legislation were passed, there is no assurance that the U.S. Supreme Court would not hold the death penalty excessive.

Chief Justice Burger and Justice Rehnquist expressed concern in the *Coker* case over the majority's decision in holding the death penalty excessive. These justices pointed out the following facts:

On December 5, 1971, Coker raped and then stabbed to death a young woman. Less than eight months later Coker kidnapped and raped a second young woman. After twice raping this 16-year-old victim, he stripped her, severely beat her with a club, and dragged her into a wooded area where he left her for dead. He was apprehended and pleaded guilty to offenses stemming from these incidents. He was sentenced by three separate courts to three life terms, two 20-year terms, and one eight-year term of imprisonment. Each judgment specified that the sentences it imposed were to run consecutively rather than concurrently. Approximately one and one-half years later, on September 2, 1974, petitioner escaped from the state prison where he was serving these sentences. He promptly raped another 16-year-old woman in the presence of her husband, abducted her from her home, and threatened her with death and serious bodily harm. It is this crime for which the sentence now under review was imposed.

The Court today holds that the State of Georgia may not impose the death penalty on Coker. In so doing, it prevents the State from imposing any effective punishment upon Coker for his latest rape. The Court's holding, moreover, bars Georgia from guaranteeing its citizens that they will suffer no further attacks by this habitual rapist. In fact, given the lengthy sentences Coker must serve for the crimes he has already committed, the Court's holding assures that petitioner (Coker) and others in his position will henceforth feel no compunction whatsoever about committing further rapes as frequently as he may be able to escape from confinement and indeed even within the walls of the prison itself. To what extent we have left States "elbow room" to protect innocent persons from depraved human beings like Coker remains in doubt.

These two dissenting justices were also concerned over the *Coker* decision because there was an indication that the majority would declare the death penalty excessive for any crime in which no murder was involved. These justices stated the following:

Since the Court (the majority) now invalidates the death penalty as a sanction for all rapes of adults at all times for all circumstances, I reluctantly turn to what I see as the broader issues raised by this holding.

The plurality acknowledges the gross nature of the crime of rape. A rapist not only violates a victim's privacy and personal integrity, but inevitably causes serious psychological as well as physical harm in the process. The long-range effect upon the victim's life and health is likely to be irreparable; it is impossible to measure the harm which results. Volumes have been written by victims, physicians and psychiatric specialists on the lasting injury suffered by rape victims. Rape is not a mere physical attack, it is destructive of the human personality. The remainder of the victim's life may be gravely affected, and this in turn may have a serious detrimental effect upon her husband and any children she may have. I therefore wholly agree with Mr. Justice White's conclusion as far as it goes that short of homicide, rape is the "ultimate violation of the self." Victims may recover from the physical damage of knife or bullet wounds, or a beating with fists or a club, but recovery from such a gross assault on the human personality is not healed by medicine or surgery. To speak blandly, as the plurality does, of rape victims who are "unharmed," or, as the concurrence, to classify the human outrage of rape in terms of "excessively brutal," versus "moderately brutal," takes too little account of the profound suffering the crime imposes upon the victims and their loved ones.

Despite its strong condemnation of rape, the Court reaches the inexplicable conclusion that the "death penalty is an excessive penalty" for the perpetrator (Coker) of this heinous offense. As pointed out by one of the dissenting justices in the *Coker* decision, Chief Justice Warren Burger, the result of the case is that the death penalty may be imposed only on the conviction of murder. Burger also pointed out that the Court's conclusion in that case was very disturbing. He stated that

the clear implication of today's holding appears to be that the death penalty may he properly imposed only as to crimes resulting in death of the victim. This case casts serious doubt upon the unconstitutional validity of statutes imposing the death penalty for a variety of conduct which, though dangerous, may not necessarily result in any immediate death, e.g., treason, airplane hijacking and kidnaping. In that respect, today's holding does even more harm than is initially apparent. We cannot avoid judicial notice that crimes such as airplane hijacking and mass terrorist activity can constitute a serious and increasing danger to the safety of the public. It would be unfortunate indeed if the effect of today's holding were to inhibit States and the Federal Government from experimenting with various remedies—including possibly imposition of the death penalty—to prevent and deter such crimes.

Burger further stated that some of the justices of the U.S. Supreme Court are inclined to interject their own feelings against the death penalty by restricting its implementation through strict imitations of its use. This same attitude has been manifested by some state supreme court justices in the strict interpretation of the *Witherspoon* case. As previously mentioned, *Witherspoon* dealt with the alleged undue exclusion of prospective jurors and the question of whether the facts of a particular case fell within the special circumstances permitting the death penalty to be imposed.

Subsequent Death Penalty Legislation

Since the *Coker* decision was handed down, the U.S. Supreme Court has invalidated the death penalty in two other landmark cases, establishing new approaches to death penalty limitations. In the case of *Godfrey* v. *Georgia*,[5] the Court held that the sentence of death amounted to cruel and unusual punishment when pronounced on the defendant Godfrey, even though two murders had been committed. The Court quoted the Georgia statute providing that the death penalty could be invoked when the offense of murder was "outrageously or wantonly vile, horrible or inhuman." The Court held that to fall within that category, the evidence must demonstrate that the offender committed the murder through torture, depravity of mind or an aggravated battery before killing the victim. In the Godfrey case, the facts indicate that the defendant shot both victims in the head with a shotgun and that they died instantly. There was no evidence of serious suffering by the victims that would justify the death penalty under the Georgia statute. There were dissenting justices in that case who felt that the killings by the defendant did fall within the statute as being outrageously or wantonly vile, horrible, and inhuman. In the case of *Enmund* v. *Florida,*[6] the facts reveal that Enmund and two other defendants entered into a conspiracy to rob a victim of money. The three went to the home of the victim, Kersey, and two of the robbers approached Kersey to commit the crime. Kersey resisted and called for help. His wife came to the rescue and wounded one of the robbers. In retaliation, the robbers killed both Kersey and his wife. During this time, Enmund was sitting in the getaway car. After the killing, the three left the scene of the crime but were later identified, arrested, and tried on a charge of first-degree murder. In accordance with the Florida statute providing that "the killing of a human being while engaged in the perpetration of or in the attempt to perpetrate the offense of robbery is murder in the first degree even though there is no intent to kill, and for which upon conviction the death penalty may be imposed," all three defendants were convicted of first-degree murder and sentenced to death.

Enmund appealed the death sentence on the grounds that the death penalty under the circumstances was in violation of the cruel and unusual punishment clause of the Eighth Amendment of the U.S. Constitution. Enmund alleged that he did not participate in the actual killing and had no intent to kill during the robbery, and as such, the death penalty as applied was disproportionate to the crime he committed. The U.S. Supreme Court agreed with Enmund that the death penalty in his instance was cruel and unusual punishment. The Court stated the following:

> We have no doubt that robbery is a serious crime deserving serious punishment. It is not, however, a crime so grievous an affront to humanity that the only adequate response may be the penalty of death. It does not compare with murder, which does involve the unjustified taking of human life. Although it may be accompanied by another crime, robbery by definition does not include the death of another person. The murderer kills; the robber if no more than that, does not. Life is over for the victim of the murderer; for the robbery victim, life is not beyond repair. As we said of the crime of rape in the *Coker* case, we have the abiding conviction that the death penalty, which is unique in its severity and irrevocability, is an excessive penalty for the robber who, as such, does not take human life.

The dissenting justices in the *Enmund* case felt that the death penalty was not disproportionate to the crime of felony murder even though Enmund did not actually kill or intend to kill the victims. They pointed out that Enmund planned the robbery and assisted in carrying it out by going with the other two defendants to the victim's home and sat in the getaway car to aid in the escape after the robbery. As such, he was as guilty of murder as the other two defendants.

The majority of the justices in the *Enmund* case did not rule out all death penalty sentences in which a coconspirator did not actually do the killing, but as stated by one of the dissenting justices, to invoke the death penalty in such instances there must be proving of intent at the time that the robbery was planned. This requirement could be most difficult, since intent is a state of mind, and proving the state of mind when a robbery was planned is troublesome. Imposing the intent phase in such cases does preclude the death penalty's being imposed in most instances.

The U.S. Supreme Court in *Tison* v. *Arizona*[7] modified the intent ruling set forth in the *Enmund* decision. The Court in the *Tison* case stated that although the defendants had no specific intent to kill the victims of their crime, their mental state was one of such "reckless disregard for human life" that the death penalty was not cruel and unusual punishment under the circumstances.

The facts of the *Tison* case indicate that Gary Tison was serving a life sentence for the murder of a guard in an attempted escape. After serving a number of years in prison, Gary Tison's wife and his three sons, Raymond, Donald, and Ricky, conspired to assist him in escaping. In furtherance of the conspiracy, they assembled an arsenal of weapons, which the Tison brothers smuggled into the Arizona State Prison, where Gary Tison was serving time. The brothers armed Gary Tison and his cellmate, Randy Greenwalt, who also was serving a life sentence for murder. The five were able to overpower the guards and forced them and the visitors who were present at the time into a closet. The five fled the prison grounds in the Tisons' Ford and proceeded to a house nearby where the brothers had secreted a Lincoln automobile.

The five abandoned the Ford and proceeded in the Lincoln toward Flagstaff, going by way of back desert roads. On the way, a tire blew out on the Lincoln, so they decided to flag down a motorist and steal his car. Raymond stood in front of the Lincoln to flag a car while the others hid beside the road.

One car passed; then a Mazda automobile containing John Lyons, his wife, his two-year-old son, and John's fifteen-year-old niece stopped to render aid. As Raymond showed John Lyons the flat tire, the others emerged and, at gunpoint, forced the Lyons family into the back seat of the Lincoln. Raymond and Donald Tison drove the Lincoln down a dirt road further into the desert, followed by Gary, Ricky Tison, and Greenwalt in the Mazda. After traveling a short distance, both cars stopped, and Gary Tison blasted the radiator of the Lincoln with a shotgun, presumedly to further disable it. The Lyons family were made to stand in front of the Lincoln, where John Lyons pleaded with the group to spare his family's life and requested that they be given water so that they could survive in the desert. He asked as well for the five to take the Mazda and go on their way. Gary Tison ordered his sons to get some water from the Mazda. The sons did not know why their father gave them that order except that he seemed to be confused about what to do because of the baby. As the boys were returning with the water, they saw Gary Tison and Randy Greenwalt brutally murder the entire Lyons family, including the baby, with blasts from shotguns. The five men then got into the Mazda and drove away. Several days later, the group encountered a police roadblock. During a shootout, Donald Tison was killed. Gary Tison escaped but died of exposure from the desert heat. Greenwalt, Ricky Tison, and Raymond Tison were captured, tried, convicted of murder, and given the death penalty.

Ricky and Raymond Tison appealed their death penalty sentence to the U.S. Supreme Court on the grounds set forth in the *Enmund* decision, alleging that their death penalty was cruel and unusual punishment, since they had no intent to murder the victims of the crime. The Court rejected their contention. The Court pointed out that the Tison brothers were major participants in a long series of events leading up to the murder of the four victims and that, after the killing, the brothers further assisted in the escape. The Court maintained that they should have anticipated that serious injury or death would occur as a result of their activities. The Court also held that the whole mental attitude of the Tison brothers was one of "reckless indifference to the value of human life" and that this reckless disregard of human life was every bit as shocking to the moral sense as an intent to kill. As such it was sufficient to justify the death penalty and was not in violation of the Eighth Amendment guarantee against cruel and unusual punishment.

Attention is called to the fact that even though an appellate court reverses the death penalty, the offender is not necessarily set free. In most instances, the sentence will be reduced from the death penalty to life imprisonment without the possibility of parole or to life imprisonment only, depending on the statutes of the particular state. A life sentence without the possibility of parole may also be changed to life imprisonment by a governor at any time. Under a life sentence, most offenders are eligible for parole after serving a term of approximately twelve years. That possibility does not mean that the offender will be paroled after that period, but an offender sentenced for life usually does not serve until his or her death.

Retarded Defendants

In 2002, the U.S. Supreme Court held, by a six-to-three decision, that the Constitution's ban on cruel and unusual punishment bars the execution of mentally retarded people. The decision was a turnaround for the Court that thirteen years earlier had found no reason to bar the execution of the mentally retarded. The *Atkins* v. *Virginia* case involved Daryl Atkins, who had an I.Q. of 59. He had been sentenced to death for a murder and a robbery committed when he was eighteen years old. The majority decision of the Court noted that the tide of public opinion had turned and that now most states either prohibit capital punishment altogether or ban its use against the mentally retarded. Also, they noted that public opinion polls have demonstrated a steadily dwindling public enthusiasm for capital punishment in general. At the time of the decision, about twenty states allowed the execution of retarded persons. The decision failed to provide guidance to the states on what constitutes mental retardation for the purposes of the capital punishment prohibition.

FINES

The origin of the fine as a form of punishment is lost in history. Its early use as a form of punishment served a dual purpose. Money or property was taken from the wrongdoer and paid to the victim of the crime or to his or her relatives. The fine was also a source of revenue for the king or church, depending on the law that was broken. As other means of reimbursing the victim of a crime became available, such as civil suits, the fine was no longer used for that purpose, but fines were levied as a source of revenue for the government. The fine is still employed as a form of punishment for minor crimes.

The use of the fine as punishment in serious cases has dwindled considerably since the decision of *Williams* v. *Illinois* was handed down by the U.S. Supreme Court.[8] The statutes of most states provide for a penalty of imprisonment plus a specific amount of money that can be imposed in the form of a fine. This provision is applicable to most felonies as well as misdemeanors. As a result, judges in the past were able to impose a maximum time of imprisonment plus a fine. If unable to pay the fine, the convicted offender was imprisoned and "worked out" the fine by being given credit in a prescribed daily amount. In the *Williams* case, the U.S. Supreme

Court held that imprisoning one who was indigent and unable to pay the fine beyond the maximum amount of imprisonment prescribed by law was in violation of the Equal Protection Clause of the Fourteenth Amendment. The facts of the *Williams* case show that Williams was convicted of petty theft and received the maximum sentence provided by law, which was one year imprisonment and a $500 fine. Williams was also taxed $5 court costs. "The judgment directed, as permitted by statute, that if Williams was in default of payment of the fine and court costs at the expiration of the one-year sentence, he should remain in jail pursuant to the Illinois Criminal Code to work off the monetary obligations at the rate of $5 per day." The Court in that case stated the following:

> . . . Thus, whereas the maximum term of imprisonment for petty theft was one year, the effect of the sentence imposed here required appellant (Williams) to be confined for 101 days beyond the maximum period of confinement fixed by the statute since he could not pay the fine and costs of $505. . . .
>
> We conclude that when the aggregate imprisonment exceeds the maximum period fixed by the statute and results directly from an involuntary nonpayment of a fine or court costs we are confronted with an impermissible discrimination which rests on ability to pay, and accordingly, we reverse.
>
> Nothing in today's decision curtails the sentencing prerogative of a judge because, as noted previously, the sovereign's purpose in confining an indigent beyond the statutory maximum is to provide a coercive means of collecting or "working out" a fine. After having taken into consideration the wide range of factors underlying the exercise of his sentencing function, nothing we now hold precludes a judge from imposing on an indigent, as on any defendant, the maximum penalty prescribed by law.
>
> It bears emphasis that our holding does not deal with a judgment of confinement for nonpayment of a fine in the familiar pattern of alternative sentence of "$30 or 30 days." We hold only that a state may not constitutionally imprison beyond the maximum duration fixed by statute a defendant who is financially unable to pay a fine. A statute permitting a sentence of both imprisonment and fine cannot be parlayed into a longer term of imprisonment than is fixed by the statute since to do so would be to accomplish indirectly as to an indigent that which cannot be done directly. We have no occasion to reach the question whether a State is precluded in any other circumstances from holding an indigent accountable for a fine by use of penal sanction. We hold only that the Equal Protection Clause of the Fourteenth Amendment requires that the statutory ceiling placed on imprisonment for any substantive offense be the same for all defendants irrespective of their economic status.

Although the U.S. Supreme Court did not rule out the alternative penalties, such as thirty days in jail or a $30 fine, some appellate courts contend that application of such alternative penalties necessarily results in different treatment for the rich offender and the poor one. The nature of the penalty actually inflicted by the thirty days in jail or $30 fine depends on the offender's financial ability and personal choice. If the offender chooses and is able to pay the fine, imprisonment may be avoided. If he or she chooses imprisonment, the fine may be avoided. If the offender is unable to pay the fine, imprisonment cannot be avoided. Thus, the indigent offender has no choice, and the alternative penalties work as a violation of the Equal Protection Clause. However, to date, the alternative penalty procedure has not disappeared from the justice system, and fines will continue to be imposed as a form of penalty for some time to come.

Capstone Cases

United States v. *Grayson*
438 U.S. 41, 98 S.Ct. 2610, 57 L.Ed.2d 582 (1978)

Chief Justice Burger delivered the opinion of the Court.

We granted certiorari to review a holding of the Court of Appeals that it was improper for a sentencing judge, in fixing the sentence within the statutory limits, to give consideration to the defendant's false testimony observed by the judge during the trial. . . .

Grayson testified in his own defense. He admitted leaving the camp but asserted that he did so out of fear: "I had just been threatened with a large stick with a nail protruding through it by an inmate that was serving time at Allenwood, and I was scared, and I just ran." He testified that the threat was made in the presence of many inmates by prisoner Barnes, who sought to enforce collection of a gambling debt and followed other threats and physical assaults made for the same purpose. Grayson called one inmate, who testified: "I heard [Barnes] talk to Grayson in a loud voice one day, but that's all. I never seen no harm, no hands or no shuffling whatsoever."

Grayson's version of the facts was contradicted by the Government's rebuttal evidence and by cross-examination on crucial aspects of his story. For example, Grayson stated that after crossing the prison fence he left his prison jacket by the side of the road. On recross, he stated that he also left his prison shirt but not his trousers. Government testimony showed that on the morning after the escape, a shirt marked with Grayson's number, a jacket, and a pair of prison trousers were found outside a hole in the prison fence. Grayson also testified on cross-examination: "I do believe that I phrased the rhetorical question to Captain Kurd, who was in charge of [the prison], and I think I said something if an inmate was being threatened by somebody, what would he do? First of all he said he would want to know who it was." On further cross-examination, however, Grayson modified his description of the conversation. Captain Kurd testified that Grayson had never mentioned in any fashion threats from other inmates. Finally, the alleged assailant, Barnes, by then no longer an inmate, testified that Grayson had never owed him any money and that he had never threatened or physically assaulted Grayson.

The jury returned a guilty verdict, whereupon the District judge ordered the United States Probation Office to prepare a presentence report. At the sentencing hearing, the judge stated:

> I'm going to give my reasons for sentencing in this case with clarity, because one of the reasons may well be considered by a Court of Appeals to be impermissible; and although I could come into this Court Room and sentence this Defendant to a five-year prison term without any explanation at all, I think it is fair that I give the reasons so that if the Court of Appeals feels that one of the reasons which I am about to enunciate is an improper consideration for a trial judge, then the Court will be in a position to reverse this Court and send the case back for re-sentencing.
>
> In my view a prison sentence is indicated, and the sentence that the Court is going to impose is to deter you, Mr. Grayson, and others who are similarly situated. Secondly, it is my view that your defense was a complete fabrication without the slightest merit whatsoever. I feel it is proper for me to consider that fact in the sentencing, and I will do so.

He then sentenced Grayson to a term of two years' imprisonment, consecutive to his unexpired sentence.

On appeal, a divided panel of the Court of Appeals for the Third Circuit directed that Grayson's sentence be vacated and that he be resentenced by the District Court without consideration of false testimony. . . . We reverse.

In *Williams* v. *New York,* 337 U.S. 241 (1949), Mr. Justice Black observed that the "prevalent modern philosophy of penology [is] that the punishment should fit the offender and not merely the crime, and that, accordingly, sentences should be determined with an eye toward the preformation and rehabilitation of offenders." But it has not always been so. In the early days of the Republic, . . . the period of incarceration was generally prescribed with specificity by the legislature. Each crime had its defined punishment. . . .   *(Continued)*

Approximately a century ago, a reform movement asserting that the purpose of incarceration, and therefore the guiding consideration in sentencing, should be rehabilitation of the offender, dramatically altered the approach to sentencing. A fundamental proposal of this movement was a flexible sentencing system permitting judges and correctional personnel, particularly the latter, to set the release date of prisoners according to informed judgments concerning their potential for, or actual, rehabilitation and their likely recidivism. . . . Indeterminate sentencing under the rehabilitation model presented sentencing judges with a serious practical problem: how rationally to make the required predictions so as to avoid capricious and arbitrary sentences, which the newly conferred and broad discretion placed within the realm of possibility. An obvious, although only partial, solution was to provide the judge with as much information as reasonably practical concerning the defendant's "character and propensities . . . his present purposes and tendencies," and, indeed, "every aspect of life." *Williams* v. *New York.* Thus, most jurisdictions provided trained probation officers to conduct presentence investigations of the defendant's life and, on that basis, prepare a presentence report for the sentencing judge.

Constitutional challenges were leveled at judicial reliance on such information, however. In *Williams* v. *New York,* a jury convicted the defendant of murder but recommended a life sentence. The sentencing judge, partly on the basis of information not known to the jury but contained in a presentence report, imposed the death penalty. The defendant argued that this procedure deprived him of his federal constitutional right to confront and cross-examine those supplying information to the probation officer and, through him, to the sentencing judge. The Court rejected this argument. It noted that traditionally "a sentencing judge could exercise a wide discretion in the sources and types of evidence used to assist him in determining the kind and extent of punishment to be imposed within limits fixed by law. . . . And modern concepts individualizing punishment have made it all the more necessary that a sentencing judge not be denied an opportunity to obtain pertinent information," indeed, "to deprive sentencing judges of this kind of information would undermine modern pedagogical procedural policies that have been cautiously adopted throughout the nation after careful consideration and experimentation." Accordingly, the sentencing judge was held not to have acted unconstitutionally in considering either the defendant's participation in criminal conduct for which he had not been convicted or information secured by the probation investigator that the defendant was a "menace to society."

Of course, a sentencing judge is not limited to the often far-ranging material compiled in a presentence report. "[B]efore making [the sentencing] determination, a judge may appropriately conduct an inquiry broad in scope, largely unlimited either as to the kind of information he may consider, or the source from which it may come." *United States* v. *Tucker,* 404 U.S. 443 (1972). Congress recently reaffirmed this fundamental sentencing principle by enacting 18 U.S.C. § 3577:

> No limitation shall be placed on the information concerning the background, character, and conduct of a person convicted of an offense which a court of the United States may receive and consider for the purpose of imposing an appropriate sentence.

Thus, we have acknowledged that a sentencing authority may legitimately consider the evidence heard during trial, as well as the demeanor of the accused. *Chaffin* v. *Stynchcombe,* 412 U.S. 17 (1973). More to the point presented in this case, one serious study has concluded that the trial judge's "opportunity to observe the defendant, particularly if he chose to take the stand in his defense, can often provide useful insights into an appropriate disposition." ABA Sentencing Alternatives and Procedures § 5.1 (App.Draft 1968).

A defendant's truthfulness or mendacity while testifying on his own behalf, almost without exception, has been deemed probative of his attitudes toward society and prospects for rehabilitation and hence relevant to sentencing. Soon after *Williams* was decided, the Tenth Circuit concluded that "the attitude of a convicted defendant with respect to his willingness to commit a serious crime [perjury] is a proper matter to consider in determining what sentence shall be imposed within the limitations fixed by statute." *Humes* v. *United States,* 186 F.2d 875 (1951). The Second, Fourth, Fifth, Sixth, Seventh, Eighth, and Ninth Circuits have since agreed. Only one Circuit has directly rejected the probative value of the defendant's false testimony in his own defense. In *Scott* v. *United States,* 135 U.S.App. D.C. 377 (1969), the court argued that the peculiar pressures placed upon a defendant threatened with jail and the stigma of conviction make his willingness to deny the crime an unpromising test of his prospects for rehabilitation if guilty. It is indeed unlikely that many men who commit serious offenses would balk on principle from lying in their own defense. The guilty man may quite sincerely repent his crime but yet, driven by the urge to remain free, may protest his innocence in a court of law. . . .

Against this background we evaluate Grayson's constitutional argument that the District Court's sentence constitutes punishment for the crime of perjury for which he has not been indicted, tried, or convicted by due process. A second argument is that permitting consideration of perjury will "chill" defendants from exercising their right to testify on their own behalf.

In his due process argument, Grayson does not contend directly that the District Court had an impermissible purpose in considering his perjury and selecting the sentence. Rather, he argues that this Court, in order to preserve due process rights, not only must prohibit the impermissible sentencing practice of incarcerating for the purpose of saving the Government the burden of bringing a separate and subsequent perjury prosecution but also must prohibit the otherwise permissible practice of considering a defendant's untruthfulness for the purpose of illuminating his need for rehabilitation and society's need for protection. He presents two interrelated reasons. The effect of both permissible and impermissible sentencing practices may be the same: additional time in prison. Further, it is virtually impossible, he contends, to identify and establish the impermissible practice. We find these reasons insufficient justification for prohibiting what the Court and the Congress have declared appropriate judicial conduct.

First, the evolutionary history of sentencing, set out [above] . . . demonstrates that it is proper—indeed, even necessary for the rational exercise of discretion—to consider the defendant's whole person and personality, as manifested by his conduct at trial and his testimony under oath, for whatever light those may shed on the sentencing decision. . . . Second, in our view, Williams fully supports consideration of such conduct in sentencing. There the Court permitted the sentencing judge to consider the offender's history of prior antisocial conduct, including burglaries for which he had not been duly convicted. . . . Third, the efficacy of Grayson's suggested "exclusionary rule" is open to serious doubt. No rule of law, even one garbed in constitutional terms, can prevent improper use of firsthand observations of perjury. The integrity of the judges, and their fidelity to their oaths of office, necessarily provide the only, and in our view adequate, assurance against that.

Grayson's argument that judicial consideration of his conduct at trial impermissibly "chills" a defendant's statutory right, 18 U.S.C. § 3481, and perhaps a constitutional right, to testify on his own behalf is without basis. The right guaranteed by law to a defendant is narrowly the right to testify truthfully in accordance with the oath—unless we are to say that the oath is mere ritual without meaning. This view of the right involved is confirmed by the unquestioned constitutionality of perjury statutes, which punish those who willfully give false testimony. Further support for this is found in an important limitation on a defendant's right to the assistance of counsel: Counsel ethically cannot assist his client in presenting what the attorney has reason to believe is false testimony. Assuming, arguendo, that the sentencing judge's consideration of defendant's untruthfulness in testifying has any chilling effect on a defendant's decision to testify falsely, that effect is entirely permissible. There is no protected right to commit perjury.

Grayson's further argument that the sentencing practice challenged here will inhibit exercise of the right to testify truthfully is entirely frivolous. That argument misapprehends the nature and scope of the practice we find permissible. Nothing we say today requires a sentencing judge to enhance, in some wooden or reflex fashion, the sentences of all defendants whose testimony is deemed false. Rather, we are reaffirming the authority of a sentencing judge to evaluate carefully a defendant's testimony on the stand, determine—with a consciousness of the frailty of human judgment—whether that testimony contained willful and material falsehoods, and, if so, assess in light of all the other knowledge gained about the defendant the meaning of that conduct with respect to his prospects for rehabilitation and restoration to a useful place in society. Awareness of such a process realistically cannot be deemed to affect the decision of an accused but unconvicted defendant to testify truthfully in his own behalf.

Justice Stewart, with whom Justice Brennan and Justice Marshall join, dissenting. [Omitted.]

Roper v. *Simmons*
125 S. Ct. 1183; 2005 U.S. LEXIS 2200 (2005)

[Christopher Simmons, a juvenile, committed murder at the age of 17. He was tried and sentenced to death.]
Justice Kennedy delivered the opinion of the Court.

This case requires us to address, for the second time in a decade and a half, whether it is permissible under the Eighth and Fourteenth Amendments to the Constitution of the United States to execute a juvenile offender who was older than 15 but younger than 18 when he committed a capital crime. In *Stanford* v. *Kentucky*, 492 U.S.

(Continued)

361, 106 L. Ed. 2d 306, 109 S. Ct. 2969 (1989), a divided Court rejected the proposition that the Constitution bars capital punishment for juvenile offenders in this age group. We reconsider the question.

At the age of 17, when he was still a junior in high school, Christopher Simmons, the respondent here, committed murder. About nine months later, after he had turned 18, he was tried and sentenced to death. There is little doubt that Simmons was the instigator of the crime. Before its commission Simmons said he wanted to murder someone. In chilling, callous terms he talked about his plan, discussing it for the most part with two friends. Simmons proposed to commit burglary and murder by breaking and entering, tying up a victim, and throwing the victim off a bridge. Simmons assured his friends [that] they could "get away with it" because they were minors.

The State sought the death penalty. As aggravating factors, the State submitted that the murder was committed for the purpose of receiving money; was committed for the purpose of avoiding, interfering with, or preventing lawful arrest of the defendant; and involved depravity of mind and was outrageously and wantonly vile, horrible, and inhuman.

The jury recommended the death penalty after finding [that] the State had proved each of the three aggravating factors submitted to it. Accepting the jury's recommendation, the trial judge imposed the death penalty.

Simmons obtained new counsel, who moved in the trial court to set aside the conviction and sentence. After these proceedings in Simmons' case had run their course, this Court held that the Eighth and Fourteenth Amendments prohibit the execution of a mentally retarded person. *Atkins* v. *Virginia,* 536 U.S. 304, 153 L. Ed. 2d 335, 122 S. Ct. 2242 (2002). Simmons filed a new petition for state postconviction relief, arguing that the reasoning of Atkins established that the Constitution prohibits the execution of a juvenile who was under 18 when the crime was committed.

The Missouri Supreme Court agreed. It held that since Stanford,

a national consensus has developed against the execution of juvenile offenders, as demonstrated by the fact that eighteen states now bar such executions for juveniles, that twelve other states bar executions altogether, that no state has lowered its age of execution below 18 since Stanford, that five states have legislatively or by case law raised or established the minimum age at 18, and that the imposition of the juvenile death penalty has become truly unusual over the last decade."

We granted certiorari and now affirm.

The Eighth Amendment provides: "Excessive bail shall not be required, nor excessive fines imposed, nor cruel and unusual punishments inflicted." The provision is applicable to the States through the Fourteenth Amendment. As the Court explained in Atkins, the Eighth Amendment guarantees individuals the right not to be subjected to excessive sanctions. The right flows from the basic "precept of justice that punishment for crime should be graduated and proportioned to the offense." By protecting even those convicted of heinous crimes, the Eighth Amendment reaffirms the duty of the government to respect the dignity of all persons.

The prohibition against "cruel and unusual punishments," like other expansive language in the Constitution, must be interpreted according to its text, by considering history, tradition, and precedent, and with due regard for its purpose and function in the constitutional design. To implement this framework we have established the propriety and affirmed the necessity of referring to "the evolving standards of decency that mark the progress of a maturing society" to determine which punishments are so disproportionate as to be cruel and unusual.

In *Thompson* v. *Oklahoma,* 487 U.S. 815, (1988), a plurality of the Court determined that our standards of decency do not permit the execution of any offender under the age of 16 at the time of the crime. The plurality opinion explained that no death penalty State that had given express consideration to a minimum age for the death penalty had set the age lower than 16. The plurality also observed that "[t]he conclusion that it would offend civilized standards of decency to execute a person who was less than 16 years old at the time of his or her offense is consistent with the views that have been expressed by respected professional organizations, by other nations that share our Anglo-American heritage, and by the leading members of the Western European community." The opinion further noted that juries imposed the death penalty on offenders under 16 with exceeding rarity; the last execution of an offender for a crime committed under the age of 16 had been carried out in 1948, 40 years prior.

Bringing its independent judgment to bear on the permissibility of the death penalty for a 15-year-old offender, the Thompson plurality stressed that "[t]he reasons why juveniles are not trusted with the privileges and responsibilities of an adult also explain why their irresponsible conduct is not as morally reprehensible as that of an adult." According to the plurality, the lesser culpability of offenders under 16 made the death penalty inappropriate as a form of retribution, while the low likelihood that offenders under 16 engaged in "the kind of cost-benefit analysis that attaches any weight to the possibility of execution" made the death penalty ineffective as a means of deterrence. With Justice O'Connor concurring in the judgment on narrower grounds, the Court set aside the death sentence that had been imposed on the 15-year-old offender.

The next year, in *Stanford* v. *Kentucky,* 492 U.S. 361 (1989), the Court, over a dissenting opinion joined by four Justices, referred to contemporary standards of decency in this country and concluded [that] the Eighth and Fourteenth Amendments did not proscribe the execution of juvenile offenders over 15 but under 18. The Court noted that 22 of the 37 death penalty States permitted the death penalty for 16-year-old offenders, and, among these 37 States, 25 permitted it for 17-year-old offenders. These numbers, in the Court's view, indicated there was no national consensus "sufficient to label a particular punishment cruel and unusual." A plurality of the Court also "emphatically reject[ed]" the suggestion that the Court should bring its own judgment to bear on the acceptability of the juvenile death penalty.

The same day the Court decided Stanford, it held that the Eighth Amendment did not mandate a categorical exemption from the death penalty for the mentally retarded. *Penry* v. *Lynaugh,* 492 U.S. 302, (1989). In reaching this conclusion it stressed that only two States had enacted laws banning the imposition of the death penalty on a mentally retarded person convicted of a capital offense. According to the Court, "the two state statutes prohibiting execution of the mentally retarded, even when added to the 14 States that have rejected capital punishment completely, [did] not provide sufficient evidence at present of a national consensus."

Three Terms ago the subject was reconsidered in Atkins. We held that standards of decency have evolved since Penry and now demonstrate that the execution of the mentally retarded is cruel and unusual punishment. The Court noted objective indicia of society's standards, as expressed in legislative enactments and state practice with respect to executions of the mentally retarded. When Atkins was decided only a minority of States permitted the practice, and even in those States it was rare. On the basis of these indicia the Court determined that executing mentally retarded offenders "has become truly unusual, and it is fair to say that a national consensus has developed against it."

The inquiry into our society's evolving standards of decency did not end there. The Atkins Court neither repeated nor relied upon the statement in Stanford that the Court's independent judgment has no bearing on the acceptability of a particular punishment under the Eighth Amendment. Instead we returned to the rule, established in decisions predating Stanford, that "the Constitution contemplates that in the end our own judgment will be brought to bear on the question of the acceptability of the death penalty under the Eighth Amendment." Mental retardation, the Court said, diminishes personal culpability even if the offender can distinguish right from wrong. The impairments of mentally retarded offenders make it less defensible to impose the death penalty as retribution for past crimes and less likely that the death penalty will have a real deterrent effect. Based on these considerations and on the finding of national consensus against executing the mentally retarded, the Court ruled that the death penalty constitutes an excessive sanction for the entire category of mentally retarded offenders, and that the Eighth Amendment "places a substantive restriction on the State's power to take the life' of a mentally retarded offender."

Just as the Atkins Court reconsidered the issue decided in Penry, we now reconsider the issue decided in Stanford. The beginning point is a review of objective indicia of consensus, as expressed in particular by the enactments of legislatures that have addressed the question. This data gives us essential instruction. We then must determine, in the exercise of our own independent judgment, whether the death penalty is a disproportionate punishment for juveniles.

As in Atkins, the objective indicia of consensus in this case—the rejection of the juvenile death penalty in the majority of States; the infrequency of its use even where it remains on the books; and the consistency in the trend toward abolition of the practice—provide sufficient evidence that today our society views juveniles, in the words Atkins used respecting the mentally retarded, as "categorically less culpable than the average criminal."

A majority of States have rejected the imposition of the death penalty on juvenile offenders under 18, and we now hold this is required by the Eighth Amendment.

Justice Stevens, with whom Justice Ginsburg joined, concurred. [Omitted.]
Justice O'Connor, dissenting.
The Court's decision today establishes a categorical rule forbidding the execution of any offender for any crime committed before his 18th birthday, no matter how deliberate, wanton, or cruel the offense. Neither the

(Continued)

objective evidence of contemporary societal values, nor the Court's moral proportionality analysis, nor the two in tandem suffice to justify this ruling.

Although the Court finds support for its decision in the fact that a majority of the States now disallow capital punishment of 17-year-old offenders, it refrains from asserting that its holding is compelled by a genuine national consensus. Indeed, the evidence before us fails to demonstrate conclusively that any such consensus has emerged in the brief period since we upheld the constitutionality of this practice in *Stanford* v. *Kentucky,* 492 U.S. 361, 106 L. Ed. 2d 306, 109 S. Ct. 2969 (1989).

Instead, the rule decreed by the Court rests, ultimately, on its independent moral judgment that death is a disproportionately severe punishment for any 17-year-old offender. I do not subscribe to this judgment. Adolescents as a class are undoubtedly less mature, and therefore less culpable for their misconduct, than adults. But the Court has adduced no evidence impeaching the seemingly reasonable conclusion reached by many state legislatures: that at least some 17-year-old murderers are sufficiently mature to deserve the death penalty in an appropriate case. Nor has it been shown that capital sentencing juries are incapable of accurately assessing a youthful defendant's maturity or of giving due weight to the mitigating characteristics associated with youth.

SUMMARY

- Blood feuds resulted when it became a family responsibility to avenge a wrong.
- Imprisonment as punishment was not used in early English history.
- Banishment was one of the first forms of punishments.
- The colonies permitted the use of whipping as a punishment.
- Today, imprisonment is one of the most common forms of punishment.
- In most states, the judge determines the sentence. In a few states, like Texas, the defendant may choose to be sentenced by a jury.
- Most states require a presentence investigation prior to the imposition of a sentence for a felony conviction.
- Probation is one of the most popular forms of punishment today.
- The U.S. Constitution prohibits cruel and unusual punishments.
- The death penalty is considered excessive punishment for the crime of rape.
- The use of fines as punishment has dwindled since the *Williams* v. *Illinois* case.

REVIEW QUESTIONS

1. What amendment includes the guarantee against cruel and unusual punishment?
2. Why was imprisonment not used as a form of punishment in early criminal procedures?
3. What contribution did William Penn make to the sentencing procedure?
4. What is the primary purpose behind sentencing an offender?
5. List the different forms of punishment that may presently be imposed upon a convicted offender.
6. Explain the significance of each of the following types of sentences:
   a. The definite sentence
   b. The indefinite sentence
   c. The indeterminate sentence
7. What is the primary purpose of granting probation?
8. Why has the alternative sentence of a fine of $30 or thirty days in jail been criticized?

LOCAL PROCEDURE

1. Which type of sentence is imposed—indefinite or indeterminate—in your home state?
2. Who sentences the defendant—the judge, the jury, or some other body?

ENDNOTES

1. 408 U.S. 238 (1972).
2. 428 U.S. 280 (1976).
3. 428 U.S. 153 (1976).
4. 433 U.S. 584 (1977).
5. 446 U.S. 420 (1980).
6. 458 U.S. 782 (1982).
7. 95 L.Ed. 2d 127 (1987).
8. 339 U.S. 235 (1970).

What we seek is the reign of law, based upon the consent of the governed and sustained by the organized opinion of mankind.
—Woodrow Wilson, on the League of Nations, in a speech at Mount Vernon, July 4, 1918

Collateral Proceedings 17

Chapter Outline

Key Words

Certiorari
Extradition
Habeas corpus

International extradition
Rendition

Unlawful Flight
Statute
Writ

Learning Objectives

After completing this chapter, you should be able to:

1. Explain the procedures involved in extradition.
2. Discuss international extradition.
3. Define rendition.
4. Explain the use of writs.
5. Explain the importance of habeas corpus.
6. Discuss the Uniform Criminal Extradition Act.
7. Explain the use of a writ of certiorari.

In this chapter, we will examine the two collateral proceedings that are essential to the judicial process. Collateral proceedings refer to those proceedings that are not part of the normal judicial process involved in the conviction and sentencing or the acquittal of a defendant but that are a necessary part of the criminal justice system. The collateral proceedings discussed in this chapter are extradition and writs.

EXTRADITION

From a sequential standpoint, **extradition** should have been included in the discussion on arrest, but in view of the technicalities involved in this subject, we believe that its discussion will be more understandable if delayed until this point. Extradition is the procedure followed in returning an accused from one state or foreign country to the state where the crime was committed for the purpose of prosecution. The extradition proceedings may be international or interstate. Interstate extradition is referred to by some legal writers as **rendition**.

Interstate Extradition

Interstate extradition is based upon Article IV, Section 2, of the U.S. Constitution. This section provides that "A person charged in any state with treason, felony, or other crime, who shall flee from justice, and be found in another state, shall on demand of the executive authority of the state from which he fled, be delivered up, to be removed to the state having jurisdiction over the crime." Because of certain deficiencies of this provision in covering all phases of extradition, most states have adopted the Uniform Criminal Extradition Act. Prior to the act's adoption, it was necessary to prove that an accused had actually fled from the state in which the crime was committed to avoid prosecution. The act makes it unnecessary to prove that the accused fled from justice. The mere presence of the accused in another state is all that is necessary. Prior to the adoption of the act,

The Arizona State Prison Complex at Buckeye. (*Source*: AP Wide World Photos.)

an accused who was found in another state to which he or she had not voluntarily gone could not be extradited. For example, in one case, a fugitive was wanted for robbery in Utah but fled to Oklahoma. While in Oklahoma, the offender committed a bank robbery and was sentenced to serve a federal sentence in the penitentiary in Leavenworth, Kansas. Utah attempted to extradite the fugitive from Kansas after the completion of the bank robbery sentence. It was held that since the fugitive did not voluntarily flee to Kansas, he could not be extradited. The adoption of the act permits extradition from any state even though the accused did not voluntarily go to that state. An accused may be extradited on either a misdemeanor or a felony charge. However, because of the expense and procedure involved, fugitives are seldom extradited on a misdemeanor charge.

Requirements for Extradition   In order to extradite an accused, there must be a warrant of arrest outstanding against that individual based on an accusatory pleading filed in the county in which the crime took place. After determining that the accused is in another state, the prosecuting attorney of the county in which the crime was committed will make an application to the governor of his or her state. The application is a request for the governor to make a demand on the governor of the state where the accused is presently located for the return of the fugitive to the demanding state for prosecution. The application must show the name of the fugitive, the crime charged, the approximate time and date of the offense, the circumstances surrounding the commission of the crime, and the state and location where it is believed that the fugitive is located. It must also be alleged that the fugitive was in the demanding state at the time that the crime was committed. The application, along with copies of the accusatory pleading and a warrant, will be submitted to the governor of the demanding state. On approval of the application for extradition, the governor of the demanding state will appoint an officer to deliver the extradition papers to the governor of the state in which the fugitive is located, with a demand that the fugitive be returned to the demanding state for prosecution. The state in which the fugitive is located is generally referred to as the asylum state.

Acting on the Extradition Request   On receipt of the papers, the governor will review them in an effort to determine whether the fugitive should be surrendered to the demanding state. The governor may request the attorney general, or any prosecuting attorney of his or her state, to conduct an investigation to assist in making the determination. The investigation may include an inquiry to determine that the person sought is actually the one charged in the demanding state, and the offender's identity must be established with certainty. An inquiry may be made by the asylum state to make certain that the accused has been substantially charged in the demanding state. This is a determination of whether or not a complaint has been filed or an indictment returned and a warrant of arrest issued. The governor of the asylum state may wish to be satisfied that the accused sought was in the demanding state at the time the crime was committed and that he or she then left the demanding state. If the investigation concludes that the fugitive should be surrendered, the governor will issue a governor's warrant of arrest directing some officer to place the fugitive under arrest. After the arrest is made, the fugitive will be taken before a local magistrate, who will set a date for an extradition hearing. If the offense for which the fugitive is being extradited is a bailable offense in the demanding state, the local magistrate may set bail in order that the fugitive may post bail and be free from custody pending the extradition hearing. The hearing is usually set within a few days after the arrest. During the hearing, two major facts will be considered. First, is the fugitive in custody the person named in the accusatory pleading of the demanding state? Second, was the fugitive in the demanding state at the time the crime was committed? If the magistrate has any reservations about either of these issues, a request may be made that the demanding state present further evidence to prove the identity and whereabouts of the fugitive. The fugitive is entitled to the assistance of counsel at the hearing and to present evidence in his or her own behalf. If the magistrate is satisfied that the fugitive at the hearing is the one named in the accusatory pleading and was in the demanding state at the time that the crime was committed, the fugitive will be turned over to the custody of an officer of the demanding state for return to that state. Evidence of the fugitive's guilt or innocence is not pertinent at the hearing and will not be presented. After returning to the demanding state, the fugitive may be prosecuted on any charge, not just the one named in the extradition proceedings. In fact, the fugitive does not even have to be prosecuted on that charge if the prosecuting attorney wishes to substitute a different charge.

The Fugitive Already Arrested Not all fugitives wanted in another state are first arrested on a governor's warrant. Frequently, an individual is arrested on a minor local charge, after which it is determined that there is an outstanding warrant of arrest for that individual in another state. The laws of most states permit a temporary detention of the arrested person until extradition proceedings can be instituted. Many times, extradition proceedings are waived under these circumstances. If the person in custody waives the right to extradition proceedings, the waiver will eliminate the application to the governor of the demanding state and the other extradition formalities previously described. Upon agreeing to waive extradition, the arrested person is taken before a local magistrate, from whom consent to be returned to the demanding state will be given. Usually, the consent is given in writing. The magistrate will then order the arrested person's return to the demanding state.

Refusal to Extradite Although the U.S. Constitution provides that a person charged with a crime who has fled a state shall, upon demand, be "delivered up" to the demanding state, there have been times when a governor of an asylum state has refused to honor this constitutional provision. Both the U.S. Supreme Court and many state courts have held that the governor of an asylum state has the duty to abide by the demand, but there is no authority that can compel the governor to extradite a person wanted for prosecution. It has been held, however, that the governor of the asylum state must, within a reasonable time, either abide by the demand or refuse to extradite. The action cannot just be postponed indefinitely. The demanding state is entitled to know whether the fugitive is to be returned or not.[1] It has also been held that the asylum state has no right to question the merits or motives of the demanding state. The guilt or innocence of the offender is the sole responsibility of the demanding state.

In one case, the supreme court of an asylum state ordered a local court to investigate the conditions of the prison in the demanding state from which the offender escaped before the asylum state would authorize the extradition of the offender. However, the U.S. Supreme Court held in the case of *Pacileo* v. *Walker*[2] that the state supreme court had exceeded its authority. The facts of the *Pacileo* case indicate that Walker, the defendant, escaped from an Arkansas prison and was later apprehended in California. The governor of Arkansas requested that Walker be extradited to Arkansas to serve the remainder of his sentence. The governor of California signed the extradition papers, but the California Supreme Court ordered a local court to investigate the conditions of the Arkansas prison system to determine whether they violated the Cruel and Unusual Punishment Clause of the Eighth Amendment to the U.S. Constitution. The local sheriff who was charged with the responsibility of making the investigation contended that the courts of the asylum

The maximum security prison Tecumseh State Penitentiary, Nebraska. (*Source*: Mikael Karlsson/Arresting Images.)

state did not have the authority to investigate the prison conditions of the demanding state. The sheriff's contention was appealed to the U.S. Supreme Court, which held that once the governor of the asylum state signs the extradition papers, the courts of that state may consider only whether or not the extradition documents of the demanding state and asylum state are in order. Any further inquiry is beyond the local court's authority. The Court held that this issue had been previously decided in other cases.

Federal Law Against Unlawful Flight

Interstate extradition proceedings are not to be confused with the procedure followed under the federal Unlawful Flight to Avoid Prosecution Statute. In the 1930s, gangsters began to plague local law enforcement officers by going into a community and committing a series of serious crimes and then immediately fleeing to parts unknown. These officers were often handicapped in their efforts to locate the gangsters, because many times they fled to another state. Because of the seriousness of the situation, Congress passed the Unlawful Flight to Avoid Prosecution Statute. This statute permits the federal government, through the Federal Bureau of Investigation (FBI), to assist in locating and arresting badly wanted fugitives. When a fugitive is identified as having left the state where a crime was committed, the local prosecuting attorney can have a local warrant of arrest issued. The U.S. Attorney for that district is then requested to file a complaint charging the fugitive with the violation of the **Unlawful Flight Statute**. A warrant is issued on the federal complaint giving the FBI the authority to locate and arrest the fugitive. In most instances, the local prosecuting attorney must agree to handle extradition proceedings, since the statute was passed to assist in locating and arresting the fugitive and not for return to the demanding state. Originally, the statute permitted assistance in only a few major crimes; however, it now permits assistance to be given for any felony violation.

International Extradition

International extradition is based entirely on treaties with certain countries; these treaties specify the crimes for which an accused may be extradited. In most instances, political crimes are excluded. If a fugitive is extradited from a foreign country, he or she may be prosecuted only on the extradition charge. This safeguard prevents countries from extraditing a political fugitive under the pretext of a specified crime and then instigating prosecution for an alleged attempt to overthrow a government or for another political or unspecified crime. International extradition is handled in the United States through the Department of State. Instead of the governor of the demanding state directly contacting the officials in the asylum country, the governor will forward the demand for extradition to the secretary of state. The secretary of state will submit the demand to the officials of the asylum country, requesting that the fugitive be surrendered to officials of the United States in order that he or she be returned to this country for prosecution. If those officials decide that extradition is in order, the fugitive will be surrendered to this country. As in the case of the governor who does not honor the constitutional provision on interstate extradition, little can be done to compel a foreign country to extradite a person wanted in this country, with the exceptions of registering a protest or breaking a treaty. In most instances, however, the asylum country honors the demand. Treaties differ somewhat among countries. Some treaties provide that any person may be extradited for the specified crimes; other treaties exempt citizens of that particular country. This provision could hamper extradition, since many countries recognize dual citizenship. The lack of a treaty between two countries does not prevent one of them from surrendering a wanted fugitive to the other. Under these circumstances, the fugitive may be prosecuted for any crime unless the two countries agree otherwise.

WRITS

A **writ** defies simple definition. Legally, a writ is defined as a mandatory precept, under seal, issued by a court, and commanding the person to whom it is addressed to do or not to do some act. One might think of a writ as a written order issued by a court directing some other court officer to do or not to do a particular act. A number of writs may be issued by a court, but only the more frequently encountered ones will be discussed here.

Writ of Habeas Corpus

The writ of **habeas corpus** has been termed the great writ because its purpose is to obtain the prompt release of one who is being unlawfully detained. The right to this writ is embodied in the U.S. Constitution and in the laws of all the states. The statutes of the states read similarly to the following: Every person unlawfully imprisoned or restrained of liberty, under any pretense whatever, may request a writ of habeas corpus to inquire into the cause of the imprisonment or restraint. The person who believes that he or she is being unlawfully imprisoned, or someone in that person's behalf, may petition the appropriate court to have a writ of habeas corpus issued. Generally, a writ of habeas corpus may be issued by a judge of the superior court or its equivalent, or by a justice of an appellate court. In most states, the judge of the inferior court has no authority to issue a writ of habeas corpus.

The petition must state the place of confinement, the officer or person doing the confining, and the facts explaining why the petitioner feels unlawfully imprisoned. If the reason is valid, the writ will be issued and served on the person holding the prisoner, commanding that the prisoner be brought before the issuing court for a hearing to determine whether there is sufficient cause to confine the prisoner. A copy of the writ is furnished to the local prosecuting attorney in order that evidence may be presented endeavoring to prove the legality of the imprisonment. But the burden of proof is on the imprisoned person to prove by a preponderance of evidence that the imprisonment is unlawful. If the offense for which the person is imprisoned is a bailable one, the person is entitled to post bail pending the habeas corpus hearing.

If, after hearing the evidence presented by the prisoner and the prosecuting attorney, the judge concludes that the prisoner is being unlawfully detained, an order for the prisoner to be set free will be issued. The prisoner may not be charged further on that offense unless additional evidence is developed showing reasonable cause for an arrest and commitment by a legal process. If the judge concludes that the imprisonment was lawful, the prisoner will remain in custody to await the appropriate judicial processes.

The early use of the writ of habeas corpus was limited to obtaining the immediate release of one unlawfully restrained. But in recent years, the use of this writ has been broadened materially to make it applicable in a number of situations. For example, if an offender believes that the bail set for release is excessive, a writ of habeas corpus may be filed in an effort to get a reduction in bail. Further, if a convicted person believes that the sentence is excessive, the writ may be filed to have a determination made on this issue. This writ has also been used to determine the effectiveness of counsel. One of the more extensive uses made of the writ in recent years has resulted from some appellate court decisions, particularly those of the U.S. Supreme Court, that affect the rights of one convicted. For example, the *Witherspoon* decision held that a prospective juror could not be challenged for cause just because the juror had reservations against the death penalty. This decision caused writs of habeas corpus to be filed by all those convicted and given the death penalty in trials in which prospective jurors had been excused for cause as being against the death penalty. These writs requested that the sentence of death be reduced to life imprisonment. This action was possible, since the U.S. Supreme Court made the *Witherspoon* decision retroactive. When a decision is made retroactive, it is effective even though a trial is completed and the appeal period has passed. If a decision is not made retroactive, only those offenders whose trial or appeal has not been completed may take advantage of it.

The writ is also the way that the death penalty in state criminal trials is traditionally attacked in federal court. In the past, convictions were voided years after the defendants were found guilty. The process has also been used to delay the imposition of the death penalty. To eliminate this possibility, in 1996 the U.S. Congress passed the Antiterrorism and Effective Death Penalty Act. This act establishes limitation periods for the bringing of habeas actions and requires that federal courts generally defer to state courts' determinations. Under the act, a habeas corpus petitioner will normally have one year in which to seek relief. If the claim has been adjudicated in state court, relief will not be available unless the state court's adjudication resulted in a decision that is either contrary to or involved an unreasonable application of clearly established federal law as determined by the U.S. Supreme Court, or was based on an unreasonable determination of the facts in light of the evidence presented in the state court proceedings. The presumption of correctness accorded state courts' factual findings was also strengthened. Second or successive habeas corpus actions presenting new claims must be dismissed unless the claim is shown to rely on a new, previously unavailable rule of constitutional law or unless the factual predicate for the claim could not have been discovered previously through due diligence and the new facts would be sufficient to establish by clear and convincing evidence that, except for the error, no reasonable fact finder would have convicted.[3]

Writ of Certiorari

This writ is issued by an appellate court to permit the review of a decision or judgment by a lower court. It is often issued when other means of appeal are not possible. The writ of **certiorari** is often granted by a state supreme court to review a lower court's decision in order to establish guidelines to be followed in future cases by either trial judges or lower appellate courts. This is particularly the case if there is some doubt concerning a law or procedure. This writ is automatically issued in most jurisdictions to review a case when the death penalty is imposed to determine whether the facts warrant a conviction and the imposition of the death penalty. The U.S. Supreme Court frequently issues this writ to review the decision of a state appellate court when there may be a possible denial of a U.S. constitutional guarantee. The *Coker* decision is a good example. Coker was convicted of forceful rape and sentenced to death in a trial court in Georgia. The Georgia Supreme Court affirmed both the conviction and the death penalty. The U.S. Supreme Court granted Coker a writ of certiorari in order to determine whether the death penalty was excessive for the conviction of rape and, thus, a violation of the Eighth Amendment.

SUMMARY

- Interstate extradition is often referred to as rendition.
- International extradition is regulated by treaties between the countries involved.
- Interstate extradition involves the governor (or a representative of the governor) of the requesting state sending a request for extradition to the governor of the receiving state (where the accused is located).
- A person being extradited has a right to a judicial hearing in the receiving state before he or she is extradited.
- The receiving state has no obligation to honor a request for extradition.
- It is a violation of federal law to cross state boundaries in order to avoid prosecution in another state.
- The writ of habeas corpus is termed the great writ.
- The writ is used to test the legality of confinement.

REVIEW QUESTIONS

1. What is extradition?
2. Upon what is international extradition based?
3. Upon what is interstate extradition based?
4. In relation to prosecution, how do international and interstate extradition differ?
5. In what way did the Uniform Criminal Extradition Act correct certain weaknesses in the extradition procedure?
6. Briefly outline the procedure that must be followed in extraditing an offender.

7. What is the purpose of each of the following writs:
   a. Habeas corpus?
   b. Certiorari?

LOCAL PROCEDURE

1. Has your state adopted the Uniform Criminal Extradition Act?
2. Does your state have statutory procedures for handling writs?

ENDNOTES

1. *State of South Dakota* v. *Brown*, 144 Cal.Rptr. 758 (1978).
2. 449 U.S. 86 (1981).
3. 18 U.S. Code 3663A.

> Rape is the only crime in which the victim becomes the accused and, in reality, it is she who must prove her good reputation, her mental soundness, and her impeccable propriety.
>
> —Freda Adler, 1975

Victims' Rights

18

Key Words

Restitution
Symbolic restitution
Victim compensation

Victim impact
    statement

Victim service
    provider

Learning Objectives

After completing this chapter, you should be able to:

1. Discuss restitution in historical perspective.
2. Explain how a typical victim's compensation program works.
3. List the various benefits that victims of crime may receive from state compensation programs.
4. Explain the various types of restitution available.
5. Explain the purpose of victim impact statements and the issues involved in their use by the courts.
6. Define and explain the various victims' service providers available.

HISTORICAL PERSPECTIVE

The majority of this book has focused on the criminal justice system and the offender. Understanding how we respond to offenders is an important part of the criminal justice process; however, we must also understand how the victim of a crime fits within this system. This chapter will examine a newly emerging trend in the United States, that of victim interaction in the criminal justice system.[1] During the late 1960s, victims of crime began volunteering to serve within various victim assistance programs. As these crime victims continued to speak out about their treatment in the criminal justice system, the states and the federal government reacted by establishing commissions to study crime and its consequences.

The federal government responded by establishing the Law Enforcement Assistance Administration (LEAA). This agency provides funds to law enforcement agencies for a variety of purposes, including the establishment of victim and witness programs.[2] In 1975, the LEAA called a meeting in Washington, D.C., of various victim advocates to discuss methods of increasing victims' rights. One of the consequences of this meeting was the formation of the National Organization for Victim Assistance (NOVA). Today, NOVA is considered by many to be one of the leading victim rights organizations in the world.

Gains and Losses

During the late 1970s and early 1980s, the movement foundered. Lack of funding by the federal government caused many community-based victim organizations and service providers to cease operations. Additionally, within the movement, issues such as professionalism and training caused increasing divisiveness. The movement began to splinter into specialized groups that focused on specific issues. Several sexual assault and domestic violence organizations, such as the National Coalition Against Sexual Assault, were established to address the specific needs of those victims.[3] Although there was tension among various service providers because of diminishing funding and disagreement regarding specific goals, there was also progress in other areas of the victims' movement during this period. Parents of Murdered Children (POMC) was founded by Robert and Charlotte Hullinger in 1978, and Mothers Against Drunk Driving (MADD) was founded by Candy Lighter in 1980. Both of these organizations continue to have an impact on victims' rights and the victims' movement.

Increased Public Awareness

From 1982 to 1986, victims' organizations began to use the media to increase public awareness of crime victim issues. President Ronald Reagan and Congress responded to this heightened awareness with actions that would eventually have long-term consequences for the victims' movement. In 1982, President Reagan appointed a Task Force on Victims of Crime. This task force published a report that has since become a platform for victims' rights.[4]

Question: "How important do you think it is for the judicial system to provide victims and their families with each of the following?"

	Very Important	Somewhat Important	Not Too Important	Not at All Important	Not Sure
Right to be notified about dates and places of trials and related hearings	84%	13%	1%	1%	1%
Right to be physically present at trials and related hearings	82	15	1	0	1
Opportunity to discuss case with prosecutor during plea bargaining	72	18	3	3	4
Opportunity to discuss case with prosecutor during trial	57	28	6	4	4
Opportunity to make statement prior to sentencing about how crime affected them	72	20	5	2	2
Right to be paid for stolen or damaged property or injuries received in crime	81	15	2	1	1

*Percentages may not add to 100 because of rounding.
Source: Kathisen Maguire and Ann L. Pastore (eds.), Sourcebook of Criminal Justice Statistics 1992. U.S. Department of Justice Statistics (GPO, Washington, D.C., 1993). p. 199, Table 2.49.*

In 1984, another key event took place when Congress passed the Victims of Crime Act (VOCA).[5] The Office for Victims of Crime (OVC) was created in the Department of Justice to implement the task force's recommendations. OVC provides grants to states for programs with direct services for victims of all crimes. VOCA also established the Crime Victims Fund to provide money to local victim assistance programs and state victim compensation programs. The fund receives money from federal criminal fines, penalties, and bond forfeitures.

Increased Professionalism

From 1984 to the present, the victims' movement has been characterized by an increase in the professionalism of its advocates and providers. In earlier years, the victims' movement was marked by strong, dynamic leaders with vision and determination. At present, it has expanded beyond the ability of any one person's ability to influence its direction. It is now a national movement with a tremendous influence on local, state, and national politics.

Universities are expanding their victim-related courses. Organizations such as NOVA are offering increased training opportunities, and in 1995 the U.S. Department of Justice sponsored the first National Victim Assistance Academy in Washington, D.C. This academy was repeated in 1996 using distance-learning technology to link three universities in a joint academic effort. It continues to be offered on various college campuses across the nation.

The public awareness of victim issues continues to grow, and victim advocates have become an acknowledged force in modern politics. **Victim service providers** are realizing that their profession requires multidisciplinary training. There is a growing awareness that to be accepted by other professionals requires continuing education, certification, or other acknowledged credentials. This increased professionalism should translate into more sophisticated interventions and a faster rate of progress within the victims' movement.

Additional Laws

Increased professionalism also means increased knowledge and insight into the problems of victims. Congress has acknowledged the plight of victims by passing a Victims' Bill of Rights. By 1990, two-thirds of the states had enacted similar types of laws protecting victims. In 1994, Congress enacted the Violent Crime Control and Law Enforcement Act. Title IV of that law is the Violence Against Women Act (VAWA). Congress mandated that various professions form partnerships and work together to respond to all forms of violence against women.

The U.S. Attorney General is required to report to Congress annually on the grants that are awarded under the act and to ensure that research examining violence against women is encouraged. The report must include the number of grants, funds distributed, and other statistical information. Additionally, the report must assess the effectiveness of any programs that are funded under VAWA.

VAWA provides funding for a variety of research-based studies. It also requires that federal agencies engage in research regarding violence against women. For example, the National Institute of Justice is mandated to conduct four important projects: (1) the development of a research agenda that will address violence with particular emphasis on underserved populations; (2) the assessment of establishing state databases to record the number of sexual and domestic violence incidents; (3) a study to determine how abusive partners obtain addresses of their victims; and (4) an examination with other agencies of the battered woman syndrome.[6]

The Concept of a "Victim" Under Alaska Law

Alaska Statutes

Section 12.55.185.   Definitions. In this chapter, unless the context requires otherwise, "victim" means:

    A. a person against whom an offense has been perpetrated;

    B. one of the following, not the perpetrator, if the person specified in (A) of this paragraph is a minor, incompetent, or incapacitated:

       i. an individual living in a spousal relationship with the person specified in (A) of this paragraph; or

      ii. a parent, adult child, guardian, or custodian of the person;

    C. one of the following, not the perpetrator, if the person specified in (A) of this paragraph is dead:

       i. a person living in a spousal relationship with the deceased before the deceased died;

      ii. an adult child, parent, brother, sister, grandparent, or grandchild of the deceased; or

      iii. any other interested person, as may be designated by a person having authority in law to do so.

Source: Alaska state legislature.

In 2000, Congress passed the Victims of Trafficking and Violence Prevention Act. Division A of the act addresses the issue of trafficking of persons into the sex trade, slavery, and slavery-like conditions through prosecution of traffickers and assistance for victims of trafficking. This act increases penalties for slavery and trafficking crimes and provides for restitution for trafficking victims. Division B of the act expands VAWA and also expands the definition of a victim of terrorism to include a person who is a national of the United States or an officer or employer of the U.S. government who is injured or killed as a result of a terrorist act or mass violence outside the United States.

Several laws that were added to aid victims of the September 11, 2001, terrorist attacks. Title IV of the Air Transportation Safety and System Stabilization Act of 2001 established the September 11th Victim Compensation Fund of 2001 to address the economic and noneconomic losses of victims of this specific act of terrorism. (The final rules regarding this act were published March 6, 2002.) The USA Patriot Act of 2001 addresses the needs and concerns of victims of terrorist acts, including immigrant victims of the attacks on September 11, 2001. The Victims of Terrorism Tax Relief Act of 2001 exempts from income taxes any individual who dies as a result of wounds or injury incurred from the terrorist attacks.

In what may become one of the most critical dates in the history of victims' rights, on June 25, 1996, President Bill Clinton proposed a Victims' Rights Constitutional Amendment to the U.S. Constitution. In a speech made in the Rose Garden of the White House announcing this amendment, President Clinton stated that after studying all the alternatives, he was convinced that the only way to fully safeguard the rights of victims was to amend the Constitution to guarantee victims certain rights.[7]

The Victims' Rights Constitutional Amendment faces a long and complex process before it becomes law. It must be approved by Congress and then adopted by three-quarters of the states to become part of the Constitution. It is not something that will happen in a few weeks or months, and there are those who already claim that the proposed amendment is too detailed and should be made broader. No matter what the outcome, the simple fact that such an amendment has actually been proposed is a significant acknowledgment of the plight of victims of crimes.

RESTITUTION

Introduction

The 1982 *Final Report of the President's Task Force on Victims of Crime* included several key points regarding restitution.[8] The report recommended that legislation be enacted requiring judges to order restitution for property loss and personal injury in all cases unless the judge explicitly finds that restitution is not appropriate. However, it went on to point out that although restitution is a proper goal to be pursued, it has limitations. The report noted that restitution cannot be ordered unless the perpetrator is caught and convicted. Even if it is ordered, the offender often has no resources with which to make any payments. Finally, those perpetrators who can make payments may take many years to finally pay off the balance. In the interim, the victim is left to bear the cost of the crime.[9]

As a result of this report and other factors influencing the victim's movement over the last two decades, a number of laws have been enacted addressing the issue of restitution. Hillenbrand reports that one of the reasons these laws have been enacted may be the change in perception regarding restitution. She states that society began to view restitution not as a way to punish or rehabilitate the offender, but as a method of bringing justice to victims.[10] Other authorities argue that laws mandating restitution have been passed as politically correct, with little or no thought given to their effect. This situation has resulted in a system that does not deliver on its promise of making victims whole. Consequently, victims become more disillusioned with the criminal justice system when they learn that the court order mandating the offender to pay restitution carries no weight or authority.[11]

Even the definition of **restitution** causes conflict. It represents many things to many people. The victim may view restitution as a way to regain financial loss and punish the offender, whereas the court may see it as a method of instilling responsibility in the offender. The agency charged with collecting restitution may view it as simply one more task for an already overburdened department. Traditionally, restitution is a court-ordered sanction that involves payment of compensation by the defendant to the victim for injuries suffered as a result of the defendant's criminal act.

Restitution as we know it today can be traced to the criminal laws that authorized suspended sentences and the use of probation. By the late 1930s, several states had passed laws that allowed judges to order restitution as a condition of granting probation.[12] This process viewed restitution as part of the correctional process. In the late 1970s and 1980s, the victims' movement began to argue that restitution should be viewed as protecting victims from suffering financial hardship rather than as punishing or rehabilitating the offender.

The modern concept of restitution in the criminal justice system serves a variety of purposes in the administration of justice. Restitution attempts to establish a relationship between the perpetrator and the victim in an effort to make the offender aware of the financial consequences suffered by the victim as a result of the offender's acts. Another purpose of restitution is to advance the concepts of personal responsibility and accountability to the victim. A third idea regarding restitution holds that though it cannot undo the wrong, it can assist the victim financially and emotionally and at the same time educate the offender. Finally, restitution serves to punish the offender. The funds used to pay restitution must come from the offender and thus have a continuing impact on him or her.[13]

Status of Crime Victim Compensation Programs in the United States

Each state in the United States, as well as the District of Columbia, the U.S. Virgin Islands, Guam, and Puerto Rico, operates a crime victim compensation program to provide financial assistance for victims of violent or personal crime. Each state administers its own program in accordance with its state statute. The U.S. Department of Justice provides supplemental Victims of Crime Act (VOCA) funding and technical support to the states. The following information is generally applicable to all state compensation programs. For information regarding specific programs, contact the programs directly.

Eligibility Requirements

Report to police. Usually within 72 hours; exceptions are made for good cause.

Filing period. One year is typical; exceptions are made for good cause.

Victims of terrorist acts. Compensation is payable through the federal Antiterrorism Emergency Reserve for residents and nonresidents who are injured or killed in acts of terrorism within the United States or for U.S. nationals, officers, and/or employees of the U.S. government who are injured or killed in acts of terrorism outside the United States. In addition, some state compensation programs provide benefits to victims of terrorism.

Claimants. The following parties are eligible for compensation in most states:

- Victims of crime
- Dependents of homicide victims
- Relatives of victims of crime
- Citizens of foreign countries

Procedures

The claimant must file an application with the compensation agency in the state where the crime occurred. Based on information submitted by the victim, the agency determines if the claimant is eligible and has suffered a financial loss. In most states, the victim can appeal the agency's decision to deny or reduce the amount of compensation.

Benefits and Award Limits

Maximum benefits available to victims from the state programs average about $25,000, though a number of states have higher or lower maximums.

Compensable costs. All states will cover the following:

- Medical expenses
- Mental health counseling
- Lost wages for disabled victims
- Lost support for dependents of homicide victims
- Funeral and burial expenses

In addition, many states cover the following:

- Travel for medical treatment
- Services to replace work previously performed by the victim
- Crime scene cleanup
- Moving expenses
- Essential medical personal property (such as prosthetic devices, glasses)
- Rehabilitation
- Attorneys' fees

Emergency awards. Some states provide emergency awards or expedite processing for victims faced with extraordinary financial needs.

Funding sources. Most states obtain their funding from fees or charges assessed against offenders. Some states receive appropriations from general revenue. OVC provides supplemental funds from federal criminal fines and penalties.

Source: Information taken from the Office for Victims of Crime, *U.S. Department of Justice's Directory of International Crime Victim Compensation Programs, 2004–2005* (Washington, D.C., Government Printing Office, 2005, pp. 81–82.)

Types of Restitution

Restitution can now be ordered for a wide variety of criminal acts, including sex crimes, child sexual abuse, telemarketing fraud, and domestic violence.[14] Restitution can also be ordered to pay for lost wages, child care, and other expenses involved in attending court hearings.[15] Additionally, there are many different types of restitution.[16]

The most common form of restitution is financial, which requires the offender to make payments directly to the victim of the crime. Financial community restitution requires the offender to make payments to a community agency such as a restitution center, which then pays the victim. Individual service restitution requires the offender to perform a service for the victim. For example, the offender might be required to repair or replace property he or she damaged during the commission of the crime. Community service restitution requires the offender to perform some beneficial service to the community. In this type of restitution, which is sometimes referred to as **symbolic restitution**, society serves as the symbolic victim. Finally, some states authorize restitution fines. Restitution fines differ from actual restitution in that they are collected and deposited in the state's crime victim compensation fund. These monies then become part of the fund's operating expenses.

Restitution may be tied to different aspects of a defendant's sentence and is frequently imposed at the earliest possible time in the criminal process. Additionally, many plea agreements call for restitution. Imposing payment as a condition of probation is the most commonly used method of collecting restitution. A court order may also follow the defendant to the correctional institution. Many states now require inmates to work while incarcerated; while working in prison, they normally receive only a minimal amount of money (usually far less than the minimum wage). Several states have passed laws requiring that a portion of that amount, no matter how small, be set aside for payment as restitution to the victim. More and more states are implementing policies that require restitution to be established as a condition of parole. States are also passing laws that provide that any restitution order in a criminal case will also be considered a civil order for remuneration from the defendant to the victim and may be processed in civil courts.

Problems with Restitution

Restitution is a complex process that involves a number of different professionals working in the criminal justice system. Unfortunately, these professionals are usually overworked and underbudgeted. Many of them claim that collecting and disbursing restitution is someone else's job.[17] This perception leads to poor communications and diminished accountability among agencies within the criminal justice system and, in turn, causes poor consultation and communication with victims. Since there may not be one agency controlling or coordinating restitution, judges may impose insufficient or excessive restitution orders.

Many victims feel dissatisfied with the restitution process. Some believe that the amount imposed in the court order was insufficient. Others feel powerless as they search for answers to their questions, only to be directed from one agency to another.[18]

Occasionally, multiple perpetrators are involved in one crime against a single victim. If the prosecution grants one of the perpetrators immunity to testify against the others, the victim will not be able to receive a court order of restitution against that defendant. By the same token, there are crimes involving single perpetrators and multiple victims. Deciding which victim should receive the perpetrator's limited funds can create great difficulties.

Another obvious problem with restitution is the socioeconomic status of the perpetrator. In a majority of cases, he or she is poor and unlikely to earn the money necessary to make full restitution. Additionally, juvenile offenders are often incapable of obtaining or holding on to jobs that might provide them with the funds necessary to pay the court-ordered restitution.

COMPENSATION[19]

Introduction

Victims often suffer physical injury, emotional and mental trauma, and financial loss as a result of a crime. The financial loss to crime victims can cause additional stress as they worry about paying hospital and doctor bills, physical recovery from their injuries, and their ability to return to work. Crime victim compensation programs exist to provide financial assistance to victims and to reduce some of these stressors. These programs exist in all fifty states, as well as the District of Columbia, and many will pay for medical care, mental health counseling, lost wages, and, in the case of homicides, funeral costs and loss of support.[20] Although no amount of money can replace the use of an arm or the loss of a loved one, it can help victims preserve their financial stability and dignity and thereby assist in the recovery process.

As we discussed, in 1984 Congress enacted VOCA, which established a Crime Victims Fund, supported by revenues from federal offenders. This revenue was based upon fines, penalty assessments, and forfeited appearance bonds. When VOCA was enacted, the fund ceiling, or amount that could be allocated to the fund, was $100 million. Amendments to VOCA occurred in 1986, 1988, 1990, and 1992, when Congress removed the ceiling. Although deposits fluctuate from year to year, the total amount deposited in the fund from its inception to 2004 was more than $3.1 billion.[21]

Some of this money is available to the Administrative Office of the U.S. Courts, which established and administers a centralized National Fine Center. This center receives all the fines, assessments, and penalties and collects money from those who failed to pay on time. Other monies are used to improve the investigation and prosecution of child abuse cases, including those child abuse acts committed against Native Americans. However, most of the money in the fund is used to support state victim compensation and victim assistance service programs. **Victim compensation** is a direct payment to, or on behalf of, a crime victim for crime-related expenses such as unpaid medical bills, mental health counseling, funeral costs, and lost wages.[22] Victim assistance includes services such as crisis intervention, counseling, emergency transportation to court, temporary housing, advocacy, and criminal justice support.[23]

VOCA also established special assessments for individual crimes that are levied on every conviction. Additionally, VOCA has a "Son of Sam" provision that requires royalties from the sale of literary rights or any other profits derived from a crime to be deposited in the Crime Victims Fund and held for five years to satisfy any civil judgment that a victim may obtain. If no judgments are filed, these funds become part of the general Crime Victims Fund.[24]

Victim assistance programs include organizations that provide a wide variety of services to victims of state and federal crimes. More than 8,000 agencies or organizations provide services to victims, and nearly 3,000 of those organizations received some VOCA funding.[25]

Program Operation

California established the first compensation program in 1965, and within three years, five other states created similar programs. California's is still the largest program in the nation; it pays out about a third of the total benefits paid by all programs combined.[26] The median annual payout per state is approximately $2 million.

Every state administers a crime victim compensation program through a central agency.[27] These agencies are organized and funded statewide, with administration, claims investigation, and decision making handled by each state's headquarters. There is an ongoing debate among those in the field regarding centralization versus decentralization of compensation services.[28]

Most victim compensation programs are small agencies employing only a handful of staff. The lack of personnel creates delays in processing claims, prevents the training of groups regarding their right to compensation, and does not allow for specialized services such as bilingual staff. Some agencies are using student interns or volunteers to carry out staff functions. These programs provide assistance to victims of both federal and state crimes. Although each state compensation program is independently run, most programs have similar eligibility requirements and offer the same types of benefits. The maximum state award generally ranges between $10,000 and $25,000.[29]

Victims applying for compensation must comply with certain requirements, including reporting the crime and filing claims by certain deadlines. In most states, the victim initiates the process by calling the compensation agency. Program staff then mail an application to the victim, who fills it out and returns it to the compensation agency. Once the claim form is received, it is processed by an investigator or a claims specialist. These employees do not go out into the field to obtain their information; rather, they collect data using letters, telephone calls, and other techniques. These investigators must verify a wide variety of information, including the fact that the crime was reported to the proper law enforcement agency and the existence of appropriate documentation of medical expenses. They must also obtain data regarding funds paid by insurance companies and determine the amount, if any, of lost wages.

Once all pertinent information is gathered, the victim compensation agency will decide whether or not to make an award and, if so, how much it should be. In most states, victims may appeal a denial of benefits. These appeals are heard by a different panel from the one that made the original determination. Some states require that the appeal be heard by a judge.

Eligibility

Not all victims of every crime are eligible for state compensation. In general, the majority of states limit compensation to victims who suffered injuries as a result of the criminal conduct of another and to survivors of homicides (i.e., relatives and friends). Additionally, there is some disparity among eligibility requirements in these programs, with some states mandating that the victim suffer some sort of physical injury and others allowing for physical or mental injures. Most of the states allow the parents of deceased victims to collect compensation.

A majority of states disallow some classes of persons from eligibility. Most states preclude firefighters and police officers from receiving victim compensation awards. The rationale for this exclusion is that if their injuries are job related, they are eligible for other state programs, such as worker's compensation. Some states exclude convicted prisoners from filing claims while they are in jail or prison, or are serving probation or parole. VOCA requires states to provide compensation to nonresidents victimized within a state as well as to persons who are subject to federal jurisdiction, such as Native Americans. Additionally, residents of one state who are victimized in another state are eligible in their home state if the state where the crime occurred does not allow those victims compensation.

In the past, domestic violence victims were summarily denied compensation. Many states denied these claims because of the belief that the victim contributed to his or her own injuries by staying in the relationship or that any award would benefit the wrongdoer if he or she was still living with the victim. In a way similar to the change in attitudes toward victims of drunk driving, our altered perception of domestic violence victims has resulted in a change in policy in most states. The great majority of all states now include domestic violence as a compensable crime.

Some state compensation programs have very few domestic violence claims. The staff of these programs believe that is the case because victims underreport this form of violence. Additionally, certain minority groups may not report because exposing male offenders to public attention violates cultural norms. Finally, many program staff believe that police add information to their reports that serves to disqualify victims of domestic violence. For instance, police officers may include details to indicate that a domestic violence victim may have contributed to his or her injuries. However, the officers might not include that same information in a barroom altercation between strangers where misconduct is far more common and likely.[30]

VICTIM IMPACT STATEMENTS

History of Victim Impact Statements[31]

A new series of rights is emerging in our judicial system. These rights confer upon the victim or upon the relatives of deceased victims the opportunity to speak out or be heard during various phases of the criminal justice process. As with many rights that converge on a single point, there is an actual or a potential conflict. How we handle this conflict is a reflection of the morals and ethics of our society. This section reviews the history of these various rights and examines the rationale behind the current status of the law as it relates to victim impact statements.

One of the most controversial "rights" bestowed upon victims is the victim impact statement. In essence, the **victim impact statement** presents the victim's point of view to the sentencing authority. Providing the sentencing authority with all relevant information is not a new phenomenon in the criminal justice system. For many years, courts have accepted information regarding the defendant prior to the imposition of a sentence. Traditionally, presentence reports have been used by judges to determine the proper punishment for criminal defendants. The report, which is normally prepared by a probation officer, details the defendant's background, education, and criminal record. Many of these reports also include information concerning the victim of the crime.[32]

Victim impact evidence is now admitted in sentencing for a wide variety of criminal acts, including those that fall within the realm of family violence. However, the law on admissibility and use of victim impact statements is based upon use of this evidence during death penalty cases. To understand the nature of victim impact statements, it is necessary to review how this evidence is used in the most serious types of criminal cases—those involving capital punishment.

The use of victim impact evidence during the sentencing phase of a criminal raises serious constitutional issues. The right to confront witnesses comes head-to-head with the right to have all relevant evidence placed before the sentencing authority. Intense feelings were aroused in the U.S. Supreme Court when it addressed this issue.

Constitutional Issues

In *Booth* v. *Maryland,* the U.S. Supreme Court initially addressed the use of victim impact statements in a sentencing jury's determination.[33] In 1983, John Booth and

Willie Reed bound and gagged an elderly couple. Believing that the couple might be able to identify them, Booth stabbed them numerous times with a kitchen knife. The trial judge in *Booth* allowed the jury to consider a victim impact statement that detailed the family's and the community's respect and admiration for the victims as well as the impact of the murder on the victims' family.[34]

The Supreme Court, in reversing the death sentence, held that it was impermissible to allow the jury access to such evidence in the sentencing phase of a death penalty proceeding.[35] The Court listed three factors that precluded the prosecution from introducing evidence of the homicide's impact on the victim's family.

First, in holding that the victim impact statement (VIS) impermissibly allows the jury to focus on the victim rather than the defendant, the Court stated the following:

> When the full range of foreseeable consequences of a defendant's actions may be relevant in other criminal and civil contexts, we cannot agree that it is relevant in the unique circumstances of a capital sentencing hearing. In such a case, it is the function of the sentencing jury to "express the conscience of the community on the ultimate question of life or death." When carrying out this task the jury is required to focus on the defendant as a "uniquely individual being." The focus of a VIS, however, is not on the defendant, but on the character and reputation of the victim and the effect on his family. These factors may be wholly unrelated to the blame-worthiness of a particular defendant.[36]

The Court was particularly moved by the fact that the capital defendant does not typically choose his or her victim and, in fixing the punishment, there should be no correlation between the murder and the grief experienced by the victim's family.

Second, the Court held that the sentence of death should not turn on the characteristics of the victim and the victim's family. Specifically, the Court recognized that the imposition of the death penalty should not be determined on the basis of the ability of the victim's family to articulate their anguish and bereavement, whether the victim did or did not leave behind a family, or on the fact that the victim was a stellar member of the community.[37] These factors focus attention on the victim and away from the central inquiry of whether the defendant's characteristics and background are such that the death sentence is warranted.[38]

Finally, the Court stated that because a VIS contains the subjective perceptions and feelings of family members, the defendant has limited rebuttal opportunity.[39] Further, to the extent that the defendant is given an opportunity to rebut such information, "[t]he prospect of a 'mini-trial' on the victim's character is more than simply unappealing, it could well direct the sentencing jury from its constitutionally required task—determining whether the death penalty is appropriate in light of . . . the crime."[40]

In summing up the Court's holding that introduction of the VIS violates the Eighth Amendment's prohibition against cruel and unusual punishment, Justice Powell stated that such evidence would serve no other purpose than to inflame the jury and divert it from its obligation to be fair and impartial.[41] It should be apparent that at the time of the decision in *Booth* v. *Maryland,* the relevant considerations at the sentencing phase of a murder trial were those aspects of the defendant's background or character, or those circumstances that extenuated or mitigated the defendant's culpability.

South Carolina v. *Gathers* followed the rationale of *Booth* and held unconstitutional the imposition of a death penalty based upon prosecutorial remarks that were considered inflammatory.[42] Demetrius Gathers and three companions sexually assaulted and killed Richard Haynes, a man they encountered in a park. During the incident, the perpetrators ransacked a bag the victim was carrying. The bag contained several articles pertaining to religion, including a religious tract entitled "Game Guy's Prayer." During the sentencing phase of the trial, the prosecutor's argument included references to Haynes's personal qualities and included a reading of the "Game Guy's Prayer." The Supreme Court reversed the sentence, stating that such references to the qualities of the victim were similar to the *Booth* holding prohibiting victim impact statements. The Court determined that such evidence was likely to inflame the jury and thus violated the defendant's Eighth Amendment rights. In a well-reasoned and logical dissent, Justice O'Connor stated, "Nothing in the Eighth Amendment precludes the community from considering its loss in assessing punishment nor requires that the victim remain a faceless stranger at the penalty phase of a capital case." The dissent by Justice O'Connor was a signal that the winds of judicial temperament might be changing.

In *Payne* v. *Tennessee,* the court completely reversed itself and allowed to stand the imposition of a death sentence that was based in part on evidence contained in a victim impact statement. In 1987, Pervis Tyrone Payne entered the apartment of Charisse Christopher and her two children. Payne stabbed Charisse and the children numerous times with a butcher knife. Charisse and her daughter, Lacie Jo, died; however, three-year-old Nicholas survived.

Payne was caught and convicted for the murders. During the penalty phase, four witnesses testified regarding the defendant's background, reputation, and mental state. All these witnesses urged the jury not to impose the death penalty. In rebuttal, the prosecution called the maternal grandmother, who was caring for Nicholas. She was allowed to testify, over the defendant's objection, that Nicholas continued to cry out, calling for his dead mother and sister. The witness was also allowed to testify regarding her personal grief over the loss of her loved ones.

During closing arguments, the prosecutor hammered on the pain and suffering that Nicholas and his deceased family had endured, stating the following:

> But we do know that Nicholas was alive. And Nicholas was in the same room. Nicholas was still conscious. His eyes were open. He responded to the paramedics. He was able to follow their directions. He was able to hold his intestines in as he was carried to the ambulance. So he knew what happened to his mother and baby sister.
>
> There is nothing you can do to ease the pain of any of the families involved in this case. There is nothing you can do to ease the pain of Bernice or Carl Payne, and that's a tragedy. There is nothing you can do basically to ease the pain of Mr. and Mrs. Zvolanek, and that's a tragedy. They will have to live with it for the rest of their lives. There is obviously nothing you can do for Charisse and Lacie Jo. But there is something you can do for Nicholas.
>
> Somewhere down the road Nicholas is going to grow up, hopefully. He's going to want to know what happened. And he is going to know what happened to his baby sister and his mother. He is going to want to know what kind of justice was done. He is going to want to know what happened. With your verdict, you will provide the answer.[43]

The jury sentenced Payne to death, and the case was then appealed to the U.S. Supreme Court. Payne contended that the trial court erred when it allowed the maternal grandmother to testify. Relying on *Booth* and *Gathers,* Payne argued that such evidence was a violation of his Eighth Amendment rights. After reviewing the principles that have guided criminal sentencing over the ages, the Court stated that the consideration of the harm caused by the crime has been an important factor in the exercise of judicial discretion. The majority opinion went on to state that neither *Booth* nor *Gathers* even suggested that a defendant, entitled as he or she is to individualized consideration, is to receive that consideration wholly apart from the crime committed. The Court stated that victim impact evidence is simply another form or method of informing the sentencing authority about the specific harm caused by the crime in question.[44]

Thus the U.S. Supreme Court overruled *Booth* and *Gathers* to the extent that they prohibited introduction of evidence or argument regarding the impact of the crime on the victim, families, and community. In addition, the Court's decision clearly stated that the decision regarding the admission of such evidence was the prerogative of the individual states. The Court ruled that it would not intervene unless the evidence introduced was so unduly prejudicial that it rendered the trial fundamentally unfair.[45] If this possibility occurred, the Court reasoned, the Due Process Clause of the Fourteenth Amendment provides a mechanism for relief.

The decision was not without heated dissent. In a dissenting opinion, Justices Marshall and Blackmun uttered words that will ring in the halls of justice and law school classrooms forevermore: "Power, not reason, is the new currency of this Court's decision making."[46] The justices went on to point out that the Court was disregarding the accepted judicial principle of stare decisis.[47]

The decision also generated controversy in the academic world when a series of articles appeared condemning the Court for both allowing victim impact evidence and appearing to repudiate its acceptance of stare decisis.[48] Although the dissent and certain individuals within the academic community may condemn the majority's opinion, it is now clearly the law of the land. In addition, the Supreme Court's decision enhances the victims' rights movement in the United States. It allows individual states to determine what is relevant evidence in the death penalty phase of a capital crime. Some would argue that the decision in *Payne* leaves prosecutors and defense attorneys scrambling to determine what type of evidence is admissible under the guise of victim impact statements. The answer is simply this: Evidence that does not result in rendering a trial fundamentally unfair is proper. This concept of fundamental fairness is not a new, untested, or ill-defined doctrine.

There is a long history defining acts by the state that are classified as fundamentally unfair. The doctrine of fundamental fairness has its roots in two early cases. In

Law in Practice

Victim's Rights Constitutional Amendment

Section 1. To ensure that the victim is treated with fairness, dignity, and respect, from the occurrence of a crime of violence and other crimes as may be defined by law pursuant to section two of this article, and throughout the criminal, military, and juvenile justice process, as a matter of fundamental rights to liberty, justice and due process, the victim shall have the following rights: to be informed of and given the opportunity to be present at every proceeding in which those rights are extended to the accused or convicted offender; to be heard at any proceeding involving sentencing, including the right to object to a previously negotiated plea, or to a release from custody; to be informed of any release or escape; and to a speedy trial, a final conclusion free from unreasonable delay, full restitution from the convicted offender, reasonable measures to protect the victim from violence or intimidation by the accused or convicted offender, and notice of the victim's rights.

Section 2. The several States, with respect to a proceeding in a State forum, and the Congress with respect to a proceeding in a United States forum, shall have the power to implement further the rights established in this article by appropriate legislation.

Source: Office for Victims of Crime (Washington, D.C.), 1996.

Powell v. *Alabama,* several black youths were accused of repeatedly raping two young white girls. They were caught, tried, and convicted. Their conviction was overturned on the ground that the failure of the trial court to appoint counsel until the day of the trial was a violation of the defendants' due process.[49] In *Brown* v. *Mississippi,* a sheriff hung the defendant from a tree and whipped him until he confessed to the murder of a white man. The Supreme Court held that such actions are revolting to the sense of justice, and the confession was suppressed.[50]

The doctrine of fundamental fairness accepts the concept that due process is a general command that requires states to provide the defendant with a fair trial. If the admission of the victim impact evidence "revolts the sense of justice" or "shocks the conscience" of the court, such admission would be error under the Due Process Clause.

Victim impact evidence is now an accepted part of the judicial process. The ability of a victim of family violence to inform the court of the impact of the offender's acts on his or her life can only benefit the victim and continue to educate the public regarding the dynamics of violence.

SUMMARY

- Historically, the victim has been a forgotten part of the criminal justice process.
- The victims' rights movement in the United States began in the late 1970s.
- In 1982, President Ronald Reagan appointed a Task Force on Victims of Crime.
- In 1984, the VOCA was enacted.
- The Final Report of the Task Force recommended that an order of restitution be required in sentencing an individual convicted of a crime against an individual.
- Today, restitution can now be ordered for a wide variety of criminal acts.
- Most states have some form of victim compensation program to reduce the trauma of victimization.
- Victims have the right to present a victim's impact statement in a criminal trial during the sentencing procedures.

REVIEW QUESTIONS

1. Explain why the historical perspective of restitution is important in understanding today's models.
2. List reasons why an incarcerated prisoner should not have to make restitution to a victim. Assume that you are the prisoner's advocate and must convince a judge of your position.
3. Explain how a typical compensation program is funded and operates.
4. Describe the various eligibility requirements for receiving compensation.
5. List the various benefits that victims of crime may receive under a state compensation program.
6. Explain and give concrete examples of fundamental fairness. Can you list ways in which a victim impact statement would violate this constitutional standard?
7. Should law enforcement officers inform the victim of a crime about victim impact statements? Prepare a form that should be given to victims outlining their rights.
8. How can we ever determine whether victim impact statements serve a valid purpose in the criminal justice system? How would you structure such a study? What are the pitfalls inherent in these types of studies?

LOCAL PROCEDURE

1. Who handles compensation claims in your county? Contact them and determine whether they have handouts that explain their duties.
2. Who coordinates restitution in your court system?
3. Are different types of restitution available in your jurisdiction? List the types.
4. Attend a sentencing hearing at your local courthouse. Was the victim present? Did he or she make a victim impact statement? Do you think it had any effect on the sentencing of the offender? Explain your reasoning.

ENDNOTES

1. Portions of this chapter have been adapted from Harvey Wallace, *Victimology: Legal, Psychological and Social Perspectives* (Allyn & Bacon, Boston), 1997.
2. Emilio C. Viano, *Victim/Witness Services: A Review of the Model* (GPO, Washington, D.C.), 1979.
3. M. Largen, "Grassroots Centers and National Task Forces: A History of the Anti-Rape Movement," 32 *Aegis*, pp. 46–52 (Autumn 1981).
4. *Final Report of the President's Task Force on Victims of Crime* (GPO, Washington, D.C.), December 1982.
5. Victims of Crime Act of 1984, 42 U.S. Code, section 10601 (1984).
6. Jeremy Travis, "Violence Against Women: Reflections on NIJ's Research Agenda," *National Institute of Justice Journal* vol. 34, pp. 34–42, (February 1996).
7. "Remarks by the President at Announcement of Victims' Constitutional Amendment," Press Release, The White House, Office of the Press Secretary, Washington, D.C., June 25, 1996, p. 2.
8. *Final Report of the President's Task Force on Victims of Crime.*
9. Ibid. at 38.
10. Susan Hillenbrand, "Restitution and Victim Rights in the 1980s." In A. J. Lurigio, W. G. Skogan, and R. C. Davis (eds.), *Victims of Crime: Problems, Policies, and Programs* (Sage, Newbury Park, Calif.), 1990.
11. Carol Shapiro, "Is Restitution Legislation the Chameleon of the Victims' Movement?" In B. Gateway and J. Hudson (eds.), *Criminal Justice, Restitution, and Reconciliation* (Willow Tree Press, Monsey, N.Y.), 1990.
12. L. F. Frank, "The Collection of Restitution: An Overlooked Service to Crime Victims," vol. 8, *St. John's Journal of Legal Commentary* 107 (1992).
13. *National Victim Assistance Academy Text* (unpublished 1998), pp. 21–105.
14. *Attorney General Guidelines for Victim and Witness Assistance, 1995* (U.S. Department of Justice, Washington, D.C.), 1995.
15. 18 U.S. Code, section 3663(b), as amended by section 40504 of P.L. 103–322 (1994).
16. *National Victim Assistance Academy Text,* pp. 21–10–8, 21–10–11.
17. Michael D. Harris, "No One Wants Responsibility for Restitution," *Los Angeles Daily Transcript,* January 6, 1995, p. A-1.
18. *National Victim Assistance Academy Text,* p. 21–10–7.
19. Much of the material that appears in this section has been adapted from various federally funded projects, including NACVCB's *Crime Victim Compensation: A Fact Sheet and Crime Victim Compensation: An Overview* (National Association of Crime Victim Compensation Boards, Alexandria, Va.), July 1, 1994; *Crime Victim Compensation,* Dale G. Parent, Barbara Auerbach, and Kenneth E. Carlson, *Compensating Crime Victims: A Summary of Policies and Practices,* Office of Justice Programs (U.S. Department of Justice, Washington, D.C.), January 1992; *Compensating Crime Victims and Focus on the Future: A Systems Approach to Prosecution and Victim Assistance,*

National Victim Center, MADD, and American Prosecutors Research Institute (U.S. Department of Justice, Washington, D.C.), no date; hereinafter, *Focus on the Future.*

20. *Crime Victim Compensation,* p. 112.
21. "Victims of Crime Act Crime Victims Fund," *OVC Fact Sheet* (Office for Victims of Crime, Washington, D.C.), 2005.
22. Ibid.
23. Ibid.
24. *Compensating Crime Victims,* p. 2.
25. Ibid.
26. *Compensating Crime Victims,* p. 2.
27. Ibid.
28. *Compensating Crime Victims,* p. 7.
29. "Victims of Crime Act Crime Victims Fund," *OVC Fact Sheet* (Office for Victims of Crime, Washington, D.C.), 1996.
30. *Compensating Crime Victims,* p. 21.
31. This section has been adapted from Harvey Wallace, *Family Violence; Legal, Medical and Social Perspectives* (Allyn & Bacon, Boston), 1996.
32. See Phillip A. Talbert, *The Relevance of Victim Impact Statements to the Criminal Sentencing Decision,* 36 UCLA L Rev 199, 202–11 (1988), and Maureen McLeod, *Victim Participation Criminal Law Bull at Sentencing,* 22 Crim L. Bull. 501, 505–11 (1986).
33. *Booth* v. *Maryland,* 482 U.S. 496 (1987).
34. Ibid. at 500–01.
35. Ibid. at 509. The Court did, however, carefully note that information typically contained in a victim's statement is generally admissible in noncapital cases and may be considered in capital cases if directly related to the circumstances of the crime. Id. at 508 n. 10. For example, the Court noted that the prosecution may produce evidence regarding the characteristics of the victim to rebut an argument made by the defendant (e.g., the victim's peaceable nature to rebut the claim of self-defense). Ibid.
36. Ibid. at 507–07 (citations omitted).
37. Ibid. at 505–07.
38. Ibid. at 507–08.
39. Ibid.
40. Ibid.
41. Ibid.
42. 490 U.S. 805 (1989).
43. 115 L.Ed.2d 728–729.
44. 115 L.Ed.2d 734–735.
45. 115 L.Ed.2d 735.
46. 115 L.Ed.2d 748.
47. 115 L.Ed.2d 756.
48. See Jimmie O. Clements, Jr., *Case Note, Criminal Law—Victim Impact Evidence: The Scope of the Eighth Amendment Does Not Include a Per Se Bar to the Use of Victim Impact Evidence in the Sentencing Phase of a Capital Trial,* Payne v. Tennessee. 23 St. Mary's L.J. 517(1991); Aida Alaka, *Note, Victim Impact Evidence, Arbitrariness and the Death Penalty: The Supreme Court Flipflops in* Payne v. Tennessee, 23 Loy. U. Chi. L.J. 581(1992); K. Elizabeth Whitehead, *Case Note, Mourning Becomes Electric:* Payne v. Tennessee's *Allowance of Victim Impact Statements During Capital Proceedings,* 45 Ark. L. Rev. 531(1992).
49. *Powell* v. *Alabama,* 287 U.S. 45, 53 S.C. 55, 77 L.Ed. 158 (1932).
50. U.S. 278, 56 S.Ct. 461, 80 L.Ed. 682 (1936).

Glossary

Abandonment: The concept that once property has been abandoned, its former owner has no reasonable right of privacy in it.

Abstract goals: The underlying principles upon which our justice system is based.

Adversary system: Our concept of justice, in which one side represents the plaintiff or state and the other side represents the defendant, while the judge acts as the independent referee.

Aggravation or circumstances in aggravation: Facts which tend to justify the imposition of a more severe punishment.

Allen charge: An instruction given a deadlocked jury in attempt to get the jury to reach a verdict.

Alternate juror: A person who sits with the jury during the trial and is prepared to serve as a jury member if one of the regular jurors is excused or disqualified.

Appointed counsel: A counsel that has been appointed by the judge to represent the defendant.

Arraignment: A hearing before a court having jurisdiction in which the identity of the defendant is established, the defendant is informed of the charges and of his or her rights, and in some states the defendant is required to enter a plea.

Arrest: The seizure of a person to answer for a criminal charge.

Atonement: A designated price to be paid or duty to be performed by an offender to the victim or victim's family when a certain crime was committed.

Bail: A form of pretrial release in which the defendant is required to post money or property to ensure his or her presence at trial.

Bailiff: An individual assigned to assist the judge and the jury and to perform other duties assigned by the judge.

Bench trial: A trial by a judge without a jury.

Bench warrant: A warrant issued by the judge during a trial. It is issued from the judge's bench.

Booking: The process that officially records an entry into detention after an arrest.

Bounty hunters: Individuals who hunt persons who have violated the terms of their bail and did not appear in court.

Boykin advisement: The required advice that a judge must give a defendant in open court before the judge can accept a guilty plea. Based on the Supreme Court case of *Boykin* v. *Alabama*.

Brady material: Material that tends to be beneficial to the defendant's case must be provided to defense prior to trial. Based on the Supreme Court decision in *Brady* v. *Maryland*.

Certiorari: A petition to an appeals court to invoke its jurisdiction.

Challenges for cause: A challenge to a potential juror based on the juror's qualifications or lack of impartiality.

Change of venue: Moving of the trial to a different geographical location.

Character evidence: Evidence of a person's character that tends to prove that the individual did or did not commit a certain act.

Charging the jury: The act of a judge in instructing the jury.

Civil contempt: The willful continuing failure or refusal of any person to comply with a court's lawful writ, subpoena, process, order, rule, or command that by its nature is still capable of being complied with.

Code of Hammurabi: One of the first-known attempts to establish a written code of conduct.

Competency: Refers to the mental state of the defendant at the time of trial. A defendant must be able to assist his or her counsel in defending of the case.

Complaint: A written statement made upon oath before a judge, magistrate, or official authorized by law to issue warrants of arrest, setting forth essential facts constituting an offense and alleging that the defendant committed the offense.

Consciousness of guilt: The concept that reflects on the defendant's knowledge of his or her level of guilt.

Constitutional right to speedy trial: The defendant's right to a speedy trial guaranteed by the Sixth Amendment. Speedy trial time starts when prosecution is commenced.

Constructive contempt: Any criminal or civil contempt other than a direct contempt. [See Direct contempt.]

Consular immunity: The limited immunity granted to consuls and their deputies as representatives of a foreign government.

Contempt: The violation of court order or disruption of court proceedings.

Continuance: The delay of a trial at the request of one of the parties.

Conviction in absentia: Conviction of a defendant in which the defendant is not present in court.

Court rules: Rules issued by the courts to regulate the process in the courts in the areas not regulated by statutes, regulations, and other rules.

Court trial: A trial by a judge without a jury.

Criminal contempt: Either misconduct of any person that obstructs the administration of justice and that is committed either in the court's presence or so near thereto as to interrupt, disturb, or hinder its proceedings; or willful disobedience or resistance of any person to a court's lawful writ, subpoena, process, order, rule, or command, where the dominant purpose of the contempt proceeding is to punish the contemptor.

Cross-examination: The examination of a witness by the party that did not call the witness; used to weaken the witness's testimony.

Cross section of community standard: The requirement that the jury panel or list be representative of a cross section of the community.

Cruel and unusual punishment: The constitutional protection contained in the Eighth Amendment that prohibits the imposition of punishment that is considered cruel or unusual.

Curative instructions: Instructions given to a jury to cure any errors caused by the jury receiving inadmissible evidence or other information.

Curtilage of a dwelling house: A space, necessary and convenient and habitually used for family purposes and the carrying on of domestic employments. It includes the garden, if there is one, and it need not be separated from other lands by a fence.

Daubert test: A test used by the courts to determine if certain scientific evidence should be admitted into evidence.

Death-qualified jury: A jury in which the members have indicated that under appropriate circumstances they would vote for the death penalty.

Declarant: An individual making a formal statement.

Definite sentence: A sentence that has a specified period of confinement or definite terms.

Deliberations: The closed sessions of a jury in which the jury attempts to reach a verdict.

Demurrer: The formal mode of disputing the sufficiency in law of the pleadings contained in the complaint.

Deposition: A form of pretrial discovery in which a witness is questioned under oath and the other parties are given an opportunity to be present and ask questions. Used more in civil than in criminal cases.

Determination of guilt: A verdict of guilty by a jury, a finding of guilty by a court following a nonjury trial, or acceptance by the court of a plea of guilty.

Deterrence: Punishment based on the goal of deterring future criminal activity.

Diplomatic immunity: The immunity granted to diplomatic officers, their staffs, and their families by which they are free from local jurisdiction and as such cannot be arrested or detained for any offense unless they are permanent residents or citizens of the United States.

Direct contempt: The disorderly or insolent behavior or other misconduct committed in open court, in the presence of the judge, that disturbs the court's business, where all the essential elements of the misconduct occur in the presence of the court and are observed by the court, and where immediate action is essential to prevent diminution of the court's dignity and authority before the public.

Direct examination: The initial questioning of a witness by the party that originally called the witness.

Directed verdict: A verdict by the judge when the judge concludes that the evidence is such that a jury could not legally find the defendant guilty.

Due process: Those procedures that effectively guarantee individual rights in the face of criminal prosecution and those procedures that are fundamental rules for fair and orderly legal proceedings.

Duplicate: A counterpart produced by the same impression as the original, or from the same matrix, or by means of photography, including enlargements and miniatures, or by mechanical or electronic re-recording, or by chemical reproduction, or by other equivalent techniques which accurately reproduce the original.

Effective counsel: An attorney who exercises the normal standards of effectiveness in representing his or her client.

Evidence relating to past sexual behavior: Such a term includes, but is not limited to, evidence of the complaining witness's marital history, mode of dress, and general reputation for promiscuity, nonchastity, or sexual mores contrary to the community standards and opinion of character for those traits.

Evidentiary hearing: A hearing held by the trial court to resolve contested factual issues.

Exclusionary Rule: The rule used to exclude evidence that was obtained by the violation of a constitutional right such as an illegal search.

Exoneration of bail: The court's act in dissolving bail after the defendant has appeared in court as required.

Expectation of privacy zone: The living area immediately surrounding a home where the residents have an expectation of privacy.

Extradition: The surrender by one state or nation to another state or nation of a person who is charged with a crime in the requesting state.

Farce or sham test: A test formerly used to determine if the defense counsel adequately represented the defendant. The defense must be more than a sham or farce.

Foreperson: The individual jury member who has been selected by the other jurors as their spokesperson.

Former acquittal: A defense based on double jeopardy in which defendant claims that he or she has been acquitted of the charged offense.

Fruit of the Poisonous Tree: Additional evidence discovered from information obtained as the result of a constitutional violation such as an illegal search.

Gag order: An order by the judge to the parties to a lawsuit to refrain from discussing the case with the press.

Grand jury: An investigative body that meets to determine whether there is sufficient evidence to support an indictment against a defendant. The grand jury may also investigate the conduct of public officials and agencies.

Habeas corpus: A writ that orders the custodian of a prisoner to appear in court and explain why the individual is being held in confinement.

Harmless error: Any error, defect, irregularity, or variance which does not affect substantial rights and shall be disregarded.

Hearsay: A statement, other than one made by the declarant while testifying at the trial or hearing, offered in evidence to prove the truth of the matter asserted.

Hung jury: A jury that cannot agree on a verdict.

Husband-wife privilege: A communication is confidential if it is made privately by any person to his or her spouse and is not intended for disclosure to any other person. An accused in a criminal proceeding has a privilege to prevent his or her spouse from testifying as to any confidential communication between the accused and the spouse. The privilege may be claimed by the accused or by the spouse on behalf of the accused. The authority of the spouse to do so is presumed. There is no privilege under this rule in a proceeding in which one spouse is charged with a crime against the other person or property of (1) the other, (2) a child of either, (3) a person residing in the household of either, or (4) a third person committed in the course of committing a crime against any of them.

Impaneled jury: A jury that has been selected and sworn in by the judge.

Impartial trial by jury: A jury that starts the case without any preconceived opinions regarding the guilty or innocence of the defendant.

Impeachment: The attempt to limit or discredit evidence that has been admitted.

Indefinite sentence: A sentence that has no fixed term and may be adjusted to fit the offender.

Independent state grounds: A decision based on a state constitution or statute that does not involve an interpretation of federal law.

Indeterminate sentence: A sentence in which the period of confinement or other punishment is to be determined based on the need of the offender.

Indictment: A written statement charging the defendant or defendants named therein with the commission of an indictable offense, presented to the court by a grand jury, endorsed "A True Bill," and signed by the foreperson. The term indictment includes presentment.

Indigent defendant: A defendant who lacks the resources to afford to hire his or her attorney.

Information: A written statement charging the defendant or defendants named therein with the commission of an indictable offense, made on oath, signed, and presented to the court by the district attorney without action by a grand jury.

Initial appearance: The first appearance by the defendant in a criminal case before a judge. Generally, at the initial appearance, the defendant is informed of the charges against him or her and advised of his or her rights. In some states it is the same as an arraignment.

Insanity: The abnormal mental state of the defendant at the time that the crime was committed.

International extradition: Extradition of a fugitive from another country subject to the extradition treaties between the two countries.

Joiner: The consolidated trial of a case by joining charges or defendants.

Judgment: The adjudication of the court based upon a plea of guilty by the defendant, upon the verdict of the jury, or upon the court's own finding following a nonjury trial that the defendant is guilty or not guilty.

Judicial notice: The act of a court in accepting certain facts without the necessity to present evidence to prove them, such as the fact that New York is a state, a fact that a court can take judicial notice of.

Jurisdiction: The power of a court to act in regard to the individual or subject matter.

Jury list: A jury panel. The list of potential jurors that have been summoned from which a jury may be selected.

Jury of one's peers: A jury composed of a cross section of the community that was selected in a fair and impartial manner.

Jury panel: The list of potential jurors that have been summoned from which a jury may be selected.

Law enforcement officer: Any person vested by law with a duty to maintain public order or to make arrests for offenses.

Lay witness: A nonexpert witness.

Legislative immunity: Statutory provisions that grant limited immunity to legislative members while attending or going to legislative sessions.

Limited admissibility: Evidence that is admitted for a limited purpose only.

Locked-down jury: A jury that has been sent to the deliberations room to start deliberations on the findings.

Magistrate: A judicial officer with the power to issue a warrant, including magistrates, district judges, superior court judges, and any other judicial officer authorized by law to conduct a preliminary examination of a person accused of a crime or issue a warrant.

Manifest necessity: In reference to a mistrial, a condition in which the judge concludes that it is necessary to declare a mistrial.

Material witness: A witness whose presence is deemed necessary for the trial of the case. A person designated as a material witness may be required to post security to ensure his or her presence at trial.

Mentally incompetent: Refers to an accused who lacks sufficient present ability to assist in his or her defense by consulting with counsel with a reasonable degree of rational understanding of the facts and the legal proceedings against the defendant.

Miranda warning: Warnings required before officers can interrogate a suspect who is in detention.

Mistrial: The act of a judge in terminating a trial before it is concluded because of errors or issues that call into question the fairness of the trial.

Mitigation or "circumstances in mitigation": Facts that tend to justify the imposition of a lesser punishment.

Motion to suppress evidence: A motion presented prior to trial to determine the admissibility of certain items of evidence.

Negotiated plea: A plea that has been agreed upon by the defendant and the state; a plea bargain.

New trial: A retrial of a defendant with a new jury.

Nolo contendere: A plea of no contest that supports a conviction if accepted by the judge.

Notice of alibi defense: A requirement that the defendant provide the prosecution with advance notice that an alibi defense will be used.

Open fields: The concept that the Fourth Amendment's restrictions on unreasonable searches and seizures do not apply to items in open fields.

Opening statements: Statements made by counsel prior to the presentation of evidence. The statements are not considered evidence and should not contain arguments on behalf of a party.

Order to show cause: An order in response to a habeas corpus petition directing the respondent (warden) to file a return. The order to show cause is issued if the petitioner (prisoner) has made a prima facie showing that he or she is entitled to relief; it does not grant the relief requested. An order to show cause may also be referred to as granting the writ.

Orientation goals: Those goals of the justice system that are oriented in one of two opposite directions— law and order or individual rights.

Original: Concerning a writing or recording, the writing or recording itself or any counterpart intended to produce the same effect by a person executing or issuing it. An original of a photograph includes the negative or any print therefrom. If data are stored in a computer or similar device, any printout or other output readable by sight, shown to reflect the data accurately, is an original.

Peremptory challenge: A challenge that a party has to eliminate a potential juror. Each side has a limited number of peremptory challenges. While the party peremptorily challenging a potential juror normally is not required to provide a reason for the challenge, the challenge may not be used to exclude one gender or race from the jury.

Petty offenses: Offenses which have a maximum jail time of six months and a fine of not more than $500.

Plain errors: Errors or defects affecting substantial rights that may be noticed, although they were not brought to the attention of the court.

Plain view doctrine: The concept that looking at items in plain view is not a search because there is no reasonable expectation of privacy concerning items in plain view.

Pragmatic goals: Criminal justice goals related to preventing crime and developing better environmental conditions in the neighborhoods that foster law-abiding behavior.

Precept: A warrant or legal document issued by a court directing a person to comply with the terms of the precept.

Preliminary hearing: A proceeding before a judicial officer to determine if a crime has been committed, whether the crime occurred within the jurisdiction of the court, and whether there are reasonable grounds to believe that the defendant committed the crime.

Preliminary questions: Basic questions like name and address asked of a witness when the witness is first called to testify.

Preponderance of evidence: The normal burden of proof required in civil cases where the moving party is required to establish that it was more likely than not that a certain event occurred or a fact exists.

Pretrial discovery: The right of parties to obtain evidence from the other parties prior to the commencement of the trial.

Pretrial diversion: An agreement between the parties to a criminal case that the charges will be dropped if the defendant successfully meets the conditions for diversion.

Private person arrest: An arrest by a person who does not have a peace officer status.

Privileged communications: Communications between individuals that are protected from discovery or use in a trial. Generally, communications between a party and his or her attorney are privileged.

Probable cause: Exists when the facts and circumstances within the officer's knowledge, and of which he or she has reasonably trustworthy information, are sufficient to cause a reasonably cautious person to believe that an offense has been or is being committed.

Probation: Placing a defendant on conditioned release subject to revocation if the defendant violates the terms of the release.

Public defender: An attorney who works for the state and has the duty of defending indigent defendants.

Public trial: A trial that the public has a right to attend.

Public's right of access to a trial: The constitutional right of the public and the press to attend a criminal trial granted by the First Amendment.

Rape shield laws: Laws designed to protect a rape victim and limit the admission of the victim's prior sexual history.

Reasonable cause to believe: A basis for belief in the existence of facts which, in view of the circumstances under and purposes for which the standard is applied, is substantial, objective, and sufficient to satisfy applicable constitutional requirements.

Reasonable doubt: The burden of proof that is required before a defendant may be convicted of a crime. The burden is on the prosecution to prove a fact with a high degree of certainty.

Reasonable suspicion: A suspicion based on facts or circumstances which by themselves do not give rise to the probable cause requisite to justify a lawful arrest, but which give rise to more than a bare suspicion, that is, a suspicion that is reasonable as opposed to imaginary or purely conjectural. A suspicion based on facts that would cause a reasonable person to conclude that criminal activity is ongoing or has occurred.

Rebuttal evidence: Evidence to rebut or negate evidence present by the other party.

Redirect examination: The examination by the party who called the witness to cover matters that were covered in the cross-examination.

Rehabilitated: The conclusion that a defendant has reformed.

Release on own recognizance: Release of a defendant without bail upon his or her promise to appear at all appropriate times, sometimes referred to as "personal recognizance."

Relevant evidence: Evidence having any tendency to make the existence of any fact that is of consequence to the determination of the action more probable or less probable than it would be without the evidence.

Rendition: Another term for interstate extradition.

Resisting arrest: The act of resisting a lawful arrest; a crime.

Restitution: Court-ordered sanction that involves payment of compensation by the defendant to the victim for injuries suffered as a result of the defendant's criminal activity.

Retained counsel: Counsel that has been selected and employed by the defendant.

Return: The law enforcement officer executing an arrest warrant shall endorse thereon the manner and date of execution, shall subscribe his or her name, and shall return the arrest warrant to the clerk of the court specified in the arrest warrant.

Right of confrontation: The constitutional right of a defendant to confront the witnesses against him or her. It includes the right to cross-examine the witness.

Right of discovery: The right of either a prosecutor or a defendant to discover certain evidence in possession of the other party.

Right to trial by jury: Right of a defendant to have his or her case decided by a fair and impartial jury.

Search: A governmental intrusion into an area where a person has a reasonable expectation of privacy.

Search warrant: A written order, in the name of the state or municipality, signed by a judge or magistrate authorized by law to issue search warrants, directed to any law enforcement officer, commanding him or her to search for personal property and, if found, to bring it before the issuing judge or magistrate.

Seizure: Taking any person or thing or obtaining information by an officer pursuant to a search or under other color of authority.

Self-representation: A defendant's acting as his or her own attorney.

Sequestered jury: A jury that has been secluded from the public and the press. Generally, a jury is sequestered during the deliberation phase of the trial.

Severance: The act of dividing multiple charges or defendants into separate trials.

Standards: Detail goals to improve the justice system.

Standby counsel: An attorney appointed by a judge to be available to consult with the defendant in cases where the defendant represents himself or herself.

Statute of limitations: The time within which criminal proceedings must commence after the commission of the crime. Some crimes, such as murder, have no statute of limitations.

Statutory right to a speedy trial: Defendant's right to a speedy trial, which is guaranteed by a statute.

Stop and frisk: The act of stopping a person for investigative purposes and frisking him or her for the presence of a weapon.

Subpoena duces tecum: A subpoena of a witness that also orders the witness to bring certain documents to court.

Subpoenas: Orders issued by the clerk of the court in which a criminal proceeding is pending at any time for witnesses required by any party for attendance at trial and at hearings, for taking depositions, or for any other lawful purpose.

Summons: An order issued by a judicial officer or, pursuant to the authorization of a judicial officer, by the clerk of a court, requiring a person against whom a criminal charge has been filed to appear in a designated court at a specified date and time.

Suspended sentence: An adjudged sentence whose imposition is suspended under certain conditions, and upon compliance with the conditions the sentence is vacated. If the conditions are not complied with, the suspension is vacated and the sentence is imposed.

Symbolic restitution: A beneficial service to the community that the defendant is ordered to perform because of his or her criminal misconduct.

Syndromes: Mental conditions that are often presented to excuse or justify the conduct of the defendant.

Temporary detention: A brief investigative detention.

Terry stop: An investigative stop by an officer to determine if criminal activity is ongoing.

Torts: A private or civil wrong or injury that is addressed in civil court.

Transactional immunity: Immunity granted to force a witness to testify in which the witness cannot be prosecuted for the criminal act covered by his or her testimony.

Trial by ordeal: An ordeal in which the accused was required to perform some physical task to prove his or her innocence.

Unlawful flight: Fleeing the jurisdiction of a court to avoid criminal proceedings.

Use and derivative immunity: Immunity granted to force a witness to testify whereby his or her testimony or any other information obtained as the result of the testimony cannot be used against him or her.

Venue: The geographic location of the court.

Verdict: A judgment by the court. In a criminal court, it refers to the finding of guilty or not guilty.

Victim: A person against whom a criminal offense has allegedly been committed, or the spouse, parent, lawful representative, or child of someone killed or incapacitated by the alleged criminal offense, except where the spouse, parent, lawful representative, or child is also the accused.

Victim impact statements: Statements which victims or victim representatives are permitted to submit for court consideration at sentencing time.

Victim service providers: Organizations that provide services to victims of crime.

Victim's bill of rights: Statutory legislation that provides certain basic rights to a victim during the trial of a criminal case.

Victim's compensation: Payments made to victims in an attempt to lessen the impact of the crime upon them.

Waiver of error: No party may assign as error on appeal the court's giving or failing to give any instruction or portion thereof, or to the submission or the failure to submit a form of verdict, unless the party objects thereto before the jury retires to consider its verdict, stating distinctly the matter in which the party objects and the grounds of his or her objection.

Work product: Discovery cannot be required of legal research or of records, correspondence, reports, or memoranda to the extent that they contain the opinions, theories, or conclusions of the prosecutor, members of the prosecutor's legal or investigative staff or law enforcement officers, or of defense counsel or defense counsel's legal or investigative staff.

Writ: A mandatory precept (warrant), under seal, issued by a court and commanding a person to whom it is addressed to do or not to do some act.

Subject Index

Case Index